S0-AII-770

BRITISH WRITERS

BRITISH WRITERS

JAY PARINI
Editor

RETROSPECTIVE SUPPLEMENT III

CHARLES SCRIBNER'S SONS
A part of Gale, Cengage Learning

MATIGNON HIGH SCHOOL LIBRARY

GALE
CENGAGE Learning™

Detroit • New York • San Francisco • New Haven, Conn • Waterville, Maine • London

Ref
820.09
S427B

British Writers Retrospective Supplement III

Project Editor: Lisa Kumar

Copyeditors: Gretchen Gordon, Robert E. Jones, Linda Sanders

Proofreaders: Susan Barnett, Gretchen Gordon

Indexer: Wendy Allex

Permission Researcher: Laura Myers

Permissions: Margaret Abendroth, Jennifer Altschul, Margaret Chamberlain-Gaston

Composition: Gary Leach

Manufacturing: Rhonda A. Dover

Publisher: Frank Menchaca

Project Manager: Janet Witalec

Copyright © 2010 by Charles Scribner's Sons

ALL RIGHTS RESERVED. No part of this work covered by the copyright herein may be reproduced, transmitted, stored, or used in any form or by any means graphic, electronic, or mechanical, including but not limited to photocopying, recording, scanning, digitizing, taping, Web distribution, information networks, or information storage and retrieval systems, except as permitted under Section 107 or 108 of the 1976 United States Copyright Act, without the prior written permission of the publisher.

For product information and technology assistance, contact us at **Gale Customer Support, 1-800-877-4253.** For permission to use material from this text or product, submit all requests online at **www.cengage.com/permissions.** Further permissions questions can be emailed to **permissionrequest@cengage.com**

While every effort has been made to ensure the reliability of the information presented in this publication, Gale, a part of Cengage Learning, does not guarantee the accuracy of the data contained herein. Gale accepts no payment for listing; and inclusion in the publication of any organization, agency, institution, publication, service, or individual does not imply endorsement of the editors or publisher. Errors brought to the attention of the publisher and verified to the satisfaction of the publisher will be corrected in future editions.

EDITORIAL DATA PRIVACY POLICY. Does this publication contain information about you as an individual? If so, for more information about our editorial data privacy policies, please see our Privacy Statement at www.gale.cengage.com.

LIBRARY OF CONGRESS CATALOGING-IN-PUBLICATION DATA

British writers. Retrospective supplement III / Jay Parini, editor.
   p. cm.
  Includes bibliographical references and index.
  ISBN 978-0-684-31599-7 (hardcover : alk. paper)
  1. English literature--Bio-bibliography. 2. English literature--History and criticism. 3. Authors, English--Biography. I. Parini, Jay. II. Title.

PR85.B688 Retro Suppl.
3 820.9--dc22   [B] 2009031917

The paper used in this publication meets the requirements of ANSI/NISO Z39.48-1992 (Permanence of Paper).

Charles Scribner's Sons
an imprint of Gale, Cengage Learning
27500 Drake Rd.
Farmington Hills, MI 48331–3535

ISBN-13: 978-0-684-31599-7
ISBN-10: 0-684-31599-8

Printed in the United States of America
1 2 3 4 5 6 7 13 12 11 10 09

Acknowledgements

Acknowledgement is gratefully made to those publishers and individuals who permitted the use of the following materials in copyright.

COWPER, WILLIAM. *The Poems of William Cowper.* Edited by John D. Baird and Charles Ryskamp. Oxford,1995. Reproduced by permission of Oxford University Press. / *The Task and Other Selected Poems.* Edited by James Sambrook. Longman, 1994. Copyright © Pearson Education Limited 1994. Reproduced by permission of Pearson Education Limited.

DRYDEN, JOHN. *The Poems of John Dryden.* Edited by James Kinsley. Clarendon Press, 1958. Reproduced by permission of Oxford University Press.

DURRELL, LAWRENCE. *Balthazar.* E.P Dutton and Company Inc, 1960. Copyright © 1958 by Lawrence Durrell. Copyright renewed 1986 by Lawrence Durrell. Used by permission of Viking Penguin, a division of Penguin Group (USA) Inc. In the UK & Canada by permission of Faber & Faber Limited. / *The Black Book.* E.P Dutton and Company Inc, 1960. Copyright © 1959 by Lawrence Durrell. Copyright renewed 1987 by Lawrence Durrell. Reproduced by permission of the author. / *Monsieur.* The Viking Press, 1975. Copyright © 1974 by Lawrence Durrell. All rights reserved. Reproduced by permission of Faber & Faber Ltd. In the U.S. by permission of Curtis Brown Ltd. / *Quinx.* Faber and Faber, 1985. Copyright © Lawrence Durrell, 1985. Reproduced by permission of Curtis Brown Ltd. In the British Commonwealth by permission of Faber & Faber Ltd.

GUNN, THOM. *Collected Poems.* Faber and Faber, 1993. Copyright © Thom Gunn, 1954, 1957, 1961, 1965, 1971, 1976, 1982, 1992, 1993. Reproduced by permission of Faber & Faber Ltd. In the U.S. by permission of Farrar, Straus & Giroux, LLC. / *Boss Cupid.* Farrar Straus Grioux, 2000. Copright © 2000 by Thom Gunn. Reproduced by permission of Faber & Faber Ltd. In the U.S. by permission of Farrar, Straus and Giroux, LLC. / *Ben Jonson.* Penguin, U.K., 1974.

HILL, GEOFFREY. *For the Unfallen.* Andre Deutsch, 1959. Copyright © 1959 by Geoffrey Hill. All rights reserved. Reproduced by permission of Penguin Books, Ltd. In the United States by permission of Houghton Mifflin Harcourt Publishing Company. /

King Log. Andre Deutsch, 1968. Copyright © 1959, 1964, 1968 by Geoffrey Hill. All rights reserved. Reproduced by permission of Penguin Books, Ltd. In the U.S. by permission of Dufour Editions Inc. / *Mercian Hymns.* Andre Deutsch, 1971. Copyright © 1971 by Geoffrey Hill. Reproduced by permission of Penguin Books, Ltd. In the United States by permission of Houghton Mifflin Harcourt Publishing Company. / *New & Collected Poems, 1952-1992.* Copyright © 1994 by Geoffrey Hill. All rights reserved. Reproduced by permission of Penguin Books, Ltd. In the United States by permission of Houghton Mifflin Harcourt Publishing Company. / *Caanan.* Copyright © 1996 by Geoffrey Hill. All rights reserved. Reproduced by permission of Penguin Books, Ltd. In the United States by permission of Houghton Mifflin Harcourt Publishing Company. / *The Triumph of Love.* Copyright © 1998 by Geoffrey Hill. All rights reserved. Reproduced by permission of Penguin Books, Ltd. In the United States by permission of Houghton Mifflin Harcourt Publishing Company. / *Scenes from Comus.* Penguin Books, 2005. Copyright © Geoffrey Hill, 2005. Reproduced by permission of Penguin Books, Ltd. / *A Treatise of Civil Power.* Penguin Group, 2007. Copyright © 2007 Geoffrey Hill. Reproduced by permission of Penguin Books, Ltd. In the U.S. and Canada by permission of Yale University Press. / *Without Title.* Penguin Group, 2006. Copyright © 2006 Geoffrey Hill. Reproduced by permission of Penguin Books, Ltd. In the U.S. and Canada by permission of Yale University Press.

JOYCE, JAMES. *James Joyce, New and Revised Edition.* Oxford University Press, 1982. Reproduced by permission of Oxford University Press.

LARKIN, PHILIP. *Collected Poems.* Edited by Anthony Thwaite. The Marvell Press and Faber and Faber, 1988. Copyright © the Estate of Philip Larkin, 1988. Introduction and editorial matter copyright Anthony Thwaite, 1988. Reproduced by permission of Faber & Faber Ltd. In the U.S. by permission of Farrar, Straus & Giroux, LLC.

ROSSETTI, CHRISTINA. *The Complete Poems of Christina Rossetti, Volume III.* Edited by R.W. Crump. Louisiana State University Press, 1979. Copyright ©

ACKNOWLEDGEMENTS

1979, 1990 by Louisiana University Press. All rights reserved. Reproduced by permission.

SMITH, STEVIE. *Collected Poems of Stevie Smith.* New Directions, 1983. Copyright © 1972 by Stevie Smith. Reprinted by permission of New Directions Publishing Corp. / *Collected Poems of Stevie Smith.* Edited by James MacGibbon. New Directions, 1983. Copyright © 1964 by Ogden Nash. Reprinted by permission of Curtis Brown, Ltd. / *New Selected Poems of Stevie Smith.* New Directions, 1988. Copyright © 1972 by Stevie Smith. Reprinted by permission of New Directions Publishing Corp. / *Me Again: Uncollected Writings of Stevie Smith.* Farrar Straus Giroux, 1981. Edited by Jack Barbera and William McBrien. Copyright © 1981 by James MacGibbon. Reproduced by permission of Virago, an imprint of Little, Brown Book Group. In the U.S. by permission of Farrar, Straus and Giroux, LLC.

TENNYSON, ALFRED. *British Writers.* Edited by Ian Scott-Kilvert. Charles Scribner, 1981. Copyright 1979 The British council. Reproduced by permission of Gale, a part of Cengage Learning. / *The Letters of Alfred Lord Tennyson, 1871-1892, Vol.3.* Edited by Cecil Y. Lang and Edgar F. Shannon. Oxford: Clarendon Press, 1991. Reproduced by permission of Oxford University Press.

THOMAS, DYLAN. *The Collected Poems of Dylan Thomas.* New Directions, 1953. Copyright 1938, 1939, 1943, 1946 by New Directions Publishing Corporation. Copyright 1952, 1953 by Dylan Thomas. Copyright 1937, 1955, 1956, 1957 by the Trustees for the Copyrights of Dylan Thomas. Copyright renewed 1981 by Caitlin Thomas, Llewelyn Edouard Thomas, Aeronwy Bryn Thomas-Ellis & Colm Garth Thomas. Reproduced by permission of the author's literary agent. / *A Reader's Guide to Dylan Thomas.* Farrar, Straus and Cudahy, 1962. Copyright 1962. Copyright renewed 1990 by Elizabeth Tindall Layton. Reproduced by permission of Farrar, Straus and Giroux, LLC.

Contents

Subjects in Retrospective Supplement III

Introduction

MATIGNON HIGH SCHOOL LIBRARY

C. S. Lewis, the British author of such enchanting and informative books as *The Chronicles of Narnia* once said: "Literature adds to reality, it does not simply describe it. It enriches the necessary competencies that daily life requires and provides; and in this respect, it irrigates the deserts that our lives have already become." Our feeling is that these essays will help to bring readers closer to some of the finest British authors —authors that have been written about in this series before—but not for some years. The idea of this series has always been that, now and then, we should revisit some of the major authors, as research and thinking about their work is constantly under revision.

British Writers itself was originally an off-shoot of a series of monographs that appeared between 1959 and 1972, the *Minnesota Pamphlets on American Writers*. These pamphlets were incisively written and informative, treating ninety-seven American writers in a format and style that attracted a devoted following of readers. The series proved invaluable to a generation of students and teachers, who could depend on these reliable and interesting critiques of major figures. The idea of reprinting these essays occurred to Charles Scribner, Jr., an innovative publisher during the middle decades of the twentieth century. The series appeared in four volumes entitled *American Writers: A Collection of Literary Biographies* (1974). *British Writers* began with a series of essays originally published by the British Council, and regular supplements have followed. The goal of the supplements has been consistent with the original idea of the series: to provide clear, informative essays aimed at the general reader. These essays often rise to a high level of craft and critical vision, but they are meant to introduce a writer of some importance in the history of British or Anglophone literature, and to provide a sense of the scope and nature of the career under review.

The articles in our series have been written by a wide range of critics, each of whom has demonstrated a thorough knowledge of the field and a sense of literary style in his or her own writing. They have all been held to a high standard of clarity and scholarship. In these retrospective essays, the goal has always been to revisit the career of a major author in a way that sheds light on the unfolding career in the light of recent scholarship. A major author, such as William Shakespeare or James Joyce, is a moving target, so to speak. That is, their work shifts in meaning with each generation. It's difficult to keep them in view. These articles are meant to aid the reader in understanding where, at present, the critical thinking has gone with each subject.

Some of the classic authors are studied here, including Shakespeare, who is a world unto himself—it was a daring task to take him on again. Other major authors are looked at, too: Aphra Behn, John Dryden, William Cowper, Anne Radcliffe, Mary Shelley, Christina Rossetti, Tennyson and Browning, Elizabeth Gaskell, Rudyard Kipling, James Joyce, Dylan Thomas, and Philip Larkin—all of them firmly within the "classic" vein, authors who will always be of interest to readers, and who have attracted the wide attention of literary scholars and historians. We also examine some modern or contemporary writers of considerable fame, such as Stevie Smith, Geoffrey Hill, Thom Gunn, and Kazuo Ishiguro—all of them writers who have been studied at length by critics already; but they are, except for Smith and Gunn, still writing, and so their work shifts again and again, the writer's vision evolving with the times. We offer fresh takes on them here. In the case of John Le Carré, we examine a "classic" writer in the mold of popular fiction: he is perhaps the best writer of spy novels we have yet had within the body of British writers.

As ever, we have kept one purpose in mind: to present critical and biographical assessments that will bring series readers back to the texts discussed, helping them in their reading. These are all, in our view, stimulating and informative

INTRODUCTION

essays that should enable students and general readers to enter into the world of these writers in a fresh way, encouraging them on their intellectual journeys. Above all, these essays should lengthen the reading list of those wishing to expand their range of reference, and to return to these classic authors in fresh ways.

JAY PARINI

Chronology

CHRONOLOGY

Paul's: founds St. Paul's School

1509–1547 Reign of Henry VIII

1509 The king marries Catherine of Aragon

1511 Erasmus' *Praise of Folly* published

1513 Invasion by the Scots defeated at Flodden Field

1515 Wolsey appointed lord chancellor

1516 Sir Thomas More's *Utopia*

1517 Martin Luther's theses against indulgences published at Wittenberg

Henry Howard (earl of Surrey) born

1519 Charles V of Spain becomes Holy Roman Emperor

1519–1521 Magellan's voyage around the world

1525 Cardinal College, the forerunner of Christ Church, founded at Oxford

1526 Tyndale's English translation of the New Testament imported from Holland

1529 Fall of Cardinal Wolsey

Death of John Skelton

1529–1536 The "Reformation" Parliament

1531 Sir Thomas Elyot's *The Governour* published

1532 Thomas Cranmer appointed archbishop of Canterbury

Machiavelli's *The Prince*

1533 The king secretly marries Anne Boleyn

Cranmer pronounces the king's marriage with Catherine "against divine law"

1534 The Act of Supremacy constitutes the king as head of the Church of England

1535 Sir Thomas More executed

Thomas Cromwell appointed vicar general of the Church of England

1536 The Pilgrimage of Grace: risings against the king's religious, social, and economic reforms

Anne Boleyn executed

The king marries Jane Seymour

1537 The dissolution of the monasteries: confiscation of ecclesiastical properties and assets; increase in royal revenues

Jane Seymour dies

1538 First complete English Bible published and placed in all churches

1540 The king marries Anne of Cleves

Marriage dissolved

The king marries Catherine Howard

Fall and execution of Thomas Cromwell

1542 Catherine Howard executed

Death of Sir Thomas Wyatt

1543 The king marries Catherine Parr

Copernicus' *De revolutionibus orbium coelestium*

1546 Trinity College, Cambridge, refounded

1547 The earl of Surrey executed

1547–1553 Reign of Edward VI

1548–1552 Hall's *Chronicle*

1552 The second Book of Common Prayer

ca. 1552 Edmund Spenser born

1553 Lady Jane Grey proclaimed queen

1553–1558 Reign of Mary I (Mary Tudor)

ca. 1554 Births of Walter Raleigh, Richard Hooker, John Lyly, and Fulke Greville

1554 Lady Jane Grey executed

Mary I marries Philip II of Spain

Bandello's *Novelle*

Philip Sidney born

ca. 1556 George Peele born

1557 Tottel's *Miscellany*, including the poems of Wyatt and Surrey, published

ca. 1558 Thomas Kyd born

1558 Calais, the last English possession in France, is lost

Birth of Robert Greene

Mary I dies

1558–1603 Reign of Elizabeth I

1559 John Knox arrives in Scotland

Rebellion against the French regent

ca. 1559 George Chapman born

1561 Mary Queen of Scots (Mary Stuart) arrives in Edinburgh

Thomas Hoby's translation of Castiglione's *The Courtier Gorboduc*, the first English play in blank verse

Francis Bacon born

1562 Civil war in France

English expedition sent to support the Huguenots

1562–1568 Sir John Hawkins' voyages to Africa

1564 Births of Christopher Marlowe and **William Shakespeare**

CHRONOLOGY

1565   Mary Queen of Scots marries Lord Darnley

1566   William Painter's *Palace of Pleasure*, a miscellany of prose stories, the source of many dramatists' plots

1567   Darnley murdered at Kirk o'Field

Mary Queen of Scots marries the earl of Bothwell

1569   Rebellion of the English northern earls suppressed

1570   Roger Ascham's *The Schoolmaster*

1571   Defeat of the Turkish fleet at Lepanto

ca. 1572   Ben Jonson born

1572   St. Bartholomew's Day massacre

John Donne born

1574   The earl of Leicester's theater company formed

1576   The Theater, the first permanent theater building in London, opened

The first Blackfriars Theater opened with performances by the Children of St. Paul's

John Marston born

1576–1578   Martin Frobisher's voyages to Labrador and the northwest

1577–1580   Sir Francis Drake sails around the world

1577   Holinshed's *Chronicles of England, Scotlande, and Irelande*

1579   John Lyly's *Euphues: The Anatomy of Wit*

Thomas North's translation of *Plutarch's Lives*

1581   The Levant Company founded

Seneca's *Ten Tragedies* translated

1582   Richard Hakluyt's *Divers Voyages Touching the Discoverie of America*

1583   Philip Massinger born

1584–1585   Sir John Davis' first voyage to Greenland

1585   First English settlement in America, the "Lost Colony" comprising 108 men under Ralph Lane, founded at Roanoke Island, off the coast of North Carolina

1586   Kyd's *Spanish Tragedy*

Marlowe's *Tamburlaine*

William Camden's *Britannia*

The Babington conspiracy against Queen Elizabeth

Death of Sir Philip Sidney

1587   Mary Queen of Scots executed

Birth of Virginia Dare, first English child born in America, at Roanoke Island

1588   Defeat of the Spanish Armada

Marlowe's *Dr. Faustus*

1590   Spenser's *The Faerie Queen*, Cantos 1–3

Richard Brome born

1592   Outbreak of plague in London; the theaters closed

Henry King born

1593   Death of Christopher Marlowe

1594   The Lord Chamberlain's Men, the company to which Shakespeare belonged, founded

The Swan Theater opened

Death of Thomas Kyd

1595   Ralegh's expedition to Guiana

Sidney's *Apology for Poetry*

1596   The earl of Essex's expedition captures Cadiz

The second Blackfriars Theater opened

ca. 1597   Death of George Peele

1597   Bacon's first collection of *Essays*

1598   Jonson's *Every Man in His Humor*

1598–1600   Richard Hakluyt's *Principal Navigations, Voyages, Traffics, and Discoveries of the English Nation*

1599   The Globe Theater opened

Death of Edmund Spenser

1600   Death of Richard Hooker

1601   Rebellion and execution of the earl of Essex

1602   The East India Company founded

The Bodleian Library reopened at Oxford

1603–1625   Reign of James I

1603   John Florio's translation of Montaigne's *Essays*

Cervantes' *Don Quixote* (Part 1)

The Gunpowder Plot

Thomas Browne born

1604   Shakespeare's *Othello*

ca. 1605   Shakespears's *King Lear*

Tourneur's *The Revenger's Tragedy*

1605   Bacon's *Advancement of Learning*

1606   Shakespeare's *Macbeth*

Jonson's *Volpone*

Death of John Lyly

Edmund Waller born

1607   The first permanent English colony

xiii

CHRONOLOGY

established at Jamestown, Virginia

1608   John Milton born

1609   Kepler's *Astronomia nova*

John Suckling born

1610   Galileo's *Sidereus nuncius*

1611   The Authorized Version of the Bible

Shakespeare's *The Tempest*

1612   Death of Prince Henry, King James's eldest son

Webster's *The White Devil*

Bacon's second collection of *Essays*

ca. 1613   Richard Crashaw born

1613   The Globe Theatre destroyed by fire

Webster's *The Duchess of Malfi*

1614   Ralegh's *History of the World*

1616   George Chapman's translation of Homer's *Odyssey*

Deaths of **William Shakespeare, Francis Beaumont, and Miguel Cervantes**

ca. 1618   Richard Lovelace born

1618   The Thirty Years' War begins

Sir Walter Ralegh executed

Abraham Cowley born

1619   The General Assembly, the first legislative assembly on American soil, meets in Virginia

Slavery introduced at Jamestown

1620   The Pilgrims land in Massachusetts

John Evelyn born

1621   Francis Bacon impeached and fined

Robert Burton's *Anatomy of Melancholy*

Andrew Marvell born

1622   Middleton's *The Changeling*

Henry Vaughan born

1623   The First Folio of Shakespeare's plays

Visit of Prince Charles and the duke of Buckingham to Spain; failure of attempts to negotiate a Spanish marriage

1624   War against Spain

1625–1649   Reign of Charles I

1625   Death of John Fletcher

Bacon's last collection of *Essays*

1626   Bacon's *New Atlantis*, appended to *Sylva sylvarum*

Dutch found New Amsterdam

Death of Cyril Tourneur

Death of Francis Bacon

1627   Ford's *'Tis Pity She's a Whore*

Cardinal Richelieu establishes the

Company of New France with monopoly over trade and land in Canada

Buckingham's expedition to the Isle of Ré to relieve La Rochelle

Death of Thomas Middleton

1627–1628   Revolt and siege of La Rochelle, the principal Huguenot city of France

1628   Buckingham assassinated

Surrender of La Rochelle

William Harvey's treatise on the circulation of the blood (*De motu cordis et sanguinis*)

John Bunyan born

Death of Fulke Greville

1629   Ford's *The Broken Heart*

King Charles dismisses his third Parliament, imprisons nine members, and proceeds to rule for eleven years without Parliament

The Massachusetts Bay Company formed

1629–1630   Peace treaties with France and Spain

1631   **John Dryden born**

Death of John Donne

1633   William Laud appointed archbishop of Canterbury

Death of George Herbert

Samuel Pepys born

1634   Deaths of George Chapman and John Marston

1635   The Académie Française founded

George Etherege born

1636   Pierre Corneille's *Le Cid*

Harvard College founded

ca. 1637   Thomas Traherne born

1637   Milton's "Lycidas"

Descartes's *Discours de la méthode*

King Charles's levy of ship money challenged in the courts by John Hampden

The introduction of the new English Book of Common Prayer strongly opposed in Scotland

Death of Ben Jonson

ca. 1638   Death of John Webster

1638   The Scots draw up a National Covenant to defend their religion

ca. 1639   Death of John Ford

CHRONOLOGY

1565 Mary Queen of Scots marries Lord
Darnley

1566 William Painter's *Palace of Pleasure*, a miscellany of prose stories, the source of many dramatists' plots

1567 Darnley murdered at Kirk o'Field

Mary Queen of Scots marries the earl of Bothwell

1569 Rebellion of the English northern earls suppressed

1570 Roger Ascham's *The Schoolmaster*

1571 Defeat of the Turkish fleet at Lepanto

ca. 1572 Ben Jonson born

1572 St. Bartholomew's Day massacre

John Donne born

1574 The earl of Leicester's theater company formed

1576 The Theater, the first permanent theater building in London, opened

The first Blackfriars Theater opened with performances by the Children of St. Paul's

John Marston born

1576–1578 Martin Frobisher's voyages to Labrador and the northwest

1577–1580 Sir Francis Drake sails around the world

1577 Holinshed's *Chronicles of England, Scotlande, and Irelande*

1579 John Lyly's *Euphues: The Anatomy of Wit*

Thomas North's translation of *Plutarch's Lives*

1581 The Levant Company founded

Seneca's *Ten Tragedies* translated

1582 Richard Hakluyt's *Divers Voyages Touching the Discoverie of America*

1583 Philip Massinger born

1584–1585 Sir John Davis' first voyage to Greenland

1585 First English settlement in America, the "Lost Colony" comprising 108 men under Ralph Lane, founded at Roanoke Island, off the coast of North Carolina

1586 Kyd's *Spanish Tragedy*

Marlowe's *Tamburlaine*

William Camden's *Britannia*

The Babington conspiracy against Queen Elizabeth

Death of Sir Philip Sidney

1587 Mary Queen of Scots executed

Birth of Virginia Dare, first English child born in America, at Roanoke Island

1588 Defeat of the Spanish Armada

Marlowe's *Dr. Faustus*

1590 Spenser's *The Faerie Queen*, Cantos 1–3

Richard Brome born

1592 Outbreak of plague in London; the theaters closed

Henry King born

1593 Death of Christopher Marlowe

1594 The Lord Chamberlain's Men, the company to which Shakespeare belonged, founded

The Swan Theater opened

Death of Thomas Kyd

1595 Ralegh's expedition to Guiana

Sidney's *Apology for Poetry*

1596 The earl of Essex's expedition captures Cadiz

The second Blackfriars Theater opened

ca. 1597 Death of George Peele

1597 Bacon's first collection of *Essays*

1598 Jonson's *Every Man in His Humor*

1598–1600 Richard Hakluyt's *Principal Navigations, Voyages, Traffics, and Discoveries of the English Nation*

1599 The Globe Theater opened

Death of Edmund Spenser

1600 Death of Richard Hooker

1601 Rebellion and execution of the earl of Essex

1602 The East India Company founded

The Bodleian Library reopened at Oxford

1603–1625 Reign of James I

1603 John Florio's translation of Montaigne's *Essays*

Cervantes' *Don Quixote* (Part 1)

The Gunpowder Plot

Thomas Browne born

1604 Shakespeare's *Othello*

ca. 1605 Shakespears's *King Lear*

Tourneur's *The Revenger's Tragedy*

1605 Bacon's *Advancement of Learning*

1606 Shakespeare's *Macbeth*

Jonson's *Volpone*

Death of John Lyly

Edmund Waller born

1607 The first permanent English colony

CHRONOLOGY

CHRONOLOGY

1639 Parliament reassembled to raise
taxes
Death of Thomas Carew
Charles Sedley born

1639–1640 The two Bishops' Wars with
Scotland

1640 The Long Parliament assembled
The king's advisers, Archbishop
Laud and the earl of Strafford,
impeached
Aphra Behn born
Death of Philip Massinger

1641 Strafford executed
Acts passed abolishing extraparlia-
mentary taxation, the king's
extraordinary courts, and his power
to order a dissolution without
parliamentary consent
The Grand Remonstrance censuring
royal policy passed by eleven votes
William Wycherley born

1642 Parliament submits the nineteen
Propositions, which King Charles
rejects as annihilating the royal
power
The Civil War begins
The theaters close
Royalist victory at Edgehill; King
Charles established at Oxford
Death of Sir John Suckling

1643 Parliament concludes the Solemn
League and Covenant with the
Scots
Louis XIV becomes king of France
Charles Sackville, earl of Dorset,
born

1644 Parliamentary victory at Marston
Moor
The New Model army raised
Milton's *Areopagitica*

1645 Parliamentary victory under Fairfax
and Cromwell at Naseby
Fairfax captures Bristol
Archbishop Laud executed

1646 Fairfax besieges King Charles at
Oxford
King Charles takes refuge in
Scotland; end of the First Civil War
King Charles attempts negotiations
with the Scots
Parliament's proposals sent to the
king and rejected

1647 Conflict between Parliament and the
army
A general council of the army
established that discusses
representational government within
the army
The Agreement of the People drawn
up by the Levelers; its proposals
include manhood suffrage
King Charles concludes an agreement with the Scots
George Fox begins to preach
John Wilmot, earl of Rochester,
born

1648 Cromwell dismisses the general
council of the army
The Second Civil War begins
Fairfax defeats the Kentish royalists
at Maidstone
Cromwell defeats the Scots at Pre-
ston
The Thirty Years' War ended by the
treaty of Westphalia
Parliament purged by the army

1649–1660 Commonwealth

1649 King Charles I tried and executed
The monarchy and the House of
Lords abolished
The Commonwealth proclaimed
Cromwell invades Ireland and
defeats the royalist Catholic forces
Death of Richard Crashaw

1650 Cromwell defeats the Scots at Dunbar

1651 Charles II crowned king of the
Scots, at Scone
Charles II invades England, is
defeated at Worcester, escapes to
France
Thomas Hobbes's *Leviathan*

1652 War with Holland
Death of Richard Brome

1653 The Rump Parliament dissolved by
the army
A new Parliament and council of
state nominated; Cromwell becomes
Lord Protector
Walton's *The Compleat Angler*

1654 Peace concluded with Holland
War against Spain

1655 Parliament attempts to reduce the

army and is dissolved

Rule of the major-generals

1656 Sir William Davenant produces *The Siege of Rhodes*, one of the first English operas

1657 Second Parliament of the Protectorate

Cromwell is offered and declines the throne

Death of Richard Lovelace

1658 Death of Oliver Cromwell

Richard Cromwell succeeds as Protector

1659 Conflict between Parliament and the army

1660 General Monck negotiates with Charles II

Charles II offers the conciliatory Declaration of Breda and accepts Parliament's invitation to return

Will's Coffee House established

Sir William Davenant and Thomas Killigrew licensed to set up two companies of players, the Duke of York's and the King's Servants, including actors and actresses

Pepys's *Diary* begun

1660–1685 Reign of Charles II

1661 Parliament passes the Act of Uniformity, enjoining the use of the Book of Common Prayer; many Puritan and dissenting clergy leave their livings

Anne Finch born

1662 Peace Treaty with Spain

King Charles II marries Catherine of Braganza

The Royal Society incorporated (founded in 1660)

1664 War against Holland

New Amsterdam captured and becomes New York

John Vanbrugh born

1665 The Great Plague

Newton discovers the binomial theorem and invents the integral and differential calculus, at Cambridge

1666 The Great Fire of London

Bunyan's *Grace Abounding*

London Gazette founded

1667 The Dutch fleet sails up the Medway and burns English ships

The war with Holland ended by the Treaty of Breda

Milton's *Paradise Lost*

Thomas Sprat's *History of the Royal Society*

Death of Abraham Cowley

1668 Sir Christopher Wren begins to rebuild St. Paul's Cathedral

Triple Alliance formed with Holland and Sweden against France

Dryden's *Essay of Dramatick Poesy*

1670 Alliance formed with France through the secret Treaty of Dover

Pascal's *Pensées*

The Hudson's Bay Company founded

William Congreve born

1671 Milton's *Samson Agonistes* and *Paradise Regained*

1672 War against Holland

Wycherley's *The Country Wife*

King Charles issues the Declaration of Indulgence, suspending penal laws against Nonconformists and Catholics

1673 Parliament passes the Test Act, making acceptance of the doctrines of the Church of England a condition for holding public office

1674 War with Holland ended by the Treaty of Westminster

Deaths of John Milton, Robert Herrick, and Thomas Traherne

1676 Etherege's *The Man of Mode*

1677 Baruch Spinoza's *Ethics*

Jean Racine's *Phèdre*

King Charles's niece, Mary, marries her cousin William of Orange

1678 Fabrication of the so-called popish plot by Titus Oates

Bunyan's *Pilgrim's Progress*

Dryden's *All for Love*

Death of Andrew Marvell

George Farquhar born

1679 Parliament passes the Habeas Corpus Act

Rochester's *A Satire Against Mankind*

1680 Death of John Wilmot, earl of Rochester

1681 Dryden's *Absalom and Achitophel* (Part 1)

CHRONOLOGY

CHRONOLOGY

CHRONOLOGY

Franklin's experiments with electricity announced

Voltaire's *Essai sur les moeurs*

1748 War of the Austrian Succession ended by the Peace of Aix-la-Chapelle

Smollett's *Adventures of Roderick Random*

David Hume's *Enquiry Concerning Human Understanding*

Montesquieu's *L'Esprit des lois*

1749 Fielding's *Tom Jones*

Johnson's *The Vanity of Human Wishes*

Bolingbroke's *Idea of a Patriot King*

1750 The *Rambler* founded (1750–1752)

1751 Gray's *Elegy Written in a Country Churchyard*

Fielding's *Amelia*

Smollett's *Adventures of Peregrine Pickle*

Denis Diderot and Jean le Rond d'Alembert begin to publish the *Encyclopédie* (1751–1765)

Richard Brinsley Sheridan born

1752 Frances Burney and Thomas Chatterton born

1753 Richardson's *History of Sir Charles Grandison* (1753–1754)

Smollett's *The Adventures of Ferdinand Count Fathom*

Birth of Elizabeth Inchbald

1754 Hume's *History of England* (1754–1762)

Death of Henry Fielding

George Crabbe born

1755 Lisbon destroyed by earthquake

Fielding's *Journal of a Voyage to Lisbon* published posthumously

Johnson's *Dictionary of the English Language*

1756 The Seven Years' War against France, 1756–1763 (the French and Indian War in America, 1755–1760)

William Pitt the elder becomes prime minister

Johnson's proposal for an edition of Shakespeare

Death of Eliza Haywood

Birth of William Godwin

1757 Robert Clive wins the battle of Plassey, in India

Gray's "The Progress of Poesy" and "The Bard"

Burke's *Philosophical Enquiry into the Origin of Our Ideas of the Sublime and Beautiful*

Hume's *Natural History of Religion*

William Blake born

1758 The *Idler* founded (1758–1760)

Mary Darby Robinson born

1759 Capture of Quebec by General James Wolfe

Johnson's *History of Rasselas, Prince of Abyssinia*

Voltaire's *Candide*

The British Museum opens

Sterne's *The Life and Opinions of Tristram Shandy* (1759–1767)

Death of William Collins

Mary Wollstonecraft born

Robert Burns born

1760–1820 Reign of George III

1760 James Macpherson's *Fragments of Ancient Poetry Collected in the Highlands of Scotland*

William Beckford born

1761 Jean-Jacques Rousseau's *Julie, ou la nouvelle Héloïse*

Death of Samuel Richardson

1762 Rousseau's *Du Contrat social* and *Émile*

Catherine the Great becomes czarina of Russia (1762–1796)

1763 The Seven Years' War ended by the Peace of Paris

Smart's *A Song to David*

1764 James Hargreaves invents the spinning jenny

Ann Radcliffe born

1765 Parliament passes the Stamp Act to tax the American colonies

Johnson's edition of Shakespeare

Walpole's *The Castle of Otranto*

Thomas Percy's *Reliques of Ancient English Poetry*

Blackstone's *Commentaries on the Laws of England* (1765–1769)

1766 The Stamp Act repealed

Swift's *Journal to Stella* first published in a collection of his letters

CHRONOLOGY

CHRONOLOGY

John Gilpin" published in the *Public Advertiser*

Choderlos de Laclos's *Les Liaisons dangereuses*

Rousseau's *Confessions* published posthumously

1783 American War of Independence ended by the Definitive Treaty of Peace, signed at Paris

William Blake's *Poetical Sketches*

George Crabbe's *The Village*

William Pitt the younger becomes prime minister

Henri Beyle (Stendhal) born

1784 Beaumarchais's *Le Mariage de Figaro* first performed (published 1785)

Death of Samuel Johnson

1785 Warren Hastings returns to England from India

James Boswell's *The Journey of a Tour of the Hebrides, with Samuel Johnson, LL.D.*

Cowper's *The Task*

Edmund Cartwright invents the power loom

Thomas De Quincey born

Thomas Love Peacock born

1786 William Beckford's *Vathek* published in English (originally written in French in 1782)

Robert Burns's *Poems Chiefly in the Scottish Dialect*

Wolfgang Amadeus Mozart's *The Marriage of Figaro*

Death of Frederick the Great

1787 The Committee for the Abolition of the Slave Trade founded in England

The Constitutional Convention meets at Philadelphia; the Constitution is signed

1788 The trial of Hastings begins on charges of corruption of the government in India

The Estates-General of France summoned

U.S. Constitution is ratified

George Washington elected president of the United States

Giovanni Casanova's *Histoire de ma fuite* (first manuscript of his memoirs)

The *Daily Universal Register* becomes the *Times* (London)

George Gordon, Lord Byron born

1789 The Estates-General meets at Versailles

The National Assembly (Assemblée Nationale) convened

The fall of the Bastille marks the beginning of the French Revolution

The National Assembly draws up the Declaration of Rights of Man and of the Citizen

First U.S. Congress meets in New York

Blake's *Songs of Innocence*

Jeremy Bentham's *Introduction to the Principles of Morals and Legislation* introduces the theory of utilitarianism

Gilbert White's *Natural History of Selborne*

1790 Congress sets permanent capital city site on the Potomac River

First U.S. Census

Burke's *Reflections on the Revolution in France*

Blake's *The Marriage of Heaven and Hell*

Edmund Malone's edition of Shakespeare

Wollstonecraft's *A Vindication of the Rights of Man*

Death of Benjamin Franklin

1791 French royal family's flight from Paris and capture at Varennes; imprisonment in the Tuileries

Bill of Rights is ratified

Paine's *The Rights of Man* (1791–1792)

Boswell's *The Life of Johnson*

Burns's *Tam o'Shanter*

The *Observer* founded

1792 The Prussians invade France and are repulsed at Valmy September massacres

The National Convention declares royalty abolished in France

Washington reelected president of the United States

CHRONOLOGY

New York Stock Exchange opens
Mary Wollstonecraft's *Vindication of the Rights of Woman*
William Bligh's voyage to the South Sea in H.M.S. *Bounty*
Percy Bysshe Shelley born

1793 Trial and execution of Louis XVI and Marie-Antoinette
France declares war against England
The Committee of Public Safety (Comité de Salut Public) established
Eli Whitney devises the cotton gin
William Godwin's *An Enquiry Concerning Political Justice*
Blake's *Visions of the Daughters of Albion and America*
Wordsworth's *An Evening Walk* and *Descriptive Sketches*
John Clare born

1794 Execution of Georges Danton and Maximilien de Robespierre
Paine's *The Age of Reason* (1794–1796)
Blake's *Songs of Experience*
Ann Radcliffe's *The Mysteries of Udolpho*
Death of Edward Gibbon

1795 The government of the Directory established (1795–1799)
Hastings acquitted
Landor's *Poems*
Death of James Boswell
John Keats born
Thomas Carlyle born

1796 Napoleon Bonaparte takes command in Italy
Matthew Lewis' *The Monk*
John Adams elected president of the United States
Death of Robert Burns

1797 The peace of Campo Formio: extinction of the Venetian Republic
XYZ Affair
Mutinies in the Royal Navy at Spithead and the Nore
Blake's *Vala, Or the Four Zoas* (first version)
Mary Shelley born
Deaths of Edmund Burke, Mary Wollstonecraft, and Horace Walpole

1798 Napoleon invades Egypt

Horatio Nelson wins the battle of the Nile
Wordsworth's and Coleridge's *Lyrical Ballads*
Landor's *Gebir*
Thomas Malthus' *Essay on the Principle of Population*

1799 Napoleon becomes first consul
Pitt introduces first income tax in Great Britain
Sheridan's *Pizarro*
Honoré de Balzac, Thomas Hood, and Alexander Pushkin born

1800 Thomas Jefferson elected president of the United States
Alessandro Volta produces electricity from a cell
Library of Congress established
Death of **William Cowper and Mary Darby Robinson**
Marie Jane Jewsbury and Thomas Babington Macaulay born

1801 First census taken in England

1802 The Treaty of Amiens marks the end of the French Revolutionary War
The *Edinburgh Review* founded
England's war with France renewed
The Louisiana Purchase
Robert Fulton propels a boat by steam power on the Seine
Birth of Thomas Lovell Beddoes
George Borrow and James Clarence Mangan

1804 Napoleon crowned emperor of the French
Jefferson reelected president of the United States
Blake's *Milton* (1804–1808) and *Jerusalem*
The Code Napoleon promulgated in France
Beethoven's *Eroica* Symphony
Schiller's *Wilhelm Tell*
Benjamin Disraeli born

1805 Napoleon plans the invasion of England
Battle of Trafalgar
Battle of Austerlitz
Beethoven's *Fidelio* first produced
Scott's *Lay of the Last Minstrel*

CHRONOLOGY

1806   Scott's *Marmion*
Death of William Pitt
Death of Charles James Fox
Elizabeth Barrett born

1807   France invades Portugal
Aaron Burr tried for treason and acquitted
Byron's *Hours of Idleness*
Charles and Mary Lamb's *Tales from Shakespeare*
Thomas Moore's *Irish Melodies*
Wordsworth's *Ode on the Intimations of Immortality*

1808   National uprising in Spain against the French invasion
The Peninsular War begins
James Madison elected president of the United States
Covent Garden theater burned down
Goethe's *Faust* (Part 1)
Beethoven's Fifth Symphony completed
Lamb's *Specimens of English Dramatic Poets*

1809   Drury Lane theater burned down and rebuilt
The *Quarterly Review* founded
Byron's *English Bards and Scotch Reviewers*
Byron sails for the Mediterranean
Goya's *Los Desastres de la guerra* (1809–1814)
Edward Fitzgerald, **Alfred Tennyson born**

1810   Crabbe's *The Borough*
Scott's *The Lady of the Lake*
Elizabeth Gaskell born

1811–1820   Regency of George IV

1811   Luddite Riots begin
Coleridge's *Lectures on Shakespeare* (1811–1814)
Jane Austen's *Sense and Sensibility*
Shelley's *The Necessity of Atheism*
John Constable's *Dedham Vale*
William Makepeace Thackeray born

1812   Napoleon invades Russia; captures and retreats from Moscow
United States declares war against England
Henry Bell's steamship *Comet* is launched on the Clyde river
Madison reelected president of the United States
Byron's *Childe Harold* (Cantos 1–2)
The Brothers Grimm's *Fairy Tales* (1812–1815)
Hegel's *Science of Logic*
Charles Dickens, **Robert Browning born**

1813   Wellington wins the battle of Vitoria and enters France
Jane Austen's *Pride and Prejudice*
Byron's *The Giaour* and *The Bride of Abydos*
Shelley's *Queen Mab*
Southey's *Life of Nelson*

1814   Napoleon abdicates and is exiled to Elba; Bourbon restoration with Louis XVIII
Treaty of Ghent ends the war between Britain and the United States
Jane Austen's *Mansfield Park*
Byron's *The Corsair* and *Lara*
Scott's *Waverley*
Wordsworth's *The Excursion*

1815   Napoleon returns to France (the Hundred Days); is defeated at Waterloo and exiled to St. Helena
U.S.S. *Fulton*, the first steam warship, built
Scott's *Guy Mannering*
Schlegel's *Lectures on Dramatic Art and Literature* translated
Wordsworth's *The White Doe of Rylstone*
Anthony Trollope born

1816   Byron leaves England permanently
The Elgin Marbles exhibited in the British Museum
James Monroe elected president of the United States
Jane Austen's *Emma*
Byron's *Childe Harold* (Canto 3)
Coleridge's *Christabel, Kubla Khan: A Vision, The Pains of Sleep*
Benjamin Constant's *Adolphe*
Goethe's *Italienische Reise*
Peacock's *Headlong Hall*
Scott's *The Antiquary*

CHRONOLOGY

CHRONOLOGY

Scott's *Quentin Durward*

Death of Ann Radcliffe

1824 The National Gallery opened in London

John Quincy Adams elected president of the United States

The *Westminster Review* founded

Beethoven's Ninth Symphony first performed

William (Wilkie) Collins born

James Hogg's *The Private Memoirs and Confessions of a Justified Sinner*

Landor's *Imaginary Conversations* (1824–1829)

Scott's *Redgauntlet*

Death of George Gordon, Lord Byron

1825 Inauguration of steam-powered passenger and freight service on the Stockton and Darlington railway

Bolivia and Brazil become independent Alessandro Manzoni's *I Promessi Sposi* (1825–1826)

1826 André-Marie Ampère's *Mémoire sur la théorie mathématique des phénomènes électrodynamiques*

James Fenimore Cooper's *The Last of the Mohicans*

Disraeli's *Vivian Grey* (1826–1827)

Scott's *Woodstock*

1827 The battle of Navarino ensures the independence of Greece

Josef Ressel obtains patent for the screw propeller for steamships

Heinrich Heine's *Buch der Lieder*

Death of William Blake

1828 Andrew Jackson elected president of the United States

Births of Henrik Ibsen, George Meredith, Margaret Oliphant, Dante Gabriel Rossetti, and Leo Tolstoy

1829 The Catholic Emancipation Act

Robert Peel establishes the metropolitan police force

Greek independence recognized by Turkey

Balzac begins *La Comédie humaine* (1829–1848)

Peacock's *The Misfortunes of Elphin*

J. M. W. Turner's *Ulysses Deriding Polyphemus*

1830–1837 Reign of William IV

1830 Charles X of France abdicates and is succeeded by Louis-Philippe

The Liverpool-Manchester railway opened

Tennyson's *Poems, Chiefly Lyrical*

Death of William Hazlitt

Christina Rossetti born

1831 Michael Faraday discovers electromagnetic induction

Charles Darwin's voyage on H.M.S. *Beagle* begins (1831–1836)

The Barbizon school of artists' first exhibition

Nat Turner slave revolt crushed in Virginia

Peacock's *Crotchet Castle*

Stendhal's *Le Rouge et le noir*

Edward Trelawny's *The Adventures of a Younger Son*

Isabella Bird born

1832 The first Reform Bill

Samuel Morse invents the telegraph

Jackson reelected president of the United States

Disraeli's *Contarini Fleming*

Goethe's *Faust* (Part 2)

Tennyson's *Poems, Chiefly Lyrical*, including "The Lotus-Eaters" and "The Lady of Shalott"

Death of Johann Wolfgang von Goethe

Death of Sir Walter Scott

Lewis Carroll born

1833 Robert Browning's *Pauline*

John Keble launches the Oxford Movement

American Anti-Slavery Society founded

Lamb's *Last Essays of Elia*

Carlyle's *Sartor Resartus* (1833–1834)

Pushkin's *Eugene Onegin*

Mendelssohn's *Italian Symphony* first performed

Death of Maria Jane Jewsbury

1834 Abolition of slavery in the British Empire

Louis Braille's alphabet for the

CHRONOLOGY

blind

Balzac's *Le Père Goriot*

Nikolai Gogol's *Dead Souls* (Part 1, 1834–1842)

Death of Samuel Taylor Coleridge

Death of Charles Lamb

William Morris born

1835 Hans Christian Andersen's *Fairy Tales* (1st ser.)

Robert Browning's *Paracelsus*

Births of Samuel Butler and Mary Elizabeth Braddon

Alexis de Tocqueville's *De la Democratie en Amerique* (1835–1840)

Death of James Hogg

1836 Martin Van Buren elected president of the United States

Dickens' *Sketches by Boz* (1836–1837)

Landor's *Pericles and Aspasia*

Death of William Godwin

1837–1901 Reign of Queen Victoria

1837 Carlyle's *The French Revolution*

Dickens' *Oliver Twist* (1837–1838) and *Pickwick Papers*

Disraeli's *Venetia* and *Henrietta Temple*

1838 Chartist movement in England

National Gallery in London opened

Elizabeth Barrett Browning's *The Seraphim and Other Poems*

Dickens' *Nicholas Nickleby* (1838–1839)

1839 Louis Daguerre perfects process for producing an image on a silver-coated copper plate Faraday's *Experimental Researches in Electricity* (1839–1855)

First Chartist riots

Opium War between Great Britain and China

Carlyle's *Chartism*

1840 Canadian Act of Union

Queen Victoria marries Prince Albert

Charles Barry begins construction of the Houses of Parliament (1840–1852)

William Henry Harrison elected president of the United States

Robert Browning's *Sordello*

Thomas Hardy and John Addington Symonds born

1841 New Zealand proclaimed a British colony

James Clark Ross discovers the Antarctic continent

Punch founded

John Tyler succeeds to the presidency after the death of Harrison

Carlyle's *Heroes and Hero-Worship*

Dickens' *The Old Curiosity Shop*

1842 Chartist riots

Income tax revived in Great Britain

The Mines Act, forbidding work underground by women or by children under the age of ten

Charles Edward Mudie's Lending Library founded in London

Dickens visits America

Robert Browning's *Dramatic Lyrics*

Macaulay's *Lays of Ancient Rome*

Tennyson's *Poems*, including "Morte d'Arthur," "St. Simeon Stylites," and "Ulysses"

Wordsworth's *Poems*

1843 Marc Isambard Brunel's Thames tunnel opened

The Economist founded

Carlyle's *Past and Present*

Dickens' *A Christmas Carol*

John Stuart Mill's *Logic*

Macaulay's *Critical and Historical Essays*

John Ruskin's *Modern Painters* (1843–1860)

1844 Rochdale Society of Equitable Pioneers, one of the first consumers' cooperatives, founded by twenty-eight Lancashire weavers

James K. Polk elected president of the United States

Elizabeth Barrett Browning's *Poems*, including "The Cry of the Children"

Dickens' *Martin Chuzzlewit*

Disraeli's *Coningsby*

Turner's *Rain, Steam and Speed*

Edward Carpenter and Gerard Manley Hopkins born

CHRONOLOGY

CHRONOLOGY

CHRONOLOGY

Wonderland
Dickens' *Our Mutual Friend*
Meredith's *Rhoda Fleming*
A. C. Swinburne's *Atalanta in Calydon*
Arthur Symons born
Death of **Elizabeth Gaskell**

1866 First successful transatlantic telegraph cable laid
George Eliot's *Felix Holt, the Radical*
Elizabeth Gaskell's *Wives and Daughters*
Beatrix Potter born
Swinburne's *Poems and Ballads*

1867 The second Reform Bill
Arnold's *New Poems*
Bagehot's *The English Constitution*
Carlyle's *Shooting Niagara*
Marx's *Das Kapital* (vol. 1)
Trollope's *The Last Chronicle of Barset*
George William Russell (AE) born

1868 Gladstone becomes prime minister (1868–1874)
Johnson impeached by House of Representatives; acquitted by Senate
Ulysses S. Grant elected president of the United States
Robert Browning's *The Ring and the Book* (1868–1869)
Collins' *The Moonstone*

1869 The Suez Canal opened
Girton College, Cambridge, founded
Arnold's *Culture and Anarchy*
Mill's *The Subjection of Women*
Trollope's *Phineas Finn*

1870 The Elementary Education Act establishes schools under the aegis of local boards
Dickens' *Edwin Drood*
Disraeli's *Lothair*
Morris' *The Earthly Paradise*
Dante Gabriel Rossetti's *Poems*
Saki born

1871 Trade unions legalized
Newnham College, Cambridge, founded for women students
Carroll's *Through the Looking Glass*

Darwin's *The Descent of Man*
Meredith's *The Adventures of Harry Richmond*
Swinburne's *Songs Before Sunrise*
William H. Davies born

1872 Max Beerbohm born
Samuel Butler's *Erewhon*
George Eliot's *Middlemarch*
Grant reelected president of the United States
Hardy's *Under the Greenwood Tree*

1873 Arnold's *Literature and Dogma*
Mill's *Autobiography*
Pater's *Studies in the History of the Renaissance*
Trollope's *The Eustace Diamonds*
Dorothy Richardson born

1874 Disraeli becomes prime minister
Hardy's *Far from the Madding Crowd*
James Thomson's *The City of Dreadful Night*

1875 Britain buys Suez Canal shares
Trollope's *The Way We Live Now*
T. F. Powys born

1876 F. H. Bradley's *Ethical Studies*
George Eliot's *Daniel Deronda*
Henry James's *Roderick Hudson*
Meredith's *Beauchamp's Career*
Morris' *Sigurd the Volsung*
Trollope's *The Prime Minister*
Death of Harriet Martineau
Birth of Flora Thompson

1877 Rutherford B. Hayes elected president of the United States after Electoral Commission awards him disputed votes
Henry James's *The American*

1878 Electric street lighting introduced in London
Hardy's *The Return of the Native*
Swinburne's *Poems and Ballads* (2d ser.)
Births of A. E. Coppard and Edward Thomas

1879 Somerville College and Lady Margaret Hall opened at Oxford for women
The London telephone exchange built
Gladstone's Midlothian campaign

xxix

CHRONOLOGY

(1879–1880)
Browning's *Dramatic Idyls*
Meredith's *The Egoist*

1880 Gladstone's second term as prime minister (1880–1885)
James A. Garfield elected president of the United States
Browning's *Dramatic Idyls Second Series*
Disraeli's *Endymion*
Radclyffe Hall born
Hardy's *The Trumpet-Major*
Lytton Strachey born

1881 Garfield assassinated; Chester A. Arthur succeeds to the presidency
Henry James's *The Portrait of a Lady* and *Washington Square*
D. G. Rossetti's *Ballads and Sonnets*
P. G. Wodehouse born
Death of George Borrow

1882 Triple Alliance formed between German empire, Austrian empire, and Italy
Leslie Stephen begins to edit the *Dictionary of National Biography*
Married Women's Property Act passed in Britain
Britain occupies Egypt and the Sudan
James Joyce born

1883 Uprising of the Mahdi: Britain evacuates the Sudan
Royal College of Music opens
T. H. Green's *Ethics*
T. E. Hulme born
Stevenson's *Treasure Island*

1884 The Mahdi captures Omdurman: General Gordon appointed to command the garrison of Khartoum
Grover Cleveland elected president of the United States
The *Oxford English Dictionary* begins publishing
The Fabian Society founded
Hiram Maxim's recoil-operated machine gun invented

1885 The Mahdi captures Khartoum: General Gordon killed
Haggard's *King Solomon's Mines*
Marx's *Das Kapital* (vol. 2)

Meredith's *Diana of the Crossways*
Pater's *Marius the Epicurean*

1886 The Canadian Pacific Railway completed
Gold discovered in the Transvaal
Births of Frances Cornford, Ronald Firbank, and Charles Stansby Walter Williams
Henry James's *The Bostonians* and *The Princess Casamassima*
Stevenson's *The Strange Case of Dr. Jekyll and Mr. Hyde*

1887 Queen Victoria's Golden Jubilee
Rupert Brooke born
Haggard's *Allan Quatermain* and *She*
Hardy's *The Woodlanders*
Edwin Muir born
Death of Richard Jefferies

1888 Benjamin Harrison elected president of the United States
Henry James's *The Aspern Papers*
Kipling's *Plain Tales from the Hills*
T. E. Lawrence born

1889 Yeats's *The Wanderings of Oisin*
Death of **Robert Browning**

1890 Morris founds the Kelmscott Press
Agatha Christie born
Frazer's *The Golden Bough* (1st ed.)
Henry James's *The Tragic Muse*
Morris' *News From Nowhere*
Jean Rhys born

1891 Gissing's *New Grub Street*
Hardy's *Tess of the d'Urbervilles*
Wilde's *The Picture of Dorian Gray*

1892 Grover Cleveland elected president of the United States
Conan Doyle's *The Adventures of Sherlock Holmes*
Shaw's *Widower's Houses*
Rebecca West, Hugh MacDiarmid, and J. R. R. Tolkien born
Wilde's *Lady Windermere's Fan*
Death of **Alfred Tennyson**

1893 Wilde's *A Woman of No Importance* and *Salomé*
Vera Brittain born
Death of John Addington Symonds

1894 Kipling's *The Jungle Book*
Moore's *Esther Waters*

CHRONOLOGY

Marx's *Das Kapital* (vol. 3)
Audrey Beardsley's *The Yellow Book* begins to appear quarterly
Shaw's *Arms and the Man*
Death of **Christina Rossetti**

1895 Trial and imprisonment of Oscar Wilde
William Ramsay announces discovery of helium
The National Trust founded
Conrad's *Almayer's Folly*
Hardy's *Jude the Obscure*
Wells's *The Time Machine*
Wilde's *The Importance of Being Earnest*
Yeats's *Poems*

1896 William McKinley elected president of the United States
Failure of the Jameson Raid on the Transvaal
Housman's *A Shropshire Lad*
Edmund Blunden and Austin Clarke born

1897 Queen Victoria's Diamond Jubilee
Conrad's *The Nigger of the Narcissus*
Havelock Ellis' *Studies in the Psychology of Sex* begins publication
Henry James's *The Spoils of Poynton* and *What Maisie Knew*
Kipling's *Captains Courageous*
Shaw's *Candida*
Stoker's *Dracula*
Wells's *The Invisible Man*
Death of Margaret Oliphant
Ruth Pitter born

1898 Kitchener defeats the Mahdist forces at Omdurman: the Sudan reoccupied
Hardy's *Wessex Poems*
Henry James's *The Turn of the Screw*
C. S. Lewis born
Shaw's *Caesar and Cleopatra* and *You Never Can Tell*
Alec Waugh born
Wells's *The War of the Worlds*
Wilde's *The Ballad of Reading Gaol*

1899 The Boer War begins
Elizabeth Bowen born
Noël Coward born
Elgar's *Enigma Variations*
Kipling's *Stalky and Co.*

1900 McKinley reelected president of the United States
British Labour party founded
Boxer Rebellion in China
Reginald A. Fessenden transmits speech by wireless
First Zeppelin trial flight
Max Planck presents his first paper on the quantum theory
Conrad's *Lord Jim*
Elgar's *The Dream of Gerontius*
Sigmund Freud's *The Interpretation of Dreams*
V. S. Pritchett born
William Butler Yeats's *The Shadowy Waters*

1901–1910 Reign of King Edward VII

1901 William McKinley assassinated; Theodore Roosevelt succeeds to the presidency
First transatlantic wireless telegraph signal transmitted
Chekhov's *Three Sisters*
Freud's *Psychopathology of Everyday Life*
Rudyard Kipling's *Kim*
Thomas Mann's *Buddenbrooks*
Potter's *The Tale of Peter Rabbit*
Shaw's *Captain Brassbound's Conversion*
August Strindberg's *The Dance of Death*
Lewis Grassic Gibbon born

1902 Barrie's *The Admirable Crichton*
Arnold Bennett's *Anna of the Five Towns*
Cézanne's *Le Lac D'Annecy*
Conrad's *Heart of Darkness*
Henry James's *The Wings of the Dove*
William James's *The Varieties of Religious Experience*
Kipling's *Just So Stories*
Maugham's *Mrs. Cradock*
Stevie Smith born

CHRONOLOGY

Times Literary Supplement begins publishing

1903 At its London congress the Russian Social Democratic Party divides into Mensheviks, led by Plekhanov, and Bolsheviks, led by Lenin

The treaty of Panama places the Canal Zone in U.S. hands for a nominal rent

Motor cars regulated in Britain to a 20-mile-per-hour limit

The Wright brothers make a successful flight in the United States

Burlington magazine founded

Samuel Butler's *The Way of All Flesh* published posthumously

Cyril Connolly born

George Gissing's *The Private Papers of Henry Ryecroft*

Thomas Hardy's *The Dynasts*

Henry James's *The Ambassadors*

Alan Paton born

Shaw's *Man and Superman*

Synge's *Riders to the Sea* produced in Dublin

Yeats's *In the Seven Woods* and *On Baile's Strand*

Frank O'Connor, William Plomer, Edward Upward and John Wyndham born

1904 Roosevelt elected president of the United States

Russo-Japanese war (1904–1905)

Construction of the Panama Canal begins

The ultraviolet lamp invented

The engineering firm of Rolls Royce founded

Barrie's *Peter Pan* first performed

Births of Cecil Day Lewis and Nancy Mitford

Chekhov's *The Cherry Orchard*

Conrad's *Nostromo*

Henry James's *The Golden Bowl*

Kipling's *Traffics and Discoveries*

Georges Rouault's *Head of a Tragic Clown*

G. M. Trevelyan's *England Under the Stuarts*

Puccini's *Madame Butterfly*

First Shaw-Granville Barker season at the Royal Court Theatre

The Abbey Theatre founded in Dublin

Death of Isabella Bird

1905 Russian sailors on the battleship Potemkin mutiny

After riots and a general strike the czar concedes demands by the Duma for legislative powers, a wider franchise, and civil liberties

Albert Einstein publishes his first theory of relativity

The Austin Motor Company founded

Bennett's *Tales of the Five Towns*

Claude Debussy's *La Mer*

E. M. Forster's *Where Angels Fear to Tread*

Richard Strauss's *Salome*

H. G. Wells's *Kipps*

Oscar Wilde's *De Profundis*

Births of Norman Cameron, Henry Green, and Mary Renault

1906 Liberals win a landslide victory in the British general election

The Trades Disputes Act legitimizes peaceful picketing in Britain

Captain Dreyfus rehabilitated in France

J. J. Thomson begins research on gamma rays

The U.S. Pure Food and Drug Act passed

Churchill's *Lord Randolph Churchill*

William Empson born

Galsworthy's *The Man of Property*

Kipling's *Puck of Pook's Hill*

Shaw's *The Doctor's Dilemma*

Yeats's *Poems* 1899–1905

1907 Exhibition of cubist paintings in Paris

Henry Adams' *The Education of Henry Adams*

Henri Bergson's *Creative Evolution*

Conrad's *The Secret Agent*

Births of Barbara Comyns, Daphne du Maurier, and Christopher Fry

Forster's *The Longest Journey*

CHRONOLOGY

André Gide's *La Porte étroite*

Shaw's *John Bull's Other Island* and *Major Barbara*

Synge's *The Playboy of the Western World*

Trevelyan's *Garibaldi's Defence of the Roman Republic*

Christopher Caudwell (Christopher St. John Sprigg) born

1908 Herbert Asquith becomes prime minister

David Lloyd George becomes chancellor of the exchequer

William Howard Taft elected president of the United States

The Young Turks seize power in Istanbul

Henry Ford's Model T car produced

Bennett's *The Old Wives' Tale*

Pierre Bonnard's *Nude Against the Light*

Georges Braque's *House at L'Estaque*

Chesterton's *The Man Who Was Thursday*

Jacob Epstein's *Figures* erected in London

Forster's *A Room with a View*

Anatole France's *L'Ile des Pingouins*

Henri Matisse's *Bonheur de Vivre*

Elgar's First Symphony

Ford Madox Ford founds the *English Review*

Ian Fleming born

1909 The Young Turks depose Sultan Abdul Hamid

The Anglo-Persian Oil Company formed

Louis Bleriot crosses the English Channel from France by monoplane

Admiral Robert Peary reaches the North Pole

Freud lectures at Clark University (Worcester, Mass.) on psychoanalysis

Serge Diaghilev's Ballets Russes opens in Paris

Galsworthy's *Strife*

Hardy's *Time's Laughingstocks*

Malcolm Lowry born

Claude Monet's *Water Lilies*

Stephen Spender born

Trevelyan's *Garibaldi and the Thousand*

Wells's *Tono-Bungay* first published (book form, 1909)

1910–1936 Reign of King George V

1910 The Liberals win the British general election

Marie Curie's *Treatise on Radiography*

Arthur Evans excavates Knossos

Edouard Manet and the first post-impressionist exhibition in London

Filippo Marinetti publishes "Manifesto of the Futurist Painters"

Norman Angell's *The Great Illusion*

Bennett's *Clayhanger*

Forster's *Howards End*

Galsworthy's *Justice* and *The Silver Box*

Kipling's *Rewards and Fairies*

Norman MacCaig born

Rimsky-Korsakov's *Le Coq d'or*

Stravinsky's *The Firebird*

Vaughan Williams' *A Sea Symphony*

Wells's *The History of Mr. Polly*

Wells's *The New Machiavelli* first published (in book form, 1911)

Death of **Rudyard Kipling**

1911 Lloyd George introduces National Health Insurance Bill

Suffragette riots in Whitehall

Roald Amundsen reaches the South Pole

Bennett's *The Card*

Chagall's *Self Portrait with Seven Fingers*

Conrad's *Under Western Eyes*

D. H. Lawrence's *The White Peacock*

Katherine Mansfield's *In a German Pension*

Edward Marsh edits *Georgian Poetry*

Moore's *Hail and Farewell* (1911–1914)

Flann O'Brien born

Strauss's *Der Rosenkavalier*

CHRONOLOGY

Stravinsky's *Petrouchka*
Trevelyan's *Garibaldi and the Making of Italy*
Wells's *The New Machiavelli*
Mahler's *Das Lied von der Erde*

1912 Woodrow Wilson elected president of the United States
SS *Titanic* sinks on its maiden voyage
Five million Americans go to the movies daily; London has four hundred movie theaters
Second post-impressionist exhibition in London
Bennett's and Edward Knoblock's *Milestones*
Constantin Brancusi's *Maiastra*
Wassily Kandinsky's *Black Lines*
D. H. Lawrence's *The Trespasser*
Death of William Thomas Stead
Lawrence Durrell born

1913 Second Balkan War begins
Henry Ford pioneers factory assembly technique through conveyor belts
Epstein's *Tomb of Oscar Wilde*
New York Armory Show introduces modern art to the world
Alain Fournier's *Le Grand Meaulnes*
Freud's *Totem and Tabu*
D. H. Lawrence's *Sons and Lovers*
Mann's *Death in Venice*
Proust's *Du Côté de chez Swann* (first volume of *À la recherche du temps perdu*, 1913–1922)
Barbara Pym born
Ravel's *Daphnis and Chloé*
R.S. Thomas born

1914 The Panama Canal opens (formal dedication on 12 July 1920)
Irish Home Rule Bill passed in the House of Commons
Archduke Franz Ferdinand assassinated at Sarajevo
World War I begins
Battles of the Marne, Masurian Lakes, and Falkland Islands
Joyce's *Dubliners*
Norman Nicholson born

Shaw's *Pygmalion* and *Androcles and the Lion*
Yeats's *Responsibilities*
Wyndham Lewis publishes *Blast* magazine and *The Vorticist Manifesto*
C. H. Sisson, Patrick O'Brian, Henry Reed, and **Dylan Thomas born**

1915 The Dardanelles campaign begins
Britain and Germany begin naval and submarine blockades
The *Lusitania* is sunk
Hugo Junkers manufactures the first fighter aircraft
First Zeppelin raid in London
Brooke's *1914: Five Sonnets*
Norman Douglas' *Old Calabria*
D. W. Griffith's *The Birth of a Nation*
Gustav Holst's *The Planets*
D. H. Lawrence's *The Rainbow*
Wyndham Lewis's *The Crowd*
Maugham's *Of Human Bondage*
Pablo Picasso's *Harlequin*
Sibelius' Fifth Symphony
John Cornford and Denton Welch born

1916 Evacuation of Gallipoli and the Dardanelles
Battles of the Somme, Jutland, and Verdun
Britain introduces conscription
The Easter Rebellion in Dublin
Asquith resigns and David Lloyd George becomes prime minister
The Sykes-Picot agreement on the partition of Turkey
First military tanks used
Wilson reelected president president of the United States
Henri Barbusse's *Le Feu*
Griffith's *Intolerance*
Joyce's *Portrait of the Artist as a Young Man*
Jung's *Psychology of the Unconscious*
Moore's *The Brook Kerith*
Edith Sitwell edits *Wheels* (1916–1921)

CHRONOLOGY

Wells's *Mr. Britling Sees It Through*

1917　United States enters World War I

Czar Nicholas II abdicates

The Balfour Declaration on a Jewish national home in Palestine

The Bolshevik Revolution

Georges Clemenceau elected prime minister of France

Lenin appointed chief commissar; Trotsky appointed minister of foreign affairs

Conrad's *The Shadow-Line*

Douglas' *South Wind*

Eliot's *Prufrock and Other Observations*

Modigliani's *Nude with Necklace*

Sassoon's *The Old Huntsman*

Prokofiev's *Classical Symphony*

Yeats's *The Wild Swans at Coole*

1918　Wilson puts forward Fourteen Points for World Peace

Central Powers and Russia sign the Treaty of Brest-Litovsk

Execution of Czar Nicholas II and his family

Kaiser Wilhelm II abdicates

The Armistice signed

Women granted the vote at age thirty in Britain

Rupert Brooke's *Collected Poems*

Gerard Manley Hopkins' *Poems*

Joyce's *Exiles*

Lewis's *Tarr*

Sassoon's *Counter-Attack*

Oswald Spengler's *The Decline of the West*

Strachey's *Eminent Victorians*

Béla Bartók's *Bluebeard's Castle*

Charlie Chaplin's *Shoulder Arms*

1919　The Versailles Peace Treaty signed

J. W. Alcock and A. W. Brown make first transatlantic flight

Ross Smith flies from London to Australia

National Socialist party founded in Germany

Benito Mussolini founds the Fascist party in Italy

Sinn Fein Congress adopts declaration of independence in Dublin

Eamon De Valera elected president of Sinn Fein party

Communist Third International founded

Lady Astor elected first woman Member of Parliament

Prohibition in the United States

John Maynard Keynes's *The Economic Consequences of the Peace*

Eliot's *Poems*

Maugham's *The Moon and Sixpence*

Shaw's *Heartbreak House*

The Bauhaus school of design, building, and crafts founded by Walter Gropius

Amedeo Modigliani's *Self-Portrait*

Patricia Beer born

1920　The League of Nations established

Warren G. Harding elected president of the United States

Senate votes against joining the League and rejects the Treaty of Versailles

The Nineteenth Amendment gives women the right to vote

White Russian forces of Denikin and Kolchak defeated by the Bolsheviks

Karel Ĉapek's *R.U.R.*

Galsworthy's *In Chancery* and *The Skin Game*

Sinclair Lewis' *Main Street*

Katherine Mansfield's *Bliss*

Matisse's *Odalisques* (1920–1925)

Ezra Pound's *Hugh Selwyn Mauberly*

Paul Valéry's *Le Cimetière Marin*

Yeats's *Michael Robartes and the Dancer*

Edwin Morgan born

1921　Britain signs peace with Ireland

First medium-wave radio broadcast in the United States

The British Broadcasting Corporation founded

Braque's *Still Life with Guitar*

Chaplin's *The Kid*

Aldous Huxley's *Crome Yellow*

Paul Klee's *The Fish*

CHRONOLOGY

D. H. Lawrence's *Women in Love*
John McTaggart's *The Nature of Existence* (vol. 1)
Moore's *Héloïse and Abélard*
Eugene O'Neill's *The Emperor Jones*
Luigi Pirandello's *Six Characters in Search of an Author*
Shaw's *Back to Methuselah*
Strachey's *Queen Victoria*
Births of George Mackay Brown and Brian Moore

1922 Lloyd George's Coalition government succeeded by Bonar Law's Conservative government
Benito Mussolini marches on Rome and forms a government
William Cosgrave elected president of the Irish Free State
The BBC begins broadcasting in London
Lord Carnarvon and Howard Carter discover Tutankhamen's tomb
The PEN club founded in London
The *Criterion* founded with T. S. Eliot as editor
Kingsley Amis born
Eliot's *The Waste Land*
A. E. Housman's *Last Poems*
Joyce's *Ulysses*
D. H. Lawrence's *Aaron's Rod* and *England, My England*
Sinclair Lewis's *Babbitt*
O'Neill's *Anna Christie*
Pirandello's *Henry IV*
Edith Sitwell's *Façade*
Virginia Woolf's *Jacob's Room*
Yeats's *The Trembling of the Veil*
Donald Davie, **Philip Larkin born**

1923 The Union of Soviet Socialist Republics established
French and Belgian troops occupy the Ruhr in consequence of Germany's failure to pay reparations
Mustafa Kemal (Ataturk) proclaims Turkey a republic and is elected president
Warren G. Harding dies; Calvin Coolidge becomes president

Stanley Baldwin succeeds Bonar Law as prime minister
Adolf Hitler's attempted coup in Munich fails
Time magazine begins publishing
E. N. da C. Andrade's *The Structure of the Atom*
Brendan Behan born
Bennett's *Riceyman Steps*
Churchill's *The World Crisis* (1923–1927)
J. E. Flecker's *Hassan* produced
Nadine Gordimer born
Paul Klee's *Magic Theatre*
Lawrence's *Kangaroo*
Rainer Maria Rilke's *Duino Elegies* and *Sonnets to Orpheus*
Sibelius' *Sixth Symphony*
Picasso's *Seated Woman*
William Walton's *Façade*
Elizabeth Jane Howard born

1924 Ramsay MacDonald forms first Labour government, loses general election, and is succeeded by Stanley Baldwin
Calvin Coolidge elected president of the United States
Noël Coward's *The Vortex*
Forster's *A Passage to India*
Mann's *The Magic Mountain*
Shaw's *St. Joan*
G. F. Dutton born

1925 Reza Khan becomes shah of Iran
First surrealist exhibition held in Paris
Alban Berg's *Wozzeck*
Chaplin's *The Gold Rush*
John Dos Passos' *Manhattan Transfer*
Theodore Dreiser's *An American Tragedy*
Sergei Eisenstein's *Battleship Potemkin*
F. Scott Fitzgerald's *The Great Gatsby*
André Gide's *Les Faux Monnayeurs*
Hardy's *Human Shows and Far Phantasies*
Huxley's *Those Barren Leaves*
Kafka's *The Trial*

CHRONOLOGY

O'Casey's *Juno and the Paycock*
Virginia Woolf's *Mrs. Dalloway* and *The Common Reader*
Brancusi's *Bird in Space*
Shostakovich's *First Symphony*
Sibelius' *Tapiola*

1926 Ford's *A Man Could Stand Up*
Gide's *Si le grain ne meurt*
Hemingway's *The Sun also Rises*
Kafka's *The Castle*
D. H. Lawrence's *The Plumed Serpent*
T. E. Lawrence's *Seven Pillars of Wisdom* privately circulated
Maugham's *The Casuarina Tree*
O'Casey's *The Plough and the Stars*
Puccini's *Turandot*
Jan Morris born

1927 General Chiang Kai-shek becomes prime minister in China
Trotsky expelled by the Communist party as a deviationist; Stalin becomes leader of the party and dictator of the Soviet Union
Charles Lindbergh flies from New York to Paris
J. W. Dunne's *An Experiment with Time*
Freud's *Autobiography* translated into English
Albert Giacometti's *Observing Head*
Ernest Hemingway's *Men Without Women*
Fritz Lang's *Metropolis*
Wyndham Lewis' *Time and Western Man*
F. W. Murnau's *Sunrise*
Proust's *Le Temps retrouvé* posthumously published
Stravinsky's *Oedipus Rex*
Virginia Woolf's *To the Lighthouse*

1928 The Kellogg-Briand Pact, outlawing war and providing for peaceful settlement of disputes, signed in Paris by sixty-two nations, including the Soviet Union
Herbert Hoover elected president of the United States

Women's suffrage granted at age twenty-one in Britain
Alexander Fleming discovers penicillin
Bertolt Brecht and Kurt Weill's *The Three-Penny Opera*
Eisenstein's *October*
Huxley's *Point Counter Point*
Christopher Isherwood's *All the Conspirators*
D. H. Lawrence's *Lady Chatterley's Lover*
Wyndham Lewis' *The Childermass*
Matisse's *Seated Odalisque*
Munch's *Girl on a Sofa*
Shaw's *Intelligent Woman's Guide to Socialism*
Virginia Woolf's *Orlando*
Yeats's *The Tower*
Iain Chrichton Smith born

1929 The Labour party wins British general election
Trotsky expelled from the Soviet Union
Museum of Modern Art opens in New York
Collapse of U.S. stock exchange begins world economic crisis
Robert Bridges's *The Testament of Beauty*
William Faulkner's *The Sound and the Fury*
Robert Graves's *Goodbye to All That*
Hemingway's *A Farewell to Arms*
Ernst Junger's *The Storm of Steel*
Hugo von Hoffmansthal's *Poems*
Henry Moore's *Reclining Figure*
J. B. Priestley's *The Good Companions*
Erich Maria Remarque's *All Quiet on the Western Front*
Shaw's *The Applecart*
R. C. Sheriff's *Journey's End*
Edith Sitwell's *Gold Coast Customs*
Thomas Wolfe's *Look Homeward, Angel*
Virginia Woolf's *A Room of One's Own*
Yeats's *The Winding Stair*

Second surrealist manifesto;
Salvador

Dali joins the surrealists

Epstein's *Night and Day*

Mondrian's *Composition with Yellow Blue*

Death of Edward Carpenter and
Flora Annie Steel

John Montague, Keith Waterhouse,
and **Thom Gunn born**

1930 Allied occupation of the Rhineland
ends

Mohandas Gandhi opens civil
disobedience campaign in India

The *Daily Worker*, journal of the
British Communist party, begins
publishing

J. W. Reppe makes artificial fabrics
from an acetylene base

John Arden born

Auden's *Poems*

Coward's *Private Lives*

Eliot's *Ash Wednesday*

Wyndham Lewis's *The Apes of God*

Maugham's *Cakes and Ale*

Ezra Pound's *XXX Cantos*

Evelyn Waugh's *Vile Bodies*

Birth of Kamau (Edward) Brathwaite and Ruth Rendell

1931 The failure of the Credit Anstalt in
Austria starts a financial collapse in
Central Europe

Britain abandons the gold standard;
the pound falls by twenty-five
percent

Mutiny in the Royal Navy at Invergordon over pay cuts

Ramsay MacDonald resigns, splits
the Cabinet, and is expelled by the
Labour party; in the general election
the National Government wins by a
majority of five hundred seats

The Statute of Westminster defines
dominion status

Ninette de Valois founds the Vic-Wells

Ballet (eventually the Royal Ballet)

Coward's *Cavalcade*

Dali's The *Persistence of Memory*

O'Neill's *Mourning Becomes Electra*

Anthony Powell's *Afternoon Men*

Antoine de Saint-Exupéry's *Vol de nuit*

Walton's *Belshazzar's Feast*

Virginia Woolf's *The Waves*

Caroline Blackwood, **John le Carré born**

1932 Franklin D. Roosevelt elected
president of the United States

Paul von Hindenburg elected
president of Germany; Franz von
Papen elected chancellor

Sir Oswald Mosley founds British
Union of Fascists

The BBC takes over development
of television from J. L. Baird's
company

Basic English of 850 words
designed as a prospective
international language

The Folger Library opens in
Washington, D.C.

The Shakespeare Memorial Theatre
opens in Stratford-upon-Avon

Faulkner's *Light in August*

Huxley's *Brave New World*

F. R. Leavis' *New Bearings in
English Poetry*

Boris Pasternak's *Second Birth*

Ravel's *Concerto for Left Hand*

Athol Fugard and Peter Redgrove
born

Rouault's *Christ Mocked by Soldiers*

Waugh's *Black Mischief*

Yeats's *Words for Music Perhaps*

Geoffrey Hill born

1933 Roosevelt inaugurates the New Deal

Hitler becomes chancellor of
Germany

The Reichstag set on fire

Hitler suspends civil liberties and
freedom of the press; German trade
unions suppressed

George Balanchine and Lincoln
Kirstein found the School of
American Ballet

Beryl Bainbridge born

CHRONOLOGY

Lowry's *Ultramarine*
André Malraux's *La Condition humaine*
Orwell's *Down and Out in Paris and London*
Gertrude Stein's *The Autobiography of Alice B. Toklas*
Peter Scupham and Anne Stevenson born

1934   The League Disarmament Conference ends in failure
The Soviet Union admitted to the League
Hitler becomes Führer
Civil war in Austria; Engelbert Dollfuss assassinated in attempted Nazi coup
Frédéric Joliot and Irene Joliot-Curie discover artificial (induced) radioactivity
Einstein's *My Philosophy*
Fitzgerald's *Tender Is the Night*
Graves's *I, Claudius* and *Claudius the God*
Toynbee's *A Study of History* begins publication (1934–1954)
Waugh's *A Handful of Dust*
Births of Fleur Adcock, Alan Bennett, Christopher Wallace-Crabbe, and Alasdair Gray

1935   Grigori Zinoviev and other Soviet leaders convicted of treason
Stanley Baldwin becomes prime minister in National Government; National Government wins general election in Britain
Italy invades Abyssinia
Germany repudiates disarmament clauses of Treaty of Versailles
Germany reintroduces compulsory military service and outlaws the Jews
Robert Watson-Watt builds first practical radar equipment
Karl Jaspers' *Suffering and Existence*
Births of André Brink, Dennis Potter, Keith Roberts, and Jon Stallworthy
Ivy Compton-Burnett's *A House and Its Head*

Eliot's *Murder in the Cathedral*
Barbara Hepworth's *Three Forms*
George Gershwin's *Porgy and Bess*
Greene's *England Made Me*
Isherwood's *Mr. Norris Changes Trains*
Malraux's *Le Temps du mépris*
Yeats's *Dramatis Personae*
Klee's *Child Consecrated to Suffering*
Benedict Nicholson's *White Relief*
Death of Lewis Grassic Gibbon
Edward VII accedes to the throne in January; abdicates in December

1936–1952   Reign of George VI
1936   German troops occupy the Rhineland
Ninety-nine percent of German electorate vote for Nazi candidates
The Popular Front wins general election in France; Léon Blum becomes prime minister
Roosevelt reelected president of the United States
The Popular Front wins general election in Spain
Spanish Civil War begins
Italian troops occupy Addis Ababa; Abyssinia annexed by Italy
BBC begins television service from Alexandra Palace
Auden's *Look, Stranger!*
Auden and Isherwood's *The Ascent of F-6*
A. J. Ayer's *Language, Truth and Logic*
Chaplin's *Modern Times*
Greene's *A Gun for Sale*
Huxley's *Eyeless in Gaza*
Keynes's *General Theory of Employment*
F. R. Leavis' *Revaluation*
Mondrian's *Composition in Red and Blue*
Dylan Thomas' *Twenty-five Poems*
Wells's *The Shape of Things to Come* filmed
Steward Conn and Reginald Hill born
Death of John Cornford

CHRONOLOGY

1937   Trial of Karl Radek and other
Soviet leaders
Neville Chamberlain succeeds Stanley Baldwin as prime minister
China and Japan at war
Frank Whittle designs jet engine
Picasso's *Guernica*
Shostakovich's Fifth Symphony
Magritte's *La Reproduction interdite*
Hemingway's *To Have and Have Not*
Malraux's *L'Espoir*
Orwell's *The Road to Wigan Pier*
Priestley's *Time and the Conways*
Virginia Woolf's *The Years*
Emma Tennant born
Death of Christopher Caudwell
(Christopher St. John Sprigg)

1938   Trial of Nikolai Bukharin and other Soviet political leaders
Austria occupied by German troops and declared part of the Reich
Hitler states his determination to annex Sudetenland from Czechoslovakia
Britain, France, Germany, and Italy sign the Munich agreement
German troops occupy Sudetenland
Edward Hulton founds *Picture Post*
Cyril Connolly's *Enemies of Promise*
du Maurier's *Rebecca*
Faulkner's *The Unvanquished*
Graham Greene's *Brighton Rock*
Hindemith's *Mathis der Maler*
Jean Renoir's *La Grande Illusion*
Jean-Paul Sartre's *La Nausée*
Yeats's *New Poems*
Anthony Asquith's *Pygmalion* and Walt Disney's *Snow White*
Ngũgĩ wa Thiong'o born

1939   German troops occupy Bohemia and Moravia; Czechoslovakia incorporated into Third Reich
Madrid surrenders to General Franco; the Spanish Civil War ends
Italy invades Albania
Spain joins Germany, Italy, and Japan in anti-Comintern Pact
Britain and France pledge support to Poland, Romania, and Greece
The Soviet Union proposes defensive alliance with Britain; British military mission visits Moscow
The Soviet Union and Germany sign nonaggression treaty, secretly providing for partition of Poland between them
Germany invades Poland; Britain, France, and Germany at war
The Soviet Union invades Finland
New York World's Fair opens
Eliot's *The Family Reunion*
Births of Ayi Kwei Armah, Seamus Heaney, Michael Longley and Robert Nye
Isherwood's *Good-bye to Berlin*
Joyce's *Finnegans Wake* (1922–1939)
MacNeice's *Autumn Journal*
Powell's *What's Become of Waring?*
Ayi Kwei Armah born

1940   Churchill becomes prime minister
Italy declares war on France, Britain, and Greece
General de Gaulle founds Free French Movement
The Battle of Britain and the bombing of London
Roosevelt reelected president of the United States for third term
Betjeman's *Old Lights for New Chancels*
Angela Carter born
Chaplin's *The Great Dictator*
Bruce Chatwin born
Death of William H. Davies
J. M. Coetzee born
Disney's *Fantasia*
Greene's *The Power and the Glory*
Hemingway's *For Whom the Bell Tolls*
C. P. Snow's *Strangers and Brothers* (retitled *George Passant* in 1970, when entire sequence of ten novels, published 1940–1970, was entitled *Strangers and Brothers*)

1941   German forces occupy Yugoslavia, Greece, and Crete, and invade the

CHRONOLOGY

Soviet Union
Lend-Lease agreement between the United States and Britain
President Roosevelt and Winston Churchill sign the Atlantic Charter
Japanese forces attack Pearl Harbor; United States declares war on Japan, Germany, Italy; Britain on Japan
Auden's *New Year Letter*
James Burnham's *The Managerial Revolution*
F. Scott Fitzgerald's *The Last Tycoon*
Huxley's *Grey Eminence*
Derek Mahon born
Shostakovich's *Seventh Symphony*
Tippett's *A Child of Our Time*
Orson Welles's *Citizen Kane*
Virginia Woolf's *Between the Acts*
Death of **James Joyce**

1942 Japanese forces capture Singapore, Hong Kong, Bataan, Manila
German forces capture Tobruk
U.S. fleet defeats the Japanese in the Coral Sea, captures Guadalcanal
Battle of El Alamein
Allied forces land in French North Africa
Atom first split at University of Chicago
William Beveridge's *Social Insurance and Allied Services*
Albert Camus's *L'Étranger*
Joyce Cary's *To Be a Pilgrim*
Edith Sitwell's *Street Songs*
Waugh's *Put Out More Flags*
Births of Ama Ata Aidoo, Douglas Dunn, Susan Hill, and Jonathan Raban

1943 German forces surrender at Stalingrad
German and Italian forces surrender in North Africa
Italy surrenders to Allies and declares war on Germany
Cairo conference between Roosevelt, Churchill, Chiang Kai-shek
Teheran conference between

Roosevelt, Churchill, Stalin
Eliot's *Four Quartets*
Henry Moore's *Madonna and Child*
Sartre's *Les Mouches*
Vaughan Williams' *Fifth Symphony*
Peter Carey, David Malouf Iain Sinclair born

1944 Allied forces land in Normandy and southern France
Allied forces enter Rome
Attempted assassination of Hitler fails
Liberation of Paris
U.S. forces land in Philippines
German offensive in the Ardennes halted
Roosevelt reelected president of the United States for fourth term
Education Act passed in Britain
Pay-as-You-Earn income tax introduced
Beveridge's *Full Employment in a Free Society*
Cary's *The Horse's Mouth*
Huxley's *Time Must Have a Stop*
Maugham's *The Razor's Edge*
Sartre's *Huis Clos*
Edith Sitwell's *Green Song and Other Poems*
Graham Sutherland's *Christ on the Cross*
Trevelyan's *English Social History*
David Constantine, Craig Raine and W. G. Sebald born

1945 British and Indian forces open offensive in Burma
Yalta conference between Roosevelt, Churchill, Stalin
Mussolini executed by Italian partisans
Roosevelt dies; Harry S. Truman becomes president
Hitler commits suicide; German forces surrender
The Potsdam Peace Conference
The United Nations Charter ratified in San Francisco
The Labour Party wins British General Election
Atomic bombs dropped on Hi-

roshima and Nagasaki

Surrender of Japanese forces ends
World War II

Trial of Nazi war criminals opens at
Nuremberg

All-India Congress demands British
withdrawal from India

De Gaulle elected president of
French Provisional Government;
resigns the next year

Betjeman's *New Bats in Old
Belfries*

Britten's *Peter Grimes*

Orwell's *Animal Farm*

Russell's *History of Western
Philosophy*

Sartre's T*he Age of Reason*

Edith Sitwell's *The Song of the
Cold*

Waugh's *Brideshead Revisited*

Births of Wendy Cope and Peter
Reading

Death of Arthur Symons

1946 Bills to nationalize railways, coal
mines, and the Bank of England
passed in Britain

Nuremberg Trials concluded

United Nations General Assembly
meets in New York as its permanent
headquarters

The Arab Council inaugurated in
Britain

Frederick Ashton's *Symphonic
Variations*

Britten's *The Rape of Lucretia*

David Lean's *Great Expectations*

O'Neill's *The Iceman Cometh*

Roberto Rosselini's *Paisà*

Dylan Thomas' *Deaths and
Entrances*

Jim Crace and Philip Pullman born

1947 President Truman announces
program of aid to Greece and
Turkey and outlines the "Truman
Doctrine"

Independence of India proclaimed;
partition between India and
Pakistan, and communal strife
between Hindus and Moslems follows

General Marshall calls for a
European recovery program

First supersonic air flight

Britain's first atomic pile at Harwell
comes into operation

Edinburgh festival established

Discovery of the Dead Sea Scrolls
in Palestine

Princess Elizabeth marries Philip
Mountbatten, duke of Edinburgh

Auden's *Age of Anxiety*

Camus's *La Peste*

Chaplin's *Monsieur Verdoux*

Lowry's *Under the Volcano*

Priestley's *An Inspector Calls*

Edith Sitwell's *The Shadow of Cain*

Waugh's *Scott-King's Modern
Europe*

Births of Dermot Healy, and Red-
mond O'Hanlon

Death of Flora Thompson,
1948 Gandhi assassinated

Czech Communist Party seizes
power

Pan-European movement (1948–
1958) begins with the formation of
the permanent Organization for
European Economic Cooperation
(OEEC)

Berlin airlift begins as the Soviet
Union halts road and rail traffic to
the city

British mandate in Palestine ends;
Israeli provisional government
formed

Yugoslavia expelled from Soviet
bloc

Columbia Records introduces the
long-playing record

Truman elected of the United States
for second term

Greene's *The Heart of the Matter*

Huxley's *Ape and Essence*

Leavis' *The Great Tradition*

Pound's *Cantos*

Priestley's *The Linden Tree*

Waugh's *The Loved One*

Death of Denton Welch

Ciaran Carson and Zakes Mda born

1949 North Atlantic Treaty Organization

established with headquarters in
Brussels

Berlin blockade lifted

German Federal Republic
recognized; capital established at
Bonn

Konrad Adenauer becomes German
chancellor

Mao Tse-tung becomes chairman of
the People's Republic of China following Communist victory over the
Nationalists

Peter Ackroyd born

Simone de Beauvoir's *The Second
Sex*

Cary's *A Fearful Joy*

Arthur Miller's *Death of a Salesman*

Orwell's *Nineteen Eighty-four*

Birth of Michèle Roberts

1950 Korean War breaks out

Nobel Prize for literature awarded
to Bertrand Russell

R. H. S. Crossman's *The God That
Failed*

T. S. Eliot's *The Cocktail Party*

Fry's *Venus Observed*

Doris Lessing's *The Grass Is Singing*

C. S. Lewis' *The Chronicles of Narnia* (1950–1956)

Wyndham Lewis' *Rude Assignment*

George Orwell's *Shooting an
Elephant*

Carol Reed's *The Third Man*

Dylan Thomas' *Twenty-six Poems*

Births of Sara Maitland, and A. N.
Wilson

1951 Guy Burgess and Donald Maclean
defect from Britain to the Soviet
Union

The Conservative party under
Winston Churchill wins British
general election

The Festival of Britain celebrates
both the centenary of the Crystal
Palace Exhibition and British
postwar recovery

Electric power is produced by
atomic energy at Arcon, Idaho

W. H. Auden's *Nones*

Samuel Beckett's *Molloy* and *Malone Dies*

Benjamin Britten's *Billy Budd*

Greene's *The End of the Affair*

Akira Kurosawa's *Rashomon*

Wyndham Lewis' *Rotting Hill*

Anthony Powell's *A Question of
Upbringing* (first volume of *A
Dance to the Music of Time*, 1951–
1975)

J. D. Salinger's *The Catcher in the
Rye*

C. P. Snow's *The Masters*

Igor Stravinsky's *The Rake's
Progress*

Peter Fallon born

1952– Reign of Elizabeth II

At Eniwetok Atoll the United States
detonates the first hydrogen bomb

The European Coal and Steel Community comes into being

Radiocarbon dating introduced to
archaeology

Michael Ventris deciphers Linear B
script

Dwight D. Eisenhower elected
president of the United States

Beckett's *Waiting for Godot*

Charles Chaplin's *Limelight*

Ernest Hemingway's *The Old Man
and the Sea*

Arthur Koestler's *Arrow in the Blue*

F. R. Leavis' *The Common Pursuit*

Lessing's *Martha Quest* (first
volume of *The Children of Violence*,
1952–1965)

C. S. Lewis' *Mere Christianity*

Thomas' *Collected Poems*

Evelyn Waugh's *Men at Arms* (first
volume of *Sword of Honour*, 1952–
1961)

Angus Wilson's *Hemlock and After*

Births of Rohinton Mistry and
Vikram Seth

1953 Constitution for a European political
community drafted

Julius and Ethel Rosenberg
executed for passing U.S. secrets to
the Soviet Union

CHRONOLOGY

Cease-fire declared in Korea

Edmund Hillary and his Sherpa guide, Tenzing Norkay, scale Mt. Everest

Nobel Prize for literature awarded to Winston Churchill

General Mohammed Naguib proclaims Egypt a republic

Beckett's *Watt*

Joyce Cary's *Except the Lord*

Robert Graves's *Poems 1953*

Death of Norman Cameron, **Dylan Thomas**

Birth of Tony Parsons

1954 First atomic submarine, *Nautilus,* is launched by the United States

Dien Bien Phu captured by the Vietminh

Geneva Conference ends French dominion over Indochina

U.S. Supreme Court declares racial segregation in schools unconstitutional

Nasser becomes president of Egypt

Nobel Prize for literature awarded to Ernest Hemingway

Kingsley Amis' *Lucky Jim*

John Betjeman's *A Few Late Chrysanthemums*

William Golding's *Lord of the Flies*

Christopher Isherwood's *The World in the Evening*

Koestler's *The Invisible Writing*

Iris Murdoch's *Under the Net*

C. P. Snow's *The New Men*

Thomas' *Under Milk Wood* published posthumously

Births of Iain Banks, Louise De Bernières, Romesh Gunesekera, Kevin Hart, Alan Hollinghurst, Hanif Kureishi, and **Kazuo Ishiguro**

1955 Warsaw Pact signed

West Germany enters NATO as Allied occupation ends

The Conservative party under Anthony Eden wins British general election

Cary's *Not Honour More*

Greene's *The Quiet American*

Philip Larkin's *The Less Deceived*

F. R. Leavis' *D. H. Lawrence, Novelist*

Vladimir Nabokov's *Lolita*

Patrick White's *The Tree of Man*

John Burnside and Patrick McCabe born

1956 Nasser's nationalization of the Suez Canal leads to Israeli, British, and French armed intervention

Uprising in Hungary suppressed by Soviet troops

Khrushchev denounces Stalin at Twentieth Communist Party Congress

Eisenhower reelected president of the United States

Anthony Burgess' *Time for a Tiger*

Golding's *Pincher Martin*

Murdoch's *Flight from the Enchanter*

John Osborne's *Look Back in Anger*

Snow's *Homecomings*

Edmund Wilson's *Anglo-Saxon Attitudes*

Janice Galloway, Philip Kerr and Kate Thompson born

1957 The Soviet Union launches the first artificial earth satellite, *Sputnik I*

Eden succeeded by Harold Macmillan

Suez Canal reopened

Eisenhower Doctrine formulated

Parliament receives the Wolfenden Report on Homosexuality and Prostitution

Nobel Prize for literature awarded to Albert Camus

Beckett's *Endgame* and *All That Fall*

Lawrence Durrell's *Justine* (first volume of *The Alexandria Quartet,* 1957–1960)

Ted Hughes's *The Hawk in the Rain*

Murdoch's *The Sandcastle*

V. S. Naipaul's *The Mystic Masseur*

Eugene O'Neill's *Long Day's Journey into Night*

Osborne's *The Entertainer*

Muriel Spark's *The Comforters*

White's *Voss*
Death of Dorothy Richardson
Birth of Nick Hornby

1958 European Economic Community
established
Khrushchev succeeds Bulganin as
Soviet premier
Charles de Gaulle becomes head of
France's newly constituted Fifth
Republic
The United Arab Republic formed
by Egypt and Syria
The United States sends troops into
Lebanon
First U.S. satellite, *Explorer 1,*
launched
Nobel Prize for literature awarded
to Boris Pasternak
Beckett's *Krapp's Last Tape*
John Kenneth Galbraith's *The Afflu-
ent Society*
Greene's *Our Man in Havana*
Murdoch's *The Bell*
Pasternak's *Dr. Zhivago*
Snow's *The Conscience of the Rich*
Greg Delanty born

1959 Fidel Castro assumes power in
Cuba
St. Lawrence Seaway opens
The European Free Trade Associa-
tion founded
Alaska and Hawaii become the
forty-ninth and fiftieth states
The Conservative party under
Harold Macmillan wins British
general election
Brendan Behan's *The Hostage*
Golding's *Free Fall*
Graves's *Collected Poems*
Koestler's *The Sleepwalkers*
Harold Pinter's *The Birthday Party*
Snow's *The Two Cultures and the
Scientific Revolution*
Spark's *Memento Mori*
Susanna Clarke and Robert Craw-
ford born

1960 South Africa bans the African
National Congress and Pan-African
Congress
The Congo achieves independence

John F. Kennedy elected president
of the United States
The U.S. bathyscaphe *Trieste*
descends to 35,800 feet
Publication of the unexpurgated
Lady Chatterley's Lover permitted
by court
Auden's *Hommage to Clio*
Betjeman's *Summoned by Bells*
Pinter's *The Caretaker*
Snow's *The Affair*
David Storey's *This Sporting Life*
Andrew Miller and Ian Rankin born

1961 South Africa leaves the British
Commonwealth
Sierra Leone and Tanganyika
achieve independence
The Berlin Wall erected
The New English Bible published
Beckett's *How It Is*
Greene's *A Burnt-Out Case*
Koestler's *The Lotus and the Robot*
Murdoch's *A Severed Head*
Naipaul's *A House for Mr Biswas*
Osborne's *Luther*
Spark's *The Prime of Miss Jean
Brodie*
White's *Riders in the Chariot*
Jonathan Coe, Meaghan Delahunt
and Jackie Kay born

1962 John Glenn becomes first U.S.
astronaut to orbit earth
The United States launches the
spacecraft *Mariner* to explore Venus
Algeria achieves independence
Cuban missile crisis ends in
withdrawal of Soviet missiles from
Cuba
Adolf Eichmann executed in Israel
for Nazi war crimes
Second Vatican Council convened
by Pope John XXIII
Nobel Prize for literature awarded
to John Steinbeck
Edward Albee's *Who's Afraid of
Virginia Woolf?*
Beckett's *Happy Days*
Anthony Burgess' *A Clockwork
Orange* and *The Wanting Seed*
Aldous Huxley's *Island*

CHRONOLOGY

Isherwood's *Down There on a Visit*
Lessing's *The Golden Notebook*
Nabokov's *Pale Fire*
Aleksandr Solzhenitsyn's *One Day in the Life of Ivan Denisovich*
Kathleen Jamie born

1963 Britain, the United States, and the Soviet Union sign a test-ban treaty
Birth of Simon Armitage
Britain refused entry to the European Economic Community
The Soviet Union puts into orbit the first woman astronaut, Valentina Tereshkova
Paul VI becomes pope
President Kennedy assassinated; Lyndon B. Johnson assumes office
Nobel Prize for literature awarded to George Seferis
Britten's *War Requiem*
John Fowles's *The Collector*
Murdoch's *The Unicorn*
Spark's *The Girls of Slender Means*
Storey's *Radcliffe*
John Updike's *The Centaur*

1964 Tonkin Gulf incident leads to retaliatory strikes by U.S. aircraft against North Vietnam
Greece and Turkey contend for control of Cyprus
Britain grants licenses to drill for oil in the North Sea
The Shakespeare Quatercentenary celebrated
Lyndon Johnson elected president of the United States
The Labour party under Harold Wilson wins British general election
Nobel Prize for literature awarded to Jean-Paul Sartre
Saul Bellow's *Herzog*
Burgess' *Nothing Like the Sun*
Golding's *The Spire*
Isherwood's *A Single Man*
Stanley Kubrick's *Dr. Strangelove*
Larkin's *The Whitsun Weddings*
Naipaul's *An Area of Darkness*
Peter Shaffer's *The Royal Hunt of the Sun*
Snow's *Corridors of Power*

Alan Warner born
Death of Ian Fleming

1965 The first U.S. combat forces land in Vietnam
The U.S. spacecraft Mariner transmits photographs of Mars
British Petroleum Company finds oil in the North Sea
War breaks out between India and Pakistan
Rhodesia declares its independence
Ontario power failure blacks out the Canadian and U.S. east coasts
Nobel Prize for literature awarded to Mikhail Sholokhov
Robert Lowell's *For the Union Dead*
Norman Mailer's *An American Dream*
Osborne's *Inadmissible Evidence*
Pinter's *The Homecoming*
Spark's *The Mandelbaum Gate*

1966 The Labour party under Harold Wilson wins British general election
The Archbishop of Canterbury visits Pope Paul VI
Florence, Italy, severely damaged by floods
Paris exhibition celebrates Picasso's eighty-fifth birthday
Fowles's *The Magus*
Greene's *The Comedians*
Osborne's *A Patriot for Me*
Paul Scott's *The Jewel in the Crown* (first volume of *The Raj Quartet*, 1966–1975)
White's *The Solid Mandala*
Peter Ho Davies born
Death of Frank O'Connor

1967 Thurgood Marshall becomes first black U.S. Supreme Court justice
Six-Day War pits Israel against Egypt and Syria
Biafra's secession from Nigeria leads to civil war
Francis Chichester completes solo circumnavigation of the globe
Dr. Christiaan Barnard performs first heart transplant operation, in South Africa

CHRONOLOGY

China explodes its first hydrogen bomb

Golding's *The Pyramid*

Hughes's *Wodwo*

Isherwood's *A Meeting by the River*

Naipaul's *The Mimic Men*

Tom Stoppard's *Rosencrantz and Guildenstern Are Dead*

Orson Welles's *Chimes at Midnight*

Angus Wilson's *No Laughing Matter*

1968   Violent student protests erupt in France and West Germany

Warsaw Pact troops occupy Czechoslovakia

Violence in Northern Ireland causes Britain to send in troops

Tet offensive by Communist forces launched against South Vietnam's cities

Theater censorship ended in Britain

Robert Kennedy and Martin Luther King Jr. assassinated

Richard M. Nixon elected president of the United States

Booker Prize for fiction established

Durrell's *Tunc*

Graves's *Poems 1965–1968*

Osborne's *The Hotel in Amsterdam*

Snow's *The Sleep of Reason*

Solzhenitsyn's *The First Circle* and *Cancer Ward*

Spark's *The Public Image*

Monica Ali born

1969   Humans set foot on the moon for the first time when astronauts descend to its surface in a landing vehicle from the U.S. spacecraft *Apollo 11*

The Soviet unmanned spacecraft *Venus V* lands on Venus

Capital punishment abolished in Britain

Colonel Muammar Qaddafi seizes power in Libya

Solzhenitsyn expelled from the Soviet Union

Nobel Prize for literature awarded to Samuel Beckett

Carter's *The Magic Toyshop*

Fowles's *The French Lieutenant's Woman*

Storey's *The Contractor*

Death of John Wyndham

Hari Kunzru and David Mitchell born

1970   Civil war in Nigeria ends with Biafra's surrender

U.S. planes bomb Cambodia

The Conservative party under Edward Heath wins British general election

Nobel Prize for literature awarded to Aleksandr Solzhenitsyn

Durrell's *Nunquam*

Hughes's *Crow*

F. R. Leavis and Q. D. Leavis' *Dickens the Novelist*

Snow's *Last Things*

Spark's *The Driver's Seat*

Death of Vera Brittain

1971   Communist China given Nationalist China's UN seat

Decimal currency introduced to Britain

Indira Gandhi becomes India's prime minister

Nobel Prize for literature awarded to Heinrich Böll

Bond's *The Pope's Wedding*

Naipaul's *In a Free State*

Pinter's *Old Times*

Spark's *Not to Disturb*

Births of Kiran Desai, Sarah Kane and Martin McDonagh

Death of **Stevie Smith**

1972   The civil strife of "Bloody Sunday" causes Northern Ireland to come under the direct rule of Westminster

Nixon becomes the first U.S. president to visit Moscow and Beijing

The Watergate break-in precipitates scandal in the United States

Eleven Israeli athletes killed by terrorists at Munich Olympics

Nixon reelected president of the United States

Bond's *Lear*

Snow's *The Malcontents*

CHRONOLOGY

Stoppard's *Jumpers*
1973 Britain, Ireland, and Denmark enter
European Economic Community

Egypt and Syria attack Israel in the
Yom Kippur War

Energy crisis in Britain reduces
production to a three-day week

Nobel Prize for literature awarded
to Patrick White

Bond's *The Sea*

Greene's *The Honorary Consul*

Lessing's *The Summer Before the
Dark*

Murdoch's *The Black Prince*

Shaffer's *Equus*

White's *The Eye of the Storm*

Death of William Plomer
1974 Miners strike in Britain

Greece's military junta overthrown

Emperor Haile Selassie of Ethiopia
deposed

President Makarios of Cyprus
replaced by military coup

Nixon resigns as U.S. president and
is succeeded by Gerald R. Ford

Betjeman's *A Nip in the Air*

Bond's *Bingo*

Durrell's *Monsieur* (first volume of
The Avignon Quintet, 1974–1985)

Larkin's *The High Windows*

Solzhenitsyn's *The Gulag
Archipelago*

Spark's *The Abbess of Crewe*

Death of Edmund Blunden, Austin
Clarke, and Nancy Mitford
1975 The U.S. *Apollo* and Soviet *Soyuz*
spacecrafts rendezvous in space

The Helsinki Accords on human
rights signed

U.S. forces leave Vietnam

King Juan Carlos succeeds Franco
as Spain's head of state

Nobel Prize for literature awarded
to Eugenio Montale
1976 New U.S. copyright law goes into
effect

Israeli commandos free hostages
from hijacked plane at Entebbe,
Uganda

British and French SST Concordes
make first regularly scheduled commercial flights

The United States celebrates its
bicentennial

Jimmy Carter elected president of
the United States

Byron and Shelley manuscripts
discovered in Barclay's Bank, Pall
Mall

Hughes's *Seasons' Songs*

Koestler's *The Thirteenth Tribe*

Scott's *Staying On*

Spark's *The Take-over*

White's *A Fringe of Leaves*
1977 Silver jubilee of Queen Elizabeth II
celebrated

Egyptian president Anwar el-Sadat
visits Israel

"Gang of Four" expelled from
Chinese Communist party

First woman ordained in the U.S.
Episcopal church

After twenty-nine years in power,
Israel's Labour party is defeated by
the Likud party

Fowles's *Daniel Martin*

Hughes's *Gaudete*
1978 Treaty between Israel and Egypt
negotiated at Camp David

Pope John Paul I dies a month after
his coronation and is succeeded by
Karol Cardinal Wojtyla, who takes
the name John Paul II

Former Italian premier Aldo Moro
murdered by left-wing terrorists

Nobel Prize for literature awarded
to Isaac Bashevis Singer

Greene's *The Human Factor*

Hughes's *Cave Birds*

Murdoch's *The Sea, The Sea*

Death of Hugh MacDiarmid
1979 The United States and China
establish diplomatic relations

Ayatollah Khomeini takes power in
Iran and his supporters hold U.S.
embassy staff hostage in Teheran

Rhodesia becomes Zimbabwe

Earl Mountbatten assassinated

The Soviet Union invades
Afghanistan

CHRONOLOGY

The Conservative party under Margaret Thatcher wins British general election

Nobel Prize for literature awarded to Odysseus Elytis

Golding's *Darkness Visible*

Hughes's *Moortown*

Lessing's *Shikasta* (first volume of *Canopus in Argos, Archives*)

Naipaul's *A Bend in the River*

Spark's *Territorial Rights*

White's *The Twyborn Affair*

1980 Iran-Iraq war begins

Strikes in Gdansk give rise to the Solidarity movement

Mt. St. Helen's erupts in Washington State

British steelworkers strike for the first time since 1926

More than fifty nations boycott Moscow Olympics

Ronald Reagan elected president of the United States

Burgess's *Earthly Powers*

Golding's *Rites of Passage*

Shaffer's *Amadeus*

Storey's *A Prodigal Child*

Angus Wilson's *Setting the World on Fire*

1981 Greece admitted to the European Economic Community

Iran hostage crisis ends with release of U.S. embassy staff

Twelve Labour MPs and nine peers found British Social Democratic party

Socialist party under François Mitterand wins French general election

Rupert Murdoch buys *The Times* of London

Turkish gunman wounds Pope John Paul II in assassination attempt

U.S. gunman wounds President Reagan in assassination attempt

President Sadat of Egypt assassinated

Nobel Prize for literature awarded to Elias Canetti

Spark's *Loitering with Intent*

1982 Britain drives Argentina's invasion force out of the Falkland Islands

U.S. space shuttle makes first successful trip

Yuri Andropov becomes general secretary of the Central Committee of the Soviet Communist party

Israel invades Lebanon

First artificial heart implanted at Salt Lake City hospital

Bellow's *The Dean's December*

Greene's *Monsignor Quixote*

1983 South Korean airliner with 269 aboard shot down after straying into Soviet airspace

U.S. forces invade Grenada following left-wing coup

Widespread protests erupt over placement of nuclear missiles in Europe

The ?1 coin comes into circulation in Britain

Australia wins the America's Cup

Nobel Prize for literature awarded to William Golding

Hughes's *River*

Murdoch's *The Philosopher's Pupil*

1984 Konstantin Chernenko becomes general secretary of the Central Committee of the Soviet Communist party

Prime Minister Indira Gandhi of India assassinated by Sikh bodyguards

Reagan reelected president of the United States

Toxic gas leak at Bhopal, India, plant kills 2,000

British miners go on strike

Irish Republican Army attempts to kill Prime Minister Thatcher with bomb detonated at a Brighton hotel

World Court holds against U.S. mining of Nicaraguan harbors

Golding's *The Paper Men*

Lessing's *The Diary of Jane Somers*

Spark's *The Only Problem*

1985 United States deploys cruise missiles in Europe

Mikhail Gorbachev becomes general secretary of the Soviet Communist party following death of Konstantin

CHRONOLOGY

Chernenko
Riots break out in Handsworth district (Birmingham) and Brixton
Republic of Ireland gains consultative role in Northern Ireland
State of emergency is declared in South Africa
Nobel Prize for literature awarded to Claude Simon
A. N. Wilson's *Gentlemen in England*
Lessing's *The Good Terrorist*
Murdoch's *The Good Apprentice*
Fowles's *A Maggot*
Death of **Philip Larkin**

1986 U.S. space shuttle *Challenger* explodes
United States attacks Libya
Atomic power plant at Chernobyl destroyed in accident
Corazon Aquino becomes president of the Philippines
Giotto spacecraft encounters Comet Halley
Nobel Prize for literature awarded to Wole Soyinka
Final volume of *Oxford English Dictionary* supplement published
Amis's *The Old Devils*
Ishiguro's *An Artist of the Floating World*
A. N. Wilson's *Love Unknown*
Powell's *The Fisher King*
Death of Henry Reed

1987 Gorbachev begins reform of Communist party of the Soviet Union
Stock market collapses
Iran-contra affair reveals that Reagan administration used money from arms sales to Iran to fund Nicaraguan rebels
Palestinian uprising begins in Israeli-occupied territories
Nobel Prize for literature awarded to Joseph Brodsky
Golding's *Close Quarters*
Burgess's *Little Wilson and Big God*
Drabble's *The Radiant Way*

1988 Soviet Union begins withdrawing troops from Afghanistan
Iranian airliner shot down by U.S. Navy over Persian Gulf
War between Iran and Iraq ends
George Bush elected president of the United States
Pan American flight 103 destroyed over Lockerbie, Scotland
Nobel Prize for literature awarded to Naguib Mafouz
Greene's *The Captain and the Enemy*
Amis's *Difficulties with Girls*
Rushdie's *Satanic Verses*

1989 Ayatollah Khomeini pronounces death sentence on Salman Rushdie; Great Britain and Iran sever diplomatic relations
F. W. de Klerk becomes president of South Africa
Chinese government crushes student demonstration in Tiananmen Square
Communist regimes are weakened or abolished in Poland, Czechoslovakia, Hungary, East Germany, and Romania
Lithuania nullifies its inclusion in Soviet Union
Nobel Prize for literature awarded to José Cela
Second edition of *Oxford English Dictionary* published
Drabble's *A Natural Curiosity*
Murdoch's *The Message to the Planet*
Amis's *London Fields*
Ishiguro's *The Remains of the Day*
Death of Bruce Chatwin

1990 Communist monopoly ends in Bulgaria
Riots break out against community charge in England
First women ordained priests in Church of England
Civil war breaks out in Yugoslavia; Croatia and Slovenia declare independence
Bush and Gorbachev sign START agreement to reduce nuclear-weapons arsenals
President Jean-Baptiste Aristide

CHRONOLOGY

overthrown by military in Haiti
Boris Yeltsin elected president of
Russia
Dissolution of the Soviet Union
Nobel Prize for literature awarded
to Nadine Gordimer
Death of **Lawrence Durrell**

1992 U.N. Conference on Environment
and Development (the "Earth Sum-
mit") meets in Rio de Janeiro
Prince and Princess of Wales
separate
War in Bosnia-Herzegovina intensi-
fies
Bill Clinton elected president of the
United States in three-way race with
Bush and independent candidate H.
Ross Perot
Nobel Prize for literature awarded
to Derek Walcott
Death of Ruth Pitter

1993 Czechoslovakia divides into the
Czech Republic and Slovakia;
playwright Vaclav Havel elected
president of the Czech Republic
Britain ratifies Treaty on European
Union (the "Maastricht Treaty")
U.S. troops provide humanitarian
aid amid famine in Somalia
United States, Canada, and Mexico
sign North American Free Trade
Agreement
Nobel Prize for literature awarded
to Toni Morrison

1994 Nelson Mandela elected president in
South Africa's first post-apartheid
election
Jean-Baptiste Aristide restored to
presidency of Haiti
Clinton health care reforms rejected
by Congress
Civil war in Rwanda
Republicans win control of both
houses of Congress for first time in
forty years
Prime Minister Albert Reynolds of
Ireland meets with Gerry Adams,
president of Sinn Fein
Nobel Prize for literature awarded
to Kenzaburo Õe
Amis's *You Can't Do Both*

Naipaul's *A Way in the World*
Death of Dennis Potter

1995 Britain and Irish Republican Army
engage in diplomatic talks
Barings Bank forced into
bankruptcy as a result of a maverick
bond trader's losses
United States restores full
diplomatic relations with Vietnam
NATO initiates air strikes in Bosnia
Death of Stephen Spender
Israeli Prime Minister Yitzhak
Rabin assassinated
Nobel Prize for literature awarded
to Seamus Heaney

1996 IRA breaks cease-fire; Sein Fein
representatives barred from
Northern Ireland peace talks
Prince and Princess of Wales
divorce
Cease-fire agreement in Chechnia;
Russian forces begin to withdraw
Boris Yeltsin reelected president of
Russia
Bill Clinton reelected president of
the United States
Nobel Prize for literature awarded
to Wislawa Szymborska
Death of Caroline Blackwood

1996 British government destroys around
100,000 cows suspected of infection
with Creutzfeldt-Jakob, or "mad
cow" disease

1997 Diana, Princess of Wales, dies in an
automobile accident
Unveiling of first fully-cloned adult
animal, a sheep named Dolly
Booker McConnell Prize for fiction
awarded to Arundhati Roy

1998 United States renews bombing of
Bagdad, Iraq
Independent legislature and Parlia-
ments return to Scotland and Wales
Booker McConnell Prize for fiction
awarded to Ian McEwan
Nobel Prize for literature awarded
to Jose Saramago

1999 King Hussein of Jordan dies
United Nations responds militarily
to Serbian President Slobodan
Milosevic's escalation of crisis in

CHRONOLOGY

Kosovo

Booker McConnell Prize for fiction awarded to J. M. Coetzee

Nobel Prize for literature awarded to Günter Grass

Deaths of Patricia Beer, Ted Hughes, Brian Moore, and Iain Chrichton Smith

2000   Penelope Fitzgerald dies

J. K. Rowling's *Harry Potter and the Goblet of Fire* sells more than 300,000 copies in its first day

Oil blockades by fuel haulers protesting high oil taxes bring much of Britain to a standstill

Slobodan Milosevic loses Serbian general election to Vojislav Kostunica

Death of Scotland's First Minister, Donald Dewar

Nobel Prize for literature awarded to Gao Xingjian

Booker McConnell Prize for fiction awarded to Margaret Atwood

George W. Bush, son of former president George Bush, becomes president of the United States after Supreme Court halts recount of closest election in history

Death of former Canadian Prime Minister Pierre Elliot Trudeau

Human Genome Project researchers announce that they have a complete map of the genetic code of a human chromosome

Vladimir Putin succeeds Boris Yeltsin as president of Russia

British Prime Minister Tony Blair's son Leo is born, making him the first child born to a sitting prime minister in 152 years

Death of Patrick O'Brian Keith Roberts and R.S. Thomas

2001   In Britain, the House of Lords passes legislation that legalizes the creation of cloned human embryos

British Prime Minister Tony Blair wins second term

Margaret Atwood's *The Blind Assassin* wins Booker McConnell Prize for fiction

Kazuo Ishiguro's *When We Were Orphans*

Trezza Azzopardi's *The Hiding Place*

Terrorists attack World Trade Center and Pentagon with hijacked airplanes, resulting in the collapse of the World Trade Center towers and the deaths of thousands. Passengers of a third hijacked plane thwart hijackers, resulting in a crash landing in Pennsylvania. The attacks are thought to be organized by Osama bin Laden, the leader of an international terrorist network known as al Qaeda

Ian McEwan's *An Atonement*

Salman Rushdie's *Fury*

Peter Carey's *True History of the Kelly Gang*

Deaths of Eudora Welty and W. G. Sebald

2002   Former U.S. President Jimmy Carter awarded the Nobel Peace Prize

Europe experiences its worst floods in 100 years as floodwaters force thousands of people out of their homes

Wall Street Journal reporter Daniel Pearl kidnapped and killed in Karachi, Pakistan while researching a story about Pakistani militants and suspected shoe bomber Richard Reid. British-born Islamic militant Ahmad Omar Saeed Sheikh sentenced to death for the crime. Three accomplices receive life sentences.

Slobodan Milosevic goes on trial at the U.N. war crimes tribunal in The Hague on charges of masterminding ethnic cleansing in the former Yugoslavia.

Yann Martel's *Life of Pi* wins Booker McConnell Prize for fiction

Nobel Prize for literature awarded to Imre Kertész

2003   Ariel Sharon elected as Israeli prime minister

Venezuelan President Hugo Chavez forced to leave office after a nine week general strike calling for his resignation ends

U.S. presents to the United Nations its Iraq war rationale, citing its Weapons of Mass Destruction as imminent threat to world security

U.S. and Britain launch war against Iraq

Baghdad falls to U.S. troops

Official end to combat operations in Iraq is declared by the U.S.

Aung San Suu Kyi, Burmese opposition leader, placed under house arrest by military regime

NATO assumes control of peacekeeping force in Afghanistan

American troops capture Saddam Hussein

J.K. Rowling's *Harry Potter and the Order of the Phoenix*, the fifth installment in the wildly popular series, hit the shelves and rocketed up the best-seller lists

Nobel Prize for literature awarded to J. M. Coetzee

Death of C. H. Sisson

2004 NATO admits seven new members—Bulgaria, Estonia, Latvia, Lithuania, Romania, Slovakia, and Slovenia

Terrorists bomb commuter trains in Spain—al–Qaeda claims responsibility

Ten new states join the European Union, expanding it to twenty–five members states total

Muslim terrorists attack a school in Beslan, Russia, resulting in over 300 civilian deaths, many of them schoolchildren

George W. Bush is re–elected president of the United States

Allegations of corruption in the election of Ukraine's Viktor Yanukovych result in the &ldquote;Orange Revolution" and Parliament's decision to nullify the first election results— the secondary run–off election is closley monitored and favors Viktor Yushchenko for president

A massive 9.0 earthquake rocks the

Indian Ocean, resulting in a catastrophic tsunami, devastating southern Asia and eastern Africa and killing tens of thousands of people

Alan Hollinghurst's *The Line of Beauty* wins Man Booker Prize for fiction

Death of **Thom Gunn**

2005 Terrorists bomb three subway stations in London, killing 52 and injuring more than 700

Pope John Paul II dies, marking the end of an era for the Roman Catholic Church. He is succeeded by Pope Benedict XVI

Hurricane Katrina hits the U.S. Golf Coast, devastating cities in Louisianna and Mississippi, and killing over 1,000 people.

J.K. Rowling's *Harry Potter and the Half-Blood Prince* sells over 6.9 billion copies on the first day of release in the U.S. alone

Nobel Prize for literature awarded to Harold Pinter

Deaths of Saul Bellow and Arthur Miller

2006 Former Iraqi President Saddam Hussein is found guilty for crimes against humanity and is executed in Iraq

Ban Ki-moon elected the next UN secretary-general

International Astronomical Union rules that Pluto is no longer seen as a planet

Fleur Adcock wins the Queen?s Gold Medal for Poetry

Kamau Brathwaite wins the Griffin Poetry Prize for *Born to Slow Horses*

2007 Oil prices skyrocket as a barrel of crude oil tops ninety dollars

Record-high mortgage foreclosures and a steep decline in the housing market strain financial industries causing multibillion-dollar losses at major banks and investment firms

Seung-Hui Cho opens fire at Virginia Tech University killing 32 and wounding several others before turning the gun on himself

The final volume of J.K. Rowling's *Harry Potter* series, *Harry Potter and the Deathly Hallows*, is released selling over 8.3 million copies in the first twenty-four hours

Nobel Prize for literature awarded to Doris Lessing

2008 Barack Obama is elected the first African-American President of the United States

A 7.9 magnitude earthquake strikes the Sichaun region of China, leaving 4.8 million homeless and over 68,000 dead

Fidel Castro resigns as President of Cuba after a record-breaking 49 years as head of state

Georgia launches a military strike against the defected region of South Ossetia, sparking the start of the short-lived South Ossetia War

2009 United States President Barack Obama orders the closure of all secret prisons and detention camps operated by the CIA, including the Guantánamo Bay facility in Cuba

The World Health Organization declares a flu pandemic of the H1N1 virus, following an initial outbreak of the illness in Mexico

Carol Ann Duffy is the first woman appointed poet laureate of the United Kingdom

Mahmoud Ahmadinejad is confirmed as the winner of a second term as president of Afghanistan, following accusations of ballot tampering and other forms of election fraud

Nobel Prize for literature awarded to Herta Müller

List of Contributors

J. C. BITTENBENDER. Professor of English, Eastern University, teaching twentieth-century British literature. Areas of specialty include modern Scottish and Irish literature, and he has published articles on Robert Burns, James Kelman, Alasdair Gray and other Scottish writers. Additional areas of academic interest include Bakhtinian theory and censorship studies. **Dylan Thomas**

SANDIE BYRNE. English literature academic and writer. Author of a number of books and articles on nineteenth- and twentieth-century authors, including *Jane Austen: Mansfield Park* and *The Unbearable Saki: The Work of H. H. Munro.* **Elizabeth Gaskell**

FRANCES A. CHIU. Instructor in history and literature, New School University. Received her Ph.D. from Oxford University. She has presented papers at the ASECs, BSECs, eighteenth- and nineteenth-century British Women Writers, and the DeBartolo conferences. Publications include (as editor) Ann Radcliffe's *Gaston de Blondeville* and J. Sheridan Le Fanu's *The Rose and the Key*; as well as contributions to *Eighteenth-century Life, Notes and Queries,* and *Romanticism on the Net.* **Ann Radcliffe**

PETER DEMPSEY. Senior lecturer in English, University of Sunderland, teaching twentieth-century Irish and American literature. Publications include essays on David Markson, Sara Paretsky, Joyce, and Ronald Firbank. Also author of fiction reviews for British and American newspapers and magazines. **James Joyce**

KIT FAN. Poet and scholar. Received his Ph.D. from the University of York. Publications include contributions to the *London Magazine, Poetry Review, Poetry Wales, The Rialto* and the *Warwick Review.* He is also a regular reviewer for *Poetry Review.* **Thom Gunn**

KATHERINE FIRTH. Visiting Research Fellow at Trinity College, University of Melbourne. Previ-

ous publications include works on modernist and 1930s poetry. **Alfred Tennyson**

JOSHUA GRASSO. Assistant Professor of English, East Central University (Ada, OK). Received his Ph.D. from Miami University, where his dissertation focused on seventeenth- and eighteenth-century travel writing. His most article, "'An Enemy of his Country's Prosperity and Safety': Mapping the English Traveler in Defoe's Robinson Crusoe" appeared in the *CEA Critic.* Additional publications include articles on Kipling, V. S. Naipaul, and Marjane Satrapi's *Persepolis.* **Rudyard Kipling**

LISA K. KASMER. Assistant Professor, Clark University. Research includes an examination of the intersection of genre and politics in women's historical fiction in the early nineteenth century. She has published on women's history writing and historical fiction. **Mary Shelley**

TADZIO KOELB. Writer and scholar. Received his M.A. in creative writing from the University of East Anglia. Regular contributor of reviews and features on books and literature to a number of UK publications, including the *Times Literary Supplement, Guardian, Literary Review, New Statesman,* and the *Jewish Quarterly.* His novella *Fate's Lieutenant* was shortlisted for the Faulkner Society's William Faulkner/William Wisdom prize. **Lawrence Durrell**

BARRY LEWIS. Senior lecturer, University of Sunderland. Received his Ph.D. in postmodernist American fiction from the University of Sunderland. Formerly held posts at University of Newcastle, the University of Trondheim, and Stavanger College in Norway. Publications include *Kazuo Ishiguro* and *My Words Echo Thus: Possessing the Past in Peter Ackroyd.* **Kazuo Ishiguro**

ELIZABETH LUDLOW. Fellow and part-time tutor in the in the department of English and Comparative Literary Studies, Institute of Advanced Studies. Her Ph.D. thesis, "'We can but spell a surface history': The Biblical Typology of Christina Rossetti" considered Rossetti's use of biblical typology in her articulation of individual and communal identity. She is also the author of book reviews and articles in the field of Rossetti scholarship. **Christina Rossetti**

THOMAS MARKS. Lecturer in Victorian and Modern English literature, Magdalen College, Oxford. Publications include articles on Alfred Tennyson and Browning, as well as regular contributions to the *Times Literary Supplement* and other literary journals. **Robert Browning**

JANET McCANN. Professor of English, Texas A&M University. Instructor in creative writing and women's literature. She is the author of *Wallace Stevens Revisited: The Celestial Possible,* has co-authored several texts and anthologies, and written five poetry collections including *Emily's Dress.* **Stevie Smith**

JULIE NASH. Associate Professor of English, University of Massachusetts, Lowell. Publications include *Servants and the Problem of Paternalism in Works by Maria Edgeworth and Elizabeth Gaskell* and (as editor) the essay collections *New Approaches to the Literary Art of Anne Brontë* (with Barbara Suess) and *New Essays on Maria Edgeworth.* Also author of articles on Behn, Maria Edgeworth, Elizabeth Gaskell, and Fay Weldon, and served as a guest editor for a special issue on servants and literature of the journal *Lit: Literature, Interpretation, Theory.* **Aphra Behn**

PIERS PENNINGTON. Graduate student, Corpus Christi College, Oxford. His thesis examines the positioning of the self in modern poetry. **Philip Larkin**

LACY SCHUTZ. Archivist, Sterling and Francine Clark Art Institute (Williamstown, MA), and poet. Received an M.A. in writing from Bennington College and an M.L.S. from Pratt Institute. Her poems have been published in many journals, including the *Colorado Review* and *Post Road,* and her essay on Kenneth Koch appeared in *American Authors.* **Geoffrey Hill**

CHARLOTTE SCOTT. Lecturer in Shakespeare, Goldsmiths College, University of London. Publications include *Shakespeare and the Idea of the Book.* **William Shakespeare**

GORDON SPARK. Postgraduate research student, University of Dundee. His thesis examines the treatment of time and history in the work of Kazuo Ishiguro and Timothy Mo. Research interests include the development of espionage fiction in the twentieth century, with particular interest in the work of Graham Greene, Ian Fleming and John Le Carré. He has published on Ishiguro and is co-editor of two edited collections on contemporary fiction and culture. **John Le Carré**

RHIAN WILLIAMS. Lecturer in nineteenth-century literature, University of Glasgow. Research interests include the uses of genre, form, and prosody, especially in the nineteenth century, but more broadly in Anglophone poetry, as explored in her book, *The Poetry Toolkit: The Essential Guide to Studying Poetry.* She has published articles on Alfred Tennyson, Elizabeth Barrett Browning, William Wordsworth and "Michael Field" and edited various collections of nineteenth-century letters and theatrical presentations. **William Cowper**

DAVID WYKES. Professor of English, Dartmouth College. He has been teaching eighteenth-century literature for over three decades at Dartmouth, and he has published a book on Dryden, among other writers of the period. **John Dryden**

BRITISH WRITERS

APHRA BEHN

(1640—1689)

Julie Nash

"ALL WOMEN TOGETHER ought to let flowers fall upon the tomb of Aphra Behn, which is, most scandalously but rather appropriately, in Westminster Abbey, for it was she who earned them the right to speak their minds." With these words from *A Room of One's Own* (p. 65), Virginia Woolf sparked a revival of interest in the career of Aphra Behn, one of the first women to earn her living by writing.

In the 240 years that elapsed between Behn's death and the publication of Woolf's celebrated feminist essay, Behn's literary reputation was eclipsed by her reputation as a writer of "rank and feculent" works, "too filthy [for decent people] to handle," in the words of the Victorian periodical *Saturday Review*. A prolific author of plays, poetry, fiction, and translations, Behn was well suited to the bawdy world of Restoration London, and her works reflect the amorous, courtly values of their author. In time, the era would come to be known for its decadence, and the English would eventually turn to King William and Queen Mary of Orange to restore respectability to the English crown. Behn died within days of their coronation. Thus one of the most colorful characters in an era known for its colorful characters fittingly left the stage just as the Restoration curtain was drawing to a close.

FROM SECRET SPY TO INFAMOUS PLAYWRIGHT: LIFE AND CAREER

If she was in fact born in 1640, as most of her biographers believe, Aphra Behn's childhood coincided with the early years of the English Civil War in which Parliament challenged and eventually overthrew the absolute monarchical rule of King Charles Stuart I. Behn's childhood was marked by national turmoil, culminating in the execution of the king in 1649. Following eleven years of Puritan rule (known as the Interregnum), Charles II was restored to the throne, setting the stage for an anti-Puritan London that celebrated the "royal" values of beauty, poetry, and opulent sensuality. These national events, as well as the long-standing English rivalry with the Dutch, would influence Behn's later writing in direct and indirect ways. As a passionate and loyal royalist, Behn embraced every opportunity to praise the Stuart dynasty and the aristocratic principles that characterized courtly life. Her works of fiction, poetry, and drama celebrate the values of love, honor, and pleasure while condemning treachery as the greatest vice. The use and misuse of power is her central theme, reflecting one of the chief preoccupations of life in Restoration London.

All of Behn's biographies—from the earliest tributes that closely followed her death to the excellent 1996 book by Janet Todd, *The Secret Life of Aphra Behn*—rely on some speculation and incomplete records to piece together details of Behn's birth and early years. Most scholars believe her birth name was Johnson and that she was born in Kent; her mother may have been Elizabeth Denham, a wet nurse to the aristocratic Colepeper family, and her father may have been Bartholomew Johnson, a barber. If so, her origins were respectable, though modest. Perhaps early connections to the Colepeper family (and their well-placed relations, the Sidneys) enabled her to have access to an education that would have been unusual for a girl of her background. Though she would later complain of a poor education, her works reveal knowledge of French, history, philosophy, and a wide variety of European literature.

How Aphra Johnson, a barber's daughter from Kent, became Aphra Behn, the woman who would one day be buried among England's greatest writers in Westminster Abbey, can perhaps be attributed to a series of early adventures that she drew upon in her fiction and plays. While in her early twenties, Behn traveled with her family to the South American colony of Surinam (which would later fall to the Dutch); Todd conjectures that Behn may have been sent there as a spy. She remained in Surinam for several months, observing the manners of the natives, colonists, and slaves, storing up images that would appear years later in her short novel *Oroonoko*. While there, she played the flute, wrote her first play, and possibly became romantically involved with William Scot, an English exile wanted for treason whose father was executed during the Civil War.

After she returned to England in 1664, Behn married and became a widow within the space of two years. Scholars know even less about the elusive Mr. Behn than they do about the circumstances of Aphra "Johnson's" birth. Some have even speculated that her husband never existed, that Aphra chose to present herself as a widow to make it possible for her to live in London with fewer restrictions. Janet Todd suggests that Aphra may have married Johan Behn, a merchant sailor and slave trader who was active at the time. There are no records of this marriage, and the writings of Aphra Behn herself are silent on the subject. Her works, however, do suggest that the match was less than ideal: throughout her writings, the merchant class is repeatedly portrayed as grasping and pretentious. In addition, a common theme in Behn's oeuvre is the disastrous fate of the young woman who marries an older man, suggesting that this may have been her experience as well. If Behn did base any of these literary matches on her own marital experience, she must have found Mr. Behn to be repulsive. For example, in her 1677 play *The Rover,* a young woman imagines going to bed with an older man who "yawns and sighs a belch or two ... throws himself into bed, and expects you in his foul sheets, and e'er you can get yourself undressed, calls you with a snore or two" (act 1, scene 1).

Whoever Mr. Behn was—young or old, merchant or gentleman—by the middle of 1666 he had apparently died and left his widow with no financial resources. Though she had been considering a career in writing, unheard of for a woman, she was persuaded to take an even more adventurous path as a spy for Charles II. England was once again at war with the Dutch, and Behn's assignment was to communicate with her old acquaintance Sir William Scot, then in exile.

Following his stay in Surinam, Scot was unable to return to England because he was still wanted for his ties to the Puritan government. He traveled instead to Holland, where he was able to obtain valuable information about Dutch uprisings against the English. The English government saw in Scot a potentially valuable informant if they could convince him to shift his loyalty to the king. But spies and double agents flourished at this time, and Scot was mistrustful of any ambassador who attempted to negotiate an agreement. Although the details are unclear, Aphra Behn was eventually selected to travel to Antwerp to meet with Scot, secure his loyalty, and obtain any information that might be valuable.

Restoration women rarely participated in public life, much less espionage, but Behn was (and would remain) fiercely patriotic. In addition, she was in need of a means of support and no doubt expected financial recompense for the very real risks she was undertaking. Her activities in Antwerp were closely scrutinized by both English and Dutch loyalists who knew of her earlier connection to Scot. This period of Behn's life was fraught with difficulty. She could never fully trust Scot, and her British contacts did not fully trust her. Moreover, both she and Scot were desperate for money. Her letters from this period describe the impoverished conditions in which she and other English agents were living. Behn was forced to pawn her jewelry to meet her daily expenses and wrote to friends asking to borrow money when there was none forthcoming from the Crown.

During her stay in Antwerp, Behn regularly furnished the English with information on the Dutch navy, spies, and other useful matters, but she was increasingly short of money and concerned about her work. In a letter to James Halsall, she wrote, "I am almost out of my witts I heare not ffrom you. Sir I am worse than dead till I am out of this expensive hous wheare I vow to god I do not rest with continuall thoughts of my debts and fears of displeasing you" (Goreau, p. 106). In another letter Behn expresses pride in the service she has performed for her country and resentment about the way she has been treated by the king's representatives: "I am very confident that no person in the world could have drawn [Scot] to a resolution of that kind, besides my self: … Being so long with out any money: I was forcd to be at very great charge where I had credit so that when I ow'd 100 and 20 pounds I had a bill of 50.... I am dayly, and howerly, abusd and threatened.... I am in extreame want and necessity.... I have pawnd all my rings, and little things I had.... I beseech you, take some pitty" (Goreau, p. 107).

When Behn finally received word that she was to return to England, she was forced to borrow money for her trip home. Her dealings in Antwerp had perhaps taught her the value of self-preservation and the need to advocate on her own behalf. It also furnished her with her pen name, Astrea, a code name she adopted to protect herself in case her letters were intercepted. Many of her later works were published under this name, and her contemporaries often referred to her by it. She had little else to show for her trouble. Although she had worked tirelessly on the king's behalf, her work was generally unappreciated and, perhaps more importantly, uncompensated. By late 1668 she was ill and in debtors' prison with no prospects and determined not to starve.

Scholars do not know how long Behn spent in prison or who enabled her release by paying her debts. Perhaps the royal government came through after all or perhaps her friends raised the money. It was not long, though, before Behn found a unique way of staying out of debt: playwriting.

Behn's first play, *The Forced Marriage; or, The Jealous Bridegroom* (1670), ran for a respectable six nights and was followed by at least nineteen more dramas. Though most of her plays were successful, she was regularly criticized for the very unfeminine act of writing for the public.

In the prologues, epilogues, and other accompanying commentaries of many of these plays, she defended her right to compete in the literary marketplace with men. In an epistle to the reader that accompanied her unsuccessful third play, *The Dutch Lover,* she explains that a classical education is not necessary to write a good play and thus women are just as capable as men in this genre. She even compares herself to Shakespeare, who, she argues, had achieved about the same level of education as most women.

In 1670 it was unheard of for a woman to make her living as a writer, but Aphra Behn had few other options and saw an opportunity in the world of Restoration theater. The Continental tastes that Charles II imported from his exile in France included a demand for original drama, but because the Puritans had closed the public theaters during the Interregnum, there were few experienced playwrights, actors, or even audience members. Behn was well suited to meeting this demand, especially because women were allowed to appear on the public stage for the first time in England. Behn would go on to create memorable, witty heroines throughout her playwriting career, parts created for individual actresses who were celebrities in their day just as movie stars are in ours. This opportunity was a double-edged sword for both female actor and playwright, however. Women who performed for the public or, in Behn's case, wrote for the public, were seen as sexually compromised. The culture of Restoration theater was racy, with prostitutes advertising their services alongside the orange sellers. Charles II plucked two actresses off the stage and made them his mistresses. One of them, Nell Gwynne, became a friend of Behn's and helped ensure her success by publicly attending her plays. Another friend of Behn's, the actress Elizabeth Barry, was the acknowledged mistress of John Wilmot, the Earl of Rochester, who purportedly coached her to greatness on a bet. Any woman associated with this sexually charged atmosphere would be automatically suspected of having loose morals, no matter how unblemished her actual life. The fact that Behn also chose to write sexually suggestive plays ensured that her reputation as a respectable woman would suffer.

It was a double standard, and she knew it. In a "Preface to the Reader" printed with her play *Sir Patient Fancy,* she writes, "I printed this play with all the impatient haste one ought to do, who would be vindicated from the most unjust and silly aspersion ... and which only my being a woman has procured me; *That it was Bawdy,* the least and most excusable fault in the men writers" (Goreau, p. 233). Of course, as Behn herself pointed out, she wrote for profit and to please a licentious age. In the same preface she notes that she is "forced to write for bread and not ashamed to own it, and consequently ought to write to please (if she can) an age which has given several proofs it was by this way of writing to be obliged" (Goreau, p. 233).

Though frequently the target of criticism, Behn also enjoyed literary success and participated in the glittering social life of Charles' court. She had many friends with whom she regularly corresponded and collaborated, and her poetry and letters suggest a rich social circle knit together by a love of theater, poetry, and Tory politics. She counted the Earl of Rochester and fellow writers John Dryden and Thomas Otway among her friends. Though fraught with complications, especially for women, love affairs were also frequent in Behn's circle, and she herself was involved with the bisexual lawyer John Hoyle for some years. Scholars believe that much of Behn's erotic poetry and her "Love Letters to a Gentleman" are addressed to Hoyle and describe a complex, intense relationship based on passionate desire on one hand and mistrust on the other. Hoyle's first appearance in her writings is as the faithless "J.H." from her poem "Our Cabal," which describes a pastoral outing among Behn and her friends.

The year 1677 marked the high point of Behn's theatrical career with the production of her comedy *The Rover.* Although she would continue to write plays throughout her life, the freewheeling lifestyle of the early Restoration era was fading amid political turmoil that affected attendance at theaters. With fourteen acknowledged children by his numerous mistresses, Charles II had no legitimate heirs. His Catholic brother, James II, was next in line to the throne, and

England feared a permanent return to Catholic rule should he inherit the crown. Many supported Charles' popular illegitimate Protestant son, James, the Duke of Monmouth, to succeed his father, creating a period of national turmoil known as the Exclusion Crisis. Behn was adamant in her support of the Stuart dynasty, however, so much so that a warrant was taken out for her arrest in 1682 for writing an epilogue to a lost play in which the Duke of Monmouth was urged to treat his father with more gratitude. (Apparently Charles II was more fond of his rebellious son than Behn was). Her dramas became increasingly political and focused on issues of loyalty and betrayal. When she was later asked to write a poem in praise of the new King William of Orange (who had ousted James in the "Glorious Revolution" of 1688), Behn remained loyal to the exiled James, stating that she "deplore[s]" the "wond'rous change" of the revolution that "leaves me unpitied far behind / On the forsaken barren shore" ("A Pindaric Poem to the Reverend Doctor Burnet, On the Honour He Did Me of Enquiring After Me and My Muse" (*Oroonoko, and Other Writings,* p. 268).

If the political instability of the 1680s left Behn's living as a playwright in doubt, it forced her to seek other ways of making a living. Behn turned to translation as a way to pay her bills and, increasingly, to fiction, a genre more suited to one without a classical education. Her first novel, *Love Letters Between a Nobleman and His Sister,* was published in three parts beginning in 1684 and (barely) fictionalized the evolution of a well-known scandal. The novel was popular and was followed by a number of subsequent works of amatory fiction, as well as *Oroonoko* (1688), the tragedy of the royal slave that would be her most lasting and famous literary work.

During her lifetime Behn was best known for her witty stage comedies, but her greatest contribution to literature was probably to the development of the novel. Although Ian Watt's influential 1957 work *The Rise of the Novel* dismisses Behn's fiction as not realistic enough to be included in his analysis of the novel's traditions, more recent critics have disagreed, seeing in Behn's fiction precursors to the detailed, plot-driven novels that would dominate the eighteenth century. Her narrators, in particular, anticipate the female narrators in recognizable ways. Behn went out of her way to claim that the stories she wrote were true, and often lays claim to being an eyewitness to certain key events such as Oroonoko's execution or the botched beheading of Prince Tarquin in *The Fair Jilt.* She thus explicitly establishes a biographical connection between herself and her narrators. Just where these connections begin and end remains a mystery. The narrator who relates Oroonoko's "history" is the same one who had inserted herself into *Love-Letters Between a Nobleman and His Sister.* We know *Love-Letters* is a work of fiction based on true events. Behn would have us assume the same is true for *Oroonoko,* but the relationship between Behn and her narrators—as well as that between history and Behn's fiction—remains unstable, as Jacqueline Pearson notes in *The Cambridge Companion to Aphra Behn.*

Though her fiction was popular, it would not be able to save her from financial distress and ill health. Of her literary accomplishments, however, she harbored little doubt. In contrast to her earlier claim that she wrote only for money, she now openly admitted that she craved respect and fame and, moreover, deserved it. In a note on a translation written a few months before she died, she expresses the hope that her writing will be granted immortality alongside that of other poets. Likewise, she concludes *Oroonoko* with the expectation that "the reputation of [her] pen is considerable enough to make his [Oroonoko's] glorious name to survive to all ages" (Introduction to *Oronooko, and Other Writings,* p. 73).

Aphra Behn died on April 16, 1689, and her reputation did survive, although probably not in ways she might have liked. *Oronooko's* immortality owes as much to Thomas Southerne's 1695 stage adaptation, *Oroonoko: A Tragedy,* which remained popular through the nineteenth century. By 1910 Behn had become a footnote in literary history. The *Short, Biographical Dictionary of English Literature* published that year by John W. Cousin has a brief entry on her that outlines her biography and tells us that her plays are "extremely gross, and are now happily little

known." In fact, her plays were no bawdier than those of her contemporaries, most of whom received similar, if less virulent, censure from successive centuries of criticism. (Cousin also calls out Behn's contemporary John Dryden for writing plays that are "deeply stained with the immorality of the age"). However, due to increasing interest in women's writing, the twentieth and early twenty-first centuries witnessed a resurgence of interest in Aphra Behn's works, from her witty stage comedies to her fictional engagement with issues such as race and colonization.

In less than two decades of writing, Behn's output was prolific, with complex and multifaceted works in a variety of genres, styles, and subjects. But over the course of her career, her drama, poetry, and fiction circle back to three major themes: sex and gender, marriage and money, and politics and power. These are overlapping issues in most of her works, but it is nonetheless useful to organize a discussion of her oeuvre by moving thematically from private (sex and gender) to semiprivate (marriage and money) to public (politics and power) matters.

A NOT-SO-GOLDEN AGE: SEX AND GENDER

Restoration London offered an alternative to the Puritan mindset that was predominant during the Interregnum. Charles II, with his multiple mistresses and illegitimate children, provided a model for sexual freedom that was followed in the worlds of the court and theater. Behn seems to have embraced this ethos and the idea of "free love," at least to a point. As a practical matter, she was well aware that this freedom had different implications for men and women.

In her poem "The Golden Age," published in her 1684 collection *Poems Upon Several Occasions,* Behn lays out her utopian vision of a pastoral world prior to the corrupting influences of court, king, or law. The title refers to the Elizabethan period, but Behn is exploring an idealized past that enables her to envision a world in which women have control over their sexuality and love freely and with abandon. Sexual expression is natural, and shame does not exist. In "The Golden Age" nature is in harmony with itself and with its inhabitants: "Calm was the Air, no Winds blew fierce and loud, / The Skie was dark'ned with no sullen Cloud" (II, ll. 1–2). Humanity's efforts to control the earth result in violence. The Golden Age is a time before "stubborn" ploughs "rape" the virgin earth (III, ll. 1–2) and monarchs, "Those Arbitrary Rulers over men" (IV, l. 4), had not yet broken the laws of nature. This poem is one of few works in which Behn overtly criticizes monarchical succession. Behn's description of the arbitrary power of kings is in opposition to her otherwise loyal support of the Stuart dynasty. Yet here Behn classifies all civilizing forces as equally constraining, particularly for women.

The nymphs and shepherds in "The Golden Age" enact courtship rituals of seduction and resistance, but the women yield willingly and without coercion. Sex is passionate and mutually pleasurable:

The Lovers thus, thus uncontroul'd did meet,
Thus all their Joyes and Vows of Love repeat:
Joyes which were everlasting, ever new
And every Vow inviolably true.

(VII, ll. 1–4)

Behn sets aside special scorn for the Restoration concept of "Honour," which, according to Behn, controls women's sexuality through religion and shame. "Cursed" Honour is a "miser" and a "tyrant" who imprisons women's beauty and desires and teaches women to be artful rather than free with their feelings (VIII, l. 3). The poem concludes with a carpe diem address to "Sylvia," urging her to join the speaker in sexual enjoyment while they are still young and able to do so.

Behn's celebration of sexual love was in keeping with the ethos of the Restoration court, but she was well aware that she was not living in a "Golden Age" and that desire was a double-edged sword for women (literally; she frequently uses images of war and battles to stand in for heterosexual relationships). In addition to the practical dangers of unwanted pregnancy and venereal disease (from which Behn herself suffered), Behn knew it was dangerous to surrender fully one's body and heart in an environment that viewed women as expendable. Angeline Goreau, among others, has written about the misogyny that underpinned the supposedly free spirit of the Restoration. The literature of the period repeatedly uses obscene epithets to describe women, refers to them as whores, resents them for withholding their sexuality from men, and then abandons them when they give in. The title of Rochester's poem "Love a Woman? You're an Ass," aptly sums up a prevailing attitude that women like Behn had to confront if they became involved with men.

The dangers of surrendering to desire appear in a number of Behn's works. In "A Ballad on Mr. J.H. to Amoret, Asking Why I Was So Sad" the speaker warns her friend "Amoret" (possibly based on the actress Elizabeth Barry) to stay away from "J.H." (most likely John Hoyle). Like "The Golden Age," this ballad is set in a pastoral world, but this is not a place where every vow is "inviolably true." The speaker writes of coming upon "Amyntas" in a secluded grove. What at first appears natural in him turns out to be artful:

His Eyes their best Attracts put on,
Designing some should be undone;
For he could at his pleasure move,
The Nymphs he lik'd to fall in Love.

(ll. 37–45 *Oroonoko, and Other Writings*, p. 215)

He seduces her with his good looks, wit, and charm. The speaker is "entirely won and lost," playing on the concept of the lost, or fallen, woman who is undone by her seducer. Similarly, in "Love Armed," first written for her tragedy *Abdelazar* and later reprinted in *Poems Upon Several Occasions,* the speaker and her lover create a deity to love in which "my poor heart alone is harmed, / Whilst thine the victor is, and free" (ll. 15–16). "A Ballad" and "Love Armed" reveal a darker side of desire in which seduction is a game played by designing men. In this game, men can love and be "free," while women are "lost" and "harmed."

Of course, it was not only men who manipulated others for their own sexual pleasure. Behn also creates dangerous, seductive females who are easily a match for her predatory libertines. Behn's first novel, *Love-Letters Between a Nobleman and His Sister,* was published in three parts. It chronicles the real-life relationship between Lord Grey, a Whig supporter of Monmouth, and his wife's younger sister, Lady Henrietta Berkeley, with whom he had been involved since she was in her early teens. At the time Behn wrote the first part of the novel, Lord Grey had been tried and convicted for "debauching" Lady Henrietta; had been subsequently arrested for his part in a conspiracy with Monmouth to kill the king and his brother James; and had avoided execution by escaping with Lady Henrietta to the Continent.

It is easy to see why this source material must have been irresistible to Behn, who was looking for a way to make a living as opportunities in the theater dried up. The scandal was well known and involved both sexual and political intrigue. The country's mood was heightened by anxieties over a permanent Stuart (and Catholic) dynasty, but there was not much appetite for violent revolution. Behn's thinly veiled account of Grey's (technically incestuous) relationship with his sister-in-law set alongside a plot to assassinate the king enabled her to capitalize on public interest and to shift her gaze away from the stage and into the more private and intimate genre of letters and narrative fiction. Behn moves the setting to sixteenth-century France and changes the characters' names but leaves many of the details from the scandal intact. The first part of *Love-Letters* is written in the epistolary style and consists of fictionalized letters mostly between Philander and his wife's sister Sylvia (a few of the letters are written by servants and one is by Philander's wife). The erotic letters reveal the emotional conflicts of the characters as they wrestle with their illicit passion and eventually succumb to it. Part 2, published in 1685, follows their exploits abroad as Philander tires of Sylvia and pursues a new mistress, the brother of whom in turn pursues Sylvia. In this section, Behn has abandoned the epistolary style and shifted to an omniscient narrator, one who assists the reader in negotiating an increasingly complex plot. Part 3 was published in 1687, two years after the real

Monmouth's execution for his rebellious invasion and attempted overthrow of King James. Behn covers these historical events by detailing the failed rebellion of "Cesario," a would-be hero who is ultimately too weak for the role. Ros Ballaster points out that Part 3 also traces Sylvia's "development as a full-blown female libertine" who seduces men for pleasure or profit (usually both) (*Cambridge Companion to Aphra Behn,* p. 137). Philander, like the real Grey, escapes retribution for his part in the treason.

In Part 1, Philander and Sylvia resemble lovers out of Behn's "Golden Age." They repeatedly assert that their love is pure, that it is the laws of the world and the binding practice of marriage that keep them apart and make their passion a guilty one. Philander writes to Sylvia, contrasting the freedom of the natural world to the unnatural constraints imposed by humanity:

> Here [in nature] is no troublesome honour, amongst the pretty inhabitants of the woods and streams, fondly to give laws to nature, but uncontrolled they play, and sing, and love; no parents checking their dear delights, no slavish matrimonial ties to restrain their nobler flame. No spies to interrupt their blest appointments; but every little nest is free and open to receive the young fledg'd lover.
>
> (*Love-Letters Between a Nobleman and His Sister*, pp. 30–31)

"Honour" once again becomes a check on passion. Despite her love for Philander, Sylvia's emotions are mixed. She longs for her lover, but she knows that in sacrificing her "Honour" she will be paying a high price. Once they do consummate their relationship (after one failed attempt in which Philander is impotent), Sylvia writes a long letter that alternates between declarations of passion and statements of regret. The ideal free love Behn advocates in "The Golden Age" is more complicated in the Restoration age. Sylvia's passion is all-consuming and thus dangerous:

> I now can think of nothing but of thee.... One thought of thee is worth the world's enjoyment, I hate to dress, I hate to be agreeable to any eyes but thine; I hate the noise of equipage and crowds, and would be more content to live with thee in some lone shaded cottage, than be a queen, and hindered

by that grandeur one moment's conversation with *Philander:* may'st thou despise and loathe me, a curse the greatest that I can invent, if this be any thing but real honest truth.

(Love-Letters Between a Nobleman and His Sister, p. 59)

Philander does not come to despise Sylvia, but he does grow tired of her and takes up with other women. As Behn notes throughout her writing, once satiated, passion often wanes. By Part 3, Sylvia is the seducer, both in order to revenge herself upon Philander for his infidelity and to enrich herself, "ready money being the joy of her heart." Sylvia even goes so far as to have sexual relations with a lover in view of her servant, "so absolutely had she depraved her reason, from one degree of sin and shame to another." Sylvia pursues pleasure and power in a traditionally masculine way, without shame and without any real consequences. Her transformation from innocent young virgin to Restoration rake is complete. As the novel concludes, Philander takes leave of Sylvia with the full belief that she has been faithful to him, and indeed a brief reunion convinces both of them that "there was a very great friendship still remaining at the bottom of their hearts for each other, nor did they part without manifold proofs of it." Sylvia, presumably, moves on to other conquests, unscathed by her own philandering ways.

In *Love-Letters Between a Nobleman and his Sister,* as well as other works, Behn depicts men and women who violate gender norms and traditional roles. As a woman writing in a man's world, Behn frankly acknowledged this transgression. Her writings regularly and ardently argue for women's rights (especially for women of the upper class, or "quality" as Behn would put it), but she also knew that the very act of writing was unwomanly. In the preface to her play *The Lucky Chance,* Behn excuses her brazen act of writing by claiming that it is not part of her feminine side: "All I ask, is the privilege for my masculine part, the poet in me (if any such you will allow me).... If I must not, because of my sex, have this freedom [to write], but that you will usurp all to yourselves, I lay down my quill, and you shall hear no more of me." (*Aphra Behn: The Rover and Other Plays,* p. 191). This assertion of her right to write expresses an androgynous view of gender in which she allows herself to be a woman with both masculine and feminine qualities. As Janet Todd writes, Behn "wanted 'Fame' in the masculine term of glory, not the feminine one of goodness, chastity and modesty, yet she also wanted to play at being a 'defenceless Woman.' She both accepted the gender divide of the time that made wit and poetry mainly masculine in the context of what a man was and could do, and mocked it when she declared that she, a woman, wanted to be a man, a hero, and display her 'Masculine Part' " (*Secret Life,* p. 362).

Many of Behn's works offer alternative ways of looking at gender that resist binary notions of male and female. One of her best-known poems is "To the Fair Clarinda, Who Made Love to Me, Imagined More than Woman," published in Behn's only collection of poetry published in her lifetime, *Poems Upon Several Occasions.* In this poem, the female speaker pursues and is pursued by the beautiful Clarinda, who, because of her strength and nobility is more "youth" (a young man) than "fair maid." The title claims that Clarinda "made love to" the speaker, performing a traditionally masculine role in courtship, and thus is "imagined more than woman." The title suggests that gender roles are not biologically determined so much as constructed, and can be transformed through the power of imagination and desire.

Restoration culture and law acknowledged heterosexual sexuality as well as "sodomy," defined as homosexuality between males (a capital crime at the time). Female-to-female desire went largely unacknowledged and thus could be "no crime," as Behn's speaker cleverly appreciates. Since the bodies of the speaker and Clarinda are both (allegedly) biologically female, sexual intercourse is technically impossible. Thus, both women are conveniently spared the loss of their virginity and reputations:

In pity to our sex sure thou wert sent,
That we might love, and yet be innocent:
For sure no crime with thee we can commit;
Or if we should—thy form excuses it.

For who, that gathers fairest flowers believes
A snake lies hid beneath the fragrant leaves.

(*Oroonoko, and Other Writings*, p. 262)

Behn suggests that the feminine part of Clarinda is merely her superficial "form" beneath which lies a phallic "snake" in the form of masculine desire. Clarinda emerges as a hermaphrodite who offers the speaker the best of both worlds: sexual fulfillment (the masculine side) and friendship (the feminine side):

Thou beauteous wonder of a different kind,
Soft Cloris with the dear Alexis joined;
When ere the manly part of thee, would plead
Thou tempts us with the image of the maid,
While we the noblest passions do extend
The love to Hermes, Aphrodite the friend.

(p. 262)

This poem is often cited as evidence of Behn's own bisexuality, although there is no suggestion beyond her literary writings to confirm that she ever had a sexual relationship with another woman. Whether she did or not, she clearly acknowledges that desire is not limited to heterosexual relationships, and gender roles are far from clearly defined.

Jennifer Frangos' provocative reading of "To the Fair Clarinda" asserts that "The theatrical dimension to 'To the fair Clarinda' is ... seen in the poem's emphasis on, and eroticization of, multiple identities coalescing around a single body" (p. 11). Like an actress on the Restoration stage, Clarinda performs various gender roles: fair maid, pursuing youth, friend. Not surprisingly, many of Behn's plays also explore performative aspects of gender. Behn's plays challenge traditional gender roles while often conversely endorsing them. Like their author, many of these plays advocate having it both ways: they suggest that women should enjoy the freedoms allowed men as long as that suits them, but that they should rely on feminine "softness" when that suits them better.

In *The Young King,* a play Behn began in Surinam but which was not performed until 1679, the Princess Cleomena takes the place of her brother as a warrior and future ruler as a result of an oracle's prophecy. She excels at "martial fop-

peries" and holds her own in battle. In the play's first scene, two characters discuss her androgyny, perplexed that, "If it were not for her Beauty, one would swear were no Woman, she's so given to Noise and Fighting" (p. 111). Like Clarinda, Cleomena is a "fair maid" who is "more than woman." Unlike Clarinda, however, Cleomena is ready to reject the masculine side of herself, blaming "the faults of education / That cozening Form that veils the Face of Nature" (act 1, scene 2, p. 115). Cleomena can easily and successfully perform the signs of masculinity, but "Nature" eventually has her way and the princess falls in love with the sleeping Thersander, inconveniently an enemy prince, though he courts her under an assumed name.

Complicated plot twists lead Cleomena to believe that Thersander (whom she only knows to be an enemy prince) has killed the man she loves (not realizing that, in fact, they are the same man). Vowing revenge, she dresses as a man, gains entry into Thersander's quarters, and stabs him nearly to death. Cleomena's education as a warrior has prepared her to fight for what she perceives to be justice. She later explains that "Love and my Revenge made me a Soldier" (act 5, scene 5, p. 184). When caught, however, Cleomena defends herself and tells Thersander's father, "And now dispose my Destiny as you please, / Only remember that I am a Woman" (act 5, scene 1, p. 175). Under the threat of torture and execution, Cleomena quickly sheds her masculine persona and reverts back to her "natural" identification of female. She has learned to maneuver between gender roles to gain what she wants—first vengeance and later freedom. Because this play is not a tragedy but a tragicomedy, Thersander recovers, explains the confusion, and the two lovers agree to marry and make peace between their kingdoms. "Thus The God of Love o'ercomes the God of War" (act 5, scene 5, p. 189) and Cleomena and her brother are restored to their gender-specific roles of wife and king respectively.

The Young King challenges traditional ideas about gender by making it clear that women can be educated for strength and power as successfully, if not more successfully, than some men.

However, the play's happy ending requires that Cleomena be returned to "Garments suitable to her Sex" before leaving the battlefield for marriage to a man to whom she has vowed to be "faithful and submissive" (act 5, scene 5, p. 182).

Cleomena's donning of men's clothing was hardly unusual on the Restoration stage. Cross-dressing was a standard convention in comedy prior to the Restoration but had less erotic charge when female roles were still played by males. In Shakespeare's time, for example, a cross-dressing Rosalind was just a male actor pretending to be a female who was wearing male clothes. Once women began playing female roles on stage, however, cross-dressing became more provocative. Many of Behn's plays feature female characters who don a male disguise to obtain information, trick a would-be lover, or simply travel from one place to another without restriction (Sylvia also cross-dresses at one point in *Love Letters Between a Nobleman and His Sister*). Behn's final play, the tragicomedy *The Widow Ranter,* performed posthumously, features an unusual cross-dressing woman who does not return to women's clothes at the end of the play. A wealthy, hard-drinking, boisterous woman, the Widow Ranter is in love with Daring, a follower of the tragic rebel Bacon. Dressed as a traditional woman, the widow fails to make progress with Daring, so she follows him into battle in men's clothes and pursues him that way. Though Daring had been in love with another woman, he is eventually won by the widow's devotion to him and her willingness to cross-dress in order to pursue him. The widow will hardly be settling down to a lifetime of faithful submission to Daring: they tease each other, pretend to duel, and look forward to a lifetime of never being "drunk out of [each other's] company" (act 4, scene 3). In the midst of war, Daring offers to marry her "while thy breeches are on, for I never liked thee half so well in petticoats." The widow is actually a rather marginal character in this play, which largely focuses on a rebellious plot in the colony in Virginia, yet the play is named after her, and her relationship with Daring is one of several concluding marriages that give the otherwise tragic plot a comic ending. At least by the end of her career, Behn was able to envision alternative roles for women that were overtly androgynous.

SELLING ONESELF: MARRIAGE AND MONEY

The Widow Ranter does not return to petticoats but does return to marriage, something the Widow Behn evidently never did. As a widow, Behn may have missed the financial security that marriage could provide, but she probably would have chafed under its restrictions. Under Restoration law, a married woman could not own property, her earnings would be turned over to her husband, she had no legal rights to her children, and she could not obtain a divorce except under conditions of infidelity combined with cruelty (something that would be difficult to prove considering that she was not allowed to testify in court). Behn's writings may have conveyed inconsistent messages when it came to matters of sexual freedom, but they consistently condemned forced marriages and marriages contracted for financial reasons.

With a few exceptions (such as when, in "The Golden Age," she condemns the arbitrary power of kings), Behn affirmed the divine right of monarchical rule. She remained loyal to Charles' brother James even when it would have been in her best interest to write a poem praising the new King William. This appreciation for patriarchal rule, however, did not extend to the rights of parents to force their daughters to marry against their will. When compared with extramarital sex, mercenary marriages are a much greater crime throughout Behn's writings, all the more so because society condemns the former while rewarding the latter.

From her first play, the tragicomedy *The Forced Marriage,* Behn explored the relationship between marriage and the subjection of women and continued to do so throughout her career in theater. Her most famous play, *The Rover,* which remained in production for over a century, is representative of her comedies, in which beautiful women outwit mercenary patriarchs and achieve control over their own lives. Like most of her plays, *The Rover* is based on an earlier script by Thomas Killigrew. Set in the Interregnum period, the play follows a group of cavaliers (exiled followers of the then-exiled King Charles II) after they land in Naples during carnival. The carnival setting allows characters to wear disguises and masks without calling attention to themselves, to "commit extravagances" they won't have to answer for, as the hero Belvile puts it (act 2, scene 1. *Oronooko, The Rover, and Other Works,* p. 174). The title character, Willmore, has just arrived and is eager to drink heavily and seduce the first woman he encounters (as well as any subsequent ones who may be willing). His friend Belvile, on the other hand, has fallen in love with the virtuous Florinda, though he is too poor to marry her. Belvile and Florinda are the romantic couple separated by patriarchal convention. Acting as a foil for this couple are Willmore and Florinda's sister Hellena, a witty virgin whose family has determined will become a nun.

The opening scene, in which Florinda and Hellena try to convince their brother Don Pedro to allow them to choose their own futures, sets up the theme of forced marriage and the relationship between marriage and money that Behn will revisit throughout the play. Florinda refers to the custom of mercenary marriage as slavery, but Don Pedro claims that she should be pleased at the prospect of "seeing all her own that meets her eyes" (act 1, scene 1. *Oronooko, The Rover, and Other Works,* p. 161). Don Pedro agrees to help her avoid marriage to a rich old man under the condition that she marry a rich younger man instead, for Belvile, he tells her, "has no fortune to bring to you" and so she must forget him (p. 162). In his father's absence, Don Pedro's power over his sisters is absolute, to the point that he orders the rebellious Hellena locked up for the duration of the carnival.

The bald acknowledgement of the mercenary purpose of marriage in act 1 is made without shame or apology. Don Pedro and his sisters are "quality," and were Florinda to be married to increase the family's fortune, no one would shun her or accuse her of immorality. Behn exposes the hypocrisy behind this practice by introducing Angellica Bianca, an expensive courtesan who is advertising for a new "gallant." Willmore (despite an earlier flirtation with an escaped Hellena) is attracted to Angellica, yet he tells her he scorns her profession: "Poor as I am, I would not sell myself," he tells her (act 2, scene 2, p. 185). By this time, Angellica has broken her vow that "nothing but gold shall charm [her] heart" and has began to fall in love with Willmore. She defends her work as a courtesan by likening it to mercenary marriages:

> Pray, tell me sir, are you not guilty of the same mercenary crime, when a lady is proposed to you for a wife, you never ask, how fair—discreet—or virtuous she is; but what's her fortune—which if but small, you cry—she will not do my business— and basely leave her.
>
> (act 2, scene 2, p. 186)

Willmore's reply, that such mercenary marriage is a "barbarous custom," helps explain why he remains a positive character in this play, despite his lechery. Though governed solely by his desire for immediate gratification (even to the point of being willing to commit rape), he is not driven by financial motives and thus can be accommodated in the play's happy ending.

Despite an affair with Angellica, Willmore remains drawn to the virginal Hellena, who must walk a fine line between wit and prudence. Marriage may have been a legally sanctioned prison for many women, but it was also their only protection from the consequences of sex. Willmore is drawn to Hellena because she appears to be a match for him. She teases him sexually, telling him that should he "divert" her from her plan to be a nun by seducing her, "I should have a new man to seek I find; and what a grief that will be—for when I begin, I fancy I shall love like anything" (act 1, scene 2, p. 170). Hellena attracts Willmore by suggesting that beneath the veneer of the respectable virgin is a sexually insatiable libertine just waiting to be let loose. Willmore is intrigued ("Oh, I long to come first to the banquet of love!"), but as a woman Hellena does not have the freedom to love just for pleasure (act 1, scene 2, p. 170). She knows that if she gives in to her passion for Willmore without the protections of marriage she will be left with "a cradle full of noise and mischief and a pack of repentance at [her] back" (act 5, scene 2, p.

242). Though Willmore would prefer to consummate their love outside of marriage, which he associates with "portion, and jointure," he eventually gives in and agrees to marry her, citing Hellena's "good nature."

This decision is by no means a foregone conclusion, because Behn had created in Angellica Bianca a sympathetic character who is undone not because she is sexually compromised but by her own passion for Willmore. As a shrewd businesswoman, her success depends upon her choosing the right protector to keep her financially secure. In falling for the impoverished Willmore, she has forfeited that security for a man unable to return her feelings. Although the nature of comedy requires that she receive her happy ending as well (she is paired off with a wealthy, handsome protector), the pathos of her final speech to Willmore, gun in hand, speaks to the risks women face when they allow themselves to be controlled by desire and forget their self-interest.

Given their shared initials, Aphra Behn may have identified with the scorned Angellica Bianca, who lived with passion in spite of the questionable wisdom of doing so. If so, that might explain the reversal of the prostitute's fortunes in *The Rover Part 2*. Capitalizing on the success of *The Rover*, Behn wrote a sequel in which a widowed Willmore arrives in Spain and is once again attracted to a witty virgin, Ariadne, and a passionate whore, La Nuche. Ariadne shares Hellena's independence. Though engaged to Willmore's friend Beaumond, she is attracted to Willmore and so follows him to learn more about him. As they flirt, she declares that she is "not one to be sold," for which Willmore praises her. He propositions her, suggesting that while she may not be one to be sold, she is probably "one to be had." She responds in financial terms, telling Willmore she is saving her charms for "one that can esteem 'em to their worth, can set a Value and a Rate upon 'em" (act 2, scene 1, p. 138). Ariadne goes out of her way to differentiate herself from La Nuche, the whore she knows Willmore to be attracted to, but her negotiation of the terms under which she will be enjoyed sounds very much like she knows she is someone with something to sell. As Willmore later tells Ariadne, virgin or whore, "you Women have all a certain Jargon, or Gibberish, peculiar to your selves; of Value, Rate, Present, Interest, Settlement, Advantage, Price, Maintenance, and the Devil and all of Fopperies, which in plain Terms signify ready Money, by way of Fine before Entrance; so that an honest well-meaning Merchant of Love finds no Credit amongst ye" (act 2, scene 1, p. 141).

For his part, Willmore condemns the practices of prostitution here just as he did in Part 1, but we learn at the beginning of the play that he mourns the loss of Hellena's jointure at least as much as he does the wife who died at sea. Easily condemning women for bartering their sexuality, he is capable of the same self-interest. This time, however, marriage proves to be too high a price to pay. Though he declares La Nuche to be a "slavish mercenary Prostitute" he offers her his love, not including his constancy or his hand in marriage (p. 182). Ironically, it is La Nuche who ultimately walks away from the wealth offered her by Beaumond and chooses "Love unadorn'd, no covering but his Wings" with Willmore (act 5, scene 5, p. 244). The respectable Ariadne prefers marriage to a man she will try to love to unmarried life with the man she does love, a libertine.

Despite the many happy nuptials that conclude Behn's comedies, she repeatedly used the stage to explore the mercenary nature of marriage and its connection to prostitution. Whether women were better off choosing the relative security of marriage to the risks of a single life is never fully resolved in her work. Certainly her plays celebrate love matches while condemning those made for financial gain, but neither resembles the ideal of free love that she portrays in "The Golden Age."

"DOGS, TREACHEROUS AND COWARDLY": *POLITICS AND POWER*

Behn knew that implicit in her condemnation of forced marriages was a criticism of the dangers of absolute power. Even her lightest comedies have indirect political implications. Some, like *The Rover*, which praise the sacrifices made by

Charles' royalist followers during his exile, are implicitly political at times. As the lighthearted 1670s gave way to the paranoid, unstable 1680s, though, politics became increasingly hard to avoid. The Stuart succession was under attack; the false "Popish Plot" of 1678 led to a massive wave of anti-Catholic hysteria that had Charles and his supporters in a bind. Charles' wife and brother were both Catholic, and he had flirted with conversion for much of his rule. Protestant England, especially the Parliament, were suspicious of Catholic influence in the country and spread rumors of a plot by the pope to assassinate the king. A witch hunt followed in which hundreds of people were accused of conspiring in the plot, including the queen. Fifteen people were executed. People stopped attending the theater and tried to stay out of each other's way to avoid being accused of harboring Catholic sympathies. Behn addressed this issue directly in her farce *The Roundheads,* in which she compares England's current crisis to the instability of the Civil War and the Interregnum period. The "Roundheads" of the play are petty parliamentarians, unable to lead in the days following Oliver Cromwell's death. In re-creating this era for her audience, Behn conjures an unappealing picture of an England without the stability of a legitimate king. Mob rule, which had played a large a part in the Popish Plot, is a likely and dangerous result of questioning the legitimacy of the king and altering the laws of succession. Even sex is depicted for political purposes, as dashing cavaliers outwit hypocritical Puritans in the bedroom. Susan J. Owen points out that in *The Roundheads,* Behn subverts her feminist agenda in favor of upholding Tory patriarchal ideals, "offering the familiar association of royalism with virtue, and rebellion with women out of place" (*Cambridge Companion to Aphra Behn,* p. 68).

Behn would remain politically engaged for the rest of her career, and would have the opportunity to comment on another crisis in her final works. By 1688, the year of *Oroonoko*'s publication, the issue of succession had been resolved. The Duke of Monmouth was dead (an event Behn would chronicle in *Love-Letters Between a Nobleman to His Sister*), but James had fled into exile only to be supplanted by his Protestant daughter Mary and her husband, William of Orange. Behn had dedicated *The Rover Part 2* to James and was clearly distressed by the revolution that marked the end of her beloved Stuart dynasty, a revolution that took place as she composed her final novel. *Oroonoko,* the tragedy of a "royal slave," would enable Behn to return to an earlier period in her depiction of Surinam while also writing a scathing parable about the usurpation and abuse of power.

Although Behn had visited Surinam as a young woman, it is not known whether she actually met and befriended a royal slave who would later be executed for leading a rebellion. The detailed description of life in Surinam, however, has been enough to convince biographers that her trip there did in fact take place, as her narrator claims. At the time of the novel, Surinam was an English colony that would soon fall to the Dutch. By 1688 the English crown would be passed to a Dutch king, a connection Behn's readers could not fail to make. In the meantime, they could temporarily escape the unrest at home by reading Behn's exotic accounts of life in Surinam and Africa.

Behn's description of the native South Americans evokes her poem "The Golden Years." Uncorrupted by civilization, these "Indians" live in harmony with the natural world and with each other:

> Though they are all ... naked, if one lives forever among 'em there is not to be seen an undecent action, or glance.... They have a native justice, which knows no fraud; and they understand no vice, or cunning, but when they are taught by the white men. They have plurality of wives; which, when they grow old, they serve those that succeed 'em, who are young, but with a servitude easy and respected,
>
> (*Oroonoko, and Other Writings,* p. 8).

Behn's readers would no doubt have been fascinated with accounts of native culture and the lush South American landscape just as they might have enjoyed, in the novel's earlier scenes, set in Africa, comparing the Coramantien court of Oroonoko's grandfather to their own treacherous royal power plays. Oroonoko's skin is black, but his features, manners, and education are European, possibly making him a more plausible hero for Behn's audiences. He falls in love with Imoinda, "the beautiful black Venus to our young Mars," and the two plan to marry until Oroonoko's centurion grandfather claims Imoinda for his harem (p. 12). Behn here returns to the theme of forced marriages, connecting the British practice of mercenary marriages to the "barbaric" customs of an African court. Eventually Imoinda is sold into slavery, while Oroonoko, months later, is tricked into it by accepting the hospitality of a white slave trader. This is one of several acts of treachery condemned by Behn's narrator in the novel.

The novel's treatment of the institution of slavery is complex. Despite Behn's unconventional life, she was never a political radical nor a supporter of democracy. Her works reveal a consistent distrust of the "common man" as unfit to lead or even to judge what is best for himself. Behn condemns Oroonoko's betrayal because he is a *royal* slave, not because the institution of slavery is necessarily wrong. He himself had engaged in the slave trade and had in fact once presented Imoinda with a number of slaves as a gift. As a prince, he is entitled to loyalty and respect and honorable dealings, something Behn felt was due her own King James.

Upon arriving in Surinam, Oroonoko is recognized as superior to his fellow slaves and treated well. His new master, Trefry, begins to "conceive so vast an esteem for him that he ever after loved him as his dearest brother, and showed him all the civilities due to so great a man" (pg. 38). He is reunited with Imoinda; they share a modest home and conceive a child. Behn's narrator recalls Oroonoko's many adventures in the colony, including his assistance in helping to broker peace between the colonists and a rebellious band of Indians. Nonetheless, as the birth of Oroonoko's child approaches, he becomes convinced that Trefry has no intention of keeping his promise to return him to Africa. Oroonoko then conceives of organizing a slave rebellion. His speech against the indignities of slavery is the earliest criticism of the institution in an English work of fiction:

they suffered not like men who might find a glory and fortitude in oppression; but like dogs, that loved the whip and bell, and fawned the more they were beaten: that they had lost the divine quality of men, and were become insensible asses, fit only to bear: nay, worse; an ass, or dog, or horse, having done his duty could lie down in retreat, and rise to work again, and while he did his duty, endured no stripes; but men, villainous, senseless men, such as they, toiled on all the tedious week till Black Friday: and then, whether they worked or not, whether they were faulty or meriting, they, promiscuously, the innocent with the guilty, suffered the infamous whip, the sordid stripes, from their fellow-slaves, till their blood trickled from all parts of their body; blood, whose every drop ought to be revenged with a life of some of those tyrants that impose it.

(*Oroonoko, and Other Writings*, p. 57).

Behn's vivid description suggests at least some outrage at the way slavery is practiced, the arbitrary ways that justice is imposed, and the lack of recognition of what is due a fellow human being. On the other hand, the narrator begins to be suspicious of Oroonoko and says, "I neither thought it convenient to trust him much out of our view, nor did the country, who feared him" (pg. 58). Behn writes with multiple voices about slavery, representing Oroonoko's antislavery views powerfully but also representing the (well-justified) fears of the isolated and outnumbered white people who benefit from the institution.

This time, it is Oroonoko's fellow slaves who betray him. With the exception of Oroonoko, Imoinda, and one friend, the slaves surrender to the whites and Oroonoko is captured; he confesses that he had been mistaken "in endeavoring to make those free who were by nature slaves, poor wretched rogues, fit to be used as Christians' tools; dogs, treacherous and cowardly" (p. 66). Here Oroonoko echoes his author's aristocratic ideals: some are "by nature" slaves while others are "by nature" kings. Class, not race, determines "quality."

Oroonoko escapes, but he knows he is doomed. Determined to die as a hero, Oroonoko plans to return to the plantation and kill those who have betrayed him. Knowing the fate Imoinda would face as his widow, he first kills her, who dies praising her killer. But Oroonoko is denied his hero's death. Mourning Imoinda, he is unable to motivate himself for one final attack. He is easily captured and dies a gruesome death, burned at the stake while his enemies chop off his body parts bit by bit. Behn's own King James would escape Oroonoko's fate, though he too would find few supporters among his so-called followers. No doubt Behn shared her hero's contempt for disloyal subjects and untrustworthy rulers. She had never lived in a "Golden Age," but *Oroonoko* presents an especially dark vision of human nature. Unfortunately, we will never know how Behn would have responded to the relatively stable reign of James's successors.

IMMORTALITY

Aphra Behn would not live to see the England of William and Mary settle into respectable stability. She would not live to see her plays bowdlerized in the name of decency and her reputation fade into obscurity for over two hundred years until Virginia Woolf and Vita Sackville-West revived interest in her life and works. Behn's tombstone carries the following epitaph:

Here lies a proof that wit can never be Defence against mortality

There are no defenses against mortality, but Behn might have felt that burial in Westminster Abbey was adequate compensation for this injustice. Her remains lie with five centuries of her beloved monarchs.

Selected Bibliography

WORKS OF APHRA BEHN

DRAMA
The Forced Marriage. 1670.
The Amorous Prince. 1671.
The Dutch Lover. 1673.
Abdelazar. 1676.
The Town Fop. 1676.
The Rover Part 1. 1677.
Sir Patient Fancy. 1678.
The Feigned Courtesans. 1679.
The Young King. 1679.

The Rover Part 2. 1681.
The False Count. 1681.
The Roundheads. 1681.
The City Heiress. 1682.
Like Father, Like Son. 1682.
The Lucky Chance. 1686.
The Emperor of the Moon. 1687.
The Widow Ranter. 1689, posthumously performed.
The Younger Brother. 1696, posthumously performed.

FICTION AND POETRY
Love-Letters Between a Nobleman and His Sister Part I. London: Printed by Randall Taylor, 1684.
Poems Upon Several Occasions. London: Printed for R. Tonson and J. Tonsons, 1684.
Love Letters from a Noble Man to His Sister Part II. London: 1685.
The Amours of Philander and Silvia (*Love Letters* Part III). London: 1687.
Oroonoko. London: Printed for William Canning, 1688.
Agnes de Castro. London: Printed for William Canning, 1688.
The Fair Jilt. London: Printed for William Canning, 1688.
The History of the Nun: or, The Fair Vow-Breaker. London: 1688.
The Dumb Virgin: or, The Force of Imagination. London: 1700.

COLLECTED WORKS AND RECENT EDITIONS
Full-text versions of Aphra Behn's works can be found on-line at Project Gutenberg (http://onlinebooks.library.upenn.edu/webbin/gutbook/author?name=Behn%2C%20Aphra%2C%201640-1689).
Love-Letters Between a Nobleman and His Sister. Charleston, SC: Bibliobazaar, 2007.
The Works of Aphra Behn, 6 vols. Edited by Montague Summers. London: William Heinemann, 1913.
The Works of Aphra Behn, 7 vols. Edited by Janet Todd. Columbus: Ohio State University Press, 1992. (Vol. 1, *Poetry;* vol. 2, *Love-Letters Between a Nobleman and His Sister;* vol. 3, *The Fair Jilt and Other Short Stories;* vol. 4, *Seneca Unmasqued and Other Prose Translations;* vol. 5, *The Plays, 1671–1677;* vol. 6, *The Plays, 1678–1682;* vol. 7, *The Plays, 1682–1696*).
Oroonoko, The Rover, and Other Works. Edited by Janet Todd. New York: Penguin, 1992.
Oroonoko, and Other Writings. Edited by Paul Salzman. New York: Oxford University Press, 1994.
The Rover and Other Plays. Edited by Jane Spencer. New York: Oxford University Press, 1995.
Love-Letters Between a Nobleman and His Sister. Edited by Janet Todd. New York: Penguin, 1996.

Oroonoko; or, The Royal Slave. Edited by Joanna Lipking. Norton Critical Edition. New York: Norton, 1997. (Includes the novel, historical background, and criticism.)

Oroonoko; or, The Royal Slave. Edited by Catherine Gallagher. Bedford Critical Edition. Boston: Bedford/St. Martin's, 2000. (Features primary sources to provide cultural background on the novel.)

BIBLIOGRAPHY

O'Donnell, Mary Ann. *Aphra Behn: An Annotated Biography of Primary and Secondary Sources.* New York: Garland, 1986.

CRITICAL AND BIOGRAPHICAL STUDIES

Conway, Alison. "Flesh on the Mind: Behn Studies in the New Millennium." *Eighteenth Century: Theory and Interpretation* 44, no. 1:87–93 (spring 2003).

Dickson, Vernon Guy. "Truth, Wonder, and Exemplarity in Aphra Behn's *Oroonoko.*" *Studies in English Literature 1500–1900* 47, no. 3:573–594 (summer 2007).

Duffy, Maureen. The *Passionate Shepherdess: The Life of Aphra Behn, 1640–1689.* London: Jonathan Cape, 1977.

Frangos, Jennifer. "Aphra Behn's Cunning Stunts: 'To the Fair Clarinda.' " *Eighteenth Century: Theory and Interpretation* 45, no. 1:21–40 (spring 2004).

Gabbard, D. Christopher. "Clashing Masculinities in Aphra Behn's *The Dutch Lover.*" *Studies in English Literature 1500–1900* 47, no. 3:557–572 (summer 2007).

Goreau, Angeline. *Reconstructing Aphra: A Social Biography of Aphra Behn.* New York: Dial Press, 1980.

Hughes, Derrick. *The Theatre of Aphra Behn.* New York: Palgrave, 2001.

Hughes, Derrick, and Janet Todd, eds. *The Cambridge Companion to Aphra Behn.* Cambridge, U.K.: Cambridge University Press, 2004.

Hutner, Heidi, ed. *Rereading Aphra Behn: History, Theory, and Criticism.* Charlottesville: University Press of Virginia, 1993.

Martin, Roberta. " 'Beauteous Wonder of a Different Kind': Aphra Behn's Destabilization of Sexual Categories." *College English* 61, no. 2:192–210 (November 1998).

Nash, Julie. " 'The Sight on't Would Beget a Warm Desire': Visual Pleasure in Aphra Behn's *The Rover.*" *Restoration: Studies in English Literary Culture 1660–1700* 18, no. 2:77–87 (fall 1994).

Pacheco, Anita. "Rape and the Female Subject in Aphra Behn's *The Rover.*" *ELH* 65, no. 2: 323–345 (1998).

Sackville-West, Vita. *Aphra Behn: The Incomparable Astrea.* London: G. Howe, 1927.

Spencer, Jane. *Aphra Behn's Afterlife.* New York: Oxford University Press, 2000.

Stapleton, M. L. *Admired and Understood: The Poetry of Aphra Behn.* Newark: University of Delaware Press, 2004.

Todd, Janet. *The Sign of Angellica: Women, Writing, and Fiction, 1660–1800.* New York: Columbia University Press, 1989.

Todd, Janet, ed. *Aphra Behn Studies.* Cambridge, U.K., and New York: Cambridge University Press, 1996.

Todd, Janet. *The Secret Life of Aphra Behn.* New Brunswick, N.J.: Rutgers University Press, 1997.

Woolf, Virginia. *A Room of One's Own.* London: P. Hogarth, 1929. Reprinted, New York: Harcourt Books, 1996.

ROBERT BROWNING

(1812—1889)

Thomas Marks

ROBERT BROWNING'S DEATH in Venice on 12 December 1889 sparked no small debate about where he was to be buried. His close family (one son, one sister) tried to arrange a plot in the English Cemetery at Florence, adjacent to his late wife, Elizabeth Barrett Browning, but greater forces were at work. After some negotiation, the poet's body was repatriated and laid to rest on 31 December in Poets' Corner amid much pomp and circumstance at Westminster Abbey. It was characteristic of Browning that the circumstances of his death should distill preoccupations about what was familiar and what was foreign, both for the poet and for his contemporaries, because so much of his work charts the intersections of these extremes.

Browning spent much of his life abroad and most of it in creative exile, achieving social and literary success in England only in his final decades. His extraordinary (and extraordinarily long) poem *The Ring and the Book,* published in four volumes in 1868 and 1869, grumbles about its potential readership, the "British Public, ye who like me not" (book 1, line 410). Browning's work introduces into Victorian poetry foreign characters, unusual rhythms and forms, and arcane language and knowledge. Even when his verse thinks fondly about England, as in "Home-Thoughts, from Abroad" (1845), it is mindful that its subtle displacements make what is familiar seem strange: "home-thoughts" is a collocation that puts a slight but noticeable pressure on the imagined autonomy of "home." G. K. Chesterton insisted that "Browning was a thoroughly typical Englishman of the middle class" (p. 5), but the poet's work is so striking and strange that Henry James could rightfully claim that, of the poets, "none of the odd ones have been so great and none of the great ones so odd" ("Browning," p. 47).

EARLY LIFE AND WORK

Robert Browning was born in the village of Camberwell, on the green southern fringes of London, on 7 May 1812. His father, Robert Browning (1782–1866), was in many ways a conventional member of the urban middle class; he was a mild Dissenter, who did not conform to the Church of England, and he spent fifty years as a clerk at the Bank of England. Nevertheless he was an independent thinker and not afraid to act on either his conscience or his instincts. As a young man he had rejected a career in the plantation business in the West Indies and had consequently been stripped of his inheritance by his stern father. In 1811 he married Sarah Anna Wiedemann (1772–1849), who was of mixed Scottish and German descent and was ten years his senior. Browning was very close to his delicate mother, whose devout nonconformist Christianity provided him with a sense of discipline and propriety that he was never to forget and would only occasionally flout. He lived with his parents until he was thirty-four, and, as his first authoritative biographer, Mrs. Sutherland Orr, notes in her *Life and Letters of Robert Browning,* "it was his rule never to go to bed without giving [his mother] a goodnight kiss" (p. 43).

At the age of eight Browning was sent as a weekday boarder to a small school in the village of Peckham, where for the next six years he was given an elementary education by the Misses Ready and later by their brother, the Rev. Thomas Ready. Browning's father was a shareholder in the new London University, and in October 1828 Browning, at age sixteen, became the sixteenth pupil to be enrolled there. He persevered for only eight months before he was lured back by the emotional magnet of home.

ROBERT BROWNING

Browning's real education—and his poetic apprenticeship—took place in his father's remarkable library, which contained some six thousand volumes. It was there that he encountered the unusual texts that inspired his obscure early verse, and there that he read the classics and literature in French, Italian, and Spanish. He was a keen reader of the flamboyant George Gordon, Lord Byron (1788–1824), and soon adopted a dandyish appearance to boot (his yellow kid gloves caused a small suburban stir). Browning's most significant early literary encounter occurred in 1826 or 1827, when his cousin James Silverthorne gave him the *Miscellaneous Poems* of Percy Bysshe Shelley (1792–1822), whose verse was still little known in the years following his premature death. Browning was struck by the mysterious visions and intense lyricism of Shelley's poetry, and he soon persuaded his mother to ferret out from book dealers in the capital the first—and only—editions of other poems that Shelley had published during his lifetime. For a rebellious period, he even borrowed Shelley's atheism—and his vegetarianism.

Browning's early poetry is a series of obscure attempts to define the function of the poet in an era when poetry seemed to have drained from the world. John Keats (1795–1821), Shelley, and Byron had all died as young men in the early 1820s, and verse had retreated to sentimental subjects. *Pauline: A Fragment of a Confession* (1833), *Paracelsus* (1835), and *Sordello* (1840) are experimental works that frustrated most of the few readers who paid any attention to them on publication. (Browning would later claim that not a single copy of *Pauline* had ever been sold.) Critics complained about their "dreamy" tone and language, and they spawned a reputation for willful difficulty that was to dog Browning until late in his career. Nonetheless they are important works that not only point toward the emergence of the distinctive dramatic energy of Browning's middle period but also negotiate with the legacy of a Romantic past whose import remained uncertain.

In this literary context, Browning's poetical career began with a nimble irony at what may well be a deathbed scene. In *Pauline* the speaker is an elderly poet who has been exhausted by age and experience and who unburdens himself to the mysterious woman named in the title:

Pauline, mine own, bend o'er me—thy soft breast
Shall pant to mine—bend o'er me—thy sweet eyes,
And loosened hair and breathing lips, and arms
Drawing me to thee—these build up a screen
To shut me in with thee, and from all fear

(ll. 1–5)

Thus we enter the nervous metaphysical world of this poem. *Pauline* eschews a conventional narrative of personal development to think in more abstract terms about difficult distinctions between "mind" and "soul"—distinctions so tortuous that John Stuart Mill was to note in the margin of his review copy of the book that its writer "seems to me possessed with a more intense and morbid self-consciousness than I ever knew in any sane human being" (Pettigrew and Collins, I, p. 1022.) The poet and his words have escapist bents:

Pauline, come with me, see how I could build
A home for us, out of the world, in thought!
I am uplifted: fly with me, Pauline!

(ll. 729–731)

Browning's sense of how speech can complicate the motives of its speaker is already traceable here: the speaker's invitation to soar away from reality is belied by the ambiguous phrasing "build / … out of the world," which tries to move away from ("out of") the mundanity of the world but cannot help also involving the very materials that make up earthly existence by building from ("out of") them. Even "fly with me" is securely anchored—it is one of many allusions in the poem to Shelley's *Epipsychidion* (1821), with which it shares the unusual subgenre of allegorical autobiography. The speaker elegizes Shelley as the "Sun-treader"—"life and light be thine for ever!" (l. 151)—whose poetry is incomparable and unsurpassable. The complex workings of poetic homage might also encourage the reader to think otherwise; Browning's poem moves away from worshipping Shelley and toward expression of a more religious faith.

The composition of *Pauline* had been inspired by the theater; the idea came to the poet after a performance of William Shakespeare's *Richard III* by the frail veteran actor Edmund Kean. Browning's interest in drama is further apparent in *Paracelsus,* a long poem published two years later, that dramatizes five scenes from the life of the sixteenth-century alchemist who, for Browning, symbolized the transition from medieval to modern systems of knowledge. Browning mined the quirky fifty-volume *Biographie Universelle* (1811–1862) in his father's library for source material, and transformed that ore into a detailed study of ambition. *Paracelsus* examines how aspiration is modified and thwarted by personal development as different kinds of knowledge are attained; the tone is best described as tragicomic. Paracelsus gains celebrity and notoriety as he thirsts for transcendence, but his quest is disappointed by his gradual discovery of what it is to be human. "I," Paracelsus proclaims, "thus insensibly am—what I am!" (part 2, l. 185). The poem lacks the pithy characterization that would become Browning's forte, and its long dialogues are short on dramatic intensity. The most memorable scene is an encounter between Paracelsus and Aprile, a lyric poet who is a further version of Shelley. His lyricism suggests a different kind of knowledge from Paracelsus' desire "to KNOW," as it investigates what it might mean "to LOVE" (part 2, l. 624)—to understand the world by drawing closer to its other inhabitants.

Browning chose not to temper his own ambition through the lessons he had taught Paracelsus. Instead he buried himself in the recondite world of medieval Italy as he worked on the enormous narrative poem *Sordello.* It is one of the most opaque poems in the English language, thanks to the remote detail of its subject matter and the elliptical syntax, esoteric vocabulary, and intellectual gymnastics that characterize the texture of its verse:

On flew the song, a giddy race,
After the flying story; word made leap
Out word, rhyme—rhyme; the lay could barely keep
Pace with the action visibly rushing past:
Both ended.

                    (book 2, ll. 84–88)

Alfred, Lord Tennyson famously declared that he understood no more than the first line ("Who will, may hear Sordello's story told") and the last ("Who would has heard Sordello's story told")—and that they were both lies. Jane Welsh Carlyle, the wife of Thomas Carlyle, damned the poem when she claimed not to understand whether its eponymous hero was a man, a city, or a book. Like the two works that precede it, *Sordello* is an intensely self-reflexive poem about the nature of poetry: in an important interlude in the third book (ll. 614–1021), the narrator turns away from his historic subject to defend difficult poetry, as opposed to poetry that aims for no more than "completeness" (l. 620). *Sordello* plots an idiosyncratic route through the wars between the Guelf and Ghibelline factions in thirteenth-century Italy (those who supported the authority of the popes and those who supported the emperors), focusing on the life and death of the troubadour poet Sordello. His struggle to balance creative integrity and popular appeal recurs as a theme, mirroring Browning's own steadfastness in the face of public opprobrium and indifference. Though it will always have its critics, *Sordello* remains a unique, indulgent tapestry of historical fantasy. Its rhyming couplets are marked by a comic facility that was to emerge more thoroughly in Browning's later work.

BELLS AND POMEGRANATES

In 1835 Browning befriended William Charles Macready (1793–1873), who had inherited Edmund Kean's mantle after the death of the great Romantic actor and theater manager in 1833. Macready galvanized Browning's dramatic inclinations, asking him to write a play for the Covent Garden Theatre. *Strafford: An Historical Tragedy* (1837) and the six plays that followed over the next decade are a lackluster collection of historical tragedies and moral dramas. Wordy, static character studies, they do not at all suit the rhythm of staged performance. As Browning's preface to *Strafford* explains, the poet was more interested in "Action in Character rather than Character in Action"—that is, the world's imprint on the developing self rather than human agency as it shapes the world. The poet's concentration on language as a vehicle for the expression of subjective experience was an embarrassment to the stage: the absence of action meant that *Strafford* quietly but insistently denied the collaborative nature of theatrical art. Browning was vexed by Macready's exacting revisions to his script, and their relationship prickled into acrimony after the relative failure of *A Blot in the 'Scutcheon* (1843).

Meanwhile Browning struggled to find a publisher for his work, even though his relatives had been meeting its expense, until Edward Moxon proposed a series of inexpensive, sixteen-page pamphlets that would contain both poetry and drama. Browning would come to fret about how this format detracted from the quality of his verse, but in 1841 he pressed ahead under the general title *Bells and Pomegranates*. In the "advertisement" printed at the beginning of the first number, he wrote, "I amuse myself by fancying that the cheap mode in which they appear will for once help me to a sort of Pit-audience again" (Pettigrew and Collins, Volume I, p. 1070) (only with a proud squint at his early career could he have imagined ever having commanded one). As he explained in the final part of the series, the enigmatic title was designed to suggest "something like an alternation, or mixture, of music with discoursing, sound with sense, poetry with thought" (Pettigrew and Collins, volume I, p. 1069). *Pippa Passes* (1841), the dramatic poem that made up the first number, juxtaposed the affecting lyrics of a silk-mill girl with the conceited rhetorical strategies of a cast of quasi-Shakespearian buffoons and scoundrels. At once experimental and accessible, it is significantly richer than Browning's plays of the period.

Browning was initially reluctant to incorporate shorter poems in the *Bells and Pomegranates* pamphlets, considering that they were foremost intended to be an outlet for his ambition as a dramatist. Nonetheless *Dramatic Lyrics* (1842) and *Dramatic Romances and Lyrics* (1845) represent one of the most important developments in Victorian poetry, as Browning's trademark dramatic monologues take to a printed page that aspires toward the conditions of the theatrical stage. Browning and Tennyson developed the dramatic monologue independently in the 1830s, drawing on a wide range of models, from the complaint poem to the Romantic lyric and the conversational poems of Walter Savage Landor (1775–1864). That said, it is less helpful to define the boundaries of the form than to celebrate its flexibility under Browning's pen. These volumes include a remarkable assortment of comparatively short poems that place their speakers in dramatized, realistic settings: "My Last Duchess," "Soliloquy of the Spanish Cloister," "Waring," "Johannes Agricola in Meditation," "Porphyria's Lover," "Pictor Ignotus," and "The Bishop Orders His Tomb at Saint Praxed's Church." The speakers of these poems have distinctive voices and psychologies. Some of them address a silent auditor (or interlocutor) who interposes between the speaker and the reader and thus complicates our understanding of their motives for speaking. In many ways these poems are like plays with only one speaking character, but they also make much of their status as printed rather than performance texts, as their speakers adopt verse forms that they appear not to be conscious of. We are cajoled into sympathy by such talkative characters, even as their words are ironically undermined by the intelligent strategies of verse; a rhyme can challenge our opinion of the speaker by bringing together what he or she means to keep apart.

The most brilliant and incisive of the early monologues was published in *Dramatic Lyrics*, the third of the *Bells and Pomegranates* series. In "My Last Duchess" a silver-tongued Italian duke displays the portrait of his dead wife to the envoy of the father of his prospective bride:

That's my last Duchess painted on the wall,
Looking as if she were alive. I call
That piece a wonder, now: Frà Pandolf's hands
Worked busily a day, and there she stands.

(ll. 1–4)

On one level, the duke's apparently effortless speech convincingly welcomes the reader into a remote yet coherent world in spite of the disconcerting knowledge that the opening of the poem tunes into the scene not as it commences, but in medias res. On another level, the duke's easy management of the situation is unsettled by the control that Browning exerts over him. Although the neat couplets emulate the duke's linguistic facility, they also make clear that Browning is the puppet master outside the world of the poem. With the words "Looking as if she were alive," the duke boasts about how lifelike the portrait is. Yet "Looking" might be an action in progress as much as a passive description here, which allows us to imagine an uncanny possibility that the picture is looking out at its viewers and really does become "alive." It is a self-reflexive moment that reminds the reader of the duke's own suspended status, between the unnerving and vivid craftiness of his speech and the delicate craft of Browning's portrait of him. A tiny wrinkle in the verse becomes an apt expression of the duke's paranoia at how much his last duchess's eyes might have roved when she was alive, "as if she ranked / My gift of a nine-hundred-years-old name / With anybody's gift" (ll. 32–34). His retrospective jealousy leads to the abrupt, macabre revelation that he was responsible for her death:

Oh sir, she smiled, no doubt,
Whene'er I passed her; but who passed without
Much the same smile? This grew; I gave commands;
Then all smiles stopped together.

(ll. 43–46)

This revelation works in a similar way to the poem itself: it is an intense, puzzling euphemism that conceals unpleasant truths.

"My Last Duchess" is like a specimen that asks us to analyze its language for traces of psychopathological behavior. The duke's language can also be taken as a measure of his psychological unrest: he is obsessed with presentation and—in what may be a rhetorical ploy but may be something more sinister—repeatedly draws attention to the fluency that he claims to lack. Browning was interested in the many psychological theories that had emerged in the early nineteenth century, and other poems in these volumes experiment further with possible congruities between disturbed mental states and modes of self-expression. The poems that were

later titled "Johannes Agricola in Meditation" and "Porphyria's Lover" appeared as a pair called "Madhouse Cells" in *Dramatic Lyrics* (Browning was often to present his poems in canny partnerships). This title suggests not so much that the speakers of these poems have been institutionalized as that they are mentally imprisoned by their own delusions. The units of verse of both poems (rhyming *ababb*) indicate modes of thought that are unable to develop beyond their limited fixations: the thought processes of their speakers get stuck, repeatedly.

In "Johannes Agricola in Meditation" the speaker is the founder of the Antinomian doctrine, which deems salvation to be predetermined regardless of the earthly deeds and misdeeds of Christian believers. Believing that he has "God's warrant" (l. 33), Agricola is revealed as no more than a stagnant solipsist:

The heavens, God thought on me his child;
Ordained a life for me, arrayed
Its circumstances every one
To the minutest; ay, God said
This head this hand should rest upon
Thus, ere he fashioned star or sun.

(ll. 15–20)

The subject of "Porphyria's Lover" is romantic and sexual obsession; what at first seems like the speaker's anxiety to protect the object of his love is revealed as murderous insanity as he strangles her, attempting to fix and possess her beauty forever:

That moment she was mine, mine, fair,
Perfectly pure and good: I found
A thing to do, and all her hair
In one long yellow string I wound
Three times her little throat around,
And strangled her.

(ll. 36–41)

The poetry puts into perspective what the speaker cannot. His description of the murder, "a thing to do," chillingly portrays how mental disturbance can short-circuit moral judgments. To him the murder weapon is no more than "string" wound around her throat "three times," as if he were performing some small household task like tying up a parcel. Yet Browning's achievement is to fuse pathos and pathology. The speaker's repetition of "mine" rephrases his delusion but also ironically insists on what can now never be his:

And thus we sit together now,
And all night long we have not stirred,
And yet God has not said a word!

(ll. 58–60)

Porphyria and her lover are a sad "we" that consists of only one person.

"Johannes Agricola in Meditation" is not the only poem in these volumes to attack religious hypocrisy. Browning mistrusted dogma and satirized it frequently. In "Soliloquy of the Spanish Cloister" an envious monk rails against the religiosity of Brother Lawrence in a way that betrays his own concerns as earthly more than spiritual (he is reading a "scrofulous French novel," l. 57). In "The Bishop Orders His Tomb at Saint Praxed's Church," an anonymous Renaissance bishop prattles on his deathbed about the design of his funerary monument (which we assume will never be built). His imaginary tomb sparkles with enough precious stones as to seem a one-man New Jerusalem:

Some lump, ah God, of *lapis lazuli*,
Big as a Jew's head cut off at the nape,
Blue as a vein o'er the Madonna's breast.

(ll. 42–44)

Preoccupied with worldly representation, the bishop participates in religious misrepresentation. His thoughts are so little concentrated on his spiritual life that he names God only in the insincere exclamation "ah God." His exuberant descriptions of the head of John the Baptist (whose name he appears to forget) and the breast of the Virgin Mary (fresco painters used the expensive blue pigment of lapis lazuli to color her cloak more often than her breast) are further indicators of his obsession with a physical order that is more human than divine. In a parody of the Catholic doctrine of transubstantiation, he even imagines that his sensory experience will persist after his death:

And then how I shall lie through centuries,
And hear the blessed mutter of the mass,
And see God made and eaten all day long,
And feel the steady candle-flame, and taste
Good strong thick stupefying incense-smoke!

(ll. 80–84)

Despite its historical Roman setting, the poem is a response to a contemporary question, as it satirizes what Browning took to be the architectural and liturgical flummery of crypto-Catholic developments in Anglicanism in the 1840s (the Oxford movement and the Cambridge Camden Society). Further poems in *Dramatic Romances and Lyrics* weigh into the intellectual and political controversies of the 1840s: "The Flight of the Duchess" examines the complications of medieval revivalism, while "The Lost Leader" regrets William Wordsworth's betrayal of British Liberal party principles "Just for a handful of silver" (l. 1) and a derisory laureateship.

"The Italian in England" and "The Englishman in Italy" are studies of political loyalty and apathy, respectively, in the climate of nationalist fervor that was spreading across Europe. Browning had first visited Italy in 1838, when the experience had provided him with fertile material for *Sordello* and *Pippa Passes*. From August until December 1844 he made a second journey that took him to Naples, Rome (including the graves of Keats and Shelley), and Florence. Browning was struck by the beautiful decay of the peninsula whose glorious past he had visited so often in Latin and Italian literature. But he was also aware of the embarrassing status of the tourist at a time of great political moment for the Italian people. "The Italian in England" responds to the revelation that the English government had been opening the correspondence of Giuseppe Mazzini, the Italian revolutionary in exile in England, and passing information to the Austrians who occupied Italy at the time. "The Englishman in Italy" is a picturesque celebration of the lush Italian landscape, spoken by an English traveler whose enthusiasm is eventually critiqued when he makes a casual defense of the oppressive Corn Laws in his own country (trade restrictions that set an artificially high price for grain in England). Browning was never so naive in his relations with foreign cultures and languages; for him linguistic and cultural translation was not a way of familiarizing what was strange, but of testing the limitations and assumptions of what was familiar.

MARRIAGE AND MEN AND WOMEN

Although *Bells and Pomegranates* did little to attract a "Pit-audience" to Browning's poetry, the pamphlets did find admirers among the literary elite. Elizabeth Barrett (1806–1861), the most celebrated woman poet of the time, had praised the poetic nourishment offered by Browning's *Pomegranates* in "Lady Geraldine's Courtship" (1844). Their mutual friend Frederick Kenyon encouraged Browning to write an appreciative response. When Browning sent his first letter to Barrett on 10 January 1845, he initiated one of the most profound correspondences in English literary history—and one of its most remarkable partnerships. The two poets exchanged 572 letters between them in the eighteen months of their courtship.

Elizabeth was a literary celebrity but a social exile, trapped in her Wimpole Street bedchamber by both physical frailty and a domineering father. She was initially reluctant to meet Browning, fearing that he would be nonplussed by their age difference—she was six years older—and her visibly poor health. But he was captivated by her, and his letters soon became passionate pleas to escape to Italy with him from climates (atmospheric and literary) that were detrimental to their happiness. He tried to encourage her in verse. "The Flight of the Duchess" is a dramatic romance that sympathizes with its heroine against domestic tyrannies. Their correspondence charts the depths of that word, as it imagines how two people might correspond with each other emotionally and intellectually, and how that private intimacy must be crafted and protected in a linguistic medium that is by its nature public. Browning hoped that these densely allusive, elliptical letters would "move & live—the thoughts, feelings, & expressions even,—in a self-imposed circle limiting the experience of two persons only" (vol. 1, p. 463). Their poetry continued to converse throughout their marriage. The male lover of "In a Balcony" (in Browning's *Men and Women*) cries out, "How I do love you! Give my love its way!" (l. 12) in antiphonal response to Barrett's *Sonnets from the Portuguese* ("How do I love thee? Let me count the ways....")

The poets' courtship might have been borrowed from a French comedy. Browning was smuggled into the Barrett house thanks to the occasional white lie and the help of Elizabeth's sister, Henrietta. In a letter to Barrett he joked that "by the time all this is over, we shall be fit to take a degree in some Jesuits college—we shall have mastered all the points of casuistry" (vol. 2, p. 951). On their wedding day, 12 September 1846, Elizabeth made the short journey to Marylebone Street Church under the pretense of a drive in Regent's Park. The only witnesses at the ceremony were her maid and Browning's cousin James Silverthorne. She returned to her father's house without her husband, and it was not until a week later that they fled to Italy together (according to Chesterton, Wordsworth was said to have commented, "I hope they understand each other—nobody else would," p. 40). They spent the winter in Pisa before settling in the cosmopolitan expatriate community in Florence, in a spacious apartment in Casa Guidi opposite the Pitti Palace. It was the place they fondly called home for thirteen years.

The courtship letters work through Browning's anxieties about his poetic reputation and articulate his growing confidence under the stewardship of Elizabeth's sympathy. He anticipates that his best work is to come, although he recognizes that he will never master the urgent sincerity typified by the best of her poems: "You speak out, *you,*—I only make men & women speak—give you truth broken into prismatic hues, and fear the pure white light, even if it is in me" (vol. 1, p. 7). His own attempt to write more directly was a false move. *Christmas–Eve and Easter–Day* (1850) contains a long dream-vision poem that undercuts its serious subject with bathetic rhymes and experimental rhythms ("Christmas-Eve") and a dry dialogue on the nature of faith ("Easter-Day").

ROBENING

ROBERT BROWNING

The early years in Italy mingled the pleasures of freedom with the regrets of exile. On 9 March 1849 Elizabeth gave birth to their only child, Robert Wiedemann Barrett Browning ("Pen"), but this happy event was marked by sadness when Browning received news of his mother's death only days later. The Brownings were keen advocates of Italian unification, which had seemed possible in the 1840s, and were disappointed by the restoration of the conservative status quo in the years following the revolutionary fervor of 1848 (this political optimism and defeat are the subjects of Elizabeth's rousing call to action in *Casa Guidi Windows*). Given his own circumstances and the political mood, it is perhaps unsurprising that Browning turned to intimacy and the endurance of art as the subjects for his next collection of poems.

Men and Women (1855) is one of the great achievements of Browning's career. Its two volumes and fifty-one poems are remarkable for their variety of tone, poetic form, and subject matter. Their ironies are softer and more ambivalent than in the Gothic scenarios of the early dramatic monologues, and they exhibit an intense, layered emotional texture that Browning learned from the complex drama of his own love. The speakers are more ambivalent than the hypocritical clergymen and monomaniacal murderers who had appeared in *Bells and Pomegranates*:

Our interest's on the dangerous edge of things.
The honest thief, the tender murderer,
The superstitious atheist, the demirep
That loves and saves her soul in new French books—

("Bishop Blougram's Apology," ll. 395–98)

The opening poem, "Love Among the Ruins" is a Theocritan pastoral that reworks the old hope that love persists despite the disintegration of man's other works. Its speaker is a young shepherd whose simple love for "a girl with eager eyes and yellow hair" (l. 55) is played out against the backdrop of a ruined "city great and gay" (l. 6) in a move that reduces political ambition to no more than "centuries of folly, noise and sin!" (l. 81). It is a brilliant technical achievement comprising couplets of long anapestic lines and

short three–syllable lines (cretics) that signal the formal innovation of the volume. Other love poems in *Men and Women* give the lie to the misconception that, for Robert and Elizabeth, love had conquered all. "A Lovers' Quarrel" and "A Woman's Last Word" need not have specific biographical sources, but they offer reminders that for love to ripen into complexity it must be open to negotiation and compromise.

"Two in the Campagna" is a pessimistic companion piece to "Love Among the Ruins." It is an anti-pastoral poem in which the seemingly sympathetic landscape warps into a metaphor for the incompatibility of two lovers:

No. I yearn upward, touch you close,
Then stand away. I kiss your cheek,
Catch your soul's warmth,—I pluck the rose
And love it more than tongue can speak—
Then the good minute goes.

(ll. 46–50)

The physical proximity of the lovers seems to promise spiritual proximity, but this is defeated by the speaker's realization that he can never share his lover's intimate sense of being. His kiss on her cheek becomes a perfunctory gesture even as it happens, as "catch" seems to signify something grasped fleetingly (like a word or phrase) rather than captured definitively (like a big fish). The good of this temporal "minute" is spatially "minute." The poem's exploration of "Infinite passion, and the pain / Of finite hearts that yearn" (ll. 59–60) is an interesting comment on Victorian ideas of interpersonal sympathy: it thinks about the potential for independent minds to affect and cultivate one another before concluding that they are irreconcilably apart, strangers to each other and even to themselves. Other poems in *Men and Women*, such as "Mesmerism," investigate the opposite extreme by imagining what might happen if minds were able to exert irrational influences on each other. In his love poems Browning tries to measure whether poetry has a special emotive power to "touch you close."

Many of the masterpieces in *Men and Women* consider not only the function of poetry but also the enduring lessons of Renaissance painting and music. Browning's great interest in the sister arts was stimulated by his Florentine surroundings. The poet's fascination with music was long-standing, and in "A Toccata of Galuppi's" and "Master Hugues of Saxe-Gotha" he displays his facility with the technical language and practice of musical composition. This partially explains why the music of his verse became an important issue in critical debates about its merit. In the *Westminster Review* of January 1856, George Eliot remarked that "turning from the ordinary literature of the day to such a writer as Browning, is like turning from Flotow's music, made up of well-pieced shreds and patches, to the distinct individuality of Chopin's Studies or Schubert's Songs" (p. 235). Others complained that Browning's poetry was distinctive because it lacked the mellifluous cadences they were wont to associate with lyric verse (hence Oscar Wilde's quip, "Meredith is a prose Browning, and so is Browning"). Nevertheless, poems from "The Pied-Piper of Hamelin" to "Holy-Cross Day" mark his ability to find meanings in sound and rhythm that are distinct from the semantic content of language. The opening lines of "Holy-Cross Day" celebrate the riotous energy of nonsense ("Fee, faw, fum! bubble and squeak!").

Browning's love of painting dated back to his childhood visits to the Dulwich Picture Gallery, and his knowledge of Renaissance art had been fostered by careful reading of Giorgio Vasari's *Lives of the Most Eminent Painters, Sculptors, and Architects* (1550/1568; trans. 1850–1852). One of the painters Browning read about was Filippo Lippi (c. 1406–1469), who became the subject of his most vivid and energetic dramatic monologue, "Fra Lippo Lippi." Apprehended by the Florentine watch in a steamy back alley ("where sportive ladies leave their doors ajar," l. 6), he makes his slight excuses ("Zooks, what's to blame? you think you see a monk!" l. 3) before relaxing into a brilliant manifesto for his naturalistic art that also defends his fleshier instincts ("flesh and blood, / That's all I'm made of," l. 61):

This world's no blot for us,
Nor blank; it means intensely, and means good:
To find its meaning is my meat and drink.

(ll. 313–315)

Browning believed in the transcendent possibility of the arts (including poetry, as "How It Strikes a Contemporary" makes clear), but although he thought that the artist's ultimate responsibility was to God, he championed painters whose aesthetic moved toward naturalism. Fra Lippo derisively mimics his ecclesiastical patrons who would have him idealize his subjects and thereby impede the progress of painting:

Here's Giotto, with his Saint a-praising God,
That sets us praising,—why not stop with him?
Why put all thoughts of praise out of our head
With wonder at lines, colours, and what not?
Paint the soul, never mind the legs and arms!

(ll. 189–193)

"Andrea del Sarto" approaches these ideas from another angle; its speaker has failed to devote himself to the dutiful work that Browning believed artists owed to their God-given ability. Where Fra Lippo displays the canny enthusiasm of an artist whose talent is still dawning (and the poem ends at dawn's "grey beginning," l. 392), Andrea del Sarto reflects on his comparative failure as a painter with a premature weariness that renders this poem a melancholy "twilight-piece" (l. 49). His uxoriousness has spoiled his artistic ambition, and the result is a moving, if pathetic, plea for his wife's loyalty in the face of his own disintegrating talent:

I often am much wearier than you think,
This evening more than usual, and it seems
As if—forgive now—should you let me sit
Here by the window with your hand in mine
And look a half-hour forth on Fiesole,
Both of one mind, as married people use,
Quietly, quietly the evening through,
I might get up tomorrow to my work
Cheerful and fresh as ever.

(ll. 11–19)

This is a slow, unhappy sentence that shows up Andrea's lack of resolve by struggling to its own resolution. His tarnished faith is rewarded by Lucrezia's faithlessness as she responds to the whistle of her "cousin" (which is probably a euphemism) below the window, and her husband relinquishes her to the night.

ROBERT BROWNING

The third dominant theme of *Men and Women* is religious faith. "Bishop Blougram's Apology" is a long dramatic monologue that has an unusual status in the volume as a poem that responds to a contemporary controversy in a contemporary setting. It is a tour de force that pits the crapulous after-dinner casuistry of an Anglo-Catholic bishop against a hack journalist named Gigadibs (who remains silent). "An Epistle Containing the Strange Medical Experience of Karshish, the Arab Physician" and "Cleon" take an oblique look at the New Testament; they parody the Epistles of Saint Paul as they cast back to a time when Christianity was a marginal cult, a small rumor amid learned Arabic and Greek cultural narratives. The most extraordinary exploration of faith in the collection occurs in "Childe Roland to the Dark Tower Came," in which a wandering knight (or "Childe") persists on a mysterious quest whose meaning remains occluded. The subject matter of the poem looks back to Romantic vision poetry, but the desiccated wasteland through which the knight travels anticipates the apocalyptic landscapes of modernist poetry:

As for the grass, it grew as scant as hair
In leprosy; thin dry blades pricked the mud
Which underneath looked kneaded up with blood.

(ll. 73–75)

As the poem concludes, the knight seems on the verge of combating an enemy as he reaches the dark tower and is confronted by a strange vision of his lost companions:

There they stood, ranged along the hill-sides, met
To view the last of me, a living frame
For one more picture! in a sheet of flame
I saw them and I knew them all. And yet
Dauntless the slug-horn to my lips I set,
And blew.

(ll. 199–204)

It is a perverse revelation, for although we assume that it does not harbinger the "last of" the narrator (because he is narrating), the poem leaves us in suspense. Even stranger, the final line seems to announce the title of the poem: Childe Roland's fate may be to continue questing in baffling—perhaps "metatextual"—circles.

MOURNING AND DRAMATIS PERSONAE

Although *Men and Women* was widely reviewed, the critiques were scathing, and worse still, as eminent a reader as John Ruskin expressed his confusion to Browning in a letter that offered a bizarre commentary on a poem called "Popularity"—which was a cruel irony, given Browning's poor literary reputation at the time. The period of dejection that followed was only partially assuaged by extended periods in London, Paris, Normandy, and Rome, by the comfortable legacy bequeathed to the Brownings by John Kenyon, and by the rapturous reception given to Elizabeth's masterpiece, *Aurora Leigh,* on its publication in 1856.

Robert and Elizabeth spent the winter of 1859 in Rome, but Elizabeth was increasingly frail. Her pulmonary condition had worsened and she was increasingly dependent on morphine. They returned to Florence, where she died in the arms in her husband on 29 June 1860. He wrote to his sister that

> My life is fixed and sure now. I shall live out the remainder under her direct influence endeavouring to complete mine, miserably imperfect now, but so as to take the good she was meant to give me.... I shall live in the presence of her, in every sense, I hope and believe.

(*Letters of Robert Browning,* p. 62)

Nevertheless, Browning seems to have shrouded his grief in the business of arrangements: first for his wife's funeral and then for his permanent removal to England. Pen's golden curls, which had so delighted his mother, had been clipped by the time father and son settled at 19 Warwick Crescent, London, in August that year.

The poems that appeared in *Dramatis Personae* (1864) make amends for Browning's stoical response to his wife's death. The speakers of "James Lee's Wife," "Too Late," and "May and Death" are fragile barometers of possession and loss; the unstable speaker of "Too Late" laments that "There's only the past left: worry that!" (the cruel irony here is that the past is no more than a record of what has already "left"). Browning had been working on some of these poems since before Elizabeth's death; a long poem that he almost certainly had kept from her was "Mr. Sludge, 'The Medium,' " a brutal critique of the spiritual medium Daniel Dunglas Home, whose table-turning and rapping she had found so compelling (to Browning's disgust). In the context of her death, however, the medium's admission that he has cheated the living by mimicking the dead also becomes a subtle reproach to the living as they cling to their mental images of the dead. By contrast, "Prospice" and "Eurydice to Orpheus" are moving lyrics that ponder whether there is any possibility of communion with the dead. Eurydice's tragic misunderstanding is to make a passionate demand for "one immortal look" (l. 6) from her husband as he leads her from the Underworld; it is her oddly human impatience that will return her to the dead and him to mortal solitude.

Dramatis Personae lacks the pithy brilliance of *Men and Women;* Sludge is true to his name as his catalog of excuses sprawls over fifteen hundred lines. The title of the volume is indicative of their speakers' waning control over language; they play roles that are assigned to them in a drama and are denied the rhetorical talent, even agency, of a Fra Lippo or Bishop Blougram. The most refined monologue in the volume, however, takes agency as one of its themes. In "Caliban upon Setebos," a simple-minded version of Shakespeare's Caliban mutters to himself in the mud ("letting the rank tongue blossom into speech," l. 23) as he considers his submission to an indifferent god ("Setebos") whom he tries to mold in his own image. His tautological theology is brilliantly rendered by Browning in a confusion of pronouns as Caliban refers to both himself and his god in the third person: for example, in line 26, "Thinketh He made it, with the sun to match," the opening verb describes what Caliban is doing, but "He" should probably be taken as Setebos. (Caliban is not a very clear thinker.) He strains for a crude animistic power that would allow him to imitate Setebos or Prospero, but his attempts to rescue any kind of agency for himself are consistently undercut by the reader's recognition that this furiously wordy character has had his messy thought

molded into blank verse by a force beyond his control (namely, Robert Browning):

Himself peeped late, eyed Prosper at his books
Careless and lofty, lord now of the isle:
Vexed, 'stitched a book of broad leaves, arrow-shaped,
Wrote thereon, he knows what, prodigious words;
Has peeled a wand and called it by a name;
Weareth at whiles for an enchanter's robe
The eyed skin of a supple oncelot; …

(ll. 150–156)

Browning's vision of primitivism is also one of the most intellectual achievements of this most intellectual of poets; it responds carefully to the debates surrounding Darwin's *Origin of Species* (1859) and satirizes the theological sophistry that attempted to usurp the scientific upheavals of the High Victorian period.

THE RING AND THE BOOK

Although Browning had settled in London, he spent the rest of the 1860s intellectually immersed in Baroque Italy as he composed the vast monologues that were to become *The Ring and the Book* (1868–1869). The twelve books and around 21,000 lines of this poem render it epic in proportion and ambition, if not in substance. It is perhaps the closest that nineteenth-century poetry comes to the complex realism of the Victorian novel, with its social panorama and challenging accumulation of historical detail. Indeed, Henry James penned an important appreciation titled "The Novel in the *Ring and the Book.*" For at least one modern critic, it epitomizes Victorian excess, "reminiscent of other and baser Victorian misunderstandings about the nature of the aesthetic, from wax-flowers under glass to models of the Crystal Palace constructed out of matchsticks" (Everett, p. 173). But it is also a sustained examination of poetry's claims to discover and represent truths that lie beyond the prosaic forms of daily life. This is clear from the first book, where a Browning-like speaker makes the brilliant self-reflexive gesture of describing his source material and its transformation by the poet's alchemical craft:

Do you see this square old yellow Book, I toss
I' the air, and catch again, and twirl about
By the crumpled vellum covers,—pure crude fact
Secreted from a man's life when hearts beat hard,
And brains, high-blooded, ticked two centuries since?

(ll. 33–37)

The poet presents his "old yellow Book" with the exuberance of a conjuror before describing this mysterious anthology of pamphlets, letters, and legal documents in Latin and Italian, happened upon in the bric-a-brac of a Florentine street market (book 1, ll. 38–83). Browning had purchased such a book in 1859 or 1860, and was soon convinced that its "Roman murder-case" provided intricate material for a long poem. (He offered it to Anthony Trollope and Tennyson before undertaking it himself.)

The so-called *Old Yellow Book* survives in Balliol College Library, Oxford, not nearly as yellow as Browning's poem would have us believe. Such artistic license is telling; it signals the Gothic quality of faded documents but also introduces a careful echo of Victorian culture. "Yellow-backs" had been a publishing phenomenon in the 1850s and 1860s, offering sharp, sensationalist thrills (including the first detective fiction) that had been marketed to railway passengers (airport fiction *avant la lettre*). That Browning's subject matter might be appropriate for a thriller—and the poem has frequently been described as a detective novel in verse—is an indicator of how his poetry continued to negotiate, sometimes ironically, what poetry might salvage from the accelerating pace of the world and the self-conscious modernity of the age.

The poem explores the aftermath of a grisly triple murder in Rome in 1698 that is the culmination of an arranged marriage between a young Roman girl, Pompilia Comparini, and an impecunious Tuscan aristocrat, Count Guido Franceschini. Her elderly parents disown her as the changeling daughter of a prostitute; her husband abuses her and demands the agreed dowry. Several years and much legal wrangling later, she escapes with a glamorous priest, Giuseppe Caponsacchi, but they are overtaken on the road to Rome and accused of adultery. Roman justice is too lenient for Guido, who cuts down Pompilia and her parents in a brutal frenzy. And so the poem begins (and does everything in its power to remind us that narrative is never so simple).

Browning's opening salvo prefaces the poem like the general prologue to *The Canterbury Tales,* with sketches of its disparate cast of speakers. Unlike *The Canterbury Tales,* however, *The Ring and the Book* reworks a single tale many times to gain new meaning in different idioms and under different moral and social pressures (the story is told three times in the opening book alone). In books 2–4, three Roman characters offer their interpretations of the murders in the immediate confusion of the attacks as Pompilia lies dying a slow death that acts as counterpoint to the compulsive retellings leading up to it. "Half-Rome" and "The Other Half-Rome" are voyeuristic gossips: the former has been loitering near the Comparini bodies all day to launch his macho defense of Guido ("Case could not well be simpler," he claims in book 2, l. 183) that doubles as a warning to any man who would cuckold him, while the latter sentimentalizes "little Pompilia" (book 3, l. 2) and inadvertently celebrates her death by indulging in a kind of pre-death hagiography ("'Tis a miracle," book 3, l. 7). His Pompilia is so pastel-colored that he can only describe the difficult crux of the story (her flight with Caponsacchi) as a "tenebrific passage" (book 3, l. 788). In book 4 "Tertium Quid," a foppish refugee from the commedia dell'arte, tries to flatter fellow salon guests with a pithy survey of the case that tars all of the players with crimes that contradict each other. His patrician's tongue is not so much acidic as base and repetitive, revealing more sympathies than he might claim with "this rabble's-brabble of dolts and fools / Who make up reasonless unreasoning Rome" (book 4, ll. 10–11).

These corrupt rhetorical strategies are mere trifles when set against the snaking obsequies of Guido (the speaker of book 5). His opening complaints about his sore body (he has been on the rack) parody the deprivation he has visited on the body of his wife, and her version of Christian martyrdom:

Thanks, Sir, but, should it please the reverend Court,
I feel I can stand somehow, half sit down
Without help, make shift to even speak, you see,
Fortified by the sip of ... why, 'tis wine,
Velletri,—and not vinegar and gall

(book 5, ll. 1–5)

"Sir" is one of the wriggling keywords he uses to assert the hierarchies that he claims to have defended in killing his wife, setting "the whole-some household rule in force again" (book 5, l. 2042). Like Othello, he is articulate in arguing his inarticulacy (though the relentless nature of his evil is much closer to that of Iago). Nowhere in Browning's oeuvre is the strange status of text that strives to represent speech made more apparent than in *The Ring and the Book,* with its focus on peculiar foreign sources and a vivid cast of speakers. At its simplest, this is a joke about a Roman legal system that required speeches to be transcribed before presentation to the court ("pleadings all in print," book 1, l. 242). More significantly, it makes real the possibility of many kinds of loss and recuperation by nudging things that exist on the brink of historical memory (gossip, idiomatic speech, the victims of crime) to the center of the literary record. Different voices compete to interpret the body of a dying girl as if it were a text, but Browning generously preserves her breath long enough to give her voice, an ironic reversal of the illiteracy that has helped to imprison her in a terrifying marriage:

How happy those are who know how to write!
Such could write what their son should read in time,
Had they a whole day to live out like me.

(book 7, ll. 82–85)

Pompilia's monologue represents a triumph for her simplicity over the preening sophistication that characterises the poem's other voices: the only polysyllabic word in these lines is "happy," an adjective as unpretentious as what it advocates.

The variety of voices and interpretations presented in *The Ring and the Book,* make it tempting to suggest that the poem anticipates the trendy relativity of the postmodern novel. But this is to underestimate the English Protestant sensibility that underpins the work. Pompilia articulates Browning's sustained faith in the perfection that follows the flaws and compromises of this existence:

Marriage on earth seems such a counterfeit,
Mere imitation of the inimitable:
In heaven we have the real and true and sure.

(book 7, ll. 1824–1827)

Relativity only operates within an earthly sphere (or "ring") for the poet who finds imperfection on earth as a sign of fulfillment to come. It is no coincidence that Browning's invocation of "lyric Love" (book 1, ll. 1391–1416)—often considered a thinly veiled elegy to Elizabeth—resounds in both the language and thought of Pompilia's monologue, or that Pompilia's words chime with Browning's "lesson" as the poem concludes "that our human speech is naught, / Our human testimony false" (book 12, ll. 834–835). Set beside these beliefs, human justice is a makeshift arrangement. The two lawyers' monologues that follow Pompilia's are extended studies of buffoonery in a context of greed, ambition, and Latin pedantry; only Browning could have countered his tragic message with a comic celebration of what it entailed.

When Pope Innocent XII assumes responsibility for Guido's life and death in book 10, he faces the impossible challenge that the poem raises: how to reconcile oneself and the world to a judgment that is provisional and imperfect. Pompilia, the pope, and Caponsacchi (book 6) advocate ways of thinking that subordinate earthly narratives to divine truths. And yet Browning privileges Guido with another monologue (book 11; he is the only character besides the poet to speak twice) that is a reminder of the trappings of realism and the seductive Gothic vision of the villain, as he tries "each expedient to save life" (book 11, ll. 852). He has no more vitality than when he imagines his own execution:

Tight you're clipped, whiz, there's the blade on you,
Out trundles body, down flops head on floor,
And where's your soul gone? That, too, I shall find!

(book 11, ll. 233–235)

Pompilia had used the word "clipped" to describe the damage she suffered at his hands; this is a characteristically cruel, if unconscious, act of linguistic usurpation. In a final panic, he makes a plea for mercy that aligns him with Marlowe's Faustus in the moments before he is eternally damned. His last appeal, to Pompilia, might recognize her innocence but might also be a final accusation of her guilt: "Pompilia, will you let them murder me?" (book 11, l. 2425).

The complex judgment represented and required by *The Ring and the Book* was rendered even more subtle by Browning's chosen method of publication. The poem appeared in four volumes over the course of three months; like many of the greatest Victorian novels, it was a serialized fiction. The final texts of the later books were not yet finalized when the first two volumes were published, so critical verdicts were delayed (much like the poem's internal postponement of sentencing). Interim reviews were favorable (which may be why, in book 12, Browning is so optimistic about the "British Public, who may like me yet," l. 831). But the reception that greeted the poem when the final volume had been published more than vindicated Browning's long-standing belief in himself. In the *Athenaeum* for 20 March 1869, R. W. Buchanan praised it as "the supremest poetical achievement of our time."

LATE POEMS

In the final decades of his life, Browning became a public figure and social fixture who nonetheless found time to compose a vast quantity of verse. The quality of this work is inferior to the concise yet complex wit of the middle period or the brilliant social and psychological investigations of *The Ring and the Book*. Few readers have ventured beyond T. S. Eliot's jibe that "one can get on very well in life without ever having read all the later poetry of Browning and Swinburne" (*On Poetry and Poets*, p. 48). The fifteen volumes that Browning published during this period form an arcane, even absurd, procession: they include *Prince Hohenstiel-Schwangau, Saviour of Society* (1871), *Red Cotton Night-Cap Country; or, Turf*

and Towers (1873), *Pacchiarotto and How He Worked in Distemper* (1876), *Ferishtah's Fancies* (1884), and *Parleyings with Certain People of Importance in Their Day* (1887). Over and again, Browning's critics were baffled.

Eliot's rejection of the late poetry is provocative, because the formal innovation and disruptions of genre that characterize much of this work in some ways anticipate the achievements of literary modernism. In *Balaustion's Adventure* (1871) and *Aristophanes' Apology* (1875), Browning inserts the "transcripts" of two plays by Euripedes (*Alkestis* and *Herakles,* respectively) into a narrative framework that comments on the creative opportunities and restrictions of reworking the classical tradition. The heroine, Balaustion, can "bring forth new good, new beauty, from the old" (l. 2425). (Her recital of *Alkestis,* a play about a loyal wife who volunteers to die in place of her husband, articulates another version of Browning's personal loss.) *The Agamemnon of Aeschylus* (1877) is the most challenging product of the poet's interest in Greek drama and among the most unusual translations of the Victorian period. It anticipates Vladimir Nabokov's endorsement of literal translation in that it refuses to bring the Greek text closer to its English-speaking audience by adopting a fluent idiom and instead attempts to stretch the English language toward Greek syntax and diction. It is the culmination of Browning's experiments with voices and texts that are simultaneously familiar and foreign.

Some of the late verse has a playful quality; it often suggests that its technical accomplishments are diversions or games. The ludic rhymes in "Of Pachiarotto, and How He Worked in Distemper" include three lines that yoke together "pooh-poohed it is," "lewd ditties," and "nudities" (ll. 103–105). This is a poem that laughs off its own bad mood, so that although it is an attack on the poet's critics, it concludes with the poet's admission that "I've laughed out my laugh on this mirth-day!" (l. 571). (Browning did not so much work in a temper as work his temper into his poetry.) The first stanza of "Pambo," a poem from the slight volume *Jocoseria* (1883), is no more than an exemplary joke about rhyme:

Suppose that we part (work done, comes play)
With a grave tale told in crambo
—As our hearty sires were wont to say—
Whereof the hero is Pambo?

(ll. 1–4)

"Crambo" is a game in which players have to find rhymes for words or lines that have been suggested by another player. In using it as the clumsy rhyme-word here, Browning signals a careful irony; it is one of few possible rhymes for "Pambo," a character who struggles to reform the ungainliness of his speech. The rhyming hexameters of *Fifine at the Fair* (1872) are less jaunty but no less audacious. They are flexible enough to beat a slow, consistent measure or an unsettled fluttering rhythm apposite to Don Juan, who speaks a poem that wavers between his love for his wife Elvire and the temptations of a "fizgig called Fifine" (l. 507). Browning attracted several wealthy, intelligent women around this time and twice rebuffed a marriage proposal from Lady Ashburton (1827-1903), who was a keen art collector and philanthropist. *Fifine at the Fair* was the poet's exploration of the obligations and complications of commitment. It is set in the "pleasant land of France" (l. 14)—where he had often summered since the death of Elizabeth—and works through serious themes of loyalty and devotion in a carnival context that is far from the workaday world.

Other playfully experimental poems revise conventional notions of genre and continue Browning's idiosyncratic remapping of the boundary between verse and prose. *Red Cotton Night-Cap Country* (1873) and *The Inn Album* (1875) are set outside the bustle of the city, the former in a "hitherto un-Murrayed bathing-place" in northern France (Murray published tourist guides) and the latter in a shabby inn in the English countryside, ironically and repeatedly described as a "calm acclivity, salubrious spot!" (l. 11). Yet these are both topical poems that examine the sprawl of the city's mental life into the country through railways, newspapers, and novels: *Red Cotton Night-Cap Country* is based on a contemporary French scandal that Browning reconstructed from legal documents, while *The*

Inn Album contains references to Ruskin, Tennyson, Benjamin Disraeli, and many others ("Tennyson take my benison," l. 2407). As with *The Ring and the Book,* these works examine whether poetry processes the messy life of realist novels in a way that is different from prose, and how the symbolic claims of verse act on modern narratives. *The Inn Album* is particularly engaging in its proximity to sensation fiction: with its submerged narrative, its examination of moral flaws, and its strange threats to selfhood and self-integrity, it reads like a sequel to the uneasy sonnets of George Meredith's *Modern Love* (1862). Where *The Ring and the Book* and *Red Cotton Night-Cap Country* are restored from textual artifacts, the characters of *The Inn Album* imagine that they are leaving written traces as they return to the inn and add to the visitors' book, to which the poem's title refers. It is a perplexing but intriguing device that demonstrates Browning's continued formal experimentation. The poet-speaker imagines fictional characters browsing the album and rebuking the style of its contributors: "That bard's a Browning; he neglects the form" (l. 17).

By the 1880s Browning had become a national institution. In 1881 F. J. Furnivall founded the first Browning Society; three years later there were twenty-two of them. Browning was reluctant to be the object of bardolatry during his lifetime, and it must have seemed to him that he was beginning to lead a posthumous existence. Much of his poetry from this period has a retrospective quality; the popular volumes of *Dramatic Idyls* (1879 and 1880) turned back toward the style of the earlier dramatic romances, with their succinct narratives and knotty moral dilemmas. His head was crowded with voices and visions of the past: "Beatrice Signorini" (in *Asolando,* 1889) seems like a late pendant poem to "My Last Duchess."

Asolando was to be Browning's last volume. He had cherished the small town of Asolo in northern Italy since his first visit there in 1838, and throughout his life he had a recurring dream about how his return there seemed always just out of reach. In 1889 he traveled there from Venice, where he had been staying with Pen at the

Palazzo Rezzonico, and was spurred into a final creative flurry. There is a conscious finality to these poems, a slow sense of preparation for something unknown that is most explicit in the "Epilogue":

One who never turned his back but marched breast
  forward,
Never doubted clouds would break,
Never dreamed, though right were worsted, wrong
  would triumph,
Held we fall to rise, are baffled to fight better,
Sleep to wake.

(ll. 11–16)

Asolando was published the morning of 12 December 1889, and Browning died later that day. His final satisfaction was to receive news of the favorable reviews that had greeted it.

CONCLUSION

The great ventriloquist lives on in the voices of twentieth and twenty-first century poetry. T. S. Eliot's aversion to Browning is belied by the speakers of his own brilliant monologues: Prufrock inherits his indecisions from Andrea del Sarto. Of the modernists, it was Ezra Pound who thought most carefully about how Browning's voices might interfere with his own: the title of *Personae* (1909) recalls *Dramatis Personae*. Other poets influenced by Browning include Robert Lowell, W. H. Auden, and Louis MacNeice (who wrote a radio play called *The Dark Tower*). More recently, Mick Imlah reworked the dramatic monologue in modern Scottish contexts in *The Lost Leader* (2008), a volume that announced its debt to Browning by borrowing one of his titles.

Even if Browning has become a keystone for our understanding of Victorian literature, the singularity of his achievement has never subsided. He brought home to his readers the odd business of living, and the great dramatic monologues are still as uncanny as they always were, as their vivid voices refuse to quiet down into aesthetic or historical slumbers.

Selected Bibliography

WORKS OF ROBERT BROWNING

POETRY

Pauline: A Fragment of a Confession. London: Saunders and Otley, 1833.

Paracelsus. London: Effingham Wilson, 1835.

Sordello. London: Edward Moxon, 1840.

Bells and Pomegranates I: Pippa Passes. London: Edward Moxon, 1841.

Bells and Pomegranates III: Dramatic Lyrics. London: Edward Moxon, 1842.

Bells and Pomegranates VII: Dramatic Romances and Lyrics. London: Edward Moxon, 1845.

Christmas-Eve and Easter-Day: A Poem. London: Chapman and Hall, 1850.

Men and Women, 2 vols. London: Chapman and Hall, 1855.

Dramatis Personae. London: Chapman and Hall, 1864.

The Ring and the Book, 4 vols. London: Smith, Elder, 1868–1869.

Balaustion's Adventure: Including a Transcript from Euripides. London: Smith, Elder, 1871.

Prince Hohenstiel-Schwangau, Saviour of Society. London: Smith, Elder, 1871.

Fifine at the Fair. London: Smith, Elder, 1872.

Red Cotton Night-Cap Country; or, Turf and Towers. London: Smith, Elder, 1873.

Aristophanes' Apology: Including a Transcript from Euripides, Being the Last Adventure of Balaustion. London: Smith, Elder, 1875.

The Inn Album. London: Smith, Elder, 1875.

Pacchiarotto and How He Worked in Distemper, with Other Poems. London: Smith, Elder, 1876.

The Agamemnon of Aeschylus Transcribed by Robert Browning. London: Smith, Elder, 1877.

La Saisiaz; The Two Poets of Croisic. London: Smith, Elder, 1878.

Dramatic Idyls. London: Smith, Elder, 1879.

Dramatic Idyls, Second Series. London: Smith, Elder, 1880.

Jocoseria. London: Smith, Elder, 1883.

Ferishtah's Fancies. London: Smith, Elder, 1884.

Parleyings with Certain People of Importance in Their Day. London: Smith, Elder, 1887.

Asolando: Fancies and Facts. London: Smith, Elder, 1890.

PLAYS

Strafford: An Historical Tragedy. London: Longman, 1837.

Bells and Pomegranates II: King Victor and King Charles. London: Edward Moxon, 1842.

Bells and Pomegrantes IV: The Return of the Druses. London: Edward Moxon, 1843.

Bells and Pomegranates V: A Blot in the 'Scutcheon. London: Edward Moxon, 1843.

Bells and Pomegranates VI: Colombe's Birthday. London: Edward Moxon, 1844.

Bells and Pomegranates VIII: Luria; and A Soul's Tragedy. London: Edward Moxon, 1846.

CORRESPONDENCE AND MANUSCRIPTS

Letters of Robert Browning Collected by Thomas J. Wise. Edited by Thurman L. Hood. London: John Murray, 1933.

The Letters of Robert Browning and Elizabeth Barrett Barrett, 1845–1846, 2 vols. Edited by Elvan Kinter. Cambridge, Mass.: Harvard University Press, 1969. (References to the courtship correspondence are to volume and page number in this edition.)

The Brownings' Correspondence, 16 vols. to date. Edited by Philip Kelley et al. Winfield, Kan.: Wedgestone Press, 1984–. (Projected 40 volumes.)

Browning's manuscripts are collected in many places. There is much material in the United States; Browning was more widely admired by Americans than by his own countrymen during his lifetime. Large collections of material related to Browning can be found in the Armstrong Browning Library, University of Waco, Texas, and in Balliol College Library, University of Oxford.

COLLECTED WORKS

The Poetical Works of Robert Browning, 16 vols. London: Smith, Elder, 1888–1889. Vol. 17, edited by Edward Berdoe, added 1894. (The final edition to be seen through the press by Browning himself).

Robert Browning: The Poems, 2 vols. Edited by John Pettigrew and Thomas J. Collins. New Haven, Conn., and London: Yale University Press; Harmondsworth, U.K., and New York: Penguin, 1981. Supplemented by *The Ring and The Book.* Edited by Richard D. Altick. New Haven, Conn., and London: Yale University Press; Harmondsworth: Penguin, 1981 (1971). (All references to Browning's poetry are to line numbers in this edition. The first volume includes poems up to and including *Prince Hohenstiel-Schwangau.*)

Editing Browning is a long journey. The Ohio *Complete Works of Robert Browning,* begun in 1969, will comprise seventeen volumes (fourteen are available to date). The Oxford *Poetical Works of Robert Browning,* begun in 1984, will comprise fifteen volumes (eight are available to date). The Longman *Poems of Browning,* begun in 1991, has so far completed three volumes (the poems to 1861; this edition will print the earliest available text of each poem).

BIBLIOGRAPHY AND CONCORDANCE

Broughton, Leslie N., and B. F. Stelter. *A Concordance to the Poems of Robert Browning,* 4 vols. New York: Haskell House, 1982. (First published 1924–1925.)

Drew, Philip. *An Annotated Critical Bibliography of Robert Browning.* London: Harvester Wheatsheaf, 1990.

CRITICAL AND BIOGRAPHICAL STUDIES

Armstrong, Isobel, ed. *Writers and Their Background: Robert Browning.* London: G. Bell and Sons, 1974.

Bloom, Harold, and Adrienne Munich, eds. *Robert Browning: A Collection of Critical Essays.* Englewood Cliffs, N.J.: Prentice Hall, 1979.

Bristow, Joseph. *Robert Browning.* New York, Harvester Wheatsheaf, 1991.

Chesterton, G. K. *Robert Browning.* London: House of Stratus, 2001. (First published 1903).

Eliot, George "Robert Browning's *Men and Women*" in *Selected Critical Writings.* Ed. Rosemary Ashton. Oxford: Oxford University Press, 1992. Pp. 234–242.

Eliot, T.S. "What is Minor Poetry?" in *On Poetry and Poets.* London: Faber and Faber, 1957. Pp. 39–52.

Everett, Barbara. "Browning Versions." In her *Poets in Their Time.* London: Faber, 1986. Pp. 159–181.

Hair, Donald S. *Robert Browning's Language.* Toronto: University of Toronto Press, 1999.

Irvine, William, and Park Honan. *The Book, The Ring, and the Poet.* London: Bodley Head, 1975.

James, Henry. "Browning in Westminster Abbey." In his *English Hours.* London: Heinemann, 1905. Pp. 44–49.

Karlin, Daniel. *The Courtship of Robert Browning and Elizabeth Barrett.* Oxford: Oxford University Press, 1985.

Langbaum, Robert. *The Poetry of Experience: The Dramatic Monologue in Modern Literary Tradition.* New York: Random House, 1957.

Litzinger, Boyd, and Donald Smalley, eds. *Browning: The Critical Heritage.* London: Routledge and Kegan Paul, 1970.

Orr, Mrs. Sutherland. *Life and Letters of Robert Browning.* Rev. ed. by Frederick G. Kenyon. London: Smith, Elder, 1908.

Reynolds, Matthew. "Browning's Forms of Government." In *Robert Browning in Contexts.* Edited by John Woolford. Winfield, Kan.: Wedgestone Press. Pp. 118–47.

Slinn, Warwick E. *Browning and the Fictions of Identity.* London: Macmillan, 1982.

Tucker, Herbert. *Browning's Beginnings: The Art of Disclosure.* Minneapolis: University of Minnesota Press, 1980.

William Cowper

(1731—1800)

Rhian Williams

THE POET, HYMNIST, and letter writer William Cowper (pronounced "Cooper") is often recognized as a "transitional" writer (Rhodes, p. 15) whose works come between the elegancies of the Augustan period—exemplified by Alexander Pope (1688-1744)—and the Romantic period's shift toward "the real language of men," called for and exemplified by William Wordsworth (1770-1850). Yet to see Cowper as one who merely "fills a gap" between more significant periods not only does him a disservice but also distorts significantly the picture of English cultural life at the end of the eighteenth century. For Cowper was far from overlooked either during his life or in the century that followed. Writing in 1905, in fact, H. S. Milford felt reassured that "Cowper [is not] one of the neglected poets whose lives have still to be written and their position in the poetic hierarchy determined" (p. xii). Yet, in a poem of 1785 (dates for poetry refer to the first publication; where this was posthumous, Milford's suggested date of composition is included) Cowper likened himself to a stricken deer:

I was a stricken deer that left the herd,
Long since; with many an arrow deep infixt
My panting side was charged when I withdrew
To seek a tranquil death in distant shades.

(The Task 3, ll. 108–111, in The Poems of William Cowper, vol. 2, p. 165)

Although Cowper characterizes himself as an outsider—separated from the herd, injured and in need of care and comfort—and he may have lived a quiet, reclusive, and secluded life in rural England, his letters and poems profoundly influenced English Romanticism and the country's ensuing literary culture. For this reason alone his works are worth exploring; however, there are more specific riches to discover. William Blake described Cowper's letters as "Perhaps, or rather Certainly, the very best letters that were ever published" (quoted in Cowper's *Letters and Prose Writings,* vol. 1, p. v; hereafter referred to as *Letters*). Samuel Taylor Coleridge celebrated his "divine Chit chat" (Coleridge, vol. 1, p. 279) and spoke to William Hazlitt of him as "the best modern poet" (quoted in Hazlitt, vol. 9, p. 107). Meanwhile Wordsworth, strikingly echoing the aspirations he had for his own poetry (to "[fit] to metrical arrangement a selection of the real language of men"; *Lyrical Ballads,,* p. 57) described the reader's "exquisite pleasure in seeing such natural language so naturally connected with metre," (ibid., p. 92) which he found in examples of Cowper's poetry such as "Verses Supposed to be Written by Alexander Selkirk" (1782):

Ye winds that have made me your sport,
Convey to this desolate shore,
Some cordial endearing report
Of a land I shall visit no more.
My friends do they now and then send
A wish or a thought after me?
O tell me I yet have a friend,
Though a friend I am never to see.

(Poems, vol. 1, p. 404, ll. 33–40)

Although Cowper's poetry has been described as "ornate" (Wu, p. 17), it is the ability that Wordsworth and Coleridge identified, of shaping a conversational tone to a regular metrical arrangement, that attracted (and continues to attract) Cowper's most ardent admirers. Yet, as even just these fragments of poetry attest, Cowper's plain style and elegant simplicity were frequently and movingly directed toward some of the most distressing and lonely of human experiences: abandonment, spiritual despair, painful empathy with injury, and madness. Sadly, this is all too easily attributed to the conditions of Cowper's life, which, although quiet and without public incident, was dogged by mental instability, spiritual strife, and apparently small yet significant changes in domestic arrangements. However, this is not the only story of Cowper's writing. Countering the melancholy of poems such as those mentioned—and the frank distress of others, such as "Hatred and Vengeance, My Eternal Portion" (c. 1774, pub. 1816)—comes the light-hearted comedy of the much-loved ballad "The Diverting History of John Gilpin" (1782); the warm affection of his "pet poems," such as "Epitaph on a Hare" (1784) and "The Retired Cat" (c. 1791, pub. 1803); and, particularly arrestingly, the unnerving satirical bite of the broadside ballads he wrote for the Committee for the Abolition of the Slave Trade, a cause that he passionately supported. In "The Negro's Complaint" (1789), for instance, he asks:

Is there, as ye sometimes tell us,
Is there One who reigns on high?
Has he bid you buy and sell us
Speaking from his throne the sky?
Ask him if your knotted scourges,
Matches, blood-extorting screws
Are the means that Duty urges
Agents of his Will to use?

(*Poems*, vol. 3, p. 14, ll. 25–32)

His letters are equally various, moving between the desperately uncertain and an attractively modest style of witty storytelling. (In a useful and engaging essay on the letter form, "Forgotten Genres," Patricia Meyer Spacks elegantly considers the "fictive structures" that Cowper employs in his correspondence.) In all cases, however—whether distressing, melancholic, satirical, or comic—it is Cowper's force of personality that has been celebrated and held in great affection. This is because—and here we can see Cowper's contribution to the ensuing Romantic movement—while his work sweeps across a range of political, religious, satirical, and ecological concerns, such vistas are winningly focused into a sympathetic individual perspective. Indeed, Duncan Wu understands the significance of Cowper's great six-book blank verse poem, *The Task*—which was to make him among the most

famous of English poets at the time—to be its "unabashed preoccupation with the self" (p. 17). Certainly a poem in which the poet "Roved far and gather'd much" (book 6, line 1012; in *Poems*, vol. 2, p. 262), moving between political and social commentary, affectionate and detailed description of a familiar landscapes, personal meditation and calls for emotional connections between people, is a significant precursor of Wordsworth's *The Excursion* (1814) and *The Prelude* (1850). However, as Simon Malpas hints, Cowper's mode is not "entirely reducible" (p. ix) to its contribution to the Romantic movement; indeed, looking backward to the likes of Pope and John Dryden as well as forward to Wordsworth and Coleridge, Cowper's is a complex poetics in which, Malpas says, the "apparent confidence and urbanity of the Augustan poetry is disrupted from within by a poetic voice that is often anything but secure or certain" (p. ix). Here we may begin to glimpse what sets Cowper's poetry apart: its capacity to mobilize the familiar as a route to the intensely personal—a characteristic that Spacks likewise explores with sophistication in her chapter on Cowper in *The Poetry of Vision* (1967).

Norman Nicholson insisted that "we always read [Cowper's poetry] with at least part of our attention on the poet rather than on the poem. To those who love Cowper, his poetry is a biography" (p. 57). Certainly Cowper's poetry connects vitally to his life, because of the way it allowed him to survive (for a time) mental strife and domestic upset. Furthermore, its attention to everyday detail—the gentle seasonal variations seen in a carefully tended garden, the playful habits of domestic animals, the witty capturing of social conversation and country callers—brings the habits of late-eighteenth-century rural English society vividly and engagingly to life. Yet it is important to recognize—as was first given book-length examination by readers such as Vincent Newey and Bill Hutchings in the 1980s and 1990s—that Cowper's style may be personal and plain, but it is not artless. Cowper, in fact, translated personal experience into art forms that could be appreciated and sympathized with by large communities of readers. In this respect

Cowper's contribution to hymn writing was an important "training" period (although, in the event, it was short-lived).

Yet this commitment to taking the variety and complexity of life and then organizing it into verse arrangements that would have particular emotional and political effects (both for readers and for the author) was one that Cowper pursued across his writing. For some, this method assaults cherished ideas about poetic inspiration, imaginative projection, and the role of the poet as passionate embracer of stupendous landscapes: Hazlitt wittily hinted at this attitude when he described Cowper "look[ing] at [nature] over his clipped hedges, and from his well-swept garden walks … He shakes hands with nature with a pair of fashionable gloves on" (vol. 2, p. 250). In fact such dismissal overlooks the power of natural imagery in Cowper's work, wherein storms (particularly at sea) are vividly evoked as indicators of divine power and strength versus mortal frailty. Even so—as Ralph Pite has suggested—Cowper's more circumspect, even horticultural, approach not only merits attention but also may even be a source of education for our own society as it addresses the impact of ecological change and globalization. In order to recognize this potential, it is helpful to be able to unravel some of the assumptions made about Cowper, his times, and the poetic styles that he used.

EARLY LIFE AND EDUCATION

William Cowper was born on November 15, 1731, at the rectory held by his father, the Reverend John Cowper (1694–1756), at Great Berkhamsted, Hertfordshire. James Sambrook tells us that the assumption mentioned in many early biographies that his mother, born Ann Donne in 1703, was related to the seventeenth-century poet, John Donne is, in fact, mistaken (p. 1). William was the elder of only two among the Cowpers' seven children who survived infancy, and his mother died giving birth to his brother John in 1737. This brought an end to Cowper's happy childhood, which he remembered being filled with his appreciation of his mother's generous love. When, more than fifty years later, a relative sent Cowper a miniature portrait of her he was prompted to write the poignant poem, "On the Receipt of My Mother's Picture out of Norfolk" (1798), which accesses the lonely bewilderment of the abandoned child in its simple listing of what was lost:

Thy nightly visits to my chamber made
That thou might'st know me safe and warmly lay'd,
Thy morning bounties e'er I left my home
The biscuit or confectionary plum
(Poems, vol. 3, p. 58, ll. 58–61)

Yet the poem also, as Hutchings perceptively notes, meditates on "the capacity of art to forge stability out of an unstable world" (p. 3): a vital consideration for all of Cowper's work. This was not the only form in which Cowper expressed this long-held grief for his mother; as Malpas asserts and Hutchings undertakes to demonstrate, "Cowper's letters are frequently as beautifully constructed as his poems" (Malpas, p. xviii). In his letter acknowledging receipt of the portrait, Cowper's careful laying out of the connection between him, his mother, and the relative who had linked them once again may seem pedantic to some, with its formal structuring of affection: "Every creature that bears any affinity to my mother is dear to me, and you, the daughter of her brother, are but one remove distant from her; I love you therefore and love you much, both for her sake and for your own" (<i>Letters,</i> vol. 3, p. 349). However, as Sambrook finds in Cowper's nature poetry, the letter has a "manner of organizing … descriptions in such a way as to direct the reader's mental eye to a series of objects in the spatial relationships of a formally composed … painting" (p. 28). Such an approach does not distance a reader from the strong feeling and divine power that lie at the heart either of the family tree or of nature's, which Cowper claims in book 6 of <i>The Task</i> is "but a name for an effect / Whose cause is God" (<i>Poems,</i> vol. 2, p. 242, ll. 223-224). Rather such organization emphasizes the solidity of his affection's framework, implies the constancy of its foundation, and renders it familiar, bringing it closer to a reader's position, maximizing its potential to draw on his or her emotional response. Yet this method also demonstrates the profound importance of familiarity and structure in Cowper's life. The loss of his mother shook that foundation, threatening Cowper's capacity for happiness and satisfaction.

Unfortunately, at the time of his mother's death Cowper was attending Dr. Pittman's School, where he was severely bullied by a boy of fifteen who "let loose the cruelty of his temper" on the previously indulged boy (*Letters,* vol. 1, p. 5). This was the start of a mixed educational experience: at age eight he was sent to live with Mrs. Disney, an oculist (on account of damage to his eyes), before attending, from 1742, Westminster School in London, known particularly at this time for educating the sons of great Whig families. Westminster provided Cowper with several valued companions and an excellent grounding in classical languages: he left with the skill of reading and also writing Latin verses (which he continued to do throughout his life). However, Westminster also informed Cowper's "Tirocinium; or, A Review of Schools" (1785), which he intended to recommend that young students be privately educated by a tutor rather than sent away to boarding school. In this poem of outrage, prompted by his having read that Westminster had needed to appoint a physician to treat venereal disease among pupils at the school, Cowper tellingly claimed that "Great schools suit best the sturdy and the rough" (*Poems,* vol. 2, p. 279, l. 341).

When Cowper left Westminster, his father desired for him to become a barrister and so, at age eighteen, and reluctant to displease his family, he left for London to be apprenticed to a lawyer, Mr. Chapman of Greville Street, with whom he also lodged. The move was ultimately to prove disastrous for Cowper, emotionally and psychologically.

LONDON

Anxious to escape lawyers' offices, to which he felt unsuited, Cowper became a frequent visitor at the London home of his uncle, Ashley Cow-

per, clerk of the parliaments: a position of wealth and influence. However, it was Ashley's three daughters who proved the main attraction, especially the middle daughter, Theadora Jane (1734?–1824). Cowper fell in love with her during 1752, and for the next couple of years their relationship followed an intense if rocky course, evident in the "Delia" poems that Cowper produced at this time. Sadly, perhaps due to the combination of personal and professional difficulty, this period also saw the first of Cowper's intense depressions: "Day and night I was upon the rack, lying down in horrors and rising in despair" (*Letters,* vol. 1, p. 8). It may have been his nephew's emotional state that influenced Ashley's decision to intervene in the cousins' romance and withhold permission for their marriage, causing them to part in 1755.

The depression seems to have passed, however—Baird describes Cowper in the late 1750s as a "lively young man about town"—and he began associating with his former Westminster schoolmates in the Nonsense Club: a group dedicated to dining, drinking, and writing comic verses. Yet, there is a melancholy cast even in those poems that Cowper wrote for the group, and his 1757 lament for the death of a school friend segues into a regretful memory of past love. Although Cowper continued to visit Ashley's home and holiday with the family, he and Theadora did not see or meet each other; her health suffered, too, from the separation. Perhaps with the intention of lifting this burden, in 1763 Ashley set about improving Cowper's professional prospects by nominating him to the position of clerk of the journals in the House of Lords. However, this necessitated a public examination, and the prospect of such scrutiny was to cause a catastrophic sense of despair.

In around 1767 Cowper set down his experiences of a mental torment, beginning with this prospect of professional scrutiny and ending with his removal to an asylum for the insane, under the care of Dr. Nathaniel Cotton at St. Albans, where Cowper was to spend eighteen months. The account—published posthumously as *Adel-*

phi in 1816 (the full text is included in *Letters,* vol. 1, pp. 3–61)—is written as a conversion narrative, reminiscent of those of St. Augustine and St. Paul, and frames his experiences with frequent references to biblical sources, especially Isaiah and the Psalms. The competing stresses that Cowper's private and professional circumstances implied—a desire to live up to family expectations and become a safe prospect for Theadora, his conviction that he could not, and the threat that his failure would damage his uncle's reputation as well as his own—began to arrange themselves in Cowper's mind into a terrible configuration of accusation: "in this situation such a fit of passion has sometimes seized me when alone in my chambers that I have cried out aloud and cursed the very hour of my birth" (*Letters,* vol. 1, p. 17). From here *Adelphi* affords the reader a compelling yet horrifying view of the irrational grip of torment in which Cowper was held: "Satan plied me close with horrible visions and more horrible voices. My ears rang with the sound of the torments that seemed to await me and inevitable damnation was denounced upon me" (p. 31). Despite several attempts at suicide—"my mind was as much shaken as my body, distracted betwixt the desire of death and the dread of it" (p. 21)—the variety of means he attempted were each foiled, and he was forced to find other means of reprieve. Although his brother John could not draw him out of his acute terror, Cowper eventually called on his cousin, the Reverend Martin Madan (a notable Methodist enthusiast), to come to his aid. Although Cowper describes Madan's "truly Christian tenderness" and felt at first that "the comfortable things he spoke to me out of the Gospel of Jesus once more prevailed with me to hope a little for mercy" (p. 31) the relief was short-lived. Cowper was taken to Cotton's asylum and only began to retreat from determined self-destruction when he opened his Bible randomly at Romans 3:25, "where Jesus is set forth as the propitiation for our sins" (p. 39). At this intervention, Cowper was, at last, suffused with joy: "immediately the full beams of the sun of righteousness shone upon me ... In a moment I believed and received the Gospel" (p. 39).

RELIGIOUS AND RURAL CONSOLATION

Following this sudden conversion and his subsequent release from Dr. Cotton's establishment, Cowper vowed never to return to London. Instead he moved—with the assistance of his brother John—to Huntingdon, near to Cambridge, and took up a life of quiet retirement and religious piety. Although this was not the end of Cowper's mental instability, it was the end of his urban experience. From 1765 until his death, Cowper remained in the countryside, inspiring his famous conviction (expressed in *The Task,* book 1, line 749) that "God made the country, and man made the town" (*Poems,* vol. 2, p. 136), and falling in with a pastoral tradition, descended from Horace, that used a rural location as a platform for satirizing the vice and folly of the age. However, this perspective was yet to come. In the immediate aftermath of the 1760s depression, Cowper sincerely embraced—in a manner not seen in his earlier work and letters—a new religious life, characterized by the earnest diligence and emotional enthusiasm of an evangelical dissenting Christian position.

Cowper's new religious life was encouraged by a new acquaintance, who became the most significant in Cowper's life. Forced by financial constraints, Cowper decided to lodge and board with the Reverend Morley Unwin, his wife Mary (née Cawthorne, 1723?–1796), and their two adult children. This home—described by Cowper as "a place of rest prepared for me by God's own hand" (*Letters,* vol. 1, p. 6)—provided a source of strength, focused particularly in the evangelical Mary, of whom Cowper wrote, "I could almost fancy my own Mother restored to Life again, to compensate to me for all the Friends I have lost and all my Connections broken" (*Letters,* vol. 1, p. 134). Falling in with the family's evangelical perspective, Cowper became dedicated to the conversion of others (the account of his brother's deathbed conversion formed the appendix to *Adelphi*), and he wrote several earnest letters of thanks during June 1765 (his first for two years) to friends who had offered Christian comfort during his illness. However, this restful home was soon to be disrupted: in 1767 Morley Unwin died suddenly, following a fall from his horse. Soon afterward, Mary and Cowper met the Reverend John Newton, curate of Olney and a notable evangelical. A man of striking personality and colorful background (he had been a sailor and a slave trader before his conversion), Newton's boisterous energy meant that his eagerness to see Mary, her daughter, and Cowper settled at Olney soon became fact: by February 1768 they were resident in a rented house called "Orchard Side." Newton set about persuading his reluctant friend to address the prayer meetings he had instigated at Olney and eventually to contribute to a joint collection of hymns: these were eventually published as *Olney Hymns* in 1779.

Despite the outward success of this period—Cowper seemed domestically settled and he was producing hymns and addresses—the letters reveal the start of a change of mood. In 1770, he had lost his brother John, and although this was softened by John's conversion, this brother had been his last remaining close relative. Letters indicate that elements of evangelical belief were beginning to cause as much concern as comfort for Cowper. For one who had previously found intense personal scrutiny difficult to bear, the dissenting Christian emphasis on the believer's personal relationship with Christ (explored in some of Cowper's extraordinary hymns), together with the legacy of Calvin's endorsement of the doctrine of predestination (especially the notion of an "elect" group of followers who would be saved), risked providing a narrative of damnation to confirm Cowper's personal tendency toward self-accusation. Furthermore, Newton's industrious example seems to form the background to letters in which Cowper berates himself for his lack of religious enthusiasm: "A seaman terrified at a storm who creeps down into the hold, when he should be busy amongst the tackling aloft, is just my picture" (*Letters,* vol. 1, p. 253–254). Adding to Cowper's distress was the fact that—in order to counter gossip about the two living together without a chaperone, following the marriage of Mary's daughter—he had become engaged to marry Mary in early 1773.

Cowper's old friend and continued correspondent, Lady Hesketh (who was in fact his cousin Harriot, sister of Theodora and now married to Sir Thomas Hesketh), attributed the mental breakdown he suffered in January of that year to the burden of "prayer meetings, and all the enthusiastic conversation" (quoted in Sambrook, p. 10). The descent was a repeat of that suffered in 1763, except that it felt more severe and was finally exacerbated by a terrible dream, which Cowper could not bear to recollect, in which a voice cried to him "Actum est de te peristi" (*Letters,* vol. 1, p. 51), meaning, "All is done with you, you have perished" (Sambrook, p. 10). However, it seems also that the prospect of marrying Mary—which Sambrook suggests perhaps converged a mother figure with that of a lover—also ignited Cowper's distress, articulated in a small collection of Latin poems written in 1774. Whatever its exact cause, Cowper retreated to the Olney vicarage to be cared for by the Newtons, where he was gradually able to let go of his most distorted hallucinations. However, he had lost all faith in public worship: from 1773 until his death he never joined in grace at table and never prayed or entered a church again. He now "believed firmly that he was the unique object of God's utter and unqualified reprobation" (Baird).

POETIC AND HORTICULTURAL CONSOLATION

Following his gradual recovery, Cowper returned to life with Mary at Orchard Side, and the idea of marriage was abandoned. Here they lived quietly until the summer of 1786, after which they continued their restrained lives in better accommodation in the village of Weston Underwood, providing a vital sense of continuity and lasting peacefulness. However, Cowper's complex relationship with faith did not provide the comfort he had at first anticipated; rather, he turned to poetry for help and remedy. From now until the 1790s, as Cowper's financial position settled (helped partly by Theodora, who continued anonymously to support him throughout his life), Cowper began to concentrate on poetry, producing his greatest works during twenty years of sustained and impressive industry. Despite the extended length (and subsequent influence) of some of these works, however, Cowper claimed only a modest ground: "I have no more Right to the Name of a Poet, than a Maker of Mousetraps has to That of an Engineer. ... But it has served to rid me of some melancholy Moments, for I only take it up as a gentleman performer does his Fiddle" (*Letters,* vol. 1, p. 290). While this image recurs later with a more anxious need to push away distressing thoughts—he claimed, "the most ludicrous lines I ever wrote have been written in the saddest mood" and likened himself to "mariners on board a ship buffetted by a terrible storm" who "employ themselves in fiddling and dancing" (*Letters,* vol. 2, p. 91)—poetry provided a calming structure that eased personal strife while also, as his dialogue poem "Table Talk" (1782) explores, containing a social and moral purpose.

This poem introduces what would become a central image for Cowper's writing: the poet as gardener. Writing to an old friend from his London days, Joseph Hill, and to Mary's son William following his recovery, Cowper speaks of the seeds he has purchased, melons and cucumbers he is cultivating, and the habits of the animals he observes, particularly three young hares (given to him by neighbors) that he named Puss, Tiney, and Bess. As Cowper gradually peeled away from the intense introspection and self-examination of his overtly religious period, his outlook broadened. Letters find him thanking correspondents for books and journals they have recommended (he developed a particular passion for travel books on America and the Indies), and he responded to pressing issues within the dissenting Christian community and in larger political life. Anticipating, and indeed fueling, the dissenting Christian concern for animal and human welfare, Cowper's poetry condemns animal cruelty in blood sports, savagely attacks slavery and the oppression issuing from English power in India, and expresses a jaded disgust for a monarchy that he considered to have abused its right to royal prerogative. While such concerns are dealt with gravely in poems such as *The Task* and a series of "moral satires" written in a burst of energy during the winter of 1780–1781, they also seep into his more arch and witty letters, which adopt an attractively ironic attitude toward

his modest occupations and those of great men in the world at large:

> Nothing of this sort has happen'd lately, except that a Lion was imported here at the Fair, Seventy Years of Age, & as tame as a Goose. Your Mother and I saw him embrace his Keeper with his Paws, and lick his Face. Others saw him receive his Head in his Mouth, and restore it to him again unhurt ... A Practise hardly reconcileable to Prudence, unless he had had a Head to spare. The Beast however was a very Magnificent one, and much more Royal in his Appearance, than those I have seen in the Tower.
>
> (*Letters,* vol. 1, pp. 285–286)

In 1782 Cowper's first book of poems was published (including the moral satires) and in 1785 he published his most diverse and well-recognized work, *The Task,* a poem of over five thousand lines that was instigated by a friend Cowper had met in the summer of 1781: the widow Lady Austen (born Ann Richardson, 1738?–1802). Lady Austen, whose lively wit and conversation provided a contrast to Mary's quieter companionship, had a profound influence on Cowper's poetic production, although his friendship with her was ultimately short-lived. During her stays at Olney she became Cowper's muse, inspiring several of Cowper's occasional verses and igniting in him an "itching" and "tingling" to write, as he notes in a poem from around 1781, "A Poetical Epistle to Lady Austen" (pub. 1803; collected in *Poems,* vol. 1, p. 453). Yet her presence was also to cause discomfort: she and Cowper had their first falling out in the summer of 1782 before finally breaking off relations for good in the summer of 1784. Sambrook summarizes the joyfulness that Lady Austen brought to Cowper during their brief comradeship, together with the difficulties she presented for his relationship with Mary. However, in poetic terms the acquaintanceship was a success: she not only provided the material for his hugely popular ballad "John Gilpin" but also recognized the signs of growing melancholy in Cowper in October 1783 and commissioned the diversion, challenging him to write a poem in blank verse on the subject of the sofa where she was sitting at the time. So began *The Task.*

WILLIAM COWPER

FINAL YEARS

In 1786, Cowper and Mary were struck by the blow of her son's death from typhus. William Unwin had been a close friend and confidant of Cowper: indeed, he was one of the very few to have known of Cowper's secret project following *The Task:* a blank-verse translation of Homer to rival that of Pope. However, Unwin's death brought about another bout of depression that lasted for several months. Despite this, Cowper recovered and managed to complete his Homeric translation by 1790. During this time he continued to produce his many occasional verses (often dedicated to some new friends at Weston, the Throckmortons), together with ballads for the antislavery commission. An additional boost came with the financial success of the Homer translation (despite its mixed reception). However, the exhaustion that work brought also ignited another period of severe mental imbalance: James Boswell reported that Cowper was now in a "strait waistcoat" and was "impressed with the most dismal doctrines of Calvinism" (quoted in King, p. 51). Although he recovered again, life continued to be very trying for the rest of the decade: Cowper described himself as a "broken fountain" (*Letters,* vol. 3, p. 10), and as Mary began to suffer severely from a series of strokes that began in 1792 he descended into a state of despair from which he never recovered. Poetry from this period is either painfully poignant (as in his verses "To Mary") or ultimately unsuccessful: an attempted edition of John Milton's *Paradise Lost* proved too distressing in its depiction of Hell for him to complete.

In their final years, Mary Unwin and Cowper were forced to move from what had become a chaotic home at Weston to be cared for by his young cousin, John Johnson, at East Dereham in Norfolk, with the assistance of Lady Hesketh and William Hayley, the patron of William Blake, whom Cowper had met during his attempted work on Milton. Cowper described himself then as having been "a poor Fly entangled in a thousand webs from the beginning" (*Letters,* vol. 4, p. 469), and manuscript letters between Hesketh and Hayley (held at the British Library) attest to the distressing circumstances in which Cowper and Mary found themselves ("a heart-:breaking Subject") as they came to rely—although without acknowledgement—on the kindness of those such as Johnson. Mary died in 1796, but Cowper displayed no reaction to this and never spoke of her again. In his final couple of years he managed some translations of classical verses and, in March 1799, he published "The Castaway," for which he is still remembered. However, these were his final poetic utterances; Cowper died on April 25, 1800, and was buried beside Mary at East Dereham church.

POETIC FORM

Having traced a woeful sense of inevitability in Cowper's life, a reader may be surprised to find that his poetry offers something alternative. It is frequently soothing, enriching, and gladdening in its evocation of domestic life and landscape, and Cowper uses wit and an ingenious eye and ear for idiosyncrasy to style himself as an observer and commentator on modern manners. Even when he is angry, Cowper's attention to detail, and his conjuring of a personality from hinted movements and gestures, can overtake his desire to condemn, producing miniature and amusing portraits of the vain and self-absorbed, as in this description of a pompous churchman in book 2 of *The Task* (ll. 445–462):

First we stroke
An eye-brow; next, compose a straggling lock;
Then with an air, most gracefully perform'd,
Fall back into our seat; extend an arm,
And lay it at its ease with gentle care,
With handkerchief in hand, depending low.
The better hand more busy, gives the nose
Its bergamot, or aids th'indebted eye
With op'ra glass, to watch the moving scene,
And recognize the slow-retiring fair.

...

But how a body so fantastic, trim,
And queint in its deportment and attire,
Can lodge an heav'nly mind—demands a doubt.

(*Poems,* vol. 2, p. 150)

The object of Cowper's condemnation here is affectation—excessively fashionable dress, fussy appearance, and wily words: slightly earlier in the poem he has announced that "in my soul I loath / All affectation" (ll. 416–417). Instead, Cowper makes a moral case for simplicity as a route to sincerity and spiritual nourishment: "I seek divine simplicity in him / Who handles things divine" (ll. 432–433). It is this principle that informs all of Cowper's poetic production and that he understood to be the poet's primary work:

> To make verse speak the language of prose, without being prosaic, to marshall the words of it in such an order, as they might naturally take in falling from the lips of an extemporary speaker, yet without meanness; harmoniously, elegantly, and without seeming to displace a syllable for the sake of the rhyme, is one of the most arduous tasks a poet can undertake.
>
> (*Letters,* vol. 2, p. 10)

Along with the fact that Cowper forms a vital precursor to Wordsworth, we can note that Cowper's *The Task* also importantly influenced Coleridge, in his "conversation poems." However, as Cowper implies, the impression of simplicity is gained at the expense of hard work and, despite appearances, Cowper's easy style did not come without strife. Furthermore, Cowper's work is characterized by variety and includes the easy, plain speaking to which he aimed, but it also reaches into the complexly coded, abstruse, and mysterious. Implying a route between the two, Cowper linked his poetic industry to his mature love of gardening and horticulture. Verse arrangements are designed not to neutralize his poetry's affective or expressive capacity but rather to provide the protective and nurturing conditions that will allow them to bloom and influence others, just as the pruning gardener judiciously shapes his plants to their advantage as described in *The Task*, book 3 (ll. 421–426):

> The rest, no portion left
> That may disgrace his art, or disappoint
> Large expectation, he disposes neat
> At measur'd distances, that air and sun
> Admitted freely may afford their aid,
> And ventilate and warm the swelling buds.
>
> (*Poems,* vol. 2, p. 173)

As Hazlitt demonstrated, however, Cowper's reputation often overlooks both his essential bid for clarity and plain speaking and the reflective ways in which he uses fixed arrangements. To provide an introduction to Cowper's poetry that emphasizes its artful, rather than slavish, attachment to form, this discussion will introduce his lyrical and satirical modes before finally considering his relationship with blank verse and its possibilities in *The Task.*

LYRICAL MEASURES

The lyrics that first established Cowper's reputation were his contributions to *Olney Hymns* of 1779. (Cowper contributed 66 hymns to the collection, while John Newton contributed 282.) This volume contributed to the contemporary expansion in evangelical hymnody, headed by Isaac Watts and the Wesley brothers, who focused on hymns as "the best mode of spreading an Evangelical message to the greatest number of people; and also as a way of illuminating the personal relationship the believer was free to forge with God" (Knight and Mason, p. 25). The hymn's simultaneous familiarity (in terms of arrangement) and idiosyncrasy (in terms of emphasizing emotion and personal relationships with God) makes it an interface between the individual and the society of which he is a part. In Cowper's case this is achieved by shifting the balance toward self-examination and strikingly direct enunciation of the trials and intensities of a personal faith, together with emphasis on the redeeming sacrifice made by Christ:

> This heart, a fountain of vile thoughts,
> How does it overflow?
> While self upon the surface floats
> Still bubbling from below.
>
> ("11: Jehovah Our Righteousness," ll. 13–16, in *Poems,* vol. 1, p. 150)

> Jesus, whose blood so freely stream'd
> To satisfy the law's demand;
> By thee from guilt and wrath redeem'd,
> Before the Father's face I stand.
>
> ("5: Jehovah-Shalem," ll. 1–4, in *Poems,* vol. 1, p. 144)

The hymns' arrangement echoes the Christian message of personal sacrifice within a loving context, since the movements between long and short lines (made clear to the ear through rhyme) install a meditative, rocking regularity around the disturbing imagery, directing the singer or reader's understanding of violence's place within a overarching framework of redemption. This notion of design and arrangement as a container and preserver of divine mystery is made evident in one of Cowper's best-known hymns, number 35 of the *Olney Hymns*, "Light Shining out of Darkness," which likens God, effectively, to a mysterious artist, whose "bright designs" are carefully structured to encourage an attentive and diligent process of unraveling on the part of the believer (perhaps by repeated hymn singing), who must be patient and trusting that this work will ultimately reveal truth:

God moves in a mysterious way,
His wonders to perform,
He plants his footsteps in the Sea,
And rides upon the Storm.
Deep in unfathomable Mines,
Of never failing Skill,
He treasures up his bright designs,
And works his Sovereign Will.

...

His purposes will ripen fast,
Unfolding every hour,
The Bud may have a bitter taste,
But *wait* to *Smell the flower.*

(*Poems*, vol. 1, p. 174–175, ll. 1–20)

This verse arrangement draws us back, perhaps surprisingly, to Cowper's earlier use of lyrical "measures" (when used in hymns, the meter and rhyme arrangements of lyric are known as "measures"). Some of Cowper's earliest surviving poetry relates to the period he spent in London studying the law and falling in love with his cousin Theadora. In a self-deprecating and humorous study titled "Of Himself," for instance (c. 1752, pub. 1825), Cowper uses ballad meter to describe how his "bashful" and rough ways were eventually brought into line with a new society's desires:

Howe'er, it happen'd, by degrees,
He mended and grew perter,

In company was more at ease,
And dress'd a little smarter.

...

The women said, who thought him rough,
But now no longer foolish,
The creature may do well enough,
But wants a deal of polish.
At length improved from head to heel,
'Twere scarce too much to say,
No dancing bear was so genteel,
Or half so dégagé.

(*Poems*, vol. 1, p. 32–33, ll. 13–32)

In employing these polished and familiar patterns, Cowper performs a sophisticated process of self-fashioning. He draws on meters associated with simple and sincere expression, in not only in hymns, but also ballads, which, following the publication of Thomas Percy's *Reliques of Ancient English Poetry* (a collection of definitive versions of songs and ballads) in 1765, were nostalgically associated with older, simpler forms of social interaction. However, he uses these forms to illustrate his move toward a more urbane, consciously constructed form of social interaction, in which he uses the language and dress of the chattering classes. Clearly, then, Cowper's attitude toward simplicity and artistry, sincerity and pose, is a complex one.

Such stimulating ideas may also be discerned in the poetry that Cowper wrote to Theadora, named "Delia" in the verses. Perhaps responding to the sense of artifice that this covering of Theadora's identity implies, Norman Nicholson describes the poems as "merely exercises in the fashion, with nothing approaching the joy or even the excitement of love" (p. 20); indeed they have received relatively little critical attention. Yet, there is more to be done with these poems. Their use of conventional codes, such as names that echo classical tradition, constitute an erudite expression of the real conditions of courtship in late-eighteenth-century society, which took place in family drawing rooms and public ballrooms, meaning that lovers' conversations often *were* nimble dances between the public and the private realm. Constructing ornate and lyrical arrangements for such expression (such as the *rime couée* stanza, associated with medieval romance tales) allows Cowper to sustain an air of light, decorous, and genteel behavior while implying beneath it a culture of passion and intensity. This mirrors the games the lovers play, such as when they pretend to argue simply so they have an excuse to make up again, all the more sincerely, as conveyed in a poem such as "This evening, Delia, you and I" (c. 1752, pub. 1825):

This evening, Delia, you and I
Have managed most delightfully,
For with a frown we parted;
Having contrived some trifle that
We both may be much troubled at,
And sadly disconcerted.

...

Happy! when we but seem t'endure
A little pain, then find a cure
By double joy requited;
For friendship, like a sever'd bone,
Improves and gains a stronger tone
When aptly reunited.

(*Poems,* vol. 1, pp. 30–31, ll. 1–24)

With Cowper having established this playful mode, it is all the more striking when his "Delia" verses turn to regret. As Cowper's relationship with Theadora became more complex, he used the ballad meter's short lines and stanzas to imply dismay, perhaps that such mischievous arrangements can turn sour, as in "Written in a Quarrel" (c. 1753, pub. 1825):

Sure in those eyes I loved so well,
And wish'd so long to see,
Anger I thought could never dwell,
Or anger aim'd at me.

(*Poems,* vol. 1, p. 39, ll. 9–12)

Increasingly the lyrical measures that once denoted joyful artifice come to denote lovers' misunderstandings and cross-purposes. Poems such as "See where the Thames" (c. 1753, pub. 1825) imply the fragility of relationships that are expressed in a public language and are exposed to public view:

While you indulge a groundless fear,
Th'imaginary woes you bear
Are real woes to me:
But thou art kind, and good thou art,

Nor wilt, by wronging thine own heart,
Unjustly punish me.

(*Poems,* vol. 1, p. 45, ll. 37–42)

Indeed, with terms such as "woe," "wrong," "unjust," and "punish," Cowper's loving vocabulary reaches forward to the language of tested personal faith that would later fill his lyrics. As Theadora and Cowper were forced to separate, the poems' lines lengthen, implying the desire to linger in the lover's presence, and where their relationship was once conducted in witty conversation and repartee, it is now indicated by intensely material and bodily exchange; in the poem "On Her Endeavouring to Conceal Her Grief at Parting" (c. 1754, pub. 1825), tears echo the bloody symbolism of the Christian Eucharist:

Since for my sake each dear translucent drop
Breaks forth, best witness of thy truth sincere,
My lips should drink the precious moisture up,
And, e'er it falls, receive the trembling tear.

(*Poems,* vol. 1, p. 35, ll. 5–8)

Theadora and Cowper parted in 1755 and did not ever meet again. But her memory appears to have continued to inform his lyrical expressions until long after their separation. In the immediate aftermath of the relationship's end, this was evident in the "Delia" mode in a poem such as "Written in a Fit of Illness 1755" (1825):

In these sad hours, a prey to ceaseless pain,
While feverish pulses leap in ev'ry vein,
When each faint breath the last short effort seems
Of life just parting from my feeble limbs;
How wild soe'er my wand'ring thoughts may be,
Still, gentle Delia! still they turn on thee!

(*Poems,* vol. 1, p. 43, ll. 1–6)

Later, the lingering memory of Theadora recurs in moments of intense lyricism; that is, when Cowper's direct and personal expressions of emotional strain shift into obscure and coded references to a lost love or to shaken limbs (an image that echoes with the lyrics of the Greek poet Sappho). So, for instance, "On the Death of Sir W. Russell" (c. 1757, pub. 1803), written for the death of a friend, fuses with grief for Theadora:

Doom'd, as I am, in solitude to waste
The present moments, and regret the past;
Depriv'd of every joy, I valued most,
My Friend torn from me, and my Mistress lost;

(*Poems*, vol. 1, p. 62, ll. 1–4)

Much later, during his halting recovery from the depression brought on by spiritual strife, an enigmatic Latin fragment, titled "Heu quam Remotuss Vescor ab Ominus" (c. 1774, pub. 1823, translation, Sambrook, p. 11) recalls the language of abandonment following the collapse of his relationship with Theodora:

Te cariorem luce vel artubus,
Te vinculo nostram jugali,
Deserui tremulam sub ense.
[You, dearer than light or limbs,
You in our conjugal bond,
I deserted you, trembling beneath the sword.]

(*Poems*, vol. 1, p. 210, ll. 6–8)

Indeed, when depressions damaged his capacity for happiness it was in lyrical arrangements that Cowper produced some of the most affecting expressions of mental strife in English poetry. As with his loving lyrics, this poetry is remarkable for being saturated with emotion whilst simultaneously adopting a reflective position that understands the discipline of verse formation. The poet experiences this as both a comfort and a torment because it lashes idiosyncrasy to familiar patterning. See, for example, Cowper's use of Sapphics in the poem "Hatred and vengeance, my eternal portion" (c. 1774, pub. 1816), in which the blunt slashing of each stanza's shortened final line (required by the classical, quantitative arrangement) repeats the punishment of which the lyric speaks:

Hatred and vengeance, my eternal portion,
Scarce can endure delay of execution:—
Wait, with impatient readiness, to seize my
Soul in a moment.

⋯

Him, the vindictive rod of angry justice
Sent, quick and howling, to the centre headlong;
I, fed with judgments, in a fleshy tomb, am
Buried above ground.

(*Poems*, vol. 1, p. 209–210, ll. 1–20)

Such painful verses recurred again toward the end of Cowper's life. "To Mary" (c. 1793, pub. 1803) is a gentle and moving paean to Mary Unwin and the care she provided for Cowper. Implying a buried connection between his own modestly constructed lyric and her domestic artistry, Cowper uses a simple arrangement of single rhymes and refrain to express the lastingness of their affection: "And all thy threads with magic art / Have wound themselves around this heart" (*Poems*, vol. 3, p. 206, ll. 18–19). However, Cowper's mood darkened with time, most notably in "The Castaway," one of his last poems (c. 1799, pub. 1803). Here the expanded ballad meter is reflected in its content as a mariner is washed away (ballads often feature sea-dog tales). Cowper's personal totem of mental fatigue, the sea storm, finds him coupling his own fate with that of the sailor, igniting a plaintive poem in which the meter's inevitable returns of rhymes and fixed arrangements parallels horrifyingly both men's inexorable path to abandonment and death:

No voice divine the storm allay'd,
No light propitious shone,
When, snatch'd from all effectual aid,
We perish'd, each, alone;
But I, beneath a rougher sea,
And whelm'd in deeper gulphs than he.

(*Poems*, vol. 3, p. 216, ll. 61–66)

LIGHT VERSE

Cowper's darkest poems appear toward the end of a poetic life that was nonetheless also filled with lighter, sociable verse, the kind that accords with Cowper's sense (expressed in *The Task*, book 2) that "There is a pleasure in poetic pains / Which only poets know" (*Poems*, vol. 2, p. 146, ll. 285–286). In the next lines, he speaks of "shifts and turns, / Th'expedients and inventions multiform, / To which the mind resorts, in chase of terms" (ll. 286–288), echoing his admission that "while I am held in pursuit of pretty images, or a pretty way of expressing them, I forget everything that is irksome" (*Letters*, vol. 1, p. 425). Particularly during the later 1770s and 1780s Cowper was engaged in producing many examples of *vers de société* (verse written to entertain a social group known intimately to the poet). Writing for friends such as Lady Austen, the Throckmortons, the Newtons, and Mary, Cowper's tripping couplet rhymes suggest not only a comfort for the poet but also a desire to reach out and deliver that comfort to others too. As the rhymes chime together in pairs, so the poems effect sympathetic friendships between friendship pairs, as in "An Epistle to the Rev. William Bull" (c. 1782, pub. 1814):

For instance, at this very time,
I feel a wish, by cheerfull rhime
To sooth my friend, and had I pow'r,
To cheat him of an anxious hour.

(*Poems,* vol. 2, p. 8, ll. 5–8)

Cowper's society was not restricted to human interaction either; it was partly through poetry that he developed his acute sympathy with animals, writing of pet hares and birds, and of animals seen in his garden and the surrounding countryside. Just as he had tended to emphasize the emotional and psychological benefit of poetic arrangement, these verses seek to devise and protect a space of care and asylum for animals who thrive on sympathetic understanding. So in "The Faithfull Bird" (1792), two finches who live together in a greenhouse are "happy Pris'ners" since, on escaping, the one "Was much too generous and sincere / To leave his friend behind" (*Poems,* vol. 2, p. 30, ll. 23–24) and "By chirp and kiss he gave him proof / That to escape alone / Was freedom little to his taste" (lines 25–26), leading Cowper to advocate the benefits of friendship, which those who appreciate it would value over abstract liberty. Fitting with his religious position, he often devised animal and gardening "fables" such as "The Pineapple and the Bee" (1782), which tells of a bee seduced by pineapples kept beneath glass, "basking hot and all in blow" (*Poems,* vol. 1, p. 418, l. 2), illustrating for Cowper, "the sin and madness of mankind" who "Consumes his soul with vain desires" (ll. 14, 16). Elsewhere, horticulture can illustrate the precious quality of human love that endures hardship, as when Cowper likens Mary's continued love for him during "turbulent years" to flowers kept alive and warm through winter thanks to

the shelter of the greenhouse ("The Winter Nosegay," 1782). Alongside such poems, Cowper also created an altogether more boisterous comic adaptation of a popular street ballad, "The Diverting History of John Gilpin" (1782), in which the meter's longer lines push the galloping narrative forward while the shorter ones pull at the reins:

Now see him mounted once again
Upon his nimble steed,
Full slowly pacing o'er the stones
With caution and good heed.
But finding soon a smoother road
Beneath his well-shod feet,
The snorting beast began to trot,
Which gall'd him in his seat.

(*Poems,* vol. 2, p. 297–298, ll. 77–84)

"John Gilpin" was published in the *Public Advertiser* and soon became immensely popular, due in part to public readings by an actor named John Henderson. It forms the backbone of Cowper's comic verse, which also included many epigrams and several "mock heroic" poems, such as "Report of an Adjudged Case" (1782) and "To the immortal memory of the Halybutt (c.1784, pub. 1824)," which address trivial and comic subjects with feigned solemnity.

SATIRE AND TRANSLATION

Cowper was, nevertheless, still committed to producing verse that was genuinely serious in tone and purpose, focused mainly in the series of "moral satires" of 1780–1781—which included the poems "Table Talk," "The Progress of Error," "Truth," "Expostulation," "Hope," "Charity," "Conversation," and "Retirement." Just before this period he had produced a lengthy "mock romance" titled *Antithelyphthora* and published strictly anonymously in 1781. This was a response to his former confidante Martin Madan's prose tract advocating polygamy, titled *Thelyphthora; or, A Treatise on Female Ruin.* These works find Cowper increasingly looking outward at the political, religious, and cultural conditions of England from a generally Whig perspective. As Vincent Newey richly explores, the satires speak to a period of war and rioting by advocating circumspection and restraint (echoing the pattern and tone of his lighter verse)—as a means, in fact, of "proclaiming genuine liberty as opposed to licentiousness" (1991, p. 123). This is stated somewhat directly in "Table Talk":

Let active laws apply the needful curb
To guard the peace that riot would disturb,
And liberty preserv'd from wild excess,
Shall raise no feuds for armies to suppress.

(*Poems,* vol. 1, p. 250, ll. 314–317)

Other poems in the "moral satires" (included in Cowper's *Poems* of 1782) take as their target corrupt uses of the press, the clergy, education, "polite" society and its profligate habits, slavery and the slave trade, political faction, drunkenness and gluttony, vanity, and exploitation. Among this exhaustive list of condemnations, Cowper also finds time to advocate good conversation (ideally emulating that between the risen Christ and his disciples), the happiness of rural retirement, and the virtues of men such as Nathaniel Cotton (who cared for him at St. Albans), John Thornton (a philanthropist), and John Howard (a prison reformer). Cowper's satirical mode is also developed in his anti–public school piece, "Tirocinium" (quoted earlier) and in occasional verses such as "Heroism" (1782). These poems have been likened to the Augustan satiric mode of Pope and Dryden, while Donald Davie reads Cowper's "plain" style in accordance with that of Cowper's favorite, Matthew Prior. Indeed, although Cowper praised Pope in moral terms for "verse well disciplin'd, complete, compact" (in "Table Talk," l. 647), his own ambition to translate Homer (in the late 1780s) was designed to reassert the "manly, bold, sublime" spirit of the original, which he felt had been lost beneath Pope's "beauties" (*Letters,* vol. 5, pp. 52–53). Despite this commendable intention, the version Cowper published in 1791—although it may have earned him considerable financial security (it attracted five hundred subscribers)—received only a lukewarm critical reception. While Cowper's satirical poems are less easy than his other work for a modern audience to access (constituting as they do a detailed commentary on the specific cultural conditions of late-eighteenth-century English life), they nevertheless contribute a vital example of literary intervention in social and political commentary, attesting to the public role of poetry as it was understood in the late eighteenth century. However, we may yet have some sympathy with Cowper's admission in "The Flatting Mill" (c. 1781, pub. 1815) that:

Alas for the Poet! who dares undertake
To urge reformation of national ill—
His head and his heart are both likely to ache
With the double employment of mallet and mill.
If he wish to instruct he must learn to delight,
Smooth, ductile, and even his Fancy must flow,
Must tinkle and glitter like gold to the sight
And catch in its progress a sensible glow.

(*Poems,* vol. 1, p. 457, ll. 13–20)

It was this move to delight that Cowper sought to effect with his most notable poem, *The Task.*

THE TASK

Cowper expressed his enduring love for John Milton's epic poem in blank verse, *Paradise Lost* (1667); he described is as music "like that of a fine Organ" combining "the deepest Tones of Majesty, with all the Softness & Elegance of the Dorian Flute. Variety without End!" (*Letters,* vol. 1, p. 307). It was this form that Cowper chose for his "map of busy life / Its fluctuations and its vast concerns" (book 4, lines 55–56) laid out in *The Task* (collected in *Poems,* vol. 2, pp. 111–263). Having cultivated and developed a range of lyrical meters, rhyming couplets, classical translations, and quantitative meters, Cowper settled on the unrhymed five-beat line in order, most comprehensively, to arrange words as if "from the lips of an extemporary speaker" (*Letters,* vol. 2, p. 10), and the speaker in this case is most openly and directly Cowper. Where previously personal circumstances had been encoded in classical reference, biblical allusion, and allegorical fable, in *The Task* the poet openly identifies himself ("I sing the Sofa. I, who lately sang / Truth, Hope and Charity," he announces in the opening lines of book 1) and, clearly setting a precedent for Wordsworth's childhood recollections in *The Prelude,* soon provides a specific sense of well-loved rural scene:

For I have loved the rural walk through lanes
Of grassy swarth close cropt by nibbling sheep,
And skirted thick with intertexture firm
Of thorny boughs: have loved the rural walk
O'er hills, through valleys, and by rivers' brink,
E'er since a truant boy I pass'd my bounds
T'enjoy a ramble on the banks of Thames.
And still remember, nor without regret Of hours that
  sorrow since has much endear'd,
How oft, my slice of pocket store consumed,
Still hung'ring pennyless and far from home,
I fed on scarlet hips and stoney haws,
Or blushing crabs, or berries that imboss
The bramble, black as jet, or sloes austere.
Hard fare! but such as boyish appetite
Disdains not, nor the palate undepraved
By culinary arts, unsav'ry deems.

(book 1, ll. 109–125)

Indeed, Mary Unwin even provides a parallel to Dorothy Wordsworth in this poem, by offering the companionship and "witness" necessary to ignite poetic meditation (see book 1, ll. 144–162). While evidently attached to the simple and colloquial, Cowper's mode is not averse to Miltonic inversions (see l. 125 above) and even mixes rough language with Latinate loftiness (see the "stercoraceous heap"—that is, compost—of book 3, l. 463), demonstrating the sophisticated construction that underpins his homely style. This fits with his temperamental attachment to a quiet, retired life, which functions not to neglect or simplify the complexities of the world but rather as a specific location for social and mental industry, allowing persons to become better equipped to withstand the corrupting and psychologically damaging effects of the world. Much of the poem is set in wintertime, providing Cowper with a rich set of contrasts between external frost and internal cozy warmth, drawing attention to the poem's larger principle of contrast: between the public and private self, domestic and international concern, individual faith and the congregational church, individual meditation and social conversation, and, indeed, humor and earnestness. A passage in which Cowper finds himself on a cold night before the hearth (book 4, ll. 272–301) is typical:

But me perhaps
The glowing hearth may satisfy awhile
With faint illumination that uplifts
The shadow to the ceiling, there by fits
Dancing uncouthly to the quiv'ring flame.
Not undelightful is an hour to me
So spent in parlour twilight; such a gloom
Suits well the thoughtfull or unthinking mind,
The mind contemplative, with some new theme
Pregnant, or indisposed alike to all.

...

'Tis thus the understanding takes repose
In indolent vacuity of thought,
And sleeps and is refresh'd. Meanwhile the face
Conceals the mood lethargic with a mask
Of deep deliberation, as the man
Were task'd to his full strength, absorb'd and lost.

While Cowper works ingeniously to trace the shifts and twists of imaginative and contemplative thought (and to intertwine them with the landscape so familiar yet temporarily distanced from him by the cold), he also wryly acknowledges his own diligent pose when he names his face the "mask of deep deliberation" possibly covering mere "vacuity of thought." The passage is a striking source—indeed template—for Coleridge's "Frost at Midnight" (1798).

Other passages in the poem provide emotional and political cues for Wordsworth's contributions to the *Lyrical Ballads:* Michael Mason has pointed out that "craz'd" Kate (at ll. 534–556 of book 1) anticipates figures such as Martha Ray in "The Thorn," while Cowper's angry denunciation of the contemporary economic upheaval wreaked on rural communities (as they increasingly became satellite properties of the urbanite merchant classes) identifies the fate of those such as Simon Lee:

Mansions once
Knew their own masters, and laborious hinds
Who had surviv'd the father, serv'd the son.
Now the legitimate and rightful Lord
Is but a transient guest, newly arrived
And soon to be supplanted.

(book 3, lines 746–751)

Passages such as this focus the underlying and repeated concern of *The Task:* insistence on humanity's duty of care. If a winter's evening provides a safe retreat for Cowper and his companions, so he advocates providing similar spaces of safety for animals (such as his hares), far from the sportsman's chase (which he loathed):

Thou mays't frolic on the floor
At evening, and at night retire secure
To thy straw couch, and slumber unalarm'd.
For I have gain'd thy confidence, have pledg'd
All that is human in me, to protect
Thine unsuspecting gratitude and love.

(book 3, ll. 343–348)

Human duty, furthermore, extends to the natural landscape that humans are privileged to share with such animals; the landscape, in Cowper's view, is also due care and protection, a duty that he considers fulfilled by the benevolent steward-ship of his patron Throckmorton, whose lands are "Rais'd by the mole, the miner of the soil" (book 1, l. 273) but grossly contravened by the celebrated landscape gardener, "The omnipotent magician, [Capability] Brown" (book 3, l. 766), before whom "Woods vanish, hills subside, and vallies rise" (l. 775). (Cowper's poem "The Poplar-Field" (c. 1784, pub. 1800) similarly mourns the loss of natural habitats to fashionable taste; its concerns anticipate Gerard Manley Hopkins's "Binsey Poplars," published 1918.) Looking yet further abroad, and stemming from his deep-rooted principle of affinity, Cowper "blush[es], / And hang[s] his head, to think himself a man" (book 2, ll. 27–28) in a world that tolerates slavery. Fundamentally appreciating a principle of interconnectedness, Cowper as-sesses British economic imperialism and cannot tolerate the hypocrisy that would provide one law at home while presiding over another abroad: "thieves at home must hang; but he that puts / Into his overgorged and bloated purse / The wealth of Indian provinces, escapes" (book 1, l. 736–738). Later, Cowper asks of the postman bringing the mail, "Is India free? and does she wear her plumed / And jewelled turban with a smile of peace, / Or do we grind her still?" (book 4, l. 28–30).

The principle that all of Cowper's targets contravene is that of providing thoughtful, ap-propriate, and even culturally sensitive care and security for those over whom a person, nation, government, clergy, or monarchy presides. Those who abuse authority, particularly by institutional-izing systems that privilege their own comfort over the individual needs of others, are the repeated scourges of Cowper's gently conversa-tional and lilting lines. But if this is the poem's constant outrage, it also provides its binding glue. For, by the same principle (bolstered by the observational talent demonstrated in his animal and character sketches), Cowper advocates responsibility, diligence, and specificity of care, a model that acknowledges rather than erases individuals as they each constitute the compo-nents of an overarching society. From this posi-tion we may be able to extrapolate the back-ground to Romantic exploration of individual subjectivity.

Yet, as Ralph Pite suggests, Cowper's is also an "alternative tradition," which nevertheless informs "Romantic ecology," in which "the self does not experience a sublime, self-extinguishing identification with the forms of nature; instead, it seeks to establish with natural things a relation 'founded on the affections'" (p. 150). The inclina-tion toward acknowledging and appreciating the frames of expression and the borders of the self (especially where such borders can become interfaces), even when founded in distress, has been seen throughout Cowper's work. However, it is in *The Task*—a poem that is well-ordered and structured into six books, executed in regular meter, and dedicated to the domestic and the rural—that this is given full freedom to blossom. For within its overarching frame of regularity—mirroring the Christian-rural society it advo-cates—it leaps and bounds from travelogue to satire, from pastoral retreat to intense interna-tional engagement, from Augustan elegance to common speech, from Romantic meditation to lighthearted humor and wit. As such, *The Task* contains within its carefully tended borders some of the most intriguing, thought-provoking, inspir-ing, and even comforting passages of conversa-tional poetry in the English canon.

INFLUENCE

In 1818, in a preface attached to the publication of *Northanger Abbey* and *Persuasion,* Henry Austen took pains to characterize his recently deceased sister, Jane Austen, as a morally upright, diligent, and commendable female author. To do this, he linked her name with that of William Cowper: "her favourite moral writers were Johnson in prose, and Cowper in verse." Indeed, at his death Cowper was one of the most widely read and cherished of English poets. Praised for his pious Christianity and modest rural morality, a combination that proved especially attractive in the ensuing decades, Cowper could provide the cultural capital that Henry Austen wished to access. However, Cowper's legacy to Austen is both more complex and more subversive than this anecdote suggests. Austen repeatedly introduced Cowper into her novels: Marianne Dashwood, Fanny Price, and Mr. Knightley all align themselves with his writing. However, where Henry Austen may have liked to insist that this constituted the conservative moral backbone of Jane Austen's writing, it is clear that Cowper was, in fact, far from quiescent on issues of politics, religion, and international relations. Thus familiarity with Cowper's work can allow us to unravel the complexities of Austen's. For once we understand his position on the economic plunder of the English countryside, the brutality of the slave trade, and his condemnatory observation of fashionable society, then we may begin to appreciate the complex ways in which Austen imports contemporary critique into her apparently artless references to a much loved poet. Cowper's presence in *Mansfield Park,* for example, is a potentially incendiary one: not only does he link to a committed antislavery position (implicitly critiquing Sir Thomas's use of slaves in the West Indies), but his condemnation of absenteeism among the clergy, irresponsible stewardship of the countryside, the corrupt morals of the city, and the damage done by landscape "improvers" implies a running commentary on the sins of the Bertrams, the Rushworths, and the Crawfords, all focused in the Cowper-loving observer Fanny Price.

Cowper's presence—either in Austen's oeuvre or in the canons we now devise—should not, therefore, be understood as neutral, merely illustrative, and certainly not minor. Rather, his work offers a unique, intense, and complexly reflective view on eighteenth-century English life, provides a vital context against which properly to assess the innovations of the Romantics, and, finally, should provoke our own times into a thoughtful, critical and responsible response to a world coming to terms with the effects of ecological damage and globalization.

Selected Bibliography

WORKS OF WILLIAM COWPER

FIRST EDITIONS

With Newton, J. *1779 Olney Hymns in Three Books.* London: W. Oliver, 1779.

Anti-Thelyphthora. A tale, in verse. London: J. Johnson, 1781.

Poems. London: J. Johnson, 1782.

The Task: A Poem in Six Books, to which are added An Epistle to Joseph Hill, Esq., Tironcinium, or a Review of Schools, and the History of John Gilpin. London: J. Johnson, 1785.

The Negro's Complaint. London: [Darton & Harvey], 1791.

The Iliad and Odyssey of Homer, translated into English blank verse, by William Cowper. (The Battle of the Frogs and Mice. Translated into English blank verse by the same hand.). 2 vols. London: J. Johnson, 1791.

Poems by William Cowper. A new edition. London: J. Johnson, 1798.

Poems, translated from the French of Madame de la Mothe Guion, to which are added Some Original Poems of Mr. Cowper not inserted in his works. Newport-Pagnell: J. Wakefield, 1801.

Hayley, W., ed. *The Life and Posthumous Writings of W. Cowper.* 3 vols. Chichester, 1803-4.

Adelphi. A sketch of the character, and an account of the last illness, of the late Rev. John Cowper … Written by his brother, the late William Cowper, Esq. … Faithfully transcribed from his original manuscript, by John Newton. London: Williams & Son, 1816.

ARCHIVES

The following archive collections include materials related to William Cowper:

Bedfordshire and Luton Archives and Records Service: 669 Higgins.

Birmingham: Archives and Heritage Service: MS 1513.

British Library, Manuscript Collections: Add MS 30801; Add MS 37059; Add MS 39673; Dep 9987; Eg MS 3662; Add MSS 24154-5.

Cambridge University: Trinity College Library: Rothschild Library Catalogue nos. 685-695, 1388, 1468, 1774.

Cambridge University Library, Department of Manuscripts and University Archives: Add 6755, 5993.

Centre for Buckinghamshire Studies: AR 80/96; AR 112/2006.

Cowper Memorial Library.

Hertfordshire Archives and Local Studies: D/Z 117; DE/P.

Huntington Library: see Guide to literary MSS, 1979.

Lambeth Palace Library: MS3534.

McMaster University Library: see Union list of MSS in Canadian repositories, suppl 1977-78.

The Morgan Library: see NUC MS 84-2144.

National Register of Archives for Scotland: NRA(S)0112 1141.

Oxford University: Bodleian Library, Special Collections and Western Manuscripts: MS Eng misc d 134; MS Eng misc d 636; MS Autogr d 21.

Princeton University Library: C0136.

Victoria & Albert Museum, National Art Library: Forster Collection.

Warwickshire County Record Office: CR 1998, 741 Throckmorton.

Yale University Libraries: Beinecke Library: c470.

MODERN EDITIONS

Baird, John D., and Charles Ryskamp, eds. *The Poems of William Cowper,* 3 vols. Oxford: Clarendon Press, 1980–1995. (All quotations from poetry are from this edition.)

King, James, and Charles Ryskamp, eds. *The Letters and Prose Writings of William Cowper,* 5 vols. Oxford: Clarendon Press, 1979–1986.

Malpas, Simon, ed. *William Cowper: The Centenary Letters.* Manchester, U.K.: Fyfield Books, 2000.

Milford, H. S., ed. *The Poetical Works of William Cowper.* 1905. 4th ed., London: Oxford University Press, 1934.

Rhodes, Nick, ed. *William Cowper: Selected Poems.* Manchester, U.K.: Carcanet, 1984.

Sambrook, James, ed. *"The Task" and Selected Other Poems.* London and New York: Longman, 1994.

BIOGRAPHICAL AND CRITICAL STUDIES

Baird, John D. "Cowper, William (1731–1800)." In *Oxford Dictionary of National Biography.* Edited by H. C. G. Matthew and Brian Harrison. Oxford: Oxford University Press, 2004. Online ed., edited by Lawrence Goldman. (http://www.oxforddnb.com/view/article/6513), May 2008.

Coleridge, Samuel Taylor. *Collected Letters of Samuel Taylor Coleridge,* 6 vols. Edited by Earl Leslie Griggs. Oxford: Clarendon Press, 1956–1971.

Hazlitt, William. *The Selected Writings of William Hazlitt,* 9 vols. Edited by Duncan Wu. London: Pickering & Chatto, 1998.

Hutchings, Bill. *The Poetry of William Cowper.* London: Croom Helm, 1983.

King, James. *William Cowper: A Biography.* Durham, N.C.: Duke University Press, 1986.

Knight, Mark, and Emma Mason. *Nineteenth-Century Religion and Literature: An Introduction.* Oxford: Oxford University Press, 2006.

Percy, Thomas. *Reliques of Ancient English Poetry,* 3 vols. Edited by Nick Groom. London: Routledge, 1996.

Newey, Vincent. *Cowper's Poetry: A Critical Study and Reassessment.* Liverpool: Liverpool University Press, 1982.

———. "William Cowper and the Condition of England." In *Literature and Nationalism.* Edited by Vincent Newey and Ann Thompson. Liverpool: Liverpool University Press, 1991. Pp. 120–139.

Nicholson, Norman. *William Cowper.* London: John Lehmann, 1951.

Pite, Ralph. "'Founded on the Affections': A Romantic Ecology." In *The Environmental Tradition in English Literature.* Edited by John Parham. Aldershot, U.K.: Ashgate, 2002. Pp. 144–155.

Spacks, Patricia Meyer. "Forgotten Genres." *Modern Language Studies* 18, no. 1: 47–57 (1988).

———. *The Poetry of Vision: Five Eighteenth-Century Poets.* Cambridge, Mass.: Harvard University Press, 1967.

Wordsworth, William, and Samuel Taylor Coleridge. *Lyrical Ballads.* Edited by Michael Mason. London and New York: Longman, 1992.

Wu, Duncan, ed. *Romanticism: An Anthology.* 3rd ed. Oxford: Blackwell, 2006.

JOHN DRYDEN

(1631—1700)

David Wykes

TO INSTRUCT AND DELIGHT

OF THE INCONTESTABLY great English poets, John Dryden is surely the least read and the most fruitfully studied. Readers whose only aim in reading poetry is "delight" will pass him by on the other side. *The Classic Hundred: All-Time Favorite Poems* (ed. William Harmon, Columbia University Press, first published in 1990 as *The Concise Columbia Book of Poetry*) comprises the one hundred "most anthologized" English poems, which do not include any poem by Dryden. The editor's explanation, that Dryden's poems are not "short, independent and compassable" as are the poems most frequently anthologized is true, but it is a summary description of a far more complex situation in Dryden's case than it is in the cases of Henry David Longfellow and Walt Whitman, who join him in the party of the excluded. Dryden is absent because his poems, by the evolution of English poetry and the change of social conditions, have become the province only of readers who seek "instruction." It will be true in ninety-nine cases out of a hundred that those reading this article are in search of information about Dryden because they are studying some of his poems "for a course." It would be perverse, therefore, not to place this account at the service of such readers, though this is not at all to concede that Dryden's poetry offers nothing to delight. For delight is essential, as Dryden knew. When he pondered the classic tag about poetry's two functions, he pointed out that poetry cannot instruct *unless* it delights.

"If the prospect of delight be wanting [lacking] (which alone justifies the perusal of poetry)," wrote T. S. Eliot in 1924, "we may let the reputation of Dryden sleep in the manuals of literature" (*Homage*, p. 13). But despite Eliot's efforts to open the prospect of delight that he saw in Dryden's poetry, and to do for Dryden what he helped do for John Donne and Andrew Marvell (both of whom appear in *The Classic Hundred*), most of the readers and poets of the twentieth century have been content to leave him to slumber under the guardianship of the professoriat. And the professoriat has done well by him; no English poet has been better served by research and scholarship. Professional readers come to Dryden to advance their careers by means of his life and work, but in the process they discover, if they did not know it before, that he offers delight in plenty. He is a fine and many-sided writer, not a Shakespeare, Milton, or Blake, but of equal standing with poets who absorbed and drew on his work, such as Thomas Gray, Byron, and Keats. (In our own day, Geoffrey Hill's allegiance to Dryden helps define his very individual stance in relation to his contemporaries and to the poetry of the past.) These professional readers are freed to take delight in Dryden's work because they have to understand that good poetry always extends beyond the confines of the taste of any one age. Dryden's poems are foreign to the taste of the early twenty-first century and so are generally rejected or ignored. Early twenty-first century popular preferences are for nineteenth-century romanticism extended to include the Metaphysical poets of the seventeenth century (or at least their more direct and dramatic poems) and modern poets with filiations (however ironic) with romanticism, such as Yeats, Frost, and Eliot. To be free to enjoy Dryden means discovering that good poetry has been written on premises very different from romanticism's and that what is needed to free us to be delighted and instructed by Dryden is a little undangerous learning.

For editors and presenters of Dryden, this necessary basis of information about him, his times, and his poetic manner has been offered in the form of the notes they supply. Notes are indispensable, but they are a poor substitute for the kind of learning that liberates readers and empowers them. What is needed is a brief guide to the important ways in which Dryden's poetry diverges from the common, mostly unconscious assumptions that govern the responses of modern readers. Such a guide will also explain in detail why he can't get into *The Classic Hundred*.

DRYDEN'S POETRY: UNCONFESSIONAL, PUBLIC, AND POLITICAL

Dryden's poetry is not autobiographical, or, as we say now, not confessional, which means that it is radically unlike most of the poetry written since romanticism and most of the poetry, both before and after romanticism, that means most to modern readers. Dryden mentions himself quite often in his work, and especially in his prefaces created a distinctive persona for himself, but he is never the main subject of his poetry. When he became a Roman Catholic, probably in 1685, he was the author of *Religio Laici* (1682), a poem defending the status of the Church of England as the true church. In 1687 he published *The Hind and the Panther*, which transfers to the Catholic Church the authority earlier vested in the Church of England. One might expect that the Catholic poem would include an account of what led to Dryden's conversion, and it does—yet it doesn't.

> My thoughtless youth was winged with vain desires,
>
> My manhood, long misled with wand'ring fires,
>
> Followed false lights, and when their glimpse was gone,
>
> My pride struck out new sparkles of her own.
>
> Such was I, such by nature still I am,
>
> Be thine the glory, and be mine the shame.
>
> Good life be now my task; my doubts are done …
>
> (part 1, ll. 72–78)

This is technically confessional, but it employs the general terms in which Catholic auricular confession was most often framed. The modern reader craves details, details, but Dryden offers very few, for essentially, to employ a crude but effective distinction, his poetry is not private but public. His opinions on public issues are found in his writing; of private matters there is hardly a trace.

In our own day, such poetic concentration on public events would be simply inconceivable, but Dryden was completely in accord with the taste and literary demands of his time. Religious antagonisms and conflicts of constitutional interpretation had led to civil wars in England. The kingdoms of Scotland and Ireland too were completely involved in war. A king of three kingdoms, Charles I, had been put on trial and executed. Parliament and puritanism had triumphed and had established their republic, the Commonwealth, which had eventually become a military dictatorship under Oliver Cromwell, Lord Protector, king in all but title. Upon Cromwell's death in 1658, the republic had staggered without direction until in 1660 a consensus was acknowledged that monarchy, in the form of King Charles II, should be restored. Dryden's great poems are of the period of the Restoration and are therefore poems of contention, debate, party politics, and vigorous, sometimes vicious, antagonism. Poets of that period were inevitably "poets militant"; they had and made enemies.

When antagonism and contention are dominant, poetry on public themes will be formulated in satire and lampoon. (Panegyric, the other side of the coin, will get plenty of exercise too.) Satire and lampoon are no longer popular genres of poetry, are often instinctively rejected as inherently unpoetical, in fact, but that judgment is historically determined and has nothing to do with poetry's "nature." Dryden's *Absalom and Achitophel,* a party political work, is a commentary on the great Exclusion Crisis of 1679–1681. It is often satirical in manner, sometimes descending to scurrilous abuse, but, all at the same time, it is civilized, urbane, majestic, superbly intelligent, and endlessly entertaining. Politics in seventeenth-century England could engage a great poet's full powers and find an eager and extensive readership. In his life of Dryden, Samuel Johnson said that his father, a bookseller in the provincial city of Lichfield, remembered that Dryden's *Absalom and Achitophel* had been one of the great best sellers of his career. To appreciate Dryden's achievement means entering in imagination a world where political issues were immediate and utterly absorbing, and where a poem upholding the right of James, Duke of York, to succeed his brother Charles II on the throne could fly off the shelves and yet instantly become part of the stable corpus of great English poetry. It is poetry's loss that it can no longer engage with such major human events.

USED BRICK

If a reviewer nowadays says of a poet's work that it is obvious that the poet has been reading a lot of Emily Dickinson, the intent is almost always derogatory. If Emily Dickinson is obviously present as an "influence," the modern poet's achievement is lessened. Influence from reading is inevitable and necessary, but it is prudent to conceal it. For Dryden and for all poets who preceded and for many who followed him, quite the opposite was the case. No one was embarrassed to reveal knowledge of his or her great and even not-so-great predecessors. Dryden often referred to his poetical work as his "studies," and the major element in his own training and practice as a poet was the studious reading of the poetry of the past and present.

In his poetry, such reading is deliberately echoed and alluded to because Dryden wished to be seen as an educated poet who was creating his own poems both in imitation of and at variance from the poetry of the past. He believed that the English language of his day had grown up to the point where it was ready to stand as a "classical" tongue comparable to Greek and Latin, and part of his program to confirm the new status of English involved both translation (see below) and all forms of allusion. To make allusions, direct and indirect, brief and extensive, to other writers put Dryden's poetry on a continuum of achievement with the past and helped greatly to characterize his ideal reader, something that all poetry

attempts. The first readers of Dryden's poems were mostly the gentry and bourgeoisie who had forgotten their Latin but knew that the Roman poets were "the classics." Dryden put them back in touch with their education, gave them Virgil and Ovid and Horace to read in a form that asserted the respectability and dignity of English, and fostered the idea that England now had a civilization comparable to Rome's. And these effects derived as much from his "original" poems as from his translations. The past is vital and present in Dryden's work, and his reader is in every way encouraged and gently chided to admire the wealth of allusion that is laid before him or her. Reading Dryden is always an education, which may be why scholars love him and why students should go willingly to his school.

Anyone who knows a little about architecture and building knows that used or recycled brick is a highly attractive material. Used brick is weathered, its color has ripened and its angles have softened—but it costs the earth. The echoes and allusions in Dryden's poetry are his version of used brick, found throughout his work, his predecessors' poetry reused and made his own with no expense spared.

ORATORY AND RHETORIC

A necessary consequence of the public and political nature of Dryden's best poetry is that it is rhetorical and that the poet's speaking voice is heard much as if he were an orator. Neither of these terms is now honorific. "Rhetorical" carries strong overtones of "empty gesture," and "oratory" suggests the efforts of speechwriters on occasions that are mostly public relations exercises. Dryden, however, was the heir of the great classical and Renaissance traditions of rhetoric and oratory, and when in a poem he had to make a case and carry through an argument, he used the skills of persuasion, encoded as methods of presentation and choices of stratagem, that his classical education and subsequent reading had opened for him.

The voice of persuasion is that of the orator, but oratory had at command a great variety of tones and levels of formality. Dryden, in fact, rarely addresses us as if we were at a public meeting. His is always a speaking voice, different from the mostly meditative voices that we "overhear" as the solitary readers of much Romantic and post-Romantic poetry, yet with the special intimacy that comes from attending to an argument subtly and consecutively unfolded by an impassioned yet entirely self-possessed speaker. If "rhetoric" and "oratory" suggest mercenary commitment only, the work of the "hired gun," Dryden's poetry will dispose of that delusion.

POEMS OF OCCASIONS

Dryden was a Poet Laureate of England (*and* Historiographer Royal), so a great many of Dryden's poems were occasional, written one may say by virtue of his government offices, such as an elegy for Charles II, *Threnodia Augustalis,* and a poem on the birth of a son (later to be the Old Pretender) to James II, *Britannia Rediviva.* These are not among Dryden's best poems, but since they are what he was expected to write by virtue of his offices they may seem less reprehensible than a poem like *Eleanora, A Panegyric Poem Dedicated to the Memory of the Late Countess of Abingdon* (1692). This was commissioned by her husband, the Earl of Abingdon, and Dryden, who was at the time short of money, undoubtedly received a substantial payment for it. Dryden had never met the Countess of Abingdon, *nor* her husband, as he admits in the preface, but he turned that circumstance to his advantage. His scholar's knowledge of English literature reminded him that John Donne had written two panegyrics upon Elizabeth Drury, whom he "had never seen" but "whom he has made immortal in his admirable 'Anniversaries.'" That was a good enough precedent for Dryden who, as the California edition of his *Works* shows, carefully modeled *Eleanora* on Donne's poems. This decision combined scholarship, professionalism, and the enthusiasm of a lover of poetry (he called Donne "the greatest wit, though not the best poet of our nation"—Donne's versification in Dryden's view was undeveloped and a tad crude). If his motive

for accepting the commission was essentially mercenary, his method of executing it was anything but perfunctory or routine. He employed all the skills he had been honing for thirty years and produced what James Winn has rightly called a "noble poem" of 377 lines.

As Dryden writes of the countess' "conjugal virtues," Milton's *Paradise Lost,* as so often in his work, is ready to hand:

A wife as tender, and as true withall,
As the first woman was before her fall:
Made for the man, of whom she was a part;
Made, to attract his eyes, and keep his heart.
A second Eve, but by no crime accursed;
As beauteous, not as brittle, as the first.
Had she been first, still paradise had bin,
And death had found no entrance by her sin.
So she not only had preserved from ill
Her sex and ours, but lived their pattern still.

(ll. 165–175)

To say that this is wickedly exaggerated and hugely insincere may be true, but not at all to the point. Dryden's poetic power is his sincerity and his inspiration. He says he had thought of calling the poem *The Pattern,* and though he has no personal knowledge of the countess as the pattern for her sex, reputation is everything and her reputation is accessible to all. To rely on what others have told him of Eleanora is therefore to trust the very best kind of testimony, and the poem's length and decent exuberance show that the poet was not forced to grind it out. It is a commissioned, occasional poem on the subject of a woman whom Dryden has never seen—but none of these circumstances means it *has* to be a bad poem, nor is it.

DOING HIS BEST: "TO THE MEMORY OF MR. OLDHAM"

Dryden's elegy for John Oldham (1635–1683) is the sole poem of his that might have expected to be included in *The Classic Hundred.* Famous critics have praised it; T. S. Eliot quotes it entire in *Homage to John Dryden* (1924), as do Geoffrey Hill in *The Enemy's Country* (1991) and Paul Hammond in his *Literary Life* of Dryden (1991).

Our object in joining this distinguished company, however, is to observe how the poem gathers in one convenient example the features of Dryden's poetry so far delineated.

To the Memory of Mr. Oldham
Farewell, too little and too lately known,
Whom I began to think and call my own;
For sure our souls were near allied, and thine
Cast in the same poetic mold with mine.
One common note on either lyre did strike,
And knaves and fools we both abhorred alike.
To the same goal did both our studies drive;
The last set out the soonest did arrive.
Thus Nisus fell upon the slipp'ry place,
While his young friend performed and won the race.
O early ripe! to thy abundant store
What could advancing age have added more?
It might (what nature never gives the young)
Have taught the numbers of thy native tongue.
But satire needs not those, and wit will shine
Through the harsh cadence of a rugged line.
A noble error and but seldom made,
When poets are by too much force betrayed.
Thy gen'rous fruits, though gathered ere their prime
Still showed a quickness, and maturing time
But mellows what we write to the dull sweets of
 rhyme.
Once more, hail and farewell; farewell thou young
But ah too short Marcellus of our tongue;
Thy brows with ivy and with laurel bound;
But fate and gloomy night encompass thee around.

Occasion. In 1684, the year after John Oldham, up-and-coming poet, died of smallpox, there appeared the *Remains of Mr. John Oldham in Verse and Prose,* prefaced by several elegiac and commendatory poems. Dryden's tribute led the list. Commendatory and memorial poems were common currency of Restoration poetry, and Dryden wrote a number of them. These were written by invitation and not usually paid for, except in terms of publicity, for it was understood that the invitation to contribute was a mark of literary status and an honor in itself.

Public and Private. Dryden's poem, moreover, reminds us that personal closeness to the deceased was not requisite. His knowledge of Oldham, on the evidence of the poem itself, seems confined to the public aspects. He has read Oldham's poetry (he even echoes a line of Oldham's in the poem), and he knows him by reputation. But there is no definite evidence of personal friendship. "Whom I began to think and call my own" may refer only to Oldham's public literary persona. It's possible that Dryden would not have recognized Oldham had he met him in the street.

Yet the poem for many readers is suffused with mournful emotion, though perhaps the admission should be made here that many *young* readers find it marmoreal, if not frigid. (It may be that the poem opens itself most to older people, as one of the benefits and regrets of aging.) The element of undemonstrative lament makes it, despite its professions, a private as well as a public poem, though "crypto-private" might be the accurate term. By beginning the poem with the similarities between Oldham and himself, Dryden soon finds himself, and finds powerful emotion, in seeing his own fate, or rather the fate of his reputation, implied in Oldham's. (This is the turn that elegies for poets by poets generally make.) No one can say that this poem does not mourn Oldham and regret his loss, but it has to connect with the sense of general mortality, and it does so by investing in Dryden's personal vulnerability.

But the most surprising element in the Oldham elegy, and the point where public and private seem to fuse, is the sixth couplet. "O early ripe! to thy abundant store / What could advancing age have added more?" A rhetorical question implies its own answer, and by the conventional rules of elegy—"Speak nothing but good of the dead"—the unspoken answer to this question has to be "Nothing." But instead, in a complete reversal of elegiac expectation, Dryden answers the question with an appraisal of Oldham's ability in versification and converts a wholly predictable panegyric into a *rara avis* indeed: a just elegy. "It might (what nature never gives the young) / Have taught the numbers of thy native tongue." In other words, "If you had lived a little longer, you might have learned how to write English verse, but young people are naturally without that ability." The shock of this for at least one contemporary is recorded in Paul Hammond's edition of the poem: "Tom Brown said that D. here had kicked over the milk that he had given: 'you tell the World that he was a very fine ingenious Gentleman, but still did not understand the cadence of the *English* tongue' (vol. 2, p. 232)." Though Dryden follows up by stating (lines 15 and 16) that "satire needs not" polished verses, he has initiated a process of taking and giving that will last till the end of the poem. (He may not have noticed that Oldham and others had defended Oldham's use of "rugged" lines in his *Satires on the Jesuits* as a deliberate artistic decision.) This concession on satire is undermined by the fact that Dryden was the known author of *Absalom and Achitophel* and *Mac Flecknoe* (the anonymity of both poems was transparent; he acknowledged both in 1693), two poems whose elegance and "correctness" of versification are combined with vigorous, even scurrilous satire. The process of taking returns in line 16, where Dryden demonstrates how to use substitution to produce ruggedness without harshness: "Through the harsh cadence of a rugged line." The first foot is perhaps a trochee, if it is not a pyrrhic, and is followed by a spondee, a pyrrhic, and two iambs. The first three feet are standard substitutions in iambic pentameter; Dryden's skill lies in using the three of them together to give Oldham a metrical lesson.

Oldham's verse, therefore, can be politely described—giving—as over-forceful, a "noble error," but—taking—an error nevertheless and one that did "betray" Oldham. The triplet that follows (ll. 19–21), with its third line extended by a foot to make it an alexandrine, in a characteristic earmark of Dryden's style, similarly gives (Oldham's fruits—his works—although picked early by death and therefore not ripe, nevertheless show "liveliness; sharpness of taste" [*OED* 5; Hammond, vol. 2, p. 233]) and takes: "and maturing time / But mellows what we write to the dull sweets of rhyme." Dryden speaks of the skills of the older, ripened poet with ironical deprecation. If Oldham had lived to be a mature poet himself, all he would have gained would have been the "dull sweets of rhyme." But rhyme is not the issue. It is the onomatopoeic beauty of those fourteen words, "and maturing time / But mellows what we write to the dull sweets of

rhyme," that is ironically represented as "dull sweets." Lines 22 and 23, by the use of allusion (see below) repeat the motion of apparently giving while really taking away that we see in the triplet (lines 19–21), as does the final couplet. Line 24 bestows on the dead poet garlands of ivy, immortality, which must be the literary immortality of his poetry's survival, and laurels, denoting conquest; again, this must be literary conquest. But the last line, the final alexandrine that Dryden loved, throws a pall over all ideas of immortality and any forms of survival: "But fate and gloomy night encompass thee around."

Allusions. Dryden employs allusions to Virgil twice in the poem, and it should be noted that both work to make arguments. These are highly functional allusions, not decoration. Allusion is chosen for arguments, however, because in each case Dryden is arguing for himself and allusion offers concealment.

To the same goal did both our studies drive;
The last set out the soonest did arrive.
Thus Nisus fell upon the slipp'ry place,
While his young friend performed and won the race.

When he published his Oldham poem, Dryden had finished or was about to finish his translation into heroic couplets, now his almost invariable choice of meter, of two passages from *The Aeneid* telling the story of the friendship and death of Euryalus and the older Nisus (from *Aeneid* V and IX, published in 1685 in *Sylvae*). For the Oldham poem he casts himself in the role of Nisus, who, during funeral games for Aeneas's father (Book V), took part in a footrace with Euryalus and other Trojans and Sicilians. "Shot from the crowd, swift Nisus all o'erpassed," but loses his lead when he slips in a pool of blood "of oxen slain" for sacrifice. Salius is about to take the lead when Nisus

caught the foot of Salius as he rose;
So Salius lay extended on the plain:
Euryalus springs out the prize to gain,
And cuts the crowd; applauding peals attend
The conqu'ror to the goal, who conquered through his
  friend.

The allusion unfolds with Nisus as Dryden setting off in his poetic career, followed by the young Euryalus, Oldham. But Nisus falls, though what this represents in Dryden's career is unknown. (The most likely speculation is that Oldham produced verse translations that antedated Dryden's beginnings in the genre.) Unlike his classical namesake, this Nisus cannot be represented as assisting Euryalus by impeding an opponent, but Dryden's meaning is clear. Oldham had a victory in poetry because Dryden somehow was out of the race.

The second allusion is to Oldham as the "young, / But ah too short Marcellus of our tongue." Marcellus was the nephew, adopted son, and putative heir of the emperor Augustus; Oldham is thus the lost heir of the empire of the English language, greatly mourned like Marcellus, but like Marcellus of small actual though great potential achievement. And if it is an Augustus we seek, the current incumbent of the throne of English poetry, who else but Dryden could come to mind? Oldham as Marcellus does not logically install Dryden as emperor, but poetry's logic is its own, and the steely determination of Dryden to complete his elegy for Oldham with exact justice in the matter of achievement can be felt to the very end, as can his mournful awareness of the fate of Oldham, Dryden, and all poets in the gloomy night of death.

BIOGRAPHY: PROFESSIONAL BEFORE PROFESSIONALISM

Dryden is the first English poet whose literary income and its sources add many informative details to his biography. He belonged to the Puritan country gentry of Northamptonshire, but his life turned in unexpected directions. His decision to live by his pen, to be both a gentleman and an author, is astonishing, given the longstanding and absolute incompatibility of paid authorship and gentility, but a respectable profession of authorship was a historical inevitability in the mid-seventeenth century, and Dryden's personality and circumstances fitted him to be the harbinger. He was not the first English professional writer—that distinction is Alexander Pope's—but as in so much else, Dryden broke trail for Pope.

Dryden was born in 1631 in the Northamptonshire village of Aldwincle and grew up in the nearby village of Titchmarsh. The families of his parents, Erasmus Dryden and Mary Pickering, were alike in their Puritan Protestantism and their "country" politics. Religion and politics were, throughout the seventeenth century, usually so closely allied as to be inseparable, and both families had suffered for their politics and their religion during Charles I's "personal rule." John Dryden's cousin, Sir Gilbert Pickering, twenty years older than the poet, had been a member of the Short Parliament and the Long. He sided with Cromwell and the army in the 1640s, and was a judge at the trial of Charles I. (It was later to his advantage that he did not sign the king's death warrant.) In the 1650s he served on the Lord Protector's Privy Council and held the important office of Lord Chamberlain at Cromwell's court. There is no absolute proof but it is a near certainty that Pickering got Dryden his first employment, so initiating his lifelong dependence on the patronage system of the seventeenth century.

Sometime in the 1640s, perhaps in 1644 when he was thirteen, Dryden entered Westminster School in London, probably after primary schooling in Titchmarsh. The Master of Westminster (from 1638 to 1695) was Richard Busby, well known for his royalist and high church opinions, but who seems to have kept his post because of the high esteem for his abilities as a teacher and scholar among those who governed the country on very different ideological principles from his own. Dryden did well under Busby's supervision and retained great affection for him; he later sent two of his sons to Westminster, but he also commented sourly on the propensity for flogging for which Busby was notorious. The best Westminster pupils could expect to be elected King's Scholars (or during the Interregnum, Westminster Scholars) of Trinity College, Cambridge, and Dryden duly proceeded to the university in 1650. His first published poem, "Upon the Death of the Lord Hastings," appeared in a collection of elegies,

JOHN DRYDEN

Lachrymae Musarum; The Tears of the Muses in 1649, after he had left Westminster and before he went to Cambridge (he signed himself "Johannes Dryden, Scholae Westm. Alumnus"). At Cambridge he wrote poetry in English and Latin and published a commendatory poem in 1650. He graduated B.A. in 1654, just before his father died.

Dryden's career after leaving Cambridge until the Restoration is generally darkness broken by three interesting facts: in October 1657 he signed a receipt for fifty pounds from John Thurloe, Cromwell's secretary of state; in November 1658 he walked in Cromwell's funeral procession alongside John Milton and Andrew Marvell, "Secretaries of the French and Latin Tongues"; and in January 1659 he published *Heroic Stanzas,* an elegy for Cromwell. The signed receipt, taken with Dryden's place in the funeral procession, seems to be reliable evidence that he was employed, in a subordinate role, of course, in the same way as the other great poets were, mainly as a translator of diplomatic documents. Unlike Milton and Marvell, however, Dryden was to change from the cautious praise of Cromwell shown in *Heroic Stanzas* to a rather fervent royalism after the Restoration, but his slight acquaintance with Milton (who was virtually retired when Dryden knew him) seems to have supported his later judgment of Milton's poetic greatness and the respect he always showed for him. Patronage had probably got him his government job, and from leaving Cambridge until his death Dryden exploited the old patronage system for the production of literature and at the same time was instrumental in bringing into being the new system of publishing that eventually replaced it.

With the Restoration of the monarchy in 1660, Dryden became a royalist (he "changed with the nation," as Samuel Johnson remarked). Like his later religious conversion, this has the appearance of opportunism and hypocrisy, but it is the appearance only. Dryden's changes of mind were sincere, for he steadfastly maintained his new beliefs when it would have been of great material advantage to abandon them. Royalism also meant, in effect a "rightward" movement in Dryden's religious observance, away from the Puritanism of his childhood and young manhood and toward the high church Anglicanism he had seen at Busby's Westminster. But we can only speculate about this, and about the reaction of Dryden's Northamptonshire kin when they learned of it. Dryden's home now was and was to remain London, but he enjoyed visits to Northamptonshire and seems to have maintained cordial relations with his family despite his conversions in politics and, later, religion.

The likeliest source of income for Dryden after the Restoration was the result of another restoration, that of the theater. A government of Puritans, however far they may have been in reality from the maypole-felling, iconoclastic miseryguts stereotype, could not be expected to tolerate public performances where men and boys routinely appeared in women's garments. The reestablishment of licensed public theaters was therefore eagerly undertaken by their victorious opponents, who thus initiated the last great era of British drama before the renaissance of the later twentieth century. (And introduced women as professional actresses to the British stage, thereby satisfying one Puritan objection by making things even worse.) Two companies were established in London, the King's and the Duke's, and within a few years they had custom-built indoor theaters with scenery and artificial lighting. Income from the theater, however, depended very directly on having an instantaneous success with the audience. Dryden's early career as a dramatist was not uniformly successful, but he was hardworking and learned fast, and when the theaters were closed by the great plague of 1665, the Theatre Royal had staged four plays by him, a comedy, a tragicomedy, and two plays of the type he would most excel in, the rhymed heroic play, namely *The Indian Queen* (written in collaboration with his new brother-in-law, Sir Robert Howard) and *The Indian Emperor.* The comedy, *The Wild Gallant,* failed on the stage and was only printed, in a revised version, in 1669. The other three plays succeeded, the heroic plays especially.

The energetic playwriting in the immediate post-Restoration years was not the entirety of Dryden's output at that time. He clearly wanted to establish himself in the eyes of the court as a reliable royalist poet for public occasions. Charles II returned to England as king in May 1660, and in June, Dryden published *Astraea Redux* [Justice Led Back], "A Poem on the Happy Restoration and Return of His Sacred Majesty Charles the Second," one poem among scores published on the occasion. In April of the next year he published *To His Sacred Majesty,* "A Panegyric on His Coronation." He also supplied during this period a couple of commendatory poems, but in terms of his financial security the most interesting is his poem *To My Lord Chancellor,* "Presented on New Year's Day" (1662).

Edward Hyde, Earl of Clarendon, had been Charles's Lord Chancellor since before the Restoration. He was in effect prime minister and also a man of literary interests. He clearly took at this time the role of patron to Dryden, but very little is known about their relationship. The poem Dryden offered Clarendon is a panegyric and its chief function from Dryden's point of view was surely to remind the chancellor that he had in Dryden a talented adherent whose loyalty and right thinking deserved reward. At a meeting of the Privy Council in the same month in which the poem appeared, January 1662, the chancellor reminded the monarch that the king's promise of a present of money to "My Lord Berkshire" had not yet been realized. In reply the king mentioned the sum of eleven thousand pounds, and in late February warrants were issued awarding three thousand pounds immediately to Lady Elizabeth Howard, daughter of the Earl of Berkshire, and eight thousand pounds, to come a little later, to her father, who had lost his fortune in the service of Charles I and Charles II. The immediate payment of three thousand pounds to his daughter was meant to supply her with a dowry. To complete the circle, John Dryden married Lady Elizabeth Howard on 1 December 1663, the marriage having been made possible, as James Winn has suggested, by Clarendon's intervention after Dryden's poetic prompt, and that in turn throws bright light on the nexus of poetry and money in Dryden's life.

In June 1665, when the plague closed the London theaters, the Drydens retreated to the estate of the Earl of Berkshire at Charlton in Wiltshire. There Dryden worked on his play, *Secret Love,* on his essay in the form of a symposium, *Of Dramatic Poesy,* the first systematic study in English of the theory of drama, and his historical poem *Annus Mirabilis,* an account, designed to support the king's government, of the naval war with the Dutch in 1665 and 1666, with an account of Charles II's heroic behavior during the Great Fire of London in September 1666. This poem was clearly intended to strengthen Dryden's credentials as a public and royalist poet, and in the spring of 1668 it looked as if all his ships were coming in. Sir William Davenant died; he had been Poet Laureate since 1638, and Dryden, having made himself the obvious candidate, was given the post and a stipend of one hundred pounds a year. His success as a playwright—five plays produced in 1667 alone—made him a very desirable property, and he apparently set up a bidding war for his exclusive services between the King's and Duke's companies. The King's bid highest and Dryden made an agreement to write for them three plays a year in exchange for one-and-a-quarter shares in the company. This share may have brought him in good years as much as three hundred pounds. The copyright of the plays remained with Dryden, so it looked as if, between the king and the King's Company, Dryden's financial future was assured.

Appearances deceived. Dryden received no payment of his stipend as Poet Laureate (and later as Historiographer Royal, a second post to which he was appointed in 1670) until 1671, and thereafter the stipend was always in arrears. (Lady Elizabeth Dryden—as an earl's daughter she retained her title on marriage—received the last payment on her three thousand pounds on 11 August 1669.) On 25 January 1672 the King's Company's building, the Theatre Royal in Bridges Street, near where Dryden had bought a house in Longacre, burned down, and thereafter his theatrical income was uncertain and spasmodic as the company strove to reestablish itself. As a contracted shareholder-playwright, Dryden had few good years. He was never able to be comfortable and complacent; he always had to be alert for an opportunity.

One that should be mentioned was his well-remunerated facility with prologues and epilogues. (In the Restoration theater, every play began with a prologue and ended with an epilogue.) Since a good prologue was thought necessary to give a play a good start, some playwrights, trusting Dryden's abilities more than their own, employed him to write (usually) the prologue or epilogue for them. His standard fee was said to be ten guineas.

After the fire of 1672, Dryden's playwriting proceeded at less than the hectic pace of the earliest years. He clearly had several plays in the pipeline which continued on to performance and publication, but it is notable that nondramatic works of controversy, in both prose and verse, begin to appear among his publications. Attacks on him as a playwright brought replies from Dryden, and a physical attack on him is a reminder that criticism was not only metaphorically violent and personal in those years. On the night of 18 December 1679, he was beaten and badly injured in Rose Alley, near Longacre. His biographers think it probable that he was thought to have been the author of a poem, *An Essay on Satire* (actually by the Earl of Mulgrave) that someone of real or self-imputed importance deemed insulting. (The form of the attack, a cudgeling by thugs, was a statement of Dryden's social inferiority to the instigator; had he been a gentleman, he would have been challenged to a duel.)

James Winn points out that if the attack was intended to make Dryden more cautious in his public utterances, it had the opposite effect. The Rose Alley ambush took place just as the great political crisis of the Popish Plot and the Exclusion project was unfolding in a way that would bring Dryden his great opportunity as a controversialist and satirist. *Absalom and Achitophel,* published in November 1681, was anonymous but few doubted who the author was. It is not a cautious poem.

In the last years of the reign of Charles II and during the short reign of James II, Dryden was as much Poet Laureate and Historiographer Royal as dramatist. Besides his political poems he wrote political pamphlets and translated works of controversy. But with the Revolution of 1688,

which established a Protestant monarchy after the expulsion of the Catholic James II, Dryden, now a Catholic himself and henceforth a largely tacit supporter of the exiled Stuarts, could no longer be openly a controversialist. His government posts were gone, and so the great achievement of *Absalom and Achitophel* could have no successors from his pen.

Need sent Dryden back to the theater. Five plays of his were staged after the Revolution, but his new chief interest and source of income had really begun to germinate back in 1679 when his version of *Troilus and Cressida* had been published by Jacob Tonson. In 1679 Tonson was just out of his apprenticeship. Dryden was forty-eight; Tonson was twenty-four and nominally a "stationer" or bookseller, but his ambition and acumen give him a strong claim to be the first "publisher" in the modern sense of the term. He initiated publishing projects, commissioned books, got advice from established writers on manuscripts, advertised his publications and in effect brought into being something like the firm of Dryden and Tonson, Publishers.

The first indication of the way things would go was the appearance in 1680 of *Ovid's Epistles, Translated by Several Hands.* Dryden translated two of the epistles and collaborated on another with the Earl of Mulgrave. In addition—and this is a sign of his developing "editorial" role in Tonson's business—he wrote the preface to the volume and made it a significant document in the theory of translation, one of his most important critical essays. Translation was to be the bulk of Dryden's production for Tonson, and in the last years of his life he became perhaps the greatest verse translator into English.

Again obviously with Dryden's advice and assistance, Tonson broke new ground in 1684 with *Miscellany Poems by the Most Eminent Hands.* This was followed the next year by *Sylvae: or, The Second Part of Poetical Miscellanies,* and in 1693 by *Examen Poeticum: Being the Third Part of Miscellany Poems.* The first Tonson miscellany included *Absalom and Achitophel, Mac Flecknoe,* and *The Medal,* all preserving the transparent fiction of their author's anonymity. Prologues and epilogues by Dryden were republished too, bringing welcome additional payment. All these poems were proven successes. The presence of two of Virgil's eclogues, an idyll of Theocritus, and an elegy of Ovid in Dryden's verse translations, as well as verse translations by the other contributors, was a way of confirming the public's interest in such versions, demonstrated earlier by *Ovid's Epistles.* In *Sylvae,* the second Tonson miscellany (1685), Dryden wrote a preface following up his essay prefatory to the Ovid. One third of *Sylvae* was his and comprised translations of Virgil, Theocritus, Lucretius, and Horace.

Dryden's late discovery of his genius for satire was not to be suppressed by the political success of his ideological adversaries. It gets full expression in his fine translation into heroic couplets of some of Juvenal's and all of Persius' satires in 1692. *Examen Poeticum* in 1693 included fifteen pieces by Dryden, most of them translations. A fourth miscellany appeared in 1694, but by then Dryden was less involved, having embarked on the ambitious project of a translation for Tonson of the complete *Works* of Virgil. (Dryden even managed to contribute to the fifth miscellany in 1704, four years after his death.)

Dryden's Virgil translation summarized conveniently the extent and nature of the changes he and Tonson brought about in the author's economic relationship with the public. *The Works of Virgil* was a grand undertaking, in the large folio format with many full-page engraved illustrations, but it was not simply a stationer's unaided publication. Patronage played a large part in the financing, for the *Virgil* was published by subscription, and although Tonson managed the subscription lists and paid Dryden two hundred pounds of the money that came in to keep him going after he started work in 1693, subscription was still a long step away from publishing as we know it today. When the enterprise was publicized, it was announced that there were to be two lists of subscribers. One list, limited to one hundred names, was to commit the subscribers to a down payment of three guineas and a final payment of two guineas on delivery of the book. The subscribers were a

gathering of the great and good of Williamite England. There were fellow Catholics and prominent Protestants. There were Whigs and Tories. Samuel Pepys, a kinsman of Dryden's and a friend from Cambridge days, was a five-guinea subscriber, as were actors, actresses, and playwrights, such as William Congreve and Thomas Southerne. There were cabinet ministers, clergymen, soldiers and sailors, and all on the five-guinea list were gentlemen and ladies. The subscribers on the second list, who were not limited in number, paid a guinea down and a second guinea on receipt of the book. The book then went on sale, on less fine paper, at Tonson's shop and his profits came mainly from those sales.

The idea of a translation of Virgil by Dryden had been mooted publicly some time before the contract was drawn up, and the subscribers and everyone interested knew that this work was "for the nation." The subscription list turned the single patron into a community of support, albeit a community in the first instance of the aristocratic and armigerous. Despite appearances, this was a decisive step toward modern publishing.

Dryden made about fourteen hundred pounds from his *Virgil,* which was no fortune for three years' work. Without knowing it, however, he had shown a way for a poet to achieve financial independence, bringing with it independence of the theater, of hack work, and of the patron. If in his lifetime he never quite established the respectability of the professional poet, he certainly opened the way to it.

"TO SETTLE THE SUCCESSION OF THE STATE":
TWO MASTERPIECES

Reputation and achievement fit tightly together in the career of Dryden. Everyone nowadays agrees that the two pinnacles of his work are *Mac Flecknoe* and *Absalom and Achitophel.* It is hard to believe that this situation will ever markedly change. It is possible to believe that Dryden will cease to be read—even in graduate schools—but if he *is* read, then *Mac Flecknoe* and *Absalom and Achitophel* will earn the most admiration for the best reasons.

JOHN DRYDEN

The higher peak is without doubt *Absalom and Achitophel,* but there is substantial sub rosa agreement that *Mac Flecknoe* is more fun. But running these two thoroughbreds in tandem seems at first sight a disservice to both, for they are markedly different breeds. They share Dryden's fine versification and the heroic couplet form, but one is vulgarly comic beneath a high-falutin' surface while the other approaches true tragic dignity. In *Mac Flecknoe,* the kingdom at issue is the Empire of Stupidity (or Dulness, which comes to mean everything negative and bad); in *Absalom and Achitophel* it is simultaneously the biblical kingdom of David and the three kingdoms of England, Scotland, and Ireland. Yet really the affiliations that link these two poems dominate their divergences. Most strikingly, they turn out to be about the same problem: succession, the question of who comes next to the throne when the present monarch shall be gathered to his fathers. This problem was the political ground bass of Charles II's entire reign, rising to startling prominence during the years of the Popish Plot and the Exclusion controversy. It is to be expected, therefore, that *Absalom and Achitophel* should have appeared in 1681, during the crisis years, since the plan to exclude the Catholic James, Duke of York, from succeeding his brother on the throne had been everywhere debated for a couple of years. What does surprise, however, is that Dryden's first poem on the succession theme should have been written in the summer of 1676, well before the idea boiled over and became the sole preoccupation of politicians and public.

MAC FLECKNOE: "IMMORTAL WAR WITH WIT"

The first reaction of a thoughtful modern reader to *Mac Flecknoe* is likely to be that it is a guilty pleasure. The whole poem is 215 lines of character assassination, powerful and hilarious but full of what are obviously low blows and personal fouls. Thomas Shadwell, the victim of this mugging, is ridiculed for being fat, a drunkard, and a drug addict, and there is a persistent note of anti-Celtic racism too. (Neither Flecknoe nor Shadwell was Scots, Irish, or Welsh—Flecknoe in fact was a Roman Catholic, born in Northampton-shire—but Dryden cheerfully exploits the prejudice that saw Ireland as a land of bog-hopping illiterates.) This nearly all-purpose political incorrectness is apt to conceal from the casual reader that a serious and worthy purpose of general importance can be found under Dryden's fanciful outpouring of abuse, but critics trying to lay bare that serious purpose may never go so far as to claim that the greater purpose negates the scurrility of what Dryden does to Shadwell. "Nothing personal" can nowise be said, but it is nevertheless true that Shadwell in Dryden's hands can be seen as a symptom of a great disease as well as the butt and occasion of this spectacularly and elegantly abusive poem.

Shadwell (1642–1692) studied at Cambridge and at the Middle Temple for a legal career, but chose the theater instead. He succeeded in comedy, where he loudly proclaimed his allegiance to the "humors" comedy of Ben Jonson while modifying and adapting the genre to the tastes of the Restoration stage. (Dryden too revered Jonson but not uncritically, and his title, "Son of Flecknoe," is intended to deny Shadwell the title he undoubtedly coveted, "Son of Ben.") In controversies over the theory and practice of comedy he had been at times allied with and often opposed to Dryden, but in the summer of 1676 he had taken positions and made utterances that led Dryden to launch at him the unavoidable and unforgettable missile of *Mac Flecknoe.* There is no doubt that it was overkill. Every reference book that includes Shadwell has to protest that he was not nearly so bad a playwright as Dryden would have his readers believe, and yet the first thing that still comes to mind when Shadwell's name is mentioned is *Mac Flecknoe.*

The poem has a formal clarity and fittingness that has always been admired, but the first thing to be noticed about it is that it has only two speakers. One is the narrator and the other is Flecknoe, the old and fading monarch of the "realms of Nonsense." This king or emperor feels he must nominate his successor, for Nonsense is not a hereditary monarchy like England, where the king's eldest legitimate son automatically succeeds to the throne, but a monarchy rather like that of biblical Israel, where the king nominates his successor from among his sons, often born of various mothers. Simultaneity, however, is Dryden's allusive method here, and if the Bible comes to mind it should be accompanied by what was then its secular equivalent, the *Aeneid*. Shadwell as an Old Testament king, an anti-Solomon, perhaps, is also Aeneas in negative, handing on his new kingdom to Ascanius-Shadwell. Less openly, but equally certainly, Flecknoe is God the Father, the Ancient of Days, bestowing an everlasting dominion and a kingdom that shall not be destroyed (Daniel 7:13–14) upon his Only Begotten Son—one of many—whose coming is preceded by his own Elijah—John the Baptist, Flecknoe himself taking this role too, "sent before but to prepare thy way" (l. 32). Flecknoe has two speeches, lines 13–59 and 139–210. Apart from a brief introduction and conclusion, the narrator's voice is heard between Flecknoe's speeches, describing the geographical empire of Nonsense, which turns out to be coterminous with the run-down and seedier parts of the City of London, and the coronation procession and coronation itself, leading to Flecknoe's speech of prophetic blessings.

Two voices, therefore, and a third eloquently absent. In the entire course of the poem, Shadwell, its eponymous hero, "Son of Flecknoe," *says not a word.* Much is said about him, nothing by him. Speech rightly employed is the agent and outward sign of reason, the divine attribute that fallen man has not wholly forfeited. Speech wrongly employed is amply displayed in Flecknoe's two orations, for he is a praiser of folly, with a system of values that takes evil for good and nonsense for sense. Flecknoe is no hypocrite; for him, stupidity is the greatest of virtues, and he finds everything to praise in his "son."

Shadwell alone my perfect image bears,
Mature in dulness from his tender years:
Shadwell alone, of all my sons is he
Who stands confirmed in full stupidity.
The rest to some faint meaning make pretense,
But Shadwell never deviates into sense.

(ll. 15–20)

But the son has nothing to say and his saying is nothing. Dryden, through Flecknoe's inverted system of values, takes sideswipes at Shadwell's bulk ("his goodly fabric fills the eye / And seems designed for thoughtless majesty") and other disadvantageous attributes, but the principal target is always and everywhere Shadwell's writings, his speech made perniciously permanent. Flecknoe has studied Shadwell's plays and their prefaces, prologues, epilogues, and dedications very closely. The poem is filled with praise that systematically deprives Shadwell of any literary virtue, and the generalizations about his writing are based on minutely detailed examination.

Like mine, thy gentle numbers feebly creep;
Thy tragic muse gives smiles, thy comic sleep.
With whate'er gall thou sett'st thyself to write,
Thy inoffensive satires never bite.
In thy felonious heart though venom lies,
It does but touch thy Irish pen and dies.

(ll. 197–202)

The disagreement about literary theory has developed into the conviction—how seriously held by Dryden is impossible to know—that Shadwell's oeuvre is the product of an active principle of anarchy and anticreativity. The structure of the poem supports this argument by undermining its advocate, Flecknoe. After his second speech, the prophetic blessings, Flecknoe is dropped through a trapdoor by two characters reenacting a scene from Shadwell's latest play, an Elijah who sinks rather than soars.

Sinking he left his drugget robe behind,
Borne upwards by a subterranean wind.
The mantle fell to the young prophet's part,
With double portion of his father's art.

(ll. 214–217)

Flecknoe-Elijah is bound for a cloacal rather than celestial destination, but his mantle nevertheless descends on his successor prophet, Elisha-Shadwell, whose work will be doubly nonsensical and stupid, twice as bad-good as his spiritual father's, in fact.

In terms of the poem's genre, Paul Hammond says that "*Mac Flecknoe* can be thought of as combining a number of modes or genres: the paradoxial encomium [such as Erasmus' *Praise of Folly*], the personal lampoon, and the satirical discussion of literary values and writers" (Hammond, vol. 1, p. 311). But he goes on to nominate a fourth type that today most often serves to characterize Dryden's poem: mock heroic. Hammond makes clear that mock heroic, as applied to *Mac Flecknoe,* is more a style, a rhetorical attitude, than a form: "heroic language and incident are applied to an unworthy subject," which certainly is Shadwell's case in Dryden's hands. One might suggest, however, that modern students of Dryden are happiest with the term "mock heroic" for *Mac Flecknoe* because of a literary historical "succession" that has turned the poem (a development that Dryden should admire but probably would not, since it turns him into a version of his own Flecknoe) into the predecessor of the greatest English poem of the early eighteenth century, Alexander Pope's mock epic *The Dunciad.*

ABSALOM AND ACHITOPHEL: *SACRED MONARCHY*

Unlike the afterlife of *Mac Flecknoe,* a mustard seed that waxed a great tree in *The Dunciad,* the reputation of *Absalom and Achitophel* is entirely unsupported by influence over subsequent poems. While there were several rejoinders to the poem, and adoption by foes and friends of its rhetoric (Hammond, vol. 1, p. 449), of influence per se there is nothing, and that fact is highly implicative. Without knowing it, in *Absalom and Achitophel,* Dryden wrote an elegy for a great idea that in his time had died, though it has never been laid to rest. The death of that idea is the explanation for *Absalom and Achitophel*'s terminal position. Dryden there has made a corpse only recently dead appear active and vital, but the illusion is sustainable only within the poem, whose success is partly indicated by the fact that even in the twenty-first century, while reading *Absalom and Achitophel,* one feels that sacred monarchy, the divine right of kings, is—for a moment—a viable political idea.

Dryden never pretended his great poem was other than a partisan performance, acknowledg-

ing in the preface "To the Reader" that he had employed his "pen for one party." *Absalom and Achitophel* gives the best possible appearance to an idea whose time had passed, and does so only shortly before the spectacular and definitive failure of that idea as a political program. Yet when the poem was published, and for a number of years thereafter, Dryden and his royalist Tory party believed quite reasonably that they had won. For the first few years of its existence, *Absalom and Achitophel* was the triumphant celebration of sacred monarchy on the English model. The Revolution of 1688 turned it into the elegy and epitaph for the divine right of kings of England.

ABSALOM AND ACHITOPHEL: *THE POLITICAL MOMENT*

On 15 June 1673, James, Duke of York, the king's brother and the heir apparent to the throne (Charles II had no legitimate children) resigned his royal appointments, including his post as Lord High Admiral, and the fat was in the fire. According to the Test Act, passed earlier that year, to keep their appointments all officeholders were to receive Anglican communion and in other ways signify that they were not non-Anglican Protestants or, more pointedly, Roman Catholics. James's resignation was final confirmation of what had long been suspected, that the kingdom's heir "and the son of a martyr for the Protestant religion" (as John Evelyn remarked) had apostasized, and that the next king of England, if he survived his brother (as everyone assumed he would and as in fact he did) would be the Defender of the Faith and head of the Church of England while belonging to the Catholic communion. James was a widower, the father of two Protestant daughters, the princesses Mary and Anne, but he greatly increased the fears of overwhelmingly Protestant England by marrying, in September 1673, the Catholic Mary Beatrice, sister of the Duke of Modena, a city not far enough from Rome, to many people's way of thinking. If the new duchess bore a son, he would take precedence in the line of succession over his

Protestant half-sisters, so the possibility of line of Catholic Stuarts became a reality.

James's publicly acknowledged conversion and his Catholic marriage made anti-Catholicism a constant presence in the politics of the later part of Charles II's reign. An element of calm was provided for a while by Mary of Modena's failure to bear a child; while the Princess Mary continued to stand second in line to the throne after her father, a Catholic succession was only a hypothesis. Yet the prospect of James's own accession to the throne was profoundly disquieting to many, especially because Louis XIV of France seemed to be giving annual demonstrations of the tyranny and religious bigotry that were popularly associated with Catholic monarchs.

Anti-Catholic sentiment was revitalized in 1678 with Titus Oates's revelation of the notorious "Popish Plot," nothing but a tissue of lies that nevertheless took a number of lives and convinced much of the population that Jesuits and Catholic laymen had plotted to kill the king and put James on the throne as their puppet. For the king's opponents, soon led by the devious and often unscrupulous Anthony Ashley Cooper, Earl of Shaftesbury (who was also the admired protector and generous patron of John Locke) the problem was to find a way to preserve the monarchy while somehow excluding the Duke of York from the succession to the throne. "Exclusion" eventually became the descriptive term for the entire, years-long crisis engendered by the maneuvers to keep James from ruling as a Catholic.

The most popular and most publicized of these stratagems involved another James: James, Duke of Monmouth, who was Charles II's eldest illegitimate child, well known to be the king's favorite, and—most important—a Protestant. (Monmouth's Protestantism, or Anglicanism, to be specific, was not a matter of special devotion. He was not a Catholic, and that was all that mattered.) The scheme that came closest to success was a proposed law, a Bill of Exclusion, that would have cut the Duke of York out of the succession by legitimizing Monmouth. It is this plan with which *Absalom and Achitophel* is concerned. Exclusion Bills were introduced into the House of Commons in 1679 and 1690. The first had its second reading but died when the king dissolved Parliament. The second bill passed in the Commons but was defeated in the House of Lords. A third was introduced in the Oxford Parliament of 1681, but the king had by then received a secret subvention from Louis XIV and, no longer dependent on supply from Parliament, was able to dissolve Parliament yet again and never had to call another during the rest of his reign.

The summer of 1681 saw the political tide turn the king's way, and he began by asserting his prerogative powers to move against the Whig opposition. He had Shaftesbury sent to the Tower on a charge of high treason, but a jury selected by Whig sheriffs rejected the evidence as insufficient. Shaftesbury tried without success to organize a revolt and in 1682 fled to Holland, where in 1683 he died.

Absalom and Achitophel was advertised for sale on 19 November 1681; Shaftesbury's trial began on 24 November. It was long held that the poem was timed to affect the trial, but Phillip Harth has shown that this is unlikely (Hammond, vol. 1, p. 445). Dryden had composed it in the summer of 1681 as a general contribution to the Tory assault and, as mentioned above, it was a best seller.

The moment of the poem, therefore, was when the Tory counterattacks had begun to tell and when Shaftesbury had been publicly identified as the Whig principal, the power behind the exclusion project, with the strongest implications that he was a treasonous plotter. Moreover, and still more importantly, Dryden's poem joined a chorus of Tory voices urging the king to be more aggressive, to assert his prerogative rights more firmly, to face the fact that his favorite son, Monmouth, was opposed to the principles of monarchy that Charles believed in unwaveringly, and the fact that Monmouth was not even loyal to Charles's own person. The project of hardening the king's resolve in the Exclusion Crisis explains why King David is the most important character, with the most important speech, in the poem—whose basic action is to show him thinking over the situation and making up his mind to act henceforth with the firmness and resolve that

Dryden and the Tories recommended, to be, in other words, the embodiment of the Tory ideal of kingship.

ABSALOM AND ACHITOPHEL: *EXCLUSION AND II SAMUEL*

The characters and action of *Absalom and Achitophel* are based on the drawn-out episode of Absalom's revolt against his father David in the Second Book of Samuel (chapters 13–19). The analogy between the royal family drama, the Exclusion Crisis, and II Samuel had been observed and exploited in sermons, speeches, pamphlets, and poems before Dryden took it up (Hammond, vol. 1, pp. 446–448). No reader would have been surprised or hampered to find that King Charles appeared as King David, Monmouth as Absalom, and Shaftesbury as Absalom's adviser, Achitophel; by November 1681 these were commonplace allusions, but Phillip Harth (1993) reminds us that there was originality in Dryden's use of them.

> Whereas [an earlier poem using the parallel] relates an Old Testament story in which the presence of a few discrepancies directs the reader's attention to an analogous contemporary situation, *Absalom and Achitophel* does just the reverse.
>
> (p. 107)

Dryden keeps the biblical story quite subservient to his purposes and changes a number of features of II Samuel to accommodate the contemporary situation as he sees it.

The most obvious adjustments concern the principal characters of the poem. Because the contemporary situation takes precedence over the biblical, we may imagine Charles, Monmouth, and Shaftesbury dressed in the seventeenth-century idea of biblical attire and following seventeenth-century notions of biblical behavior. Dryden's David is not the weary and capricious monarch of II Samuel, with seven wives and an official establishment of concubines. He is the overindulgent father of his people with one wife only and she barren (Catherine of Braganza, Charles' queen consort). His love affairs and bastard children are the vices of his virtues, of philoprogenitive paternal affection. Dryden's David has flaws and faults, but he clearly has no history of murder or bloody ruthlessness. In fact, the only real similarities between David-Charles and David as characters is that they are both the Lord's anointed and each is overindulgent to a favorite son to the point of misgovernment with national political implications. The king of II Samuel is more stupidly indulgent toward his Absalom because Absalom there is *not* stupid. His ambition, daring, and ruthlessness are all his own, an inheritance from his father, in fact, though the Bible is careful not to say so. Dryden's Absalom is a beautiful but empty vessel into which his Achitophel (Dryden prefers the Vulgate's spelling to the King James Version's "Ahithophel") pours wicked counsel that stirs up Absalom's native ambition and that conceals parricidal consequences. He is putty in the hands of Achitophel.

In II Samuel, Ahithophel is Absalom's counselor who gives good if wicked advice that if followed would bring success to the rebellion. But David has begged God to "turn the counsel of Ahithophel into foolishness" (II Samuel 15:31), and when his advice is not taken Ahithophel goes home and hangs himself. Dryden's Achitophel is modeled on the disguised Satan of Milton's *Paradise Regained* and proves far more successful in his temptations. Absalom-Monmouth eventually commits himself to high treason, but he is led there and wholly manipulated by Achitophel-Shaftesbury. He cannot escape blame, but he is a follower and a dupe, and not very bright. If Dryden cannot save him from treason and filial ingratitude, he does "save" him from intelligent malevolence.

The "parallel" of II Samuel and *Absalom and Achitophel* runs, then, for only a short distance, and that suggests that the parallel was only of limited use to Dryden. That, of course, is not the case. Dryden adopted the analogy from others, but he put it to prodigious use. Allowing Dryden to write of the contemporary crisis without "naming names," by using the biblical ones instead, is an obvious advantage. Less obvious but perhaps greater is the fact that the parallel permits Dryden to avoid elements of the Exclusion Crisis that would have weakened his case, perhaps fatally. Most notably, and most impudently, he can ignore Catholicism as the main cause of the crisis. Without James's Catholicism and Monmouth's Protestantism there would have been no political crisis, yet Dryden manages to produce his poem without ever alluding to the religious schism that underlies the crisis, and it is his recourse to the scriptures that enables this great absence in his poem.

The English Catholics are mentioned in the poem (ll. 85–103, segueing into a discussion of the Popish Plot). They are the Jebusites, from whom David captured Jerusalem, and they are nearly harmless.

Thus worn and weakened, well or ill content,
Submit they must to David's government:
Impov'rished and deprived of all command,
Their taxes doubled as they lost their land.

If Catholics initiated the plot (and Dryden believed in 1681 that there was no smoke without fire) it is the Whigs who have blown it up into a national calamity. The Jebusites-Catholics then virtually disappear from the poem.

James, Duke of York, does appear in the poem, but the faint presence we are shown in no way represents the focal point of the crisis that in fact he was. He is not given a biblical name by Dryden and is referred to only by Absalom-Monmouth in the speech (ll. 315–372) in which the favorite son of the king admits that he has no lawful or moral claim at all to the throne but will nevertheless pursue his ambition: "Desire of greatness is a godlike sin." David-Charles's lawful successor takes no part in the action of the poem and is mentioned by Absalom as part of his self-indictment.

His brother, through oppressed with vulgar spite,
Yet dauntless, and secure of native right,
Of ev'ry royal virtue stands possessed,
Still dear to all the bravest and the best.
His courage foes, his friends his truth proclaim;
His loyalty the king, the world his fame.
His mercy e'en th'offending crowd will find;
For sure he comes of a forgiving kind.

(ll. 353–360)

The Duke of York figure is almost omitted altogether and his Catholicism (in the poem's terms he has converted to "Jebusitism") has vanished.

The effects of this great omission from a poem dealing with the Exclusion Crisis are manifold. In totally avoiding the one element of the crisis that was historically circumstantial and politically entangled, Dryden has made a declaration, firmly endorsing Tory policy, that James's religion was really no problem. It was a Whig phobia that when he came to the throne James would subvert the ancient constitutional arrangements of England, behave like the Catholic tyrant in France, and seek to advance Catholicism at the expense of the Church of England. The poem declares, by finding in II Samuel no equivalent for this phobia, that such foolishness is beneath reasonable consideration.

Dryden thus freed himself to ascribe to his characters motives and rationalizations that really have little to do with politics. They are motives that in Dryden's view and in that of his readers were universal, applying to all humanity at every period of history. Such motives were the structure beneath politics, and those who claimed to be acting on political grounds were in fact concealing the real motives that led to their actions. "But when to sin our biased nature leans / The careful devil's still at hand with means" (ll. 79–80). All the more reason, therefore, to ignore the pretense of politics, such as the implications of James's Catholicism, to concentrate on the ambition, envy, and malice that were the true motives of political claims. The poet who had written best of them in Christian context was John Milton, and so *Paradise Lost* and, more importantly, *Paradise Regained* are major influences on the poem.

The true nature of motive for political action in *Absalom and Achitophel* can be concisely indicated in the famous "character" of Zimri (ll. 543–568). Like the epic poems to which it is related, *Absalom and Achitophel* contains catalogs of heroes on each side of the conflict, David-Charles's party and those who follow Achitophel-Shaftesbury. Unlike Homer or Virgil, Dryden sees no purpose in balancing these lists, having real heroes on both sides. This is political warfare; the king's supporters are the party of virtue, and Achitophel's are a motley (and much more interesting) crew of villains and failures. Notable among them is Zimri, representing George Villiers, Duke of Buckingham (1628–1687), notorious for the rapidity of his shifts of allegiance and enthusiasm. Dryden was retailing the general opinion that instability was Buckingham's dominant characteristic, but no one else who wrote about him (and there were many) approached Dryden's brilliant epigrammatic finality. His Buckingham displays all the negative possibilities of the "Renaissance man" stereotype.

A man so various that he seemed to be
Not one, but all mankind's epitome:
Stiff in opinions, always in the wrong;
Was everything by starts and nothing long;
But in the course of one revolving moon,
Was chemist, fiddler, statesman, and buffoon:
The all for women, painting, rhyming, drinking,
Beside ten thousand freaks that died in thinking.

(ll. 543–552)

Nothing need be said about Zimri's political principles because he has none. Like all of Achitophel's followers (and the king's) he has adopted his politics and joined his party because of his moral character. Good men stand with the king, and those of various degrees of evil with his Satanic opponent. The contingent and circumstantial nature of real-world politics has been comfortably bypassed, and Dryden can concentrate entirely on the "eternal verities" of human nature, a political maneuver to abjure politics that has also kept his poem accessible and dramatically gripping for over three hundred years.

ABSALOM AND ACHITOPHEL: *THE ACTION OF THE POEM*

The Prologue. In choosing as his subject a particular historical moment—the king's ultimate decision to reassume the full powers delegated to him by God—Dryden was faced with the task of making dramatic an inherently undramatic idea: a change of mind as yet unaccompanied by action.

Most of his poem is retrospective. It shows how the kingdom got into the predicament from which the king's freshened resolve will save it, and this retrospective survey, in the voice of Dryden's indispensable narrator, is immensely witty and uniformly entertaining—so much so that the reader hardly notices that nothing really happens for 230 lines.

Action, however, there is in *Absalom and Achitophel,* but it is mental action; action is speech, and so the action begins when Achitophel begins his first speech to Absalom (ll. 230–302). When the poem reaches that first speech, Dryden has completed an impressive work of scene setting that has effectively disposed of any political, historical, and personal reasons that might be offered for Absalom as successor to David. All that is left is sinful ambition.

The scene setting is, of course, totally biased toward Dryden's Tory point of view, but its wit, its astonishing rhetorical self-possession, and its frequent humor carry all before them. He tackles first what seems to be the weakest element in the king's case, the promiscuity that is entangled with the problem of the successor. Charles had many (eventually fourteen) illegitimate offspring, but his queen was barren, "A soil ungrateful to the tiller's care" (l. 12), as the narrator less than chivalrously puts it. This full quiver establishes that David is not "to blame" for his legitimate childlessness, but it is also a dangerous argument since it implacably proves David's promiscuity. But Dryden's wit and rhetoric effectively draw the fangs of this grave sin (and indeed crime).

… nature prompted, and no law denied
Promiscuous use of concubine and bride;
Then Israel's monarch, after heav'n's own heart,
His vigorous warmth did variously impart
To wives and slaves; and, wide as his command,
Scattered his maker's image through the land.

(ll. 5–10)

Dryden has deftly turned sin into obedience—"after heav'n's own heart"—not expecting to be taken seriously but working to put things in what he sees as proper proportion. David's nature, like God's, is to (pro)create, and so his sins amazingly become evidence of his role as God's vicegerent. His philoprogenitive activities, exactly like his "mildness," are divine attributes that have got out of line and need to be brought under control. The triumph of Dryden's rhetoric in the opening lines of the poem—and he was always a great beginner—is that David's regal standing is increased by this discussion of his sins. In every respect, he is more than most men, and his excesses are the more excusable because they punish him most. This is especially true with respect to his favorite son, Absalom.

The first lines devoted to Absalom (ll. 18–40) seem to be only eulogistic. "Of all this num'rous progeny was none, / So beautiful, so brave, as Absalom." But as the description unfolds, it becomes clear that the narrator is carefully limiting his praise. Absalom's bravery has been demonstrated on the battlefield, and "In peace and thoughts of war he could remove, / And seemed as he were only born for love." His claim to "imperial sway" seems to be based entirely on his "manly beauty." Vague but apparently serious crimes ("Amnon's murder") have been overlooked. All in all, David ought to be possessed by the kind of misgivings that Henry IV has about Prince Hal, but here the king refuses to see his son's limitations and vices. But his brief, first description of Absalom should be enough to convince the reader that this prince is nothing but a playboy, and a dangerous one by reason of his father's favoritism. Could "indulgent David" possibly choose Absalom as his heir?

Having put Absalom in what was for Dryden the proper light, the poem next takes care of the English political and religious nations,

The Jews, a headstrong, moody, murm'ring race,
As ever tried th'extent and stretch of grace;
God's pampered people, whom, debauched with ease,
No king could govern and no God could please....

In twenty-two lines (45–66) Dryden attributes all the constitutional and religious turmoil of the tormented seventeenth century in Britain to the instability of a large proportion of the English people. The century had seen the rise to importance of popular politics, and with that had come the importance of public opinion. Dryden and the Tories despised the public opinion of the unprop-

ertied and less propertied (he always used "democracy" to mean "ochlocracy," mob rule), so he has the chutzpah here to blame their fickle opinions and enthusiasms for the troubles of his lifetime. Fortunately, "The sober part of Israel, free from stain, / Well knew the value of a peaceful reign" and shied away from the memory of the civil wars. Dryden trusted—wrongly—that the sensible majority of the ruling class would always prefer peace to more revolution.

But there remained Catholicism and the Popish Plot. In lines 79 to 149, Dryden deals with the events that precipitated the Exclusion Crisis with the brisk rhetorical ingenuity he has used heretofore. The Catholics, the "Jebusites," are now, whatever they might have been, downtrodden and harmless. The Plot has some truth to it, but it has been turned to more evil purposes by factions of the innately discontented. None of these factions is by itself powerful enough to overthrow royal government, but together, and under the direction of an inspired leader ...

That leader is "the false Achitophel"—Shaftesbury—and Dryden writes a "character" of him (ll. 150–229) that is perhaps the most brilliant passage of character assassination in English literature, certainly on a par with Pope's characters of Sporus and Atticus, and more extensive. When Dryden's character of him ends, nothing Achitophel can say could possibly persuade the reader that he is anything but pernicious. The sheer power of Dryden's language in large parts of *Absalom and Achitophel* is Shakespearean, but he is not writing drama and he is unwilling to take the great Shakespearean risk of letting characters speak mostly for themselves. The narrator's voice in the prologue section of the poem takes no chance that the reader might not follow the path Dryden has chosen for him.

The "Temptation Scene" (ll. 230–490). On the analogy of the temptation of Eve by Satan in *Paradise Lost,* it has become customary to describe the speeches of Achitophel (ll. 230–302), Absalom (ll. 315–372), and Achitophel again (ll. 376–476) as the "temptation scene." This is misleading, however, as to the nature and procedures of the two works. In *Paradise Lost,* the reader has a difficult, though not of course impossible, task to refute on Eve's behalf the arguments of the disguised Satan, who is truly seductive. Dryden takes no chances with Achitophel; he has as much likelihood of success as Satan has with Messiah in *Paradise Regained*. All he says is instantly rejected by the reader, whom Dryden has prepared in the preceding lines. Like Satan with Eve, he flatters, but so egregiously and so blasphemously that Absalom's refusal to reject this view of himself is either tacitly but massively incriminating or the sign of radical stupidity. Achitophel pours it on:

Thy longing country's darling and desire;
Their cloudy pillar and their guardian fire:
Their second Moses, whose extended wand
Divides the seas, and shows the promised land;
Whose dawning day in ev'ry distant age
Has exercised the sacred prophet's rage:
The people's prayer, the glad diviner's theme,
The young men's vision, and the old men's dream!
Thee, savior, thee, the nation's vows confess,
And never satisfied with seeing, bless.

(ll. 232–241)

The absurd Old Testament analogies culminate in a repetition of Peter's use of Joel (2:28–32) in the second chapter of Acts (2:16–21) to announce that the Messiah's time has come.

The arguments follow torrentially to match the excess of the flattery. Achitophel resorts to the emblem book, where Fortune "spreads her locks before her as she flies," but is bald at the back of her head. Absalom must seize her by her hair as soon as she approaches; once past, his handhold and his chance are gone. This banal exhortation, however, deftly conceals a great lie. Fortune did not call David to be king (l. 263); God did, and Achitophel's encouragement for Absalom to seize his fortune is a blasphemous denial of the source of David's authority. Achitophel's chutzpah reaches one of its several peaks in lines 273–274, where David's alleged decline in popularity has him tumbling like Satan from heaven: "Like the prince of angels, from his height / Comes tumbling downwards with diminished light." Satan fell because of ambition, and in *Absalom and Achitophel* the concept is essentially the same as it is in *Macbeth, Julius Caesar,* or *Paradise Lost:* the sin of refusing to

accept one's ordained place in the scheme of things, of believing oneself too good to serve. The individual set up to fall here is Absalom, who like Satan or Phaeton is aspiring beyond his nature and capacity, his ambition fueled by pride. By stupidly applying this analogy to David, Achitophel inadvertently shows who really is like the tumbling prince of angels.

Achitophel's first speech ends with some lines that could be the definition of speciousness:

And nobler is a limited command,
Giv'n by the love of all your native land,
Than a successive title, long and dark,
Drawn from the moldy rolls of Noah's ark.

(ll. 299–302)

How much better to be an "elected" head of state, popular with the populace, than a truly hereditary monarch who relies on his patriarchal succession. (Achitophel's language is another blunder, bringing back into the light patriarchal theory and the definition of legitimate succession.)

Absalom alone. Dryden's narrator seems to be doing his best for Absalom, but the terrible word *ambition* sounds again and again. "What cannot praise effect in mighty minds, / When flatt'ry soothes and when ambition blinds!" (ll. 303–304).

Th'ambitious youth, too covetous of fame,
Too full of angels' metal in his frame,
Unwarily was led from virtue's ways,
Made drunk with honor and debauched with praise.

Absalom's reply is in some ways odd. He appears not to have heard what Achitophel has said, but this must be a shortcut by Dryden. Absalom has heard and absorbed it all, and he now begins a speech (it must be heard by Achitophel but it feels like a soliloquy) that effectively eliminates every conceivable shred of justification there could be for rebelling against David over the matter of succession (ll. 315–372). He begins with a question that he hopes is *not* a rhetorical question—"And what pretence have I / To take up arms for public liberty?"—but as he enumerates David's virtues as monarch—"Mild, easy, humble, studious of our good; / Inclined to mercy, and averse from blood"—the question becomes unavoidably rhetorical: he has no just claim against David (or his brother) and cannot posture as the people's champion against a tyrant. That conclusion is reached in a rhetorical question that amounts to a self-indictment for treason: "Why should I then repine at heav'n's decree, / Which gives me no pretense to royalty?" No justifications, even specious ones, are left standing. All that remains is sinful ambition, cast in Absalom's words into the familiar Satanic mode.

I find, I find my mounting spirits bold,
And David's part disdains my mother's mold.
Why am I scanted by a niggard birth?
My soul disclaims the kindred of her earth;
And, made for empire, whispers me within,
"Desire of greatness is a godlike sin."

(ll. 367–372)

This is the first real step of action in the poem. Absalom has rejected reason and justice and will follow his ambition—to his destruction.

Achitophel's long reply (ll. 376–476) in turn seemingly takes no account of Absalom's speech, though it too must have been heard (ll. 373–374). Achitophel outlines plans to weaken David, and manages to denigrate both paternal and filial love (ll. 423–436). The speech keeps up the self-destructive tic of inadvertently telling the truth, as when Achitophel remarks that the king's brother, the heir to the throne, "Sees through the thin disguises of your arts" (l. 443). The conclusion of the speech is Achitophel's suggestion that the king secretly or perhaps subconsciously wishes Absalom to succeed him, but is afraid of his brother.

If so, by force he wishes to be gained,
Like women's lechery, to seem constrained;
Doubt not, but when he most affects the frown,
Commit a pleasing rape upon the crown.
Secure his person to secure your cause;
They who possess the prince, possess the laws.

(ll. 471–476)

That Absalom accepts the idea of taking his king and father prisoner as merciful and sensible indicates the extent of his delusion. The abhorrent image of the captive Charles I, sold by the Scots to Parliament in 1647, persisted promi-

nently in the English memory of the civil wars. Here as elsewhere, when Dryden seems to be "protecting" Absalom—his "mild nature" recoils from harming David—it turns out that sharp barbs are placed out of sight.

At almost the midpoint of the poem, what has happened is that Absalom has committed himself to evil and has almost unknowingly put himself in the power of his Mephistopheles, Achitophel. The remainder of the poem's action will come about when the implications of Absalom's "fall" have been allowed to ferment in the reader's mind.

The king's foes and Absalom's campaign. Beginning at line 487, Dryden moves away from the title characters of his poem, leaving the memory of their tableau and Absalom's decision until Absalom reenters the poem at line 682. The intervening lines, some of the most memorable in the poem, are devoted to the description of the alliance of the deluded, the self-serving, the fickle, and the fanatical that opposes the king. The account given renders line 682 savagely sarcastic: "Surrounded thus with friends of ev'ry sort, / Deluded Absalom forsakes the court." He leaves the court to go, as would now be said, campaigning. There is a wholly modern air to the account of Absalom traveling the country, gathering "votes" by knowing the names of those he meets, relying heavily on his good looks, and delivering his "stump speech." Absalom's journey, based on Monmouth's "progress" through the West Country, is planned by Achitophel (ll. 739–746) as a sounding-out strategy, and nowadays it would be perfectly routine for Achitophel or his adherents to compose the stump speech for Absalom to deliver six times a day. But speechwriters were not then an institutional feature of political life. Even had they been, Dryden would not have wished for anyone to put words into Absalom's mouth at this point. The speech (ll. 698–722) precedes the account of the "moving court" of the progress (ll. 723–750) and his own words serve chiefly to convict Absalom, to show that he is wholly committed to Achitophel's scheme in pursuit of his own wicked ambition. He presents himself as suffering for the liberties of the people, loyal to his father who is, alas, old, misguided by himself and others, and is about to be succeeded by his vaguely menacing brother.

"Take then my tears" (with that he wiped his eyes),
'Tis all the aid my present pow'r supplies:
No court informer can these arms accuse;
These arms may sons against their fathers use,
And 'tis my wish the next successor's reign
May make no other Israelite complain."

The speech is action in that it is Absalom's crossing of this Rubicon. Hitherto his words have been unpublished, but this speech to crowds of Englishmen sets in motion public events which, at the time the poem was published, had yet to be played out to their fatal conclusion and therefore can only be hinted at by Dryden, though with chilling accuracy.

The "passage on government." Lines 751–810 seem to bring the poem to a stop as Dryden's narrator thinks aloud about the unstable English, their monarchy, the upheavals of his century, and the present challenge to the established manner of succession to the throne. In the strategy of the poem, this intervention functions to build tension a little before the king's friends and the king himself enter the poem, and it introduces a note of common sense and practicality into a discussion that has hitherto been conducted on a princely level against an allusive background of the war in heaven in *Paradise Lost* and the temptations of *Paradise Regained*. "What shall we think!" asks the narrator, pondering the problems of succession, arbitrary government, contract and covenant, and the sovereignty of the people. His answer avoids most theorizing about government and power, and concentrates wholly on practicality and prudence.

Yet, grant our lords the people kings can make,
What prudent men a settled throne would shake?
For, whatsoe'er their suff'rings were before,
That change they covet makes them suffer more.
All other errors but disturb a state,
But innovation is the blow of fate.

(ll. 795–800)

"Innovation" means making all things new, starting from scratch, and this voice of common sense relies on popular memory of the civil wars to reject revolutionary solutions. Nothing is likely to be as bad as a wholly fresh start in government.

To change foundations, cast the frame anew,
Is work for rebels who base ends pursue,
At once divine and human laws control,
And mend the parts by ruin of the whole.

(ll. 805–809)

The passage on government completes the rejection of Achitophel's aims. All principle and all prudence are against him. The poem awaits the king's response: "Now what relief can righteous David bring?"

The king's friends and the king's word. Yet Dryden withholds the king's speech for a while longer by providing a catalog of the king's friends to balance the earlier list of his enemies. Balance, however, is not really possible; the king's friends are few and outnumbered; they cannot save the king. David only can save David by action that is primarily mental.

With all these loads of injuries oppressed,
And long revolving in his careful breast
Th'event of things, at last his patience tired,
Thus from his royal throne, by heav'n inspired,
The godlike David spoke: with awful fear
His train their Maker in their master hear.

(ll. 933–938)

As throughout the poem, there is interesting ambiguity about the circumstances of this speech. It is made from the throne, as if an English king were addressing his two Houses of Parliament, but it is heard apparently only by "his train," his courtiers and adherents. Again, however, the speech sounds like a soliloquy and despite the fact that it is "by heav'n inspired" and is heard "with awful fear" it is a very human speech. David complains that his forgiving nature, his "tenderness of blood," is taken advantage of, and that his power of enduring wrong assumptions about himself is taken for weakness when it is in fact strength. His rebelliously inclined subjects have no real idea of what a king should be. "Kings are the public pillars of the state, / Born to sustain and prop the nation's weight." Absalom is ominously called "my young Samson." If he is willing to pull down the edifice of kingship, "let him share the fall" and be crushed as Samson was. Dryden added lines 957–960, "But oh that yet he would repent and live," to the second edition to reintroduce David's affection for Absalom, for the speech as a whole is decidedly "tough love," though in fact it makes little mention of Absalom (18 lines out of 86) and perhaps none of Achitophel. ("His old instructor" of line 971 might conceivably be Achitophel, but is more likely the fallen angel, Satan.) David's animus is mostly directed at "th'offending age" and "haughty subjects" in general, the whole range of his opponents, and "they" will feel the force of his reluctantly but resolutely resumed power.

Oh that my pow'r to saving were confined:
Why am I forced, like heav'n, against my mind,
To make examples of another kind?
Must I at length the sword of justice draw?
O cursed effects of necessary law!
How ill my fear they by my mercy scan:
Beware the fury of a patient man.

He ends with a prediction of his victory, and there follows a swift wrap-up that startled Samuel Johnson, who wrote of the poem that because "an approach to historical truth was necessary, the action and catastrophe were not in the poet's power," resulting in "an unpleasing disproportion between the beginning and the end" (Johnson, *Works,* London 1825, vol. 8, p. 323). Indeed, the ending still startles today. But Dryden, as Johnson saw, had little choice. In the event, the abject and humiliated Monmouth had to beg his life in vain from his uncle, James II, who had succeeded Monmouth's father, Charles II, in a smooth succession largely made possible by the assertion of royal power that *Absalom and Achitophel* records and recommends. The poem in effect predicts Monmouth's rebellion and execution, but they took place almost four years after the publication of the poem.

LYRIC POEMS

With romanticism, lyric forms of poetry became once again dominant, as they had been in the early seventeenth century. In twentieth-century English poetry they became overwhelmingly dominant as blank verse, the other staple form of Romantic verse, fell away. Narrative became generally uninteresting to poets. Keats's odes, for example, had shown how lyric forms could take on the burden of philosophical and meditative discourse, and the way was cleared for lyric forms, albeit in a nonformal age, to become virtually the only forms of verse.

Dryden's lyric poems, but only two of them, do participate in the historical movement sketched above. For the most part, his lyrics are his minor poems, some of them admirable only for their uniform craftsmanship.

For Dryden, "lyric" is to be literally interpreted; these were poems meant to be set to music. Most of them were written for his plays, where musical interludes were demanded. However, the song "Farewell, fair Armida" was published anonymously in four separate miscellanies in 1672 and does not seem to have been intended for a play.

Farewell, fair Armida, my joy and my grief;
In vain I have loved you and find no relief:
Undone by your virtue, too strict and severe,
Your eyes gave me love, and you gave me despair.
Now, called by my honor, I seek, with content,
A fate which in pity you would not prevent:
To languish in love, were to find by delay
A death, that's more welcome the speediest way.
On seas, and in battles, in bullets and fire,
The danger is less than in hopeless desire.
My death's wound you gave me, though far off I bear
My fate from your sight, not to cost you a tear.
But if the kind flood on the wave should convey,
And under your window my body should lay,
The wound on my breast when you happen to see,
You'll say with a sigh,—
It was given by me.

Dryden never acknowledged this poem, but the evidence for his authorship, though complex, is strong (Hammond, vol. 1, pp. 254–255).

In many respects this lyric is quite conventional. Armida, a name from pastoral and romance, refuses to do more than look amorously on her lover and so she will cause his death. Instead of dying slowly of love, he will find swift death in battle, consoling himself with the hope that she will acknowledge her responsibility and his love if and when she gazes on his dead body. Dryden's submission to the conventions, however, comes with some individual touches. This stanzaic poem has no reason to be stanzaic. It is in couplets, and the indentation of the last two lines of each stanza is a typographical device to give it a stanzaic necessity. The meter, however, is not the iambics of most of Dryden's couplets. Each line comprises an initial iambic foot followed by three anapests, and the rapidity of this meter gives an irresistible lightness to the poem. These people are playacting, and death is part of the play.

Such a meter in such long lines would seem difficult to set to music, though one setting was done almost immediately on publication (Hammond, vol. 1, p. 254). Dryden seems always to have treated his musical collaborators, even Henry Purcell, as decided subordinates. He sent his lyrics and librettos to be set much as he would have sent a picture to be framed or a book to be bound. His verse, in fact, tended to be so musical as to forestall composers, and he would probably have enjoyed what Horace Walpole wrote much later about Handel's music for the 1687 ode: "Though I like Handel, I am not bigoted. I thought Dryden's *Ode* more harmonious before he set it than after."

"Farewell, fair Armida" adds little to and subtracts nothing from Dryden's reputation, but its professionalism and individual touches give it some distinction. Two others of his lyrics, however, are pillars of his reputation and had parts to play in the evolution of lyric forms to their later dominance.

Twice, in 1687 and 1697, Dryden was commissioned to work with a composer to produce an ode to be performed for the annual celebration of St. Cecilia's day, 22 November. Since Cecilia was the patron saint of music, he chose in each case to make music itself the subject, and he dramatized it by employing in both poems two theories of music, one very old, the other more recent.

"Speculative music" is the ancient idea that music is the embodiment of the universal principle of harmony, the "music of the spheres" that,

in the earth-centered Ptolomaic system, sounded among the crystalline spheres of the outer, uncorrupted cosmos. The more modern theory of music's power was the doctrine of *rhythmus* or "affective music" that Dryden had picked up from a 1673 book by Isaac Vossius, who argued that music attained "significance" by imitating in its rhythms the "motions" produced in the mind by the passions and affections. Dryden interpreted this to mean that music had power to control the emotions and thus the motivic impulses of humans, and that various instruments were especially suited to producing specific "affections" in listeners.

These quite complementary theories are present in both the 1687 and 1697 poems, but the first embraces both equally and balances them. *A Song for St. Cecilia's Day, 1687* is a Pindaric ode, in the manner Englished by Abraham Cowley and many times used by Dryden. It has stanzas and lines of irregular length and varied meters, all designed to suggest the not-easily-controllable impulses of passion. (Pindaric odes are poems in praise of someone or something, and Pindaric praise was assumed to be always a tad ecstatic. Horatian odes are far less "wild.") The 1687 "libretto" begins with a stanza on the power of "speculative" music.

From harmony, from heavenly harmony,
This universal frame began:
When nature underneath a heap
Of jarring atoms lay,
And could not heave her head,
The tuneful voice was heard from high
"Arise, ye more than dead."
Then cold, and hot, and moist, and dry,
In order to their stations leap,
And music's power obey.

Nature in its chaotic, unformed state is given form—"created"—by the harmonious voice of God saying (or chanting?) "Let there be light." Chaotic nature is "more than dead" because as yet it has never lived, being never yet formed. The old theory of the four universal elements—it lived longer in poetry than in science—is employed to dramatize music's power, causing the atoms to bound to their assigned places. Dryden's poetry of universal creation and destruction is always magnificent, invalidating any idea that he was successful only in the quotidian of *Mac Flecknoe* or the mythical-historical of *Absalom and Achitophel*.

Stanzas 2 through 7 are devoted to "affective" music: "What passion cannot music raise and quell?" Virtuosity here is the poet's, as he varies his sound effects, especially his meters, to give the "affective" characters of various instruments.

The trumpet's loud clangor
Excites us to arms,
With shrill notes of anger
And mortal alarms. The double double double beat
Of the thundering drum,
Cries "Hark! the foes come:
Charge, charge! 'tis too late to retreat."

(Music here acts *like* a voice, but this is not actually vocal music.) After the tribute to St. Cecilia and the organ, the instrument she was believed to have invented (stanzas 6 and 7), Dryden ends with a "Grand Chorus," one of the most splendid passages in all his work, in which the end of the world is shown to be, paradoxically, quite as harmonious as its beginning.

As from the power of sacred lays
The spheres began to move,
And sung the great creator's praise
To all the blessed above;
So when the last and dreadful hour
This crumbling pageant shall devour,
The trumpet shall be heard on high,
The dead shall live, the living die,
And Music shall untune the sky.

God will signal the end of the earth-centered cosmos with the "last trump," so that music will be the means to "untune" by destruction the "harmonious" universe with its music of the spheres. The final paradox is given great splendor by the triplet, and Dryden finds a superb epithet and metaphor for the collapsing universe: "this crumbling pageant."

In *Alexander's Feast* (1697) "speculative music" makes only a token appearance with St. Cecilia at the end, for most of the poem is one

great demonstration of *rhythmus*. But Dryden introduces some significant changes from the 1687 ode. The poem is very like the libretto of a baroque opera or cantata. (Dryden's verse, however, was here even more difficult for a composer to work with.) It has a dramatic setting. Alexander the Great has completed the conquest of Persia and is holding a feast of celebration, surrounded by his generals and accompanied by his mistress, Thais. The court musician, Timotheus, provides the music at the feat, though the nature of the music is a little vague. A "tuneful choir" is mentioned (l. 21) and Timotheus plays the lyre and, apparently (l. 158) the flute. The trumpets, drums, and hautboys (oboes) of stanza 3 may or may not be played at the feast. The significant fact, however, is that Timotheus' music is primarily vocal. His accompanying instrument is his lyre. *Rhythmus* here is presented as the effect of the poet's sung *words* on the emotions of the conqueror, Alexander, and it is clearly *what* Timotheus sings, rather than the musical accompaniment, that makes Alexander react as the poet's emotional puppet. When Timotheus' song in stanza 3 has raised the king to near madness by reanimating him with drunken victory,

The master saw the madness rise,
His glowing cheeks, his ardent eyes;
And while he heaven and earth defied,
Changed his hand, and checked his pride.
He chose a mournful muse,
Soft pity to infuse....

Timotheus is the "master" of the king's music, of course, but Dryden takes pleasure in showing that he is the master of the king's mind, too ("his glowing cheeks" are Alexander's; "his hand" is Timotheus's, but "his pride" is Alexander's). It can be fairly concluded that by 1697 Dryden was seriously fed up with musicians who rated music as equal to words (composers who found it hard to defer to the poet) and would-be conquerors like Alexander (or, closer to home, William of Orange, who as William III had led Britain into his war with Louis XIV). *Alexander's Feast* establishes the supremacy of the poet over the musician and the king. The poem is routinely subtitled "The Power of Music," but poetry, *articulate* music, emerges as the real power.

JOHN DRYDEN

Most of the nondramatic verse Dryden published is translation, which causes a quite unnecessary problem for his overall reputation and status as a poet. Even verse translation is unthinkingly assumed to be subservient, a lesser kind of thing and therefore to be largely discounted in the estimate of a poet's worth. But subservience in the case of Dryden's translations is nugatory. To translate a tale from Boccaccio's prose to the heroic couplets of late seventeenth-century England (as Dryden did three times in *Fables*) is to employ Boccaccio as a "source" rather than to serve him as a translator. In truth, Dryden did not compose *The Aeneid,* but Homer and Virgil must be translated anew for every age, and Dryden's translation in heroic couplets was the English voice of Virgil for over a hundred years. Verse translation in the last fifteen years of Dryden's life was, however, much more rewarding to him than as a source of income and a way to keep busy writing. After the Revolution of 1688 and his refusal to take the oaths of allegiance to William and Mary, he was to some degree obnoxious to the government and certainly saw himself, to use the modern term, as a "dissident," though both parties were very well-mannered about it. Dryden continued to utter opinions on aspects of the political and church situations in original poems, but he seems to have taken a special pleasure in adapting translations to this purpose. *The Character of a Good Parson; Imitated from Chaucer, And Enlarged* (included in *Fables,* 1700) carries the Parson to the late seventeenth century and positions him to serve as a virtuous contrast to clerical enemies who had attacked Dryden and as an exemplary "non-juror," an Anglican clergyman who refused to swear allegiance to William and Mary. Translation in such a mode (note that Dryden calls it "imitation," and see below, on Dryden's Criticism) goes a long way toward originality and away from subservience, and Dryden's practice as a translator leads to the paradoxical conclusion that in it he found freedom. Ovid, Boccaccio, Chaucer, and Homer served to screen Dryden and to permit him to express himself without appearing in pro-

pria persona, thus strengthening his sense of himself as a dissident.

Dryden's translations now seem to be again getting their due as some of his very best work, and his last volume, *Fables* (1700), has in some degree reclaimed its reputation as his crowning achievement. He himself, however, said (in the preface to *Sylvae,* 1685) that his "masterpiece in English" (which perhaps means "as a translation" and perhaps not) was the version of Horace's Twenty-Ninth Ode of the Third Book, "Tyrrhena regum progenies, tibi...." This is one of the great English poems, the definitive statement of the advantages of "retirement" from the world and of an attitude of philosophical skepticism to the powers of fortune over life.

Happy the man, and happy he alone,
He who can call today his own;
He who, secure within, can say:
"Tomorrow do thy worst, for I have lived today.
Be fair, or foul, or rain, or shine,
The joys I have possessed, in spite of fate, are mine.
Not heav'n itself upon the past has pow'r;
But what has been has been, and I have had my hour."

Dryden's subtitle states that the ode is "Paraphrased in Pindaric Verse" (for "paraphrased" see below, on Dryden's Criticism). By switching the poem from the regular stanzas of the Horatian ode to the irregular and unrepeating Pindaric form, Dryden claimed he was gaining "more latitude," and indeed he was. But most of all it was a step that gave him possession of Horace's poem, made it his own. What we may have here is a poem based on an earlier poem, presented as a translation, but treated with great freedom, that has become as great and as independent a poem as its original. Not that precedence matters. What does matter is that "Odes III, 29" is now a poem by Horace and a poem by Dryden that is far more than a "mere" translation. And there are signs that the translations are now being accorded the respect they should have. Paul Keegan's *New Penguin Book of English Verse* (2000) includes twelve selections from Dryden, seven of which are translations, including Horace's Twenty-Ninth Ode of the Third Book complete.

PLAYS

For most of his professional life, Dryden drew his basic income from the theater. He published more than twenty-five plays in just about all the genres employed on the Restoration stage. Taken all round, his career as a playwright justifies the claim that he was the best of the Restoration writers for the stage. Yet it is a strange truth that his plays make almost no contribution to his modern reputation. They are now the province of specialists in Restoration drama and naturally a great resource for thesis writers, but one has to wait a long time and travel a long way to see a play of Dryden's performed.

This strange situation is owing to circumstances of dramatic history and fashion. Dryden wrote a number of comedies, but several Restoration playwrights wrote comedies that are better than any one of Dryden's. The same applies to tragedy, although *All for Love* is probably the most frequently (though still very rarely) performed of Restoration tragedies. He was successful in mixed genres such as tragicomedy, and worked in masque and opera. His greatest success, however, came in a genre he virtually invented, the "heroic play." Heroic plays were set in remote times and/or remote places: Montezuma's Mexico, the Mogul empire in India, ancient Sparta and Egypt. Their subject is greatness, and their heroes are supermen whose superiority is their eloquence; their greatness is the power of their speech. This form of play has most of the trappings of tragedy but usually has a "happy ending" in that the hero at the end is not dead but victorious, though perhaps a trifle subdued. The universal eloquence of these plays is reinforced in most cases by their being written in iambic pentameter couplets, the "heroic couplets" that became Dryden's (and Pope's) almost invariably chosen meter.

Heroic plays, however, teeter always on the brink of absurdity, and this ever present possibility was perceived from the first by Dryden's critics. A group of them, led by the Duke of Buckingham, produced the burlesque play *The Rehearsal* (1671) in which Dryden appears as the loopy playwright Mr. Bayes, commenting on his absurd heroic drama *The Two Kings of Brentford* for the benefit of two men of common sense, the voices of the audience, Smith and Jones. *The Rehearsal* is far more famous than any of the "straight" heroic plays it burlesques, and Dryden was "Bayes" for a long time afterward. (He had his revenge on Buckingham in *Absalom and Achitophel.*)

When a play of Dryden's does make it to the stage, it is usually *All for Love,* his version of the Antony and Cleopatra story. But *All for Love* taken alone, since it obeys the conventions of neoclassical tragedy, is apt to be a rather dispiriting experience. Dryden's Cleopatra, for instance, can have none of the malice and deviousness that are part of her Shakespearean character. She is a queen, and according to the neoclassical rules of decorum she can never behave like a tart. All the unsuitable aspects of her character are given to her scheming eunuch, Alexas. So the way to appreciate what Dryden achieves in *All for Love* is to take it in the sequence of Shakespeare's *Antony and Cleopatra,* Dryden's play, and G. B. Shaw's *Caesar and Cleopatra.* That would display the three main streams of British drama, but where is the repertory company that could stage those three plays in one season?

CRITICISM

Dryden has a place of importance in the development of English criticism, but in writing criticism he was always first attentive to the advancement of his career. The *Essay of Dramatic Poesy* (1668) is the only "freestanding" work among his critical writings; everything else is "prefixed to," a "preface to" or "a defence of" one of Dryden's works. Thus his ideas about the nature and procedures of poetic satire are to be found in "A Discourse Concerning the Original and Progress of Satire" prefixed to *The Satires of ... [Juvenal] ... Together with the Satires of ... Persius* (1693), as well as more incidentally in such items as the preface "To the Reader" before *Absalom and Achitophel.* His first objective was to guide his readers to a sympathetic understanding of his poetry and plays or to refute the criticisms that came forth so abundantly in the Restoration literary world. His lasting worth as a critic is measured by the degree to which his criticism survives its primary, apologetic purpose and contributes to the lasting corpus of critical discourse.

Dryden's ideas about translation provide a convenient example of the manner in which he served his immediate end of shaping his reader's responses and of laying down the principles of his own practice. Dryden's major statement on translation is found in the preface to *Ovid's Epistles Translated by Several Hands* (1680). (Dryden translated Epistles II and XVIII, and collaborated with Mulgrave on XIII.) He begins briskly and imperiously: "All translation I suppose may be reduced to these three heads," and they are *metaphrase,* or literal, word for word, line by line translation; *paraphrase,* "or translation with latitude, where the author is kept in view by the translator, so as never to be lost, but his words are not so strictly followed as his sense, and that too is admitted to be amplified, but not altered" (Saintsbury, p. 16); and *imitation,* which is very free indeed, and "where the translator (if now he has not lost that name) assumes the liberty not only to vary from the words and sense, but to forsake them both as he sees occasion" (Saintsbury, p. 16). Dryden is clearly comfortable with the tripartite division, for it places the subject of translation in the framework of ethical decision making that was so commonplace as to be instinctive in the seventeenth and eighteenth centuries. It derives distantly from the *Nicomachean Ethics* of Aristotle, and in its common form is a method of finding the reasonable and correct course of conduct by defining the unacceptable extremes on either side of that middle path. Dryden's decision for "paraphrase, or translation with latitude" is arrived at by dismissal of literal translation and "imitation." "Imitation and verbal version are ... the two extremes which ought to be avoided: and therefore when I have proposed the mean betwixt them, it will be seen how far this argument will reach" (Saintsbury, p. 22). The dismissal of imitation and "servile literal translation" is undertaken with gusto, but it is noteworthy that in describing his middle way, paraphrase, Dryden is not really concise or apparently anxious to produce a hard-edged definition. The

author's meaning, his "sense," is sacrosanct; that much is certain, but the translator has liberty to choose those words and expressions that best convey the author's meaning in the translation language. Dryden in fact is codifying common sense and allowing himself the freedom necessary to produce a readable translation that does not stray much from the original's ideas and not too much more from its words. That is the practice he adopted for his Virgil and his other translations. And it is the course that Pope too followed in his translation of Homer.

The firmness, even fierceness, with which Dryden the critic speaks against imitation, however, is misleading when one looks at the bigger picture. His 1680 opinion was later substantially modified by experience, particularly political experience. We have noted above that he found imitation to be a convenient way of supporting the position of the "non-jurors" of the Church of England (*The Character of a Good Parson; Imitated from Chaucer ...*), where his disapproval of imitation changes to complete acceptance. He seems to have intended when he wrote it that his definition should warn off would-be imitators, but in fact circumstances made imitation one of the great genres of eighteenth-century English poetry. In Dryden's discussion of it, his expanded definition roughly describes the practice of Pope in his *Imitations of Horace* and of Samuel Johnson in his two imitations of Juvenal, *London* and *The Vanity of Human Wishes.* "I take imitation of an author ... to be an endeavour of a later poet to write like one who has written before him on the same subject: that is, not to translate his words, or to be confined to his sense, but only to set him as a pattern, and to write as he supposes that author would have done had he lived in our age and our country" (Saintsbury, p. 19). Dryden here as usually elsewhere is writing criticism that is more prescriptive than descriptive, and like most prescriptive criticism it fails to make a close fit with any particular text. His prescriptive criticism will always be of great value to specialists, but for more general readers his descriptive criticism is more amiable and inspiring; it inspires one to read, which is a critic's greatest power.

The preface to *Fables* (1700), which consciously adopts the discursive manner of Montaigne and discusses the writers included in the volume, conveys above all "gusto," delight in the poets' achievements. At the present time, when criticism seems to aspire to the status of a science, this will seem sentimental and naive, but it is nonetheless Dryden's best criticism.

But enough of this [his discussion of Chaucer's breadth of characterization]; there is such a variety of game springing up before me, that I am distracted in my choice, and know not which to follow. 'Tis sufficient to say, according to the proverb, that here is God's plenty. We have our forefathers and great grand-dames all before us as they were in Chaucer's days; their general characters are still remaining in mankind, and even in England, though they are called by other names than those of Monks, and Friars, and Canons, and Lady Abbesses, and Nuns. For mankind is ever the same, and nothing lost out of nature, though everything is altered.

(Saintsbury, p. 230)

Selected Bibliography

WORKS OF JOHN DRYDEN

EDITIONS

The Works of John Dryden. Edited by George Saintsbury, 18 vols. Edinburgh: W. Paterson, 1882–93. (All page citations in the text refer to this edition, cited in this article as "Saintsbury.")

The Letters of John Dryden. Edited by Charles E. Ward. Durham, N.C.: Duke University Press, 1942.

The Works of John Dryden, 20 vols. Edited by E. N. Hooker, H. T. Swedenberg, Jr., and others. Berkeley: University of California Press, 1956–2000. (Almost completed, this is the standard scholarly edition. Old spelling, good annotation.)

The Poems of John Dryden. Edited by James Kinsley. Oxford: Clarendon Press, 1958. (Old spelling, sparse notes. Poems in this article are cited from Kinsley, thoroughly modernized.)

John Dryden: Selected Criticism. Edited by James Kinsley and George Parfitt. Clarendon Press: Oxford, 1970.

The Poems of John Dryden, 5 vols. Edited by Paul Hammond and David Hopkins. London and New York: Longman Annotated English Poets. 1995–2005. (Modernized text, extensive, indispensable notes. Cited in this article as "Hammond.")

Virgil's Aeneid: Translated by John Dryden. Edited by Frederick M. Keener. London and New York: Penguin Classics, 1997.

John Dryden: Selected Poems. Edited by Stephen N. Swicker and David Bywaters. Penguin Classics, 2001. (Modernized text. Good introduction, selection, and notes.)

CRITICAL AND BIOGRAPHICAL STUDIES

Bywaters, David A. *Dryden in Revolutionary England.* Berkeley: University of California Press, 1991.

Eliot, T. S. *Homage to John Dryden: Three Essays on Poetry of the Seventeenth Century.* (1924). London: Hogarth Press, 1927.

———. *John Dryden, the Poet, the Dramatist, the Critic: Three Essays.* New York; Terence and Elsa Holliday, 1932.

Frost, William *Dryden and the Art of Translation.* New Haven, Conn.: Yale University Press, 1955.

Garrison, James D. *Dryden and the Tradition of Panegyric.* Berkeley: University of California Press, 1975.

Haley, K. D. H. *The First Earl of Shaftesbury.* Oxford: Clarendon Press, 1968. (A factual account of Dryden's fictional Achitophel.)

Hammond, Paul. *John Dryden: A Literary Life.* New York: St. Martin's Press, 1991. (Covers Dryden's entire literary career.)

———. *Dryden and the Traces of Classical Rome.* Oxford: Clarendon Press, 1999.

Harth, Phillip. *Contexts of Dryden's Thought.* Chicago: University of Chicago Press, 1968.

———. *Pen for a Party: Dryden's Tory Propaganda in its Contexts.* Princeton, N.J.: Princeton University Press, 1993.

Hill, Geoffrey. *The Enemy's Country: Words, Contexture, and Other Circumstances of Language.* Palo Alto, Calif.: Stanford University Press, 1991.

Kinsley, James, and Helen Kinsley, eds. *Dryden: The Critical Heritage.* London: Routledge and Kegan Paul, 1971.

McFadden, George. *Dryden, the Public Writer, 1660–1685.* Princeton, N.J.: Princeton University Press, 1978.

Reverand, Cedric D., II. *Dryden's Final Poetic Mode: The "Fables."* Philadelphia: University of Pennsylvania Press, 1988.

Winn, James Anderson. *John Dryden and His World.* New Haven, Conn.: Yale University Press, 1987. (The standard biography. Indispensable.)

Zwicker, Steven N. *Dryden's Political Poetry: The Typology of King and Nation.* Providence, R.I.: Brown University Press, 1972.

———. *Politics and Language in Dryden's Poetry: The Arts of Disguise.* Princeton, N.J.: Princeton University Press, 1984.

LAWRENCE DURRELL

(1912—1990)

Tadzio Koelb

ONCE REGULARLY COMPARED to Marcel Proust and widely expected to win the Nobel Prize for Literature, Lawrence Durrell is today something of a cult author, as earnestly admired by a small but durable group of fans as he is derided by his critics. To some extent the victim of changing fashions, his reputation was tarnished even during his lifetime by a series of later books written perhaps too fast, under the increasing influence of alcohol, and in any case with little regard for the market. Meanwhile, the suicide of his second daughter, Sappho, resulted in public accusations of cruelty that long blackened the author's name.

Now best remembered for *The Alexandria Quartet,* the first of his several multivolume works of fiction, Durrell's initial reputation was made as a poet, and his income as an author was chiefly assured by his travel memoirs of Mediterranean islands; a series of Wodehousian short stories also sold well. In addition, Durrell published verse plays, criticism, and an adventure novel.

Durrell benefited throughout his career from the support of such giants of modernism as T. S. Eliot, who became his editor at Faber & Faber, and Henry Miller, with whom he began a lasting friendship after reading *Tropic of Cancer* (1934); he also enjoyed close but sometimes stormy relations with Anaïs Nin. Born twenty to twenty-five years later than most of his closest literary "colleagues," and achieving his earliest renown only in middle age (he published *Justine,* the first volume of *The Alexandria Quartet,* in 1957, when he was forty-five), Durrell wrote at a time and in a style that sat uncomfortably between movements in literature, and the title "last of the modernists," bestowed by Philip Howard, his obituarist in the London *Times* (quoted in Bowker, p. 426), might well turn out to be only half the

story, with much of his later work now reclaimed for postmodernism.

ESCAPING THE ENGLISH DEATH

Lawrence George Durrell was born February 27, 1912, in Jullundur (now Jalandhar), in what was then the Indian Empire. His parents were Indian-born British colonials, and despite a successful career, his father suffered from a lifelong sense of inferiority: he had never been to university and, worse still, spoke with a colonial accent. In order to save his son from inheriting this class anxiety, he sent young Larry to attend boarding school at "home" in England. Durrell despised everything about the mother country, which he and his brother Gerald nicknamed "Pudding Island": the weather, the confined spaces, and, above all, the middle-class propriety, the "useless and ineradicable lumber—the proverbs, practices, and precepts of a dead life in a dead land" (*The Black Book,* p. 44).

Durrell's father died in 1928. Durrell's mother, Louisa, brought Larry's two brothers and his sister to England; they all lived together while Larry repeatedly failed his university entrance exams. It wasn't always easy, but Durrell enjoyed being with his family and had even found some things to love about Pudding Island. He began collecting editions of the Elizabethan dramatists, whose ribald humor matched his own, and he enjoyed being a part of London's lively bohemian scene, playing jazz and exchanging poetry with a group of colorful characters from the literary demimonde. Better still, he brought out three volumes of verse and was preparing to publish his first novel, *Pied Piper of Lovers* (1935): Larry was becoming a professional author.

His father's death had left the family in a precarious financial state, however, and his mother was not good with money. Larry, "designed by Providence to go through life like a small, blond firework, exploding ideas in other people's minds" (Gerald Durrell, p. 15), moved the whole Durrell clan—now including his first wife, Nancy—to the Greek island of Corfu. Life there was sunny, relaxed, and blissfully cheap. The family enjoyed a regular flow of visitors, and Larry made many lasting Greek friends, including such literary figures as George Katsimbalis and George Seferis. It was from Corfu that Durrell first wrote to Henry Miller, the overture to a friendship that was to prove of immediate professional and lasting personal importance, and it was here, also, that he began making notes for a major work of fiction under the working title "The Book of the Dead."

Despite the fact that Durrell never returned to the country of his birth (which in an important sense ceased to exist with the end of the Raj in 1947), he always defined himself by his colonial childhood, even if some of what he recalled—for example, his claim that Everest was to be seen from his school dorm window—was invention. Indeed, much of his adult life was spent looking for a place where he could recapture the sense of youthful wonder he felt had been taken from him prematurely. For many years, that place was Greece, which he perceived as England's virile opposite, "a wild garden with everything running to ruin—violent, vertical, sky-thrusting … undomesticated" (*The Greek Islands*, p. 15).

The outbreak of World War II ended this idyll. Louisa and the others returned to England immediately, but Larry and Nancy stayed on. They were eventually forced to make a complicated escape, taking their young daughter, Penelope, by boat via Crete to Egypt, a voyage that brought them dangerously close to patrolling German ships. Nancy and Penelope continued on to British Palestine, effectively ending what had become a difficult and unhappy marriage. The composition of Durrell's first important novel, *The Black Book* (1938), had played a major role in the breakup, Larry writing in a frenzied state punctuated by vicious outbursts.

Remaining in Egypt, Durrell landed a position as a British press attaché and successfully redirected government resources to produce a literary magazine to which he and his friends could contribute. Thus began a career in His Majesty's employment that lasted for many years to come, Durrell's vocal distaste for England notwithstanding.

Durrell claimed not to like Egypt, either, but his time there was fertile. He wrote a good deal of poetry and published his first major collection, *A Private Country* (1943), while living in Cairo. More importantly, he discovered multicultural Alexandria, "the capital of memory" (*Clea*, p. 11), which a decade later became the backdrop to what was then still called "The Book of the Dead." It was also where he met his second wife, Yvette Cohen (known as Eve), on whom he based the most famous character of his career, a woman "gorged upon introspection" (*Justine*, p. 202), the Alexandrian Jewess and femme fatale, Justine.

After the war ended in Europe, Durrell stayed with the British government, moving to Rhodes to accept a job as public information officer with the British military protectorate. His reputation as a writer continued to grow: he published the poetry collection *Cities, Plains, and People* (1946) and a minor novel, *Cefalû* (1947; later retitled *The Dark Labyrinth*), and was able on the strength of this to land a position with the British Council in Argentina. In 1949 he returned to Europe and the diplomatic corps as press attaché to the British embassy in Yugoslavia.

If Durrell disliked Egypt, he hated Argentina and despised Soviet Europe. In reaction to what he saw of life under Communism, he sometimes afterward declared himself a Fascist, even if his politics remained essentially Tory and his life and writing both apolitically antiestablishment. (This was typical of his love for shocking statements. He also claimed to be an anti-Semite, despite marrying two Jewish women and writing many important—and, by and large, sympathetic—Jewish characters into his work.) His time in Belgrade was made especially wretched when the birth of a daughter, Sappho Jane, sent Eve, already unhappy, into a debilitating depression. Eve left in search of treatment; offered a job on Cyprus, Durrell rushed back to the comfort of the Mediterranean. An attempted reconciliation there with Eve failed, and Larry once again found himself alone. He threw himself into his work.

Durrell became first director of information services and then government press censor with Britain's administration on the island, which was a crown colony. At first it seemed the perfect opportunity to return to the Greek culture he loved while maintaining an income large enough to provide for his children, but later he came to worry that his public association with an unpopular occupying power had made him persona non grata, not just on Cyprus, but in Athens, which had vainly sought sovereignty over the island. Durrell began sleeping with a pistol, and he ultimately fled following violent anti-British demonstrations during which a bomb exploded near where he was staying. A house that he purchased on Cyprus would remain empty for decades, and it was years before he found the courage to revisit Greece.

While his departure from the Greek world was wrenching, he did bring away with him the future third Mrs. Durrell, Claude-Marie Forde, and the final draft of the manuscript he had been preparing for twenty years, "The Book of the Dead," now called after its central character: Justine. In fact, Durrell was in the midst of an incredibly prolific period. In 1957 he published not only *Justine* but also his first collection of Antrobus stories, *Esprit de Corps,* comic vignettes about diplomatic life in a Belgrade-like Balkan capital (which for the next several decades was considered required reading for anyone embarking on a life in the Foreign Service); *Bitter Lemons,* the third of his well-received travel books (this one, about Cyprus, awarded the Duff Cooper Memorial Prize); several poems; and an adventure novel, *White Eagles over Serbia.* In addition, his verse play, *Sappho* (published by Faber in 1950), a heavily fictionalized episode from the life of the poet, had its first performance on BBC radio.

Claude was certainly fundamental to this creative explosion. Half-French, half-Jewish, raised in Alexandria, and herself a novelist, she understood what Durrell what trying to do and knew intimately the city about which he was writing. She also seemed to withstand better than his first two wives the violent furies to which he was increasingly prone while working. She may have served as a model for Clea, the bisexual painter in *The Alexandria Quartet* by whose grace the narrator, L. G. Darley, earns redemption through sex and art.

The couple needed a new base, one that was less expensive than England. They finally chose Provence, which Claude knew well, and settled down in a local farmhouse, a *mazet* without indoor plumbing, to write their respective novels. Durrell worked hard, in 1958 producing both *Balthazar* and *Mountolive*—the second and third installments of the *Quartet*—and a new Antrobus collection, *Stiff Upper Lip. Clea,* the last Alexandria book, appeared in 1960, and Durrell was encouraged by a successful German production of *Sappho* (he received numerous curtain calls) to return to drama as well; he published *An Irish Faustus* in 1963 and *Acte* in 1964. As interest in the author grew, publishers responded with a *Collected Poems* (1960) and two volumes of correspondence.

Durrell quickly came to love France, and he would live there for the rest of his life. His adopted home returned the affection: *Justine* and *Balthazar,* both treated with some skepticism by early reviewers in the U.K., were met with ecstatic praise in France, and each was awarded a Prix du Meilleur Livre Étranger. In 1989, he was the first recipient of the Grand Prix Littéraire de la Ville d'Antibes.

The pace at which Durrell was working eventually proved unsustainable. Although written at speed—he claimed that *Justine* was completed in only four months—his *Quartet* was nevertheless the result of two decades' contemplation and research. It was perhaps to be expected, then, that his next novel, the two-volume distopian satire *The Revolt of Aphrodite,* took nearly ten years to materialize: *Tunc* appeared in 1968 and *Nunquam* in 1970.

He released two other books in the meantime. One was a new collection of poetry, *The Ikons and Other Poems* (1960). The other, a third Antrobus collection called *Sauve Qui Peut* (1966), was a lackluster affair suggesting the vein had been depleted; the character was duly retired.

The Revolt of Aphrodite fared little better, receiving a chilly reception from most critics.

Claude suffered a long illness, ending with her death in 1967, which goes some way to explaining this apparent falling off. Durrell was devastated by the loss. His behavior became more erratic—for nine years he kept Claude's ashes in a plastic Air France bag in a closet—his drinking and violence more ferocious. His fourth wife, Ghislaine, although deeply in love with him, rarely lived in his house during their brief marriage—not surprising, considering that Durrell had threatened her at gunpoint.

Durrell decided to press ahead with another ambitious multivolume work, *The Avignon Quintet*. With the institutional lag that often sees inventive and challenging artists rewarded only for later work, *The Avignon Quintet*—comprising *Monsieur* (1974), *Livia* (1978), *Constance* (1982), *Sebastian* (1983), and *Quinx* (1985)—was, despite meeting with almost universal critical disappointment, given a great deal of attention by the British literary establishment, attention his Alexandria books had not received: *Monsieur* won the James Tait Black Memorial award, and *Constance* was short-listed for the Booker Prize. Whatever pleasure he may have had from this was short-lived: as he was finishing *Quinx,* his daughter Sappho hanged herself in the wake of her fifth abortion and a series of broken relationships.

Throughout the 1970s and 1980s, Durrell continued to write travel books, and he was also involved in the publication of several collected works, including an omnibus edition of his Antrobus stories, volumes of correspondence, and *Collected Poems 1931–1974* (1980), spanning practically his entire career. He was still writing when he died on November 7, 1990, of emphysema, aged seventy-eight. His final book, *Caesar's Vast Ghost* (1990), completed not long before his death, is an unusual mixture of autobiography, poetry, and travelogue, all genres in which he worked, the skills gathered from which he had mixed with such potency to create the *Quartet.* And indeed, it is the *Quartet,* for most readers, that stands as "the splendid culmination of Durrell's work," as Carl Bode wrote in 1961, for

which every available source was put to use, "the brightly decorated travel books, the crude early novels, the elegant, allusive poetry: Durrell drew on all these … He levied on everything, it would seem, that he had ever thought to write about. He levied on his life" (Bode, p. 531).

INTO THE LABYRINTH

It may indeed be said that while Durrell worked in many genres, he hardly ever worked in just one; even his travel books were probably to some extent fictional, for example, insofar as they featured colorful characters invented to act as spokesmen for what Durrell considered the *spiritus loci,* which was so important to all his work. This disregard for boundaries reflected Durrell's apparent intent to break what he saw as artificial barriers in art, whether between genres or between the artist and his work. As he wrote in his *Key to Modern British Poetry,*

> Literature is only one facet of the prism which we call culture. All the arts and sciences are simply different dialects of the same language, all contribute towards an attitude to life. What is this "culture"? I take this word to mean the sum, at any given time, of all the efforts man is making to interpret the universe about him. Ideas from the various departments of thought cross fertilize each other, and it is sometimes a good idea to discuss one kind of thought in terms of another.
>
> (pp. 1–2)

It also meets the urgent and, in his final novels, all-consuming demands of Durrell's sense of the self as fragmented or recurring: these invented others speak, after all, on behalf of the author and are therefore parts of him.

Starting with *The Black Book,* it becomes especially difficult to extract Durrell from his fiction: the author is now implicated not just as a source of material but to some extent as a character in his own work. After all, as he asserted in an interview with John Hawkes at Pennsylvania State University, "One creates and recreates other people and is in turn recreated by them" (Hawkes and Durrell, p. 414). To further associate the author with his fiction, clearly labeled versions of Durrell turn up regularly in his work: as the narrators Lawrence Lucifer in *The Black Book* and L. G. Darley in *The Alexandria Quartet* (Durrell's given names were Lawrence George) and, although Felix Charlock is generally considered the "Durrell" character in *The Revolt of Aphrodite,* most straightforwardly in that book as a poet named Durrell.

By the end of *The Avignon Quintet* we are confronted with a novel about a novelist, Blanford, who has written a novel about himself in the guise of a character, Sutcliffe, also a novelist, who is writing a novel featuring a novelist, with other writers entering the equation at various levels. This group includes Durrell, who writes himself into the story in "Envoi," the blank-verse postscript to *Monsieur,* as D.—he who "begat / Blanford (who begat Tu and Sam and Livia) / who begat / Sutcliffe" (p. 309). It is not surprising perhaps that the last line of fiction Durrell ever published conjures the ghost, if not the fact, of a looping circle bringing us away again from fiction, and that this eviction from the imaginary does little or nothing to establish consistency: "It was at this precise moment that reality prime rushed to the aid of fiction and the totally unpredictable began to take place!" (*Quinx,* p. 201).

HIS REAL VOICE

While *The Black Book: An Agon* doesn't attempt this level of complexity, it is the first instance in which Durrell used many of the techniques that later allowed him to investigate issues arising from his vision of the discontinuous self, most notably the layering of multiple narrative voices, and it demonstrates a growing fascination with many of the themes that occupied him for the rest of his life.

An impressionist rather than strictly plot-based novel, *The Black Book* presents the chaotic reminiscence of a former schoolteacher and fledgling writer who has escaped moribund England for a small Greek island. Calling himself "Lawrence Lucifer," he describes his past residence at the Regina Hotel, a London lodging house, and the people he knew there, particularly the girl he loved and to whom the story is in some parts addressed. Lucifer also quotes at length from the diaries of a former Regina resident, Herbert "Death" Gregory, whose relationship with a prostitute suffering from tuberculosis becomes a terrible obsession. While Lucifer has escaped by retreating to the Mediterranean and a more primitive but honest life, Gregory appears to have lived up to his chosen name, Death, and succumbed.

First appearing in an Obelisk Press edition in Paris in 1938, *The Black Book* was not published in the United States until 1960 or in the U.K. until 1977, and it was long the missing link in the public record of Durrell's growth as an artist. Durrell had already brought out two minor novels, *Pied Piper of Lovers* (1935) and *Panic Spring* (1936), the second under a pseudonym. It was while writing *The Black Book,* however, that he "first heard [his] real voice" (*The Black Book,* p. 14). It is certainly his first major accomplishment as a novelist, and it is probably a masterpiece in the original sense of the word: a demonstration that his apprenticeship was complete. Although it contains some derivative passages—mostly showing the influence of Miller—it also serves as an important template for his later work. Added to the model of his first two novels—autobiographical stories strongly influenced by location—were the strong, highly poetic prose style that afterward marked his fiction, the large multinational cast of characters, a vein of dark humor, and an insistence on explicit sexuality.

Durrell famously sent Henry Miller his only copy of the manuscript and asked that after reading it, Miller throw it into the Seine. Miller instead praised the pages and returned them. When Faber & Faber suspected *The Black Book* would break UK indecency laws, and was unwilling to publish without substantial cuts, Miller arranged for the novel to be released in France by the fearless Jewish publisher (and sometimes pornographer) Jack Kahane, whose Villa Seurat series included the "indecent" work of both Miller and Nin. T. S. Eliot wrote for *The Black Book*'s jacket that it was "the first piece of work by a new English writer to give me any hope for the future of prose fiction." It seemed that Durrell's talent had at last emerged—but only partly so: since it could not legally be sold in Britain, *The Black Book* went mostly unnoticed there.

THEN OR NEVER

It is hard to imagine any contemporary author of ambition beginning an important work exactly as he had begun a previous one twenty years earlier, but that is precisely what Durrell did with the first novel of *The Alexandria Quartet*: *Justine* opens with a British former schoolteacher and would-be novelist, isolated on a Greek island, recalling his past.

Given Durrell's success as a travel writer and his growing reputation as both novelist and poet, the first pages of *The Alexandria Quartet* might seem like a step backward. In some ways this makes perfect sense: the work, in the form of dozens of notebooks, had been gestating since the 1930s as "The Book of the Dead," intended to be, much like *The Black Book,* an examination of a lifeless England. Durrell's vision had naturally evolved with time, however, influenced by his travels, the disintegration of two marriages, and the long and painful separation from his daughters, and this return to the beginning of *The Black Book* launches a very different kind of novel—or rather, it initiates a series of novels meant to follow a new form.

In Alexandria, a "spiritual city underlying the temporal one" (*Justine,* p. 95), Justine herself has lost a child, taken from her not long after it was born; she also lost her own childhood to rape by a distant male relative. These misfortunes haunt her and impede any normal relationship. She has married the Coptic banker Nessim Hosnani, to whom she cannot be faithful, on the understanding that he will use his wealth and power to locate her child.

The narrator, as yet unnamed (we will later learn he is called L. G. Darley), lives with Melissa, a cabaret dancer, and is in love, but nevertheless begins an affair with Justine. It becomes clear that Nessim knows of their relationship, and they expect him to take revenge, probably at the annual duck hunt on Lake Mareotis, where an excess of firearms will easily make Darley's death look accidental. In the end, however, it is Capodistria, now revealed as the rapist of Justine's childhood, who is killed. Her vengeance enacted, Justine disappears.

The story is told in a highly fragmented way, jumping across time as the narrator follows different paths through his memory. This concern with the fragmentary is woven into the writing in various ways (in fact, it is a trademark of Durrell's writing that even the most seemingly insignificant events offer important thematic ties to the work as a whole), as when Justine says of her own multiple reflections in a group of mirrors: "Look! five different pictures of the same subject. Now if I wrote I would try for a multidimensional effect in character, a sort of prism-sightedness. Why should not people show more than one profile at a time?" (p. 27).

Durrell's language is masterfully lush, with many passages (particularly those devoted to landscape) poetic and even flamboyant—too much so for critics trained, according to George Steiner in his defense of Durrell's style, "to the harsh, impoverished cadence and vocabulary of Hemingway" (p. 282). A large cast is introduced, and several subplots coalesce over the course of the book, some of which will become more important as the *Quartet* advances. We meet Scobie, for example, a cross-dressing English sailor who becomes an officer in the secret service and hires the narrator to spy on his friends when they meet to study kabbalah with the old homosexual physician, Balthazar. We learn that Pursewarden, the famous, urbane, and condescending English novelist against whom the narrator must measure himself, will commit suicide.

Meanwhile, Nessim and Melissa have an affair of their own, and it is Nessim's daughter the narrator carries away with him to Greece after Melissa dies in childbirth. The book ends on a note that sets the tone for all that is to come: "Does not everything depend on our interpretation of the silence around us?" (p. 245).

As if to underline this question, the second volume, *Balthazar* (1958), begins with the arrival on Darley's island of the old doctor. Balthazar has read the manuscript readers know as *Justine*, and he intends to set the record straight. He returns the copy Darley sent him, now covered with a detailed handwritten commentary; it is, Balthazar says, like a "medieval palimpsest where different sorts of truth are thrown down one upon the other, the one obliterating or perhaps supplementing another" (p. 183). It seems Darley must revisit events a second time and make what he knows of the past fit with what Balthazar reveals in his "Interlinear," including several incidents that took place after Darley quit Alexandria for the Cyclades.

Reading Balthazar's commentary, Darley learns he must again take a backseat to Pursewarden. According to the Interlinear, Justine began her relationship with Darley to put Nessim off the track: it was Pursewarden she truly loved, and she feared what would happen to him if their affair were discovered.

It seems as well that Scobie might have been right to suspect Darley's friends: *Balthazar* centers on a plot led by Nessim and his brother Narouz to recreate Egypt as a Coptic state with the help of Zionists fighting the British Mandate in Palestine. Scobie himself has not lived to know of this—British sailors murdered him when he was discovered cruising the port in drag. Alexandria won't let him disappear entirely, however: locals who believe the old man's bathtub can impart fertility revere him as a saint, El Skob.

The book again eschews a linear approach, and Darley's reconstruction of events based on the Interlinear causes him to remember and relate the death at a costume ball of Toto de Brunel, a diplomat and probable spy. Darley understands now that the murder was a case of mistaken identity. This revelation, so in keeping with the book's themes, seems to imply that finally the hidden motives behind each action have been revealed—and yet the reader must judge carefully how much of this to accept: the truth, according to Balthazar, "is what most contradicts itself in time" (p. 23), and Pursewarden suggests that "there are only as many realities as you care to imagine" (p. 152). If this is the case, then what,

the reader must ask, can really be known of the events that took place in Alexandria?

The next volume, *Mountolive* (1958), seems at first glance to answer this. A much more chronologically simple account, it is the only volume presented in the third person and not narrated from the point of view of Darley, which seemingly isolates it from the sense of subjectivity that has been so central to the work thus far. In this ostensibly direct way we learn the early history of the Hosnani brothers and follow their relationship with the diplomat David Mountolive. As a young man stationed in Egypt, Mountolive had an affair with their mother, Leila, and the two remain friends, corresponding by letter as Mountolive travels the world for his work.

Mountolive returns now as ambassador, but his tenure begins badly when he decides to place his trust in Pursewarden: many at the embassy believe Pursewarden has willingly overlooked evidence of a Hosnani conspiracy against the closely linked British and Egyptian governments. When the cult of personality developing around the increasingly fanatical Narouz finally makes the situation impossible to ignore, Pursewarden admits his treachery to Mountolive, warns Nessim that the British have been alerted, and, overwhelmed by his double betrayal, commits suicide.

The Egyptian government comes down hard on the conspirators. Narouz is killed, and Nessim loses his fortune. If Nessim's fate is not worse, it is because Leila pleads on his behalf with Mountolive; the ambassador yields but, in a scene that comes to represent his experience of Egypt, is shocked to see his former lover's once beautiful face destroyed by illness.

As later emerges, it would be wrong to think of this "authoritative" account as the final word. Seemingly the most straightforward, *Mountolive* is also in some ways the most mysterious section of the *Quartet*. The sudden absence of first-person narration raises above all the question of voice: is there, in such a work, a "narrator"—and if so, who? Could it be Mountolive himself, for example, rehearsing the official version of the story as he will present it to his superiors at the Foreign Office? Most intriguing is the possibility that *Mountolive* could and indeed should be interpreted as a novel by the author L. G. Darley, the guiding consciousness of the other three books, using his memories as the basis for a fictional (or at least conjectural) interpretation of the events readers already know. In this light, the novel can be viewed as Darley's attempt to shape and thereby control the past and as an important breakthrough in his quest to step out of the shadow of Pursewarden, whose suicide is a major plot point in the book.

In an introduction to *Balthazar*, Durrell laid out his plan for the *Quartet*, a "'science-fiction' in the true sense." He suggests that since "modern literature offers us no Unities," he has turned to science, specifically relativity, for the structure of his "sibling" novels: "The first three parts ... are not linked in serial form. They interlap, interweave, in a purely spatial relation. The fourth part alone will represent time and be a true sequel" (p. 5). He specifies that his method is neither Proustian nor Joycean, both of which "illustrate Bergsonian 'Duration' ... not 'Space-Time'" (p. 5).

Of course that there exists a "purely spatial relation" is not strictly accurate: time enters the equation even as *Balthazar* begins (the manuscript of *Justine* must after all exist before Balthazar can impose his Interlinear commentary), and the fall of the Hosnanis in *Mountolive* postdates the first two books by some time; Durrell's approach is both more complex and less correctly "scientific" than he admits. The fourth novel, *Clea* (1960), nevertheless advances the story much further in time than do the others.

It has been some years, and Darley returns to Alexandria. Things have changed: Pursewarden and Scobie are dead, and Justine is no longer an obsession for him. Nessim, fallen from power and persecuted by the government, has lost an eye. He now drives an ambulance as part of the war effort. Even Balthazar, once a mere observer, has thrown himself into Alexandria's "great wine-press of love" (*Justine*, p. 14) and had his heart broken. Pursewarden in death talks to Darley as he never did before, speaking through his notebooks, a series of commentaries addressed to "Brother Ass," a sibling in the brotherhood of

art. We also learn that the narrator of *Mountolive* was sometimes wrong: Pursewarden may have killed himself not because of conflicting loyalties but to end his incestuous relationship with his sister.

In these new circumstances it is to Clea, the painter, that Darley is drawn. They become lovers and create an oasis of happiness against the backdrop of the waning war, spending their days swimming through beautiful waters in which sometimes float the bodies of the dead. While underwater one day, Clea is pinned by a harpoon; to save her from drowning Darley must cut her free, destroying her hand in the process. Darley fears that this may end Clea's career as a painter, but in fact her prosthesis liberates her to become a new kind of artist.

Darley senses in himself the same kind of rebirth, and in typically Durrellian fashion, the final sentences of *The Alexandria Quartet* build to a beginning rather than an end: "I wrote: 'Once upon a time ... ,'" Darley concludes. "And I felt as if the whole universe had given me a nudge!" (p. 282).

THE REVOLT OF A MODERNIST

Despite Durrell's protests that his mode is not Joycean, this burst of optimism recalls the last words of *Ulysses*, "yes I said yes I will Yes." Art here is not loss but, in the modernist tradition, recovery from loss, the ordering of acknowledged chaos.

The Alexandria Quartet was a great critical and popular success. Any problems with its parts—including those aspects of Durrell's approach that might have been "pompous," as he himself admitted in his introduction to *Balthazar* (p. 5)—were often forgiven in view of the tremendous accomplishment of the whole. George Steiner, for example, criticizing *Clea* as a "distinct failure of nerve," nevertheless maintains that "there can be little question of the fascination of Durrell's novel" (p. 287). If Durrell was indeed "the last of the modernists," it is by the *Quartet* that he proves it.

Durrell's next book went some way to unmaking that same reputation. Reed Way Dasenbrock has called *The Revolt of Aphrodite* "Durrell's most interesting and successful work of fiction" (p. 516), but as he admits, the two volumes, *Tunc* and *Nunquam*, "not only fail to conform to these modernist modes within which *The Alexandria Quartet* can be placed; they deliberately confront, mock, and subvert them" (p. 521).

Felix Charlock, who narrates, is a prisoner in his job as house inventor to Merlin, an enormous, sinister, Istanbul-based organization run by his brothers-in-law, Julian and Jocas. The firm has a controlling hand in aspects of practically every market and an almost God-like power over the lives of its employees: "The firm has given and the firm has taken away, blessed be the name of the firm" (*Tunc,* p. 16).

Charlock is also a prisoner in his unhappy marriage to the mentally unstable Benedicta. He wistfully recalls a life of contented poverty in Athens before his association with Merlin: his affair with the prostitute Iolanthe, now a movie star, nights of drunken carousing with the brilliant architect Caradoc and his sidekick, Sipple, a retired clown. Charlock first comes into contact with Merlin when Sipple's lover, Iolanthe's brother, is found dead in the clown's sordid rooms, and a plan is quickly hatched to smuggle him from the country. (It is in fact Iolanthe who murdered the boy, an honor killing on behalf of their father.) Charlock's relationship with Benedicta, one of the firm's owners, coupled with the limitless funding Merlin can offer for his research, mean he is quickly convinced to join. It is a decision he comes to regret.

When Caradoc disappears in a plane crash, Charlock spies an opportunity: he formulates a plan to fake his own death and thereby secure his freedom. It will mean losing his son, as well as giving up any and all professional activity, but his liberty seems worth the price, and he is not sure if he will have the opportunity again. Charlock even sabotages his own greatest creation, a machine capable of predicting the future, in order to cover his tracks. *"Aut tunc, aut nunquam,"* as the book's epigraph says: it was then or never.

Tunc ends as this scheme unfolds; *Nunquam* begins with Charlock in an insane asylum. His

escape has been a failure, and he is now being treated with drugs for paranoia. Caradoc has also been found and retrieved. Both Caradoc and Charlock come to accept their situation because it is only at Merlin that they can pursue their work: just as they cannot escape the firm, they cannot escape themselves, the "ribonucleic hangover" (*Tunc,* p. 16) that makes them what they are.

Whereas faked deaths, it seems, cannot bring freedom, real death does: Iolanthe forever escapes Julian's attempts to control her when she dies of cancer. Julian's obsession does not cease with her passing, however, and with Charlock's help he sets out to create a mechanical reproduction of the woman he loved, even down to the implantation of her memories. The robotic Iolanthe is a miraculous invention, but triumph turns to catastrophe when the automaton discovers its true, synthetic, nature, and as a result goes insane. The robot kills Julian in a spectacular fall from inside the dome of St. Paul's, and Charlock must in turn destroy the robot. This shocking anticlimax presents creativity not as modernist antidote to chaos but as a cog in the wheel of something enormous, spiritless, and deadening. The thematic insistence on the inability of art to transcend the commoditization of modern life is a pessimistic dismissal of the modernist vision so essential to *The Alexandria Quartet.*

Nunquam's finale sees Charlock and Benedicta, now reconciled, become Merlin's directors. In a low-tech version of hacking, Charlock plans to destroy the enormous library of microfilm that is the firm's institutional memory, but even as the book ends, it is unclear if this will have any effect: "Either everything will disintegrate, the firm will begin to dissolve; or else nothing ... it will be either/or once again; it will be now or never" (p. 318).

In a postface to the book, written as a letter to his dead wife Claude, Durrell calls his novels "inquests with open verdicts" (p. 319). Much of *Revolt*'s intent is nevertheless made clear through Charlock's reflection on his situation: the obsessions of Durrell's characters often mirror the author's own.

The evident reversal of intentions between *The Alexandria Quartet* and *The Revolt of Aphrodite* could not have occurred without the resolve of the author, whose work is always intellectually constructed—perhaps increasingly so. If *The Alexandria Quartet* feels to some extent like a great novel sometimes altered to indulge a theory, *The Revolt of Aphrodite* reads in long sections rather like a grand, albeit unfocused theory—eschatological, quasi-Marxist, and strongly Freudian—fashioned unconvincingly to resemble a novel. The change certainly did not go unnoticed by his readers, who were in general displeased, or by his American publisher, who refused the manuscript.

There may have been other reasons for the book's poor reception, however. One is that Durrell's obvious lack of familiarity with—or even interest in—international business beyond its symbolic value to the novel means that *The Revolt of Aphrodite* is always tinged with an irremediable implausibility. Merlin is hard to swallow not because it is too powerful (in fact, it is in many ways prophetic of the contemporary multinational), but because, despite its power, its influence is strangely limited and its concerns remarkably petty. How is it possible, in a notable instance, that a company seemingly in control of all world industry nevertheless fails to take over Iolanthe's film career?

The same can be said for the science part of this science-fiction story: if Charlock invents a series of revolutionary machines, why is there no revolution—no change, that is, to the nature of society? Readers may have found the space in which the story takes place, however clearly and intentionally anachronistic, somehow incomplete. Whatever the case, *The Revolt of Aphrodite* is a complex, demanding, and difficult work of art, one that does not fall easily into any category, and one that confounded readers and critics alike.

PRETENDING TO PRETEND

Durrell often claimed that lack of money made him work faster than he would have liked. As he aged, a growing sense of mortality may have given him a new reason to hurry. From the time of Claude's death he had grown morbid: along with Claude's ashes in the closet, he kept a list on his wall of dead friends, and it was lengthening rapidly. A long-term drinker and smoker in fading health, Durrell almost certainly did not have twenty years to spend in contemplation prior to beginning his next book, as he had done with *The Alexandria Quartet*.

He nevertheless decided to undertake a five-volume novel of startling conceptual complexity. Called *The Avignon Quintet,* it would be a quincunx, four elements centered on a fifth, as the four sides of a pyramid are centered on its apex. The series would reexamine many of the same issues as the *Quartet* from a different perspective, highlight Durrell's fascination with gnosticism and the Knights Templar, and reflect his creeping uncertainty about the relative value of art and life. Work on the *Quintet* began quickly after the release and critical failure of *Nunquam,* but the final volume did not appear until 1985.

Durrell had written about India from England, about England from Corfu, and about Egypt and Yugoslavia from France. His new work would be about Provence, where he still lived, but historical distance would provide the detachment on which his work seemed to depend. Although not always recounted chronologically, the action begins during the interbellum and ends just after World War II; the theme of the Templars anchors the work firmly in a historical context extending well beyond living memory.

Monsieur; or, The Prince of Darkness (1974), the first book of the *Quintet,* opens with the recollections of Dr. Bruce Drexel as he travels to Provence following the suicide of his beloved brother-in-law, Piers de Nogaret: "The southbound train from Paris was the one we had always taken from time immemorial—the same long slowcoach of a train, stringing out its bluish lights across the twilight landscapes like some super-glowworm" (p. 3). This scene will be repeated, sometimes word for word, as a kind of marker: he who utters it is at that time the work's central creative voice—a position of authority that shifts frequently. While Bruce revisits the scenes of his younger days, he recalls in detail his past: his courtship of Piers's sister, Sylvie, now mad and committed to an asylum; the friends' long visit to Egypt, where Piers became involved in a gnostic sect whose highest sacrament is ritual suicide—the only way to escape a demiurge (whom they call Monsieur) holding all life in an evil grip.

Bruce recalls his sister Pia, and the emotional collapse of her husband, the novelist Rob Sutcliffe, after Pia left him for her lesbian lover. Sylvie has in her possession many of Sutcliffe's notes for a novel he wrote about Bruce and his friends. *Monsieur* reproduces these notes; it seems they are the basis for none other than the book we have been reading—or would be, except that we suddenly learn Sutcliffe himself is a fictional character in the work of another author, Aubrey Blanford. Blanford is nevertheless in communication with his creation, Sutcliffe, as he is with his dead lover, Constance. As *Monsieur* ends, Blanford busily discusses one with the other.

The next volume, *Livia; or, Buried Alive* (1978), seems to be more naturalistic, describing Blanford's life before the war; Blanford and Sutcliffe continue to speak, but their relationship as creator and creation (something like an imaginary friend) is apparently fixed and clear, a result of Blanford's lonely childhood and poetic disposition. Through their discussions, the reader learns how various people Blanford has known were shuffled and split to form the characters encountered in *Monsieur:* Pia, for example, is based on Livia, whom Blanford marries; Piers on Livia's brother Hillary; Sylvie, in part, on a random encounter with a madwoman.

Blanford's life is filled with friends: an Egyptian prince, a Jewish peer, an impoverished British consul, a French clerk obsessed with finding the lost treasure of the Templars. Throughout a gentle summer they have adventures, visit brothels, and throw parties, but they know it cannot last: war is coming. In one sense it has already arrived, for Livia has embraced National Socialism and openly worships Hitler. She disappears, and for many years no one will see her except on film, one face in the crowd at Nazi rallies.

Constance; or, Solitary Practices (1982) follows the characters from *Livia* through their experiences of the war and introduces new characters, including Von Esslin, a German general who oversees the occupation of Avignon. Blanford moves to Egypt as secretary to the Prince and is wounded during a training exercise. Sam, Constance's husband, is killed—something she learns only after aborting their child.

While the narrative remains straightforward within the novel itself, strange things nevertheless occur that affect the series as a whole. Most disturbing to the suspension of disbelief is the revelation that Sutcliffe in fact exists; Constance is treating his wife, Pia, for depression. Who is fictional and who is not becomes, suddenly, impossible to tell. As the war ends, Constance falls in love with Sebastian Affad, an Arab banker (and presumably the original for Blanford's character Akkad, the cult leader in *Monsieur*), and Livia commits suicide.

The next volume does not attempt to solve or explain the crossing of barriers between the invented and the "real" within the fictional world of Durrell's Avignon; if anything, *Sebastian; or, Ruling Passions* (1983), serves only to make the situation more confusing by further confounding levels of "fiction" (Blanford introduces Constance to Dr. Bruce Drexel, for example) while treating the effect as unimportant. As Sutcliffe himself says, "Instead of fretting about *changing* the world, why not realise and accept it as it is, admitting that its order is divine, that reality, of which we are a part, realises itself *thus*" (p. 17).

Europe is recovering from the war, but suffering the shock of revelation as reports of the concentration camps spread. Sebastian Affad, torn between his love for Constance and his belief in the Gnostic creed of ritual suicide, feels obliged to leave her. A letter from his sect specifying the time and circumstances of Affad's death falls in the hands of Constance's patient, Mnemidis, a homicidal Egyptian man who always carries a woman's alligator handbag. Dressed as a nun, Mnemidis escapes the Swiss asylum where he is being treated and, thinking he is killing his analyst, murders Affad, potentially stripping his death of its ceremonial aspect.

Another psychiatrist, Schwarz, learns that Lily, a woman he had abandoned in Vienna while escaping the Anschluss, is alive, victim of the camps. Unable to face what has happened to her, Schwarz also kills himself. As the book ends, British police are carrying out raids, arresting members of the Gnostic suicide cult for seditious activities. The Prince escapes, and practically the entire cast—including those previously considered "fictional"—makes its way to Provence.

The final book in the series therefore starts, as did the first, on the southbound train to Avignon. That the barriers between the different layers of fiction have been completely destroyed is suggested on the very first page of *Quinx; or, The Ripper's Tale* (1985), when Blanford thinks of his fellow passengers, "Be ye members of one another" (p. 11), and confirmed when he says that he would like his writing—some of which we have read as a part of the *Quintet,* and which may itself be the fictional counterpart to Durrell's own—to "point the finger at the notion of discrete identity being very much in question" (p. 15).

To underline this, the relationship between Blanford and Sutcliffe is again redefined, now as something like a conjoined consciousness: "the two men, if that is what one can call them" (p. 35) are writing a novel, and although their pasts are separate—it was Sutcliffe alone who rescued Freud's sofa from Vienna, for example—the characters seem almost undividable in the present. In a novel short on plot and long on aphorism, puns, and experimentation, the issue of what this melding means becomes central. As Sutcliffe himself jokingly asks, "What shall we do with our alter ego?" (p. 140).

Frustratingly, there is to be no answer. The book ends on a purposefully anticlimactic note as Blanford and the others approach what they believe to be the underground hiding place of the Templar treasure. Whether the treasure is there or not, or whatever else happens to them in the caves, is left unwritten. Blanford's own thoughts on how to write such an event are the novel's last: "The lovers gave a shiver or premonition and Blanford thought that if ever he wrote the scene he would say: 'It was at this precise moment that reality prime came to the aid of fiction and the totally unpredictable began to take place!'" (p. 201).

Despite (or even perhaps because of) its innovative structure, startling approach to the question of character, and truly Durrellian array of secondary players—the deformed, the obsessed, the socially marginal—the *Quintet* was poorly received by the critics. *Monsieur* was nevertheless honored with the James Tait Black Memorial award, the only British award for fiction Durrell ever received, and *Constance* was included on the Booker Prize shortlist for 1982 (the award went instead to the Australian author Thomas Keneally).

THE WINEPRESS OF ART

The *Quintet* can be a curious experience for a reader. Taken alone, each volume might seem rather bloodless, while the series as a whole either refuses or fails to find a focus. There was a sense that Durrell had painted himself into a corner. As he writes of the conjoined Blanford and Sutcliffe (and thereby, the reader may freely imply, of himself), "It was obvious that in common with most of us they were hunting a spontaneity which had once been innate, given, and to which the key had been mislaid" (*Quinx,* p. 34).

It is perhaps for this reason that some of the most interesting passages may also be the most opaque, with Durrell appropriating outright the conventions of other genres. Throughout his career as a prose writer, Durrell had leveraged his other capabilities, especially in poetry, which he began writing when he was fifteen years old, and his final work shows the effect most bluntly:

"I am writing a defense of Inklings."

going "Inklings of what?" dying

going "Of the absolute, silly." dying

gone "And what, pray, may that be?" dead

"An inkling."

(*Quinx,* p. 35)

Indeed, Durrell sometimes felt that he had expended too much of his poetic gift on his prose and thereby missed the opportunity to become a much finer poet; it was after all his verse that first brought him to the attention of Faber & Faber, and the publication, in 1943, of the collection *A Private Country,* which brought him to the attention of the critics. As the title suggests, many of the poems in *A Private Country* highlight and assert the centrality of individual experience, but they also attest to Durrell's delight in the portraiture of place. This is not a contradiction: Durrell believed strongly that landscape was the crucible in which both culture and character were formed.

While some complained that the book's title was perhaps too apt, and the poems private to the point of hermeticism, Durrell's facility with language and his seemingly innate mastery of form (some earlier, developmental collections had been published only privately and in strictly limited numbers) easily won over most readers. The poet Peter Porter has argued that *A Private Country* is one of the best first collections of the twentieth century, comparable to W. H. Auden's *Poems* (1930), and at the time it was certainly accorded very serious attention. Although now less well known, the collection includes "The Death of General Uncebunke: A Biography in Little" (1938), a work subject to perennial rediscovery.

Cities, Plains, and People (1946) returned again to similar themes, investigating the poetic intersection between location and the personal. The title poem is, like "Uncebunke," a biography in little, this time of the poet himself, examining the *spiritus loci* of India and Greece, recording Durrell's search for liberation from England, and celebrating his triumphant escape to Corfu.

On Seeming to Presume (1948) and *The Tree of Idleness and Other Poems* (1955) demonstrated similar occupations and were very much in the "Durrell" style—too much so for some critics, who worried his work was not evolving. At this time the limited availability of *The Black Book* and the minor nature of 1947's *Cefalû* meant Durrell was still considered a poet who occasionally wrote novels. When his next collection, *The Ikons and Other Poems* (1966), appeared, this was no

longer the case: *The Alexandria Quartet* eclipsed his every previous—and subsequent—effort.

Although verse would show up now and then amid the prose, Durrell's main poetic output after *The Ikons* was to be his verse plays; these met with very little success outside Germany. He released only one more collection of new poems, *Vega and Other Poems*, in 1973. Despite what he evidently saw as a failure to maintain his practice and reputation as a poet, Durrell nevertheless lived to see three collected editions of his work, the last of which, *Collected Poems 1931–1974,* included every poem he had ever published, excluding only the verse plays and some lines embedded in the novels.

Durrell also drew for his fiction on a strong and successful background as a travel writer (or "residence writer," since he wrote only about places where he had lived; *Sicilian Carousel* in 1977 was the unsuccessful exception proving the rule). When work on his fiction went badly or his coffers ran low, Durrell turned to travel writing for creative and financial relief. If his later attempts were above all intended to boil the pot, his earliest work is among the best to be found in the genre. Part memoir, part history, works such as *Prospero's Cell* (1945), *Reflections on a Marine Venus* (1953), and *Bitter Lemons* (1957) brought the average English reader to places— Corfu, Rhodes, and Cyprus, among others— which were still, at that time, exotic locales, both culturally and physically remote, however geographically near, and served their author well as sources of both income and inspiration.

And yet while Durrell's Antrobus sketches can be seen as practice for the bawdy humor of his novels (particularly the creation of Scobie, one of modernism's most effectively comic characters), his poetry as a source to mine for the near-mannerist richness of his prose, and his travel writing as a rehearsal for his depiction of place, Durrell himself would have opposed the idea that the different genres were anything other than parts of a single artistic and cultural entity. If, ultimately, the "last of the modernists" failed to overcome the barriers that gate these parts from one another, it was perhaps a matter of timing, for while "Poetry is the raw material of sensibility, and the poet's job is to go on making poetry, not to think too much about why or wherefore," nevertheless, he says in *A Key to Modern British Poetry,* "poets belong to an age. They have ancestors and pedigrees like their poems. And they register the general drift of things by their work" (p. 64).

Lawrence Durrell was one of very few important writers to belong so specifically to the age that suffered the vacuum left by modernism's dwindling, and, in registering its drift, he occupies a unique position as Britain's only high-modernist author to have turned so fully against the creed of modernism. Little wonder that, whatever the state of his popular reputation, academic interest in Durrell has never waned.

Selected Bibliography

WORKS OF LAWRENCE DURRELL

Please note that where reprints are given, citations in the text are from that edition.

NOVELS AND SHORT STORIES

Pied Piper of Lovers. London, Cassell: 1935.

Panic Spring. London: Faber & Faber, 1936. (Under the pseudonym Charles Nordstrom.)

The Black Book: An Agon. Paris: Obelisk Press, 1938; New York: Dutton, 1960.

Cefalû. London: Editions Poetry, 1947. Reissued as *The Dark Labyrinth.* London: Faber & Faber, 1961.

White Eagles over Serbia. London: Faber & Faber, 1957.

Esprit de Corps: Sketches from Diplomatic Life. London: Faber & Faber, 1957.

Justine. London: Faber & Faber, 1957; New York: Dutton, 1960.

Balthazar. London: Faber & Faber, 1958; New York: Dutton, 1960.

Mountolive. London: Faber & Faber, 1958; New York: Dutton, 1959.

Stiff Upper Lip. London: Faber & Faber, 1958.

Clea. London: Faber & Faber, 1960; New York: Penguin, 1991.

Sauve Qui Peut. London: Faber & Faber, 1966.

Tunc: A Novel. London: Faber & Faber, 1968; New York: Dutton, 1968.

Nunquam: A Novel. London: Faber & Faber, 1970; New York: Dutton, 1970.

Monsieur; or, The Prince of Darkness. London: Faber & Faber, 1974.

Livia; or, Buried Alive. London: Faber & Faber, 1978.

Constance; or, Solitary Practices. London: Faber & Faber, 1982.

Sebastian; or, Ruling Passions. London: Faber & Faber, 1983.

Quinx; or, The Ripper's Tale. London: Faber & Faber, 1985.

POETRY AND VERSE PLAYS

A Private Country. London: Faber & Faber, 1943.

Cities, Plains, and People. London: Faber & Faber, 1946.

On Seeming to Presume. London: Faber & Faber, 1948.

Sappho. London: Faber & Faber, 1950.

The Tree of Idleness and Other Poems. London: Faber & Faber, 1955.

Selected Poems. London: Faber & Faber, 1956.

Collected Poems. London: Faber & Faber, 1960; rev. ed., 1968.

An Irish Faustus: A Morality in Nine Scenes. London: Faber & Faber, 1963.

Selected Poems, 1935–1963. London: Faber & Faber, 1964.

Acte: A Play. London: Faber & Faber, 1965.

The Ikons and Other Poems. London: Faber & Faber, 1966.

The Red Limbo Lingo: A Poetry Notebook. London: Faber & Faber, 1971.

Vega and Other Poems. London: Faber & Faber, 1973.

Selected Poems of Lawrence Durrell. London: Faber & Faber, 1977.

Collected Poems, 1931–1974. London: Faber & Faber, 1980.

TRAVEL WRITING

Prospero's Cell: A Guide to the Landscape and Manners of the Island of Corcyra. London: Faber & Faber, 1945; new ed. 1975.

Reflections on a Marine Venus. London: Faber & Faber, 1953.

Bitter Lemons. London: Faber & Faber, 1957.

Spirit of Place: Letters and Essays on Travel. London: Faber & Faber, 1969.

Sicilian Carousel. London: Faber & Faber, 1977.

The Greek Islands. London: Faber & Faber, 1978.

"Egyptian Moments." *New York Times Magazine,* June 11, 1978, p. 11.

Caesar's Vast Ghost. London: Faber & Faber, 1990.

ESSAYS

Key to Modern Poetry. London: Peter Nevill, 1952. Published as *A Key to Modern British Poetry.* Norman: University of Oklahoma Press, 1952.

Blue Thirst. Santa Barbara, CA: Capra Press, 1975.

CORRESPONDENCE

The majority of Durrell's papers are collected in the British Library and in the Lawrence Durrell Papers at Southern Illinois University at Carbondale.

Lawrence Durrell and Henry Miller: A Private Correspondence. Edited by George Wickes. New York: Dutton, 1963.

Art and Outrage: A Correspondence About Henry Miller Between Alfred Perles and Lawrence Durrell with an Intermission by Henry Miller. London: Village Press, 1973.

"Letters to Henry Miller." *Twentieth-Century Literature* 33, no. 3:359–366 (autumn 1987).

"Letters to T. S. Eliot." *Twentieth-Century Literature* 33, no. 3:348–358 (autumn 1987).

Literary Lifelines: The Richard Aldington–Lawrence Durrell Correspondence. Edited by Ian S. MacNiven and Harry T. Moore. New York: Viking, 1981.

The Durrell-Miller Letters, 1935–80. Edited by Ian S. MacNiven. London: Faber & Faber, 1988.

BIOGRAPHY

Bowker, Gordon. *Through the Dark Labyrinth: A Biography of Lawrence Durrell.* New York: St. Martin's, 1997.

Durrell, Gerald. *My Family and Other Animals.* London: Hart-Davis, 1956.

MacNiven, Ian. *Lawrence Durrell: A Biography.* London: Faber & Faber, 1998.

BIOGRAPHICAL AND CRITICAL STUDIES

Begnal, Michael H., ed. *On Miracle Ground: Essays on the Fiction of Lawrence Durrell.* Lewisburg, Pa: Bucknell University Press, 1990.

Bode, Carl. "Durrell's Way to Alexandria." *College English* 22, no. 8:531–538 (May 1961).

Dasenbrock, Reed Way. "Lawrence Durrell and the Modes of Modernism." *Twentieth-Century Literature* 33, no. 4:515–527 (winter 1987).

Dickson, Gregory. "Setting and Character in *The Revolt of Aphrodite*." *Twentieth-Century Literature* 33, no. 4:528–535 (winter 1987).

Friedman, Alan Warren. "A 'Key' to Lawrence Durrell." *Wisconsin Studies in Contemporary Literature* 8, no. 1:31–42 (winter 1967).

Gifford, James. "Lawrence Durrell's *Alexandria Quartet* and Colonial Knowing: Implicating Friedrich Nietzsche and Edward Said." In *Lawrence Durrell Borderlands and Borderlines.* Edited by Corinne Alexandre-Garner. Paris: Presses Universitaires de Paris 10, 2005. Pp. 95–112. (A 2001 draft of this text is available online at http://www.ualberta.ca/˜gifford/textsvictoria.htm.)

———. "Reading Orientalism and the Crisis of Epistemology in the Novels of Lawrence Durrell." *CLCWeb: Comparative Literature and Culture* 1, no. 2 (http://docs.lib.purdue.edu/clcweb/vol1/iss2/3), June 1999..

Hawkes, John, and Lawrence Durrell. "Lawrence Durrell and John Hawkes: Passages from a Dialogue at Pennsylvania State University." *Twentieth-Century Literature* 33, no. 3:411–415 (autumn 1987).

Johnson, Buffie. "Personal Reminiscences of Lawrence Durrell." *Twentieth-Century Literature* 33, no. 3:287–292 (autumn 1987).

Kersnowski, Frank L., ed. *Into the Labyrinth: Essays on the Art of Lawrence Durrell.* Ann Arbor: UMI Research Press, 1989.

Lemon, Lee T. "*The Alexandria Quartet*: Form and Fiction." *Wisconsin Studies in Contemporary Literature* 4, no. 3:327–338 (autumn, 1963).

Lennon, John M. "Pursewarden's Death: 'A Stray Brick from Another Region.'" *Modern Language Studies* 6, no. 1:22–28 (spring 1976).

Markert, Lawrence W. "'The Pure and Sacred Readjustment of Death': Connections Between Lawrence Durrell's *Avignon Quintet* and the Writings of D. H. Lawrence." *Twentieth-Century Literature* 33, no. 4:550–564 (winter 1987).

McNelly, Willis E. "Lawrence Durrell's 'Science Fiction in the True Sense.'" *Rocky Mountain Review of Language and Literature* 30, no. 1:61–70 (winter 1976).

Menuhin, Diana. "Lawrence Durrell in Alexandria and Sommieres." *Twentieth-Century Literature* 33, no. 3:308–311 (autumn 1987).

Moore, Harry T., ed. *The World of Lawrence Durrell.* New York: Dutton, 1964.

Nichols, James R. "Ah, the Wonder of My Body: The Wandering of My Mind: Classicism and Lawrence Durrell's Literary Tradition." *Twentieth-Century Literature* 33, no. 4:449–464 (winter 1987).

Pierce, Carol. "'Wrinkled Deep in Time': *The Alexandria Quartet* as Many-Layered Palimpsest." *Twentieth-Century Literature* 33, no. 4:485–498 (winter 1987).

Raper, Julius Rowan. "The Philosopher's Stone and Durrell's Psychological Vision in *Monsieur* and *Livia*." *Twentieth-Century Literature* 36, no. 4:419–433 (winter 1990).

Ridler, Anne. "Recollections of Lawrence Durrell." *Twentieth-Century Literature* 33, no. 3:293–297 (autumn 1987).

Spencer, Sharon. "The Ambiguities of Incest in Lawrence Durrell's Heraldic Universe: A Rankian Interpretation." *Twentieth-Century Literature* 33, no. 4:436–448 (winter 1987).

Steiner, George. *Language and Silence.* New York: Atheneum, 1976.

Stern, James. "Lawrence Durrell: A Celebration." *Twentieth-Century Literature* 33, no. 3:334–336 (autumn 1987).

Unterecker, J. "Lawrence Durrell." In *Six Contemporary British Novelists*. Edited by George Stade. New York: Columbia University Press, 1976.

Wedin, Warren. "The Artist as Narrator in *The Alexandria Quartet*." *Twentieth-Century Literature* 18, no. 3:175–180 (July 1972).

Weigel, John A. "Lawrence Durrell's First Novel." *Twentieth-Century Literature* 14, no. 2:75–83 (July 1968).

ELIZABETH GASKELL

(1810—1865)

Sandie Byrne

ELIZABETH GASKELL WAS a prolific and professional author of fiction; a near contemporary of the Brontës and an enduring influence on Victorian social realist fiction. She was born Elizabeth Cleghorn Stevenson, at 93 Cheney Walk, Chelsea, in London, on September 29, 1810. She was the eighth child of William Stevenson and his wife, Elizabeth Holland, both of whom were Unitarians. The following year, Elizabeth Stevenson died, and the thirteen-month-old Elizabeth was sent to be cared for by her Aunt Lumb at Knutsford, now a suburb of the city of Manchester but then a quiet country village, near her grandfather's farm and other family members. Her early schooling was at home, where, in keeping with the practice of Nonconformist families, her gender did not debar her from a good education. At age twelve she was sent to Avonbank, a school kept by the Byerley sisters, initially at Barford and later at Stratford-on-Avon. There she continued her studies in French, began to learn Italian and Latin, and flourished in an environment that was liberal and freethinking intellectually as well as clean and healthy physically. During these years she seems to have seen her father, who remarried, infrequently.

In 1827 Gaskell returned to Knutsford, but the following year a family tragedy took her back to London and her father and stepmother. Her only surviving brother, John, had left to join the East India Company but was lost at sea. The sorrow and anxiety this caused can be seen in the repeated motif of the lost brother in Gaskell's writing—Peter, brother of Miss Deborah and Miss Mattie in *Cranford,* and Frederick, brother of Margaret Hale in *North and South.* There seems to have been instant antipathy between Elizabeth and her stepmother, and after the death of William Stevenson in 1829, she left the family home. After some family visits, including several to a connection, William Turner, an influential Unitarian and educationalist in Newcastle in the north of England, she settled again in Knutsford until her marriage. She met her future husband, William Gaskell, on a visit to Manchester, where he was assistant chaplain of the Unitarian Cross Street Chapel. The couple married in August 1832.

Following her marriage, Gaskell had to exchange country-town Knutsford, surrounded by salubrious countryside, for industrial Manchester. Though she came to have both affection and respect for the city and its people, the culture shock must have been extreme, as it is to Margaret Hale when she arrives in the fictional Milton in *North and South,* and Gaskell found her mental and physical health affected.

Elizabeth joined William Gaskell in his work in Manchester and, apart from a few poems and other short pieces, wrote little during the first fifteen years of her marriage. These were, however, years of activity, a seemingly happy union of equals, and some sorrows. In 1836 Gaskell bore a stillborn child; in 1837 Aunt Lumb died, leaving her niece a legacy that brought her £80 a year; and in 1845 her nine-month-old son died. Four daughters of the marriage survived: Marianne, Margaret Emily (Meta), Florence Elizabeth, and Julia Bradford, but Meta in particular was the cause of anxiety through ill health and a broken engagement.

A year after the publication (1848) of *Mary Barton,* the name of its author was known, even though it had not been advertised on the book itself, and Elizabeth Gaskell was famous. She was asked to write for the first issue of Dickens' new periodical, *Household Words,* and produced in quick succession a number of short stories for periodicals as well as a longer story, *The Moorland Cottage* (1850). She met a number of literary stars of the day, including, in 1850, Charlotte Brontë, with whom developed a friendship that was to last for the rest of Brontë's life. Dickens was keen for Gaskell to publish a full-length narrative in serialized form, but before starting work on her next novel Gaskell wanted to travel. She visited the Brontës in Haworth and a new friend, Madame Mohl, in Paris. Gaskell traveled again after the publication of *North and South* (serialized in *Household Words* from September 1854 to January 1855), and was away in March 1855, when Charlotte Brontë died. A trace of this friendship perhaps survives in the name of the companion/governess to a Gaskell heroine, Molly Gibson, in *Wives and Daughters:* Miss Eyre.

Gaskell was away again when the furor about her *Life of Charlotte Brontë* broke out in 1857. In February of that year she was invited to spend some time in Rome as the guest of American artist William Wetmore Story. There she met Charles Eliot Norton and formed a friendship that would last a lifetime and generate a correspondence that provides valuable insights into Gaskell's life. Back in Manchester, Gaskell began a period of prolific productivity, mostly work commissioned by Dickens, which financed further travel. From 1860 she began to write for George Smith's new periodical, the *Cornhill Magazine,* whose format she found more congenial and suited to her style of writing than Dickens' *Household Words* and its successor, *All the Year Round.* Her time was divided between her family responsibilities and the duties of a minister's wife, her work, and the travel she found necessary to refresh her health and spirits. Her trips abroad and within Britain were as often as not working holidays or research trips. A stay in Whitby, Yorkshire, in November 1859, for example, provided the setting for *Sylvia's Lovers* (1863).

A payment of £2,000 from George Smith for Gaskell's *Wives and Daughters* enabled her to fulfill a long-held ambition, to buy a country-house retreat. It was during a visit to the new house, still kept as a surprise for the Reverend

William Gaskell, that Elizabeth Gaskell died on November 12, 1865.

GENRES AND THEMES

In an essay for *Household Words,* Gaskell wrote that the art of telling a story was born with some people, "and these have it to perfection" ("Company Manners," *Household Words* 9, 20 May 1854, p. 329). It took a little while for her to discover that she was a born storyteller. In January 1837, "Sketches Among the Poor" was published by *Blackwood's Magazine* under the names of Gaskell and her husband, and in 1840 she contributed an account of a visit to Clopton Hall to *Visits to Remarkable Places,* written by William Howitt. She does not seem to have attempted prose fiction, however, until recommended to start a novel by her husband, who suggested it as a possible distraction from her grief at the death of her infant son from scarlet fever. The result was *Mary Barton: A Tale of Manchester Life,* which was published anonymously in October 1848. After the publication and success of this novel, she was urged by her publisher, Chapman & Hall, to write another, but she initially resisted, claiming that there was not another novel in her. This was patently not so, however, and though a few years separate *Mary Barton* from Gaskell's next major work, *Ruth,* her other works quickly followed. Though best remembered for her novels, she was also the author of the first biography of Charlotte Brontë and of more than sixty short stories.

Gaskell's earliest fiction was published anonymously, or, as with "Lizzie Leigh," attributed to Charles Dickens, as editor of the periodical in which the story appeared. The identity of the author was soon known, however. In the early stages of her career, she had been much at the mercy of her publisher. When her first novel was published she was obliged to acquiesce to requests for the change of title from "John Barton" to "Mary Barton," the addition of a preface, a glossary for some terms of Lancashire dialect, and extra pages to bulk out the novel to the requisite length. Growing fame and a change of publisher eventually enabled her to gain autonomy over her own work.

Gaskell's major works are often described as "social problem" novels, though this places them within a genre to which they are by no means restricted. The "social problem novel" refers to a number of different kinds of fiction that sought to publicize a range of social ills. A number of social problem novels were written during or about the "hungry forties" (including Charles Kingsley's *Alton Locke* [1850] and Charles Dickens' *Hard Times* [1854]), but the genre continued and could be said still to be in existence today. Subcategories of the social problem genre include the industrial novel, generally set in a mill town or factory town, and the "condition of England" novel, which reveals ills at a national rather than local level, sometimes through a setting that is a microcosm of the country, though the terms are often used interchangeably of the whole genre. The phrase comes from the first chapter of Book I of Thomas Carlyle's *Past and Present* (1839).

"The woman question" (women's issues) also features as an overt or covert theme in many social problem novels, including Gaskell's *Mary Barton, Ruth,* and *North and South,* and a number of the best known social problem novels were written by women. Since women were discouraged from entering the public/political arena and encouraged to participate in a demarcated "women's sphere," we might be surprised to find interventions by women in public debates about, for example, the working conditions in mills and factories. Throughout the Victorian period, however, a number of women authors did publicize, and dramatize through fiction, problems of industrial conditions and industrial relations.

Some social problem novels are overt calls for political action, whereas others suggest that the remedy lies in personal charity, in the benevolence of the rich and powerful, and in reform, rather than in radical change to the social system that produced the poverty and other problems the novels depict. *Mary Barton* and *North and South* certainly lay bare the social ills of inequality and unfairness written into the system, but the reform they advocate is not a radical, root-level redesign. Gaskell does not call for the leveling of the social hierarchy, for the end of the social and economic system that generates poverty and great wealth, power and disempowerment. What she does is what most of the English social problem or industrial or "condition of England" novelists did: she appeals to the conscience of those in power, their humanity and their Christianity, to create better conditions for the powerless, to regard those in their power as human beings, and to treat them well. This is, to treat the effects of the system rather than do away with the system. Of course, it is hard to see what else Elizabeth Gaskell or any other Victorian social problem novelist could have done and still be read in large enough quantities to make a difference. Within the constraints of her time and milieu, Gaskell produced works that forced readers to look at unpalatable and shameful aspects of English society that they might otherwise have been ignorant of or have ignored.

Victorian Britain had more than enough social problems for authors to represent. Many were legacies of earlier periods; some were consequent on the social, cultural, and economic changes brought by the Industrial Revolution. Many commentators on these problems called for reform, and many people were active in measures designed to introduce reform, but clearly this was never enough. Although many people in the middle and professional classes prospered in the Victorian period, and some working-class people advanced into the middle classes, social mobility worked downward as well as upward. Many people barely survived on subsistence wages and in unsafe and inhumane conditions, and there was an enormous underclass of unemployed or unofficially employed, criminal, and destitute people whose sufferings were often terrible.

Gaskell was a prolific author of short stories, most of which were published in periodicals and later collected in a series of volumes. In this form, she produced fiction in a range of genres, including social realism, historical fiction, romance, the supernatural, and the mystery.

ELIZABETH GASKELL

MARY BARTON

Mary Barton: A Tale of Manchester Life (1848) is unusual in mid-Victorian fiction in having a working-class hero and heroine, and most of its secondary and background characters are also working-class. Unlike Gaskell's later heroines, Margaret Hale of *North and South,* Mary Smith of *Cranford* (1851–1853) and Molly Gibson of *Wives and Daughters* (1864–1866), Mary Barton is not outside looking in, albeit in genteel poverty, but suffers the privations created by the system that the novel examines.

Set in Manchester, in the industrial north of England, the novel presents a disaffected and increasingly rebellious workforce in a sympathetic light. The workers are struggling to survive on below-subsistence pay, at the mercy of factory and mill owners who can lay them off at any time and who are happy to replace as many of them as possible with faster and better machinery.

During the "hungry forties," when *Mary Barton* was written and published, the pay for a skilled worker fell below subsistence level, but following a series of bad harvests, the price of corn, and therefore bread, was high. There were punitive Poor Laws and restrictive Corn Laws. Working men had no vote and, they felt, no voice in Parliament. Times, as Charles Dickens and others illustrated, were hard, and bleak. Gaskell dramatizes the larger economic and social issues through the lives of individuals, representing the suffering that social and economic system generated. Among the many images of great pathos in the novel is the spectacle of the wealthy Mrs. Hunter going past John Barton in all her wealth and finery, preoccupied with petty materialist considerations, on the day his son has died from want of food.

The eponymous heroine, Mary Barton, has the chance to escape privation. She must choose between two suitors: Harry Carson, the son of the factory owner who is causing hardship and suffering among her family and friends; and Jem Wilson, a local man without Harry's education, privilege, or fortune. Before Mary has acted, the local trade unionists have decided to take action against Mr. Carson by assassinating his son, and the person who draws the straw for the task is Mary's father, John Barton.

The murder of Harry Carson may have been based on a real event, the killing of Thomas Ashton, also by a group of workers on strike, in January 1831. That murder was fictionalized by Elizabeth Stone in her novel *William Langshawe, The Cotton Lord* in 1842, and contemporary speculation made her also the author of the anonymously published *Mary Barton.*

If the novel is social realist in genre and realist in style, in the story of the murder and its consequences a mythical or fabulous, and specifically Christian, structure is imposed. Both the murderer and the bereaved and vengeful father achieve redemption, John Barton by true repentance and Mr. Carson by true forgiveness, learned from the Bible. Barton dies in Carson's arms, and thereafter Carson is a changed man, benevolent and humanitarian.

It is not difficult to see why Elizabeth Gaskell initially named her novel for the heroine's father: John Barton is a powerful and tragic character, a strong, thoughtful, and intelligent man who under different circumstances could have claimed an important position in the world. His involvement in trade unionism and Chartism, however marginal, makes him part of the great political movements of the day. Barton's character is not simply a mouthpiece for Gaskell's message of social reform, and he is neither simply romanticized as a working-class hero nor demonized as a murderer. The reader follows Barton's metamorphosis, via the death of his wife and his immersion in politics, from caring, loving husband and father to a man no longer bound to individuals by ties of kinship and affection but rather to something larger, impersonal, and to an extent abstract, in the cause of which he sublimates his individuality and even his humanity.

John Barton's is not the only tragedy in the novel. His sister-in-law, the once innocent, betrayed Esther, a broken butterfly, returns home to die; she is one of a number of "fallen women" in Gaskell's work. Jem and Mary, however, emigrate, and at the end of the novel they are with their son, awaiting the arrival of friends from England and the start of a new life.

Mary Barton, as with all of Gaskell's work, is a novel worth reading for more than its political message. The strong characterizations of John Barton and Jem Wilson and the interaction in the working-class social network produces strong readerly engagement with and interest in the characters. Tension and suspense are generated by the interrelated assassination and romantic plots and by dramatic, even melodramatic narrative climaxes, such as Jem Wilson's daring rescue of men trapped inside a burning mill, involving a perilous climb along a rickety ladder stretching between tall buildings, with the unconscious body of his elderly father on his shoulder.

RUTH

Ruth, following minor works including *The Moorland Cottage,* was published in 1853. Gaskell sent a draft of the novel to her friend Charlotte Brontë, who was impressed enough to make her publishers delay publication of her own next novel, *Villette,* so that *Ruth* would be given ample critical space in the periodicals. Whereas Mary Barton was an unusual heroine in that she was working-class, Ruth is even more unconventional for the time in that she was a "fallen woman," that is, an unmarried mother. Many "fallen women" were represented in Victorian fiction, but before *Ruth* they were almost always marginal figures. The novel was partly based on a true story—the experience of a clergyman's young daughter who was orphaned at an early age, seduced and abandoned, forced into crime, and, imprisoned and ill, faced with her seducer in the form of the surgeon called to her case. Ruth is born into a respectable family but left penniless when orphaned. Apprenticed to a dressmaker, her life is hard and almost friendless, and she is therefore ready to turn to the man who seems to offer her love. That man, the local squire, Richard Bellingham, seduces her and takes her first to London and then, far from her home and acquaintances, to Wales, where he abandons her. Ruth, pregnant and alone, is about to commit suicide but is saved by Mr. Benson, a minister of a Dissenting sect, and taken to live with him and his

sister in the north of England. As "Mrs. Denbigh," a governess, Ruth lives quietly and respectably for a number of years with her son, Leonard, while her lover meanwhile becomes a member of Parliament. An unfortunate coincidence exposes Ruth's identity and past, and she and the Bensons are disgraced. Ruth devotes her life to good works and becomes an angel of mercy to local people during an outbreak of cholera. When her lover contracts the disease, she nurses him, saving his life at the expense of her own.

Reaction to the novel was mixed. Although some critics were admiring, many readers were outraged, suggesting that the suffering and death undergone by Ruth were insufficient, and that her fate should have been made an example to other women. Others, Gaskell wrote, burned their copies of the first volume of the novel, and the unkind comments made about it kept her awake at night, in tears (*The Letters of Mrs. Gaskell,* p. 221). Gaskell had anticipated the controversy but had written of her determination to face the subject, even though it was so painful that "it requires all one's bravery not to hide one's head like an ostrich" (*Letters,* p. 227). Other readers were more tolerant and more sympathetic to Ruth. Charlotte Brontë, among others, questioned the necessity of Ruth's having to die and the book's having to be a tragedy, asking why readers were to shut up the book, weeping (Easson, ed., 1991, p. 200). Today we would see the extremely naive and ignorant Ruth as a victim, innocent of sin and therefore not in need of redemption, yet at the time she was to an extent perceived as a sinner whose subsequent actions could redeem her but who perhaps throws away a chance of redemption when, on meeting Bellingham again, she refuses to marry him. Part of the controversial message of *Ruth* is that its heroine is not in need of the forgiveness that comes from penitence but rather in need of understanding and fair treatment.

Although Ruth does suffer and eventually die, she does not undergo the appalling privations and miseries of other fallen women in Victorian fiction, even that of Gaskell's own fiction (for example, Esther in *Mary Barton*).

Similarly, though Bellingham abandons Ruth, rather than abuse her or thrust her out onto the streets in a snowstorm, he does so almost passively, by falling ill and being taken away by his mother. Gaskell resists a melodramatic treatment of the subject in favor of a lower-key, measured realism.

Whereas in *Mary Barton* the reader's focus is divided among Mary, John Barton, Jem Wilson, and, as its subtitle suggests, a strong supporting cast of secondary figures and interesting subplots, *Ruth* has a central protagonist whose story is almost the sole focus of the novel.

CRANFORD

The final book-length version of *Cranford* (1853) developed in several stages. Gaskell wrote an essay titled "The Last Generation in England," which was published in the United States in 1849 and later fictionalized as "Our Society at Cranford" and published in *Household Words* (13 December 1851). This became the first two chapters of the novel. "Mr. Harrison's Confessions" also contributed to the final version of the novel. Dickens liked the writing so much that he included an extract in the first *Household Words,* and it was serialized sporadically in that periodical until the year the book-length version was published. A further episode, "The Cage at Cranford," a short satirical observation of contemporary fashion as viewed from Cranford, appeared in 1863 and is included with some editions of *Cranford.*

The characters of *Cranford* are those marginalized, despised, ridiculed, or ignored figures in much Victorian fiction: impoverished spinsters and widows. Though in this novel they may sometimes be comic, they are represented with affectionate respect as "the Amazons." Cranford society is composed of women who might be thought to be disenfranchised and disempowered, in Victorian terms to have passed or failed in the chief duties of a woman's life. These ladies do not, however, acknowledge failure or (except fleetingly) yearn for lost possibilities. They manage the affairs of the small town they dominate perfectly well, and they rarely find a need for male company except when there is a tree to be pruned or a heavy object to be shifted. They agree that men get in the way in a house, and men are the catalysts for change and chaos in the town and the novel. The arrival of an attractive young doctor generates ill feeling, rivalry, confusion, and misunderstanding; another new arrival brings the railway with all its disruption and dislocation in his wake; and the reappearance of a third awakens old dreams and desires, only to dash them again almost immediately.

Cranford can be seen as a nostalgic portrait of an England that was already vanishing in Gaskell's time: the rural or semirural, slow-paced, strongly regional way of life even then being eroded by faster transport and communication and the spread of industrial centers. The ladies of Cranford—Miss Jenkyns and Mattie and their friends Mrs. Forrester, Miss Pole, and Mrs. Barker—are old-fashioned and live by old-fashioned notions of propriety, economy, and courtesy. But they are also prejudiced, sometimes petty, sometimes small-minded, and always far too interested in other people's business. We learn that an old-fashioned sense of social form has left Miss Mattie, one of the kindest and most virtuous of women, bereft of her chance of love, and an old-fashioned insistence on propriety and forms of manners maintains a distance between Miss Jenkyns and her closest friends and neighbors. The use of a narrator, Mary Smith, who, though familiar with Cranford from an early age, is an outsider, enables Gaskell to criticize as well as idealize, but the frailties as well as the virtues of the Cranford ladies are always chronicled with wit and humor.

Mary Smith's prolonged visits to Cranford are in some ways more like journal entries or anecdotes than a single strong plot line. Longer plot strands are created by the arrival and death of one interloping male, Captain Brown; the arrival and fluttering generated by another, the young doctor; and the restoration to Cranford of its lost son, Peter Jenkyns, who, after a misdeed results in a flogging, has run away to seek his fortune in India before the narrative opens. The matter of Mary Smith's narrative is, however, largely made up of the small events of Cranford life: the arrival of new cloth at the haberdasher's; minor accidents; the social round; news, gossip and speculation. Even so, Gaskell creates a plausible world with plausible, if eccentric and remote to us, systems of belief and behavior, as well as plausible characters whose respective stories produce both bathos and pathos.

NORTH AND SOUTH

North and South (1855) was published in serial form in *Household Words* between September 1854 and January 1855 and as a full-length novel in three volumes by Chapman & Hall in 1855. It was Dickens who had encouraged Gaskell to write a full-length novel for serial publication, but *North and South*, which has complicated personal histories and subplots and lacks the larger-than-life characters, cliff-hangers, and mnemonic name tags of Dickens' work, was not well suited to this format. Every episode submitted was longer than its allocated space; Dickens tried to prune Gaskell's prose style, and the ending had to be compressed. The ending was revised for book publication but perhaps still feels a little stylized and abrupt.

As its title suggests, *North and South* is a novel about opposites. The conjunction "and" does not imply connection; it might as well be "versus." The oppositions represented include the north of England and the south; the industrial city and the rural village or estate; rich and poor; hardship and comfort; work and leisure, or in fact work and desperate unemployment; the "male" sphere of industry and the "female" sphere of the domestic. Gaskell's polarities comprehend man and woman, youth and age, faith and doubt, ignorance and experience, and much more.

North and South is a love story or courtship ordeal novel; that is, it involves a man and a woman who must overcome obstacles (not least, their mutual antipathy) before they can be united. Therefore, it is about how opposites attract, or perhaps more pertinently, how opposites find common ground. It is, however, much more than a love story. It is in a sense a regional novel, like *Mary Barton,* in that the real problems of rural poverty in the south are largely ignored and the focus is on a northern industrial town. But the town of Milton is more than a fictional Manchester: it is synecdochic of industrial England. Significantly, the heroine of *North and South,* Margaret Hale, is at first ignorant, then contemptuous of Milton and its inhabitants. At first she sees the latter as a homogeneous lump—the working masses. Only as she comes to see them as individuals does she gain respect for them and become interested in their concerns and welfare. Just so does the social problem novel educate the reading public. It illustrates the problem; it represents the victims of and sufferers from the problem as human, as individuals, and as deserving of sympathy; and it demands from the readers a sympathetic response. It does not necessarily lay down a course of action for the remedy of the problem, and it very rarely demands the obliteration of the social system that engendered the problem; to do so could be to question the provenance of the income that enabled the reader to purchase or have leisure and ability to read the novel.

Margaret Hale lectures one of the chief oppressors of the workers in the fictional Milton, John Thornton, a mill owner, on the condition of the workers, and she demands that he take action to improve those conditions. She tries to soften Thornton's approach to and treatment of his employees, which she believes is based only on the profit motive. She appeals to his conscience; she appeals to him on the basis of the treatment of fellow human beings. To the extent that she is able, she also ameliorates the condition of the workers (and nonworkers). She does not—cannot—change the system that oppresses the workers. In fact she joins the system, at the level of chief oppressor. Just as, in George Eliot's *Middlemarch,* the schemes of Dorothea Brooke for social improvements will never come about after she gives up her fortune and her ideas of philanthropic employment in order to marry and further her husband's career, so Margaret gives her fortune to her husband (voluntarily or not, since the novel is set long before the Married Women's Property Act) and becomes a mill owner's wife.

Margaret Hale and John Thornton, the novel's heroine and hero, represent two different social and geographical origins and outlooks, almost two different nationalities. Margaret Hale is the daughter of a clergyman, from the prosperous and rural south of England. John Thornton is a self-made businessman in the industrial north. Thornton at first believes Margaret to be a snobbish and standoffish busybody, ignorant of business practice yet believing herself entitled to interfere in it. Margaret thinks of him as a boorish bully only interested in squeezing the last ounce of profit from his workers. Each must come to understand something of the other's viewpoint and something of each other's motives and aims, and each must modify prejudice against the other's world before they can reach an understanding.

As a newcomer to the industrial north, Margaret Hale is a useful character because in describing her discovery of Milton and her attempts to help some of its citizens, the narrative introduces readers to some of the town's social problems and those who suffer from them. When Margaret needs to have something explained or interpreted, readers get that explanation or interpretation as well. In a sense Margaret becomes the reconciliation or merging of the two oppositions at the heart of the story. Just as Mary Smith, in *Cranford,* "vibrates between" Manchester and Cranford, so Margaret "vibrates" between the south and the north. She is removed from her home at an early age to live with her more prosperous aunt and uncle, but she remains in the wider home, the south, until she moves with her father and mother to Milton. There, at first, her heart vibrates with the south, but on a return visit, it is the concerns of Milton that preoccupy her, and she discovers that she has become acclimatized to the industrial north. If we choose (though there are dangers in this), we can see the experience of Margaret Hale as a fictionalized representation of those of Elizabeth Stevenson, who in 1832, as the new wife of the Unitarian Minister of Cross Street Chapel, the Reverend William Gaskell, had to leave the small country town of Knutsford for the city, only sixteen miles but a world away, of Manchester.

The focus of the narrative is on individuals and individual responses (emotional, rational, intellectual, moral) to circumstances rather than on abstract and larger concepts and issues. This enables readers to feel that they have access to characters' inner lives—their motivations, fears, and desires—and allows readers to empathize or identify with the central protagonists. The characters of *North and South* are three-dimensional, well drawn, and convincing. They have strengths and weaknesses, virtues and failings. The points of view of both workers, principally that of Nicholas Higgins, and industrialists, principally John Thornton, are aired, and the apportioning of guilt is less one-sided than in *Mary Barton*.

John Thornton echoes contemporary comments, and perhaps alienates our sympathy, when, in response to a demand that he share his reasons for lowering workers' wages, he refuses, citing his right to order his affairs as he wishes without explanation. In capitalist terms his reasons are valid and are explained to the reader, but Thornton sees no reason to take his employees into his confidence. Before he is reformed by Margaret Hale, Thornton adheres to the conviction that poverty is a concomitant of character failings, probably laziness and fecklessness—a fault rather than a condition, from which follows the idea that in helping to alleviate poverty, one simply encourages it. In the nineteenth-century age of "self-help" and utilitarianism, people who were regarded as unwilling rather than, as was much more probable, unable, to exert themselves to climb the social and economic ladder were at risk of being told that they deserved to be poor and did not deserve help.

Gaskell illustrates how lack of communication and mutual understanding produce terrible results. Without knowledge of the factory owners' reasoning, and of the larger economic system, the workers cannot understand the causes of their hardship and attribute it to greed. Without an understanding of the effects of the low wages and working conditions on the workers, the capitalists attribute the workers' complaints to ignorance and greed. The kindly Mr. Hale proposes a solution: that the kinder and wiser of the "masters" would meet with the workmen and have a good talk. Though this never materializes, the difficulties are eventually ameliorated by some communication and a greater degree of mutual respect and understanding.

In the England of the 1850s workers and owners were indeed communicating a bit more, and contemporary newspaper reports were advocating such communication. Reform was slowly advancing: the Manchester Free Library opened in 1852, the Corn Laws were repealed in 1854, and the Chartist movement was under way, but there was a long way to go.

As it plays out in the novel, the industrialists' greater understanding of the workers comes from seeing that "the hands" are not brutes but experience the same emotions they do. Just as, in Kazuo Ishiguro's novel *Never Let Me Go* (2005), an institution that raises clones exhibits these children's artwork in order to claim the status of humanity for them, so Gaskell's narrative exhibits the suffering, endurance, love, and passions of the workers to the masters to claim equal humanity for them. The enlightened masters respond with a form of Christian capitalism; they accept that they have a responsibility for their employees' well-being, and they allow their consciences to override the profit motive. This is not socialism—the hierarchy is firmly in place— but it is reform.

The masters' attitude to the workers is summed up in Thornton's use of the term "the hands," which indicates that the only part of the men of interest to their employees is the part that works for them. Hands are a significant motif in the narrative, as Jenny Uglow has noted. Thornton is fascinated by Margaret's delicate white hands and the way her father takes her hand and uses her thumb and finger as tongs to lift sugar lumps to his teacup. When Thornton proffers his hand, she refuses it, though of course later she metaphorically gives her hand to him in marriage. It takes the major part of the novel and a good deal of experience before Thornton takes the hand of Nicholas Higgins, the workers' leader, in the "good grip" of equals.

The novel's Christian, liberal, reformist ethos and the coming together of the two apparently opposed main characters are dramatized through dialogue. Some characters in *North and South* are exposed to several different registers of the English language. Margaret Hale's expanded social horizons and excursions into a public domain have led to an expanded lexicon, but when she introduces a new term into the domestic, female domain, her mother determinedly resists the term's incorporation into the register that marks the family as educated, southern, and not involved in trade. Mrs. Hale deplores Margaret's use of the phrase "very slack of work," which she regards as a provincialism that would offend Margaret's wealthy Aunt Shaw. Margaret points out that her cousin Edith has "picked up all sorts of military slang from [her fiancé] Captain Lennox, and Aunt Shaw never took any notice of it." To Mrs. Hale, there is a world of difference between the slang of a military office and a factory. The exchange that follows is revealing.

"And if I live in a factory town, I must speak factory language when I want it. Why, mamma, I could astonish you with a great many words you never heard in your life. I don't believe you know what a knobstick is."

"Not I, child. I only know it has a very vulgar sound; and I don't want to hear you using it."

"Very well, dearest mother, I won't. Only I shall have to use a whole explanatory sentence instead" (p. 281).

The more long-winded version could have defined *knobstick* as a "name given by workmen to one who during a strike or lockout continues to work on his master's terms" (*Oxford English Dictionary*), a term metonymically derived from "knobbed stick"—though, perhaps significantly, the word was also applied to a master "who employs men on terms not recognized by a trade-union." That Margaret refers to John Thornton's hired nonunion laborers ("scabs" in twenty-first-century usage) and not to John Thornton is suggested both by her reticence on the subject of her feelings for Thornton at this stage of the novel and by Gaskell's earlier use of the word in the first of its meanings cited above.

Mrs. Hale is subliminally shocked because the term is indicative of Margaret's subconscious sexual interest in John Thornton, who is in part responsible for her newly expanded lexicon. Thus in *North and South,* "knobstick" is relegated to a shockingly or perhaps amusingly vulgar expression that Mrs. Hale attempts to banish from the domestic register. In *Mary Barton,* however, Gaskell uses the term in the context of an attempt to eradicate a member of the group of people it signifies. "Jonas Higginbotham; him as was taken up last week for throwing vitriol in a knob-stick's face" (*Mary Barton,* Penguin 1996, p. 188).

The conversation between mother and daughter ends in the daughter's apparent acquiescence to her mother's wishes, but the reader is made aware that Margaret will continue to use the register she has picked up from John Thornton and workers of Milton because she will need them. She will at least in part participate in the social and linguistic domain her mother resists so firmly. That domain, that register, is localized, and the Hales are largely oblivious of its wider significance. John Thornton, however, is aware that the discourse of economics is a powerful determinant of the whole nation and that the lexicon of industry is rapidly becoming diffused into the parent language. In employing the register of industry, Margaret reflects the growing diglossia of her society, but as a woman, she is not empowered by her knowledge or its application. Her knowledge and understanding will not make her an industrialist or a worker.

Both Margaret Hale and John Thornton keep their registers distinct. Margaret spares her mother the alleged vulgarities of industry and falls into the style of a Bible-quoting Lady Bountiful in her encounters with impoverished and, later, angry workers. Mr. Thornton, like Mr. Hale, employs the language of industry and the alleged male sphere for communication with superior hands and other working males. Margaret's changing and expanding lexicon is an indicator of her changing sympathies. The well-bred, upper-middle-class girl who knew very little of and wished to know even less about trade and industry has encountered both those who are familiar with words such as "fluff" (p. 118) and the circumstances attendant upon their familiarity (that is, the suffering and sometimes death that resulted from workers' constant inhalation of cotton-derived downy particles—"fluff"—in the mill). The *OED* connects the word with "flue," as perhaps an onomatopoeic imitation of the action of puffing away some light substance. The earliest example given in the *OED* is from 1790, from Francis Grose's *Provincial Glossary,* and the earliest literary usages given are 1818 and 1825. Significantly, the word is not in Dr. Johnson's eighteenth-century *Dictionary.* Margaret's habitual humanitarian thinking and sense of duty prompt her to include the mill workers in her acts of charity, as habit leads her to incorporate items from the workers' register into her own. The construction of sentences in which she uses words such as "fluff" and "knob-stick," however, foregrounds those terms as imports against her habitual register, and her affiliations remain with her mother, a lady who stepped down a rung to marry a parson, and John Thornton, the well-off businessman. Though representative of very different social groups, these two are not as polarized by class (and therefore language) as are Margaret and Bessy, Nicholas Higgins, or the undiscriminated group represented through synecdoche as "the hands." Mr. Thornton, as Cousin Edith hopes, is "able to sound his *h*'s ... not a common Darkshire accomplishment" (p. 511). He is also a convert to some of Margaret's humanitarian projects, though never to radical reform. As he says, it is "common interest which invariably makes people find means and ways of seeing each other, and becoming acquainted with each other's ... tricks of temper and modes of speech" (p. 515). The common interests of the capital-owning classes unite Margaret Hale and John Thornton, as does the common interest of their mutual attraction, and by the end of the novel they are drawing attention to their mutual register by playful syntactic repetition, as they imagine the reaction of the redoubtable Aunt Shaw to their coming union.

"I can guess. Her first exclamation will be, 'That man!' "

108

"Hush!" said Margaret, "or I shall try and show you your mother's indignant tones as she says, 'That woman!' "

(p. 521)

THE LIFE OF CHARLOTTE BRONTË

The father and husband of Gaskell's friend Charlotte Brontë, the Reverend Patrick Brontë and the Reverend Arthur Bell Nicholls, chose Gaskell to be the author of Brontë's biography. This was probably because they hoped that she would correct the inaccuracies of the obituaries and other press reports that had appeared since the death of Charlotte Brontë, and that her portrait would help to correct the aspects of the public image of Brontë that they considered undesirable.

Gaskell's *The Life of Charlotte Brontë* (1857) was not entirely hagiographic. She clearly did not see Brontë as a saint. She wrote that the difference between herself and her friend was that Charlotte Brontë put all her "naughtiness" into her writing, whereas Gaskell put in all her goodness. Brontë, she wrote, worked off a great deal of morbidity into her writing and out of her life, whereas her own books were so much better than she was that she felt like a hypocrite for having written them (*Letters,* p. 154). Nonetheless, the *Life* did suppress aspects of Charlotte Brontë's life and character that could have been considered less than suitable for an eminent authoress. No mention is made of Brontë's unrequited passion for Constantin Héger, the husband of the proprietress of the Brussels school that Charlotte and Emily Brontë visited as pupil-teachers. Gaskell worked on the biography for more than a year before it was published in 1857, while she was abroad again.

Gaskell's *Life* was the first full-length biography of a female author by a fellow female author. Though it brought her £800 and seems to have been very much a labor of love, its publication brought trials and tribulations that nearly included a literal trial: some of those featured in her *Life* complained vociferously, and Lady Scott, implicated in an adulterous relationship with Branwell Brontë, threatened to sue for libel. With the help of her husband and the publisher of the *Life,* George Smith, Gaskell managed to avert legal action but was forced to publish a retraction concerning the story of Branwell Brontë's employment and subsequent dismissal. The second edition of the *Life* was withdrawn, and a revised (both cut and expanded) edition was substituted for it in August 1857.

The *Life* is written as a linear narrative interspersed with extracts from letters and quotations from the memories of Charlotte's friends and remaining family. It is preceded by a quotation from *Aurora Leigh,* Elizabeth Barrett Browning's claim for women's capacity for artistic achievement, but the lines chosen refer to the loneliness of the woman artist who sits alone, hearing her praises sung far off. As with all of Gaskell's work, it sites its heroine in her social and geographical context, emphasizing the effect of the environment on the outlook and character of its inhabitants, and opens with an extended portrait of Haworth and its surroundings.

SYLVIA'S LOVERS

Sylvia's Lovers (1863) is dedicated to the Reverend William Gaskell: "My Dear Husband," by "her who knows his true value." Its epigraph is taken from Tennyson's *In Memoriam:*

Oh for thy voice to soothe and bless!
What hope of answer or redress?
Behind the veil, behind the veil!

The "evolution" section of the poem expresses the Victorian ambivalent attitude to Darwinian and other theories of evolution: pride in the scientific discoveries of the day in tension with anxieties about their implications. It is significant that Gaskell omits the line that opens the quatrain: "O life as futile, then, as frail!"

Where *Ruth* is set in an indeterminate recent past, *Sylvia's Lovers* is a historical novel set during the French Revolution. Although the location is far geographically and, even more, socially from Revolutionary France, the Revolution has a huge impact on the lives of the protagonists, the inhabitants of the small Yorkshire port of

Monkshaven in the north of England. Fears of invasion are rife; the war against France is still largely being fought at sea; the nation needs a strong navy; the navy needs sailors. As the whaling ships come into port, the "press gangs" are waiting to grab the men and carry them off to enforced service. The repercussions of war reach Sylvia Robson and the two men who are rivals for her: her cousin, the cautious and conventional Philip Hepburn, and the more forceful and dynamic Charley Kinraid. Hepburn adores and idolizes Sylvia; this idolatry leads a good man to a desperate act. Sylvia loves her father; his ruin leads her to abandon every precept of Christian forgiveness.

When Kinraid is abducted and pressed into service, he writes to Sylvia, assuring her of his constancy, and entrusts the letter to Hepburn, who withholds it, allowing people to believe that Kinraid has drowned. When Daniel Robson, Sylvia's father, is hanged following an abortive rebellion against the press gang's headquarters, Sylvia and her mother, made destitute, are taken in by Hepburn. The deceived Sylvia submits to Hepburn from a sense of obligation, and the resulting marriage is false; deadening to Sylvia and riddled with the terror of exposure for Hepburn. Exposure comes with the return of Kinkaid. Disgraced and despairing, Hepburn enlists in the army. After saving the life of Kinraid in battle, he returns to Monkshaven but so battle-scarred as to be unrecognizable. Like Ruth, Hepburn has a kind of redemption that results in death. He saves his daughter from drowning and dies of the consequences. His is not the real tragedy, however. The tragedy is that of Sylvia and all that is successively stripped away from her: the man she loves, her father, her mother, the family livelihood, her home, and the man she has married. She comes to forgive Hepburn, and to value his constancy, but it is on his deathbed.

As with *Mary Barton* and *North and South,* in *Sylvia's Lovers* the personal and individual is inseparable from the public and political. Male authority, possessiveness, and aggression on a local scale are inseparable from the contemporary aggression and struggle for authority and possession being waged across Europe and in America.

The object of the desire to possess and control is women, in particular Sylvia, and the novel represents that desire, that form of love or passion, as overmastering all other forms of learned, acceptable behavior: self-restraint, loyalty, honesty. It is not just men who in *Sylvia's Lovers* are rendered bestial by strong emotion. The women who are bereft of their men by the press gangs become maenads: enraged, fiery, engorged; howling and shrieking with bared teeth.

Monkshaven has as great an impact on its inhabitants and plays as great a part in the story as the industrial cities do in *Mary Barton* and *North and South.* It is isolated from the rest of the world by the sea on one side and an expanse of wild moorland on the other. Modeled on Whitby, a whaling port on the Yorkshire coast with an ancient abbey on an adjacent clifftop, Monkshaven and its surroundings are depicted as remote, bleak, and almost beyond the reach of civilization, an impression of Yorkshire that Gaskell seems to have taken away from her visits to the Brontë home in Haworth.

The novel ends on a sad but strangely subdued note, many years after the main events of the story. An anonymous traveler hears the "legend" of Philip Hepburn and his widow, who, pale and dressed in black, was seen around the town for years after his death but who died young, before her daughter had grown up.

WIVES AND DAUGHTERS

On her death, Elizabeth Gaskell left an unfinished novel, *Wives and Daughters,* which had been serialized in *Cornhill Magazine* between August 1864 and January 1866. She had enjoyed the greater length allowed for each extract in the *Cornhill* (corresponding to about three chapters of the full-length edition) in contrast to the restrictions placed on her by Dickens, and the novel expanded accordingly. The expansion was not from any kind of padding; the details are all functional and always significant. Sometimes these details are scientifically minute and exact, sometimes sensuous and impressionistic; sometimes they are reflective of the heroine's state of mind, or of Dr. Gibson's surgery, the village of

Hollingford, the Towers, the Hamleys' house, the estates, gardens, and countryside in which the story is set.

As the title suggests, the novel explores the lives of women, principally in the roles that are assumed to define them, that place them in relation to men. In doing so, it covertly challenges the woman's duty of obedience and the man's right of authority. The subtitle of the novel is "An Every-Day Story," and indeed the narrative does include many details of everyday nineteenth-century provincial life which for later readers provide fascinating local color. It also, however, represents those things that were endured day by day and hour by hour, generally in silence, by ordinary people, and the strategies those people use to enable that endurance. Those strategies are mostly the suppression of personal desires and of self. We see the conscientious Dr. Gibson bury his disappointed hopes for a supportive helpmeet for himself and loving mother for his child, hopes pushed to the back of his mind by a ruthless focus on practical matters and the unending labor of his medical practice. We see his daughter, Molly, suppressing her own maturation and development to please her father and surviving the pain of unrequited love by self-sacrifice and devotion to the interests of others. We see Molly's stepsister, Cynthia, insulating herself from an ever-present torment by the distractions of dress and the power granted by her looks. We see Roger Hamley— large, clumsy, considered dull—in the shadow of his elegant, gifted, more favored brother and doggedly working himself into achievement and standing (his scientific interests parallel those of Gaskell's cousin, Charles Darwin).

The backdrop for the novel is the wide canvas of provincial society in the decades preceding the date of the novel's publication. In the foreground are two young women growing from daughters to wives. Each girl has two fathers. Cynthia Kirkpatrick's real father has died long before the story opens but has had a father- or avuncular-figure, and she has a stepfather in Molly's real father, Dr. Gibson. Molly Gibson becomes close to Squire and Mrs. Hamley, and after the death of his wife she is like a daughter to the squire. Each of these father figures fails the girls in some way. Cynthia is hounded and harassed by hers; the squire takes action to prevent a suspected attachment between Molly and his son; and even Dr. Gibson, a good and kindly father, fails to understand and support his daughters.

The squire calls Molly "little Molly," and Dr. Gibson keeps her ignorant, even of her own financial independence, and is still calling her "little girl" and "little one" when she is fully grown and they are discussing her possible marriage (pp. 397–399). Molly accepts this infantilization with apparent meekness, but when the squire breaks down on the death of his son, she reverses the roles, taking his head on her breast and spoon-feeding him as though he were a baby. Cynthia resists such treatment. She breaks off her engagement to an eligible suitor rather than have to make her apologies for a lapse of behavior "and stand before him like a chidden child to be admonished and forgiven" (p. 548). Even more revealing of the habitual infantilization than the diminutives bestowed on Molly is the habit of both "fathers" of thinking of her in terms of amusing domesticated animals. Dr. Gibson calls her "silly little goosey" (p. 121) and Squire Hamley thinks of her as "a little four-legged doggie" running after him.

Wives and Daughters features one of Gaskell's greatest creations, the appalling Mrs. Hyacinth Kirkpatrick, said to be modeled on Gaskell's own stepmother. The masterly characterization manages to make clear that Mrs. Kirkpatrick is scheming, manipulative, greedy, vain, superficial, affected, a social-climbing snob, entirely self-centered, and yet not an entirely bad woman. The portrait of her marriage to the educated, intellectual, and somewhat austere Dr. Gibson is a study in error and self-deception which, in being more detailed and less comic, outdoes even that of Mr. and Mrs. Bennet in Jane Austen's *Pride and Prejudice*.

Mrs. Kirkpatrick's daughter, Cynthia, is similarly subtly characterized. Readers are led to expect a hard-hearted, gold-digging flirt who will damage or betray Molly, or a fallen Magdalen whom Molly will rescue, but neither stereotype is employed. Pam Morris, in her insightful introduction to the Penguin edition of *Wives and Daughters,* observes that Cynthia, having escaped indoctrination into the role of dutiful daughter, has avoided the doctrine of automatic self-abnegation and service that has been absorbed by Molly and is thus equipped to pursue her own desires. Unlike Molly, Cynthia is awake to what Morris refers to as the fictionality, that is, the constructedness of social roles such as "daughter" and "wife" (p. xix). When Roger Hamley, love of Molly's life but in love with Cynthia, is away on an expedition, it is Molly who eagerly devours his letters and sets herself to learn the discourse of Darwinian science in order to be actively involved in his interests, while Cynthia displays only boredom. On first reading, this looks like a clue to the inappropriateness and one-sidedness of the match and a further confirmation of Molly as heroine and Cynthia as antiheroine, but on a closer reading it is revealed as a product of Cynthia's continued resistance to the forces that would channel her into the approved role that Molly embraces.

RECEPTION

In spite of the controversies and occasional negative criticisms, Gaskell's writing was an immediate and continued success both popularly and critically. Although her work has been perhaps unfairly overshadowed by that of George Eliot, it has never been without readers and champions. Its reissue in paperback editions by Penguin and Oxford World Classics and introduction to the academic curriculum of both nineteenth-century and feminist studies have brought it to a wide readership. That audience was increased by television adaptations and associated tie-in editions of *Wives and Daughters* (1999), *North and South* (2004), and *Cranford* (2007).

Charles Kingsley wrote in *Fraser's Magazine* in April 1849 that *Mary Barton* should be posted in public places and read aloud from pulpits until the nation was brought to act "upon the awful facts contained in it," and that it would bring to the remedying of the social inequalities "energy of shame and repentance proportionate to the hugeness of the evil" (Easson, ed., 1991, p. 153).

John Ruskin was a fan of *Cranford,* which pleased Gaskell, because it was her avowed favorite among her novels. In a letter to Ruskin, she confessed that it was the only one of her books she could read again, and that whenever she was ill she would take the novel and be made to laugh afresh (*Letters,* p. 562.) It is in her capacity to make the reader both laugh and cry, sometimes almost simultaneously, that Gaskell is at her strongest and perhaps the appeal of her work is at its most enduring.

Selected Bibliography

WORKS OF ELIZABETH GASKELL

NOVELS AND STORIES

Mary Barton: A Tale of Manchester Life (Published anonymously), 2 vols. London: Chapman & Hall, 1848. Later editions: Macdonald Daly, ed., Harmondsworth, U.K.: Penguin, 2003; Shirley Foster, ed., Oxford: Oxford World's Classics, 2006.

The Moorland Cottage. (Published anonymously.) London: Chapman & Hall, 1850. Later edition: Suzanne Lewis, ed., *The Moorland Cottage and Other Stories.* Oxford: Oxford World's Classics, 1995.

Libbie Marsh's Three Eras: A Lancashire Tale. (As Cotton Mather Mills.) London: Hamilton, Adams, 1850.

Ruth (Published anonymously), 3 vols. London: Chapman & Hall, 1853. Later editions: Alan Shelston, ed., Oxford: Oxford World's Classics, 1985 (reprinted 1991); Angus Easson, ed., Harmondsworth, U.K.: Penguin, 2004.

Cranford. (Published anonymously.) In *Household Words* (1851–1853). London: Chapman & Hall, 1853. Later edition: Elizabeth Porges Watson, ed., Oxford: Oxford World's Classics, 1972 (reprinted 1980).

Lizzie Leigh and Other Tales. (Published anonymously.) London: Chapman & Hall, 1855. Earlier edition: *Lizzie Leigh, A Domestic Tale.* New York: Dewitt & Davenport, 1850.

North and South. (Published anonymously.) In *Household Words,* September 1854–January 1855. London: Chapman & Hall, 1855. Later editions: Patricia Ingham, ed., Harmondsworth, U.K.: Penguin, 2003; Sally Shuttleworth and Angus Easson, eds., Oxford: Oxford World's Classics, 2008.

My Lady Ludlow and Other Tales. London: Smith, Elder, 1859.

Right at Last, and Other Tales. London: Low, 1860.

Sylvia's Lovers, 3 vols. London: Smith, Elder, 1863. Later edition: Andrew Sanders, ed., Oxford: Oxford World's Classics, 1982 (reprinted 1999).

A Dark Night's Work. London: Smith, Elder, 1863.

Cousin Phillis: A Tale. New York: Harper, 1864. Later editions: Angus Easson, ed., Oxford: Oxford World's Classics, 1981; P. J. Keating, ed., Harmondsworth, U.K.: Penguin, 1995.

Cousin Phillis and Other Tales. London: Smith, Elder, 1865.

The Grey Woman and Other Tales. London: Smith, Elder, 1865.

Wives and Daughters: An Every-day Tale. In *Cornhill Magazine* (August 1864–January 1866). In 2 vols, London: Smith, Elder, 1866. Later editions: Angus Easson, ed., Oxford: Oxford World's Classics, 1987 (reprinted 2008); Pam Morris, ed., Harmondsworth, U.K.: Penguin, 1996.

OTHER WORKS

"Sketches Among the Poor." *Blackwood's Edinburgh Magazine,* January 1837, pp. 48–50.

"Clopton House." In *Visits to Remarkable Places, Old Halls, Battlefields, and Scenes Illustrative of Striking Passages in English History and Poetry,* by William Howitt. London: Longman, 1840.

The Life of Charlotte Brontë, 2 vols. London: Smith, Elder, 1857. Later editions: Elisabeth Jay, ed., Harmondsworth, U.K.: Penguin, 1997 Angus Easson, ed., Oxford: Oxford World's Classics, 1996.

JOURNALS, CORRESPONDENCE, AND MANUSCRIPTS

The primary source of the personal papers and correspondence of Elizabeth Gaskell is the John Rylands Library of the University of Manchester, in England, but these have been reproduced as a 13-reel set of microfilms by Primary Source Microfilm.

The Letters of Mrs. Gaskell. Edited by J. A. V. Chapple and Arthur Pollard. Manchester, U.K.: Manchester University Press, 1966.

BIOGRAPHICAL AND CRITICAL STUDIES

Bonaparte, Felicia. *The Gypsy-Bachelor of Manchester: The Life of Mrs. Gaskell's Demon.* Charlottesville: University Press of Virginia, 1992.

Craik, W. A. *Elizabeth Gaskell and the English Provincial Novel.* London: Methuen, 1975.

Cunningham, Valentine. *Everywhere Spoken Against: Dissent in the Victorian Novel.* Oxford: Clarendon Press, 1975.

Easson, Angus. *Elizabeth Gaskell.* London: Routledge & Kegan Paul, 1979.

Easson, Angus, ed. *Elizabeth Gaskell: The Critical Heritage.* London and New York: Routledge, 1991.

Flint, Kate. *Elizabeth Gaskell.* Writers and their Work Series. London: Northcote House, 1995.

Foster, Shirley, *Elizabeth Gaskell: A Literary Life.* Houndmills, Basingstoke, U.K.: Palgrave Macmillan, 2002.

Gallagher, Catherine. *The Industrial Reformation of English Fiction: Social Discourse and Narrative Form, 1832–1867.* Chicago: University of Chicago Press, 1985.

Gérin, Winifred. *Elizabeth Gaskell: A Biography.* Oxford: Clarendon Press, 1976.

Kestner, Joseph. *Protest and Reform: The British Social Narrative by Women, 1827–1867.* London: Methuen, 1985.

Matus, Jill L., ed. *The Cambridge Companion to Elizabeth Gaskell.* Cambridge, U.K., and New York: Cambridge University Press, 2007.

Schor, Hilary M. *Scheherezade in the Marketplace: Elizabeth Gaskell and the Victorian Novel.* Oxford and New York: Oxford University Press, 1992.

Stoneman, Patsy. *Elizabeth Gaskell.* Manchester: Manchester University Press, 2007.

Uglow, Jenny. *Elizabeth Gaskell: A Habit of Stories.* London: Faber and Faber, 1993.

FILMS BASED ON THE WORKS OF ELIZABETH GASKELL

Wives and Daughters. Four-part miniseries. Directed by Nicholas Renton, screenplay by Andrew Davies. British Broadcasting Corporation, 1999.

North and South. Four-part miniseries. Directed by Brian Percival. British Broadcasting Corporation, 2004.

Cranford. Five-part miniseries. Directed by Simon Curtis. British Broadcasting Corporation, 2007.

THOM GUNN

(1929—2004)

Kit Fan

WITH THE COLLECTION *Fighting Terms* (1954), Thom Gunn appeared on the poetic scene as part of a movement of tough realism and renovation in postwar British poetry. From the outset he was associated with the strenuous seriousness of F. R. Leavis's Cambridge and what came to be called the Movement, symbolized by Robert Conquest's *New Lines* anthology (1956). He ended his career half a century later, after the appearance of his final book, *Boss Cupid* (2000), a valedictory collection that reflected back on the poetic journey embodied in *Collected Poems* (1993). By then he had become a very different kind of poet, representing a different world than any dreamed of in F. R. Leavis's or Robert Conquest's philosophy. In the intervening years Gunn had established himself in California as a chronicler of homosexual experience in the era of gay liberation, AIDS and its aftermath, and as a poet who moved freely between Britain and the United States, poetic formalism and experimentalism, the academic and the "way.out." Though he still paid allegiance to his early conservative mentors Yvor Winters and Donald Davie, Gunn wrote with increasing candor of areas of experience associated with a newer world of gay bars, drugs, AIDS, rock and roll, casual sex, and alternative forms of social relationships associated with post-sixties California.

BIOGRAPHY AND INFLUENCES

Born in Gravesend, on the southern bank of the Thames estuary, on August 29, 1929, Gunn spent his childhood mostly in Hampstead. His parents Herbert Smith and Ann Charlotte Thompson Gunn were both journalists; they divorced when he was ten, and his mother committed suicide when he was fifteen. Gunn started military service in 1948 and enrolled at Trinity College, Cambridge, in 1950, where he met his lifelong partner, Mike Kitay, in 1952. Having completed his English degree at Cambridge during the heyday of Leavis, in 1954 Gunn followed Kitay to the United States and studied poetry under the stern guidance of Yvor Winters at Stanford. In 1958 he began teaching creative writing and poetry at the University of California at Berkeley, and in 1960 he moved to San Francisco with Kitay. He settled there permanently, teaching at Berkeley for twenty-five years until his retirement in May 1999. He died at his home on Cole Street in San Francisco's Haight-Ashbury neighborhood on April 25, 2004.

After his death, the shape of Gunn's career became visible in a new way. His second book was called *The Sense of Movement* (1957), and in its opening poem, "On the Move," he said, "One is always nearer by not keeping still" (p. 40; all quotations of poetry in this essay are from the 1994 *Collected Poems*). As a poet, Gunn was indeed restlessly mobile, committed to moving on, but his quest for poetic identity involved identity in many other senses too. His career coincided with a battle over different notions of poetry—competing notions about poetic tradition and the individual talent—but also spanned a period of ferocious conflict over identity politics, fought out in terms of race, gender, and sexuality, particularly in the United States. In these contexts, it is plausible to view Gunn's writing in terms of the dialectic between poetic and sexual identity, as he moved from the shadowy world of the literary closet into the clear light of day of gay politics in the post-Stonewall era. It involved a transition from the fraught, coded poetics of *Fighting Terms* to the candid, autobiographical reports of sexual life in *The Passages of Joy*

(1982) and the terrifying realism of the AIDS elegies of *The Man with Night Sweats* (1992). The same development can be described as a move away from the Movement, and the kind of postwar British poetry represented by Philip Larkin and others, to the West Coast poetry scene in the United States represented by City Lights bookstore, the Beat Generation, Robert Duncan, and the tradition of William Carlos Williams.

Gunn's career is thus in part a classic coming-out story, analogous to Christopher Isherwood's in *Christopher and His Kind* (1976) or Edmund White's in *The Beautiful Room Is Empty* (1988). That said, the poet refused to portray his development in triumphantly progressive terms, and he remained in many ways true to the ideas of poetry (and some of the icons) he espoused at the start. In fact he was neither interested in developing a "unique poetic personality" or investing in any overt aesthetic, cultural, or political identity. His art was born out of a struggle between the personal and impersonal, the intimate and the anonymous, the candid and the masked. Rather than being another version of the poetics of identity, Gunn's oeuvre offers a poetics of shifting identifications. The poetry never suggests the consolation of secured selfhood or existential affirmation. As intimated by the title of his first book of essays, *The Occasions of Poetry* (1982), Gunn was more interested in "occasions" than the self. Although Gunn's career reads in part as a coming-out story—"Tom Goes to San Francisco," say—or its negative double—"The Rake's Progress"—the poet's development from *Fighting Terms* to *Boss Cupid* was more oscillating and unsettled than these stories suggest. Though Gunn was one of the most eloquent reporters from gay America, he refused to be its spokesperson, and he never wrote as anyone other than himself, a self that he imagined as almost anonymous. In his introduction to the selected poems of Ben Jonson, Gunn spoke of occasional poetry as "elicited by external events," giving the examples of "a birthday" and "a war" (p. 9). That word "elicited" suggests that the motive for the poem comes from outside rather than inside and that the outside is defined in terms of the poet's "situation" in a local and more general sense, not

the "self." "A Sketch of the Great Dejection," from *The Man with Night Sweats,* for example, is a situation report from the heart of the AIDS crisis that is "elicited" by it.

Gunn's poetry offers a strange mix of realism and stylization, candor and disguise. It is also an unlikely hybrid of the raw and the cooked, contemporary and traditional, played out behind an unswerving allegiance to the poets of Elizabethan and Jacobean England under whose aegis he began his career, and whose spell persisted long after his seduction by American poets like William Carlos Williams. Gunn's editions of Ben Jonson (1974) and Fulke Greville (1968) are as essential to his poetic project as the investment in the modern represented by his selection of Ezra Pound (2000) and his essays on Basil Bunting and Robert Duncan. One of the most powerful sources of his poetic force is the tension between traditional poetic decorum and the journalistic stuff of everyday life on the streets of San Francisco—and his simultaneous identification with both.

Gunn's "Unsettled Motorcyclist" in *The Sense of Movement* is committed to movement but not necessarily development, to journeys rather than destinations. This is not a version of the gospel according to postmodernism but rather a reflex of the founding identifications of Gunn, as he pondered the contradictory nature of his sexual and cultural identity. Even after his chronicles of gay liberation, Beat culture, and hallucinogenic experiment in coming-out books like *Moly* (1971), Gunn the poet appears to have been strangely disenchanted by his own cult of hedonistic enchantment. One of his last critical essays was on John Wilmot, second earl of Rochester, one of the great erotic explorers in verse but also one of the most skeptical of English poets. Gunn's poetry of sexual, imaginative. and hallucinatory liberation was succeeded by saddened reflections on the vanity as well as the beauty of human wishes. The moment of *Moly, Jack Straw's Castle* (1976), and *The Passages of Joy* gave way not only to the beautifully freighted elegies of *The Man with Night Sweats* but also to the disenchanted lyrics from the domain of *Boss Cupid.*

Gunn was wary of his biographical self. In his postscript to the essay "My Life up to Now" he wrote that "the danger of biography, and equally of autobiography, is that it can muddy poetry by confusing it with its sources" (*The Occasions of Poetry,* p. 187). As an example, he cited Christopher Isherwood's *Christopher and His Kind,* a book he said he "wouldn't wish unwritten" but thought likely to "confuse his novels and stories" with their biographical sources (p. 187). In contrast, he argued that a poem's "truth" may be "its faithfulness to a possibly imagined feeling, not to my history" (p. 187). It may be that Gunn protests too much here; nevertheless, his words suggest a tension between his commitment to candid explorations of personal experience, including sexual pickups, erotic friendships, fantasies, and drug trips, and a fundamental sense of anonymity in his work, a lack of interest in himself *as* a "self." The data Gunn worked on, in poem after poem, at each stage of his career, were turned into "occasions of poetry," while largely sidestepping the categories of biography. It is as if his poetry depended on his treating himself as if he were someone else, or nobody in particular, an occasional person. Gunn never claimed the Orphic privileges of "the poet" or a "poet's life"—like Robert Lowell or Sylvia Plath, say—but was content to operate within the republic of contingency.

Gunn's approach to his medium is pragmatic, rather than programmatic. In formal terms, when he is set beside his English contemporary Philip Larkin, he might look a wild boy. Set beside American peers such as Allen Ginsberg, however, he can look tame or academic. If Gunn proved himself an intensely original poet, it was not because of innovations in the medium. Though he wrote obsessively about risk, he was not formally a risk taker. Though there was a marked stylistic breakthrough with *My Sad Captains* (1961) and *Moly,* which broadened his technical repertoire, Gunn continued to write within earshot of his early mentors, Shakespeare, Jonson, and Greville. He never jettisoned his commitment to traditional closed forms, and in many ways his last book, *Boss Cupid,* was also his most traditional.

Gunn used what Robert Lowell calls those "blessed structures," plot and rhyme, to process his experiences with drugs, gay liberation, and AIDS. Gunn did experiment with free verse during the period he was also experimenting with sex, drugs, and rock and roll, but his free verse is never "free" in the expansive manner of Ginsberg, Charles Olson, or Duncan. It reads more like a controlled experiment. Whether using the studious syllabics of "My Sad Captains," the hallucinatory free verse of "The Geysers," or the traditional metrics of "Moly," Gunn always keeps a sense of investigative distance, like his hero Stendhal. His originality, in other words, had more to do with his capacity to respond to the changing situations and occasions of poetry, than to the imperative to make it new. It was the imperative to adapt to the cultural and historical situations he lived in that generated the ongoing "sense of movement" in his work.

Gunn's career is not a unified poetic journey in the usual sense. Nor does it suggest a unitary self beyond its own occasions. His refusal to be "identified" in terms of styles and movements, of different poetic "camps" (or camp), make Gunn a uniquely mobile reporter from the front line of gay America in the later twentieth century, but also hard to "place." The density of his medium in this sense is a reflex of the density of the social experience it records. In retrospect, Gunn has become—perhaps paradoxically—a more public poet, an occasional poet in the mold of Ben Jonson or even Samuel Johnson, than his skeptical commitment to personal experience might lead one to believe. With its tough fidelity to "touch," the body, the realm of personal encounters, the small change of the life in the streets and bars of the modern city, his work offers an unparalleled history of modern sociability and desire.

FIGHTING TERMS

At the outset, as a postwar poet writing in peacetime, Gunn established a curious association between the roles of poet and soldier. Looking back on his first book, *Fighting Terms* (1954), in *The Occasions of Poetry,* Gunn defined the act of writing in martial terms: "Writing poetry became the act of an existentialist conqueror, excited and aggressive. What virtues this collection possesses, however, are mostly to be found in an awareness of how far I fell short of being such a conqueror" (p. 173). That title *Fighting Terms* confronted the ambivalent language of warfare in postwar Britain, as well as representing poetic language in terms of a battle. The book captures a paradoxical kind of martial virtue, however, and most of the soldiers in the book are resigned, wounded, frustrated, or some combination of these—"unsoldierly" but humanely tender. In poems such as "The Court Revolt," "The Right Possessor," "Captain in Time of Peace," and "Incident on a Journey," the poet soldier serves as an iconic model for the apprentice poet—a model that is simultaneously intellectual, erotic, and poetic, recalling the literary legacy of First and Second World War Poetry, Shakespearean drama, French existentialism, and Homeric legend, as well as Gunn's experience in the British National Service.

The opening poem, "The Wound" (p. 3), is a postwar poem in which Gunn explores warfare as a metaphor for other kinds of contest and risk. The poem's wound is one of the most mysterious in English poetry. The speaker is simultaneously Achilles, a real soldier in a real war, and at the same time someone who dreams of or poses as Achilles. From the private bed to the public battlefield, the poem swings backward and forward between the convalescent bedroom and the turbulence of the Trojan War. Gunn's iambic pentameters, tight rhymes, and trimmed stanzas create a closed, claustrophobic world, in which a modern sickroom resonates to the aftermath of the heroic line of Elizabethan blank verse. We are ushered into the ancient Greek war scene at the beginning of the second stanza when the speaker's "mind returned to Troy." "Returned" uncannily suggests mental repetition and even the possibility that the speaker could be Achilles or confuse himself with the Greek hero. The speaker's head wound is not only a hangover from the poetry of World Wars I and II but also implies a traumatized imaginary soldier gripped by memories of the battlefield. "The Wound" symbolically launched the young Gunn as a poet

of shields, armor, body, and skin (themes he never left behind). Instead of simply affirming these masculine sites, however, the speaker offers a sense of risk and vulnerability that is at odds with many critics' view of Gunn's toughness and intellectualism. At the poem's end, the speaker calls for armor but "did not reel," as if the iconic physical shield alone could provide security against his psychological turmoil. By articulating the soldier's vulnerability, Gunn draws attention to his own need for armor, suggesting that his own concealed sexual identity (implicit in the identification with Achilles as lover of Patroclus) plays a part in the internal battlefield in the background of the soldier poems. Soldiers haunt Gunn's whole career, but their iconic status gradually diffuses in later collections as Gunn incorporates the iconic figure of the soldier into erotic, autobiographical poems about times of "peace."

Many poems in *Fighting Terms* stage violence and conflict in a postwar arena—"Lazarus Not Raised," "Helen's Rape," "The Court Revolt," "The Right Possessor," "The Beach Head," "Tamer and Hawk," and "Captain in Time of Peace." At the core of the book is a cast of anonymous soldiers, who reflect on the poet's estranged contemporary masculinity through the lens of Renaissance literature. A good example is "A Mirror for Poets" (pp. 24–25), in which Gunn explicitly returns to the Elizabethan age and looks back to that time as not only a "mirror for poets" but also a distorted image of the present, "a violent time," when "wheels, racks and fires" were "in every writer's mouth." Chronicling "Hacks in the Fleet and nobles in the Tower," it names Shakespeare and Jonson and invokes the "diseased and doubtful Queen" Elizabeth, insisting that Philip Sidney's long poem "Arcadia" as well as Shakespearian and Jonsonian dramas all need to be seen as mirrors of a society where "the boundaries met / Of life and life, at danger." The poem suggests that the "huge magnanimity" of the "Paphlagonian King" in Sidney's "Arcadia" (and in *King Lear*) is a product of that "violent time" but also that that earlier period mirrors Gunn's own time of conflict.

The early Gunn loves poses and poseurs. Among the many mythical, heroic, literary, and pop idols he adopts in his first books are Achilles, Lazarus, Percy Bysshe Shelley, Shakespeare, Elvis Presley, a wolf boy, and motorcyclist. In *Fighting Terms,* Gunn's soldier icon serves as a mirror of his troubled relationship to his masculinity and sexuality. It embodies a clandestine battle being fought out not on behalf of, but against, his own society. Gunn's half-sublimated, half-stifled attraction to the masculine icon of the soldier also suggests something about his literary love affair with the heroic poetry of Homer and of the sixteenth century. Gunn's anonymous soldiers are often haunted by an imaginary heroic war, and in these poems, the poet finds ways to explore the "forbidden" zone of homoerotic masculinity. The rhetorical world of the early Gunn is often highly literary, but it is also, as Gunn's early life was, overshadowed by a sense of war. Even though he is not in any sense a war poet, he is from the outset of his career a postwar one, alive to the reality of conflict. He naturally dramatizes the world in "fighting terms."

THE SENSE OF MOVEMENT

"On the Move" (pp. 39–40) opens Gunn's second book, *The Sense of Movement* (1957), inviting us to look at "movement" from the perspective of an iconic motorcyclist. For Gunn, the motorcyclist had something of the dangerous masculine glamour of the image of the soldier in war. Indeed his biker is a civilian, Beat variant of the soldier. Gunn's motorcyclists, in their unlikely way, are as much courtiers as motorcyclists; they are secular reincarnations of Fulke Greville and adepts of philosophical speculation. The biker's image is drawn, however, from the more modern iconography of Marlon Brando, James Dean, and Elvis Presley; he is a creature of the 1950s and 1960s. With his dark studded leather jacket, tight leather pants, black leather boots, and thunderous Harley Davidson, the motorcyclist wore the armor of a postwar urban soldier, becoming an unlikely knightly emblem of heroic masculinity. Gunn's intellectual motorcyclist is a variant on his soldier icon. As a streetwise existentialist,

fighting amid the marshy fertility of "the natural," the biker is a cryptic emblem of the hidden autobiographical self that surfaced later in the last section of *Jack Straw's Castle.*

"On the Move" frames the motorcyclist within a philosophical context, presenting him as an intellectual rebel moving "with an uncertain violence." Packed into the poem's firm iambic pentameters, there is a sense of uncertainty, emptiness, a thwarted urge toward meaning. The impersonal pronoun "one" runs through the whole poem, making the motorcyclist a representative of "us" in general as well as the singular existential "one." The motorcycles offer neither "noise" nor "sound," but "a baffled sense" and "the dull thunder of approximate words"—an experience of language under a veil or in the process of formulation. The motorcyclist's movement is situated against a larger sense of "movement in a valueless world." Even though the poem clearly conjures up mobility, its rhythmic flow is half-halting, interrupted by commas, and burdened with a reiterative obsession with moving "toward, toward." It ends with an image of an existentialist quest that is simultaneously a critique of existentialist will, as the poet proclaims, "One is always nearer by not keeping still." In this way, the poet generates a Sisyphean myth of movement, in which "not keeping still" is a way to get "nearer" to the limitless (or "absolute"). It also suggests that one is perpetually condemned to movement, "reaching no absolute" and "not keeping still." "On the Move" has been one of Gunn's most anthologized poems. Though the heyday of the biker has since gone, Gunn, in turning him into a strange hybrid of Andrew Marvell, Brando, and Jean-Paul Sartre, converted a marginal 1950s subcultural icon into a figure of capable imagination.

"Elvis Presley" (p. 57) looks at another pop icon as an incarnation of youth, style, rebellion, and the homoerotic. Though not a motorcyclist, Elvis's glossy, tasseled leather jacket resembles the biker's. "Panting, stretches out / In turn, promiscuously, by every note," Gunn's Elvis is an erotic embodiment of the new rock music, which, with its "rebellious tone" and "appeal to young people," captured both the anxious instability and dynamism of postwar youth. Turning "revolt into style," Elvis "poses," but his "revolt into style" also offered a style of cultural revolt. "The pose held is a stance," Gunn says. He is speaking of Elvis, but his words also refer to his own attraction to such hip poseurs and others. The poem is full of fighting terms. Elvis's pose "wars on" the world, and he sings in a "posture for combat" in which he "wields" a guitar like a machine gun. The poet's Elvis is not only a rock icon, in other words, but an alternative version of the embattled soldier. Despite the poem's stylized rhythm, the rhymes intensify a clash between the serious and the trivial—as "combat" is rhymed with "cat," "stance" with "chance," destabilizing Elvis's vigorous certainty and directing the reader toward the uncertainty of "may be" in the last line. The poem thrives on the clash and convergence between Elvis's "revolt into style" and its own "Movement" good manners.

Though *The Sense of Movement* continues to deploy many "fighting terms"—in the seasonal violence of "Autumn Chapter in a Novel" or on the ancient Roman battlefield of "The Silver Age"—a number of poems show a new interest in more personal and autobiographical subjects. These include "In Praise of Cities," a sensual Baudelairean night scene; "To Yvor Winters, 1955," a tribute to his critical mentor; "The Inherited Estate," an account of his relationship with Mike Kitay; and the anecdotal "Thoughts on Unpacking." Such poems intimate the directions in which Gunn was moving. After *The Sense of Movement,* Gunn effectively abandoned the motorcyclist icon, but something of the motorcyclist's bodily and intellectual athleticism, his high-risk balancing of life and death, resurfaced in later work. "From the Wave" (pp. 198–199), for example, in *Moly,* recasts the motorcyclist gang as a group of Californian surfers who "poise their weight / With a learn'd skill." The existentialist conflict between "the chosen instrument" and "the mere embodiment" (in "The Unsettled Motorcyclist's Vision of his Death," p. 54) gets internalized and resolved as the surfers are "Half wave, half men," Proteus-like figures whose "sheathed bodies slick as seals / Loosen and tingle." The wave-riders' movement is not

"manufactured" by the machine, as in the earlier poem, but initiated by people responding to the rhythms of the natural world. "From the Wave" can be read as a coda to the "movement complex" voiced in the last line of "On the Move." For the wave-rider, the aim is not to be "nearer" but "right." In his later books, Gunn explored very different senses of movement.

MY SAD CAPTAINS *AND* TOUCH

In 1960 Gunn settled in San Francisco, one of the literary capitals of the 1960s. Gunn's next two books represent a stylistic movement into new territory. Of the two, *My Sad Captains* (1961) reads in many ways as a farewell to his earlier iconographic repertoire, written in a freer manner, while *Touch* (1967) seems a not-quite-achieved prelude to the shape of things to come, groping toward a new idiom, born of his encounter with LSD and sexual liberation, on the one hand, and the American verse post William Carlos Williams, on the other.

"Considering the Snail" (p. 117), like other syllabic poems in the second section of *My Sad Captains,* represents an important stylistic breakthrough. It translates the iconographic legacy of the soldier and the motorcyclist into new terms. Though the snail struggles to move on the "heavy" grass, with each line tidily trimmed to seven syllables, Gunn achieves a freer sense of movement here than in his previous iambic pentameters. The rhythm is freer (almost free verse), though occasionally punctuated by iambic echoes. The snail's silent crawl is captured in two long relative clauses, which delay the delivery of meaning and mimic the snail's slow motion. This poem's subtle, exploratory idiom mirrors the snail finding its way through space, riding the resistance of rigid metrics. The active verb "pushes" gives the snail a sense of force, as it struggles to penetrate the heavy grass. Nature, for the first time in Gunn's work, is described as independent of human interference, "where / rain has darkened the earth's dark." The color contrast between "the bright path" and "the earth's dark" underlines the snail's unspectacular progress, which is nothing like the "dull thunder of approximate words" associated with the motorcyclist. Nonetheless the snail iconically relates back to the soldier and the motorcyclist, not because they all meet on the common ground of a similar landscape, but because the snail is an armored hunter, fighting for his survival as he "moves in a wood of desire," his "antlers barely stirring" as he "hunts." The snail's phallic "antlers" and semen-like trail subliminally evoke a world of homoerotic fantasy in "a wood of desire."

Most of Gunn's syllabic poems in *My Sad Captains,* such as "Waking in a Newly Built House" and "The Feel of Hands," offer a contrasted sense of swiftness and agility, with the shortness of their lines subtly accelerating their sense of tonal movement. In "Considering the Snail," however, the speaker's "I" refocuses the poem, giving the emblematic portrait a more personal intensity as the poem considers both "what power is at work" and the snail's "fury." The first-person pronoun here signals the emergence of a new reflective voice. Gunn's "I" here, though impersonal, invites the reader to identify with the semidetached speaker. "Drenched there / with purpose" echoes the drenched war-devastated landscape featured in "Adolescence," (p. 125) another syllabic poem, in which the speaker walks "through the wet spring," with his knees "drenched from high grass charged with water," thinking of himself as "part, still, of done war."

The snail seems an unlikely warrior, but the investment in martial figures evident in Gunn's first three collections is intimately bound up with his fight for poetic identity. It also suggests the dilemma of Gunn as a homosexual poet unable explicitly to identify his erotic interests. What he developed was a poetry of identifications rather than identity, drawn to theatrical postures of assertive masculinity but aware of the degrees of impersonation this involves. In his first books, the poet himself remains a curiously anonymous figure, submerged behind his account of glamorously anonymous others, like the bikers or soldiers in "Black Jackets" and "The Byrnies." Though *My Sad Captains* marks a new poetic beginning, it too is haunted by historical "cap-

tains" who displace Achilles (from "The Wound") as well as "Rastignac at 45" (from *The Sense of Movement*). They include St. Paul in "Santa Maria del Popolo" ("Resisting, by embracing, nothingness," p. 94)—another of Gunn's "metaphysical poems," this time built around a painting by Caravaggio—and "Claus Von Stauffenberg," an existential poem about a hero of the Nazi Resistance movement. Besides these Gunn sets dodgier modern icons of masculinity, including "Blackie the Electric Rembrandt" and "The Fallen Rake" of "Modes of Pleasure," figures associated with the equally dangerous world of contemporary selfhood.

In all of these poems, the image of the anonymous soldier is never far away. In Gunn's first narrative sequence, "Misanthropos," in *Touch,* the poet explores the experience of "The Last Man," a postmilitary survivor who wanders in a bleak, ruined earth in the wake of nuclear holocaust. This is both a reflex in response to the nuclear threat of the 1960s and a legacy of Gunn's coming to adolescence during the war years, when notions of masculinity were inevitably dominated by the image of the soldier in uniform and a sense of devastating conflict. World War II comes directly into play in "Innocence" and "Claus Von Stauffenberg" from *My Sad Captains,* whereas in the first two books, the omnipresent sense of violence, battle, and danger was strangely unspecific (or a reflex of Gunn's reading of Homeric epic and Shakespearian historical drama). The poem becomes fused, however, with the drama of self-invention and masculine identification, associated with Gunn's discovery of existentialism, and the risk of self-identification as a homosexual in a postwar Britain where homosexual acts were still illegal.

"My Sad Captains" (p. 129), like some of the early poems, offers an account of men that he is attracted to. They are restaged as "sad captains" on the model of the soldiers addressed by Shakespeare's Mark Antony before the battle of Philippi. They include anonymous "friends" and a few with "historical names," and even in this syllabic poem, they are wrapped in a heroic Shakespearian aura. In some ways the poems prefigures the more candid, openly homoerotic mode of the later verse culminating in *Boss Cupid,* but it also a subliminal farewell to the heroic mode of his early work, with its strange theater of obscure conflicts and theatrical displacements, where soldiers, kings, saints, pop stars, and bikers strut their existentialist parts on the poetic stage, though with something palpably missing from the script.

MOLY

Dream and risk, the California sun, and LSD dominate Gunn's next book, *Moly* (1971), a hallucinatory chronicle of 1960s liberation. The book records the poet's experiences with drugs, as well as waking dreams about such phantasmagoric subjects as men turning into horses and swine, the heartbroken Phaedra, "half wave, half men" Californian surfers, centaurs, a pastoral landscape full of pagan gods, Odysseus meeting Hermes, LSD, and sunlight. These are no longer the tough-guy dreams of *Fighting Terms* and *The Sense of Movement,* nor the nightmare no-man's-land of "Misanthropos." The dreams recorded in *Moly* are set within and against the currents of the everyday world. The poems stretch out in search of clarity and definition in a psychedelic world of flow, with Gunn's reverberating meters marching to a new pulse. *Moly* is a book of daring dreams and wakefulness that risks recovering what is lost in myth, pastoral, childhood, primal language. It is a book that takes us through the darkness of Circe's sty to the brightness of moly (a magical herb given to Odysseus by Hermes to protect him from Circe's incantation) and the sunflower in sunlight.

Moly opens with the magical "Rites of Passage" (p. 185), about a man metamorphosing into a horse. The poem records the slow process of transformation ("something is taking place"), putting stresses on the dialectics of skin ("skin that was damp and fair / Is barklike and, feel, rough") and the protean nature of light ("My blood, it is like light"). The idea of metamorphosis, like the elements of skin and light, are developed throughout the book, as in "Tom-Dobbin" (pp. 200–201), in which the two men's bodies are depicted as a centaur in orgasm ("light is in the pupil /

luminous seed"). In other poems Gunn also explores resistance to metamorphosis. This is the subject of the title poem "Moly" (pp. 186–187), in which the speaker rises "to skin" and "human title," "putting pig within." Underlining the swine's humanity, Gunn suggests we all have it in us to be Circe's pigs, if we lose consciousness of ourselves. We need moly not because of the animal in us, but because of our humanness. If moly is the virtuous plant that protects Odysseus from Circe's spell, it is also, in Gunn's words, "Cool flesh of magic," a phrase that keep the protective plant as fleshly as the sensuous abandon it protects Odysseus from. It is this magical emphasis on flesh, rather than the didactic force of morality, that gives "Moly" its enigmatic power as a poem. Aligning the Homeric story of rescue through drugs with the LSD experience, Gunn generates a high voltage of urgency, consummated in the rhyme of "greed" and "need." The poem itself, however, has a chastened, intricately shaped feel, and its sense of magical emancipation is married to an eerie formality.

Gunn's LSD poems offer new versions of pastoral as well as myth. Under the heady influence of Ginsberg, Gunn succeeded in writing his own unique pastoral poems, such as "The Fair in the Woods" (pp. 209–210), in which he creates a lucid sylvan idyll, apparently independent of any modern geographical reference. He pictures a serene rural landscape where woodsmen dwell and "close the day," as if in Sidney's "Arcadia." For all its echoes of Sidney's Renaissance pastoral, however, Gunn's wooded landscape is also the "Landscape of acid."

In other poems, such as "Apartment Cats," "The Rooftop," "Street Song," "Flooded Meadows," and "Words," Gunn appears as a poet who dreams of different heroic lives and discovers heroism in everyday life. His reticence about showing his own life in relation to the heroic dreams and discoveries makes his poetry a striking exploration of the ambiguous domain between anonymity and autobiography, as the compulsion to "rewrite" his childhood in "Being Born." Though Gunn is open to all kinds of risk in life and verse, he prefers to be a master of risks than a blind risk-taker. This form of mastery is shown in his deliberate play between control and release in his use of rhyme and free verse, and his adventurous exploration of new forms and experiences in every book, like the surfers who "balance" triumphantly in "From the Wave." *Moly,* therefore, can be seen as an example of mastery over the risk of LSD, as Gunn explained in *The Occasions of Poetry,* "metre seemed to be the proper form for the LSD-related poems" as a way "to render the infinite through the finite, the unstructured through the structured" (p. 182).

Gunn's openness to LSD owes something to earlier poets such as Allen Ginsberg, but his insistence on the role of the conscious mind seeking to shape drugs experience within metrical forms makes his verse very different from the no-holds-barred spontaneity of Ginsberg and the Beat poets. Gunn is characteristically most formally disciplined when his material is most dangerous. This sets him apart from the post-Poundian tradition of postwar American poetry, represented by Black Mountain poets like Charles Olson and Robert Creeley and later the transgressive poetics of the Beats. In this respect, "Moly" is emblematic of Gunn as a 1960s poet. He embraces the risk of taking LSD as a source of poetic release, but he does so armed with the deeper magic of meter, mastering the danger of formal and intellectual dissolution by sheer metrical control. In doing so, he gave traditional meter a new role and new life.

JACK STRAW'S CASTLE

In *Jack Straw's Castle* (1976), the mood darkens, and the poet's dreams of liberation turn to nightmare. In the process Gunn comes out for the first time as a "gay poet," writing for the first time as an autobiographical self. In the title poem, Jack Straw is obsessed with nightmarishly claustrophobic spaces and haunted by figures such as Charles Manson and Medusa. In it Manson says: "dreams don't come from nowhere: it's your dream … you dreamt it. So there's no escape" (p. 276). The murderous Manson, a psychopathic embodiment of West Coast dreams, turns the

poet's nightmare back on its author. Despite that, the poem ends with Jack Straw's escape: "With dreams like this, Jack's ready for the world" (p. 279).

As Jack's nightmares "don't come from nowhere," the dream of "Jack Straw's Castle" asks to be read as encoded autobiography. The early Gunn identified with a series of pop and cultural idols but never with "Thom Gunn" himself. Gunn's 1976 book includes a poem called "Autobiography," and there are many Gunns in *Jack Straw's Castle*—as well as many different worlds and forms—making it the poet's most challenging and contradictory collection to that point.

The book is divided into three sections. The first section begins with taut stanzaic poems, which include portrayals (mostly in couplets) of construction workers, the Statue of Liberty, and another iconic soldier ("The Corporal"), and it ends with a dizzying account of an open-air Californian bathhouse in "The Geysers." The second section is in more exploratory "American style" free verse, typified by the jagged, episodic record of an archaeological discovery in "Bringing to Light" and climaxing in the elongated nightmare of "Jack Straw's Castle." The last section, heralded by "Autobiography," introduces a more overtly autobiographical self entangled in the process of self-definition, offering flickering memories of Hampstead in London (Gunn's childhood places) as well as recent Californian snapshots. The book concludes with "Breaking Ground" and "The Release," poems that remember "the sense of mild but constant risk" (p. 302). As the titles intimate, these last poems signal the poet's venture into a new poetic territory, a voice that is more released (and relaxed) in many senses, offering candid accounts of his sexual identity (or identities), intermixing meter and free verse, and embodying a distinctly autobiographical self.

Jack Straw's Castle makes use of heroic couplets, rhymed stanzas, free verse, and Elizabethan song, as well as expansive Whitmanesque lines and condensed, enjambed verse, reminiscent of Williams and Robert Creeley. In this sense *Jack Straw's Castle* is Gunn's most experimental book. The sense of experiment is not, however, only limited to the medium but carries over into the territory explored in the poems themselves, from the politics of the Nixon era in "Iron Landscapes" to the gay bathhouse culture of 1970s California in the dreamy but disturbing long poem "The Geysers."

The title poem, "Jack Straw's Castle" (pp. 270–279), is definitely not a ballad but has a macabre balladic quality, with its references to Charles Manson and Medusa, its narrative abruptness, and its linguistic grotesquery. A series of interlocking literary allusions provide the key to its cloistral architecture, as the sequence takes us through different sections, meters, rhyme schemes, rooms, and voices. It is prefaced by an epigraph from Charles Dickens's *Life and Adventures of Martin Chuzzlewit* (1843–1844) that recalls the moment when Jonas Chuzzlewit is haunted by the memory of the "ugly chamber" where he poisoned his father. Gunn juxtaposes Jonas's "ugly chamber" (and murderous mind) with "Jack Straw's castle" (and Charles Manson). Like Jonas and other Dickensian outcasts, Jack Straw exists as an isolated, demented consciousness removed from any community. Gunn's epigraph suggests the Dickensian gothic, but his take on gothic is analytical and disturbingly self-reflexive. The infernal room, the murderous, and the mad all feature in the poem, as well as Jack Straw's "dream sponsors," Charles Manson and the Furies. At the same time, the protagonist is also another of Gunn's heroic personae, seized by an identity crisis.

The poem ends in the bedroom where Jack is sleeping with a man "from outside the castle," a "real" man not "a dream of that same man" who lies "sheetless," "bare and close" with Jack. "Leaning ass to ass," they face apart but are connected by a "sufficient touch" like "a hinge" that "separates but not too much." If this "hinge" image paradoxically seems to align Gunn with the literary tradition of the homosexual poet, a deadly label that he tries hard to resist, it also offers him a sense of release, as he emerges from the closet of nightmare—the nightmare of the closet—toward the freer poetic voice from which some of his finest poems in *Jack Straw's Castle,* such

as "Autobiography," emerge. The hinge also prefigures the Gunnian embrace that we find everywhere in his 1992 collection, *The Man with Night Sweats.* Jack Straw is a metaphor for Gunn's nightmarish sexual crisis, but the nightmare also generates the giddy architecture of "Jack Straw's Castle," in which Gunn's biographical portrait of the imaginary Jack Straw offers a distorting autobiographical mirror of himself. Gunn's final line—"With dreams like this, Jack's ready for the world" (p. 279)—suggests that the explicit exploration of homosexual desire and terror in the sequence is in some way cathartic or preparatory, preparing a way back from the nightmare castle, named after a gay pub in Gunn's native Hampstead, to the larger world.

If Jack Straw's castle is Gunn's big imaginary closet, when he emerges from it in the final section of the book, we don't return to the steamy San Francisco bathhouses of "The Geysers" but rather to "the sniff of the real" in the childhood Hampstead of "Autobiography," (p. 285–286) where he remembers reading the poetry of Alphonse Lamartine and riding between horse chestnut trees with his brother, in a world of sweet memories free from nightmare. Gunn's directly autobiographical poems suggest release—as in the playful "Courage," celebrating the anxieties and triumphs of masturbation, and "Trust," a complex fable about a thief—but poems like "The Cherry Tree," "Behind the Mirror," and "The Release" (p. 361–362) are curiously twisted and self-thwarted investigations into autobiographical territory. In the last, he catches "the eyes of another" in a dark restaurant, only to find they were his "own eyes from a recessed mirror." Narcissus "glares into a pool" but, if "someone glares back," it is not clear what autobiographical self it might be.

THE PASSAGES OF JOY

The title of Gunn's 1982 collection, *The Passages of Joy,* playfully transposes Samuel Johnson's take on Juvenal's critique of transient fleshly pleasure to San Franciscan gay life in the

1980s. Moving from the imaginary confinement of "Jack Straw's Castle," Gunn's seventh collection explores the geographical specificity of San Francisco and London, evoking the erotic "sniff of the real" on the streets. The idea of "passages" is multiple. It suggests, among other things, the action of passing through Gunn's experience of gay history—his transit from the summer-of-love bathhouse drugs and orgies in *Moly* to the tormented self-confined in *Jack Straw's Castle,* and beyond. "Passages" also suggest bodily orifices, of course, and "passageways," the narrow, seedy, bumpy streets of San Francisco, which are playgrounds for cruising and meeting old and new friends. It also suggests the passing of people and the things that pass between people in the crowded flow of San Francisco streets.

Many of the poems are about "real" people, but "re-performed" through an anonymous third-person voice, as if Gunn were partially erasing his own presence. "Another All-Night Party" and "At the Barrier" record his sociable gay life and recreate a complex sense of friendship and carnivalesque pleasure without explicit sex. Other poems, such as "sweet Things," "The Miracle," "Song of a Camera," and "San Francisco Streets," record anonymous sex, the tearoom trade (seeking out impersonal sex in public places), sadomasochism, and promiscuity. Beside all this, other poems evoke the darker passages of urban life: an unexplained suicide in "Elegy," a familial deceit and breakdown in "Adultery," Elvis Presley's overdose in "Painkillers," and early cases of AIDS in "Transients and Residents." If the book offers a sense of the risky pleasures of street lives, Gunn playfully investigates the complexities of the sexual labyrinth, bringing together the worlds of Shakespeare, Donne, Jonson, and Rochester, alongside the contemporary taste for Bunting, Duncan, and Isherwood. In Gunn's tour of the modern city, the tension between his unchaste subject matter and his exceptionally chaste, lean, unadorned poetic form is starker in *The Passages of Joy* than ever before.

In fact *The Passages of Joy* is largely written in free verse and reads more like Robert Duncan than Yvor Winters. At the time of its publication, this approach caused some consternation among Gunn's readers, especially British ones. Poems such as "Slow Walker," "The Girls Next Door," "Donahue's Sister," and "At an Intersection" are flat, prosaic third-person reports. Instead of highlighting key experiences, Gunn's verse at times loosens narrative momentum to such a point that it offers only a series of anecdotal passing moments. If the aesthetic risk he runs in such poems is banality, however, it is one that, like his mentor William Carlos Williams, he was content to run.

Gunn's street poems in the book, with their precise naming of gay streets and landmarks, provides a vivid record of the homoerotic topography of pre-AIDS San Francisco. "San Francisco Streets" (p. 355) is typical. It portrays a boy's transition from farmer in "peach country" to middle-class salesclerk in Castro Street—a social transformation that involves an unsentimental education in gay life. From victim to hustler, from "towel boy" to "kept" boy, the unnamed protagonist rises up the pole, playing a series of assigned roles in the hierarchy of the city's homosexual culture. Mimicking Elizabethan ballad meter, the poem's loosely rhymed stanzas (*abcbdefe*) explore sensitive modern subjects—tattoos, hustlers, and bathhouses—generating a playfully stereotypical narrative that is part satire, part documentary.

The Passages of Joy opens with a poem titled "Elegy," and this and others revisit not only Gunn's own London backgrounds but also a London poetry that is far from the hedonism of San Francisco in the 1970s and 1980s. Two poems evoke specific London neighborhoods, Highgate and Talbot Road, as sites of loss and memory. They also record two memorable literary encounters, one historical, the other biographical. "Keats at Highgate" (p. 350) takes the form of a well-trimmed sonnet and records the famous chance meeting between the English sonneteers John Keats and William Taylor Coleridge in April 1819. It ends with a celebration of Keats, Gunn's Hampstead predecessor, putting "everything to use" and being "not well-dressed but oh not loose." "Talbot Road," in contrast, is a loose sequence in free verse, an exploratory city poem that returns to Gunn's stay in London from mid-1964 to 1965, when he lived opposite his friend Tony White (the dedicatee of "Innocence"). The elegiac poem reflects on moments from different decades before and after White's death in 1970s, shaping and reshaping Gunn's relationship to the "glamorous and difficult friend," and celebrating a time of complete access "to air, to street, to friendship" (p. 380).

There is a thrilling moment toward the end of "Talbot Road" where Gunn remembers a boy "in his teens, from the country," sitting "in his white shirt at the window," "in the house opposite" (p. 385). Like Gunn, the boy is a keen gazer, absorbed in "the human traffic, of all nations" in a "fine public flow" (p. 385). Moving the poem's focus from Tony to this anonymous boy, Gunn shifts our attention from the dead to the living, injecting a sense of continuity into this anecdotal, interrupted elegy. *The Passages of Joy* illustrates Gunn's investments in the "public flow" and "human traffic" of the modern city. It also confirms his vocation as a city poet. In a way the London (Hampstead and Notting Hill) he left constantly reappears in his poems, intermixing with the sexual thrills of San Francisco. It may be a coincidence that "passages" is the same word Walter Benjamin uses in his master study of Parisian urban modernity, but Gunn's book gives Samuel Johnson's word a new currency in the homoeroticized cities mapped in *The Passages of Joy.*

THE MAN WITH NIGHT SWEATS

Ten years passed before Gunn's next book, *The Man with Night Sweats* (1992), a collection that contains some of his most moving and breathtaking poems. During the interval, the erotic city had been transformed by the epidemic of AIDS, which engulfed the homosexual world recorded in Gunn's previous books and posed an unprecedented challenge to the poet as a man—and as a writer committed to the body and the city and their passages of joy.

Unlike many heroic shields and amours in Gunn's early poetry, the "shield" in this book's title poem is the speaker's own flesh; no longer one of Gunn's poses, it is a "reduced and wrecked" (p. 461) human body. The poem exposes the nightmarish opposite of the kind of trusted, erotic, and defensive shield celebrated earlier: the breakdown of the human body, its immune system and biological defenses. Instead of adopting the language of war to articulate political responsibility in time of emergency, Gunn restores the martial language surrounding AIDS to its metaphorical base, making "flesh" "the given shield" that is now "cracked" (p. 461). The "man" repeatedly summons himself as "I" in the poem, as if to bolster but also expose the singular and exclusive pronoun that highlights his isolated existence in face of shared catastrophe. Even though the meter and rhyme are surgically precise, the poem plays out the ambiguity between the fear of contagion and its reality; we do not know whether the speaker is sweating from AIDS or in terror of it, about and for himself or for his friends.

The Man with Night Sweats was published in the early 1990s when the idiom of AIDS activism permeated poetic and critical language. Gunn's monitoring of the AIDS lexicon in his verse is like a policy of linguistic quarantine, steering clear of the routine vocabulary associated with the medical crisis. The closest he comes to it are "plague," "risk," "family," and "spread." There is no direct mention of the words "AIDS," "HIV," "virus," or "homosexual" in the book. Gunn uses the word "love" (fourteen times) in preference to "sex," "trouble" rather than "crisis," and "friend" (twenty-one times) and "companion" rather than "partner." Likewise in the place of the privileged term "witness," he uses the more neutral "record," "remember," and "recognize." This is a writer committed to recording and remembering accurately, and this means not hiding behind the shield of conventional political and poetic rhetoric. Gunn was writing at a time when AIDS elegy proliferated on all fronts, but in his poems Gunn turns away from the ceremonies of public mourning and protest typical of the genre, with its hypnotic insistence on consolation and survival. In elegy after elegy, Gunn's simple and controlled language refuses large-gestured self-dramatization, touching instead on the tacit anguish of both the sufferers and witnesses, bringing the whole weight of his skeptical, formal intelligence to bear upon the crisis of AIDS in San Francisco.

Gunn's elegies create a unique record of his dead and dying friends, but they do so by suppressing his elegiac self. Focusing on the second- and third-person pronouns, Gunn initiates a difficult dialogue between the "I" and the multiple "you"s and "he"s of the book, evoking a sense of solidarity between the poet and the dying or dead. Though Gunn's readers were immediately moved and shocked by the scale of human suffering in the collection, this was in large measure because it avoids shock tactics, offering just a tough record of facts, presented without emotive rhetoric or conspicuous poetic armor. By "back-grounding" the names of the dead in the end-notes and using the anonymous pronouns "you" and "he," Gunn found a convincing way to speak as an impersonal "self" whose "I" could evolve a language of personal mourning in public without writing sentimentally or conventionally mournful poems. In refusing to speak as a public spokesperson for any group, and speaking quietly only in his own voice and that of his friends, Gunn paradoxically became the most searching "witness" to the crisis of grief and identity experienced by the gay world he was part of. The book indeed rethinks the notion of elegy, asking the reader: Is it possible to write an elegy without an explicit elegiac self? What happens to elegy if the elegiac self has either consciously retreated to the background or, as often in Gunn's case, gone missing? What happens to mourning when the mourner has absented himself?

"Your dying is a difficult enterprise" (p. 465), Gunn begins his difficult "Lament," a poem that gives primacy to the second person. In a world overcome by a vertiginous sense of disappearance, the plunge into the second person asks us to experience head-on the fraught relationship between the poet and the unnamed "you" out there engaged in the "difficult enterprise." The idea that Gunn's "you," though defined by his friends, needs to be imagined as "one of us," is central to the struggle of the book. "Memory Unsettled" (p. 479) is a plain yet memorable

poem, recording the urgent need to remember and be remembered in a world of imminent disappearances. Told from a first-person perspective, the tightly knitted stanza addresses the second person (the sufferer and "your death"), before moving on to the third person (the comforter and "a friend"). Gunn introduces the directed speech of "you," speaking as an "I," asking his friends to "Remember *me.*" "We will remember you" seems to be a direct answer to the dying friend's request, but the line is un-marked by quotation marks, creating a disorien-tating effect that suggests both timelessness and an assertion of collective memory, as well as registering the fact of death. In second-person poems such as "The Reassurance" and "Memory Unsettled," Gunn speaks through an absent "I," conveying an implicit, imaginary sense of distance between them. It is as if by "not being there," the unbridgeable distance between "I" and "you" were cancelled, freeing the "you" from "the other" and extending the pronoun's potential inclusiveness.

While Gunn suppresses the "I" in the second-person poems, he becomes more vocal and self-aware in the poems in the third person. Gunn's "he" predominates in the elegiac sequence. While his second person includes the dying and the dead, his third person is strictly restricted to the dying or the living dead. In third-person poems such as "Terminal," "Still Life," "Courtesies of the Interregnum," and "The J Car," the "I" is neither absent nor an uninvolved seer or listener but instead actively reaches out to connect with the "he," trying to establish a precarious sense of intimate identification and yet distance between the "survivor" and the dying. In the third-person poems, Gunn speaks through a more present "I," exploring an explicit distance between the unin-fected "I" and the dying "he," both of whom are caught up in this struggle toward solidarity. On the one hand, the "I" underlines the "he"—the sense of otherness, vulnerability, and grief sponsored by the disease. On the other hand, the "I" is desperate to find ways to cancel this widen-ing distance between the living and dying. Even though the speaker in the "he" poem is often as reticent and resigned as in the second–person poems, the "I" is at least literally present, reminding us of the reality of speaking as "the speaker" in the face of silence and exploring the idea of what speaking means when the "he" becomes speechless while still alive, like Gunn's friend Larry Hoyt in "Still Life."

Published in the 1990s climate of self-surveillance and suspicion toward bodily pleasure, *The Man with Night Sweats* records not only the desperate self-hug of the title poem, but many other kinds of embrace: those between lifelong lovers, casual sexual partners, the mythological Philemon and Baucis, the living and the dead, AIDS patients, and a father and his adopted son. The image of the embrace is a protean and recurring theme throughout Gunn's oeuvre, but it becomes a central organizing figure in *The Man with Night Sweats*. It is first announced in the opening poem, "The Hug," which celebrates a world based on trust and intimacy between lovers and friends. Prompted by the occasion of a birthday celebration for Gunn's lover Mike Kitay, it has a strong autobiographical edge without being confessional. In the last section of the book, however, the image of the embrace changes drastically. In "The Reassurance," "Memory Unsettled," "The Missing," "Death's Door," and "A Blank," the limiting embrace of rhyme is used to explore protean forms of embrace, creating a sense of solidarity not only between the living and the dead, the sick and the healthy, but also within the community of the sick and the dead.

Wherever there is an embrace between bodies, there is an embrace between pronouns: the "you" hugging the "I" in "The Hug," the "I" and "you" not knowing the half-embrace caught between them in "The Differences," the "he" and "she" being turned into an eternal embrace of "it" in "Philemon and Baucis," the dead "you" coming back to hug the "I" in a dream in "The Reassurance," the terminal "you" climbing into the sickbed of the dying "he" in "Memory Unsettled," the "image of an unlimited embrace" between an implicit "we" in "The Missing," and finally, the dead ("they"—the third-person plural) loosely hugging the dead in "Death's Door." While the title poem is about a self-hug, in the rest of the book Gunn's variations on hugging

literalize the human connectedness between pronouns and people, celebrating, in the midst of an epidemic caused by erotic contact, one of the most primal, intimate, comforting if not consoling human touches, the embrace, in its many forms.

BOSS CUPID

Borrowing Cupid's mysterious gift of desire, Gunn's last book, *Boss Cupid* (2000), explores his struggle as an aging poet whose life and poetry is deeply invested in the sense of risk and trust he relishes in his erotic San Francisco. Moving on from the predominantly elegiac world of his previous book, *Boss Cupid* is Gunn's most diverse and vocally erotic book. It also acknowledges and pays debts to Gunn's literary friends, family, lovers, ghosts, and impersonations. These become like Gunn's sad captains, less heroic but equally constellation-like, charged with "each hot convulsion" and waiting from a distance like Cupid, to "spurt / Out of the intersection" (p. 98) where Gunn composes his amorous scripts. Retitling Ovid's "Sir Cupid" and Edmund Spenser's "Dan Cupid" as "Boss Cupid," Gunn resuscitates the Roman god's earlier poetic career as erotic master, recasting the "devious" love god as "the source" of homoerotic desire in the wake of the AIDS epidemic in the 1980s and 1990s.

Torn between desiring and being desired, the aging poet creates a privileged but embarrassed position for himself, as someone happy to be living at the mercy of Cupid's random but dominant presence. Many poems in *Boss Cupid* record a sense of erotic privilege about encounters with younger men. Under the guise of flirtatious gossip and casual promiscuity, *Boss Cupid* also captures a sense of estrangement. The poems celebrate sexual conquest but also elegize the aging body, flirt with the crowd but commemorate domestic intimacy, gossip about casual sex but ultimately revolve around the idea of trust. The book captures this difficult, complicated struggle between authority and subordination, between flattery and embarrassment, as well as the painful erotic division between the young and old. Although in a sense Gunn struggles to find a new footing after the terrifying emptiness of his AIDS elegies, *Boss Cupid* also contains some of Gunn's finest elegies. These include "The Gas-Poker" (for his mother, referring to her suicide) and some of his riskiest songs of love and death, such as "Troubadour," his sequence about the necrophiliac gay serial killer Jeffery Dahmer.

Confronted with these dilemmas, Gunn resuscitates Cupid as a troublemaker and mediator of desire. Though Cupid can be read as just the latest of Gunn's poses or a metaphor for his troubled self, Cupid is given a sense of autonomy and bossiness that overrides authorial control. Or this at least is what the poet wants to believe. It is as if Gunn had finally discovered a refuge under the regime of Cupid, speaking from his own experience as a happy but confused victim. "American Boy" (pp. 45–46) is a fine example. In this poem, Gunn records being advised by a lover to ration their meetings ("You say I might get tired of you"). As a result they arranged their "games for such and such a date," as if in a "bicoastal romance." The poem addresses the "affectionate young man" flirtatiously and celebrates the way his "wisdom feeds" the speaker's "dried-up impulses" with "energy and juice." It ends with a sense of fine balance, a mutual pact, in which the speaker is maintained "expertly" by the boy, "At the exact degree / Of hunger without starving."

Boss Cupid's diverse, "miscellaneous" shape is unprecedented in Gunn's oeuvre. While the first section, written mainly in meter and rhyme, introduces literary and familial elegies ("Duncan," "Shit," and "My Mother's Pride"), it also explores many kinds of secular and classical desire—not only in poems like "American Boy" but in lyrics about the Greek goddesses Arethusa and Arachne. There is also a set of self-reflective, self-mocking poems about aging, grouped under the heading of "Gossip." They demonstrate a new freedom in Gunn's free verse, interlacing anecdotal jokes with catchy dialogue. Many recount sexual adventures in public places, going beyond "The Miracle," a poem that draws on George Herbert's devotional idiom, to describe two strangers having sex in a McDonald's restaurant. The final section begins edgily with the five

"songs for Jeffery Dahmer" under the title "Troubadour," then gradually relaxes into "Rapallo" and "In Trust," two of Gunn's most intimate poems, which celebrate his long-term relationship with Mike Kitay, and then sustained portraits of Cupid and King David. With its elegies, celebrations, and revisitations, in some ways *Boss Cupid* raises questions about the continuity of Gunn's entire career. That said, it also resists any sense of the finality to be found in *The Man with Night Sweats* and *Collected Poems* (1993) and finds new poetic possibilities in familiar places.

"A Wood near Athens" (pp. 102–104), near the end of the collection, derives from one of Shakespeare's most famous stage directions, from *A Midsummer Night's Dream*. It evokes a sense of both a journey and an artistic work, opening with a lost traveler struggling "through a wood" who is also paradoxically "at home," as if had "never left." At one level it offers itself as a seductive image of the poet's own journey (that wood remembers not only Shakespeare and Dante but also Gunn's own "The Fair in the Woods" from *Moly*), but it is also one of *Boss Cupid*'s most alluringly plural allegories of love. It suggests that the "conflicting trails" are also "the various trails of love." Indeed the whole poem reads as a reflection, not only on Shakespeare's great Arcadian comedy of the erotic forest but also on a poetic career, consistently driven by a vision of Eros. Though it invokes "biological necessity," it also ponders the traditional iconography of love poetry ("Love makes the shoots leap from the blunted branches") and raises a series of tantalizing questions about literary and other lovers:

But who did get it right? Ruth and Naomi,
Tearaway Romeo and Juliet,
Alyosha, Catherine Earnshaw, Jeffrey Dahmer?
They struggled through the thickets as they could

(p. 103).

The poem ends with an apotheosis of the dance ("their work was dance")—an image that runs through *Boss Cupid* as a whole—constructing a scene of "A thousand angels making festival," a modern pagan version of Dante's or John Milton's angelic host, where "Each one distinct in brightness and in function" was there to "choreograph the universe." It is a wonderfully unmisgiving, cosmic image of "work as dance," a rewriting of the stellar vision of "My Sad Captains" in the light of the later vision of *Moly*, which also incorporates the new sexually driven universe of *Boss Cupid*. Though the vision is no doubt partly mischievous, a generous travesty of Christian angelology, it is also a hymn to what he calls in its final line, "The intellect as powerhouse of love" (p. 104).

Dante believed that love was the powerhouse of intellect, but the poem asserts "The intellect as powerhouse of love." This demonstrates Gunn's continued fidelity to the inspiration of Donne and the metaphysical poets with whom he identified at the start of his oeuvre, and also to the homoerotic Shakespeare, whose sonnet "They that have power to hurt and will do none" echoes through "A Wood near Athens." In a sense, Gunn at the end of his career is as traditional a poet (in terms of cadence, stanza, line, and form) as at the beginning, but he has forced traditional poetic forms to respond to contemporary conditions and modern occasions with an intellectual suppleness and emotional candor that is almost unprecedented. His work holds its ground in comparison with the work of more overtly experimental or "radical" poets like Ginsberg or Frank O'Hara. Gunn's combination of Winterslike rigor and Duncan's openness to new experience makes his "struggle" through the wood a journey. In refusing so many of our confident labels about styles and movements and in resisting the poetics and politics of "identity," Gunn has left us a unique body of work. Paradoxically using an American spelling that is retained in the Faber edition of *Boss Cupid,* Gunn says in "A Wood near Athens," "The traveler is at home. He never left." Gunn's work equates traveling and home in a way that suggests he is at home traveling, and rather than aiming for any fictional stability of identity, remaining true to what he calls (in an image that suggests writing as well as travel) "conflicting trails / Scribbled with light" (p. 102).

Selected Bibliography

WORKS OF THOM GUNN

POEMS

Page references in the text are to *Collected Poems* (London: Faber & Faber, 1994), which includes poems from these earlier volumes:

Fighting Terms. Oxford: Fantasy Press, 1954.

The Sense of Movement. London: Faber & Faber, 1957.

My Sad Captains. London: Faber & Faber, 1961.

Moly. London: Faber & Faber, 1971.

Jack Straw's Castle. London: Faber & Faber, 1976.

The Passages of Joy. London: Faber & Faber, 1982.

The Man with Night Sweats. London: Faber & Faber, 1992.

Other collections not included in *Collected Poems* are: *Positives.* London: Faber & Faber 1966.

Touch. London: Faber & Faber, 1967.

Boss Cupid. New York: Farrar, Straus and Giroux, 2000.

ESSAYS AND CRITICISM

The Occasions of Poetry: Essays in Criticism and Autobiography. Edited by Clive James. London: Faber & Faber, 1982.

Shelf Life. London: Faber & Faber, 1993.

"St. John the Rake: Rochester's Poetry." In *Green Thoughts, Green Shades: Essays by Contemporary Poets on the Early Modern Lyric.* Edited by Jonathan F. S. Post. Berkeley: University of California Press, 2002. Pp. 242–256.

EDITIONS EDITED BY GUNN

Poetry from Cambridge, 1951–52. London: Fortune Press, 1952.

Five American Poets: Edgar Bowers, Howard Nemerov, Hyam Plutzik, Louis Simpson, William Stafford. Edited with Ted Hughes. London: Faber & Faber, 1963.

Selected Poems of Fulke Greville. London: Faber & Faber, 1968.

Ben Jonson. Harmondsworth, U.K.: Penguin, 1974.

Poems by Charlie Hinkle. Edited with William McPerson. San Francisco: Eos Press, 1988.

Ezra Pound: Poems Selected by Thom Gunn. London: Faber & Faber, 2000.

Yvor Winters: Selected Poems. New York: Library of America, 2003.

CORRESPONDENCE, MANUSCRIPTS

Thom Gunn's papers are archived in Special Collections, Bancroft Library, University of California, Berkeley,

California. The archive at Berkeley is unprocessed. It contains material from 1952 to 1984. It is comprised of three categories:

Manuscripts of Poems, 1952–1984: The majority of these handwritten and typescript drafts and proofs relate to poems published in *Moly* and *Jack Straw's Castle*.

Notebooks, 1968–1973 (8 lin. Ft.): Fourteen volumes, contained in two boxes, include drafts, revisions, notes and journal entries. Inserts of loose manuscripts and typescripts remain in these notebooks.

Letters, 1968–1969 (1 portfolio): Including correspondence between Gunn and Richard Gilbertson.

BIOGRAPHICAL AND CRITICAL STUDIES

Conquest, Robert, ed. *New Lines*. London: Macmillan, 1955.

Bergman, David. *Gaiety Transfigured: Gay Self-Representation in American Literature*. Madison: University of Wisconsin Press, 1991.

Davie, Donald. *Under Briggflatts: A History of Poetry in Great Britain, 1960–1988*. Manchester, U.K.: Carcanet, 1984.

Dodsworth, Martin. *The Survival of Poetry: A Contemporary Survey*. London: Faber & Faber, 1970.

Dyson, A. E., ed. *Three Contemporary Poets: Thom Gunn, Ted Hughes and R. S. Thomas (Casebook Studies)*. London: Palgrave Macmillan, 1990. pp. 20-101.

Gregson, Ian. *The Male Image: Representations of Masculinity in Postwar Poetry*. London: Macmillan, 1999.

Hagstrom, Jack W. C., and George Bixby, eds. *Thom Gunn: A Bibliography 1940–1978*. London: Bertram Rota, 1979.

Powell, Neil. *Carpenters of Light: A Critical Study of Contemporary British Poetry*. Manchester, U.K.: Carcanet New Press, 1979.

INTERVIEWS

Campbell, James. *Thom Gunn in Conversation*. London: Between the Lines, 2000.

Haffenden, John. *Viewpoints: Poets in Conversation*. London: Faber & Faber, 1981.

Hennessy, Christopher. *Outside the Line: Talking with Contemporary Gay Poets*. Ann Arbor: University of Michigan Press, 2005.

Hamilton, Ian. "Four Conversations: Thom Gunn." *London Magazine,* no. 4:6 (November 1964).

Hiller, Alan. "Writing in a Style: An Interview with Thom Gunn." *Amherst Student* (Amherst, Mass.), April 30, 1981.

Jones, Chris. "A Transit of Thom." *Poetry Review* 86:3 (October 1996).

Kleinzahler, August, and John Tranter. "Interview with Thom Gunn." *Scripsi* 5:3 (April 1989).

Leith, Sam. "A Writer's Life: Thom Gunn." *Telegraph,* April 12, 2003.

Lux, Billy. "Billy Lux Interviews a Poet of the Century." *Gay and Lesbian Review* 7:3:41 (summer 2000).

Powell, Jim. "An Interview with Thom Gunn." *PN Review* 16, no. 2:56 (autumn 1989).

Sarver, Tony. "Thom Gunn." *Gay News* (London), January 1978.

Scobie, W. I. "Gunn in America." *London Magazine,* no. 17:6 (December 1977).

Wilmer, Clive. "Thom Gunn: The Art of Poetry LXXII." *Paris Review* 37, no. 135:149–150 (summer 1995).

GEOFFREY HILL

(1932—)

Lacy Schutz

FROM HIS FIRST volume of poetry onward, the poet Geoffrey Hill has remained true to a central project: an articulation of the ethics inherent in language. Hill believes the erosion of language in twentieth-century poetry is not only expressive of but also a causal factor in the decay of ethics. This effect extends beyond literature and into civil discourse, politics, and the media onslaught. The expression of this belief winds its way through themes of Christianity and faith; the moral landscape; skepticism, especially toward the physical and metaphoric monuments civilization builds; colonialism; war; and desire and its agonies. His poetry is located in his experience coming of age during the Second World War and the revelations of the Holocaust; in the landscape and history (both ancient and recent) of Worcestershire; in sixteenth- and seventeenth-century English literature, philosophy, and religion; and in the civil discourse of the twentieth and early twenty-first centuries. All of this comes wrapped in varied and exquisitely rendered prosodies.

BIOGRAPHY

Geoffrey Hill was born in Bromsgrove in Worcestershire on June 18, 1932 to William George Hill and Hilda Beatrice Hill and raised in nearby Fairfield. His father was the village constable and his mother came from a family of artisans who made nails. Though his parents both left school at age thirteen, Hill studied at the local grammar school and won a scholarship to Keble College at Oxford, where he read English literature. He published his first poems in 1952 at the age of twenty: one was chosen by the poet Donald Hall for his small journal, *Isis;* a pamphlet was published, also by Hall, in the Fantasy Poets series; and two poems appeared in *Poetry Oxford.*

Hill began teaching at University of Leeds in 1954 and married Nancy Whittaker in 1956. Their first child, Julian, was born in 1958. The couple would have three more children before divorcing in 1983. Hill published his first book, *For the Unfallen,* in 1959. He taught at Emmanuel College, Cambridge, from 1981 to 1989. In 1987 he married Alice Goodman, an American poet, opera librettist, and Anglican priest. Their daughter, Alberta, was born shortly thereafter.

From 1988 to 2004 he was codirector of the Editorial Institute, which he cofounded with the literary critic and scholar Christopher Ricks, at Boston University, with the purpose of training students in the process of editing scholarly editions. Hill retired from Boston University in 2006 and was named Professor Emeritus. Other honors and awards include the Whitbread Award for Poetry for *Mercian Hymns* (1971); Fellow of the Royal Society of Literature, London; Churchill Fellow, University of Bristol (1980); recipient of the Loines Award of the American Academy and Institute of Arts and Letters (1983); Clark Lecturer, Trinity College, Cambridge (1986); an honorary D. Litt. from University of Leeds (1988); Honorary Fellow of Emmanuel College; W. H. Heinemann Award for *The Triumph of Love* (1999); Ingersoll Foundation's T. S. Eliot Award for Creative Writing (2000); Le grand prix, 23ème Biennale de Poésie, le prix Sabam, in Belgium (2003); and many others. He has published sixteen collections of poetry, four collections of critical essays, and numerous articles.

EARLY WORK

The dominant conflict in mid-twentieth-century British poetry was between nominalist and realist writing. The nominalists, simply put, believed that language could not, in the end, represent reality, could not bridge the gap between an individual's experience and the telling of it; the realists disagreed. Nominalism was the girder for postmodernism. Ten years older than Hill, Donald Davie was one of the poets at the forefront of the Movement, a group of realists that included Thom Gunn and Philip Larkin. Rejecting the devotion of the earlier generation of poets to imagism and symbols, the members of the Movement turned to the formal diction and moral content they perceived in Romantic poetry. Though Hill too admired Romantics such as W. B. Yeats, he recognized the contradictions inherent in the tradition: the disjunction between the transcendence of nature and its brutality; the promise of freedom and democracy within the nastiness of capitalism and industry. Davie's books, especially *Purity of Diction in English Verse* (Chatto & Windus, 1952), were influential to Hill, but as much for his reaction against them as for the credibility of their arguments.

While at Oxford, Hill did not associate himself with any particular school or movement of poetry. When an interviewer asked Hill about the influence of his peers and teachers on his writing, Hill denied any such influence. He found his tutors encouraging but felt that his formal studies were separate from his creative pursuits. He credited convivial conversation with his fellow students as helpful but acknowledged that they were all aware his poetic interests were very different from theirs:

> The poetry written by most of the "promising" poets of the fifties seemed to me to stem from a basic misconception about the nature of poetry and language, and I must say that my views have changed very little since then. It seemed to me that young poets of that time were writing poetry of one or two kinds, neither of which was my kind. They were either Empsonian in the most arid sense, writing cerebral conundrums, a travesty of Empson's real gifts; or they were narrating amorous adventures and travel anecdotes in language that was the equivalent of painting-by-numbers. I sensed intuitively that I really cared for neither of those alternatives. My basic intuitive sense has remained remarkably consistent in the succeeding thirty years.
>
> (Haffenden, pp. 78–79)

Like William Empson, the influential literary critic and poet, Hill had a deep interest in John Milton and in Metaphysical poets such as John Donne, as well as a regard for the ambiguities of language and the possibilities within that ambiguity for creating richly layered meaning within poetry. Though Empson was saddled with the mark of New Criticism he, like Hill, resisted being corralled into a single rubric. *Milton's God* (1961), Empson's famous criticism of *Paradise Lost,* argued that the moral ambiguity and complex contradictions in the poem are precisely what make it great, a thesis valuable to Hill's own poetic project.

Other early literary influences were A. E. Housman (for whose Shropshire locales Hill felt an intuitive affinity having been raised so nearby), other Metaphysicals such as Henry Vaughan and George Herbert, Christopher Smart, and William Blake. Of the Metaphysicals, Hill said, "It was their fusion of intellectual strength with simple, sensuous and passionate immediacy which drew me to them …" (Haffenden, p. 80).

The first poem in Hill's first book, *For the Unfallen* (1959), is aptly titled "Genesis." The American critic Harold Bloom noted in his introduction to *Somewhere Is Such a Kingdom: Poems 1952–1971,* a collection of Hill's first three volumes, that Hill had by that time come to disdain his early work, this opening salvo in particular. Bloom also calls Hill a "difficult" poet, an adjective used unrelentingly by Hill's critics, both those who praise him and those who read him with a greater skepticism. The dense language and insistent prosody of these early poems, the elements that earn the label of "difficult," are the unshakable foundation on which Hill builds the great structure of his life's work; each story, each turret and rampart in the ongoing project, is new and unique and more impressive than the last while still embracing this original style. Vincent Sherry, in his book *The Uncommon Tongue,* argues that Hill was working through the conflict of whether to write civil verse or vatic, oracular verse. The poems that make up this first volume were written between 1952 and 1958, throughout Hill's twenties. In them, one can discern movement from the civil tongue to the prophetic voice.

One also sees this motion in the titles of the first books: *For the Unfallen* evokes the public and moral, *King Log* the mythical, and *Mercian Hymns* and *Tenebrae* the incantatory.

Hill later in life identified the great task of the poet as reconciling the irreconcilable. He manifests this irreconcilability in the syntax, grammar, and punctuation of his early poems and throughout his work. Poems with fluid scansion are irregularly punctuated or composed of sentence fragments. Henry Hart, in *The Poetry of Geoffrey Hill*, draws a line between Hill's battles with standard syntax and his ambivalence toward social customs and literary traditions. On "The Distant Fury of Battle," Hart writes, "[the poem] retains traditional grammar and syntax, but forces them to the breaking point. The poem enacts what it describes. Its tortuous syntax, winding around commas, dashes, and semicolons, mimes an individual's desperate struggle to leave tradition in the grave but also to resurrect it and make it new" (p. 30).

Hill's use of prosody and grammar both invokes and revokes traditional poetic forms. In "Two Formal Elegies," Hill addresses what will become a recurring theme throughout his work: the Holocaust. The elegies are loosely rhymed sonnets, their iambic pentameter affirming Hart's point about syntax and demonstrating Hill's effort to sculpt traditional structure into a form of his own.

The wilderness revives,
Deceives with sweetness harshness. Still beneath
Live skin stone breathes, about which fires but play,
Fierce heart that is the iced brain's to command
To judgment—(studied reflex, contained breath)—
Their best of worlds since, on the ordained day,
This world went spinning from Jehovah's hand.

(*For the Unfallen*, p. 31)

Tracing the transformation of Hill's voice through the poems in this first volume, one witnesses language warping into new shapes and new constructions.

For the Unfallen was largely ignored by critics, and Hart describes a strained relationship between Hill and his audience that comes out of its simmer and to a boil in *King Log* (1968). The title of this second book refers to Aesop's fable "The Frogs Who Desired a King," in which a group of frogs ask Zeus to provide them with a ruler. Zeus tosses a log into their midst, declaring it their new king. Though initially afraid of it, the frogs become dissatisfied with the log and complain to Zeus. Aggravated, Zeus sends a new king: a stork that promptly begins to devour the frogs. Hill's allusion is layered. Many poems in this volume excoriate the lazy and complacent who must look outside themselves for guidance, those who would complain of Hill's "difficulty." Others lament the miseries caused by murderous tyrants.

Hill softens his contempt for the failures of humanity and the failure of those who are the consumers of literature to be more intelligent and self-sufficient by reminding us and himself in the poem, "Ovid in the Third Reich," "not to look down / So much upon the damned. They, in their sphere, / Harmonize strangely with the divine / Love" (*King Log*, p. 13). What follows are meditations on suffering, compassion, and what happens when compassion is unattainable in which Hill acknowledges that the moral shortfalls characteristic of human nature must also be characteristic of the lyric poet.

The parallels between the log king myth and the poems are reinforced by the title Hill gives a postscript: "King Stork." The postscript contains an essay on the sequence titled "Funeral Music." The sequence, composed of eight sonnets, addresses the horrors of tyranny and the resultant executions of three fifteenth-century members of the nobility. Hill read the *Henry VI* plays just as he was beginning to think about this series of poems and cites Shakespeare's rhetoric in the plays as important to the evolution of his own rhetorical project. The last sonnet, coming after a sort of oratory of anger, disgust, and lamentation that Hill has conceived in response to both the brutality of the murders and the brutality of the political climate in which they occurred, expresses weariness and despair, final notes common to Hill:

Not as we are but as we must appear,
Contractual ghosts of pity; not as we

Desire life but as they would have us live,
Set apart in timeless colloquy:
So it is required; so we bear witness,
Despite ourselves, to what is beyond us,
Each distant sphere of harmony forever
Poised, unanswerable. If it is without
Consequence when we vaunt and suffer, or
If it is not, all echoes are the same
In such eternity. Then tell me, love,
How that should comfort us—or anyone
Dragged half-unnerved out of this worldly place,
Crying to the end "I have not finished."

(King Log, p. 32)

Hill has also worked out, in *King Log*, some of his earlier conflicts with language, introducing more colloquial speech amid the formal and employing elements of prose. In the intervening years between publication of the first volume and the second, Hill struggled to write poems. This may have been owing partially to depression that went undiagnosed and untreated until he moved to Boston in the 1990s. Hill has said that he wrote only seven or eight poems between 1959 and 1964.

Hill's third volume, *Mercian Hymns,* was published in 1971 (later reprinted in its entirety in *Somewhere Is Such a Kingdom,* published in 1975). Easily the most accessible of Hill's books, it was selected by a majority of participating writers and scholars at a symposium held by the *New Review* as the most important book of poetry of the decade. *Mercian Hymns* represented a departure for Hill. It was well liked both by his admirers and by his detractors, and the format was experimental. Many have referred to its poems as "prose poems," but Hill prefers "versets" and points to their rhythm and pitch as factors distinguishing them from the looser prose poems of other writers.

The book was composed quickly by Hill's standards: it was completed in three years. The poems take as their subject a merging of the story of the powerful eighth-century Anglo-Saxon king Offa with a twentieth-century childhood, a mythic version of Hill's own. Offa was the ruler of Mercia, an area coinciding with the modern West Midlands where Hill grew up, and serves in Hill's rendering as a synecdoche for the tragicomic brutality and brilliance of English history. "As Hill glances over his shoulder at the past, his despair serves only to sharpen his sense of irony and comedy. His poem is an indictment, but often a funny one, of a particularly English inheritance" (Hart, p. 153). Hill draws parallels between Offa's struggles for power and Britain's participation in World War II. Having witnessed, at age eight, the Nazi bombing that destroyed Coventry, Hill is mining a particularly salient and personal topic. As is the case throughout his work, Hill strives to make language into a monument of a more significant variety than those erected in physical space. Hill has said that "every fine and moving poem bears witness to this lost kingdom of innocence and original justice. In handling the English language the poet makes an act of recognition that etymology is history. The history of the creation and the debasement of words is a paradigm of the loss of the kingdom of innocence and original justice" (Haffenden, p. 88).

The language, as always with Hill, is highly particular, and, in keeping with his subject matter, he chooses words with Germanic roots and seeks to echo both the alliteration of Anglo-Saxon poetry and the incantatory qualities of early Christian canticles. From the fifth poem in the sequence:

So much for the elves' wergild, the true governance
of England, the gaunt warrior-gospel armoured in
engraved stone. I wormed my way heavenward for
ages amid barbaric ivy, scrollwork of fern.
Exile or pilgrim set me once more upon that ground:
my rich and desolate childhood. Dreamy, smug-faced,
sick on outings—I who was taken to be a king of
some kind, a prodigy, a maimed one.

(Somewhere Is Such a Kingdom, p. 99)

Hill's pride in being a member of the working class comes through in these poems as well. On two occasions as a child his mother was ill and he was cared for by his maternal grandmother, the nailer. He felt very close to her. Poem XXV in *Mercian Hymns* reads, "I speak this in memory of my grandmother, whose / childhood and prime womanhood were spent in the / nailer's darg" (*Somewhere Is Such a Kingdom,* p. 119). The entire sequence pays homage to this personal history even as it ruminates on and criticizes the political history.

Tenebrae (1978) returns to the prosody and the challenging diffidence of Hill's earlier work. Many critics did not care for this book, finding the formalism antidemocratic, aristocratic, and conservative. Henry Hart senses, instead, a turn from the stentorian tone of previous poems to something more delicate and lyrical. "He finds the passion of the artist and lover crucifying, but his reaction is now more quietly modulated, twilit" (p. 194).

The title of the book refers to a largely obsolete Roman Catholic religious rite observed on the final three eves of Holy Week. During the ceremonies, fifteen psalms are read, and as each one is finished a candle is snuffed out until the sanctuary is in total darkness, symbolizing the extinguishment of Christ's light from the earth. The final candle, which has been hidden, is then brought forth again to indicate the resurrection and the return of hope. The poems in this volume tend toward the moody and gloomy, an ongoing winter of the spirit, but they also hint at spring's reappearance. The poems move through cycles of withering and rebirth, through the agonies and ecstasies of love's journey, and through Christ's crucifixion and resurrection. In "Lachrimae; or, Seven Tears Figured in Seven Passionate Pavans," one of several longer sequences of poems in the book, Hill toys with all of these themes, as well as with the ambiguity of the word "passion" in both its secular and religious definitions. In the seventh and final sonnet in the series, "Lachrimae Amantis" (Latin for "lover's tears"), the addressee of the poem remains unclear: it is either a lover or Christ or both. The poem evokes the biblical tales of the bridesmaids who fall asleep awaiting the bridegroom, as well as the apostles who fall asleep in Gethsemane, as the speaker drowses, meditating on the addressee's return. This book of poems is particularly heavy with allusions to Christianity, although it never becomes didactic in its religious concerns. Moreover, despite the Christian overtones, Hill, throughout this and other work, never allows either himself or the reader to garner any of the consolation one might expect to find in religious belief.

The centerpiece of *Tenebrae* is "An Apology for the Revival of Christian Architecture in England," a series of thirteen sonnets that took Hill six years to write. The title of the sequence is from a treatise by the nineteenth-century Catholic architect A. Welby Pugin extolling Gothic architecture as an antidote to emerging industrialism. Gothic architecture itself was, however, enabled by the exploitation of the lower classes and the spoils of imperial expansion. The title, therefore, is ambiguous: the apology is less a justification of the nineteenth century and more an atonement, a plea for forgiveness. The sequence returns to themes of religion and civics, examining nineteenth-century England's simultaneous political imperialism and cultural achievements and the contrast between the beauty of the countryside and the system of tenantry. Capturing that ambivalence, Hill writes in the ninth sonnet, "The Laurel Axe,"

Platonic England, house of solitudes,
rests in its laurels and its injured stone,
replete with complex fortunes that are gone,
beset by dynasties of moods and clouds.
It stands, as though at ease with its own world,
the mannerly extortions, languid praise,
all that devotion long since bought and sold, ...

(p. 30)

Prior to its publication as a stand-alone volume in 1983, Hill's book-length poem *The Mystery of the Charity of Charles Péguy* was broadcast on BBC Radio and published in both the *Times Literary Supplement* and the *Paris Review*. Charles Péguy was a French poet who died in battle in World War I. He was deeply influenced by socialism, nationalism, and an intensely conflicted relationship with Roman Catholicism. As the editor and primary contributor to the literary magazine *Les Cahiers de la Quinzaine,* Péguy published many of his own poems and essays, including, in 1914, an excoriation of the socialist leader Jean Jaurès, whom he had previously admired. Jaurès was promptly assassinated by a young nationalist, leaving Péguy with an all too real impression of the power of words.

Péguy loved the mystical aspects of the Roman Catholic faith, though he had a tortured relationship with the church itself. He particularly admired Joan of Arc, and his verse drama *La mystère de la Charité de Jeanne d'Arc* provides the reference for Hill's title. Hill found Péguy compelling enough to write 100 quatrains about him, most likely because Péguy was a man of deep incongruities. Hart wrote, "Péguy joins Hill's army of martyrs, whose devotions are noble as well as vicious and whose acts of faith are as condemnable as they are commendable. But if Jeanne d'Arc provides Péguy with a paradigm of self-sacrifice and charity, Péguy provides Hill with a model that remains, after much communing, deliberately elusive" (p. 256).

The poem begins literally with a bang: the shot that kills Jaurès. It is divided into ten sections, comprising loosely rhymed quatrains in iambic pentameter. In the fourth quatrain, Hill asks if Péguy is responsible for Jaurès' death, and the poem goes on to explore a variety of tensions: between the power of words to both incite and to atone; between moral belief and the morally ambiguous actions required by daily life; between innocence and worldliness. The poem discursively traces the evolution of Péguy's philosophy and poetry, laments his loss, and examines imagination and ethics in the light of politics and revolution. Thirteen years passed between the publication of *The Mystery of the Charity of Charles Péguy* and *Canaan* (1996). Hill was teaching at Emmanuel College, Cambridge, and it was during this time that his mental health problems worsened and became public. Hill has by and large avoided speaking about these issues, in keeping with a general reticence to discuss matters related to his personal life. His colleagues relate tales of a man suffering from serious depression, however, and Hill himself has referred in passing to obsessive-compulsive disorder and debilitating anxiety (Potts). He had a heart attack in 1988 that required triple-bypass surgery. He then moved to Boston, and it was in the United States that he finally received concerted treatment for mental illness. The antidepressants unknotted Hill's poetic imagination, and, helped along by the touch of mortality, he entered an incredibly prolific period that has continued through the present day. Another heart attack in 2001 convinced him to begin eating more carefully and exercising.

LATER WORK

The title of *Canaan* evokes the vengeful God of the Old Testament. In the biblical tradition, Canaan is the Philistine land promised to the Jews who have fled Egypt and wandered the desert for forty years. In this land some of the Jews have forgotten their own laws and joined the Canaanites in the worship of false idols, thus drawing down the fury of God. One of the epigraphs to Hill's book quotes Zephaniah 2:5 from the Geneva Bible of 1560: "o Canaan, the land of the Philistims, I wil euen destroy thee without an inhabitant." The Geneva Bible was a translation accomplished in Switzerland by Protestant British exiles forced to flee their country by the Roman Catholic queen of England, Mary Tudor. Their translation was overtly political, with marginal notes adopting a distinctly Calvinist tone, and was considered a great threat to Roman Catholicism and to the Catholic monarchy. In referencing this edition of the Bible at the beginning of his book, Hill, himself a British expatriate during the time the poems were written, signals that he will spare England no criticism or doomsaying. With this gesture, Hill returns to the public realm full of urgent wrath.

In Hill's vision, the twentieth century has transformed England into a land of philistines, voided of moral integrity by war and greed and ill-motivated alliances with other nations. Five of the poems, scattered throughout the volume, bear the title "Mysticism and Democracy;" three are addressed "To the High Court of Parliament." The first to bear this latter title opens the volume with these searing lines:

Where's probity in this—
the slither-frisk
to lordship of a kind
as rats to a bird-table?
England—now of genius
The eidolon—
unsubstantial yet voiding
substance like quicklime:
privatize to the dead

her memory:
let her wounds weep
into the lens of oblivion.

(Canaan, p. 1)

Hill also draws a direct line between poets and politicians, making the point that both must consider the words they use on many different levels. Such a thesis had been in development since Hill was a young man, and he cites his early reading of Simone Weil as confirming this "intuition" of his (Mounic interview). He also acknowledges the difficulty of writing politically engaged poetry without succumbing to dogma.

Some of the poems in *Canaan* first appeared as the new poems in the 1994 collection *New and Collected Poems.* The Canadian poet Peter Sanger looked closely at "Sobieski's Shield," which appeared in the first volume and was revised for the second. (Hill has a long history of revising poems between publications, an activity he frowned on when performed by John Crowe Ransom. See the essay "What Devil Has Got Into John Ransom?" in *The Lords of Limit.)* Hill characteristically and meticulously packs a tremendous amount of allusion and intent into a poem of a mere five dozen words, which Sanger unravels with equal carefulness. Hill exploits the ambiguity of language for its fullest possibilities, beginning with the title. The name "Sobieski" refers to a seventeenth-century Polish monarch whose victory over the Turks at Vienna, perceived at first to be a great triumph for the Polish and the Roman Catholics, eventually led to the domination of Poland by foreign powers (a tale with parallels to the rise and fall of the British Empire), as well as to a constellation that was named in Sobieski's honor but is now generally called simply "the Shield." The final lines of the poem read:

as one might assert
Justice Equity
or Sobieski's Shield even
the names
and what they have about them dark to dark.

(p. 3)

Sanger reasons that Hill is addressing those of the earlier referenced "star-gazing planet" who have lost not only the knowledge of Sobieski but also knowledge of the real meaning of justice and equity.

The Triumph of Love (1998), a book-length poem of 150 numbered stanzas, was widely reviewed and commented on. It is perhaps the most explicitly humorous of Hill's work to date and full of surprising postmodern tics that drop unexpectedly into a language that is less controlled than in previous poems. For instance, there is the repeated construction "for X read Y": "For wordly, read worldly; for in equity, inequity; / for religious read religiose; for distinction / detestation" (*The Triumph of Love,* p. 20), or in a further play on the theme of mishearing, "For definitely the right era, read: deaf in the right ear" (p. 54). There are frequent notes from a supposed editor dropped parenthetically throughout, correcting, commenting on, and/or mocking the speaker. In a review for the *Los Angeles Times,* the American poet John Hollander noted that the facility with which Hill moves between the solemn and the funny is a sign of true seriousness.

The poem, indeed, has a serious agenda, revealed in Hill's recurring use of the Latin term *laus et vituperatio.* Translated as "praise and blame," the term refers to an ancient rhetorical mode that intends to present both the positive and negative aspects of an argument. The poem juxtaposes a dialectic of history intertwined with a dialectic of the self. Hill looks back at the twentieth century, especially the victims of the world wars, and he looks back at the individual life, presumably his own. The title of the work alludes to Petrarch's poem *Trionfi,* in which a series of allegories represents the soul's progress through love and other carnal matters to a penitential state suitable for meeting God. Hill has been accused at various points in his career of engaging in pastiche—assembling poems out of a multitude of references, creating a sort of collage of works and ideas that came before. What distinguishes his work from mere pastiche, however, is the extent to which each reference, in what is an otherwise severe economy of words, enriches the poem. So when, in stanza CXXXV, a speaker breaks in to ask, "So what about the dark wood, eh? / When do we come to the dark wood?" (p. 73), the astute reader will recognize Hill's acknowledgment of the Petrarchean wood as a Renaissance device, echoing Dante, for representing the struggle of the soul with sin. After invoking this ghost he immediately revokes it by stating that we are already in the dark wood and have been there all along.

Amid this heavy lifting Hill requires of his readers, there are moments of relief. At one point in the poem Hill defines the Dutch word *boeren-verdriet* as "peasant sorrow" and later dismisses that sorrow and affliction by revising the definition and stating that the word refers simply to a type of Dutch liverwurst. In the antepenultimate stanza, Hill pulls back the curtain for just a moment to reveal the purpose of all the vituperation, the raw memory, the carping.

What
ought a poem to be? Answer, *a sad
and angry consolation.* What is
the poem? What figures? Say,
a sad and angry consolation. That's
beautiful. Once more? *A sad and angry
consolation.*

(p. 82)

Finally, as if performing an act of mercy, Hill ends the poem with nearly the same compact and lyrical line that began it: "Sun-blazed, over Romsley, the livid rain-scarp" (p. 82).

In a further testament to his faith in the power of language, Hill describes his process as never beginning with an argument. He denies any inclination toward dialectic or ratiocination. Hill begins his poems, instead, with a subject in which he discovers his argument only by discovering what words to use, pursuing inspiration and rejecting what he calls the "vulgar notion" that inspiration comes to an artist as he or she sits passively awaiting it. Rather, it "comes at the end of a work, when maybe only a word or a phrase or a few sentences are wanting, and they will not come, and you struggle for hours, days, even weeks, in agony of mind trying a hundred variants, and suddenly the word or phrase is there ..." (Haffenden, p. 82). *Speech! Speech!* (2000) addresses, more explicitly than any of Hill's

earlier work, what he has been getting at all along: that language has deteriorated, and ethics, linked inextricably with language, have declined with it.

Like *The Triumph of Love,* this too is a poem in numbered parts, clocking in at 120, one for each day of Sodom. It is a dizzying journey without mile markers or road signs, unless one takes the unusual typographical devices Hill deploys in this volume as guides. Some words have stress accents to indicate emphasis. A vertical line hovering slightly off the horizontal line of the text signifies a pause or a stutter, a shift or a turn of some sort, a double entendre, or a combination thereof. Words rendered in all capital letters seem to be an interjection, another form of emphasis, and/or sometimes a sort of found phrase from the blitz of media dropped into the discourse. Jeffrey Wainwright, in an essay on *Speech! Speech!* in his volume *Acceptable Words: Essays on the poetry of Geoffrey Hill,* calls this poem a "cacophony" and compares it to "the frantic, irritated twiddling of a radio-tuner" (p. 97).

Hill, in his search for and insistence upon an ethically consistent language, flings cultural references about, including mentions of the Internet, condoms, brake fluid, and Tarzan. There is something of John Berryman's recalcitrant Henry of the *Dream Songs* in these pieces, raging against a less-than-ideal world that is likely to triumph regardless of the individual's resistance to it. Hill calls out to the visual artists Honoré Daumier and Anselm Kiefer by name as fellow resisters and as artisans whose methods of gouging and layering are similar to his approach in this poem. Wainwright calls attention to Hill's choice of a Daumier sketch for the cover of the book: a gullible audience applauds an unseen performer, "the image for Hill's view of the uncritical sycophancy that is part of the soundtrack of contemporary culture" (p. 98).

Exactly halfway through the poem, Hill comments on his progress and checks in with the reader, acknowledging the effort required to navigate the verse. He ends the poem practically succumbing to the near impossibility of sorting out the individual voice from the dissonance of modern life, of distinguishing the complexity of individual thought, and of forming a strong sense of ethics amidst the conflicting signs of media and politics.

Adam Kirsch, a young literary critic for conservative publications such as the *New York Sun* and the *New Republic,* wrote an extensive review of Hill's next book, *The Orchards of Syon* (2002), for the *New Republic,* which he later developed into a chapter in his book on modern poetry, *The Modern Element.* He dismisses Hill's earlier work out of hand as "unwitting" (p. 31) and lacking in "specificity and humaneness" (p. 66); he uses the word "literary" pejoratively. He praises the later work, however, beginning with *Canaan,* as redeeming Hill from the critical trash heap the critic imagines history would have left him upon had he not found this new voice. Hill has had his share of detractors over the years, and even his supporters have rarely been able to resist applying the epithet of "difficult." At this late point in Hill's career, however, the overwhelming majority of critics acknowledge the achievement of his entire body of work. The British writer A. N. Wilson called him "the best writer alive" in the *Spectator* and he is "the finest British writer of our time" in the words of the poet John Hollander. Kirsch's credibility, moreover, is undermined when he notes the "ragged free verse" of *The Orchards of Syon* and fails to notice the book he is reviewing is composed almost entirely in blank verse (p. 66).

Hill departed from the merciless linguistic penitentiary he had created in *Speech! Speech!* and returned to older themes and modes in *The Orchards of Syon.* He returned to his concerns about English architecture, in particular the English country house; to meditation, lyricism, and the oracular; and to a recognizable prosody. The volume is composed of seventy-two twenty-four-line blank verse stanzas that call to mind soliloquies and eclogues. The ghosts of T. S. Eliot, William Wordsworth, Gerard Manley Hopkins, and Ezra Pound hover over the text. The word "Goldengrove" appears again and again, invoking Hopkins' original coinage of it to name an idealized rustic haven.

The Syon of the title refers to Syon Park in London, home to a fifteenth-century manor house and 200 acres of rare trees and gardens. It is not unintentional, however, that "Syon" is nearly a homophone for "Zion." The cover of the book is based on a drawing done by D. H. Lawrence and shows a rural idyll in the forefront, with a cramped industrial scene in the rear. Over all, a rainbow arches, indicating hope perhaps for some better future.

In addition to the Hopkins allusions, a number of other motifs underpin the verse. The seventeenth-century Spanish play *La vida es sueño* by Pedro Calderón de la Barca is mentioned several times. The play examines the conflict between free will and destiny and suggests that life is a dream from which only death can awaken us. It also deals with the civic and ethical responsibilities of political leadership. Music, the Bible, Greek myth, and Milton are likewise present. With these myriad references, and with the influx of contemporary culture in the prior three volumes, one might begin to think that Hill has embraced postmodernism and joined its most skilled practitioners. As he did as a young man at Oxford, however, Hill continues to resist labeling, his mix of the modern and postmodern interweaving with the styles of the classical, the late Renaissance, and the early modern periods. The work is simply too richly layered and complex to accord fully with any single movement.

There is a sense of autumn passing into winter in these poems, and they hark back in some ways to *Tenebrae* and its long winter passing into a tentative spring. In the intervening decades, if Hill has not made peace with the shortcomings and incongruities of human life, he rages less against them and looks instead for the beauty within the destruction, the wisdom within the weariness. Syon and its orchards are a sort of refuge for Hill, a serene place amid the clutter of London from which to contemplate all that he has observed and learned. In the end, the value is in the search, however hopeless, for beauty, wisdom, a faith that extends beyond mere awe. If Hill has not found these things, he continues to hope for them, and by doing so finds a type of redemption that, if not sweet, is at least palatable.

Scenes from Comus came out in 2005 and puts the previous four books into the context of a sort of quartet from which this volume signals a departure. Hill engages in a sustained dialogue with John Milton in this and the later *A Treatise on Civil Power* (2007), titled after Milton's 1659 tract. In a 2008 lecture at Cambridge University entitled "Milton as Muse," Hill stated that Milton's work has played a substantial role in his creative imagination for more than twenty-five years. He recalled that Samuel Johnson referred to the "repulsive harshness" of Milton's poetry and noted that great work is often repulsive to the prevalent tastes of the time in which it appears. He cited William Wordsworth's *Prelude* and T. S. Eliot's *The Waste Land* as examples, but the same could be said of the best of Hill's own work. One need only look to Hill's detractors to find ample use of words such as "unbearable," "intransigent," and "rarefied."

The title of this book comes from Milton's *Comus (A Mask Presented at Ludlow Castle, 1634),* in which a maiden is abducted by Comus, a reveling satyr who is the offspring of Bacchus and Circe. He attempts to debauch the lady, but she refuses the sensual pleasures he offers in order to maintain her chastity and virtue. Her reward for this steadfastness is eventual rescue by her two brothers and the divine intervention of a character called the Attendant Spirit and a river spirit named Sabrina. Hill's book is dedicated to the composer Hugh Wood, an exact contemporary of Hill's who wrote a piece of music based on Milton's mask.

Near the end of Hill's 1977 lecture titled "Poetry as 'Menace' and 'Atonement,' " delivered at the University of Leeds and later reproduced in *The Lords of Limit: Essays on Literature and Ideas* (1984), he observed that at some point the true poet will come up against the realization that poetry is a vain expression of the self, no matter how thoroughly the poet attempts to position his or her work as an "altruistic responsibility." It is at this moment, Hill notes, that the poet realizes the "irredeemable error in the very substance and texture of his craft and pride" (*Lords of Limit*, p.

17). The poet must come to terms with his or her complicity in a long history of the use of language that includes both abuse and glories.

> It is here that he knows the affliction of "being fallen into the 'they'" and yet it is here that his selfhood may be made at–one with itself. He may learn to live in his affliction, not with the cynical indifference of the reprobate but with the renewed sense of a vocation: that of necessarily bearing his peculiar unnecessary shame in a world growing ever more shameless.
>
> (*Lords of Limit,* pp. 17–18)

The literary critic Brian Phillips, in a review of *Without Title* (2006) and *Scenes from Comus* for *Poetry*, restated this premise: "The poet, by committing himself to his corrupt medium, offers himself, Christlike, to a condemnation from which only his own power of moral transfiguration can save him" (p. 141). Hill has offered himself up in book after book as the sacrificial lamb on an altar to which he is by no means certain redemption will accrue. Phillips takes issue with such uncertainty and finds Hill's vacillation between his commitment to the power and beauty of language and his concomitant anger and mistrust of it to be his primary flaw. He also finds Hill's allusions a barrier to appreciating the remarkable power of his work, comparing them to a hedge that obscures the view of an extraordinary mansion.

Phillips feels, however, that Hill has overcome these defects in *Scenes from Comus* and the book that follows it by striking a balance between aesthetics and ethics. Hill leaves behind the political badgering of prior volumes and focuses instead on nature and on the tension between the sensuous and the chaste. The book is divided into three sections. In the first, titled "Argument of the Masque," Hill signals the themes of the book in the opening verse:

Of the personality as a mask;
of character as self-founded, self-founding;
and of *the sacredness of the person.*
Of licence and exorbitance, of scheme
and fidelity; of custom and want of custom;
of dissimulation; of envy
and detraction. Of *bare preservation,*
of *obligation to mutual love;*

and of our covenants with language
contra tyrannos.

(Scenes from Comus, p. 3)

The Latin phrase *contra tyrannos* translates as "against tyrants" and covers the well-trod ground of Hill's previous work attempting to wrest language from the clutches of politicians and others whose abuse runs the gamut from the glib to the heinous. The difference this time is that Hill has come to suspect, or perhaps recognize, that there may be something of the tyrant in himself. As Milton's *Comus* illustrates the tension between the sensuous and the chaste, Hill's *Comus* explores those tensions as they play out in the individual persona, in love, in Hill's own struggle to reconcile his obviously sumptuous love of language with the virtue he insists it possess. Uncharacteristically, Hill touches on the personal, making reference to a marriage he claims to have destroyed, presumably his first to Nancy Whittaker.

The second section is called "Courtly Masquing Dances." It is the longest section: eighty stanzas in seven or nine lines each. Among Hill's predominant subjects in this section are sex, love, marriage, and nature, and the coexisting miseries and joys of both. Hill seems to identify with Comus, ruled by sensuous imagination but stymied by an environment that turns this imagination against itself into something corrupt. He notes the near impossibility of achieving happiness in this predicament and underscores the parallels between this situation and the strangeness of sexual desire, the "alchemy" of it, in late life and in marriage. In stanza 30 he writes:

Say that I ám gifted—and I'll touch you
for ordinary uncommon happiness. What
a weirdo, you think. Well, yes, I was wired weird.
Back to the forest, then, where still so much
is the matter of legend. I see us getting down
to something long since hallowed and
nuptial, nuptial or nothing, angrily desired.

(p. 29)

The final section is "A Description of the Antimasque." Traditionally, the antimasque is a comedic and/or grotesque parody of the masque, sometimes taking the form of a dance. For Hill, guilt stands in for both the comic and the misshapen. In poem 19 Hill writes,

Well,
let well alone. The gadgetry of nice
determinism makes, breaks, comedians.
All the better if you go mad like Pound
(*grille,* a grasshopper; *grido,* a cry from the fields.)
The grief of comedy [1] you have to laugh.

(p. 66)

Hill had an increasingly difficult time getting his work published in the United States at this point in his career. His relationship with his American publisher ended after *The Orchards of Syon,* and *Scenes from Comus* was never actually published outside the U.K. That text remains difficult to find, and the entire interlude created something of a scandal in the world of poetry. *Without Title* was picked up by Yale University Press and published in the United States in 2007. It appeared in England the previous year. Yale seems to have made an ongoing commitment to Hill's work, releasing his next book of poetry, *A Treatise of Civil Power,* also in 2007.

Without Title departs from the long, book-length format of the prior six volumes and is Hill's first collection of all new individual poems since *Tenebrae.* In these poems, Hill has turned his attention to nature and to the consolation and perhaps even epiphany to be found there. He is also struggling to understand the poet's, and therefore his, place in the world. If there was something manic in the recent books, especially *Canaan* and *Speech! Speech!,* these poems are calmer, more recognizably prosodic. The season has resolved itself into a definite winter.

The book is divided into three sections, the middle of which is a collection of twenty-one Pindaric odes. The first and last are made up of individual poems, a few of which are sequences of up to seven sections. Like Milton, Hill loves music. He sang in his church choir as a boy, and allusions to music have appeared and reappeared throughout his work, but nowhere so consistently as in *Without Title,* where references to hymns coexist with a poem titled "Improvisations for Jimi Hendrix." The opening poem is an "improvisation" on the fifteenth-century German chorale piece "O Welt ich muss dich lassen," which translates as "Oh World, I must leave you." Though these poems revisit lust, ethics, language, politics, love, childhood, mortality, and loss, they do so with more serenity, less of what John Keats called "irritable reaching after fact and reason" in an 1817 letter. The poem "Wild Clematis in Winter" represents the kind of honed lyricism Hill brings to the description of nature in this book, as well as the taut eroticism that enters and disappears again throughout the poems. It is dedicated to William Cookson, the Ezra Pound scholar and founder of *Agenda* literary magazine who was a contemporary of Hill's at Oxford and died in 2003.

Old traveller's joy appears like naked thorn blossom
as we speed citywards through blurry detail—
wild clematis' springing false bloom of seed pods,
the earth lying shotten, the sun shrouded off-white,
wet ferns ripped bare, flat as fishes' backbones,
with the embankment grass frost-hacked and hackled,
wastage, seepage, showing up everywhere,
in this blanched apparition.

(*Without Title*, p. 21)

The centerpiece of the book is the set of Pindarics, which Hill has written "after Cesare Pavese." Pavese was an Italian poet who killed himself in 1950. Each of the poems in this section begins with a brief epigraph from Pavese's diaries and meditates both on Hill's life and the Italian poet's. It is in these poems that Hill's most concentrated meditation on the role of the poet in history and society takes place. The twelfth Pindaric spins out from Pavese's observation, "The artist labours under restrictions that will be valueless in the eyes of posterity." It begins,

Lateness is palpable and I no longer
read in the expectation of chance greatness
as formerly I hoped for blurred encounters
transforfeiting my life.
How strange you have to be to stay faithful.

(p. 46)

In the tenth, Hill discusses his experience composing a loose translation of Eugenio Montale's poem "La Bufera," which appears in the final section of the book as "The Storm." Many reviewers highlighted this translation as one of the standout poems in the book, and in fact the volume is dedicated to Montale.

Another poem singled out for praise by critics is "The Jumping Boy." It is one of the least dense of the poems, in this volume or in any of Hill's work. The poet observes a boy jumping up and down, "winning / a momentous and just war / with gravity" (p. 7). There is a lightness to the lyricism, and a poignancy, as the boy Hill remembers himself to have been cheers on this other boy across the span of a half-dozen decades. The final poem in the book, a companion to the opening poem, is "Improvisation on 'Warum ist uns das Licht gegeben,' " which translates to "why is the light given to us." One reviewer called this Hill's swan song, but with a new book of poetry following immediately on the heels of *Without Title,* one wonders how many final elegies Hill will have. In this one, Hill harks back to his inheritance from his grandmother and her family of nailers. He writes, "I also am a worker in iron" (*Without Title,* p. 82).

A Treatise of Civil Power (2007) continues the concentrated dialogue Hill began with Milton in *Scenes from Comus.* The full title of Milton's tract, from which Hill has taken his title, is *A Treatise of Civil Power in Ecclesiastical Causes; Showing That It Is Not Lawful for Any Power on Earth to Compel in Matters of Religion.* Written during Cromwell's reign, the tract is essentially a plea for religious freedom and a pitch that the individual should answer to his or her conscience rather than the edicts of church or state. Hill's work draws on this and what are generally called Milton's "political" sonnets but which Hill prefers to think of instead as "contentious."

When he was a younger man, Hill rejected the notion that poetry should be overtly political, but upon further study and consideration decided that because it was the right of any private citizen to dispute public matters, it could only follow that the poet was also allowed to do so. He looked not only to Milton for an effective example but also to Wordsworth and Pound. Hill reasoned that the effective energy behind a poem may in fact be malign, a notion that plays out in the bursts of anger that turn up throughout the later work.

Though one might assume from the title that the poems collected in this book would strictly take up civil matters, there is a fair portion of the personal, rendered reflectively and lyrically. More than in any previous collection, these poems register disappointment, a fatigued version of the previously high-pitched fury; sorrow and regret; bathos. One of the quietest and yet most powerful poems in the book is "In Memoriam: Gillian Rose." Hill addresses, among other things, his mental illness and its effects on those around him. It is tempting to see the poem as addressed to a former lover, unless one has the kind of specific knowledge Hill so often requires of his readers, or the fortitude to dig deeper. Rose was, in fact, a British scholar and philosopher. One of her primary subjects was the Holocaust, a topic Hill has revisited frequently in his own work, and, like Hill, her work, which frequently attacked postmodernism, was often marked by anger. Hill and Rose had a quarrel that was apparently unreconciled at the time of her death in 1995. The first of the three stanzas reads:

I have a question to ask for the form's sake:
how that small happy boy in the seaside
photographs became the unstable man,
hobbyist of his own rage, engrafting it
on a stock of compliance, of hurt women.
You do not need to answer the question
or challenge imposture.
Whatever the protocol I should still construe.

(A Treatise of Civil Power, p. 35)

Though Hill never abandons his core themes of government, language, and ethics, this collection includes a number of meditations on the books Hill has been reading, ranging from the Milton of the title and a book on William Blake to Elias Canetti's *Crowds and Power,* a paragraph of which he paraphrases directly in "On Reading *Crowds and Power."* Near the end of Hill's book is a poem titled "Coda," a musical reference to the closing section of a composition. Hill invokes his grandfather who made nails and hopes that "we shall accountably / launch into death on a broad arc," and, for a moment, Hill's language breaks down, revealing some version of the real, raw man he is:

I fear to wander in unbroken darkness
even with those I love. I know that sounds
a damn-fool thing to say.

(p. 50)

CRITICAL WORK

Hill has published three volumes of critical essays: *The Lords of Limit* (1984), *The Enemy's Country* (1991), and *Style and Faith* (2003). In 2008 Oxford University Press brought out his *Collected Critical Writings.* The latter volume reprints all of the older essays, many in revised forms, as well as thirteen new pieces. It is to be expected, with the dense and wide-ranging allusiveness of Hill's poetry, that his critical writing would be similarly demanding. The subject matter is unsurprising as well. Hill moves from the sixteenth century through the twentieth, focusing primarily on poetry and, occasionally, on theology and semantics. There are essays appraising the work of John Dryden, Walt Whitman, Ezra Pound, A. E. Housman, John Crowe Ransom, and other poets. Hill is especially interested in Gerard Manley Hopkins and T. S. Eliot, and he pursues the civil and social aspects of their work with a heedfulness that suggests he finds them particularly relevant to his own poetic project. Paul Dean, in a review of the collected work for the *New Criterion,* wrote that he found in Hill's voice an odd combination of the Old Testament and a *"fin-de-siècle* aestheticist" (p. 71).

Hill once said in an interview, "form is not only a technical containment, but is possibly also an emotional and ethical containment. In the act of refining technique one is not only refining emotion, one is also constantly defining and redefining one's ethical and moral sensibility" (Haffenden, p. 87). This is as much true of his poetry as it is of his critical work, and the essays bear what can sometimes feel like a tremendous weight in the moral responsibility Hill assigns both to the authors he examines and to the pitch of his own examination. In his review of the second edition of the *Oxford English Dictionary,* Hill writes that "principle is inseparable from nuance" (*Style and Faith,* p. 10), and one understands that Hill really is judging each and every nuance for its ethical and moral pitch, a potentially exhausting prospect. In Hill's assessment of the seventeenth-century metaphysical poet Henry Vaughan, he writes, "Vaughan's embroilment in national and personal distress makes him doubly conscious: of impetus and impediment; of a world hastening to catastrophe; of humanity fearfully laggard in its recognition of the apocalyptic signs" (*Style and Faith,* p. 74). As writers often do when ostensibly writing about the work of others, Hill here reveals a core aspect of his self and his own writing.

The essays can be, at times, impenetrable, manifestations of a mind in serious argument with itself and its motivations. They can also provide a finely nuanced perspective on writers, especially of the seventeenth century. Their most valuable function, however, is providing a sort of architectural map to the foundations on which Hill has built his own poetry.

CONCLUSION

In the 1980s Christopher Ricks suggested that scholars, rather than undertaking critical studies of Hill's work, should instead focus on producing annotated volumes. He was referring specifically to *Tenebrae,* but annotated versions would be appropriate to any of Hill's books. The allusions, instead of obscuring the work, as some have suggested, have the potential to reveal manifold layers of meaning, exposing Hill's economies of language for the riches that lie beneath the surface. Though Hill has lamented the difficulty of finding a place for poetry among the "market interests" and "celebrity culture" of our times, he has produced a powerful body of work that looks unflinchingly at the times in which we live, our historical inheritance, the role of the poet, and a paradigm of ethics and conscience.

Many writers, finding early praise for their work, labor to produce a subsequent body that sounds the same, employs the same winning formula. Hill's style ranges across a vast spectrum of poetic utterance, evolving radically over the decades. Though the split between the early and

later work is most extreme, the differences between the versets of *Mercian Hymns* and the tightly wrought poems in *Tenebrae,* or between the ranting tone of *Speech! Speech!* and the subdued lyricism of *A Treatise of Civil Power,* are also notable. David Yezzi, the poet and editor, looked back at the body of Hill's work in a 2008 article for the *New Criterion.* In it, he laments that Hill's readers largely feel compelled to choose between the old work and the new, pointing out that it seems to him "reckless" to ignore anything Hill has written.

Selected Bibliography

WORKS OF GEOFFREY HILL

POETRY

For the Unfallen: Poems 1952–1958. London: Deutsch, 1959.

King Log. London: Deutsch, 1968.

Mercian Hymns. London: Deutsch, 1971. (Quotations in this essay refer to text reprinted in *Somewhere Is Such a Kingdom: Poems 1952–1971,* cited below.)

Somewhere Is Such a Kingdom: Poems 1952–1971. Boston: Houghton Mifflin, 1975. (Includes *For the Unfallen, King Log,* and *Mercian Hymns.*)

Tenebrae. London: Deutsch, 1978; Boston: Houghton Mifflin, 1979.

The Mystery of the Charity of Charles Péguy. London: Agenda, 1983. New York: Oxford University Press, 1984. (Quotations in essay refer to later edition.)

Collected Poems. Harmondsworth, Middlesex, U.K., and New York: Penguin, 1985; New York: Oxford University Press, 1986.

New and Collected Poems, 1952–1992. Boston: Houghton Mifflin, 1994.

Canaan. London and New York: Penguin, 1996. Boston: Houghton Mifflin, 1997.

The Triumph of Love. Boston: Houghton Mifflin, 1998.

Speech! Speech! Washington, D.C.: Counterpoint, 2000.

The Orchards of Syon. Washington, D.C.: Counterpoint, 2002; London and New York: Penguin, 2002.

Scenes from Comus. London and New York: Penguin, 2005.

Without Title. New Haven, Conn.: Yale University Press, 2007.

A Treatise of Civil Power. New Haven, Conn.: Yale University Press, 2007.

OTHER WORKS

The Lords of Limit: Essays on Literature and Ideas. New York: Oxford University Press, 1984.

The Enemy's Country: Words, Contexture, and Other Circumstances of Language. Stanford, Calif.: Stanford University Press, 1991.

Style and Faith. New York: Counterpoint, 2003.

Collected Critical Writings. Oxford and New York: Oxford University Press, 2008.

Brand...A version for the English stage. Minneapolis: University of Minnesota Press, 1981.

BIOGRAPHICAL AND CRITICAL STUDIES

Bolton, Jonathan. "Empire and Atonement: Geoffrey Hill's 'An Apology for the Revival of Christian Architecture in England.' " *Contemporary Literature* 38, no. 2:287–306 (summer 1997).

Dean, Paul. "Pitch Highly Strung." *New Criterion,* December 2008, p. 71. (Review of *Collected Critical Writings.*)

Edwards, Michael. "Quotidian Epic: Geoffrey Hill's *The Triumph of Love.*" *Yale Journal of Criticism* 13, no. 1:167–176 (spring 2000).

Geoffrey Hill Study Centre (http://www3.sympatico.ca/sylvia.paul/geoffrey_hill_index.htm).

Hart, Henry. *The Poetry of Geoffrey Hill.* Carbondale: Southern Illinois University Press, 1986.

Hollander, John. "The Angel of History." *Los Angeles Times,* September 20, 1998, p. 9. (Review of *The Triumph of Love.*)

Kirsch, Adam. "The Plantagenet Poet." *New Republic,* May 27, 2002, pp. 30–35. (Review of *The Orchards of Syon.*)

———. "Geoffrey Hill." In his *The Modern Element: Essays on Contemporary Poetry.* New York: Norton, 2008. Pp. 53–78.

Knottenbelt, E. M. *Passionate Intelligence: The Poetry of Geoffrey Hill.* Amsterdam: Rodopi, 1990.

Phillips, Brian. "A Colder Spell to Come." *Poetry,* May 2006, pp. 139–147. (Review of *Without Title* and *Scenes from Comus.*)

Potts, Robert. "The Praise Singer." *Guardian,* August 10, 2002. Available online (http://www.guardian.co.uk/books/2002/aug/10/featuresreviews.guardianreview15).

Roberts, Andrew Michael. "Geoffrey Hill and Pastiche: "An Apology for the Revival of Christian Architecture in England" and *The Mystery of the Charity of Charles Péguy.*" *Yale Journal of Criticism* 13, no. 1:153–166 (spring 2000).

Robinson, Alan. "History to the Defeated: Geoffrey Hill's *The Mystery of the Charity of Charles Péguy.*" *Modern Language Review* 82, no. 4:830–843 (October 1987).

Sanger, Peter. "Sobieski's Shield: On Geoffrey Hill's *The Enemy's Country* (1991) and *New and Collected Poems* (1994)." *Antigonish Review* 109 (http://www.antigonishreview.com/bi-109/109-sanger.html).

Sherry, Vincent. *The Uncommon Tongue: The Poetry and Criticism of Geoffrey Hill.* Ann Arbor: University of Michigan Press, 1987.

Wainwright, Jeffrey. *Acceptable Words: Essays on the Poetry of Geoffrey Hill.* Manchester, U.K.: Manchester University Press, 2006.

Yezzi, David. "Geoffrey Hill's Civil Tongue." *New Criterion,* March 2008, pp. 22–26.

INTERVIEWS

Haffenden, John. "Geoffrey Hill." In his *Viewpoints: Poets in Conversation with John Haffenden.* London: Faber and Faber, 1981.

Mounic, Anne. "The Poem 'Moulin mystique': A Discussion with Geoffrey Hill." Geoffrey Hill Study Centre (http://www3.sympatico.ca/sylvia.paul/ghill_interview_by_AnneMounic.htm). 2008.

KAZUO ISHIGURO

(1954—)

Barry Lewis

KAZUO ISHIGURO IS the Marcel Proust of his generation. Not in terms of quantity, certainly: his six novels (to date) could fit comfortably into one of the three volumes of the Penguin edition of *Remembrance of Things Past*. Rather, Ishiguro is like Proust because of the way he intertwines three essential themes: memory, time, and place. His writing is invariably focalized through a first-person narrator who ruminates over an earlier stage of his or her life. In doing so, the characters find that their remembrances are sometimes faulty, tinged with hindsight and self-deceiving revision. As Etsuko says toward the end of her own recollections in *A Pale View of Hills*: "Memory, I realize, can be an unreliable thing; often it is heavily coloured by the circumstances in which one remembers, and no doubt this applies to certain of the recollections I have gathered here" (p. 156).

Ishiguro was born in Nagasaki, Japan on November 8, 1954. The city suffered terrible devastation after it was struck by the second atomic bomb dropped by the U.S. Air Force at the end of World War II. Its wasteland was to form the backdrop of his first novel. His father, Shigeo—married to Shizuko (maiden name, Michida)—was an oceanographer. It was his father's work that brought the family to Guildford, Surrey, in England in 1960. Ishiguro's eldest sister, Fumiko, came with them, and a second sister, Yoko, was later born in the U.K. It was supposed to be a temporary stay while his father carried out two years of research on North Sea oil fields at the National Institute of Oceanography, but ultimately the family made the decision to settle permanently in England. Ishiguro missed his grandparents and found everyday aspects of English life exotic, such as double-decker buses and squashed hedgehogs on the road. Gradually, though, his memories of Japan faded and England became his real home. He finally became a British citizen in 1983 and did not visit his country of birth again until 1989. Throughout his novels (the first two of which are set in Japan), there is a strong sense of displacement or uprootedness. Characters such as Etsuko in *A Pale View of Hills* and Christopher Banks in *When We Were Orphans* have lost all sense of belonging and are in search of a more stable identity. No doubt this can partly be attributed to the circumstances of his own upbringing.

Ishiguro attended Stoughton Primary School (1960–1966), where he was the only child from an ethnic background. In order to fit in he became something of a ventriloquist, imitating the speech and manners of his friends. His secondary education at Woking County Grammar School for Boys (1966–1973) was less fraught with feelings of difference, although he still often found himself split between two cultures. By the time he studied at the University of Kent, Canterbury (1974–1978), Ishiguro had developed distinctive interests in literature and popular music. He had already spent a "gap year" hawking demo tapes of his own songs around record companies in the United States and Canada. He wished to emulate the success of singer-songwriters such as Bob Dylan, Leonard Cohen, and Joni Mitchell. He enjoyed reading Edna O'Brien, V. S. Naipaul, J. G. Farrell, and Margaret Drabble (whose *Jerusalem the Golden* was an important influence). Anton Chekhov and Fyodor Dostoevsky were held by him in particularly high regard. It is noticeable that Ishiguro's own fiction veers between the poles of Chekhovian minimalism and a stylistic and imaginative excess associated with the author of *Crime and Punishment*.

After graduating with a B.A. (honors) in English and philosophy, Ishiguro drifted among a

149

number of temporary jobs. His stint as a grouse beater for the Queen Mother at Balmoral Castle, Scotland, in 1973 furnished him with some direct experience of the upper echelons depicted in *The Remains of the Day*. In 1976 he became a community worker at Renfrew Social Works Department, also in Scotland. Between 1979 and 1980 the West London Cyrenians, a charity in Notting Hill that helped resettle the homeless, employed him. It was during this period that he met his future wife, Lorna Anne MacDougall. Following a brief spell at a bedsit (a one-room apartment) in Cardiff, Wales, Ishiguro settled with Lorna in the London suburb of Sydenham in 1981.

The most crucial step Ishiguro took was to study for the M.A. in creative writing at the University of East Anglia (1979–1980). Although such courses were common in the States and elsewhere, this was the first academic course of its kind in Britain. The amount of actual hands-on instruction he received was negligible. Nevertheless, the availability of mentors such as Malcolm Bradbury and Angela Carter, combined with the validating presence of other aspiring writers, galvanized Ishiguro. His M.A. dissertation became the basis of his first novel. In the summer of 1980 he rented a farmhouse in Cornwall and wrote three short stories that Faber published in *Introduction 7: Stories by New Writers* (for which he received £1000).

Things moved fast at this juncture. Bill Buford, the editor of the prestigious *Granta* literary journal, showed an interest in Ishiguro's work after receiving one of his short stories. Then Robert McCrum, editor at Faber, commissioned Ishiguro to write a novel, and *A Pale View of Hills* was published in the United Kingdom and United States in 1982. The inclusion of Ishiguro in the *Granta* "Best of Young British Novelists" issue in 1982, and the accompanying campaign by the Book Marketing Council the year after, sealed his initial success. The list of twenty writers proved to be an accurate harbinger. It included names such as Graham Swift, Pat Barker, Salman Rushdie, Rose Tremain, Martin Amis, Ian McEwan, and Julian Barnes, who, like Ishiguro, were to become leading lights of contemporary British fiction in the decades to follow.

A PALE VIEW OF HILLS

A Pale View of Hills (1982) is a remarkably poised first novel. It is partly set in Nagasaki in the years of postwar reconstruction and American occupation. Though it does not deal directly with the dropping of the atomic bomb, it manages to present a powerful objective correlative of the horrors of that time. The book presents two deftly intertwined narratives. A frame tale, set in the notional present, concerns a middle-aged Japanese woman named Etsuko and the visit of her daughter, Niki, to her house in the English countryside. Keiko, Niki's younger stepsister, had committed suicide some years earlier in a Manchester bedsit. Etsuko is still struggling to come to terms with the death of this other daughter, who was born in Japan and never really adapted to life in England. She is reluctant to talk things over with Niki, and vice versa, so some tension exists between them. Apart from a couple of short conversations, the suicide is not mentioned. Nevertheless, both mother and daughter are haunted by this tragic episode.

Several motifs associated with the ghost story are discernible in this outer tale. For instance, when Niki sleeps in her former bedroom on the first night of her stay, she feels uncomfortable because it is situated opposite Keiko's old room. She recalls how Keiko would stay cocooned in her "fanatically guarded domain" (p. 53) for weeks at a time, emerging only for the odd meal. When Niki asks Etsuko if she can move to the spare room, her mother is annoyed, although she also has some misgivings: "I too had experienced a disturbing feeling about that room opposite" (p. 53).

There is an unsettling incident in the house some five days after Niki arrives. Etsuko wakes up early in the morning and believes she hears sounds coming from Keiko's room. She is reluctant to open the door. When she does so, she finds nothing there other than Keiko's belongings. The next night, Etsuko is again disturbed, as if somebody was walking past her and into the hall. She gets up to investigate, uncertain what to think, and is relieved when she realizes the noise came from her daughter moving about in the kitchen. It is Niki's turn to get a fright when she sees Etsuko unexpectedly. She also has had distressing dreams but will not discuss them with her mother. As they continue talking, Etsuko reveals that she feels guilty about Keiko's suicide: "I knew all along she wouldn't be happy over here. But I decided to bring her just the same" (p. 176).

Niki refuses to allow her mother to take the blame and protests that her father, Keiko's stepfather, could have shown more concern with Etsuko's daughter from a previous marriage. The late Mr. Sheringham is a very shadowy figure in the novel: all we know is that he was a writer, possibly a journalist, and that his parental skills were wanting. Niki decides to return to London, where she lives with her partner, David, and Etsuko tells her she has decided to sell the house and move elsewhere. It is imbued with too many unpleasant memories.

The outer tale, then, of Etsuko and Niki is largely uneventful but conveys a frisson of eeriness. The associations of the house with Keiko's death, the nightmares, the strange "bumps" in the night, and the unnatural ambience of Keiko's room make it a haunted house. This is all extremely understated, though. In *A Pale View of Hills* it is memory itself that is the ghost, as it covers the past with its white shroud.

The second, inner story of the novel is conveyed in tandem with the outer story and concerns Etsuko's recollections of her life in Nagasaki not long after the war. At that time, the inhabitants of the city did what they could to rebuild their shattered existences. The widespread destruction wreaked by the bomb and the death of loved ones it entailed had traumatized the survivors. Etsuko herself had lost her fiancé, Nakamura, and her family. In her deranged state of the immediate aftermath, she would play the violin in the middle of the night to combat her demons.

By the 1950s, though—the period of the inner story—some stability has returned as she is married to Jiro (a gruff careerist) and expecting their first child. Etsuko befriends Sachiko. This woman hailed from a wealthy family background before the war but is now in reduced circumstances with her young daughter, Mariko. Deter-

mined to escape from Japan, Sachiko pins her hopes on a feckless American sailor, Frank. The situation has echoes of the famous opera *Madame Butterfly* (1904) by Giacomo Puccini (tellingly set in Nagasaki), in which the heroine also has dreams of fleeing Japan with her American lover, Lieutenant Benjamin Franklin Pinkerton. Although she has his child, the naval officer lets her down, so Madame Butterfly kills herself.

Mariko is willful and unpredictable after her traumatic wartime experiences. As her mother carouses with Frank, Mariko is left to fend for herself during the day in their shabby cottage. Instead of going to school, she roams the waste ground near the river: this is "several acres of dried mud and ditches.... All year round there were craters filled with stagnant water, and in the summer months the mosquitoes became intolerable" (p. 11). Etsuko finds herself thrust into the position of unofficial guardian for Mariko but finds it difficult to control the little girl, who is forever running away. On several occasions Mariko refers darkly to a mysterious woman from across the river with whom she has had some contact. This is especially troubling because there has been a spate of child murders in and around Nagasaki.

One time when Mariko runs away, Etsuko finds the little girl lying in the grass by the riverbank with a superficial leg wound. Later on, after yet another flight—this time at night—Etsuko again finds Mariko by the river. The little girl is scared by a piece of old rope that tangles around Etsuko's ankle. In chapter 9, Etsuko sees a figure dressed in black approach the cottage. She is already on edge because she had been thinking about a news report of a child found hanging from a tree, so she rushes over to see what is happening. It turns out not to be the murderer but Sachiko's elderly cousin, who has attended a funeral.

Mariko's last attempt to run away occurs in chapter 10. Sachiko has drowned her daughter's kittens in the river, with Mariko watching. She has plans to move to Kobe to wait for Frank to whisk them away to a better life. Etsuko finds Mariko, who is extremely upset, sitting on a wooden bridge. She tries to comfort her by saying that things will be fine in America with Frank and her mother. She makes several significant slips of the tongue in doing so: "If you don't like it over there, we'll come straight back. But we have to try it and see if we like it there. I'm sure we will" (p. 173). The repetition of the plural nominative pronoun confirms the suspicions of the reader that the story of Sachiko and Mariko is a disguised version of the relationship between Etsuko and Keiko. Throughout, parallels between their situations have surfaced. Sachiko wishes to take Mariko away from Japan; Etsuko took Keiko to England. Mariko is a disturbed child, prone to fits of temper and brooding; Keiko was depressed as a teenager and eventually killed herself. Sachiko knows she is not a good mother; Etsuko suspects this is true of herself too.

A Pale View of Hills resists closure and haunts us with its unresolved silences. In fact, the key feature of the book is its refusal to speak directly about its most vital subjects. The most obvious example of this is its reticence about the destruction of Nagasaki. The bomb itself receives only a handful of discreet references. This muted approach was to characterize all of Ishiguro's subsequent novels.

AN ARTIST OF THE FLOATING WORLD

In *An Artist of the Floating World* (1986), Ishiguro focuses on a painter named Masuji Ono who colludes with the imperialist fervor that gripped Japan in the 1930s by producing propaganda posters and informing on those who are not loyal to the cause within his own profession. During the years of the American occupation after World War II, his past has become a liability as the political climate has turned toward democracy. His dubious associations and activities threaten to mar the marriage negotiations that are taking place between his youngest daughter, Noriko, and her potential husband, Taro Saito.

Ishiguro drew upon two main sources for this tale of guilt and self-doubt. The first is the subplot of his previous novel, *A Pale View of Hills,* in which Etsuko's Japanese father-in-law, Ogata, is subject to slurs after the war in relation to his

teaching career. The second source for *An Artist of the Floating World* is Ishiguro's short story "The Summer After the War," which shares a similar setting and features several of the same characters.

It is important to note that the first section of *An Artist of the Floating World* (which constitutes almost half of the book) takes place in October 1948. At this time, the military dictator General Tojo and his cohorts were on trial for war crimes, culminating in Tojo's execution in December of that year. Although the novel does not explicitly refer to this, it forms the context in which Ono's own self-examination can be understood. In the course of his musings on the forthcoming marriage negotiations, Ono reviews his life and career up to the point when he first meets Chishu Matsuda, the sinuous representative of the Okada-Shingen Society who steers Ono's artistic ambitions in a political direction.

Ono's apprenticeship as a painter begins in 1913, when he churns out cheap canvases of little merit in a small room above a Furukawa restaurant for the export market. His teacher, Master Takeda, is in charge of fifteen artists who take little pride in what they do. As long as the cherry trees, carp, and golden temples that they are asked to draw looked sufficiently "Japanese" to a foreigner, they will pass muster and be rapidly shipped out.

A far better post is offered to Ono when he is invited to be part of a colony of artists under the direction of Seiji Moriyama (known as Mori-san). Ono spends seven years at Mori-san's run-down villa in the Wakaba prefecture, painting subjects in the traditional ukiyo-e or "floating world" style: geisha women in elegant poses, gentle falls of rain and suchlike. Ukiyo-e became popular in the Japanese Edo period (1603–1867, when artists such as Okumara, Utamaro, Hokusai, and Hiroshige made woodlock prints depicting courtesans, musicians, Kabuki actors, and sumo wrestlers. The name derived from the "sorrowful world" of Buddhism, the transient and illusionary realm of day-to-day activity. The style became influential when Japan opened up to the West in the mid-nineteenth century. Artists such as James McNeill Whistler and the Impressionists Edgar Degas and Claude Monet admired the emphasis upon the impermanence of form and its celebration of fleeting pleasures.

The community of floating world artists of which Ono is part often carouses with the very actors and musicians who are their subjects. During one party, Ono sidles off alone to a storeroom. Mori-san follows him there and asks his pupil why he is not taking part in the revelry. Ono replies that he is having doubts about the value of the floating world. Mori-san tries to reassure him by saying: "When I am an old man, when I look back over my life and see that I have devoted it to the task of capturing the unique beauty of that world, I believe I will be well satisfied. And no man will make me believe I've wasted my time" (pp. 150–151). Ono is not convinced and remains disenchanted with the limitations of this approach and the dissolute behavior of the other artists. He believes that this form of art is disengaged from the wider world and devotes too much attention to unimportant matters.

Ono is therefore ripe for indoctrination and is approached by Matsuda, a recruiting agent for the nationalist cause, who persuades him that aestheticism is pointless at a time of imperialist expansion: "We are now a mighty nation, capable of matching any of the Western nations. In the Asian hemisphere, Japan stands like a giant amidst cripples and dwarfs" (p. 173). Under Matsuda's sway, Ono then paints a propaganda piece called *Complacency*. This depicts three boys, standing defiantly in impoverished surroundings, while above their heads three businessmen are laughing in a bar. When he shows this new work at the villa, Ono is branded a traitor for betraying his master's principles and forced to leave the community.

Ono decides to pursue a form of art that is politically motivated and more involved in real affairs. He sets up his own school of committed artists and, with the backing of Matsuda, is elected to the Cultural Committee of the Interior Department. He also acts as official adviser to the Committee of Unpatriotic Activities. His biggest success comes with the reworking of *Complacency* into the poster *Eyes to the Horizon*. In this

version, a trio of obese politicians replaces the businessmen, while the boys from the slums are transformed into soldiers looking toward mainland Asia. Ono even betrays his most gifted pupil, Kuroda, to the authorities, leading to the student's arrest and the mindless destruction of his paintings.

Issues such as these from his past trouble Ono when he enters into marriage negotiations for his daughter. The Japanese custom of investigating the family background of potential wedding partners threatens to reveal some skeletons better left in the closet. Prompted by his eldest daughter, Setsuko, Ono takes the "precautionary steps" (p. 49) of urging former acquaintants to remain silent, if approached. At the formal meeting of the families involved in the engagement, known as the *miai*, Ono confesses that his dalliance with the military powers was a mistake. His admission is greeted with a baffled silence. It appears that the Saito family was unaware of Ono's dubious history, after all, and that the artist has overestimated his importance in the overall scheme of things. It is unclear what Ono's shameful confession was meant to achieve. It could be that he believed that admitting to his sense of guilt face-to-face would forestall a later scandal. Alternatively, perhaps he momentarily lost perspective and blurted out his secrets without thought for the consequences. In either case, the response of the Saitos is surprising, although Ono is not made aware of their puzzlement until some six months later. While visiting her father, Setsuko discloses that her sister Noriko could not understand why Ono behaved so strangely during the *miai*. Setsuko also claims that she has no recollection of inciting her father to take "precautionary steps" before the marriage negotiations. Ono's memory of both recent and past events is thus exposed as unreliable. Ironically, his moment of revelation during the *miai* served only to lessen the tension between the two families. The marriage between Noriko and Taro Saito went ahead and, within a year, they were due to have a child.

The novel ends on a regretful note with a memory that chimes with the exchange between Ono and Mori-san at the floating world villa. In

May 1938 Ono makes a return to the Wakaba Prefecture. By this time he has found real success through his propaganda paintings after winning the prestigious Shigeta Foundation Award. His plan is to meet his former sensei, or teacher, on an equal basis. When he nears the villa, however, he no longer feels the need to confront Mori-san and is content to sit on a hill, bathe in the sun, and bask for a while in his own self-satisfaction. He is possessed by a feeling of triumph that expresses itself in the very tones of the master he had disowned. He describes it as "a profound sense of happiness deriving from the conviction that one's efforts have been justified; that the hard work undertaken, the doubts overcome, have all been worthwhile; that one has achieved something of real value and distinction" (p. 204). His efforts seem to him to have been vindicated. Yet Ishiguro makes it plain by the placement of this vignette, coming as it does after Ono's fall from favor and postwar disillusionment, that this sense of triumph is deluded.

THE REMAINS OF THE DAY

The Remains of the Day (1989) moves away from the Japanese settings of Ishiguro's first two novels to focus on England. At the center of the novel is a butler, that quintessential English symbol. Through Stevens and his unswerving devotion to Lord Darlington, Ishiguro conducts an enquiry into the nature of Englishness itself. He had already experimented with such a figure in his television play *A Profile of Arthur J. Mason* (1984). *The Remains of the Day,* though, was to reach a much wider audience, especially because it was later made into a major film by the Merchant Ivory team in 1993. It starred Anthony Hopkins as Stevens and Emma Thompson as Miss Kenton and received eight Oscar nominations.

The story is skillfully managed. Stevens decides to take a motoring tour of the West Country in 1956, with the ulterior motive of luring former housekeeper Miss Kenton (now Mrs. Benn) back into service at the stately home of Darlington Hall. As he travels around the country-side and stops overnight at picturesque places such as Salisbury and Moscombe, near Tavistock, Devon, he looks back with nostalgia and regret over his life and career. Darlington Hall has passed into the hands of the American Mr. Farraday and is not what it once was. Its previous owner, Lord Darlington, was a man of wealth and distinction. Unfortunately, he supported the idea of appeasement with Hitler's Germany before World War II and was subsequently disgraced by a newspaper exposé once the war was over. Stevens comes to realize that he has made two big mistakes. He has remained loyal to an unworthy employer and, as a consequence, has rejected the proffered love of Miss Kenton.

Stevens is often blind to his own shortcomings, and the novel as a whole presents a textbook example of the unreliable narrator. For example, when the butler remembers the 1923 conference set up by Lord Darlington to discuss the injustices of the Versailles Treaty, it is clear that he exaggerates his role. The same is true when he relates the tale of his assistance in the visit of Herr Ribbentrop (Germany's foreign minister) to Darlington Hall some years later. The reader gleans that these "triumphs" were, in fact, disasters. In the second chapter, Stevens coldly dismisses the fact that his father has had a stroke in the room upstairs and continues with his professional duties. Similarly, in the fifth chapter, he loses his last chance of preventing Miss Kenton from leaving Darlington Hall as he is too preoccupied with "matters of global significance taking place upstairs" (p. 219). By acting in this tunnel-visioned manner, Stevens believes he is only fulfilling his role as a butler, but it is at the expense of his emotional fealties.

While excavating these painful memories, Stevens muses on the concept of "dignity" and its application to the butlering profession. He asserts that this is the most important ingredient and quotes the admission requirements for the (fictitious) Hayes Society as evidence: "the most crucial criterion is that the applicant be possessed of a dignity in keeping with his position. No applicant will satisfy requirements, whatever his level of accomplishments otherwise, if seen to fall short in this respect" (p. 33). Stevens cites anecdotal examples of how his father, also a butler, possessed such dignity. On one occasion, while Stevens Sr. was serving in India, he managed to dispatch a tiger that had wandered into the dining room without "any discernible traces of the recent occurrence" (p. 36). Stevens connects the quality of dignity directly with both the English temperament and the English landscape: neither is demonstrative, yet both possess a considerable understated power and poise. Here is how he explains (pompously, as usual) his reasoning:

> I would say that it is the very *lack* of obvious drama or spectacle that sets the beauty of our land apart. What is pertinent is the calmness of that beauty, its sense of restraint. It is as though the land knows of its own beauty, its own greatness, and feels no need to shout it. In comparison, the sorts of sights offered in such places as Africa and America, though undoubtedly very exciting, would, I am sure, strike the objective viewer as inferior on account of their unseemly demonstrativeness.
>
> (pp. 28–29)

By the end of Stevens' journey, however, he has begun to question the values he has so painstakingly upheld. The reunion with Miss Kenton/Mrs. Benn in the tea lounge of the Rose Garden Hotel in Little Compton is subdued. Far from wishing again to take up her old position, she expresses a certain degree of contentment with her lot, even though she thinks she probably would have been happier if things had worked out with Stevens. It is an admission that penetrates even the sturdy butler's steely emotional armor: "at that moment, my heart was breaking" (p. 239). All that remains of his day is more work. Moreover, he now sees that his service to Lord Darlington has been misplaced. Far from having served through "loyalty *intelligently* bestowed" (p. 201), he now admits that he had deceived himself about his lack of agency and has been in a constant state of denial ever since. Still, there is a glimmer of hope. While sitting on a bench by the pier at Weymouth, observing the switching-on of the lights and the fellow feeling this creates among the assembled crowd, he has an illumination of his own. He decides that bantering, a social skill that he has always dismissed as beneath him,

may be "the key to human warmth" (p. 245) and he determines to improve at it.

As with *An Artist of the Floating World, The Remains of the Day* is a novel about time, memory, nostalgia, and regret. The inner landscapes of Ono and Stevens are so similar that they are like the two faces of the one coin. Their outer circumstances would appear to be worlds apart, and England's genteel society of the 1920s and 1930s would seem to have nothing in common with the imperialistic cauldron of Japan in the same period. Yet the apparent disparities between their sociohistorical contexts should not blind us to the substrata that bind their far-flung islands together. Both the English and the Japanese peoples are noted for their repression; both of their cultures have traditionally placed great emphasis upon decorum and manners; and their nations have remained largely immune from the many invasions that have affected other countries in Europe and Asia. Consequently, the temperaments of Ono and Stevens have much in common. They are both dutiful; they strive to give their lives wider significance by devoting their energies to larger causes; and they are both ultimately unable to accept that they made profound errors by refusing to challenge the received notions of their moments in history. When the tide of public opinion turns, they are left stranded on the sandbanks of their former convictions.

Stevens is as strained as Ono when it comes to hiding his misgivings behind a linguistic facade. His habitual periphrasis and circumlocutory way of talking tries to mask the recognition of his own mistakes. For instance, on the occasion when he ignores his dying father in order to attend to the petty requests of the guests at Lord Darlington's 1923 conference, he states:

> if you consider the pressures contingent on me that night, you may not think I delude myself unduly if I go so far as to suggest that I did perhaps display, in the face of everything, at least in some modest degree a 'dignity' worthy of someone like Mr Marshall [a fellow esteemed manservant]—or come to that, my father. Indeed, why should I deny it? For all its sad associations, whenever I recall that

evening today, I find I do so with a large sense of triumph.

(p. 110)

Indeed, why should he deny it? After all, he has only abandoned his father on his deathbed for the sake of replenishing the port in the smoking room and easing the sore feet of an irate French diplomat. His refusal to respond to the advances of Miss Kenton betrays a further inversion of priorities. On the evening when the housekeeper reveals to Stevens that she has received a marriage proposal from Mr. Benn, the butler says nothing to her that might make her change her mind. He throws away the opportunity of a lifetime of personal happiness for the sake of his professional duties. The crushing irony is that the butler, by serving Lord Darlington, is far from being at the hub of world affairs as he supposes. Rather, he is the flunky of a man whom history will condemn as a Nazi sympathizer.

THE UNCONSOLED

The Unconsoled (1995) appeared six years after *The Remains of the Day* and two years after that novel was adapted for the big screen. His next project was eagerly awaited by both public and critics, many of whom anticipated something similar to the fictions that had preceded it.

Yet in many respects, *The Unconsoled* (1995) represents a radical break from Ishiguro's previous three novels, and reviewers received it with much bafflement. It lacks his trademark stylistic restraint; it eschews traditional narrative structures; and it revisits his familiar themes of memory and regret in a strikingly fresh way. His earlier books were united by a common thread. Their unreliable narrators strove to repress and revise the past in an attempt to deny full responsibility for earlier mistakes. With Ryder, the central figure of this fourth novel, the unconscious bursts through his defenses and displaces itself onto his present circumstances. There is no escape from the consequences of his errors. Ryder's fears and anxieties are displaced onto the people he meets and the places he encounters. This creates a world that is more akin to the surreal canvases of Salvador Dalí or Max Ernst than to the realistic settings of earlier books.

The plot, insofar as the nonlinear sequence of events can be effectively summarized, revolves around a prestigious pianist, namely Ryder. He arrives at an unnamed central European town on a Tuesday to give a performance on the following Thursday evening. He is without a schedule. More importantly, he does not seem to have a properly functioning memory. His amnesia even leads him to forget that he has a wife (Sophie) and child (Boris) living in this locality. He encounters many interruptions to his concert preparations. The population of the town, most of whom seem obsessed with musical matters, see him as a savior who can redeem their cultural fortunes and intervene in their personal difficulties. Ryder is passively acquiescent to their demands and struggles to cope with the chaos that increasingly surrounds him. However, as if in compensation he possesses some unexplained extrasensory powers. He reproduces word-for-word conversations at which he was not present; he is somehow privy to the innermost fears and hopes of the townspeople; and his tolerance for absurd requests is far above the average.

The novel has a dreamlike atmosphere and features many displacements of space and time. Ryder is frequently lost in the winding, looping labyrinth of the town, and his trips outside its confines confirm the impression of a place that does not obey the rules of three-dimensional geography. When he finally gets the chance to rehearse his music, he does so first on a piano stuffed into a toilet cubicle and then in an abandoned hut miles from the town center. His justified complaints fall on the deaf ears of Hoffman, the hotel manager.

The irregularities of time in this town are obvious from the outset. When Ryder arrives at his hotel in chapter 1, the elevator ride to an upper floor is endless. During the ride, Gustav the porter (whom, it is later revealed, is actually Ryder's father-in-law) regales the musician with a long monologue in which he drones on about his professional philosophy of carrying suitcases. In some respects Gustav is a parody of both the dutifulness of Stevens the butler from *The*

Remains of the Day and the standards of perfection professed by Ono in *An Artist of the Floating World.* Throughout *The Unconsoled,* Ishiguro subverts his own predilection for writing in a highly compressed and elliptical manner, a feature in his earlier works that was invariably praised by the critics.

The town invests an inordinate value in its music, as Ryder discovers. The hotel manager, Hoffman, confides to his guest that his marriage was based on a sham: his wife had been under the mistaken apprehension that he was an accomplished musician when she married him. For twenty-five years, Mr. and Mrs. Hoffman have put pressure on their son, Stephan, to become a great pianist. They believe they have failed, although Ryder praises Stephan's prowess. Indeed, Stephan gives an outstanding performance on the day of the concert, but his parents are deaf to his talents. The two leading musicians of the town, Brodsky and Christoff, have lost favor with their audience. After a bright start, Brodsky ruined his subsequent career through alcoholism. Christoff alienated the townspeople by his penchant for avant-garde compositions. Hoffman, Stephan, Brodsky, and Christoff represent aspects of Ryder, either as he was or might have been in a parallel universe. Through this device (similar to the displacement of Etsuko's story onto that of Sachiko in *A Pale View of Hills*), Ishiguro is able to explore issues relating to the tension between Ryder's commitment to his art and his personal life.

Through the course of the novel, Ryder has come to realize that his wife and child are living in the very town he is visiting. Ryder's family is a constant source of anxiety to him. He frets about the arrangements made for his parents, who are visiting the town to watch him play for the first time. Needless to say, everything goes awry. He is concerned about Gustav's health. The elderly porter, as mentioned above, habitually carries more luggage than he can handle—a state of affairs that is reenacted in the hilarious "Porter's Dance" in chapter 22—and the overexertion eventually kills him. His dying wish is for Ryder to make amends on his behalf with his daughter Sophie, to whom he has not spoken for many years.

Ryder has his own difficulties with Sophie. He knows that his long months away from home on tour have strained the marriage. He is also estranged from his son. A gift he gives the boy, a tattered do-it-yourself manual that teaches decorating, housepainting, and tiling, is woefully inappropriate. Despite a common interest in soccer, father and son never talk about it together. A long-awaited family night at home with a board game and some tasty snacks in chapter 20 is a disaster. Ryder buries himself in a newspaper and inwardly grumbles about Sophie's cuisine.

Meanwhile, the preparations for the concert are a fiasco. Ryder is forever diverted from his priorities by trivial requests and time-consuming favors. Hoffman wants the musician to look though his wife's album of press cuttings; Brodsky enlists Ryder in his quest to restore favor with Miss Collins; and Fiona Roberts, a childhood friend of Ryder's, who now works as a tram ticket-inspector, persuades him to visit the Women's Arts and Cultural Foundation (an appointment he initially fails to meet). When Thursday evening finally comes, the night descends into farce. Brodsky insists on taking the stage, despite a car accident earlier in the day that led to his leg being amputated with a saw. After a brave attempt to conduct the orchestra, using an ironing board as a crutch, he collapses into a heap. By the time Ryder is ready to perform, it is the early hours of the morning. Not only has the audience departed but all the seating has been dismantled too.

When Ryder finds out in chapter 38 that Gustav has died, he chases after Sophie and Boris to offer his condolences. He catches up with them on a tram, where he sees them hugging each other. His sympathies are bitterly rejected by Sophie: "Leave us. You were always on the outside of our love. Now look at you. On the outside of our grief too. Leave us. Go away" (p. 532). Boris protests, but Sophie turns the knife by revealing that Ryder is not Boris' genetic father (a circumstance hinted at throughout the book).

Therefore, at the novel's close, there is no consolation for Ryder, just as there has been no consolation for the inhabitants of the town. There is consolation for the reader, however: *The Unconsoled* may be frustrating and sprawling, but it never ceases to fascinate and surprise. Although not autobiographical, the book is partly a satire and distortion of Ishiguro's experiences of book tours. It is not primarily a work of fantasy, despite the nods to *Gulliver's Travels* and *Alice in Wonderland*. It echoes Kafka in its bewilderments and postponements and is postmodern in the widest sense of that term: an uncategorizable mix of the realistic and the bizarre.

WHEN WE WERE ORPHANS

When We Were Orphans (2000) is, as English soccer managers are fond of saying, "a game of two halves." The novel has seven titled sections. In part 1, "London, 24th July 1930," Christopher Banks is on the verge of making a name for himself as a detective. At a Claridge's banquet, he encounters Sarah Hemmings, an upwardly mobile siren to whom he is attracted. His bond with her is destined to be as futile as that of Stevens and Miss Kenton, though at this stage he is content to watch from the wings as Sarah attaches herself to a prominent diplomat, Sir Cecil Medhurst. Banks focuses on his upbringing in part 2, dated "London, 15th May 1931." His father was an employee of the colonial enterprise Morganbrook and Byatt. His mother, Diana, discovered the insidious role that the firm played in the Far East opium trade and began a campaign against its shady dealings. Both parents disappeared in a suspicious manner. When his father went missing, the young Banks tried to compensate for his loss through a game he played repeatedly with his Japanese friend, Akira. The two boys pretended to be detectives who track down and rescue Mr. Banks. The games came to an end when, after his mother's disappearance, Christopher was sent over to England to be cared for by a Shropshire aunt.

In part 3, "London, 12th April 1937," Banks is well established as a famous detective. He is far from satisfied, however, as the unsolved case of his parents increasingly nags at him. He researches old newspapers to search for clues and spends much time brooding over his loss. The unstable state of Europe and Asia is somehow mixed up in his mind with his own personal agenda. When he accidentally meets Sarah at a friend's wedding, he discovers that she is leaving for Shanghai with Sir Cecil (now her husband). Banks, on an impulse, decides to leave for the Far East too. He places the care of Jennifer, his adopted daughter, in the hands of a nanny.

Banks returns to the International Settlement in part 4, "Cathay Hotel, Shanghai, 20th September 1937." It is here that the novel starts to shift into a different mode. The officials he meets appear to believe that the detective can improve their own predicament. China is under attack from its Japanese enemy and there are deep internal divisions between the Nationalists and the Communists. This makes the position of the International Settlement at Shanghai, a neutral enclave for the British and American concessions, particularly vulnerable. Strangely, everybody around Banks encourages the detective to find his long-lost parents, as if this would resolve the chaotic state of the city and world affairs in general. The transition of the novel into a kind of mad fable continues in part 5, "Cathay Hotel, Shanghai, 29th September 1937." On a visit to the house of a Chinese family, arranged by his former school friend Anthony Morgan, Banks suddenly realizes that he is in his old home. The seepage of the past into the present is comparable to those episodes in *The Unconsoled* when Ryder becomes aware that the town he is visiting is, in fact, the place where he lives. The climactic part 6, "Cathay Hotel, Shanghai, 20th October 1937," presents a scenario that is an absurdist tour de force. Banks has met Sarah Hemmings several times in Shanghai, and they have planned to flee the city together. Sarah is desperate to escape a failing marriage that is marred by Sir Cecil's addictions to gambling and alcohol. However, Banks is distracted into making one last attempt to find his parents before he leaves. With the help of Lieutenant Chou from the local police force, Banks steps out from the safety of the

International Settlement and heads for the zone where the battle between the Chinese and the Japanese is at its most intense. They stumble their way through the warren, an area of bombed-out tenements, searching futilely for the house where he thinks his parents are still held captive.

At a certain point Chou abandons the ill-equipped detective to continue the pursuit unaided. Banks finds a wounded Japanese soldier and rescues him from certain murder by a gang of crazed Chinese civilians who are bent on revenge for the loss of their loved ones and their property. In his deluded state, Banks convinces himself that this soldier must be Akira, his friend from years ago. Such is the intensity of the detective's conviction that the soldier—barely aware of what is happening—plays along with this pretense. The sequence ends with one of the most nightmarish scenes in all of Ishiguro's fiction. When they eventually reach the house where his parents are supposed to be, what Banks finds is indescribable devastation and suffering. The mutilated remains of a Chinese family caught up in the bombing are strewn around the rubble. The sole survivor is a young girl who, trauma-tized, is concerned only with the fate of her dy-ing pet dog.

On his return to the International Settlement, Banks meets his Uncle Philip (who is actually a family friend and not a relative). Philip discloses what had really happened to Banks's parents. It transpires that Banks's father had simply run away with another woman. His mother had indeed been kidnapped—but not quite in the circumstances that Banks had imagined. During the course of her protests against Morganbrook and Byatt, Diana Banks had insulted one of the Chinese opium warlords, Wang Ku. To protect Christopher from possible retribution (and also to assuage his darkest sexual fantasies), Philip had brokered a deal with Wang Ku whereby Mrs. Banks would be forced into sexual slavery as one of the warlord's concubines. In return, Wang Ku promised to pay an allowance for Christopher. This denouement echoes *Great Expectations* by Charles Dickens, in which the central character eventually finds out that his financial benefactor was not Miss Havisham, as he had assumed, but the convict Magwitch, to whom he had once showed kindness.

In the final chapter of Ishiguro's novel, part 7, "London, 14th November 1958," the narrative jumps forward over twenty years. Banks has returned from a visit to Hong Kong, where he finally was reunited with his mother at Rosedale Manor, an institution for the mentally ill run by nuns. In a poignant scene, Diana fails to recognize her own son. Once back in London, Banks talks about the future with Jennifer and reflects upon a letter he had received from Sarah Hemmings in 1947. Although Sarah declared herself to be happy and to harbor no regrets about how things had turned out, Banks is unsure about her sincer-ity: "for those like us, our fate is to face the world as orphans, chasing through long years the shadows of vanished parents" (p. 313).

The protagonist of *When We Were Orphans* recalls, then, those of Ishiguro's earlier novels. Like Etsuko, Ono, and Stevens, Banks is forever looking backward into the past to find out where it all went wrong. His musings are nostalgic and tinted with regret and he is wont to deceive himself in his recollections in order to shore up his fragile sense of self. Like Ryder, his reshap-ing of experience tips over into a much more sinister amnesia and an aberrant condition in which he displaces onto the world around him his own neuroses and manias. It is a bold experi-ment that Ishiguro attempts, to blend the two poles of his stylistic spectrum (the Chekhovian and Dostoevskyan), but there is a sense of unfin-ishedness in the execution. The "realistic" chapters that chart Banks's career as a detective pay mere lip service to the genre that Ishiguro pastiches. We never really take Banks seriously as a detective at all. The later chapters, saturated in Banks's delusions, are more impressive but leave the reader stranded in an uncertain (perhaps postmodern) textual space that then zaps back toward realism in the final chapter. It is rather like the magician who, while performing a complex trick, reveals the mechanisms of the illusion. If there is then a return to a simple sleight of hand, it is hard to suspend our disbelief for a second time.

KAZUO ISHIGURO

NEVER LET ME GO

Ishiguro has often spoken in interviews of how he felt protected as a child from the horrific reality of the destruction of Nagasaki. It was not until he was ten or eleven years old that he realized that not every city had suffered from an atomic bomb. *Never Let Me Go* (2005) looks closely at the bubble of innocence that surrounds childhood and how society hides from itself its darker underpinnings. This fiction is set in an alternate England of the late twentieth century. In this world, major scientific advances in the field of genetic engineering have led to the production of a large number of clones whose organs are vital for the health of the rest of the population. These clones are brought up to give "donations" until they have "completed": euphemisms that disguise the fact that they are reared for their livers, kidneys, and other organs. It is a novel, then, that flirts with elements of both the science fiction and dystopian genres, without being fully committed to either—reminiscent, in some ways, of Margaret Atwood's *The Handmaid's Tale* (1985) or John Wyndham *The Chrysalids* (1955). Clones may be its putative topic, but the novel (like all of Ishiguro's works) is really about memory, time, and place.

The book is narrated by one such clone, namely the thirty-one-year-old Kathy H. She is currently a "carer" for the donors but will soon be surgically ransacked herself. Most of Kathy's thoughts revolve around the friendships and petty squabbles with her peers, and their education with the "guardians" at Hailsham, a benevolent institution created to provide as normal an existence as possible for children who will later die like cattle. In particular, she sifts through her recollections of the triangular relationship between herself, Ruth, and Tommy as she has been "getting this urge to order all these old memories" (p. 37).

At the opening of the story, Kathy remembers voicing her concerns about Tommy's sporadic rages and tantrums while at Hailsham, which begin for him when his poor drawing skills lead to a certain amount of bullying and exclusion by his classmates. The young Kathy is puzzled by a sudden abatement of his temper. In an intimate conversation by the duck pond, Tommy tells her that one of the guardians, Miss Lucy, has reassured him that art is not all that important. When Miss Lucy later admits that she has made a mistake, she is dismissed from the school and Tommy falls back into his old behavior.

An unspoken rivalry develops between Kathy and Ruth over Tommy's affections. Ruth, always the dominant one in the friendship, becomes Tommy's girlfriend. When they later split up, she asks Kathy to act as a go-between to help them get back together. While these shifting allegiances take place, the students are largely blind to their unique predicament. Kathy, like the reader, is not fully aware of the fate that awaits them all. They are too busy building up their "collections" of personal belongings (such as pencil cases and cassettes) via the regular "Sales" and "Exchanges" at Hailsham to see what is really happening in their lives.

The novel takes its title from a song Kathy likes on a cassette by Judy Bridgewater. One day at Hailsham, she dances alone in the dormitory to "Never Let Me Go," and hugs a pillow to her, as if it was a baby. Madame happens to observe this sad sight and starts crying. When they meet again many years later, the former guardian discloses that she was upset because it symbolized for her a young child clasping a way of life that was soon to disappear. The image of holding tight is intensified by another passage in which Tommy tells Kathy of a dream he had. The two of them were standing in a river and clasping each other close but had to let each other go because of the strong currents.

The curiosity of the students sharpens when they move from Hailsham to the Cottages, another institution set up for the clones. Here, without the guardians to monitor their every move, they are free to speculate and inquire further about their futures. Ruth and Tommy are still together, while Kathy explores her sexuality with several boys. She confides in Ruth about her one-night stands. Meanwhile, Ruth—who, like the others, is now self-conscious about her lack of biological parents—comes under the sway of two older students, Chrissie and Rodney. They convince her that they have spotted the woman from whom she was cloned. The three of them set off on a day trip, with Kathy and Tommy, to track down this "possible" to an office in Cromer. Ruth is very upset when it turns out that her hopes were raised in vain.

Chrissie and Rodney have a hidden motive for feeding Ruth's fantasies. They have heard rumors that couples from Hailsham can obtain a "deferral" of three to four years before they are forced to become donors. The trip to Cromer was merely a ruse to obtain more information about this opportunity. In a bid to become eligible for such a deferral, Tommy tells Kathy that he has secretly begun drawing again. Ruth has not been told about these "imaginary animals," but when she finds out she humiliates him in front of Kathy. She also betrays Kathy by telling Tommy about her one-night stands. By this double stroke, she effectively sunders their friendship. Not long after, Kathy leaves the Cottages to become a "carer."

Part 3 of the novel relates what happens when Ruth, Tommy, and Kathy reunite at a later stage of their lives. Kathy becomes Ruth's "carer" and their friendship is reestablished. They meet up with Tommy again, who is stationed at a different "recovery centre," and drive out on a day trip to see a boat that is stranded inland. On the return journey, Ruth confesses that she deliberately kept Tommy and Kathy apart when they were younger. To make amends, she urges them to try for a deferral. She reiterates this wish just before her fourth donation, which leads to an untimely death.

Kathy becomes Tommy's "carer" and they finally establish a physical relationship together. They approach their old guardians, Madame and Miss Emily, about a deferral, but their illusions are shattered. The benign Hailsham project has been superseded by a much more callous attitude toward the clones upon which society depends. With all hope of redemption lost, on their way back home Tommy asks Kathy to stop the car. He runs into a field and under the cover of night unleashes all the rage and frustration that has built up inside him. Kathy relates:

> I caught a glimpse of his face in the moonlight, caked in mud and distorted with fury, then I reached for his flailing arms and held on tight. He tried to

shake me off, but I kept holding on, until he stopped shouting and I felt the fight go out of him. Then I realised he too had his arms around me. And so we stood together like that, at the top of that field, for what seemed like ages, not saying anything, just holding each other, while the wind kept blowing and blowing at us, tugging our clothes, and for a moment, it seemed like we were holding on to each other because that was the only way to stop us being swept away into the night.

(p. 269)

The England that is presented in *Never Let Me Go* is a miserable place of secondhand shops, bland motorway service stations, and rundown seaside cafés. The bleakness is reinforced at the very end of the novel. Kathy, mourning the death of Tommy just three weeks earlier, returns to the flat, featureless landscape of East Anglia. She notes the bits of plastic bags clinging to the branches of trees and, looking over the forlorn fields, imagines that all the things we lose in life eventually end up in this "lost corner" of England. For a moment, she entertains the fantasy that she can see Tommy running toward her in the distance. It is a wistful close to a harrowing story.

OTHER WORK

Just as Proust devoted his energies largely to one work, Ishiguro has published very little apart from his novels. There are a handful of early short stories from the 1980s. The three that appeared in Faber's *Introduction 7: Stories by New Writers,* mentioned earlier, are "A Strange and Sometimes Sadness," "Getting Poisoned," and "Waiting for J." A sketch for *An Artist of the Floating World,* "The Summer After the War," was featured in *Granta.* Another story from that time, "A Family Supper," has been anthologized. The *New Yorker* printed "A Village After Dark" in 2001. Ishiguro's *Nocturnes: Five Stories of Music and Nightfall* is a story cycle published in 2009.

In addition to *A Profile of Arthur J. Mason* (1984), Ishiguro's television screenplay *The Gourmet* was broadcast in the U.K. in 1993. He had no direct involvement for the film of *The Remains of the Day,* but he provided the first screenplay for *The Saddest Music in the World*

(2003), although the final script (rewritten by George Toles and Guy Maddin) was very different from the original. He also wrote the script for *The White Countess* (2005), a film that shares its Shanghai interwar setting with *When We Were Orphans.*

CONCLUSION

Since the publication of his first novel, Kazuo Ishiguro has been festooned with honors and acclaim. *A Pale View of Hills* was awarded the Winifred Holtby Prize from the Royal Society of Literature in 1983. *An Artist of the Floating World* earned him the Whitbread Book of the Year Award and was short-listed for the Booker Prize in 1986. *The Remains of the Day* was awarded the Booker Prize in 1989 and appeared on the short list of the Best of the Booker award in 2008. The year 1995 was particularly successful: in addition to *The Unconsoled* gaining the Cheltenham Prize and being short-listed for the Whitbread Novel Award, Ishiguro received the Order of the British Empire (OBE) for services to literature and the Italian Premio Scanno prize. *When We Were Orphans* was short-listed for the Booker Prize and the Whitbread Novel Award. *Never Let Me Go* proved to be one of his most popular novels yet. It was on the short lists for the Man Booker Prize, the Commonwealth Writers Prize, and the James Tait Black Memorial Prize.

Awards are awards, and the judgment of a generation may not outlast that generation. Who now reads, let alone rates highly, the work of Pearl S. Buck, who was granted the Nobel Prize for Literature in 1938? With Ishiguro, though, it seems like a good bet that his reputation will be sustained. He is, in many ways, the consummate English novelist. Although he first came to attention because of his exotic name and background, at a time when publishers were looking to duplicate the success of Salman Rushdie, he has since proven himself to be far more than just a marketing opportunity. In *The Remains of the Day* we have a novel whose phrasing is so crystalline it was used as material by the BBC World Service for a series on the English

language. With *The Unconsoled,* he has articulated many of the pressures that characterize our harried, globalized existences. Yet his real achievement lies not just in what his books tell us about ourselves but also in what they refrain from saying. Silences and inference are woven into the texture of his writing in a way that recalls the pregnant use of the blank canvas in a Japanese ink drawing. Proust may have sought to fill every line of the page with detail, but Ishiguro cherishes the value of the unsaid.

The comparison with Proust may seem far-fetched, especially as Ishiguro admits to having only read a small portion of the Frenchman's magnum opus. What he gleaned from his cursory examination of Proust, however, is that a novel need not be dependent upon plot for its momentum. It can engage the reader by demonstrating how time shapes our expectations, accomplishments, and disappointments. Individuals can only do their best to achieve their goals in situations where their options are circumscribed by the larger sways of society and history. Above all, Ishiguro shares Proust's ability to evoke vividly an emotional atmosphere: the ruins of postwar Japan, the confinements of service in a stately home, or the disturbing ambience of a school for genetic clones in an England that never was. His style is certainly not Proustian: rapturous prolixity is countered by a glorious haziness and delicacy of touch that is nonetheless striking in its fidelity. These qualities—along with his patient excavations of memory and mastery of the first-person singular narrative—have contributed to Ishiguro's status as one of our most acute rememberers of things past.

Selected Bibliography

WORKS OF KAZUO ISHIGURO

Novels
Page references in this essay are to the Faber & Faber editions.

A Pale View of Hills. London: Faber & Faber 1982; New York: Putnam, 1982.

An Artist of the Floating World. London: Faber & Faber, 1986; New York: Putnam, 1986.

The Remains of the Day. London: Faber & Faber, 1989; New York: Knopf, 1989.

The Unconsoled. London: Faber & Faber, 1995; New York: Knopf, 1995.

When We Were Orphans. London: Faber & Faber, 2000; New York: Knopf, 2000.

Never Let Me Go. London: Faber & Faber, 2005; New York: Knopf, 2005.

Nocturnes: Five Stories of Music and Nightfall. London: Faber & Faber, 2009; New York: Knopf, 2009.

SHORT STORIES

Introduction 7: Stories by New Writers. London: Faber & Faber, 1981. (Contains "A Strange and Sometimes Sadness," "Getting Poisoned," and "Waiting for J.")

"A Family Supper." In *The Penguin Collection of Modern British Short Stories.* Edited by Malcolm Bradbury. Harmondsworth, U.K.: Penguin, 1987.

"The Summer After the War." *Granta* 7:121–137 (1983).

"A Village After Dark." *New Yorker,* May 21, 2001, pp. 86–91.

TELEVISION SCREENPLAYS

A Profile of Arthur J. Mason. Script for television play. Directed by Michael Whyte. Skreba/Spectre, 1984.

The Gourmet. Script for television play. Directed by Michael Whyte. Skreba/Spectre, 1986. Published in *Granta* 43:89–127 (1993).

BIOGRAPHICAL AND CRITICAL STUDIES

Lewis, Barry. *Kazuo Ishiguro.* Manchester: Manchester University Press, 2000.

Petry, Mike. *Narratives of Memory and Identity: The Novels of Kazuo Ishiguro.* Frankfurt, Germany, and New York: Peter Lang, 1999.

Shaffer, Brian W. *Understanding Kazuo Ishiguro.* Columbia: University of South Carolina Press, 1998.

Sim, Wai-Chew. *Globalization and Dislocation in the Novels of Kazuo Ishiguro.* Lewiston, N.Y.: Edwin Mellen, 2006.

Wong, Cynthia F. *Kazuo Ishiguro.* Tavistock, U.K.: Northcote House, 2000.

FILMS BASED ON THE WORKS OF KAZUO ISHIGURO

The Remains of the Day. Novel adapted for film by Ruth Prawer Jhabvala. Directed by James Ivory. Merchant Ivory Productions, 1993.

The Saddest Music in the World. Script rewritten for film by George Toles and Guy Maddin. Directed by Guy Maddin. IFC Film/MGM, 2003.

The White Countess. Script for film. Directed by James Ivory. Sony Pictures Classics, 2005.

JAMES JOYCE

(1882—1941)

Peter Dempsey

THAT JAMES JOYCE, Ireland's most prestigious literary figure, appears in this volume devoted to British authors is curiously appropriate. In the very year of the publication of *Ulysses* (1922), his most influential novel (and possibly the most influential novel of the twentieth century), this profoundly anticolonialist writer was a British citizen who by default also became a citizen of a newly independent Ireland. *Ulysses* was published in February 1922. By October of that year, after a tumultuous war of independence against the British, the Irish Free State came into being. Furthermore, *Ulysses'* first chapter is set in a British military installation and its last takes the form of a monologue by the daughter of a major in the British army. One important aspect of Joyce's innovative work is its dialogue with and interrogation of the English language and the products of British culture, as seen from the farthest western point of a British Empire that was at its zenith in the year *Ulysses* is set: 1904. Joyce's thoroughgoing transformation of the character and range of the novel—of what novels could actually do—along with his extensive battles against the censorship of his work pushed back the boundaries of what could be said in fiction and opened up the novel form for his contemporaries and for many who came after him, from the likes of Virginia Woolf and William Faulkner to writers who emerged in the late twentieth century such as Richard Powers and Zadie Smith.

LIFE

James Augustine Aloysius Joyce was born on February 2, 1882, in Rathgar, a well-to-do suburb of Dublin. He was the eldest surviving son of John Stanislaus Joyce (1849–1931) and Mary (May) Jane Joyce (1859–1903), who had ten children: six daughters and four sons. John Joyce, originally from Cork city in the west of Ireland, owned property there left to him by his family. Though May Joyce (née Murray) was born in Dublin, her family were also from the west of Ireland. At the time of James Joyce's birth, his father was living on the income from his properties and later had in addition an undemanding job as a tax collector. He was well-known as a raconteur and wit, and he had a compelling singing voice, something his eldest son inherited. He was, however, profligate with money, and with the sudden loss of his job and the regular sale of his Cork properties, the Joyce family began its slow but steady descent into poverty. Nevertheless, James Joyce's early years were comfortable. In 1888 at the age of six he was sent as a boarder to the Jesuit-run Clongowes Wood College in County Kildare, considered to be the best Catholic school in the country.

The Joyces were members of a newly emerging Catholic nationalist middle class, who expected to see home rule in Ireland in the near future and whose hopes for political and economic independence were largely tied to the titanic figure of Charles Stewart Parnell, known by supporters as "the uncrowned king of Ireland." The independent Irish parliament had been dissolved in the Act of Union of 1800, which led to the steady decline of the country, as power and influence moved back across the Irish Sea to the UK parliament. Parnell agitated in the British House of Commons, where he was an MP and leader of the Irish Parliamentary Party, for "home rule" (or devolution), a limited form of political independence. In 1889, at the height of his fame, Parnell was cited as a corespondent in a divorce case, and in predominantly Catholic Ireland the ensuing public scandal (followed by the inevitable condemnation of the Catholic Church) destroyed Parnell's career and divided opinion in the country. Within two years, Parnell was dead of pneumonia at the age of forty-five.

In 1891, the year of Parnell's death, John Joyce lost his job—and saw the beginning of his family's slide into impecuniosity. One immediate consequence was that he was forced to remove his academically gifted son from Clongowes Wood. However, two years later the Jesuits allowed the boy to take up his studies free of charge at Belvedere College in central Dublin, an area where the family now lived in genteel poverty. Joyce's father saw the fall of Parnell as the great betrayal of his lifetime, and this political catastrophe for Ireland was forever linked in his own mind with the decline in his family's fortunes. The bitterness and divisions that the treatment of Parnell generated among the Irish is caught with dramatic brilliance in the Christmas dinner scene in Joyce's 1916 novel *A Portrait of the Artist as a Young Man*. It might be said that if a reader new to Joyce's fiction had to know just one thing about Irish history, knowing who Parnell was would take that reader quite a long way. The death of Parnell was also the occasion of the embryonic litterateur's first work. The nine-year-old wrote a poem, "Et Tu, Healy," on the subject of Parnell's betrayal by his former supporters. Parnell's betrayal (as the Joyces saw it) becomes the model for all other betrayals in the novelist's work.

Joyce underwent profound intellectual and personal development during his six years at Belvedere. In 1896, the precocious fourteen-year-old had his first sexual experience, with a prostitute, and began to frequent the red–light district of Dublin. A weekend religious retreat and a hellfire sermon inspired a period of religious fervor, when Joyce considered studying for the priesthood, but this was followed by an equally intense rejection of organized religion. The place Catholicism had occupied in the formidable imagination of the young Joyce began to be filled by a new divinity: here were the beginnings of his vocation to be an artist. These dramatic episodes in the young man's life were to be reworked and depicted with considerable

sympathy but not a little irony in *A Portrait*. Most importantly for Joyce's literary development, he discovered the drama of Henrik Ibsen. In the Norwegian playwright's work, Joyce found an important example of the fearless artist of integrity: one who was willing to examine human nature outside the accepted frameworks of religious, aesthetic, and moral conventions; one who had suffered at the hands of censors yet who had made an international reputation among admirers of contemporary literature. Fired by his admiration for Ibsen's drama, he rather optimistically submitted an article on the playwright to the prestigious English journal the *Fortnightly Review*. Surprisingly, it was published in April 1900, while Joyce was an undergraduate at University College Dublin. The great playwright read it with pleasure, and his English translator wrote to Joyce with this news. A stunned but happy Joyce replied, "I am a young Irishman, eighteen years old, and the words of Ibsen I shall keep in my heart all my life" (quoted in Ellmann, 1983, p. 74).

Joyce graduated from University College in 1902, and during this period he met many of the leading figures in what was called the "Irish literary revival," a movement that sought to develop an indigenous literature that would be energized by its use of Irish myth and legend and by the creative use of both the English and the Irish languages. Joyce himself was of a resolutely internationalist outlook, both politically and artistically. Although he was scathing about the Irish revival because of what he saw as its sentimentalizing of Ireland's past and its peasantry, its moral conservatism, its sometimes xenophobic nationalism and its kowtowing to the Catholic Church, he was even more implacable in his hostility to British imperialism. The records left by members of the Irish revival show Joyce as an ambitious and prickly young man, the author of a handful of unpublished poems but convinced of his own talent. After his meeting with the poet and editor George Russell, the older man wrote, "There is a young boy named Joyce who may do something. He is as proud as Lucifer and writes verses perfect in their technique and sometimes beautiful in quality" (quoted in Ellmann, 1983, p. 100). William Butler Yeats was initially enthusiastic about Joyce's poetry, but after meeting Joyce, Yeats was less complimentary: "Such a colossal self-conceit with such a Lilliputian literary genius I never saw in one person" (Ellmann, 1983, p. 101).

After graduation Joyce needed a job, and he decided to leave parochial and stultifying Ireland and study medicine in Paris. He managed to get to Paris in December 1902 but could not afford the fees for medical training. He stayed on in the city, however, living on money earned from teaching English, from book reviews, and on money sent from home. He read voraciously in the city's National Library, developing ideas about literature that would sustain him throughout his career. But then suddenly, literature would have to wait. On April 10, 1903, the impecunious young poet received a telegram with the following blunt message: "Mother dying come home father." He left Paris for Dublin the next day. Soon after Joyce arrived home, his dying mother asked him to go to confession and take Holy Communion, but he steadfastly refused. In her last hours, May Joyce went into a coma and her brother asked Joyce and his brother Stanislaus to kneel and pray at her bedside. Both refused. Joyce used this episode in *Ulysses,* but sharpens it by having his character Stephen Dedalus refuse his conscious mother's dying wish; a recurring source of tremendous guilt he feels throughout the novel. May Joyce died of cirrhosis of the liver on August 13, 1903, aged forty-four. With the mother's death and an unemployed, heavy-drinking father, the family moved rapidly toward destitution in the way so movingly described in the scenes about them in *Ulysses.*

The next year proved to be a turning point in Joyce's life. In January 1904 he had written a brief sketch called "A Portrait of the Artist," and though it was turned down for publication, it gave Joyce the idea for an autobiographical novel. By the next month, he had finished the first chapter of a novel called "Stephen Hero." When Joyce finally abandoned it a number of years later, it was one thousand pages long. After ten years of heavy revision, it would be published as Joyce's first novel, a groundbreaking work

that abandoned many of the conventions of nineteenth-century fiction: *A Portrait of the Artist as a Young Man.* Joyce later destroyed the majority of "Stephen Hero." However, a two–hundred–page fragment remained and was published in 1963. Later in the year, he even had a poem published in the well-known journal the *Saturday Review.* Most momentously however, out walking in central Dublin on June 10, he met Nora Barnacle (1884–1951) a young woman from Galway who was working as a chambermaid in a nearby hotel. They walked out together for the first time a few days later, on June 16. Joyce's novel *Ulysses* is set on June 16 as a tribute to Nora. The day is now known the world over as "Bloomsday" after the unlikely hero of the novel, Leopold Bloom. Though little interested in art or literature, Nora was witty, attractive, and, most importantly for a man who saw betrayal everywhere, trustworthy. She became Joyce's lifelong companion. On October 8, unmarried, they left Ireland together.

In subsequent years, before he made his reputation as the leading fiction writer of his time, Joyce earned money teaching English. The couple had two children, Georgio (1905–1976) and Lucia (1907–1982) and lived for a decade in Trieste in northern Italy and nearly twice as long in Paris, only leaving in 1940 for Zurich when the Nazi invasion threatened. Apart from a number of brief visits in the years just after leaving, the couple never returned to Ireland. Joyce died on January 13, 1941, of a perforated duodenal ulcer.

In July 1904, not long after the beginning of Joyce's relationship with Nora, George Russell suggested to Joyce that he try his hand at writing a short story for Russell's paper, the *Irish Homestead.* Joyce then began a series of stories that eventually was published as the collection *Dubliners* (1914), which remains one of the most influential books of stories published in English, inaugurating a whole new era in short fiction writing. Also in July, Joyce saw one of his poems in print, and on August 13, exactly one year after his mother's death, his story "The Sisters" was published. He signed the story "Stephen Daedalus," the fictional hero of his enormous work in progress. Russell's paper went on to publish two more of Joyce's stories, until readers' complaints about these strange, unresolved tales grew too numerous to ignore. And so it was that by the end of 1904, Joyce was a resident of Europe, had a life partner, was a book reviewer, a teacher of English, and a published poet. Most importantly, he was also a writer of stories that would change the way stories are both written and read. Joyce began to write stories that would require a new kind of reader. His life's work would be to both find and ultimately create that readership. That he did so with all but the last of his mature works is an indication of his success.

CHAMBER MUSIC

Soon after settling in Trieste, Joyce began once again to work on his long, autobiographical novel and on his collection of stories. Gifted with languages, he wrote articles on Irish subjects, including what he saw as the Irish betrayal of Parnell and Oscar Wilde, for the local Italian newspaper, and he gave lectures on Hamlet, Daniel Defoe, and Irish literature. This work deepened his interest in Irish politics and in anti-colonialists such as Arthur Griffiths, the leader of the Sinn Féin movement, about whom Bloom often ruminates in *Ulysses.* Joyce's plan to publish his Italian writings as a book came to nothing, but though Joyce would eventually have an international reputation as a novelist, his first published book was *Chamber Music* (1907), a volume of poetry. The verse, which includes cliched imagery and archaic language, holds little interest for the contemporary reader. While the usually astringent critic Hugh Kenner seems to admire *Chamber Music* in his study *Dublin's Joyce,* Anthony Burgess called the fourth poem in the volume "one of the most atrocious lyrics ever penned by a great writer" (p. 71), but he notes acutely that the poems are not simply a collection, but that they form a sequence to tell a story, and clearly the arranging of seeming fragments into a coherent whole is exactly what Joyce does in *Dubliners* (1914) and in *A Portrait.* While some of Joyce's poems, including "Ecce Puer," demonstrate that he could write simply and eloquently, his poetic gift was for satirical and comic verse, which he wrote all his life. With Joyce, even this early in his career, the scatological is never far away; he later claimed (possibly because he had abandoned his ambitions to become a serious poet) that once when reading his unpublished verses in the home of a young woman, she interrupted him, went behind a screen, and loudly relieved herself in a chamber pot. As Bloom thinks in *Ulysses,* "Chamber music. Could make a kind of pun on that" (p. 364). In *Finnegans Wake* (1939), the volume becomes "chambermade music" (p. 184). Joyce later said to a friend, "I am not a poet" (Ellmann, 1983, p. 231). Later he published the less ambitious occasional verse of *Pomes Penyeach* (1927), when he was a novelist of international reputation. He earned that reputation with the fiction he wrote during his time in Trieste.

DUBLINERS

The first of these reputation-building, startlingly original books was *Dubliners,* and the sorry nigh-on ten-year saga of its long-delayed publication, involving pusillanimous publishers in dread of the blue pencil of the censor and of prosecution, and God-fearing printers who refused to set the book or who went as far as to destroy proofs of the work, is one with which Joyce became all too familiar. What was it about the book that upset the printers and publishers? At issue was Joyce's fidelity to reality, his uncompromising desire to show how ordinary people really lived, which brought him into conflict with the moral and literary conventions of the early twentieth century—and in Ireland with those who wished to see new writing portray the Irish as proud and noble people. Joyce's book seemed to coolly do the very opposite. Finally, in 1914, ten years after the first story was published, *Dubliners* saw the light of day, to be overlooked with the outbreak of the First World War. The collection has a four-part structure—stories of childhood, of adolescence, of maturity, and of public life—and the overarching theme of the work is varieties of paralysis—physical in the first story, but social, political, and moral in the others. It is instructive, as many commentators on Joyce have done, to examine the famous first piece in the collection, "The Sisters," as it offers the reader a way of looking at Joyce's fiction as a whole.

The subject matter of "The Sisters" is a death and its immediate aftermath for those closest to the deceased. This enigmatic story has drawn generations of readers into its uncomfortable and forbidding orbit, unsettling many long-held beliefs about the nature of narrative and setting out the terms in which the author's future work will be read. So, at the beginning of the twentieth century we have one of the most enigmatic stories of that century launching a literary career of one of the most profoundly enigmatic of novelists. Joyce's second novel, *Ulysses,* let it not be forgotten, is named after a Homeric hero who—in a work of over a quarter of a million words, we should remember to be shocked to contemplate—is mentioned only once, yet whose deeds apparently shape the text at every level. The story is no anomaly in Joyce's fiction. "The Sisters" contains, *in ovo,* many of the techniques to be found in the rest of *Dubliners* and in Joyce's fiction generally. They were to become part of the literary DNA of modernism and of what followed. As Richard Ellmann says, "[Joyce] cradles here the technique which has now become a commonplace of modern fiction" (p. 84).

"The Sisters" tells, in a cool and rather cold-blooded way, of a death and the responses of those closest to the deceased. It begins with the young, unnamed narrator of the story considering the impending death of Father Flynn, a priest with whom he had formed a close bond and who we are led to think entertained hopes that the boy would one day enter the priesthood. Father Flynn had already suffered a number of paralyzing strokes, and the boy dwells on the word "paralysis" when thinking of the priest's inevitable fate. On the boy's return to his aunt and uncle's house, he is told that Father Flynn is dead. His uncle and Old Cotter, a family friend, discuss the boy's relationship with the priest, and it is clear that Old Cotter disapproved of it, though he is unwilling to spell out the nature of his disapproval. Later, the boy visits the priest's house with his aunt. Father Flynn's two elderly sisters, one of whom recalls her brother's progressively bizarre behavior, an instance of which was the discovery of her brother shut in a confessional box, laughing to himself. With this curious and troubling image, the story comes to an abrupt end.

Popular theories about the cause of the mysterious paralysis of the priest run from his illness as representative of a moribund Catholic Church, or of the state of a whole city and by extension a nation, to the quite plausible argument that its source was syphilis, known in Ireland at the time as "general paresis of the insane." With this interpretation comes a slew of possibilities, all centering on forms of sexual corruption, some of them involving the young narrator, others not. Old Cotter's hesitations and verbal ellipses, his refusal to say what his objections were to the boy's relationship with the priest hints, at the very least, at some form of possibly corrupt knowledge the boy has in advance of his years. For seventy years or more, critics have been vigorously holding the story's textual feet to the fire in an attempt to get it to yield up its enigmas, but over the years there has developed a broadly consistent agreement on the story's very resistance to interpretation. "The Sisters" is, as Father Purdon says of a biblical passage in the collection's penultimate story, "Grace," "one of the most difficult texts ... to interpret" (p. 173).

The quiet allusion to Dante's *Inferno* in the story's first line ("There was no hope for him") and the boy's contemplation of the word "paralysis" is a proleptic hint about the impossibility of escape for the characters in the stories to follow. They are in their own circles of hell, from the eponymous Eveline's failed attempt to run away, to cornered Bob Doran's weary decision to marry Polly the landlady's daughter in "The Boarding House." Others feel trapped by the routine of work and the responsibilities of family life, such as Chandler in "A Little Cloud" and Farringdon in "Counterparts." In "Ivy Day in the Committee Room," Mr. Tierney and his helpers are paralyzed by political inaction because of their nostalgia for the days of Parnell's greatest successes. The entire collection, which Joyce began in 1904, can be seen in terms of entrapment and stasis. In keeping with his theory of art, Joyce could also blur the moral and the literary. He argued against the censorship of *Dubliners*'s candid depiction of sexual, social, and political relations in Victorian and Edwardian Dublin; at the same time, the work represented a dramatic upending of literary conventions. The characters in the stories are trapped in the circles of hell that is Joyce's Dublin, and though some still harbor dreams of escape, we suspect that they have as much chance of achieving them as the souls in Dante's *Inferno*. In a rather sinister story that leads us into a collection concerned with moral, political, and emotional paralysis and the hopelessness of escaping from it, "The Sisters" gets its vibrancy from its lugubrious but dynamic narrative style.

Joyce added a final story to the collection that had a rather different tone. "The Dead" is just as enigmatic as the others, just as concerned with paralysis and entrapment, and considered by many to be one of the greatest short stories of the century. By the time Joyce came to write "The Dead" in 1907, his feelings for his home country had began to soften. In the story Joyce gives us a highly complex picture of a New Year's gathering of food and music at the home of two old sisters. Nostalgia and sentiment is indulged in. The literary journalist Gabriel Conroy is to make a speech of thanks after the meal, and in it he celebrates "the tradition of genuine warm-hearted courteous Irish hospitality" (p. 204). Although ruffled by a nationalist friend and saddened by the knowledge that his aged aunts who are hosting the event will surely soon die, his complacency is shattered when he notices his wife moved to tears by a song that reminds her of a dead lover she must have had in Galway, the west of Ireland. Moved by her distress, he empathizes with her, knowing he has never had such strong feelings himself. As the story closes, he watches from the window as the snow falls across Ireland and in his imagination we are told "the time has come for him to set out on his journey westward" (p. 225). Though the story is profoundly ambiguous, there is an understanding

and a sympathy that seems to be withheld in the earlier stories in the collection.

A PORTRAIT OF THE ARTIST AS A YOUNG MAN

Joyce's experiments with narrative are carried further in his first novel, *A Portrait of the Artist as a Young Man* (1916), begun in Dublin in 1904 as "Stephen Hero" and completed in a radical new style in 1914 in Trieste. The decade-long effort to bring his novel to completion involved Joyce in reducing and rewriting the original thousand-page manuscript, which he finished in 1906. He spent two years condensing the material down and then revised it between 1908 and 1914. Why did it take Joyce so long to produce a novel of under three hundred pages? Because Joyce was not simply rewriting his novel, he was rewriting the way novels could be written. Novels about the growth of a sensitive, artistic young man could never be the same after Joyce's book, though the full implications of its originality would not be felt for decades. Like 1904, 1914 was another landmark year for Joyce. The poet Ezra Pound accepted one of Joyce's poems for a collection of contemporary ("Imagist") verse he was editing and was able to get *A Portrait* serialized in the avant-garde journal the *Egoist*. Pound became a tireless supporter of Joyce's work over the next decade. The year 1914 also saw the much-delayed publication of *Dubliners*, and Joyce made notes for his play *Exiles*. Most significantly, he began work on *Ulysses*. After its serialization, *A Portrait* was published in 1916. The book was reviewed by many of the leading critics and writers of the day in Europe, Britain, and the United States, most of whom were impressed by the obvious skill and originality of the book but repulsed by the frankness of the depiction of life in Dublin at the turn of the century. The novel is in five sections and takes the familiar form of the growth and development of a young man. What then was the nature of the novel's originality? The opening sentences tell us a good deal about that:

Once upon a time and a very good time it was there was a moocow coming down along the road and this moocow that was coming down along the road met a nicens little boy named baby tuckoo …

His father told him that story: his father looked at him through a glass: he had a hairy face. He was baby tuckoo.

(p. 3)

No adult novel before had opened in such a fashion. Although the narration is in the third person, there appears at first to be very little distance between narrator and character. A more conventional novel would have a clear temporal and linguistic division here between the narrating voice and the subject, between past and present selves. Not so with Joyce's novel. We get a highly condensed series of vignettes, often with large temporal gaps between them. Here we have the experience of the growing child both in its immediacy and with a slowly developing ironic distance that will become more and more important as the novel develops. The child begins to get a sense of identity through seeing itself in the story his father tells him. A few lines later we get the following:

He hid under the table. His mother said:
—O, Stephen will apologise.
Dante said:
—O, if not, the eagles will come and pull out his
  eyes.
Pull out his eyes,
Apologise,
Apologise,
Pull out his eyes.

(p. 4)

We are not told for what Stephen must apologize, but in the brief sections quoted are many of the recurring elements to be found throughout the novel. As Hugh Kenner was the first to point out, on the first page of the novel Stephen experiences the world using all of the five senses in turn: touch, sound, smell, taste, and sight. We infer his resistance to authority, his disobedience in the hypnotic but chilling chant, and his fascination with words and their sound.

The book, though built out of a number of dramatic scenes and set pieces, is structured in such a way as to highlight the development of the young man. Chapter 1 gives us Stephen's early childhood and school experiences, his witnessing of the political divisions in the family, and his experiences with an unjust beating at school. He does, however, get the injustice acknowledged. In chapter 2, through Stephen's limited perceptions, we see the beginnings of the financial decline of the Dedalus family as they move from house to ever-more-dilapidated house, in poorer and poorer districts of Dublin. At the end of this chapter, in his effort to experience everything the world has to offer and to rebel against the stultifying morality of Victorian Ireland, the fourteen-year-old begins to visit prostitutes. In chapter 3, Stephen repents his sinful ways after hearing a terrifying hellfire sermon. Chapter 4 sees him mortifying his senses to stave off physical desire. His devoutness is noticed by his Jesuit teachers, and he is encouraged to become a priest. He refuses and soon after he has an ecstatic vision on seeing a girl on the beach, vowing to accept a life of the senses. This is a stage on his way to seeing that his real vocation is that of an artist. In chapter 5 he states the terms of his rebellion against all kinds of orthodoxies—political, social, and religious—argued in three highly charged conversations with three friends. Finally, Stephen comes up with his own theory of art and writes his own verse. He knows now that to be a serious artist, he must escape from the narrow-mindedness of provincial Ireland, and the book finishes with a series of diary entries in which the young artist girds himself for the heroic task ahead.

Stephen sees himself as heroic: after all, the early draft was called "Stephen Hero." Joyce abandoned that draft because it saw its protagonist as heroically as he saw himself. *A Portrait* is a much more ambiguous representation of the familiar tale of the artist-figure testing the limits of the social and aesthetic conventions of his culture, and not just in its use of vivid set pieces rather than continuous scene-and-summary narration. The published novel often takes a subtly ironic attitude toward its main character. As the novel progresses, we begin to see a gap develop between the narrative voice and Stephen's thoughts and actions. Not only that, but Joyce does something that had never been done in fiction before. While it is clear, even from the short excerpts above, that the novel gives us a startling portrait of the developing consciousness of the young boy, this is not the most innovative element of the novel; what Joyce goes on to do is have the third-person narrative voice use the kind of language to be found in the books the young Stephen would be reading. For example, when Stephen visits the rector, we find the following sentence: "Stephen's heart began slowly to fold and fade with fear like a withering flower" (p. 115). We have Stephen's genuine feelings here, but the rather self-conscious alliteration of the sentence is the kind of thing the budding poet would write at this time of his life. It is important to say that Joyce is not simply mocking Stephen's pretensions to high artistic achievement. There is no authoritative narrative voice telling us what to think about Stephen. What we have is a double perspective running through the book. Stephen is in many ways brave. He is willing to stand up for what he believes in, regardless of the consequences. As an embryonic writer, language fascinates him. Do we have any evidence to support what seems to be his very high opinion of his abilities? On this score the novel leaves it to us to decide. The rather poor poem he writes doesn't inspire the reader's confidence in his abilities, but we should remember that a similarly gifted poet wrote the extraordinary book we are reading.

Stephen's keen awareness of language has its political aspect too. As an Irishman, he speaks a foreign tongue, English. He is well aware of the history of brutal military and cultural repression that has brought this about, and there are others in the book who have ideas about how to set this right. Stephen listens to them and answers them in his own way. When the English dean of Belvedere tells Stephen he has never heard the word "tundish" (a funnel), a word Stephen has just used, Stephen reflects, "The language we are speaking is his before it is mine ... his language, so familiar and so foreign, will always be for me an acquired speech" (p. 205).

Yet to take on the Irish language, as his nationalist friend Davin suggests, is not an option. Though conscious of his position as subject of the British crown, Stephen has little faith in Ireland's ability to throw off the yoke of colonialism. The Irish, he says, "threw off their language and took another ... they allowed a handful of foreigners to subject them. Do you fancy I am going to pay in my own life and person debts they made? What for?" Davin replies, "For our freedom." Stephen's response is charged with the emotion sparked by a sense of historical betrayal: "No honourable and sincere man...has given up to you his life... but you sold him to the enemy or failed him in need or reviled him.... And you invite me to be one of you. I'd see you damned first" (p. 220). We have seen the Jesuits attempt to win Stephen for the Church. Davin wishes to win the independent and brilliant young man for the nationalist cause. Riled by once more by another who wishes to win him over, Stephen says to Davin, "When the soul of man is born in this country, there are nets flung at it to hold it back from flight. You talk to me of nationality, language, religion. I shall try to fly by those nets" (p. 220).

Stephen's metaphor of flight here is no accident; it is a feature of his very name. "Stephen Dedalus" is a name made up of St. Stephen, the first Christian martyr and speaks to the self-dramatizing young man's obsession with notions of betrayal and martyrdom. His surname echoes that of Daedalus, the great artist-inventor of Greek myth who was the builder of the labyrinth, itself an emblem of the complex art Stephen wishes to create. When punished by being imprisoned in his own labyrinth, the cunning Daedalus makes two sets of wings and, along with his son Icarus, simply flies out to freedom. Icarus, meanwhile, has been warned not to fly too close to the sun, but the overreaching young man approaches the sun anyway. The wax in the wings that sustain his flight melts, and he falls to his death in the sea. Through the novel's imagery of flight, Joyce brilliantly oscillates between the stories of the father and the son. Stephen wishes to fly by the nets of social convention, but is he the father Daedalus, the great artificer, or is he Icarus, the arrogant son? Images of flight pervade the book, but so do images of the fall. When he visits the brothel districts, the incorrigibly self-dramatizing Stephen sees himself not just as falling into sin, but he identifies with Lucifer, the rebel angel cast out of heaven to fall into hell, according to the famous hellfire sermon in the novel, for his proud refusal to serve God: "*Non serviam—I will not serve*. That instant was his ruin" (p. 126). Stephen tells his friend Cranly that he has refused his mother's request to do his Easter duty: "'Why not?' Cranly said. 'I will not serve' answered Stephen. 'That remark was made before' Cranly said calmly" (p. 260).

The imagery of flight and fall are brought together in the climactic scene at the end of the book's penultimate chapter, when Stephen is walking on the beach and comes to see the significance of his name, while regarding a young woman. Some school friends call out his name, and he thinks, "Now at the name of the fabulous artificer … he seemed … to see a hawk-like man flying sunward above the sea … He would create proudly out of the freedom and power of his soul, as the great artificer whose name he bore" (pp. 183–184). He will create as Daedalus did, but "proudly," in Luciferian defiance of authority. In Stephen's mind, a young woman he sees on the beach is transformed into a vision of flight, "one whom magic had changed into the likeness of a strange and beautiful sea-bird … to live, to err, to fall, to triumph, to create life out of life!" (pp. 185–186). The famous description of the young woman contains a crescendo of poetic prose: "But her long fair hair was girlish: and girlish, and touched with the wonder of mortal beauty, her face" (p. 186). The eccentric punctuation and the inversion of conventional word order points to the seriousness of the passage. Where then is the Joycean irony? Firstly, Stephen's passionate and earnest assertion of his Daedalusian identity can be seen as comically undercut by the unconsciously Icarus-like comments of his school friends' boisterous playing on the seashore: "O, cripes, I'm drownded!" (p. 183). Secondly, the very earnestness and grammatical tortuousness of the language has been often criticized as a dated version of late-nineteenth-century "purple prose," not the kind of writing you would expect a new young avant-garde novelist to be attempting in 1916. But as Hugh Kenner (once again) was the first to observe, "It is not immature prose … rather, it is a meticulous pastiche of immaturity" (p. 120). In other words, it is another example of Joyce's ironic double perspective. Stephen is sincere, but the narrative technique allows us a little critical distance from Stephen's powerful experiences and his equally committed and extravagant prose. In one last conversation with his friend Cranly, Stephen sets out his credo: "I will not serve that in which I no longer believe, whether it call itself my home, my fatherland, or my church: and I will try to express myself … as freely as I can, using for my defence … silence, exile and cunning." (pp. 268–269)

The novel ends with Stephen taking flight to Paris. He wishes to forge "the uncreated conscience of my race" and calls on his spiritual artist-father for aid. The last of the diary entries and the last line of the book reads, "Old father, old artificer, stand me now and ever in good stead" (p. 276). In Joyce's next novel, the priggish and rather humorless young would-be artist will meet a different, but equally important, kind of father figure, by common consent the most fully rounded of all fictional characters, Leopold Bloom.

EXILES

While working on the early chapters of his second novel, Joyce wrote *Exiles* (1918), a play about the status of the artist in his own land, about the complexities of married love, about jealousy and desire. Unfortunately it is wordy and undramatic, and if it is read at all today, it is for the light it sheds on Joyce and his other works. In it, Richard Rowan, a writer who has been in exile for nine years, returns to Dublin with his wife, Bertha, and his child, Archie, to take up a post at a university, secured for him by his oldest friend, the journalist Robert Hand.

The heart of the play concerns Richard's attitude toward a liaison between his wife and his best friend. He seems to encourage it in the name of spiritual freedom. Bertha and Robert do meet in Robert's cottage, but Richard turns up and the relationship is not consummated. The piece has never held a place in the theater, but the notion of a husband allowing his wife to have an affair with another man did come to inform *Ulysses,* though in a much-transformed way.

ULYSSES

The English painter Frank Budgen, Joyce's great friend of his Zurich years, tells us that "Joyce, if asked what he did during the Great War could reply: 'I wrote *Ulysses*'" (p. 191). Joyce knew that he was writing a challenge and a goad to both novelists and readers. The basic story is very simple. Stephen Dedalus has breakfast and goes off to work for a half-day at a private school for boys. After collecting his wages, he wanders along the beach and then heads into Dublin to deliver a letter to the newspaper offices. After drinks with some pressmen, he goes to the National Library and delivers his theory of Shakespeare's *Hamlet* to some Dublin intellectuals. We next meet him late at night, drunk with friends in a maternity hospital. He goes from there to the red-light district and is punched to the ground by a British soldier. He is helped to his feet and looked after by Leopold Bloom, an advertising canvasser of Jewish descent, who takes him for some coffee in a nearby shelter and then to his home.

The two men discuss a range of topics and finally Stephen politely refuses an offer of a bed for the night and wanders off toward the end of the novel, we know not where. As Stephen had been eating his breakfast at 8 a.m., Bloom had been cooking his at the same time, and he brings his wife, Molly, a professional singer, hers in bed. Bloom leaves to get a bath and attend the funeral of an acquaintance. He has some lunch, has an altercation with a bigot in a pub, and later wanders on the same beach Stephen trod that morning. He arrives at the maternity hospital some time after Stephen and from then on their paths are intertwined, until Stephen leaves Bloom's house in the early hours of the morning. Bloom then goes to bed next to his wife, and the novel ends with Molly's reminiscences both of the day (which had included the consummation of an affair) and of her past, especially her early

girlhood in Gibraltar, where she was born, and of her life with her husband Bloom.

The plot, though full of all kinds of ordinary, everyday human interest, is not the reason the book has the reputation of being the greatest novel of the twentieth century. That reputation is because of the story's audaciousness in representing human thought and because of its stylistic and narratological daring, developing in all kinds of ways the literary techniques Joyce had used in *Dubliners* and *A Portrait*. Joyce began work on the novel in 1914, and it was finally published in 1922 in France by the American expatriate Sylvia Beach, a bookshop owner and supporter of Joyce. The American editors of the *Little Review* had been prosecuted for obscenity by the U.S. government for publishing *A Portrait* serially, so there seemed little possibility of publishing the book in the English-speaking countries. On publication, the book was promptly banned in the United States and the U.K., and copies shipped in were destroyed. It wasn't until more than a decade later that *Ulysses,* quickly recognized by many as a modern masterpiece, could be read legally in either country. The book was banned for showing those aspects of human life that had not been shown in literature before, although it treated such aspects not pruriently but occasionally comically and as part of everyday life: urination, defecation, masturbation, the onset of a female period, and the like. The part of the book one would expect to cause censorship problems would be Molly's sexual encounter with her lover, Blazes Boylan, yet ironically, that event is never narrated. We have a report of it in Molly's monologue in the last chapter of the book. The very frank depiction of sexual fantasy that occurs in the chapter set in the brothel district is just that: a fantasy concerning Bloom's guilt over his sexual neglect of his wife. The encounter we do have in great detail is the one to which the book has been leading us for hundreds of pages. Bloom sees Stephen Dedalus from the window of a funeral carriage; he passes him outside the newspaper offices in central Dublin and again on the steps of the National Library. They finally speak when Bloom picks the recently assaulted, drunken Stephen up from the street outside the brothel and takes him to a cabman's shelter for coffee to sober up. The penultimate chapter features only Stephen and Bloom. At this point, many a potential reader will ask two questions. Firstly, as nothing much seems to come of it, why is this meeting so important? And secondly—why on earth is a book set on one day in Dublin called *Ulysses*? The answer to the first question comes out of answering the second and explains the underlying the structure of the book, which runs through each chapter like invisible ink.

When Bloom brings his wife her breakfast, she asks him the meaning of a word she's found in a book she's reading: "metempsychosis." Bloom explains, "It's Greek: from the Greek. That means the transmigration of souls" (p. 77). Joyce's hidden structure is, as Bloom says, "from the Greek." Joyce uses Homer's story of a husband and father's journey home to his family as a structuring device for his novel of a young man brought home by a compassionate father figure. Joyce operates a continuous parallel between Homer's epic poem *The Odyssey* and the events on one day in Dublin. In Homer's poem, Ulysses takes many years and has many adventures before he gets back to his wife and son. He and his men set sail from Troy, are nearly eaten by cannibals, are drugged on the island of the Lotus-eaters, avoid the clutches of the deadly sirens, and when nearly home are blown back to the island of the king of the winds, Aeolus. Ulysses himself saves his men from the one-eyed Cyclops and with help escapes from the seductress goddess Circe. He even journeys to Hades, the land of the dead, and comes back alive. Home at last, he and his son kill all the suitors for his wife's hand, who have been waiting impatiently for news of Ulysses' death. How does Joyce carry out the parallel between this story and the events of his novel? What Bloom doesn't know when he describes "metempsychosis" is that he himself is a reincarnation of the Greek hero Odysseus or Ulysses (the Latin name Joyce used for him), that his wife is a version of both faithful Penelope and the goddess Calypso, and that Stephen is a kind of Telemachus, the son of Ulysses.

At first glance, Bloom seems an unlikely Ulysses: A middle-aged Dubliner with a very un-Penelope-like, soon-to-be-unfaithful wife. A source of suspicion and sometimes contempt because of his Jewish background. A lifelong outsider. A generous, curious, and thoughtful man, though far from what we might call heroic. In the novel, we will see Bloom, unlike Ulysses, trying to stay away from home for as long as possible, to avoid confronting Molly and Boylan, though the liaison occupies his thoughts all day. Nevertheless, he attends a funeral (a journey to Hades), he goes about the city doing his job, he faces down a myopic nationalist (a Cyclops figure), he visits a brothel (the equivalent of Circe's island) but only to look after someone he begins to see as a surrogate son, Stephen Dedalus. He returns home and goes to bed beside his wife, the evidence of her infidelity everywhere in the bed. He kills no suitors, but it is he who finally lies with his wife and it is he who takes up the majority of Molly's night thoughts that complete the novel. So Joyce doesn't hold Bloom up to ridicule, though characters and the narrative at times certainly do. Sometimes the Homeric parallel is used for comic purposes. The cannibal island is the Burton restaurant; Ulysses' loyal servant's hut is the cabman's shelter; the rock the blinded Cyclops hurls at Ulysses' departing ship becomes a biscuit tin hurled by a sun-blinded angry citizen as Bloom is taken off on the back of a cab. But the parallel works the other way too. By the end of the novel, Joyce bestows a kind of Ulysses-like heroism on Bloom.

Stephen too gains from the parallel with Telemachus inasmuch as his final meeting with Bloom shows him someone who has displayed a kind of paradoxically disinterested paternal care toward him. We left him in *A Portrait* taking flight to France to become an artist. He had been summoned back by his father as his mother was dying. He refused her request to pray at his bedside. "You could have knelt down, damn it … when your dying mother asked you," his friend Mulligan says (p. 4). For all his ambition he has produced nothing in the way of art; he writes just four lines of poetry in the whole of the novel, and those are derivative. His day begins in the first chapter (called "Telemachus" by Joyce) As Stephen's credo in the previous novel was *non serviam*—"I will not serve"—he finds his present situation rather paradoxical in a number of ways. He is staying with Mulligan and an English visitor, Haines, in a Martello tower, a small fortress built one hundred years before by the British to defend their Irish colony against French invasion. Haines speaks fluent Irish, which Stephen certainly can't, and the language goes unrecognized by the old milkwoman who calls by. Stephen, wearing clothes borrowed from Mulligan, sees himself as "this dogsbody" (p. 5) and "a server of a servant" (p. 12). Only half in jest, he says to Haines, the English visitor, "I am the servant of two masters ... the imperial British state and the holy Roman catholic ... church" (p. 24). The anticolonial frame of reference is there right through to the end of the novel, as it is a British soldier who knocks Stephen to the ground outside the brothel for what the soldier believes is an insult to his king.

Bigotry is to be found at the outset of the story, too. Haines tells Stephen that he fears England will fall "into the hands of German jews" (p. 25), just as the headmaster at Stephen's place of work in the next chapter says Ireland never let the Jews in. In retrospect, the anti-Semitism we find in the first two chapters tells us how Bloom will be treated by many in the rest of the book. In fact, many of the key scenes only take on their full meaning in retrospect. So quite apart from *Ulysses* being the very acme of realism, in showing us aspects of our lives not seen in fiction before, in an exceptionally daring and enormously demanding move, Joyce also expects the reader to read his novel twice—that's a novel of over seven hundred pages in its first edition. Joyce demands a new kind of reader who will be open to a new kind of narration. In an influential and helpful book-length analysis published in 2002, Michael Seidel argues that *Ulysses* has four different modes of narration: traditional third-person narration, interior narration, spoken narration, and what he calls "fourth estate narration" (p. 88). Contemporary readers were familiar with third-person and spoken narration. Interior narration, or what is widely called interior monologue,

is what many find most innovative about the novel, and certainly it is the narrative technique that was most influential both on Joyce's contemporaries (e.g., Virginia Woolf) and on the next generation of novelists (e.g., William Faulkner) for its impressive psychological realism. Though Joyce didn't invent the technique, he used it with the greatest flexibility and subtlety, as for example when Bloom's thoughts turn to what will be happening in his own bed later in the day. He tries not to think about it, but unsurprisingly it comes unbidden to him. Remembering the mail delivered that morning, he thinks, "Mrs. Marion Bloom. Not up yet ... torn strip of envelope" (p. 91), which he knows is from Boylan. Later again Bloom is dwelling on ads for cures for syphilis and thinks, "If he ... O! Eh? No ... no" (pp. 193–194), and though he doesn't articulate the thought, we understand what crosses his mind. When a serving girl counts out Bloom's four pennies change and says, "and four," he thinks, "At four she." And the careful (or more likely the second-time) reader needs no further details. Four p.m. is the time of Molly's assignation with Boylan.

Joyce's dexterous and innovative representation of thought passing through a mind achieves its apotheosis in Molly Bloom's forty-page interior monologue, which finishes the book, but Joyce's other great innovation in fiction was what Seidel calls "fourth estate narration." What he means by this term is all those elements of the novel that show the novel experimenting with the forms of fiction. This would include the Homeric parallels and what might be called the more "metafictional" elements of the text: things that make us notice that we are reading a novel. Joyce uses this technique in a radical form in the second half of the novel. Briefly, the chapter set in a hotel has barmaids who are Homeric "sirens," and it therefore exploits the musical properties of language. The chapter set in a maternity hospital parallels the nine-month gestation of a fetus with an astounding tour de force of a prose style that develops from early English to contemporary slang. The chapter set in the red-light district is set out like a play, with stage directions and speeches, but often veers off into fantasy. The chapter in which a young woman sees Bloom on the beach is written in the style of a girl's magazine of the time. The late-night visit to the cabman's shelter is written in a tired, clichéd prose. Stephen's and Bloom's long chapter together in Bloom's kitchen is done in a strangely objective-seeming question-and-answer form, similar to the Catholic penny catechism, but determinedly rational in its manner. And so on.

Is Joyce therefore just an ironist, a parodist, a *pasticheur* sending up our attempts to catch the world in a verbal form and the way we fall into clichés to describe our profoundest feelings? That is certainly an important element of the novel, but the psychological acuity of Joyce's astonishingly detailed attempt to catch thought passing in interior monologue argues for a broader ambition. Finally we might ask, what is the novel about? Whatever else it may be about, it is about love. When Bloom is confronted by an anti-Semite in a pub who asks him, "What is your nation if I may ask?" Bloom replies, "Ireland ... I was born here. Ireland" (p. 430). Bloom, for the only time before he meets Stephen, talks about his Jewish history and the persecution of the Jews "at this very moment." Asked why he doesn't stand up against injustice, he replies, "That's no use ... force, hatred, history, all that ... That's not life for men and women ... and everybody knows it's the very opposite of that that is really life ... Love ... I mean the opposite of hatred" (p. 432). And though earlier Bloom has called love and hate just "names" (p. 368)—and though the characters in the pub, the mean-spirited narrator, and one of the many grandstanding interpolated passages in the narrative itself all mock Bloom—it is impossible to say Bloom doesn't mean what he says and tries to live by this precept. So while the novel injects a kind of viral or bacteriological irony over the characters, some including Bloom have built up a certain amount of antibodies to combat it. Though seriously compromised in all kinds of ways, Molly and Bloom love each other. The difficult and suspicious Stephen has been treated kindly by Bloom and seems to have benefited from the experience, though he hardly treats Bloom with much respect. As the novel ends, we know that the very next day what Molly and Boylan did will be the talk of Dublin, and Bloom will be a laughingstock. Yet while a friend calls out to Boylan, "See the conquering hero comes," the narrative continues, "between the car and window, warily walking, went Bloom, unconquered hero" (p. 340). So, though we don't know what will happen between Bloom and Molly even on June 17, Bloom in bed with Molly could be seen as a happy ending.

While the novel was met with a large amount of understandable incomprehension, Joyce began to set about building the kind of readership his work needed, and through sympathetic critics the book came to be seen not just as a staggeringly scatological and erudite jumble of scenes but as a highly structured piece of fiction. Early essays by the indefatigable Pound and the influential T. S. Eliot helped here, and Stuart Gilbert's landmark study of 1930 established *Ulysses* as a formidable modern classic. It had already influenced contemporary writers while in serial form, and it soon established its reputation, though it wasn't until 1934 and 1936 that the novel was legally published in the United States and the U.K., respectively. The Joyce family had seemingly ended their constant traveling by settling in Paris in 1920. They would remain in France until 1940, when they left for neutral Switzerland. Almost immediately on finishing what came to be acknowledged as one of the greatest novels of the century, Joyce began his next work, which was seventeen years in the writing, the forbidding *Finnegans Wake*.

FINNEGANS WAKE

Many a critic has quailed at attempting a summary of this extraordinary 1939 novel. The default position is to say (with some justice) that it is unsummarizable, but what we can say is that at its basic level, it is the story of a family, and as *Ulysses* was a book of one day, we can see *Finnegans Wake* as a book of the night—in other words, a dream work. As a character says near the end of the book, "You mean to see we have been hadding a sound night's sleep?" (p. 597). The family at the heart of the book are the Earwickers. H. C. Earwicker is a Dublin publican.

He has a wife, Anna Livia Plurabelle, two disputatious sons, Shem and Shaun, and a daughter, Isabel. The rest of the cast include Kate and Joe, who work in the pub, and the pub's customers. In another sense, the rest of the cast is everyone, because Joyce has this family play dozens of roles, from historical, biblical, and mythic figures, to something beyond the individual consciousness, blending and condensing characters as happens in dreams. In a memorable section of the book, Anna is even the river Liffey. Her middle name is "Livia," after all. The publican's initials H. C. E. echo through the book in dozens of permutations, most famously as "Here Comes Everybody" (p. 32), probably as good a summary of the book as any.

This complex play of character, place, and action draws its structure from Giambattista Vico's cyclical theory of history, *The New Science* (1725), and its language from everywhere in the world. Although the base language of *Finnegans Wake* is English, it is like no other English encountered before, "nat language at any sinse of the world" (p. 83). The style of the book takes as its main literary trope the most humble form of wordplay, the pun. In his title and in the book's first line, we can see the whole of Joyce's method. *Finnegans Wake* is a comic Irish American song about a building worker, Tim Finnegan, who falls from a ladder and is presumed dead. At his wake—the traditional drink around the open casket to celebrate the deceased's life before they are buried—a fight breaks out, and whiskey splashes on the body. The taste rouses the "corpse" and the mourners realize Tim was merely unconscious. In other words, the song is a comic version of the resurrection, and Joyce milks this droll cycle of life, death, and rebirth for all he's worth. The book is named for the song, but not only because of the pun in the word "wake," associated as it is with both dying and rising. There is no possessive apostrophe in the book's title because it's plural. It means "Tim Finnegan wakes," but also "Finn wakes again," after the Irish mythic hero Finn MacCool, who represents the Irish people themselves. "Fin" means to finish, too, with the implication here that things will begin again.

The title is a kind of fractal of the whole, as is the first line: "riverrun, past Eve and Adam's, from swerve of shore to bend of bay, brings us by commodius vicus of recirculation to Howth Castle and Environs" (p. 3). The river running is Anna Livia, Dublin's Liffey river. Adam and Eve were of course the first family in the Bible, but the reference also alludes to the Church of Adam and Eve church in Dublin. All through the book we will find the universal and the particular enmeshed. Bay and shore is the seaside that leads from Dublin north to Howth hill, and in the initial letters of those last few words, the reader can see the publican's initials, H. C. E. This isn't really the end of the first line, though. In a book based on a circular theory of history, we find the beginning of this first line 627 pages later, on the last line of the last page: "A way a lone a last a long a loved a long the …" (p. 628). Even in that short extract we can hear the rhythmic, incantatory quality of the prose. And it is a very funny book, too, if not exactly like the joke book on Bloom's bookshelf, "1000 pages and a laugh on everyone" (pp. 793–794).

Joyce has had the very great fortune to have attracted the cleverest and most passionate of critics, and many have staunchly defended the *Wake* since its publication, but it remains the least-read well-known book in the literary canon. If you find you groan at such punning wordplay, then at 628 pages, as Samuel Johnson said of John Milton's *Paradise Lost,* "None ever wished it longer than it is." That said, many find the Anna Livia Plurabelle section and much else in the book beautiful, and it is intensely so when read aloud. It seems, though, that in this last novel, Joyce has yet to create a significant readership willing to tackle its difficulties. Joyce lost a number of his greatest admirers over the *Wake,* including Pound, and Joyce's great supporter Harriet Weaver was so puzzled by the prose that Joyce sent her a letter explaining the opening of the novel in great detail. However, there seems to be no letup in the interest in Joyce's last novel, and some of the most influential critics and theorists of the last thirty years have been drawn to the book, including the likes of Jacques Derrida, Umberto Eco, Julia Kristeva, Jacques Lacan, and Hélène Cixous. But even a sympathetic Joycean such as Michael Seidel has little to say about the *Wake,* and the brilliant Kevin Dettmar has a chapter in his 1996 book on Joyce called "On Ignoring *Finnegans Wake.*" Dettmar seems to miss the variety of styles to be found in *Ulysses* and so finds the later work, for all its humor and wide-ranging field of interest, a one-note performance—it starts as it means to go on. However, it seems very unlikely that Joyce's other works will fall from readers' favor. In *Ulysses,* the critic John Eglinton remarks that "After God, Shakespeare has created most" (p. 273). After Shakespeare, we might say Joyce has created most.

Selected Bibliography

WORKS OF JAMES JOYCE

NOVELS AND SHORT STORIES

Dubliners. London: Grant Richards, 1914; London and New York: Penguin, 1992. (With an introduction by Terence Brown.) (All page citations in the text refer to the most recent editions listed here and below.)

A Portrait of the Artist as a Young Man. New York: B. W. Huebsch, 1916. 2nd ed. London: Egoist Press, 1917. Reprint, London and New York: Penguin, 2000. (With an introduction by Seamus Deane.)

Ulysses. Paris: Shakespeare & Co., 1922; London and New York: Penguin, 2000. (With an introduction by Declan Kiberd.)

Finnegans Wake. London: Faber & Faber, 1939; New York: Viking, 1939; London and New York: Penguin, 2000. (With an introduction by Seamus Deane.)

Stephen Hero. Norfolk, Conn.: New Directions, 1963. (Edited by Theodore Spencer [Harvard College Library], and John J. Slocum and Herbert Cahoon [Yale University Library and the Cornell University Library] from manuscript editions of *A Portrait of the Artist as a Young Man.*)

POETRY AND DRAMA

Chamber Music. London: Elkin Matthews, 1907. Reprinted in *The Essential James Joyce.* Edited by Harry Levin. New York and London: 1967. (Poetry.)

Exiles: A Play in Three Acts. London: Jonathan Cape, 1921.

Reprint, New York: Viking Press, 1951. London: Jonathan Cape, 1952.

Pomes Penyeach. Paris: Shakespeare & Co., 1927. Reprinted in *The Portable James Joyce.* Edited by Harry Levin. New York and London: Penguin, 1967. (Poems.)

CRITICAL WRITINGS

The Critical Writings of James Joyce. Edited by Ellsworth Mason and Richard Ellmann. New York: Viking; London: Faber & Faber, 1959.

Occasional, Critical, and Political Writings. Edited by Kevin Barry. Oxford: Oxford University Press, 2000.

LETTERS

Letters of James Joyce. Vol. 1. Edited by Stuart Gilbert. New York: Viking; London: Faber & Faber, 1957.

Letters of James Joyce. Vol. 2. Edited by Richard Ellmann. New York: Viking; London: Faber & Faber, 1966.

Letters of James Joyce. Vol. 3. Edited by Richard Ellmann. New York: Viking; London: Faber & Faber, 1966.

Selected Letters of James Joyce. Edited by Richard Ellmann. New York: Viking; London: Faber & Faber, 1975.

BIOGRAPHICAL AND CRITICAL STUDIES

Adams, Robert M. *Surface and Symbol.* New York and Oxford: Oxford University Press, 1962.

Atherton, James. *The Books at the Wake: A Study of Literary Allusions in James Joyce's "Finnegans Wake."* New York and London: Faber & Faber, 1959.

Bishop, John. *Joyce's Book of the Dark: "Finnegans Wake."* Madison: University of Wisconsin Press, 1986.

Blamires, Harry. *The New Bloomsday Book: A Guide through Ulysses.* 3rd ed. New York and London: Routledge, 1996.

Budgen, Frank. *James Joyce and the Making of "Ulysses."* Bloomington: Indiana University Press, 1960.

Burgess, Anthony. *Here Comes Everybody.* London: Faber & Faber, 1965.

Campbell, Joseph, and Henry Morton Robinson. *A Skeleton Key to "Finnegans Wake."* London: Faber & Faber: 1947. Reprint, New York: Viking, 1961.

Cheng, Vincent. *Joyce, Race, and Empire.* Cambridge, U.K.: Cambridge University Press, 1995.

Davison, Neil R. *James Joyce, Ulysses, and the Construction of Jewish Identity: Culture, Biography, and "the Jew" in Modernist Europe.* Cambridge, U.K.: Cambridge University Press, 1996.

Deming, Robert H., ed. *James Joyce: The Critical Heritage.* 2 vols. London: Routledge, 1970.

Dettmar, Kevin J. H., *The Illicit Joyce of Postmodernism: Reading against the Grain.* Madison: University of Wisconsin Press, 1996.

Devlin, Kimberly J., and Marilyn Reizbaum, eds. *"Ulysses": En-gendered Perspectives: Eighteen New Essays on the Episodes.* Columbia: University of South Carolina Press, 1999.

Ellmann, Richard. *James Joyce.* New and rev. ed. New York: Oxford University Press, 1982.

French, Marilyn. *James Joyce's "Ulysses": The Book as World.* Cambridge, Mass.: Harvard University Press, 1976.

Gilbert, Stuart. *James Joyce's "Ulysses."* 1930. New ed., New York: Random House, 1952.

Groden, Michael. *Ulysses in Progress.* Princeton, N.J.: Princeton University Press, 1977.

Hart, Clive, and David Hayman, eds. *James Joyce's "Ulysses": Critical Essays.* Berkeley: University of California Press, 1974.

Kain, Richard. *Fabulous Voyager.* Chicago: University of Chicago Press, 1947.

Kenner, Hugh. *Dublin's Joyce.* 2nd ed. New York: Columbia University Press, 1987.

Kershner, R. B., ed. *Joyce and Popular Culture.* Tampa: University Press of Florida, 1996.

Lawrence, Karen. *The Odyssey of Style in Ulysses.* Princeton, N.J.: Princeton University Press, 1981.

Levin, Harry, ed. *The Portable James Joyce.* New York and London: Penguin, 1967.

MacCabe, Colin. *James Joyce and the Revolution of the Word.* Basinstoke, U.K.: Macmillan, 1978.

McHugh, Roland. *Annotations to "Finnegans Wake."* Baltimore, Md.: Johns Hopkins University Press, 1980.

Mahaffey, Vicki. *Reauthorizing Joyce.* Tampa: University Press of Florida, 1995.

Peake, Charles H. *James Joyce: The Citizen and the Artist.* Stanford, Calif.: Stanford University Press, 1977.

Seidel, Michael. *James Joyce: A Short Introduction.* Oxford: Blackwell, 2002.

RUDYARD KIPLING

(1865—1936)

Joshua Grasso

IN HIS AUTOBIOGRAPHY, *Something of Myself: For My Friends, Known and Unknown* (1937), Rudyard Kipling records a conversation with his parents as he worked on a particularly troublesome verse he couldn't quite "get." His mother (whom he calls "the Mother" throughout) cuts him off by saying, "You're *trying* to say: 'What do they know of England who only England know.' The Father confirmed" (p. 97). The poem was completed speedily after this inspiration, and Kipling remembered the event keenly enough to record it at the end of his life, even reflecting, "In the talks that followed, I exposed my notion of trying to tell the English something of the world outside England—not directly but by implication" (p. 98).

Nothing could be more revelatory of his methods or his craft, particularly as Kipling was one of the first major British writers not born in England. His works continually find the author on the very peripheries of empire (however much he might sympathize with the empire personally), viewing the machinations of "the white man's burden" (the phrase he coined for his famous poem of 1899) from the perspective of a cockney soldier, a harried colonial newspaper editor, and a half-caste boy flirting with imperial espionage. Despite all his attempts to embrace his mother country, Kipling was haunted by the Indian landscape and returned "home" throughout his literary career, often writing most searchingly of Anglo-India when he was farthest away. What he *knew* of England was the very fact of not being English, a rare condition that allowed him to "look in" at a world he could never truly belong to. His inherent otherness may have prevented him from writing the "great English novel" he yearned for, but it also allowed him to write—by implication—of England's stamp on an ancient world. The muse of India, and her legendary stories in particular, profoundly shaped Kipling's writing and its cheeky obsession with frame stories, fables, mythologies, and anecdotes. Though Kipling is incontestably an English (and certainly a British) writer, he is one that India continues to claim, and figures as diverse as Salman Rushdie, V. S. Naipaul, and R. K. Narayan have all written of their debt to him. Indeed, in *An Area of Darkness*, his 1964 account of his travels in India, Naipaul goes so far as to say that, with Kipling, "a journey to India was not really necessary. No writer was more honest or accurate" (London: Vintage, 2003, p. 191).

EARLY YEARS

Kipling was born in Bombay (now Mumbai) on December 30, 1865, to John Lockwood Kipling and Alice MacDonald Kipling, who had married in England in 1863. John Lockwood Kipling was a man of many talents (he illustrated many of his son's works), who rose from humble ranks to a gain a scholarship studying design and modeling. He soon found employment with the firm of Pinder, Bourne & Co., where he famously contributed to the facade of the Wedgwood Institute in Staffordshire. (His work remains visible today.) Shortly after his marriage in 1863, he was appointed professor of architectural sculpture at the Jeejeebhoy School of Art in Bombay, necessitating the move that would shape his son's career. Alice Kipling shared her husband's artistic bent but came from more prominent stock—indeed, she and her sisters all ran in impressive social and artistic circles. Her father, George MacDonald, was a noted English Methodist minister, and her sister, Georgiana, married the pre-Raphaelite painter Edward Burne-Jones; the household of his aunt "Georgy" became a haven for the adolescent Rudyard Kipling during his traumatic years in Portsmouth. Yet Alice needed no familial calling card to trumpet her worth: she was an amateur dramatist and a writer herself, and even in later years Kipling would submit his work for her approval. Rudyard Kipling was born during his parents' first year in India, and a second child, Alice (but affectionately called Trix), was born in 1868 during a visit home at the Burne-Joness'. A third child, John, was born in 1870 but died shortly thereafter.

Kipling's reminiscences of his Indian childhood are extremely positive, almost fictional in their evocation of character and atmosphere. As he writes in *Something of Myself*, "My first impression is of daybreak, light and colour and golden and purple fruits at the level of my shoulder. This would be the memory of early morning walks to the Bombay fruit market with my *ayah* and later with my sister in her perambulator, and of our returns with our purchases piled high on the bows of it" (p. 3). By all accounts he lived a charmed and somewhat spoiled life, stuffed with the sweets and stories of his *ayah* (a Portuguese-Catholic nursemaid), who taught him to dream in the vernacular. We can recognize something of the protagonists from future novels—Kim, and maybe a bit of Mowgli—in remembered accounts of the young Rudyard, who reportedly shocked his English relatives during their 1868 visit (when Trix was born). Perhaps his "native" wildness was part of the reason that, when their son was age six, his parents decided to send him and Trix back to England. It is difficult to imagine the two young children being sent alone to England, and then not even into the care of relatives but rather to complete strangers. However, it was accepted in Kipling's day for parents to send children back home as much for education as for escaping the disastrous Indian climate (epidemics in Anglo-Indian society are well documented in Kipling's stories). What has puzzled Kipling biographers is who Rudyard and Trix went to live with: a certain Captain and Mrs. Holloway, who kept a house in Portsmouth for the children of British nationals in India. The Kiplings had no acquaintance with the Holloways, having learned of their services through a newspaper advertisement. Their recent visit home may have been a failed attempt to install Kipling with members of his own family, who found young Rudyard simply too "wild" to take in. Choosing strangers might have been a safer—or less burdensome—way to undertake Kipling's English education.

At any rate, the business was quickly concluded, and brother and sister, with little explanation, soon found themselves alone in a strange new world. Recalling his impressions of the voyage—which for a six-year-old must have been quite memorable, if not traumatic—he writes, "There was next a dark land, and a darker room full of cold, in one wall of which a white woman made naked fire, and I cried aloud with dread, for I had never before seen a grate" (*Something of Myself*, p. 6). Life for Kipling at Lorne Lodge became a well of misery and abandonment, forming the basis for several later stories as well as some of the most moving passages of his autobiography, written in his seventies. Mrs. Holloway disliked Kipling intensely, perhaps seeing him as wild as his relatives did, and persecuted him through her own punishments and those of her twelve-year-old son. Calling her simply "the Woman" in his autobiography, Kipling credits her with introducing him to the concept of hell and all its associated horrors, as well as to the hypocrisy of religious instruction. If Mrs. Holloway in these pages assumes something of the air of a Dickensian villain, it is only fair to note that Trix had a much easier time of it, and in later life she tempered Kipling's recollections of Mrs. Holloway's savagery.

Rudyard and Trix arrived at Lorne Lodge in 1871 and would remain until 1877, when Alice returned from India to reestablish the family in England. In this period, the only glimpse of salvation came from holidays at The Grange, where his Aunt Georgiana and her husband, Sir Edward Burne-Jones, held court to a who's who of Victorian luminaries including Robert Browning and William Morris ("Uncle Topsy"). Here Kipling was loved and indulged, and even invited into the adults' world through childish play—including elaborate games based on the *Arabian*

Nights. He never betrayed the horrors that awaited him upon his return to Lorne Lodge, however, as "children have a clear notion of what they are likely to get if they betray the secrets of a prison-house before they are clear of it" (*Something of Myself,* p. 17). When his mother finally returned to take him away from what he calls the "House of Desolation," he reportedly held up an arm to fend off her embrace—expecting more cudgels from "the Woman." If the twin poles of Lorne Lodge and The Grange gave birth to the future artist, his true education would begin in an environment that initially promised to upstage the misery of Mrs. Holloway's lodgings—the United Services College at Westward Ho! Devon.

The oddly named village (named after Charles Kingsley's novel) housed the United Services Proprietary College, which was founded in 1874 by retired army officers as a cheap way to educate their sons for service. Contemporary reports of the school are not particularly endearing, nor are some of Kipling's own vignettes from his 1899 collection, *Stalky & Co.,* based on his years at the school. Besides the sons of various officers, troublesome boys who had been turned out of other schools made up the rest of the student body, creating a rough-and-tumble environment for a relatively sheltered youth like Rudyard. After an initial period of bullying and misery, Kipling made lasting friendships with two other boys, immortalized as Stalky (Arthur Lionel Corkran) and M'Turk (G. C. Beresford), whose hijinks became the basis for the Stalky tales and inspired his earliest writings. During this time Kipling continued to visit his sister, who had returned to Lorne Lodge, and fell deeply in love with her fellow boarder, Florence Garrard. Though this relationship followed a predictably sentimental course, Kipling would later use her as the model for Masie in his first—and to some critics, problematic—novel, *The Light That Failed* (1890). This period is also notable for his first publication, a collection of verse titled *Schoolboy Lyrics,* which his parents published privately in Lahore in 1881.

By 1882, when it became clear that Kipling was not Oxford-bound, his parents made other arrangements: namely, that he return to India to join his father and pursue a career in journalism. Kipling left England on September 20 of that year and arrived in India in October to take up his post as assistant editor of the *Civil and Military Gazette* in Lahore. A few years earlier, Lockwood Kipling had relocated to Lahore from Bombay because of his appointment as principal of the Mayor College of Art and curator of the Lahore Museum. Upon his return to India, Kipling noted later that "I found myself at Bombay where I was born, moving among sights and smells that made me deliver in the vernacular sentences whose meaning I knew not" (*Something of Myself,* p. 45). Here, he was truly "home," and he would find in the hill stations and clubs of Anglo-India his most enduring theme—a Jane Austenish "bit of ivory" to embellish with the flourish of art. During his career at the *Civil and Military Gazette,* which ran from 1882 to 1887, he worked at a furious pace, traveling throughout India and writing about the domestic dramas, colorful anecdotes, and sinister goings-on of the colonial empire. Yet what in other hands might have been bland reportage became, in Kipling's enthusiasm, sharply observed and often satirical portraits of Englishmen and women as only a "foreigner" could see them.

Perhaps the most vital ingredient for Kipling's literary recipe was the club: here, in a congenial gathering of men from all branches of the empire, Kipling learned the dialect of each profession and, more importantly, how to shape a crisp, oral narrative for an appreciative audience. His routine stories for the *Gazette* on bridge openings and communal riots quickly began filtering into a more artistic endeavor: a series of stories called *Plain Tales from the Hills* (started in 1885 and collected as a volume in 1888) that were used as "padding" between the news of home and abroad. At roughly the same time, he began writing the verses that were collected in his first true volume of poetry, *Departmental Ditties* (1886). With such a wealth of material at his disposal, a deadline, and a flesh-and-blood audience at the club, Kipling embarked on his literary career. As he later reflected,

I made my own experiments in the weights, colours, perfumes, and attributes of words in relation to other words, either as read aloud so that they may hold the ear, or, scattered over the page, draw the eye. There is no line of my verse or prose which has not been mouthed till the tongue has made all smooth, and memory, after many recitals, has mechanically skipped the grosser superfluities.

(*Something of Myself,* p. 78)

In short, like his contemporary Anton Chekhov, Kipling made his work his art, and he learned to view writing as a skill that could be perfected bit by bit, word by word. His resulting style is marked by a vigorous yet beautiful flow that makes Kipling, for all his popularity, a true "writer's writer."

APPRENTICESHIP

Kipling's first published work of prose, *Plain Tales from the Hills* (1888), might have been stifled in its cradle had the *Gazette's* readership not taken it to heart. Indeed, it is unclear at what point Kipling realized he had the makings of a book before him. Though not a novel or even a unified collection of stories, it is best described as a series of vignettes—some comic, some serious, most satirical—unified by a consistent sense of place and narration (in this case, anecdotal). The stories arose from Kipling's intimate acquaintance with the "hill life" of the hill stations scattered throughout northern India, the most famous of which was Simla, which became the government's summer residence. The title of the collection itself is a bit of a pun, since "plain" signifies not only plain, unembellished tales in a colloquial style but also the "plains" where Anglo-Indians served until the brutal summer months. From April to September, life necessarily shifted to the hill towns such as Simla, where the altitude offered a more temperate, and even "English," climate. Hill-town life became a microcosm of the British Raj itself and was something of a literary buffet for a budding writer like the scarcely-out-of-his-teens Kipling. He first visited Simla in 1883 as a guest of the *Civil and Military Gazette*, and he returned year after year, as much for his health as his literary rejuvenation. Though Kipling spent the majority of the "hot season" in Lahore, suffering miserably in body and mind, he lived vicariously through his creations, walking the streets of Simla and finding himself at mysterious locales, such as the "Gate of a Thousand Sorrows." Writing about his impressions of Simla, Kipling recalls, "Simla was another world. There the Hierarchy lived, and one saw and heard the machinery of administration stripped bare" (*Something of Myself*, p. 63). Not surprisingly, the majority of these sketches—only a few aspire to the title of a full-blown story—focus on the "machinery of administration stripped bare" and reveal the petty jealousies, ridiculous pranks, and confusion of identity that revealed itself in this imperial oasis. Yet for all the modesty of its individual stories, *Plain Tales from the Hills* is nearly a work of genius, finding inexhaustible variety in the simplest of means, and tracing the outline of an India never before read in English (and certainly not in England, which may have accounted for their popularity). Though written for a very select audience—the Anglo-Indian club with its stock of jargon and in-jokes—the stories themselves are universal and calculated in their language and purpose. They are an incontestable sign of the writer to come and, in many ways, set a standard that he could only match, but never completely transcend.

When the collection was published in 1888, it collected forty "plain tales," thirty-two of which were from the 1886–1887 run of *Plain Tales from the Hills* in the *Gazette*, with a few new ones thrown in for good measure. As suggested, the range of the stories is astonishing, flittingly effortlessly between the native and the Anglo-Indian perspective. Kipling had a chameleon-like ability to capture dialogue and narrative voice, and much as in Charles Dickens's novels, the narrator assumes various levels of discourse, making it hard to pinpoint the writer amid the masks. What does come across is his sincere admiration for native life and those who can accept, rather than shield themselves from, its mystery. While selected tales can be said to adopt a colonial perspective, the overwhelming sense is satirical—and often at the expense of the empire. This is nowhere better seen than in the first story in the volume, and perhaps the most powerful of the entire series, "Lisbeth." The story traces the career of a young Himalayan girl who is "saved" by a chaplain's wife for her extraordinary beauty, less it be "wasted" among heathen savagery. While working for the family, she rescues a wounded Englishman and announces that she has found her future husband. Needless to say, neither her mistress nor the Englishman take this at all seriously (the Englishman has a fiancée at home), but both amuse her until his leave-taking, when he is instructed to make her sugary promises. Lisbeth wastes away as his absence lengthens, until, feeling things have gone far enough, the chaplain's wife tells her the truth. Lisbeth refuses to believe it, since the chaplain's wife—a true Christian—verified the Englishman's words. Upon learning that she was merely placated, her feelings beneath their contempt, Lisbeth abandons her English ways and disappears among the hills of her people. The wife's response is to lament that "there is no law whereby you can account for the vagaries of the heathen … and I believe that Lisbeth was always at heart an infidel" (p. 11). The attention Kipling lavishes on Lisbeth, even in a handful of pages, is astonishing; we see her obsessing over an "old puzzle-map of the World," since it is her sole image of the world beyond India—and of the mysterious blob called England. Studying it, she "put it together of evenings, and cried to herself, and tried to imagine where her Englishman was" (p. 10). The satire found in many other stories in the volume is entirely absent here; Kipling's scorn for the "lying" English is keenly felt, all the more so when we encounter Lisbeth at the end of her days, a "bleared, wrinkled creature, exactly like a wisp of charred rag" (p. 11). In microcosm, we see the outsider's view of the British Raj, chomping away at the roots of an ancient and noble civilization for a convenient lie.

Other stories belie the author's age and experience and show profound insight into the darkness of empire—notably the famous "The Gate of the Hundred Sorrows," about an Anglo-Indian opium addict and his den of choice, the aforementioned gate. Though utterly without humor, the story deftly satirizes the Anglo-Indian perspective, which seeks to create class and racial hierarchies even in the depths of oblivion. As the narrator (as with most *Plain Tales*, the story employs a frame narrative—the narrator tells the story to the transcriber, who presents it to his audience) explains, "Mind you, though, the Gate was a respectable place in Fung-Tching's time, where you could be comfortable and not at all like the *chandoo-khanas* where the niggers go. No; it was clean, and quiet, and not crowded" (p. 204). The idea of a "respectable" opium den is also embraced by a half-caste woman who is considered a memsahib in the den (typically a term of respect used by a servant to address an Anglo-Indian woman of class), and by the owner himself, who boasts that the superior quality of his "Black Smoke" could pass muster even in London. Yet the true sting of the piece is the fate of the narrator, an Anglo-Indian who has sold both wife and culture for the dark promise of a "foreign" drug. His greatest wish is to "die like the bazaar woman—on a clean, cool mat with a pipe of good stuff between my lips" (p. 206). Again, the lie of British superiority goes up in smoke, rotting in an opium den with the very people he sought to control.

The majority of the other vignettes in the volume document the insular world of Anglo-Indian society and reveal Kipling's great gift for comedy—a very "Earnestian" world of appearances and deceptions. In "Thrown Away," two soldiers must cover up the suicide of a fellow soldier to his family back home, erasing the horror of his colonial desolation with the portrait of a brave soul cut down by cholera. Recounting their deception, the narrator writes, "Then began one of the most grimly comic scenes I have ever taken part in—the concoction of a big, written lie, bolstered with evidence, to soothe The Boy's people at Home" (p. 21). The obligation "the Boy's" family later gives to the writer only underlines the tenuous nature of duty in Anglo-India. Other stories involve Anglo-Indians who, like Kim in Kipling's later novel, have mastered the art of native dialects and disguises, able to blend in with the "teeming masses." In possibly the most humorous story in the volume, "The

Bronckhorst Divorce-Case," the master of disguises, Strickland, infiltrates the servants' quarter of a local household to expose trumped-up charges of adultery. The court case that follows is high comedy worthy of Oscar Wilde himself, yet with the unpleasant aftertaste of a colonial beating the natives at their own game. The servants are noticeably less sympathetic here than in other stories, and the portrayals reflect Kipling's divided nature—evident in many of his later works—between "Eastern" wisdom with "Western" education.

All of the *Plain Tales* were completed by 1887, by which time Kipling was transferred from the *Gazette* to the *Pioneer*, a "sister paper" at Allahabad, far to the south. Here Kipling was transferred from modern-day Pakistan (then as now largely Muslim) to the predominately Hindu North-Western Provinces, which Kipling initially found "strange air and water to me" (*Something of Myself*, p. 75). And yet the new diet must have suited him, since he began writing at a furious rate, quickly filling out several volumes of stories in the ensuing years: *Soldiers Three, The Story of the Gadsbys, In Black and White, Under the Deodars, The Phantom Rickshaw,* and *Wee Willie Winkie* (all of which were initially collected and published in 1888 by Kipling in the newly founded A. H. Wheeler Indian Railway Library, a venture to offer "cheap" reading material to travelers). Partially this output was the result of the newfound freedom the *Pioneer* offered him, where he could experiment with longer stories with less taxing editorial duties. However, many of the stories he was now publishing were written earlier, betraying the artistic mutation of the "plain tales": stories such as "The Phantom Rickshaw," which might have originated as a three-page anecdote, now became a starker, more indicting portrait of the Anglo-Indian officer. Yet perhaps his greatest achievement at this time—and one of the high-water marks of his entire career—is the story later collected in the volume *Wee Willie Winkie and Other Stories* (1895), the much anthologized "The Man Who Would Be King" (1888). Here Kipling elevates the frame narrative to the level of art, using both inner and outer stories to underline the fragility—and cardsharp mentality—of the British Raj.

The story opens with the humble story of a colonial newspaperman, giving us a bird's-eye portrait of Kipling's life at the *Pioneer*. The narrator slaves over copy while the various factions of Anglo-Indian society treat the paper as their official mouthpiece and the editor as their personal servant. Meanwhile, Kipling writes,

> the telephone-bell is ringing madly, and Kings are being killed on the Continent, and Empires are saying, "You're another," and Mister Gladstone is calling down brimstone upon the British Dominions, and the little black copy-boys are whining, "*kaa-pi chay-ha-yeh*" (copy wanted) like tired bees, and most of the paper is as blank as Modred's shield.
>
> (p. 245)

Such passages read like Kipling's personal journal, and they brilliantly contextualize the story proper, which is a fantastic drama that never makes the news, while the editor struggles to keep up with developments in the outside world—so "outside" the life of the plains and hills that it is often unclear whether "A King or courtier or courtesan or a Community was going to die or get a new Constitution" (p. 245).

The story proper concerns two former soldiers, Carnehan and Dravot, who decide to carve up a slice of the empire for themselves in the far-flung regions of Kafiristan. This largely unmapped corner of the empire (near the border of modern-day Afghanistan and Pakistan), though extremely dangerous, boasts the mythical descendants of Alexander the Great, thus making it a proper place to propagate a new "European" race. The two hucksters, trained in the arts of native disguise, masquerade as a traveling priest and his servant transporting a cart of mud toys to a village. The toys, however, actually hide twenty Martini guns and are the means by which the Englishmen hope to secure their new Alexandria. Once the tribes are subjugated by sheer force of arms, Dravot (the mastermind of the plot) uses Masonic rituals to dazzle the populace and perhaps forge a dubious link with Alexander. This Masonic touch adds to the humor, as Kipling himself became a Mason in 1885, despite being underage (he claims the local lodge simply needed a good secretary). In this context, the Masonic reference is fascinating for the soldiers' willingness to abuse knowledge and ritual for the ends of empire—a mere confidence trick from a colonial carpetbagger.

However, the greatest satire comes from the absurd pact the two men draw up for their "business venture," a three-point contract by which they agree (1) to be co-kings of Kafiristan, (2) to forswear women and liquor, and (3) to conduct their rule with "Dignity and Discretion" (p. 253). The plot falls apart not, surprisingly, from native resistance but rather from Dravot's own inability to be bound by the contract and curb his ambition. As he proclaims to Carnehan (who tells the story to the narrator), "I won't make a Nation ... I'll make an Empire! These men aren't niggers; they're English! Look at their eyes—look at their mouths ... They're the Lost Tribes, or something like it, and they've grown to be English ... Two million people—two hundred and fifty thousand fighting men—and all English!" (pp. 261–262). This racist diatribe shines a deadly light on colonial ambition, particularly as it was played out in the so-called great game of empire waged between England and Russia throughout much of the nineteenth century, when Britain and Russia struggled to rewrite the map of Asia, seeking strongholds in the modern nations of Pakistan, Afghanistan, India, and Mongolia. The great difficulty of hanging on to colonial possessions was the very idea of nation itself; Britain had no wish to assimilate with Indians or any other race, as the line between colonized and colonizer would become hopelessly blurred. What Dravot sees in Kafiristan (which, as he explains, was populated by the armies of Alexander the Great) is the possibility to begin a truly *English* Indian empire—one that is racially "white" and untouched by the stain of savagery. Seeing himself as a reincarnation of Alexander himself, Dravot insists on marrying a local girl, which terrifies the local population (how could a mortal survive such a wedding night?). Ultimately the Code falls away and he insists on the match, which leads to his terrified bride biting him and drawing blood. Invoking, perhaps, the fabled end of Captain Cook on the shores of Hawaii, the sight of blood proves

Dravot's mortality, and the populace stages a mutiny.

The comedy abruptly ends here, as this is not England nor Anglo-India: the native states, as the narrator reminds us, "are the dark places of the earth, full of unimaginable cruelty, touching the Railway and the Telegraph on one side, and, on the other, the days of Harun-al-Raschid" (p. 245). Dravot is made to walk to the middle of a rope bridge, which is then cut loose, while Carnehan is crucified for an entire day before being released with Dravot's severed head as a gift (or a message). Though Carnehan manages to return to civilization, it is only to tell his story to the narrator and be interred in an asylum (though the head mysteriously goes missing). The story is Kipling's darkest parable of empire building, suggesting the "darkness" that Englishmen project into the forgotten—and far more ruthless—empires of the ancient world. It is fascinating to compare this story with his later works, particularly poems such as "The White Man's Burden," and ask whether the older Kipling revised his views or whether the same voice, complete with satiric mask, continues to hold sway.

AN INTERNATIONAL CAREER

In 1889, Kipling became involved in a dispute with the *Pioneer* just as he was gaining an international reputation. Kipling felt ready to strike off on his own, particularly as he felt underappreciated in India; he famously records his former boss's last words in his autobiography: "Take it from me, you'll never be worth more than four hundred rupees a month to anyone" (*Something of Myself*, p. 81). However, as Kipling cheekily admits, he was drawing closer to seven hundred at the time—and would command even greater sums in England. En route to London, Kipling landed in San Francisco and traced a path throughout the United States and Canada, eventually winding up in New York. His impressions of the "new world" were collected in articles for the *Pioneer*, which subsequently turned up in his volumes *From Sea to Sea* (1899) and *Letters of Travel* (1920). Once in London, Kipling quickly made his way in artistic society, making lasting friendships with H. Rider Haggard (author of the 1885 African adventure, *King Solomon's Mines*) and Henry James. However, he never felt quite at ease with London society, and he developed a particular distaste for the "wide-mouthed Liberals, who darkened council with pious but disintegrating catch-words, and took care to live very well indeed" (*Something of Myself*, p. 99). He was also incensed by British opinions of India and their stereotypes of colonial government. This may have inspired his first major collection of poetry, *Barrack-Room Ballads* (preceded only by the *Departmental Ditties* of 1886), which were a series of "dramatic monologues" and songs of the common solider in India and abroad. Published in 1890, the collection contains many of his most famous poems and verse, including "Gunga Din," "Mandalay," "Danny Deever," and "The Widow at Windsor." In the latter poem, Kipling uses his keen ear for dialect to immortalize the soldier's lament about the human cost of the empire, which sends them to distant lands without hope of return. For all its musicality, the poem is among Kipling's most bitter, as the soldiers warn the world to

Walk wide o' the Widow of Windsor,
For 'alf o' Creation she owns:
We 'ave bought 'er the same with the sword an' the
    flame,
An we've salted it down with our bones.
(Poor beggars!—it's blue with our bones!)
Hands off o' the sons o' the Widow,
Hands off o' the goods in 'er shop,
For the Kings must come down an' the Emperors
    frown
When the Widow at Windsor says "Stop"!
(Poor Beggars—we're sent to say "Stop"!)

                                                            (lines 16–25)

Here are soldiers who have long since lost their appetite for patriotism and naive gallantry, seeing the entire world as an imperial "shop," with themselves as the hapless storekeepers for Queen Victoria's colonial souvenirs. In language that eerily foreshadows the World War I poetry of Siegfried Sassoon and Wilfred Owens, the soldiers drearily inspire others to

Take 'old o' the Wings o' the Morning'
An' flop round the earth till you're dead;

But you won't get away from the tune that they play
To the bloomin' old Rag over'ead.
(Poor beggars!—it's 'ot over'ead!

                                                            (lines 36–40)

For this, alas, is the last they will ever see of home—a "bloomin' old Rag" that reminds them of the false promises of heroism and the bitter reward of doing one's duty. Similarly, the famous "Mandalay" speaks of a soldier intoxicated with the East, who returns home to England and finds it empty, cold, and foreign. The poem records a communal longing among soldiers once stationed in the East, who claim that

No! you won't 'eed nothing' else
But them spicy garlic smells,
An' the sunshine an' the palm-trees an' the tinkly
    temple-bells;
On the road to Mandalay ...

                                                            (lines 35–39)

The love the soldier has left behind, as well as his love for the exotic sights and smells of Mandalay, have ruined him for England forever. Here, perhaps, we sense Kipling's own disdain of the capital, which for all its civilization lacked the pungent "spice" of the hills. In the double voice of the soldier and Kipling himself, the soldier laments,

I am sick o' wastin' leather on these gritty pavin'-
    stones,
An' the blasted Henglish drizzle wakes the fever in
    my bones;
Tho' I walks with fifty 'ousemaids outer Chelsea to
    the Strand,
An' they talks a lot o' lovin', but wot do they
    understand?

                                                            (lines 40–43)

This dissatisfaction with polite society, which seems to gloss everything over (whether by paving stones or genteel love patter) colors many of Kipling's early poems and stories. He laments the lack of artless humanity in the capital, which he savors among the "plain" conversation of soldiers or the exotic "*Kulla-lo-lo!*" of a Burmese maid. Not surprisingly, the years spent away from India evoked some of his most "exotic" fictions, his exiled homeland inspiring stories that "sounded" in his *ayah*'s dialect but translated for a surprisingly international audience.

Flush from his international success, Kipling was introduced to an unlikely collaborator: Charles Wolcott Balestier, an American agent for the publishing firm of John Lovell, newly arrived in London. This native New Yorker immediately struck a chord with Kipling, and for somewhat less than a year the two were inseparable. In early 1889 they began collaborating on a novel, *The Naulahka: A Story of West and East* (1892), which combined two "frontiers" Kipling admired—the American West and India. Naturally, the American scenes are written by Balestier, with Kipling taking over for India, making for a somewhat disjointed novel. However, the book remains a fitting testament to their personal and literary friendship, the only friendship he would preserve in this manner. Meanwhile, Balestier's sister, Caroline, also caught Kipling's fancy, and she became his wife almost immediately after Balestier's death from typhoid fever in 1891.

Despite these two "romances," the early 1890s were a difficult time for Kipling emotionally, as he felt tremendous pressure to prove himself and write a novel. The result, *The Light That Failed* (1890), was judged by many to be inferior to his previous work, and even Kipling, writing in *Something of Myself*, refers to it as an "inverted, metagrobolised phantasmagiora based on *Manon*" (p. 244). This sense of artistic failure drove Kipling to a nervous breakdown, which prompted a new round of international travel. In 1891, while spending time with his family in Lahore, Kipling received news of Balestier's death. The depth of his grief—which he never wrote about—must have been profound, as he immediately left his family and departed for England. Shortly thereafter Kipling proposed to Balestier's sister, Caroline, a shock for many of his close friends and family, who either didn't predict a match or, in the case of his mother, disapproved. The two were married on January 18, 1892, at All Souls, Langham Place, a few weeks after his beloved friend's death. It was a somber affair, as an influenza epidemic was sweeping the city (the bride's mother and sister were still recovering), the bride wore mourning

for her dead brother, and Kipling's side of the family was necessarily absent. No less a figure than Henry James gave away the bride (though he, too, had reservations about the match), and the married couple left almost immediately for America. Surprisingly, Kipling avoids the subject of Balestier entirely in his autobiography, and even Caroline ("Carrie") only makes her debut on the day of their wedding. Some have speculated that Kipling sought something of the brother in Balestier's sister, or perhaps felt it his duty to "rescue" his friend's older sister (then twenty-nine to his twenty-six). Whatever the reason (and it certainly may have been as simple as love), the two sailed to America, visiting the family estate in Vermont, before sailing off again for Japan and another world tour.

Unfortunately, their honeymoon ended almost as soon as it began, because of a financial disaster: the Oriental Banking Company, in which Kipling had invested heavily, collapsed. The couple decided to retire to Vermont and establish a house near the Balestier family home in Brattleboro. A short search uncovered a suitable house, popularly known as Bliss Cottage, which offered the Kiplings both solitude and economy. However, life there was far from idyllic: besides the New Englanders' hearty contempt for "Britishers," Kipling and his wife were cut off from the "civilized" world. As he writes, "It would be hard to exaggerate the loneliness and sterility of life on the farms … What might have become characters, powers and attributes perverted themselves in that desolation as cankered trees throw out branches akimbo, and strange faiths and cruelties, born of solitude to the edge of insanity, flourished like lichen on the sick bark" (*Something of Myself*, p. 127).

Like many artists and writers before him, however, he found that severing himself from the distractions of London had a restorative affect on his art: he began writing prolifically, including some of his most perennial stories, collected in *The Jungle Book* (1894) and *The Second Jungle Book* (1895). The two books were largely inspired by his own children, the first of whom, Josephine, was born on the night of December 29, 1892. Shortly after her birth, bolstered by the sales of his previous books, Kipling and his family moved from Bliss Cottage to a newly built house they called "Naulahka" in honor of Charles. It was here that Kipling further developed the modern notion of "children's literature" that could be equally appreciated by adult readers. This technique, which he used again in *Puck of Pook's Hill* (1906) and *Rewards and Fairies* (1910), he described as working the stories "in three of four overlaid tints and textures, which might or might not reveal themselves according to the shifting light of sex, youth, and experience" (*Something of Myself*, p. 205). As he makes clear, these "children's" tales were meant for adults—or rather, the adults the children would gradually become. The stories were meant to be "lived in," yielding new insights and stories as the children matured, while satisfying the adults who read them night after night. Though Kipling may not have invented this technique, he became its most influential proponent, and the *Jungle Book*s in particular prompted a host of admirers, most notably Edgar Rice Burrough's famous *Tarzan of the Apes* (1914).

The *Jungle Book*s began life as a single volume published in 1894 to which a second volume was added in 1895. The first volume consisted of seven stories, the first three of which introduced the character of Mowgli, while the following four consisted of related stories of the animal kingdom in an Indian setting (except for the somewhat uncharacteristic "The White Seal," which takes place in the Bering Sea). The second volume added five more Mowgli stories, with only three additional tales of Indian and Arctic life. According to Kipling, the origin of these works came from three sources: a half-remembered book about Masonic lions he read as a child, a sketch he wrote during his newspaper days about a child raised by wolves, and a line from his friend Haggard's novel *Naga the Lily* (1892). Yet these diverse materials forged a distinctly Kiplingesque work, and in many ways became the novel he was unable to write in London (like all Kipling's greatest works, it defies easy categorization). The first story, "Mowgli's Brothers," introduces the abandoned infant, Mowgli, who is taken in by a family of

wolves, all adherent followers of the "law of the jungle," which states: "Ye may kill for yourselves, and your mates, and your cubs as they need, and ye can; / But kill not for pleasure of killing, and *seven times never kill Man!*" (p. 170). The adoption incurs the wrath of the story's antagonist, the great wolf Shere Khan, who vows to devour the child as revenge. In the first three stories, Mowgli is taught the laws of the jungle by his two mentors, Baloo the bear and Bagheera the panther. In most of the *Jungle Book* tales, the animals are anthropomorphized, acting like humans in animal form, embodying mythic roles and offering folklike dictums as advice to our superhuman "everyman." In this, the stories seem like successful imitations of an older Indian tradition, such as the animal fables of *The Pancatantra*, while at the same time embodying the ethos of the Uncle Remus stories, which Kipling knew and admired. Kipling's animals are at once mirrors of human society and disguised avatars, whose teachings prepare Mowgli for the "great game" of human life.

One of the most fascinating qualities of the Mowgli stories is their treatment of man's domination of the natural world allied with his general ignorance and misery. Aside from Mowgli, the humans in the stories are a pitiful lot, either because of their own arrogance or the cruelty of others. While the animals walk in fear of man and his command of the "red flower" (fire), they also despise his disrespect for the natural world. Mowgli, as a creature of both worlds, illustrates this duality in the early story, "Tiger, Tiger!" Here, tempted by curiosity and hunger, he ventures into a village and notices the first thing that separates man from animal: the construction of gates. He then suffers himself to be led inside a house, another creation that upsets him, as it replaces forest and sky with another set of barricades, a thatch roof. Kipling humorously illustrates the claustrophobia and self-delusion that goes hand in hand with civilization (since Mowgli notes that he—or any animal of the wild—could easily tear through the roof and escape, or vice versa). However, humans are chiefly represented in this story by the priest and the old hunter, Buldeo, two individuals who judge both man and beast despite their own considerable failings. Kipling uses Mowgli's "innocence" to cast a ray of conspicuously adult cynicism on the priest's chosen calling:

> when the village priest told [Mowgli] that the god in the temple would be angry with him if he ate the priest's mangoes, he picked up the image, brought it over to the priest's house, and asked the priest to make the god angry and he would be happy to fight him. It was a horrible scandal, but the priest hushed it up, and Messua's husband paid much good silver to comfort the god.
>
> (p. 59)

Naturally, the priest's threat is intended to allow him to keep the mangoes for himself, a position that Mowgli finds unlawfully selfish (particularly as it conflicts with the law of the jungle). Mowgli's challenge is hilarious in its audacity, yet it makes perfect sense in a world where all differences are settled wolf to wolf; no "god" can hold an entire village in thrall without someone challenging his right to rule (and indeed, this very scene is mirrored in "Mowgli's Brothers," where the wolves challenge Akela, the aging monarch). As the god's wrath is not forthcoming, the priest "hushed it up," though not before extorting blood money from Messua and his wife, the couple that have "adopted" Mowgli.

This passage invites one of the work's greatest questions, and one that not even Mowgli's mentors can answer: if man is the greatest of all animals, why does he live by no law or creed? Indeed, the race most resembling man in the animal kingdom is that of the Bandar-log (the monkeys), whom all animals detest for their solitude (like men, they hide from the other animals) and lawlessness (they do not recognize—or perhaps comprehend—the law of the jungle). Mowgli struggles to understand the laws of man but can only see pain and fear instead of respect and understanding. Kipling applies an extra "tint" to his story in the second volume, "Letting in the Jungle," which returns to the village of "Tiger, Tiger!" After the disappearance of the "Devil-child" Mowgli, the village priest imprisons and tortures Messua and her husband, Mowgli's adoptive parents. Mowgli vows revenge on the entire village and calls on Hathi, the great white elephant, to let in the jungle—or trample the village, dwellings, crops and all, into oblivion (p. 208). This demand is notable in the series of Mowgli stories because Hathi is the "king" of the animal world, and Mowgli asks Bagheera to send for him, as one might a servant. Chagrined, Bagheera responds, "But, indeed, and truly, Little Brother, is it not—it is not seemly to say 'Come' and 'Go' to Hathi. Remember, he is the master of the jungle, and before the man pack changed the look on thy face, he taught thee the master-words of the jungle" (p. 204). Mowgli replies that he will now teach Hathi a master-word—one that will set the entire jungle on its ears.

The audacity with which Mowgli confronts the ancient master of the forest, and the subsequent humiliation this elephant feels when Mowgli exercises his power over him, is proof positive that he has "crossed over." Yet it also reflects the chief distinction between the world of the jungle (the ancient world) and the world of man (the modern world): the change of "we" for "me". As in the Hindu creation myth, Mowgli suddenly becomes an entity, passionately aware of his wants, needs, and desires. His selfish desire for revenge conflicts with the law of the jungle, and by disobeying it, he is setting himself above the law (which forbids the killing of men) as a man himself. When Hathi deliberates, protesting, "But I—but we have no quarrel with them, and it needs the red rage of great pain ere we tear down the places where men sleep" (p. 207), Mowgli substitutes his rage for theirs—suggesting that it speaks for all. Even Bagheera shrinks at this blatant display of power, as "Mowgli the Frog" has become both savior and devil—but for which side and for what cause is uncertain. As with all human wars, the teeming masses (who have no common quarrel with the opposing side) are pressed into service to destroy an individual's foe. Mowgli quickly warms to his role as commander, promising Hathi his destruction will be even more fruitful than in the days of old, "for the reason that there is a man to direct" (p. 206). Only man can plan destruction on such a vast scale, and following Mowgli's command, the collected might of the jungle eradicates the village, sending the hapless villagers fleeing to all ends of the earth.

However, Kipling does not utterly condemn the human race in the balance of a simpler, pantheistic creed. Even in "Letting in the Jungle," Mowgli's parents ask for safe passage to an English village thirty miles away. When Mowgli asks what "tribe" they are, his mother responds, "They be white, and it is said that they govern all the land, and do not suffer people to burn or beat each other without witnesses" (p. 199). A familiar imperial bias creeps into the story, as Kipling suggests some men do follow a "law of the jungle," invisible to the cruder natives of India. Here the "animal versus Bandar-log" distinction is revisited, as some humans are truly savage, while others (the British) navigate life and death through a steadfast creed. Mowgli's training has prepared him to "shed his skin" as a wolf and emerge as a true British subject—one who can lead armies and rule the people of India. In this he seems like a prototype for Kim, the Irish urchin in Kipling's 1901 novel who emerges from the lower classes to play a pivotal role on the imperial stage. For as Kipling promises us in "Kaa's Hunting," "A man's cub is a man's cub, and he must learn *all* the Law of the Jungle" (p. 32). Mowgli must return to the world of men after his Peter Pan–like adventures in the wild, where he will find another "tribe" to lead; one, we can only imagine, worthy of the great line of Hathi, Baloo, and Bagheera.

Also similar to the novel *Kim* is the element of spirituality that creeps into the work and betrays Kipling's divided nature on India. An alternative career for a protagonist such as Mowgli or Kim is offered in one of the greatest (and least juvenile) works in the *Jungle Book* series, "The Miracle of Purun Bhagat." In this story, a certain Dewan Sir Purun Dass, K.C.I.E., renounces his globe-trotting career as a politician and becomes a *sannyasi* (ascetic) in his old age. Here he follows the creed of Hinduism and abandons his former self as an illusion, living austerely and seeking truth among the signs and secrets of nature. As Kipling writes,

> time stopped, and he … could not tell whether he were alive or dead: a man with control of his limbs,

or a part of the hills, and the clouds, and the shifting rain and sunlight. He would repeat a Name softly to himself a hundred hundred times, till, at each repetition, he seemed to move more and more out of his body, sweeping up the doors of some tremendous discovery.

(p. 178)

There is no hint of mockery or irony here: Kipling invests the man's spiritual quest with some of his most poetic imagery and sharpest prose. While we might not typically connect Kipling, the writer of adventure and empire, with the story of a man seeking transcendence, it clearly develops the theme of man's role as conqueror and savior. Even after "checking out" of the human world and conversing solely with the animal world (in effect, taking the reverse journey as Mowgli), Purun acts swiftly to save a Himalayan village from an avalanche. Though he ultimately dies from the effort, the villagers enthrone him as a local deity and commemorate his action as a "miracle" of mythic proportions. To underline this "mythic" element in our lives, Kipling ends the story with the remark that "[the villagers] do not know that the saint of their worship is the late Sir Purun Dass, K.C.I.E., D.C.L., Ph.D., etc.," who was once an "honorary or corresponding member of more learned and scientific societies than will ever do any good in this world or the next" (p. 185). In other words, the illusion of his former career has passed away, leaving the great man remembered not for his titles but for his humanity—the only true *law* of the jungle. The story stands as a testament to Kipling's belief in man's potential, particularly as filtered through the uniquely Indian quest for enlightenment.

THE NOBEL LAUREATE

Life seemed to be set for Kipling: his daughter Elise was born in February 1896, and his works enjoyed wide—and protected—circulation from the American firm of Scribners, as represented by a young agent named Frank Doubleday (soon to establish his own publishing empire). However, when the United States became involved in a territorial issue between Britain and Venezuela, sentiment against the "Britishers" soured. Additionally, Kipling's brother-in-law, Beatty, long a source of friction in the family, became more than a nuisance.

After a heated public encounter with Kipling, Beatty was arrested, although the resulting ill will against Kipling made him decide that "Naulakha, desirable as it was, meant only 'a house' and not 'The House' of our dreams" (*Something of Myself*, p. 142). In the spring of 1896 the family left America and settled in Torquay (in Devon). As if to cement his return to England, he began writing stories of his childhood friends at Westward Ho! which were collected as the volume *Stalky & Co.* in 1899. Soon after his son John was born in 1897, Kipling and his family traveled to South Africa and wintered in Cape Town, a favorite spot that subsequently became a family tradition. Unfortunately, on a return visit to America in 1899 Kipling and his daughter Josephine fell ill with severe pneumonia. Though Kipling eventually recovered, his daughter died of the illness. As with his friend Wolcott Balestier's death some years earlier, Kipling made little recorded comment about losing Josephine, and the event is noticeably absent from his autobiography. Perhaps hoping to lose himself in his work, Kipling became a correspondent for an army newspaper in the Second Boer War (1899–1902) and wrote many stories and poems of the common soldiers stationed there.

Yet these personal details pale compared to his greatest achievement in this period: the composition of easily his finest novel, *Kim,* published in 1901. The work had long been germinating in his mind, largely in the form of a very different novel composed at Bliss Cottage. Back in England, Kipling talked over the work with his father (who appears as the model of the museum caretaker in Lahore), and he gradually cobbled together his most original work about India—ironically, while nestled in the English countryside. However, he later insisted that "there was a good deal of beauty in [*Kim*], and not a little wisdom; the best in both sorts being owed to my Father" (*Something of Myself*, p. 152). On the surface, *Kim* is a riveting adventure story told against the backdrop of the British Raj. However, from quite a different perspective, it is the most

ancient story of all—the quest for enlightenment and escape from "the wheel of life." Our hero, Kim, is an Irish urchin who has learned to imitate and personify all walks of life in Lahore—from Hindus to Muslims to the English. In the opening chapter, he becomes attached to a Tibetan lama, who mistakes Kim's "shape-shifting" as a sign that the youth is a divine messenger, a *chela*, or disciple, to aid him in his search for the sacred River of Enlightenment. However, Kim's help is also sought by the British, notably the secret agent Mahbub Ali, who hopes to use him in the great game of empire. As a fellow agent, Kim can secretly walk among the contested lands that adjoin British and Russian possessions, mapping them for the impending clash with Russia or other, unnamed, infidels.

Much of the work reflects Kim's inner awakening to both worlds—the spiritual, "eternal" India that surrounds him and the modern world of British imperialism and espionage. Kim's education as a *chela* is cut short when the British reclaim him and the lama, reluctantly, allows him to receive an "English" education. However, the lama sees this as a temporary setback, as he explains, "We have not altogether parted, but the time is not ripe that we should take the Road together. He acquires wisdom in another place. We must wait" (p. 133). As a lama of almost mythic stature (resembling the legendary characters of the Ramayana, etc.) he is willing to wait years—even lifetimes, if necessary. In the end, the separation is of a much shorter duration. Shortly after their reunion, the lama remarks:

The Search, I say, is sure … I acquired merit when I sent thee to the Gates of Learning, and gave thee the jewel that is Wisdom. Thou didst return, I saw even now, a follower of Sakayamuni, the Physician, whose altars are many in Bhotiyal. It is sufficient. We are together, and all things are as they were— Friend of all the World—Friend of the Stars—my *chela*!

(p. 162)

Though this passage is somewhat humorous, since it is prompted by Kim's "miraculous" healing of a sick villager (through English medicine), the comedy is not what remains. It is the profound faith of the lama that emerges, a faith that sees his actions—and more importantly, Kim's wisdom—as part of a cosmic plan. The lama abandoned his *chela* to the "Gates of Learning" believing that he would return, not merely as Kim but as something greater—the calf that could free him (and India, perhaps) from the shackles of illusion. The character of the lama persuades us that Kim is more than an Anglo-Indian Huckleberry Finn; like the lama, he, too, is a mythical "type" whose journey unfolds in an India both ancient and modern. And like all mythic heroes, Kim must pass his final test before he can join the lama's quest for salvation.

We know Kim is tested because of his childish love for the intricate workings of the Game, a quality prized by Mahbub Ali and his boss, Lurgan Sahib, among others. Indeed, the irony of the novel is that both camps view Kim as a superhuman creature, wielding the fate of an entire realm. Mahbub Ali admits as much to Colonel Creighton when he says, "Only once in a thousand years is a horse born so well fitted for the game as this our colt" (p. 167). The reference to Kim as a "colt" mirrors the lama's vision of him as a "calf" that can fulfill an ancient prophecy. However, Kim cannot see the connection, and he continues to be more impressed by Mahbub's heroism than by the lama's asceticism. As he says again and again on the journey: "I hope to play the Great Game" (p. 220). As a young man he stands at a crossroads between his love of life's illusion and its purpose; his love for the lama does not translate into understanding, and even worse, he believes the lama's quest will further his advancement in the Game.

The ending of the novel is perhaps Kipling's most definitive statement about the nature of India. As with *The Second Jungle Book*'s "Miracle of Purun Bhagat," the lama is taken at his word as a true miracle worker. After scuffling with Russians and being saved from drowning by Huree Babu, the lama actually finds his River—and thus, enlightenment. However, the passage also suggests a far more worldly reading. For the first time in the novel, the lama is able to "see" what Kim has noticed all along: namely, the beauty and possibility of India. His river is not in

one sacred spot, as he assumed, but in every tree and hill in the countryside—and more specifically, in Kim. Like Buddha himself, the lama returns from the River (instead of departing the world) to lead others on the path of enlightenment. Considering Kim's fate in the empire, the lama says, "Let him be a teacher; let him be a scribe—what matter? He will have attained Freedom in the end. The rest is illusion" (p. 285). In a work ostensibly celebrating the ingenuity of the British empire, this is a significantly anti-imperialist pronouncement. Kim's ultimate career, his role in the Game, is unimportant, because he is destined for salvation beyond the "wheels" of life and death. Mahbub Ali comically misunderstands the lama, responding, "Now I see! That is the right gait for the colt ... He is somewhat urgently needed as a Scribe by the State, for instance" (p. 236). What is interesting here is the reversal of roles: previously, the lama misunderstood information about the Game in terms of his quest; now Mahbub Ali (representative of the Game) can see nothing of the world beyond statistics and paperwork. Yet far from negating his words, Mahbub Ali fades away and the lama dominates the closing pages, even pronouncing the final utterance in the novel: "Come!" Mahbub Ali, along with the formerly the cynical voice of the narrator, is silenced. Perhaps similarly out of his depth, the narrator simply concludes the work with the reverent, yet laconic sentence: "He crossed his hands on his lap and smiled, as a man may who has won salvation for himself and his beloved" (p. 240). It seems we are no longer in the world of "shakers and babblers," as the narrator once flippantly remarked, but of true visionaries in a world of timeless wonder.

After the publication of *Kim,* Kipling's career reached its highest zenith, a reputation that was cemented by winning the Nobel Prize for Literature in 1907. The early years of the century were extremely productive for him, producing the final works that would survive his death: The *Just So Stories* (1902), delightful inventions in the manner of *The Jungle Books*; *The Five Nations* (1903) and *Traffics and Discoveries* (1904); and the once-famous children's books *Puck of Pook's Hill*

(1906) and *Rewards and Fairies* (1910), which celebrate the Sussex countryside. The latter contained one of his most important poems, though written many years earlier, "If." Admired—or vilified—for its characterization of English stoicism and "stiff upper lip" sensibility, the poem is all the more curious for appearing in a volume of children's stories. The poem was modeled on a friend and contained, in his words, "councils of perfection most easy to give" (*Something of Myself*, p. 206). However, it is important to remember Kipling's technique in using several shades (or "tints") often invisible to the young (or naive) reader. In "If," too, it is easy to sense a certain cynicism and satirical intent familiar from Kipling's earliest stories, particularly in the poem's exhortation to "make one heap of all your winnings / And risk it on one turn of pitch-and-toss" (pp. 17–18). As the poem is ostensibly about what makes a British boy a "man," the chief characteristics of such a person seem to be gambling, suspicion, and a generally cold disposition: "If neither foes nor loving friends can hurt you / If all men count with you, but none too much" (pp. 27–28). Such councils are quite easy to give but hard for all but the most hardened political animal to practice; nevertheless, the poem continues to be anthologized as the embodiment of the imperial ethos. Kipling was amused by its popularity, especially as schoolchildren once complained to him of having to write it out endlessly for exams.

RECESSIONAL: LAST YEARS AND CRITICAL FORTUNES

In the early decades of the twentieth century Kipling's personal life seemed more settled as well: the family took a permanent house in Sussex, which in his memoir he called "the very-own house." However, the coming years brought a quick succession of tragedies: his father's death in 1911 and the beginning of World War I in 1914. Kipling energetically visited the front and wrote extensively of the war in journalistic reports and fiction. However, this work could little prepare him for the loss of his son in the Battle of Loos on September 27, 1915. Tragi-

cally, this was John's first day in action with the Irish Guards (a commission Kipling helped his son obtain), and his body was never identified or recovered. Kipling's bitterness toward the war—and those he held responsible for the war, such as the pope, the kaiser, and Germans in general—revealed itself through his writings of the period. In the story "Mary Postgate," from the collection *A Diversity of Creatures* (1917), for instance, a spinster takes revenge for the death of a young girl (killed by a bomb) by letting an injured German soldier die, despite his pleas for help. Though this particular story was written before John's death, it reflects the sense of helplessness Kipling felt as an artist, forced to watch and write. However, he did not exactly sit idly by; in 1917 he joined the Imperial War Graves Commission, responsible for setting up graves for the fallen throughout the Western Front and elsewhere. Kipling was very active on their behalf, and after visiting the graves at Rouen, he wrote a moving memorial of his own, the story "The Gardener," about a woman looking for her illegitimate son's grave in France. The story is a strong contrast to the anger and revenge of "Mary Postgate," perhaps reflecting the closure he had reluctantly come to with his son and the war.

Kipling's last years were spent with a singular disregard for the approaching end: he continued to travel widely and write prodigiously in all forms. Unlike other writers, his later works do not betray a loss of ability or vigor; on the contrary, though he may have written no "masterworks" in the sense of *Kim* or his earlier stories, the works are unmistakably Kipling—and often at his finest. His late autobiography, published posthumously in 1937, contains brilliant observations on the craft of writing and his own "making" as a writer. The work is also fascinating for what he leaves out, making it less an autobiography than a series of sketches about his own personal and artistic maturation. Kipling died of an intestinal hemorrhage on January 18, 1936, on the very cusp of World War II. However, he made his sympathies quite clear by removing the swastika, an ancient Buddhist symbol for luck, from his books. (He had been using the symbol for decades before it came into use by the Nazi

Party.) Had he lived to see the horrors of World War II, Kipling would likely have ignored ill health and thrown comfort aside to document the realities of war and write vigorous verse and prose in defense of England. But although he was gone, his works continued to speak of the struggle and conflict of empire, particularly for those storm-tossed in its wake. As he wrote in his famous 1897 poem, "Recessional,"

> Far-called, our navies melt away;
> On dune and headland sinks the fire:
> Lo, all our pomp of yesterday
> Is one with Nineveh and Tyre!
> Judge of Nations, spare us yet,
> Lest we forget—lest we forget!
>
> (lines 13–18)

Though Kipling urges his reader "not to forget," Kipling himself was quickly abandoned by his fellow writers, viewed conveniently as an anachronism from a bygone age. Though he was warmly acclaimed when he arrived in London in the late 1890s, he never ingratiated himself with the leading literary circles. Even Henry James, a close friend, remained guarded about Kipling's work, recognizing considerable talent in his stories but never feeling he was quite a member of the "club." Partially this was because of the unorthodox nature of his talent: Kipling was not a traditionalist, in that he wrote no "textbook" novel or one definitive work. (Kipling is best appreciated for a smorgasbord of works, rather than a single volume.) Rather, his works were by nature sketches or hybrids, borrowing from many traditions without belonging entirely to this or that genre. His attempts to follow convention, such as the early novel *The Light That Failed*, were largely considered failures, while the later, less conventional works, such as *Kim* or the *Jungle Books*, remain vitally alive, however unclassifiable they remain to posterity. For this reason, the post–World War I generation has largely focused on works that can be classified—and thus easily dismissed—such as his patriotic poems and stories. This Kipling certainly has little in common with writers such as T. S. Eliot, D. H. Lawrence, or Doris Lessing, and to call him unfashionable would be an understatement. Of course, several writers have paid him grudg-

ing respect, including Eliot, who admired Kipling's voice, although he felt that the elder author wrote "verse" rather than true poetry. In the decades following Kipling's death, his reputation survived largely on the strength of his "children's literature": works such as the *Jungle Books*, the *Just So Stories*, and the "novel" *Captains Courageous* (1897) were widely read and imitated. This interest is most clearly seen in the famous Disney animated film *The Jungle Book* (1967), which follows only the loosest thread of the Mowgli outline. Nevertheless, his works never faded entirely from view, and he remained in anthologies as a figure like Alfred Tennyson—respected from a distance, if not entirely read in the best circles.

All of this legacy took a dramatic change with the dawn of the scholarly field of postcolonialism, which quickly recognized the importance of his Indian works as offering an "outsider's" view of the imperial machine (even if debate remains on where his sympathies truly lie). Edward Said has written extensively on Kipling, particularly in his book *Culture and Imperialism* (1993), which discusses how Kim embodies the "pleasures" (p. 132) of imperialism that Kipling (in Said's view) was trying to evoke. Salman Rushdie, in his essay collection *Imaginary Homelands* (1992), writes of the conflict of the "English" and "Indian" Kipling, a duality that produced one of the first truly "Indian" novels—*Kim*. Many other writers, notably V. S. Naipaul, have echoed this sentiment along with offering tempered admiration of his works; Naipaul found much of Kipling's writing about India to be still current when he visited for the first time in the 1960s, and he praised Kipling's ability to capture a distinctly Indian atmosphere and character (while recognizing its limitations). Similarly, scholars such as Sara Suleri Goodyear in *The Rhetoric of English India* (1992) and Zohreh T. Sullivan in *Narratives of Empire: The Fictions of Rudyard Kipling* (1993) have placed Kipling at the center of the postcolonial debate, underlying his importance in tracing how England understood India and how the new nation wrote about itself after independence (in 1947).

All of Kipling's earlier works are now available in new editions. The once-hard-to-find *Plain Tales from the Hills* was published in its entirety by Oxford University Press in the 1990s, and many volumes of his complete poems have appeared since the 1980s, forcing us to reevaluate the writer of "verse." Paradoxically, his children's works are possibly less in circulation today than they were in the mid-twentieth century, and the modern reader is more apt to know him by *Kim* or "The White Man's Burden" than by the *Jungle Book*s or the sadly forgotten *Puck of Pook's Hill*. Nevertheless, the grudging acceptance that preserved his reputation has grown into a new-found understanding of his literary innovations, as well as the distinct power of his writing, which treated no two subjects alike but, rather, remained uniquely his own. If the test of a great artist is the literary thumbprint that his or her works betray, then Kipling is an artist of rare stature, recognizable in a single sentence and unmistakable in any lineup of the great nineteenth- and twentieth-century British writers.

Selected Bibliography

WORKS OF RUDYARD KIPLING

COLLECTED WORKS

The Writings in Prose and Verse of Rudyard Kipling. 36 vols. New York: Charles Scribner's Sons, 1897–1937. (The Outward Bound Edition.)

The Bombay Edition of the Works of Rudyard Kipling. 31 vols. London: Macmillan, 1913–1938.

The Sussex Edition of the Complete Works in Prose and Verse of Rudyard Kipling. 35 vols. London: Macmillan, 1937–1939.

SHORT STORY COLLECTIONS

Plain Tales from the Hills. London: Thacker, Spink, 1888. (All page citations for this work in the text refer to the modern edition listed below.)

Under the Deodars, The Phantom Rickshaw, Wee Willie Winkie (published individually as above), later in *Wee Willie Winkie and Other Stories.* London: Macmillan, 1895.

Life's Handicap. London: Macmillan, 1891.

Many Inventions. London: Macmillan, 1893.

The Jungle Book. London: Macmillan, 1894. (All page citations for this work in the text refer to the modern edition listed below.)

The Second Jungle Book. London: Macmillan, 1895.

The Day's Work. London: Macmillan, 1898.

Soldiers Three; The Story of the Gadsbys; In Black and White. London: Macmillan, 1895. (The stories in this collection were individually published in A. H. Wheeler & Co.'s Railway Series in 1888.)

Stalky & Co. London: Macmillan, 1899.

Just So Stories. London: Macmillan, 1902.

Traffics and Discoveries. New York: Doubleday, Page, 1904.

Puck of Pook's Hill. London: Macmillan, 1906.

Actions and Reactions. London: Macmillan, 1909.

Rewards and Fairies. London: Macmillan, 1910.

A Diversity of Creatures. London: Macmillan, 1917.

Debits and Credits. London: Macmillan, 1926.

Thy Servant a Dog. London: Macmillan, 1930.

Limits and Renewals. London: Macmillan, 1932.

NOVELS

The Light That Failed. London: Macmillan, 1891. (Originally published in *Lippincott's Monthly Magazine* in 1890.)

The Naulahka: A Story of West and East. London: Heinemann, 1892.

Captains Courageous: A Story of the Grand Banks. London: Macmillan, 1897.

Kim. London: Macmillan, 1901. (First serialized in *McClure's Magazine,* December 1900–October 1901; all page citations for this work in the text refer to the modern edition listed below)

POETRY

Departmental Ditties, Barrack-Room Ballads, and Other Verse. New York and Chicago: United States Book Company, 1890.

The Seven Seas. London: Methuen, 1896.

The Five Nations. London: Methuen, 1903.

Collected Verse of Rudyard Kipling. Garden City, N.Y.: Doubleday, Page, 1907.

Songs from Books. London: Methuen, 1912.

The Years Between. London: Methuen, 1919.

NONFICTION

A Fleet in Being: Notes of Two Trips with the Channel Squadron. London: Macmillan, 1898.

From Sea to Sea: Letters of Travel. New York: Doubleday and McClure, 1899.

France at War on the Frontier of Civilization. Garden City, N.Y.: Doubleday, Page, 1915.

The New Army in Training. London: Macmillan, 1915.

Sea Warfare. Garden City, N.Y.: Doubleday, Page, 1917.

The War in the Mountains. Garden City, N.Y.: Doubleday, Page, 1917.

The Graves of the Fallen. London: Commonwealth War Graves Commission, 1919.

Letters of Travel, 1892–1913. London: Macmillan, 1920.

The Irish Guards in the Great War. London: Macmillan, 1923.

Souvenirs of France. London: Macmillan, 1933.

Something of Myself: For My Friends, Known and Unknown. Garden City, N.Y.: Doubleday, Doran, 1937.

Brazilian Sketches. New York: Doubleday, Doran, 1940.

Rudyard Kipling's Uncollected Speeches. Edited by Thomas Pinney. Greensboro, N.C.: ELT Press, 2008.

CORRESPONDENCE, MANUSCRIPTS

The Letters of Rudyard Kipling. 6 vols. Edited by Thomas Pinney. Iowa City: University of Iowa Press, 1990–2006.

In addition to some materials from 1888-1892 in the Marlboro College (Vermont) Rudyard Kipling Papers collection, the primary archive of Kipling's papers is the Wimpole Archive in the University of Sussex Library.

MODERN EDITIONS (EDITIONS AS CITED ABOVE)

The Jungle Books. Edited by Marcus Cunliffe. New York: Signet, 1961.

The Complete Verse. New York: Anchor, 1988.

Just So Stories: For Little Children. Oxford: Oxford University Press, 2009.

Kim. Edited by Alan Sandison. Oxford: Oxford University Press, 2008.

The Man Who Would Be King and Other Stories. Edited by Louis L. Cornell. Oxford: Oxford University Press, 2008.

Plain Tales From The Hills. Edited by Andrew Rutherford. Oxford: Oxford University Press, 1996.

BIOGRAPHICAL AND CRITICAL STUDIES

Allen, Charles. *Kipling Sahib: India and the Making of Rudyard Kipling.* London: Little Brown, 2007.

Bloom, Harold, ed. *Rudyard Kipling.* New York: Chelsea House, 1987.

Carrington, Charles. *Rudyard Kipling: His Life and Work.* Rev. ed. London: Macmillan, 1978.

Cornell, Louis L. *Kipling in India.* London: Macmillan, 1966.

Gilmour, David. *The Long Recessional: The Imperial Life of Rudyard Kipling.* Farrar, Straus and Giroux, 2002.

Goodyear, Sara Suleri. *The Rhetoric of English India.* Chicago: University of Chicago Press, 1992.

Green, Roger Lancelyn. *Kipling and the Children.* London: Elek Books, 1965.

Keating, Peter. *Kipling the Poet.* London: Secker & Warburg, 1994.

Moran, Neil K. *Kipling and Afghanistan: A Study of the Young Author As Journalist, Writing on the Afghan Border Crisis of 1884–1885.* Jefferson, N.C.: McFarland, 2005.

Orel, Harold, ed. *Critical Essays on Rudyard Kipling.* Boston: G. K. Hall, 1989.

Ricketts, Harry. *Rudyard Kipling: A Life.* New York: Carroll & Graf, 2000.

Rutherford, Andrew, ed. *Kipling's Mind and Art: Selected Critical Essays.* Stanford, Calif.: Stanford University Press, 1964.

Said, Edward. *Culture and Imperialism.* New York: Vintage, 1994.

Sullivan, Zohreh T. *Narratives of Empire: The Fictions of Rudyard Kipling.* Cambridge, U.K.: Cambridge University Press, 1993.

Tompkins, Joyce Marjorie Sanxter. *The Art of Rudyard Kipling.* London: Methuen, 1959.

Wilson, Angus. *The Strange Ride of Rudyard Kipling.* London: Secker & Warburg, 1977.

PHILIP LARKIN

(1922—1985)

Piers Pennington

IN HIS POEM "I Remember, I Remember," Philip Larkin famously looked back on his childhood. Gazing out of his train's window on the familiar surroundings of Coventry, the poem's speaker is prompted by a question from his traveling companion to catalog in his mind the place's many disappointments before bringing the poem to its close. With its long list of missed ideals, this poem is typical of the negating tendency that runs throughout Larkin's work. But "I Remember, I Remember" also does something other than lament a dull and uneventful childhood. Even though it draws on biographical fact, the presence of the traveling companion within the poem's world means that the speaker's words to him are presented as performance: as well as having access to his private thoughts, we see what the speaker chooses to make public to his friend, and so we also see the drama of the difference between the private and the public. Larkin's poem, then, is about the public presentation of the self as much as a childhood now privately recalled for what it was not, and in this chance return to his roots he touches on a concern that is fundamental to all of his writing: the relation of the self to others. This is a theme that is explored in detail in his two novels and in many of his mature poems, and following his death the question of the writer's relation to his writing became the unavoidable subject of critical discussions of Larkin's work, because the private man was revealed to be much different from the public personality he had chosen to present.

Born in Coventry on August 9, 1922, Philip Arthur Larkin was the second child and only son of Stanley Larkin (1884–1948), who was made city treasurer in the year of his son's birth, and Eva Emily Day (1886–1977). Larkin had an older sister, Catharine, but the difference in their ages of almost ten years led him to write in an unpublished fragment of autobiography that he felt very much like an only child when he was growing up. Life at home was lonely, and not particularly loving. Larkin's father, an authoritative man who admired the recovery in Germany and kept a statue of Hitler on the mantelpiece (taking his teenage son to visit the country twice), grew ever more distant from Larkin's mother, who became increasingly dissatisfied. Larkin had the run of his father's well-stocked library, though, and this stimulated an early love for the writing of D. H. Lawrence. He attended King Henry VIII School, Coventry, where in 1940 he took his higher school certificate, and later that year he went up to St. John's College, Oxford, to read for a degree in English language and literature. Highly productive in his youth, he published poems and stories in the *Coventrian,* his school's magazine, and in the summer between school and university he sent four of his poems to a national magazine, the *Listener,* which published "Ultimatum" in his first term as an undergraduate. He later remembered life in college during the war as a time when "events cut us ruthlessly down to size" (*Required Writing,* p. 18), but he was still able to pursue his interest in jazz, something he shared with Kingsley Amis, the most famous of his Oxford friends. Amis later dedicated his novel *Lucky Jim* to Larkin, and their names were brought together again in two anthologies: D. J. Enright's *Poets of the 1950s* (1955) and Robert Conquest's *New Lines* (1956) both crystallized the Movement, the literary group now best remembered for being more of a journalistic invention than a genuinely cohesive school of writing. Having been exempted from military service owing to his poor eyesight— Larkin also suffered from a stutter, which only really abated when he reached his thirties—he stayed at Oxford for the full three years, graduating with a first class degree.

From these beginnings, Philip Larkin went on to become one of the most popular poets of the latter half of the twentieth century. For some he is a major poet whose influence is inescapable, while for others he is a minor poet whose lowered sights (to use Donald Davie's words) sold poetry short—for all, though, he remains a controversial and contradictory figure. He could gloomily state that "deprivation is for me what daffodils were for Wordsworth" (*Required Writing,* p. 47), yet his understanding of poetry was closely bound up with a belief in pleasure. He wrote an essay titled "The Pleasure Principle," which regretted the way that the roles of poet and critic and scholar had merged into one, making difficulty in poetry desirable, and in the preface to his 1971 edition of *The Oxford Book of Twentieth-Century English Verse* he described himself as someone who had tried to assemble an anthology that would give its readers pleasure, above all. Although that anthology allocated a substantial number of its pages to the great modernist poets W. B. Yeats and T. S. Eliot, Larkin believed modernism to be something of an aberration, and in the introduction to *All What Jazz,* the book that collected the record reviews he wrote throughout the 1960s for the *Telegraph* newspaper, he made his views on this period of artistic innovation clear. "It helps us neither to enjoy nor endure," he stated, and challengingly experimental works such as those by Ezra Pound, Charlie Parker, and Pablo Picasso he saw as "irresponsible exploitations of technique in contradiction of human life as we know it" (p. 17). In a key statement of 1955, in which he set down his views on his poetry, Larkin explained that "my prime responsibility is to the experience itself," and that "every poem must be its own sole freshly created universe" (*Required Writing,* p. 79), a world complete in itself. Modernist writers, and those now writing in that tradition, are difficult and fragmentary where Larkin is accessible and absolute: his poems, written largely in formal stanzas and dealing for the most part with everyday subjects from an individual perspective, allow their reader unusually close contact with the personality they present. His books have sold thousands of copies. Among his formal recognitions, he received the Queen's Gold Medal for poetry in 1965, and he was awarded the CBE in 1975. He turned down the offer to become poet laureate in the year before his death, but for many people this was a role he already unofficially held.

LARKIN THE NOVELIST

Although Larkin is now best remembered for his poetry, his ambition as a young man was to be known for his prose. "I wanted to 'be a novelist' in a way I never wanted to 'be a poet,' " he remembered in a late interview: "Novels seem to me to be richer, broader, deeper, more enjoyable than poems" (*Required Writing,* p. 63). *Jill,* his debut in the genre, was published in 1946, and just a year later *A Girl in Winter* appeared on the Faber and Faber list, garnering favorable reviews. After leaving Oxford, Larkin returned to Coventry to live with his parents, and it was here that he began work on the first story, which draws loosely on his undergraduate experience. He had experimented with prose while he was at St. John's, and in his final year he found imaginative escape from the pressures of exams by writing under the female pseudonym Brunette Coleman—his most conspicuous assumption of a literary personality obviously different to his own. Larkin composed freely as Brunette, completing one novella (*Trouble at Willow Gables*) and starting another (*Michaelmas Term at St. Bride's*), while also producing a short sequence of poems, a literary essay, and the first pages of an autobiography. Written for a coterie of friends, these pieces were never made publicly available during his lifetime. Larkin would later describe *Willow Gables* as an "unclassifiable story" (*Required Writing,* p. 24), disguising the fact that it belonged to the genre of schoolgirl fiction, in which he was well read, while also covering up the riskiness of its lesbian scenes. As James Booth notes in the comprehensive introduction to his 2002 edition of these stories, critics have debated the degree to which they should be "classified as pornography" (p. vii).

Trouble at Willow Gables centers on a five-pound note that Marie Moore is sent for her birthday. The note is confiscated by the school's headmistress and subsequently stolen back by Marie. She admits to the theft and is strongly encouraged to donate the money to the school's gymnasium fund, which, as a result, reaches the amount necessary to secure a further contribution from the wealthy Lord Amis. Safely in the fund, the note is then stolen again, this time by Marie's friend Margaret Tattenham, who wants the money to bet on a hotly tipped horse. The story proceeds to unravel the mystery of the missing note, coming to its conclusion with a harmonious resolution—which sees Hilary Russell expelled from the school for her inappropriate behavior.

Michaelmas Term at St Bride's, Larkin's hybrid sequel to *Willow Gables,* transplants his characters to a fictional Oxford women's college. The draft of this unfinished story makes greater play with its intended audience, as Larkin introduces a subversive undergraduate who shares her initials with one of his contemporaries (Diana Gollancz, a student at the Slade School of Fine Art), and includes a cameo appearance by another (fellow undergraduate Bruce Montgomery, whose pseudonymous detective novel *The Case of the Gilded Fly* is also mentioned). Larkin brings something of himself to the story too, making light of his early interest in psychology through Marie's well-intentioned efforts to cure her sister of her obsession with belts. In Brunette's literary essay, a manifesto on the writing of schoolgirl fiction, Larkin states that "the world of the school story ... is a private world" (p. 262) and that we are "not writing about the real, everyday world" (p. 266). Tellingly, though, the manuscript of *St. Bride's* breaks off just after Marie and Philippa, who have finally resorted to trying the erasing powers of alcohol, gaze into the very different world that is closed behind the doors of the pub's smoke room: "'If this was reality,' [Marie] decided, 'she would rather keep in the story'" (p. 230). This momentary and artfully contained introduction of the everyday alters the scope of Larkin's story in an important way, and he would soon retire his female alter ego in order to turn his attention to *Jill.*

This novel, which makes another imaginative return to Oxford and also briefly returns to Willow Gables, explores at length the gap between the private world of imagination and the real, everyday world of circumstance. In his autobiographical essay "Not the Place's Fault," a memoir of his childhood, Larkin remembered a friend's cousin, "a gentle, slightly older boy in whom I recognized for the first time the power to create and sustain private worlds" (*Further Requirements,* p. 8). The creative problem Larkin encountered in the writing of *St. Bride's* is localized in *Jill*'s wartime world in the character of John Kemp, who, in attempting to come to terms with the unfamiliarity of his new life as an Oxford undergraduate, comes up against "the enormous disparity ... between his imagination and what actually happened" (p. 151).

We first see John on the train to Oxford, so shy that he struggles even to eat his sandwiches in front of the other passengers in his carriage. He arrives in his college to find a tea party taking place in his shared rooms, hosted by his roommate, the confident, selfish, and socially comfortable Christopher Warner, who has smashed open John's crate of china to use his things. With no space to be himself, and unimpressed by the earnest eagerness of his fellow scholar, Whitbread—who, like him, has come to Oxford from a modest background, and whose first name, significantly, we never learn—John is seduced by Christopher's blinkered assertiveness, and we see him experiment with his personality as he tries to become more like Christopher. He even has a mildly flirtatious encounter with Elizabeth, who will become Christopher's girlfriend, but when she is together with Christopher the two of them leave him feeling "like a waiter in an expensive restaurant," their friendliness "like the tips they would give a waiter" (p. 91). His image of himself is shattered completely when he overhears them ridiculing him, and as he replays this moment in his mind his distorted reconstruction moves him away from the exact details of the original episode, as Larkin emphasizes the constant flux of the internal world of memory and imagination in which nothing can ever be fixed.

John's invention of his fictional sister Jill follows in response to this moment, and it creates one of the few occasions in the novel when Christopher acknowledges his roommate on his own terms: "John saw with gathering amazement that he had said something that made Christopher envious of him—only for this moment, perhaps, but none the less envious" (p. 99). What Christopher envies here, though, is something John envies too: the ideal of a close connection, which his fabricated memories of Jill have suggested but which is actually absent from his world. John holds onto the idea of Jill, though, writing a short story that imagines her at school at Willow Gables before filling out the details of her days in a diary. As Andrew Motion suggests in his critical book *Philip Larkin,* imaginative writing is of real fixing importance here, being for John "not a refuge but an action—an attempt to understand and control" (p. 45).

What control he exerts over his creation soon disappears, though, as she frees herself from his pages and makes her way into his world—or so he imagines: "as he was absently fingering the edges of an uncut page with a transient sense of frustration ... he received a shock that could not have been greater if a brick had been thrown through the plate-glass shop-window" (p. 137). This is a very carefully constructed moment: it happens in a bookshop, a place full of fictions, where the uncut page hints toward the pristine promise of the unknown, and the image of the brick breaking through the window suggests the irruption of the real into the imaginary. Like the stories Larkin wrote as Brunette Coleman, *Jill* is structured around a single term, and John spends what remains of it trying in vain to integrate the similarly named Gillian into his life. After his attempt to host her to tea is halted by the interfering Elizabeth, he gets drunk at the end of the term and kisses her at a party—before being thrown into a fountain.

Just as *Jill* draws on aspects of Larkin's undergraduate experience, so *A Girl in Winter* draws on aspects of his professional experience as it follows a working day in the life of Katharine Lind, a young librarian. After twice trying for entry into the civil service, Larkin applied for and won a position at a local library in Wellington, Shropshire, which he took up in

December 1943. He would remain a librarian for the rest of his life, doing his writing only in his spare time. He moved to the University College of Leicester in 1946, and it was here that he first met Monica Jones, a young lecturer in English, with whom he would have the most important and long-lasting of his relationships. The general basis in autobiography is not the only continuity between the two novels, though, as Larkin explained in a letter to an old school friend: "it is a deathly book and has for theme the relinquishing of live response to life. The central character, Katharine, picks up where John left off and carries the story on into the frozen wastes" (*Selected Letters,* p. 109).

A Girl in Winter is divided into three parts: the first and the third are both set in the same wartime present, while the second flashes back to the time Katharine spent in England as a schoolgirl, when she stayed with her pen pal Robin Fennel and his family. Like John and his experience of Oxford, Katharine finds England unfamiliarly new. But where Christopher Warner had imposed himself on the world around him, Robin, on the train from Dover, "seemed perfectly adjusted to all his surroundings—including her—and able to withdraw his real personality elsewhere" (p. 77). This second part of the novel is much concerned with manners, the familiar customs that facilitate smooth personal relations but do so at the expense of real individuality: Robin's true self is what Katharine longs to see as she allows herself to acknowledge her feelings for him, not the perfectly mannered gentleman he unfailingly presents. When will he "start behaving naturally" (p. 90), she wonders on the first night of her stay, and only on her final evening does he manage to express his innermost feelings.

Katharine's later experience in England is similarly confusing. Having moved from her home in an unnamed European country because of the war, she now works in a gloomy library run by the petty Mr. Anstey, a man who never fails to make the most of his small authority. We first meet him in a scene that introduces the novel's fundamental concerns with the difficulty of individual assertion and the struggle of personal relations: his "usual performance" (p.

16) gradually subsides as he lectures Katharine about a misplaced book, until she is finally able to hear "the voice that was natural to him" (p. 18). This tension between performance and natural behavior is explored in further detail when Katharine is asked to accompany home her colleague Miss Green, who is suffering from a toothache. They pass a dentist, and Katharine persuades Miss Green—like Whitbread in *Jill*, we never learn her first name—to have the hurting tooth taken out. As Miss Green undergoes the procedure, though, Katharine realizes that her lonely need to involve herself with a vulnerable other is causing something to happen whose consequences are irrevocably real: she "could almost feel the pain exploding beneath the anaesthetic, and nerved herself against a shriek. It seemed impossible for the girl to feel nothing" (p. 48). The novel's final section shifts the focus to more intimate relations as circumstance forces Katharine to visit Veronica Parbury, a woman who cares permanently for her invalid mother and who is revealed to be romantically involved with Mr. Anstey, before it returns to Katherine in the closing pages. Robin, now in the army, visits her unexpectedly on embarkation leave, and the book ends with their thinly resurrected relationship approaching a decisive moment.

Larkin too was approaching a decisive moment in his creative life. He started work on a third novel in the autumn of 1947, but he would never finish another story again. Drafts survive of two of the books he attempted in this period, *No for an Answer* and *A New World Symphony*; he had planned that both were to conclude in America. Early in 1950 he wrote a despairing letter to his agent, Alan Pringle: "I have been trying to write novels and failing either to finish them or make them worth finishing," he confessed (*Selected Letters*, p. 158).

LARKIN THE POET: EARLY POETRY

While he was struggling with his attempts toward another novel, Larkin sent his agent the manuscript of a new volume of poems. "In the Grip of Light" went around London's publishers, but it was accepted by none of them, and the news came as a keen disappointment to a young writer already beginning to worry that his best work would soon be behind him. It was a time of emotional turmoil too: his father died in March 1948, and two months later Larkin became engaged to Ruth Bowman, his girlfriend of four years. The arrangement caused Larkin much personal anxiety until he finally broke it off, in 1950, and although he would have relationships with other women—most notably with Monica Jones—he would never marry, living for most of his life in rented rooms. In the unpublished poem "To My Wife," which dates from 1951, he imagines married life as "Another way of suffering" (l. 13), and the question of marriage is one to which he would return in his writing a number of times, if not always in a direct way. Just as the complexity of personal relations holds the focus of *A Girl in Winter*, many of his poems stage discussions about solitude and sociality, selfishness and selflessness, and in 1951 he also wrote a dramatic debate ("Round Another Point") whose two characters argue for and against marriage. If this was a time when Larkin came up against the limits of his personality, and a time when he came up against the limits of his creative imagination, it was also a time when he was forced to accept those limits, and the rejection of "In the Grip of Light" in 1948 ultimately started him working toward the poems on which his reputation now rests.

Larkin had published his poems while he was at school and university, and a collection of his early pieces, *The North Ship*, appeared in 1945, a year after a selection of his writing was included in the anthology *Poetry from Oxford in Wartime*. In a preface he wrote for the reissue of *The North Ship* in 1966, he sought to position the book's contents as the miscellanies of a young writer yet to develop a consistent style, finding in them the various influences of W. H. Auden, Dylan Thomas, and most strongly of all, W. B. Yeats. He traced the beginning of this infatuation with the music of Yeats back to hearing the poet Vernon Watkins address the Oxford English Club, and he also thought of it as something that had been relatively short-lived and come to its end—he would later say that his reading of Thomas

Hardy's poetry in 1946 had been revelatory, bringing the happy realization that "One could simply relapse back into one's own life and write from it" (*Required Writing*, p. 175). James Booth in *Philip Larkin: Writer* (1992) has suggested that the example of Yeats imposed on Larkin "a mythic rhetoric which was untrue to his sensibility" (p. 66), while Andrew Motion argues in his critical study that this early source of inspiration was more profoundly lasting, and he traces aspects of it through to the poems of Larkin's final collection, *High Windows* (1974).

Although there is a brief reminder of Brunette Coleman in poem XX ("I see a girl dragged by the wrists"), whose speaker yearns to "be that girl" (l. 42), a number of these pieces anticipate aspects of Larkin's later work. As well as looking back to the Yeats he was reading in Shropshire, the italicized refrain of the poem that begins the book ("All Catches Alight") looks forward to the counterpointing style he would develop into conversational ease in his major collections, as the wonderful promise of spring is repeatedly muted by the deathly line *"A drum taps: a wintry drum"* (l. 9). It is poem XXX ("So through that unripe day you bore your head") that provides one of the most immediate points of connection, though: here the "severed image" of the speaker's addressee "grew sweeter" (l. 4), until over time the image became "only a name" (l. 8), one signifying nothing more than a belief "embedded in the static past" (l. 10). The distance between words and images and the world, representation and reality, is similarly the subject of a number of the poems Larkin would collect into his first major book of poetry, *The Less Deceived*, which he dedicated to Monica Jones.

THE LESS DECEIVED

Larkin took up a position at Queen's University, Belfast, in September 1950, and this was one of the happiest periods of his life, following the personal and creative troubles of the previous two years. Chastened by the rejection of "In the Grip of Light," he had a pamphlet 'XX Poems' privately printed in 1951, and many of these would make their way into *The Less Deceived*.

The fledgling Marvell Press had approached Larkin about the possibility of publishing a collection of his poems, and the book appeared in 1955, financed initially by subscription.

Beginning to give up on his novels, he made a breakthrough in his poetry by writing "At Grass," which he completed in January 1950. That poem was inspired by a television documentary about racehorses, but many of the book's other poems show Larkin writing directly out of personal experience. He had met Ruth Bowman while he was working in the library at Shropshire, and it was in the library at Belfast that he met Winifred Arnott, a young graduate working there for a year. He soon felt strongly toward Winifred, and she is remembered in the poem that opens the collection, "Lines on a Young Lady's Photograph Album." The poem follows the thoughts of its speaker as he pores over the album's pictures, aware that he looks at these images of the past without risk, since this solitary activity is very different from a live exchange with the album's subject. The description of photography as an inadequate recording art hints toward the creative unfaithfulness of written representation, and "Maiden Name," which Larkin wrote after Winifred's marriage, reframes the theme of "Lines on a Young Lady's Photograph Album" with a specifically linguistic focus. In the same way that the album's photographs persist through time, keeping past images continually alive, so the newly redundant name suggests someone who no longer exists.

The fixing power of language and representation more generally is also the subject of "At Grass," which Larkin placed at the very end of the book. This poem begins with its speaker struggling to see the retired horses in the quiet countryside that now surrounds them, before meditating on the difference between their former fame and present anonymity. The poem emphasizes the distance between the freedom of the horses' present and the classifying world of almanacs and stopwatches and other means of measuring and recording that was their past. Some critics have suggested that "At Grass" holds a deeper meaning than is initially apparent: Blake Morrison, for instance, in his study *The*

Movement, writes that Larkin allows the horses to "symbolize loss of power," thereby tapping "nostalgia for a past 'glory that was England' " (p. 82), but this poem can also be seen to celebrate the new sense of escape that was beginning to manifest itself in many aspects of Larkin's life.

Indeed, not all of the book's poems are concerned with the representation of others. "If, My Darling" calls attention to the contrast between the way things seem on the outside and the way they actually are on the inside, taking for its subject the one thing about which the speaker has some sure knowledge—himself. What, Larkin's poem wonders, would this speaker's darling see were she to look not into his eyes but through them, and into his consciousness? A similar questioning of the self occurs in "Reasons for Attendance," but in this poem the difficulty of truly knowing oneself is Larkin's theme. Drawn by the sound of a jazz trumpet, the poem's speaker looks through a window into a party and proceeds to convince himself that although those inside are happy with music and the promise of sex, he is much happier with art. It was suggested to Larkin in an interview that the final line of the poem doubles the entire work back onto itself, and later in that conversation he admitted the need for tension in his poems, saying, "I think one has to dramatize oneself a little" (*Further Requirements,* p. 23).

"Reasons for Attendance" is a miniature drama of the self, and while many of the poems in *The Less Deceived* take their speaking selves for their subject, there is a further tension between the dramatized personalities presented in the poems and the complex personality of the poet behind them. As John Bayley suggests in *The Uses of Division* (1976): "We know, and the poet knows we know, how little honest the poetic art of the self can be. Which makes it all the more remarkable that Philip Larkin has contrived to make it so, or to seem so" (p. 166). What Bayley here calls the poetic art of the self is something always constructed: even though many of Larkin's poems draw their inspiration from his personal experiences, the self he presents in the poems can only be a version of himself, one

which has slipped the original experience for the drama of literary representation. Larkin's notebooks reveal the many drafts he would work through—sometimes over a period of years—before arriving at the final versions of his poems, and although the complex formal structures he often employs advertise the artifice of his poetry, the conversational tone of many poems maintains the illusion that he is speaking through them directly.

This is true of "Church Going," which is based on a visit Larkin (an agnostic) made to a church outside Belfast and which illustrates how he was able to make this focus on the self more widely relevant. The poem begins by concentrating on its solitary speaker, who enters the church only once he is sure he will be alone. After his awkwardly reverent appearance has been briefly and memorably described, the element of performance comes strongly to the fore as he reads aloud from the lectern and pronounces a verse more loudly than he had intended. Having completed his visit, the speaker then meditates on the role of churches in a society that has less and less use for them. Ultimately, Larkin had found a way of making use of personal experience and a way of broadening personal experience into general truth—and he would perfect this way of speaking to and for his readers in his next collection.

THE WHITSUN WEDDINGS

Larkin's second major collection of mature poetry was published by Faber and Faber in February 1964, and like *The Less Deceived* it was a slim book, gathering together just over thirty poems. The book consolidated Larkin's reputation and made him one of the country's most popular poets. To use the words of Andrew Motion's biography, *The Whitsun Weddings* turned Larkin's voice into "one of the means by which his country recognised itself" (p. 343). He made an audio recording of the poems for the Marvell Press (as he had done for *The Less Deceived*), and he also agreed to the making of a film about his work, which would later be shown on national television. Here was a poet writing about the real, everyday world around him, and writing about it in an accessible way. In the poem "A Study of Reading Habits," Larkin dismisses books as "a load of crap" (l. 18), finding the disappointments of minor characters to be far more real than the exaggerated glories of heroes and rogueries of villains, but he still has one eye on the ideal. In a radio broadcast about his poetry he made for the BBC later in 1964, Larkin described his fondness for billboards: "they seem to me beautiful and in an odd way sad" (*Further Requirements,* p. 81), he said, and two poems in the book are written about the world of advertising while others discuss consumer culture more generally. "Sunny Prestatyn" describes a railway poster's image of a bathing girl defaced in an aggressive way as "too good for this life" (l. 21), while "Essential Beauty" explores the contrast between the shiny pictures that show "how life should be" (l. 6) and the drab environments in which they are often displayed. The gap between the real and the ideal is also invoked from a more intimate perspective in the book's poems about love.

Larkin moved to Yorkshire in 1955 to become librarian at the University of Hull, and he would hold the position and live in Hull for the rest of his life. It was a time of expansion, and his job became a demanding one as he oversaw two major extensions to the library. Larkin was proud of his professional achievements, but he later admitted in an interview to wondering what his poems would have been like had he written them in the freshness of the morning rather than after a tiring day at work. Although Hull looms large in *The Whitsun Weddings,* Larkin looks back on his years in Belfast in "The Importance of Elsewhere." This poem feels relief that "Strangeness made sense" (l. 2) in the difference of another country, even if anxiety returns with the knowledge that being separate back in England has grave consequences: "Here no elsewhere underwrites my existence" (l. 12), the poem concludes, raising the possibility that its speaker will never find anywhere to call home. Hull, though, was the place where the reclusive Larkin finally chose to stay, and here the Hermit of Hull (as he later became known) could hide himself

away from mainstream culture and feel on the outside of things.

In "Here," the poem that begins the book, Larkin takes his readers on an imaginative journey to this remote part of Yorkshire. Three repetitions of the word "swerving" in the poem's opening stanza approach the city through the window of a train's carriage, as the magnificent opening sentence, which swerves its way through three quarters of the poem, slows its rush of descriptive detail for the "surprise" of a large town and eventually comes to rest in the hinterland immediately before the North Sea, "where removed lives // Loneliness clarifies" (ll. 24–25). In a personal continuation of the quiet provinciality celebrated by "At Grass," the three repetitions of the word "here" in the poem's closing stanza create a sense of presence that is undercut by the possibility of "unfenced existence" remaining "out of reach" (ll. 31, 32).

There are moments, though, where wonder is present in the book's poems. If not being in control is frequently a source of despair for Larkin, then unknowing is a state of being in which there is always the possibility for happy surprise as well as sadness. "First Sight" imagines such an experience as its worldly speaker reflects that lambs newly born into the hostile environment of winter snow will soon know the comforts of spring's rejuvenation. A personal moment of unexpected wonder is similarly celebrated in the "The Whitsun Weddings." Like "Here," the poem is written around a train journey, a mode of travel that frees the solitary speaker to focus on his surroundings and describe the country he sees flashing past his window. Discussing the poem in his book *Thomas Hardy and British Poetry,* Donald Davie writes that the England in Larkin's poems is "the England we have inhabited" (p. 64) and goes on to single out Larkin's "scrupulously neutral" voice, which refuses to suggest a meaning to "the way preindustrial things like farms, cattle, hedges, and grass are interspersed with industrial things like chemical froth and dismantled cars" (p. 65), preferring simply to accept the world observed. Based on a trip Larkin took from Hull to London in 1955, the poem—which he only completed three years later—remembers the congregation at station after station of newly married couples boarding the same train, all racing to the capital to begin their honeymoons. From start to finish "The Whitsun Weddings" is narrated from the speaker's seat by the window, and this is a work of realistic description for all but its last two lines, in which Larkin introduces a symbolic image that attempts to concentrate the power of the journey's "frail / Travelling coincidence" (ll. 74–75) and make it last beyond the train's termination. As the train pulls into the station, there swells "A sense of falling, like an arrow-shower / Sent out of sight, somewhere becoming rain" (ll. 79–80). With this concluding vision, the poem transcends the particularity of the afternoon's journey by suggesting something beyond the speaker's immediate comprehension: this shower of arrows is "sent out of sight" to somewhere other than the station, "becoming rain" at another time.

Larkin once revealed in an interview that he ordered the poems in his collections very carefully, and he does this to great effect in *The Whitsun Weddings,* often placing two poems that present contrasting perspectives alongside one another, so that each complicates the other. Immediately following "Here," for instance, is "Mr. Bleaney," a poem that undercuts the expansive natural possibility of "unfenced existence" with the dreary reality of a life lived in rented rooms and inescapable proximity to others, while "Self's the Man," a poem that describes the less glamorous side of love, is placed after the poem that gives the book its title. This brief meditation on selfishness deflates the promise of married bliss with a reality of hassle, before concluding that bachelor and married man are ultimately alike in the selfish pursuit of their own, different ends. The poem arrives at its conclusion, though, only for the speaker's final doubt to double it back on itself—once again dramatizing the question of just how well one can really know oneself.

Something similar happens in "Dockery and Son," which ponders the question of marriage and children. In this poem, which was inspired by a visit Larkin made to his old Oxford college, the speaker learns that one of his contemporaries now has a son studying there. The element of

private performance is strongly present in the opening stanza, as the speaker retreats from the dean's conversation into the internal world of memory, recalling having to give "'Our version' of 'these incidents last night'" (l. 7). But his assurance disappears in the solitude of the train journey back home, as he finds himself unable to come to terms with the reality of Dockery's actions: "Well, it just shows / How much … How little …" (ll. 18–19). These two ellipses prepare the way for a third ellipsis, which marks the poem's turning point: the speaker shifts from a potentially sympathetic view of Dockery to one that sees him in somewhat caricatured terms, and Larkin brings the poem to its conclusion with one of his plainest and bleakest big finishes as he describes the passing of time as leaving only "what something hidden from us chose, / And age, and then only the end of age (ll. 47–48).

The short poem "Ignorance," which follows on from "Dockery and Son," describes how even "our flesh / Surrounds us with its own decisions" (ll. 11–12), and *The Whitsun Weddings* is full of instances of individuals not being their own centers of gravity. The speaker of "Mr. Bleaney" knows only too well the habits of his room's former occupant, to the extent that Mr. Bleaney's habits have become his own, while "Afternoons" makes the point most clearly in its concluding observation about the young mothers whose lives it has described and imagined: "Something is pushing them / To the side of their own lives" (ll. 23–24). The poem makes it clear that the mothers are being pushed, but it refuses to say what exactly is doing the pushing. "Afternoons" foregrounds the element of time—in its title and in its opening line, which situates the poem at the end of summer, mapping the decline of the day onto the decline of the year—and a number of poems follow "Dockery and Son" by taking the inevitability of time's passing as their subject. "Ambulances," a poem about death, focuses on the ultimate end, while "Love Songs in Age," one of two poems written around music, idealizes love as the permanent "brilliance" (l. 17), which promises always to "solve, and satisfy" (l. 20) but which never has done so and never will for the woman whose life it describes.

"An Arundel Tomb," the poem that brings *The Whitsun Weddings* to its close, similarly takes the idea of love for its subject. Positioned at the very end of the book because of its uplifting final line, the poem describes the "faithfulness in effigy" (l. 14) the tomb's hand-holding figures display, a faithfulness which was originally "just a detail friends would see" (l. 15) but which has, over time, taken on a transcendent meaning that is resonantly sounded as the poem's conclusion: "What will survive of us is love" (l. 42). If the two repetitions of the word "almost" in the poem's penultimate line qualify the finality of this closing statement through their suggestion of hesitation, then the word "almost" also describes another poem about love Larkin was writing at this time but never finished, "The Dance." He had worked in the library with Maeve Brennan ever since he first arrived in Hull, but it was only in 1960 that their relationship became a romantic one, and "The Dance" remembers a university gathering Larkin had unwillingly attended, only to be there with Brennan. Where "The Whitsun Weddings" celebrates the love of others, and where "An Arundel Tomb" finds comfort in the idea of love, "The Dance" records the coming together of "me / As I am now" (ll. 61–62) with "you as you are now" (l. 62), before a third repetition, almost of disbelief, suggests the presence of the moment: "And now" (l. 63). In an excerpt from a letter Maeve Brennan published in her memoir *The Philip Larkin I Knew*, Larkin described the poem as "a great obstacle in my creative life" (p. 58), and he wondered whether he would be able to write anything else until he had finished it. He ultimately abandoned it, and the poems he wrote after this would be very different.

HIGH WINDOWS

After finally giving up on "The Dance," Larkin started work on "Solar." This brief lyric, a hymn to the sun, typifies a tendency that emerges strongly in his third and final collection, which was published by Faber and Faber in June 1974. Where many of the poems in Larkin's previous two books had taken their speaker for their subject, "Solar" attempts to disguise the presence of the speaking self. "The eye sees you / Simplified by distance" (ll. 8–9), the second stanza begins, carefully avoiding the pronoun, and although its personification of the sun as "you" suggests a reciprocal "me," only in the concluding stanza is the speaker's presence tacitly acknowledged: the individual becomes part of the wider community, and the singular becomes part of the plural in the poem's description of "our" needs. "The Trees," which also takes the natural world for its subject, works in much the same way. Larkin wrote this poem about the view from the high windows of his flat in Hull, and its last lines, which celebrate spring's return in newly growing leaves, sound an archetypal message of hope: "Last year is dead, they seem to say, / Begin afresh, afresh, afresh" (ll. 11–12), where the word "seem" admits the particularity of the perspective. If his creative inability to finish "The Dance" was symptomatic of his personal inability to commit to a close relationship with Maeve Brennan, then Larkin was forced to take a different approach to the writing of these poems, using the self more sparingly and more questioningly than before. That failure results in a book whose poems are angrier, more fragmented, and less immediately personal than anything he had previously chosen to publish.

"Solar" wanted to make a new start by returning to an elemental source, and the book's opening poem, "To the Sea," also reaches back in time: Larkin not only revisits childhood memory but also goes imaginatively back to the place where his parents first met. Summer holidays by the sea are "half an annual pleasure, half a rite" (l. 18), and the older self who recalls searching the sands for famous cricketers in his younger days now exults at finding others living out a similar experience: "Still going on, all of it, still going on!" (l. 10). This is the first of the book's many exclamations. Larkin had used them to especially ambiguous effect in the last line of "Absences" (from *The Less Deceived*), and they appeared occasionally in *The Whitsun Weddings,* but throughout *High Windows* they pose a very real problem of interpretation. What is the tone, exactly, of this exclamation? Is it one of happiness, for instance, or one of surprise? The poem refuses to decide either way, and if this line stands out from those that surround it, then something similar happens to the poem's speaker in the concluding stanza. Where in previous books personal experience had provided a singular example of a general truth common to all, Larkin uses the word "these" to describe the holidaymakers on the beach, keeping the speaker separate from this temporary community.

The rituals of English society are also the subject of "Show Saturday," and in place of the neutral voice that passively recorded the world seen from the window of a railway carriage, these poems openly praise the traditions they record and delight in their detail. "Show Saturday," like "To the Sea," describes the fragile events of a single day, as its speaker documents the many attractions of an agricultural show, its capacious lines struggling to cram everything in. The speaker is just a visitor to the show, though, an outsider enjoying the spectacle: again, it is "something they share / That breaks ancestrally each year into / Regenerate union" (ll. 62–64) and not something shared by everyone. By concluding the poem with the wish for the show to "always be there" (l. 64), Larkin pledges his belief in these everyday customs, even as he acknowledges that they are not his own.

These moments of local community are especially prized by Larkin because they have continued to exist throughout the momentous social changes of the previous decade, and a number of the poems in *High Windows* make clear reference to the time of their writing, sometimes bitterly so. The satirically titled "Homage to a Government," the only one of Larkin's poems to be published with its date of composition, objects to a decision to bring home soldiers "For lack of money" (l. 2), while "Going, Going," a reactionary poem written for a government report about the environment, is angry about the disappearance of the England its speaker has always known: the crowd in the motorway café whose "kids are screaming for more" (l. 21) are signs of the change that will lead, he worries, to his idea of England becoming the stuff of ideals—something found only in books.

Social change is not always a bad thing for Larkin, though, and "Annus Mirabilis" describes how in 1963 the shame of sexual desire suddenly disappeared, making every life "A quite unlosable game" (l. 15). The only problem, for the poem's speaker, is that it all happened "just to late for me" (l. 18), and its sardonically jaunty rhythm and rhymes give way in "High Windows" to an angrier treatment of the subject, which makes use of a harsh demotic idiom. "When I see a couple of kids / And guess he's fucking her" (ll. 1–2) the poem begins, before going on to compare the newfound sexual freedoms of the present day to the religious ones of the speaker's generation. The speaker here is older than the people in his poem, and rather than force a harmonizing conclusion there comes instead an image that the poem refuses to explain: high windows, the glass of those windows, and beyond that glass "the deep blue air, that shows / Nothing, and is nowhere, and is endless" (ll. 19–20). This is a kind of inverse ideal: there is nothing to be seen, as Larkin fails to find a solving explanation for his speaker's situation.

Larkin said in an interview that the demotic language of "High Windows" and "This Be the Verse" was intended to shock. The latter poem, with its harsh and crudely ambiguous opening line—"They fuck you up, your mum and dad"—is one of several poems in the book in which "readers are confronted with severely partial viewpoints," to use Stephen Regan's words in his critical study *Philip Larkin* (p. 130). The poem replaces the personal "I" with the impersonally general "you," and its monosyllables settle down into a formal pattern that reinforces the reductive simplicity of the speaker's perspective. The pattern is upset, though, momentarily, in the line that begins the third and final quatrain: "Man hands on misery to man" (l. 9). The stress, which has to be placed on the first "man," works against the metrical expectations the poem has established, thus beginning the line on a more serious footing, while the close repetition of sound in "man" and "hands" suggests confinement. The alliteration of "m" sounds along the line creates a sense of forward movement even as the final repetition of "man" circles it back onto itself, giving it a formal complexity lacking in the rest of the poem. Following the death of his father in 1948, Larkin became increasingly supportive of his mother until her death in 1977, and he lodged with her in Leicester for two years before he left for Belfast. He was sometimes frustrated by her aging, though, and had feared death himself from an early age. Two poems in *High Windows* address these universal subjects. "The Old Fools" takes an unsympathetic view of old people as its lengthy stanzas formally suggest the lack of focus it describes, a consequence of not being able to live in the here and now, while "The Building" is a study of hospitals, places that finally come to mean "a struggle to transcend / The thought of dying" (ll. 60–61).

Two more poems in *High Windows* complicate Larkin's ongoing debate about selfishness and selflessness, each concluding with a sense of weary resignation—and the poems had to remain finally inconclusive because the tension they explore is one Larkin would never finally resolve. Christopher Warner in *Jill* thanks John Kemp for a favor with the words "That's white of you, old man," and that word "white" forms the foundation of "Sympathy in White Major," a poem that documents Larkin's unlikely appropriation of French writing, as revealed by Barbara Everett's influential 1980 article "Philip Larkin: After Symbolism." In debates about contemporary poetry, Larkin's work is frequently seen as an exemplary case of accessibility, but when *High Windows* was first published a number of readers found some of the poems to be obscure. As Everett writes in her article, the difficulty of "Sympathy in White Major" lies in "how to take it," since there is "the absence of a sense of why the man and the drink and the fantasies of praise frankly matter at all" (p. 230).

Not only do those fantasies constitute yet another manifestation of the ideal, but the poem is significant in this volume because it focuses attention back onto the self. Its speaker soliloquizes on his altruistic behavior as he mixes himself a gin and tonic, before vainly imagining the tributes from others that gather to a toast in his honor at the poem's end: *"Here's to the whitest man I know"* (l. 23) the voices finally chorus,

before the speaker regretfully continues the sentence "Though white is not my favourite colour" (l. 24). For all his selflessness, he is still alone, and the implication is that he should have been more selfish. "Vers de Société" sees the situation in slightly different terms: this poem's speaker would rather indulge his desire to be solitary than spend meaningless time with others, but "Beyond the light stand failure and remorse" (l. 35), and he finds himself accepting the invitation to the sherry party.

Just as Larkin as an undergraduate had written under the female pseudonym Brunette Coleman, so his early poem "Wedding-Wind" (from *The Less Deceived*) was written from the perspective of a newly married young woman, and he similarly writes as other people in *High Windows*. "Posterity," which returns to a favorite theme by satirizing the professional study of literature, shows Larkin's movements in this direction. The poem begins with its speaker situating his biographer Jake Balokowsky into his academic context before allowing him to address the reader directly. No initial placing is involved in the three poems collected together under the title "Livings," though, as Larkin collapses the distance between speaker and character so that we are addressed by three very different people. The first poem is spoken by someone who deals "with farmers, things like dips and feed" (l. 1), while the second seems to be spoken by the solitary keeper of a lighthouse. In the third, spoken by someone dining in a university setting, the contrast of the poem's formal elements (the regularity of its iambic rhythm and the fixity of its rhyme scheme) with its forensic language creates a pleasurably light verse, which unexpectedly gives way to a conclusion of natural beauty, as "Chaldean constellations / Sparkle over crowded roofs" (ll. 23–24). These three poems present us with three brief glimpses into three very different lives, and we are forced to work out an understanding of the speakers and their situations through the incidental details they are each made to mention.

In his previous two books, Larkin's poems had presented characters in the first person not noticeably different from himself, and in other poems in this book, such as "This Be the Verse," he resigns that conversational persona to present a blinkered speaker who has no time for second thoughts. Here, though, he adapts his technique to allow the first person to present obviously different characters. When Larkin introduced the book's concluding poem, "The Explosion," on a radio program that celebrated his fiftieth birthday, he said that he wanted to write "different kinds of poems that might be by different people" (*Further Requirements,* p. 92). The poems of *High Windows* begin to fulfill that aim.

CONCLUSION

Larkin wrote only a handful of poems after the publication of *High Windows,* and many of these were merely occasional pieces, such as "Bridge for the Living," words for a cantata which he was commissioned to write for the completion of the Humber Bridge near Hull. The major "Aubade," one of the last poems he chose to publish, extends the concern with old age by taking death as its subject, that "special way of being afraid / No trick dispels" (ll. 21–22). After four stanzas of unflinching personal meditation, the closing lines open out to reveal perspectives broader than the speaker's own, as "all the uncaring / Intricate rented world begins to rouse" (ll. 46–47). The fineness of the language here, the delicate blending of sounds across the break and along the line, gives a formal grandeur to the new day's beginning: "Work has to be done" (l. 49), and some temporary solace at least is found in the rhythms of the natural world and the connections of human enterprise, as the speaker's singularity is once again placed into a wider context of community. Isolation is inescapable, though, in "Love Again," a brutal piece about the loneliness of sexual jealousy, which was included only in Anthony Thwaite's posthumous edition of the poems. Larkin here attempts to work out "why it never worked for me" (l. 15)—why, that is, he was never able to settle for the sort of life and love that many of his poems suggest he so badly desired. As in "Dockery and Son," the past is seen to shape the present in ways now hopelessly beyond individual control, and "Love Again"

comes to its close with its speaker searching for some kind of explanation:

Something to do with violence
A long way back, and wrong rewards,
And arrogant eternity.

(ll. 16–18)

This was the last substantial poem Larkin wrote. A year before his death he said in an interview that "I haven't given poetry up, but I rather think poetry has given me up" (*Further Requirements,* p. 112). As a young man, he turned back to poetry when his novels began to fail him, but after these words were broadcast in March 1984 he published no more creative work. Having lived almost all of his life in rented rooms, needing to feel free from the fixity of attachment, he had bought his first and only house in 1974, and it was there in Hull that he lived out his final years, latterly with Monica Jones, before his death from esophageal cancer late in 1985. A memorial service was held in Westminster Abbey.

The years following Larkin's death have been nothing if not controversial, as private revelation has complicated the public personality Larkin presented in his poems, interviews, and other published pieces. Anthony Thwaite's edition of the *Collected Poems* (1988) drew on the notebooks in which Larkin composed his poetry to set the work he chose to collect alongside a number of unpublished and unfinished pieces. If poems such as "The Dance" and "Love Again" divulged just how deeply personal his writing could sometimes be, then Thwaite's subsequent selection of Larkin's letters (1992) provided a far more disturbing glimpse into the writer's private life: here, to the great shock of many, was the correspondence of a man variously sexist, racist, and reactionary. Further revelation followed just a year later with the publication of Andrew Motion's superb biography, *Philip Larkin: A Writer's Life* (1993), which revealed for the first time the full extent of his relationships with Monica and Maeve and his few other affairs. From the outside, this dour librarian led a dull life, traveling to mainland Europe only twice as an adult (latterly to receive the Shakespeare Prize in Hamburg), but, as Motion writes in the biography, it was "a much more dramatic and intense life than he let on, though it was performed on an inner stage rather than before the wide world" (p. xix).

Two further publications have appeared. James Booth's edition of *Trouble at Willow Gables* (2002) presents the pieces the young Larkin wrote under the pseudonym Brunette Coleman, along with the two surviving attempts toward a third novel. *No for an Answer* draws loosely on his broken engagement with Ruth Bowman, while the fragments of *A New World Symphony* are based on Monica Jones and her life as a lecturer at the University College of Leicester. Also included in this volume are two dramatic debates (on the subjects of writing and marriage), and two early verse dramas (one tellingly titled "Behind the Façade") are similarly included in A. T. Tolley's edition of Larkin's *Early Poems and Juvenilia* (2005)—youthful anticipations of the dramatic method he would perfect in his mature poetry. Tolley's volume follows the young writer's early development, from his schoolboy beginnings through to the publication of his first book, *The North Ship,* and he justified his edition by appealing to Larkin's continuing popularity and wide study. These books will no doubt be augmented by further revelatory publications, and further controversy will no doubt follow too.

Several studies have sought to rehabilitate Larkin's reputation after the backlash that followed the publication of the *Selected Letters.* Stephen Cooper's *Philip Larkin: Subversive Writer* (2004) places its emphasis on the early work, suggesting that Larkin's fundamental concern was to "unsettle many of those … reactionary attitudes that he expresses in some of the published letters" (p. 2), whereas John Osborne's purpose in *Larkin, Ideology, and Critical Violence* (2008) is "not so much to annihilate biographicalism" but rather to "dislodge it from a monopoly position" on critical work by focusing attention onto the careful construction of the poems (p. 25). We know a great deal about Philip Larkin: although he asked for his diaries to be destroyed on his death, he was a voluminous correspondent, and he wrote a number of autobio-

graphical vignettes about significant periods in his life. These critical books have begun the process of working out how full a role biographical knowledge should play in the interpretation of his poetry, and in doing so they engage with the situation "I Remember, I Remember" presents, in which public speech is a selective performance of private thought. Larkin wrote in a late letter that he wanted to live under a pseudonym, but his true self will more than likely remain as finally elusive as it is now.

Selected Bibliography

WORKS OF PHILIP LARKIN

NOVELS

Jill. London: Fortune Press, 1946. Reissued, London: Faber, 1964.

A Girl in Winter. London: Faber, 1947.

POETRY

The North Ship. London: Fortune Press, 1945. Reissued, London: Faber, 1966.

The Less Deceived. Hessle, U.K.: Marvell Press, 1955.

The Whitsun Weddings. London: Faber, 1964.

High Windows. London: Faber, 1974.

PROSE

All What Jazz: A Record Diary, 1961–1968. London: Faber, 1970.

Required Writing: Miscellaneous Pieces, 1955–1982. London: Faber, 1983.

AS EDITOR

The Oxford Book of Twentieth-Century English Verse. Chosen by Philip Larkin. Oxford: Clarendon Press, 1973.

AUDIO RECORDINGS

Philip Larkin Reads "The Less Deceived." Marvell Press, 1958.

Philip Larkin Reads "The Whitsun Weddings." Marvell Press, 1965.

POSTHUMOUS SELECTIONS AND COLLECTIONS

Collected Poems. Edited by Anthony Thwaite. London: Faber, 1988. (Contains unpublished and unfinished material with contents chronologically arranged; all poetic extracts in the essay are taken from this edition.) 2nd ed., London: Marvel, 2003. (Contains published poems by collection, with appendices of the published by uncollected poems written between 1940 and 1974, and the published by uncollected poems written after 1974.)

Selected Letters of Philip Larkin, 1940–1985. Edited by Anthony Thwaite. London: Faber, 1992.

Further Requirements: Interviews, Broadcasts, Statements, and Reviews. Edited by Anthony Thwaite. London: Faber, 2001.

Trouble at Willow Gables and Other Fictions. Edited by James Booth. London: Faber, 2002.

Early Poems and Juvenilia. Edited by A. T. Tolley. London: Faber, 2005.

CORRESPONDENCE, MANUSCRIPTS

Larkin donated the first of the workbooks in which he composed his mature poems to the British Library. The remaining seven workbooks (with a microfilm of the first) are held in the substantial Philip Larkin Collection at the Brynmor Jones Library, University of Hull, along with other of Larkin's literary, personal, and professional papers.

CRITICAL AND BIOGRAPHICAL STUDIES

Bayley, John. *The Uses of Division: Unity and Disharmony in Literature.* London: Chatto & Windus, 1976.

Bloomfield, B. C. *Philip Larkin: A Bibliography, 1933–1944.* Rev. and enlarged ed. London and New Castle, Del.: British Library and Oak Knoll Press, 2002.

Booth, James. *Philip Larkin: Writer.* Hemel Hempstead, U.K.: Harvester Wheatsheaf, 1992.

———. *Philip Larkin: The Poet's Plight.* Basingstoke, U.K.: Palgrave Macmillan, 2005.

Bradford, Richard. *First Boredom, Then Fear: The Life of Philip Larkin.* London: Peter Owen, 2005.

Brennan, Maeve. *The Philip Larkin I Knew.* Manchester, U.K.: Manchester University Press, 2002.

Cooper, Stephen. *Philip Larkin: Subversive Writer.* Brighton, U.K., and Portland, Ore.: Sussex Academic Press, 2004.

Davie, Donald. *Thomas Hardy and British Poetry.* New York: Oxford University Press, 1972.

Everett, Barbara. "Philip Larkin: After Symbolism." *Essays in Criticism* 30, no. 3:227–242 (1980).

Morrison, Blake. *The Movement: English Poetry and Fiction of the 1950s.* Oxford and New York: Oxford University Press, 1980.

Motion, Andrew. *Philip Larkin.* London and New York: Methuen, 1982.

———. *Philip Larkin: A Writer's Life.* London: Faber, 1993.

Osborne, John. *Larkin, Ideology, and Critical Violence: A Case of Wrongful Conviction.* Basingstoke, U.K.: Palgrave Macmillan, 2008.

Regan, Stephen. *Philip Larkin.* Basingstoke, U.K.: Macmillan, 1992.

Rossen, Janice. *Philip Larkin: His Life's Work.* Hemel Hempstead, U.K.: Harvester Wheatsheaf, 1989.

Swarbrick, Andrew. *Out of Reach: The Poetry of Philip Larkin.* Basingstoke, U.K.: Macmillan, 1995.

Thwaite, Anthony, ed. *Larkin at Sixty.* London: Faber, 1982.

Tolley, A. T. *Larkin at Work: A Study of Larkin's Mode of Composition as Seen in His Workbooks.* Hull, U.K.: University of Hull Press, 1997.

———. *My Proper Ground: A Study of the Work of Philip Larkin and Its Development.* Edinburgh: Edinburgh University Press, 1991.

Watt, R. J. C., ed. *A Concordance to the Poetry of Philip Larkin.* Hildesheim, Zurich, and New York: Olms-Weidmann, 1995.

Whalen, Terry. *Philip Larkin and British Poetry.* Basingstoke, U.K., Macmillan, 1986.

JOHN LE CARRÉ

(1931—)

Gordon Spark

JOHN LE CARRÉ is that rarest of creatures, a writer of best–selling espionage novels who has transcended the narrow bounds of genre fiction to be recognized as one of the finest British writers of the postwar period. His powerful and often satirical prose and his willingness to experiment with form and genre single out le Carré as one of the most accomplished and innovative of contemporary writers. His novels can, of course, be read simply as "entertainments" (to borrow Graham Greene's label for his own espionage novels). Indeed, in many ways le Carré has helped to define and develop the genre, his novels mapping the historical contexts and technical minutiae first of the cold war and then of the uncertain world that followed in the conflict's wake. But, like Greene and Joseph Conrad before him, le Carré uses the secret world as a means of exploring very human themes: the nature of loyalty and betrayal, the search for self and national identity, the struggle to live an ethical life in an increasingly unethical world.

Le Carré was born David John Moore Cornwell on October 19, 1931 in Poole, Dorset. His father, Richard Thomas Archibald (Ronnie) Cornwell (1906–1975), was a flamboyant con man who would unwittingly provide much of the context for le Carré's subsequent writing. Le Carré's mother, Olive (Gassy) Cornwell, abandoned the family when le Carré was five; he would eventually be reunited with her when he was twenty-one. Le Carré has a brother, Tony, two years his senior, and a half-sister, Charlotte (b. 1949), an actress who would provide the inspiration for Charlie, the protagonist in *The Little Drummer Girl*. Such cold facts, however, fail to do justice to the central role that le Carré's childhood has played in his novels. All writers draw on their own lives to some extent, but rarely can an author's early experiences have had such an influence on his work as in the case of le Carré, whose novels are replete with orphaned offspring, absent parents, and chaotic childhoods.

His mother's flight saw le Carré dispatched at an early age first to St. Andrew's preparatory school in Berkshire and then to Sherborne School in Dorset. The socially stratified air of boarding school, where his lower-class roots would render him something of a perpetual outcast, would also provide a rich and enduring context for his later work. Le Carré sought refuge from the chaos of his family life but found only a cold, hierarchical world of emotional detachment and institutionalized brutality. This ambiguous relationship with institutions—a simultaneous dependency and sense of alienation—is another element of his childhood that le Carré would draw heavily upon in his fiction. In 1947 he escaped Sherborne, spending a year studying foreign languages at the University of Bern. It was here, in the German-speaking corner of Switzerland, that his enduring love of the German language and culture was born. Here too, le Carré claims to have taken his first faltering footsteps into the secret world, running trivial errands for a Bern-based British diplomat. After Bern, he further flirted with the intelligence world when he completed his national service with the Intelligence Corps in postwar Austria. In 1952 he returned to another of England's great institutions, resuming his education at Lincoln College, Oxford. Family life once again intruded, and he was forced to suspend his studies for a year when his father was declared bankrupt, leaving his son's tuition fees unpaid. Le Carré spent the year fruitfully, marrying Alison Ann Veronica Sharp in 1954; they would go on to have three sons before divorcing in 1971. After graduating in 1956, le Carré spent the next two years teaching languages at the prestigious public school Eton, the model—along with Sherborne—for Carne School, the setting for *A Murder of Quality*.

It is not clear precisely when le Carré was recruited to the British Intelligence service. He owns to having carried out errands for a diplomat in Bern and was involved in intelligence work in Austria during his national service. He also claims to have carried out espionage activities at Oxford, a traditional recruiting ground for the British Secret Services. What is known is that he left his teaching post at Eton in 1958 to join MI5, the British Security Service concerned with domestic security, and that he later transferred to MI6, the British Secret Intelligence Service. It would be in the latter agency that le Carré's finest creation, George Smiley, would pass his brilliant career. Le Carré was sent to Bonn in 1961 under cover as second secretary in the British embassy and to Hamburg in 1963 as political consul. His cover was blown in 1963 by the British defector Kim Philby, an experience that would contribute to his study of betrayal in *Tinker Tailor Soldier Spy*. By that point, however, le Carré's third novel, *The Spy Who Came In from the Cold*, had become an international best seller, and a new career beckoned.

THE 1960S: BEGINNINGS

John le Carré's literary career began on the commuter train from Missenden to London, in an attempt to stave off boredom during the commute to the Foreign Office; the result was *Call for the Dead* (1961). The novel introduces George Smiley, the spy who will come to personify one of the enduring themes of le Carré's work: the individual's struggle to maintain integrity in the face of larger political necessities. The opening chapter, "A Brief History of George Smiley," gives early notice of the author's gift for characterization and sets out the type of secret world le Carré intends to portray: Smiley, described variously as "a shrunken toad" (p. 9), "fleshy" (p. 10), "bespectacled" (p. 10), and "frog-like" (p. 15), is the antithesis of the suave, sophisticated James Bond. Le Carré also introduces, with brilliant economy, Smiley's unlikely and troubled marriage to the errant and eternally absent Lady Ann Sercombe. The "incongruity of the match" (p. 9) will be turned against Smiley in subsequent novels such as *A Murder of Quality* and *Tinker Tailor Soldier Spy*.

Although *Call for the Dead* has an espionage background, it is essentially a detective novel, a vehicle that allows le Carré to establish Smiley's impressive deductive intellect. The "call" in the title refers to the alarm call placed by the Foreign Office official Samuel Fennan that makes a lie of his apparent suicide. Seizing on this anomaly, Smiley unravels a trail of deception involving the East German agent Hans Dieter Mundt, the murdered man's wife, Elsa Fennan, and most significantly, Smiley's protégé and wartime agent Dieter Frey. As Smiley unravels the trio's deception, so le Carré ponders the moral tangle of espionage. Elsa, in particular, is sympathetically portrayed. A concentration camp survivor, her treachery emerges out of a fear of the past and a determination that fascism must never rise again. Similar sympathies might be afforded the Byronic figure of Frey, but his blind faith in ideology over individualism—demonstrated in his willingness to murder Elsa to ensure her silence—makes him a far more ambiguous character. These ambiguities are highlighted in the novel's climactic confrontation between Smiley and Frey. After a Holmesian pursuit through the fogbound streets of London the two grapple, but the armed German refuses to fire upon his former friend and plunges to his death in the Thames in a scene that recalls the fatal encounter between Holmes and Moriarty at Reichenbach Falls. The novel ends with Smiley wracked by guilt and questioning the validity of his actions: "Dieter was dead, and he had killed him.... And Dieter had let him do it, had not fired the gun, had remembered their friendship when Smiley had not.... 'Oh God,' said Smiley aloud, 'who was then the gentleman ... ?'" (pp. 147–148). The novel thus ends with le Carré musing on the nature of betrayal—both the public betrayal of one's nation and the personal betrayal of one's friend—and on the ethical dilemma at the heart of espionage. Smiley is left to wonder whether the sacrifice of one's friend is justified in the protection of one's country. It is a dilemma to which le Carré will return again and again.

In *A Murder of Quality* (1962) le Carré draws on his own experiences at Sherborne and Eton to depict the insular world of Carne School into which Smiley, as an outsider, is welcomed with deep suspicion. Perhaps the most interesting element of the novel is le Carré's critique of British class prejudice, to which Smiley himself falls victim—the viperous Shane Hecht knows she has her man when she comments that the only Smiley she had heard of had made a "curious" and "quite unsuitable" (p. 86) union with Lady Ann Sercombe, foreshadowing the much more damaging exploitation of Smiley's broken relationship with Ann undertaken by the Soviet spymaster Karla and the treacherous Bill Haydon in the later Smiley novels. The novel also further establishes Smiley's intellectual and deductive abilities as he competes against local prejudice to identify the murderer. Le Carré also takes the opportunity to further demonstrate Smiley's liberal temperament: the innate decency within Smiley leaves him shaken by the realization that the man he has exposed will be hanged for his crimes, meaning that *A Murder of Quality* ends on much the same note of moral ambiguity as does *Call for the Dead,* with Smiley pondering the human cost of acting in the public good.

By the early 1960s le Carré was based in Bonn and was on hand to witness the reaction as the East Germans began construction of the wall that would come to symbolize the cold war for a quarter of a century. The Berlin Wall bookends le Carré's breakthrough novel, *The Spy Who Came In from the Cold* (1963), providing the setting for both the tense opening scene and the novel's bleak climax. In between, le Carré suggests that the ideologies operating on either side of that wall are far from polarized; as the head of British Intelligence, "Control," observes, "our methods—ours and those of the opposition—have become much the same" (p. 20). Recalled from East Berlin to the Circus (le Carré's name for the headquarters of British Intelligence) after the death of the last double-agent under his control there, the spy Alec Leamas is treated to a cynical

discourse from Control into the moral justifications of their trade:

> We do disagreeable things, but we are *defensive....* We do disagreeable things so that ordinary people here and elsewhere can sleep safely in their beds at night.... Of course, we occasionally do very wicked things.... I mean, you can't be less ruthless than the opposition simply because your government's *policy* is benevolent, can you now?
>
> (p. 20)

Control's motive is to recruit the wretched Leamas into a plot to do "disagreeable things" to the head of East German Intelligence, Hans Dieter Mundt (last seen fleeing Britain in *Call for the Dead*). Faking his drunken and criminal decline after dismissal from the service, Leamas is picked up by the East Germans and "defects" with information designed to discredit Mundt.

But all is not as it seems. Ambiguity and misdirection are the tools of le Carré's trade, a requirement of the genre but also a fitting metaphor for the moral confusion that genre depicts. Both Leamas and the reader discover that they have been double-crossed. Leamas has in fact been sent to discredit the astute Fiedler, an intelligence officer who is set to expose Mundt as a British spy. Confronted by another of the novel's pawns, his girlfriend Liz Gold, as to the treachery of what has passed, Leamas is depressingly resigned:

> What do you think spies are: priests, saints and martyrs? They're a squalid procession of vain fools, traitors too, yes; pansies, sadists and drunkards, people who play cowboys and Indians to brighten their rotten lives. Do you think they sit like monks in London balancing the rights and wrongs?
>
> (p. 231)

It is worth pausing, in light of Leamas' comments, to consider the small but significant role played in the novel by George Smiley. Smiley disapproves of the "distasteful" (p. 56) operation, as Control explains to Leamas: "He sees the necessity but he wants no part in it" (p. 56). Despite what Control describes as Smiley's "fever" (p. 56), he haunts the novel, a shadowy figure here "silhouetted in the shifting mist" (p. 38), there lurking in the newspaper kiosk at the

Dutch airport through which the East Germans exfiltrate Leamas. Significantly, before Leamas' departure for the Continent, Control briefs him in Smiley's flat—a residence that both Smiley and Control know is likely to be under surveillance. Later in the novel Smiley calls upon Liz out of apparent concern for her well-being, thus linking her to the operation and providing Mundt with the witness he requires to trap Fiedler. These actions lead, indirectly, to the deaths of both Liz and Leamas—individuals sacrificed for the greater good, just as Smiley's own feelings toward the operation must be sacrificed in the name of political expediency. As the novel reaches its desperate denouement, Smiley stands on the Western side of the Wall, urging Leamas over. Le Carré leaves it to the reader to decide whether this is born out of a sense of guilt for his complicity in the double-cross or out of a more cynical desire to see the operation through to its bitter end.

It was perhaps inevitable given the huge success of *The Spy Who Came In from the Cold* that le Carré's subsequent novels would suffer by comparison. Yet both *The Looking-Glass War* (1965) and *A Small Town in Germany* (1968) confirm le Carré's alchemic touch with plot while also pointing to an experimental approach to narrative technique that will characterize much of his later work. Like the novel it follows, *The Looking-Glass War* concerns the preparations for, and execution of, an operation in East Germany. However, le Carré eschews the traditional demands of the genre, focusing less on the execution of that operation than on its preparation. The shadow of betrayal once more hangs over Smiley and Control, who appear to offer assistance to the Department, an entirely fictional offshoot of the Circus created by le Carré, while privately realizing that the operation is doomed from the outset. Formed during the war and increasingly marginalized in the two decades since, the Department wallows in nostalgia for those heady days. Amateurism abounds, from the bungled handover of secret film that sets the novel in motion to reactivated wartime agent Fred Leiser's needless killing of a border guard which dooms the mission almost as soon as it has begun.

Despite the failure of the mission, however, the team led by Leclerc—Control's counterpart in the Department—appears satisfied at the novel's conclusion. The game has been played out to its end. And here lies the novel's central theme: that espionage is no more than a game, played out by agents who pine for an England, and for a war, that no longer exists. With this war cold by definition, these players must create the very conflicts that justify their existence. Their detachment from the human cost of such activities is encapsulated by the cynical technocrat Adrian Haldane, who responds to the young and naive agent John Avery's pleas that they must do something to save Leiser with the hateful words, "We sent him because we needed to; we abandon him because we must.... We're technicians, not poets" (p. 229). For the cold war technician, le Carré seems to say, the people matter less than the process.

In his next novel, *A Small Town in Germany,* le Carré draws upon his own time in Bonn to explore, once again, the tensions between loyalty, betrayal, and political necessity. Dispatched to Germany to track down Leo Harting, an assumed defector from the British embassy, Alan Turner discovers that he must complete his task against a background of competing political pressures and venal self-interest. The mist that permanently shrouds the town stands as a metaphor for the ethereal world in which human principals are sacrificed in the name of political expediency. Peter de Lisle, the callous and superficial face of British diplomacy, describes the city as "an island cut off by fog ... a very *metaphysical* spot [where] the dreams have quite replaced reality" (p. 57). He continues, "We live somewhere between the recent future and the not so recent past." The "recent future" is the seven days that Turner has to locate Harting before the German nationalist politician Klaus Karfeld stages his political rally in the city. The "not so recent past" is the ghost of Nazism and Karfeld's own role during the war, uncovered first by Harting and subsequently by Turner. Le Carré illustrates his willingness to experiment with narrative technique by presenting much of the novel as undiluted dialogue as Turner goes about the business of interrogating various embassy officials. In large portions of the novel, the narrator dissolves into the background, allowing the dialogue to reveal and conceal in equal measure. Slowly, however, Turner pieces together the truth: Harting has uncovered the war crimes in Karfeld's closet and, motivated by the same fear of a rejuvenated Nazi party as that which compelled Elsa Fennan to betray her husband and her adopted country in *Call for the Dead,* intends to assassinate him. This is a contingency that the British cannot countenance because they are reliant upon German support for their imminent bid for membership in the European Economic Community. Thus *A Small Town in Germany* ends by exploring the same territory that has begun to fascinate le Carré throughout his first decade as a writer, with Harting (and the truth he has discovered about Karfeld) buried in a cynical attempt to protect Britain's larger political interests.

THE 1970S: THE FALL AND RISE OF GEORGE SMILEY

By the turn of the decade, le Carré was firmly established as one of Britain's most successful authors. But just as his professional life was going from strength to strength, so his personal world was falling apart. The breakdown of his first marriage, and his dalliance with the married couple James and Susan Kennaway, are explored in his first novel of the new decade, *The Naive and Sentimental Lover* (1971). It is difficult not to read the novel as an autobiographical work; in it, the protagonist, Aldo Cassidy, is attempting to escape his unsatisfactory marriage through his involvement with the artistic Shamus and his beautiful partner, Helen. But *The Naive and Sentimental Lover* was not a critical or commercial success: if it is true to say that the critics seemed unduly disconcerted by *Lover*'s departure from the espionage field, and reluctant to accept le Carré as anything other than a genre writer, then it is equally fair to suggest that le Carré's step beyond the confines of the spy novel fails to reach the heights attained by the novels with which he made his name in the preceding decade. But having divorced Alison in 1971 and married

Valerie Jane Eustace in 1972 (the couple has one son, Nicholas, also an author), le Carré was free to refocus his energies on the fictional landscape he knew best. Over the remainder of the decade he would produce three novels that would come to stand at the center of his oeuvre. Retrospectively repackaged as the "Quest for Karla" trilogy, *Tinker Tailor Soldier Spy, The Honourable Schoolboy,* and *Smiley's People* would come to stand as perhaps le Carré's finest body of work.

In *Tinker Tailor Soldier Spy* (1974), le Carré tapped into a particular aspect of the secret world that had long gripped the British psyche. Ever since the exposure in the 1950s of a circle of Soviet spies recruited at Cambridge before the war, the British public had been in turns fascinated and appalled by the idea of the highly placed Soviet mole at the heart of the British establishment. Cast out of the Circus in the power struggle that follows a disastrous mission orchestrated by the late Control, Smiley is called upon by Oliver Lacon, "Whitehall's head prefect" (p. 30), to identify Merlin, the Soviet mole operating at the highest level of the Circus. Like the Department in *The Looking-Glass War,* the Circus is starved of success and meaningful action, sidelined in the increasingly bipolar cold war dominated by the two superpowers. There is something of the larger decline of Britain present in the marginalization of the Circus, as the former Circus researcher Connie Sachs avers: "Poor loves. Trained to Empire, trained to rule the waves. All gone. All taken away" (p. 102).

In a novel of parallels, the dilapidated world of the Circus is mirrored in that of Thursgood's, the school to which the badly wounded field agent Jim Prideaux is quarantined in the guise of a French tutor upon his return from Czechoslovakia. The school represents the Circus in miniature, a microcosm of the class divisions, rigid hierarchy, and covert allegiances that characterize the adult world of the Circus. Prideaux's arrival in the first chapter of the novel, a comic tour de force that would hardly be out of place in a Dickens novel, goes unobserved save for the attentions of the misfit pupil Bill "Jumbo" Roach, the "best watcher in the whole damn unit" (p. 191). There is more to Prideaux's compliment than mere flattery: just as the school represents the Circus in miniature, so Roach stands as a younger version both of Prideaux and of Smiley.

The success of *Tinker Tailor* lies in the way in which the hunt for the traitor is depicted. Investigating the Circus from the outside, Smiley is forced to rely upon the occasional file pilfered from the archives by Lacon or his protégé Peter Guillam, upon his own interrogation of other marginalized former Circus players, and upon the fragments of his own remarkable memory. Smiley's investigations are interrupted by frequent analeptic episodes that serve to reveal much of the recent history of infighting within the Circus, as well as longer reaches back into the careers of the chief protagonists. Slowly these fragments come together to reveal the mole. Typically, Smiley must balance his sense of anger at Bill Haydon's treachery against his own humanitarian nature. But while his liberal tendencies may lead him to conclude that "nothing is worth the destruction of another human being" (p. 297), deep down he acknowledges that the traitor must be condemned: "Haydon had betrayed. As a lover, a colleague, a friend ... in every capacity Haydon had overtly pursued one aim and secretly achieved its opposite" (p. 297). Le Carré emphasizes Haydon's treachery by denying him a voice for much of the remainder of the novel, instead reporting his interrogation indirectly. The effect is to distance the reader from Haydon, so that his justification for betrayal ("He hated America very deeply," p. 306) and his snobbish self-importance ("He wanted to arrive [in Moscow] *looking* like someone," p. 309) serve only to heighten the lack of sympathy toward him. For Haydon, there is no tension between loyalty and betrayal, no redemption in the balancing of ethics and politics. His treachery is absolute and his death at the hands of Prideaux—whom he has perhaps betrayed more than any other—is as inevitable as it is deserved.

Despite his central place in the le Carré canon, Smiley is something of a marginal figure. He resigns twice during the course of *Call for the Dead*, and in *A Murder of Quality* he is very noticeably the outsider in the cloistered world of Carne. In both *The Spy Who Came In from the Cold* and *The Looking-Glass War*, Smiley lurks in the shadows, and in *Tinker Tailor* he is able to investigate the mole only because he has been cast out of the Circus in the power struggle following Control's death. In *The Honourable Schoolboy* (1977), Smiley finally takes center stage, assuming control of the Circus in the aftermath of Haydon's exposure. But Smiley's grip on power is fragile. His tenure is, from the outset, in the capacity of "caretaker chief" (p. 15), and the Circus he inherits has been left in ruins, staffed by a ragtag if occasionally brilliant collection of minor characters left over from the Haydon era or else dragged out of retirement to help steer the service through the squall. As the Foreign Office mandarin Roddy Martindale chimes, "only George Smiley ... could have got himself appointed captain of a wrecked ship" (p. 52). But captain he is, and so he must make the difficult decisions that were once Control's province. There is a certain hardening in Smiley's outlook: it is necessary "to be *inhuman in defence of humanity ... harsh in defence of compassion ... single-minded in defence of our disparity*" (p. 471, original emphasis). And yet, as Guillam astutely observes, the self-flagellation remains: "One day ... he'll cease to care, or the paradox will kill him. If he ceases to care, he'll be half the operator he is. If he doesn't, that little chest will blow up from the struggle of trying to find an explanation for what we do" (p. 470).

The novel lacks the tight, economical structure of *Tinker, Tailor,* the looser form and occasionally meandering plot reflecting perfectly something of the chaos of the Circus in those troubled days. Eschewing the more familiar European theater, *The Honourable Schoolboy* takes a postcolonial turn, with one of the bedraggled Circus survivors, Jerry Westerby, dispatched to Hong Kong to investigate a money-laundering operation run by Karla's agent Drake Ko. Westerby, lacking Smiley's ability to subsume personal feelings in the interests of professional expediency, warns Ko of his imminent capture and attempts to rescue Lizzie Worthington, Ko's mistress, with whom he has fallen in love. In another of le Carré's familiarly bleak denouements, however, Westerby is killed alongside

Drake, while the real prize—Drake's brother Nelson—is snatched off by the all-powerful Americans, who have lurked in the novel's background throughout. The setting of Hong Kong, soon to be returned to China and with larger conflicts raging on its doorstep, reflects the decline of Britain as a world power and hints at the larger global forces that will occupy le Carré's fiction after the end of the Cold War. That sense of change is felt keenly in the Circus, which no longer has room for Smiley's gentlemanly generation, recruited from Oxbridge and the public schools in the years before the war. The novel ends with Smiley once again consigned to retirement and a new pro-American regime in place at the Circus, headed by the Foreign Office bureaucrat Saul Enderby, representative of the new breed of politically aware espiocrat that will increasingly become the focus of le Carré's attention. But not before George Smiley's last hurrah.

Critics have generally viewed Smiley as a sympathetic character, a rare liberal conscience in an increasingly amoral world. But his practice of putting professional concerns ahead of his own personal ethics means that he is also an ambiguous character, whose actions often contribute to the demise of others. This ambiguity reaches its peak in *Smiley's People* (1980). *Smiley's People* is, like *Tinker Tailor,* a world of mirrors, no more so than in the blurred distinction between East and West: the great game has become, in the words of Connie Sachs, one of "half-angels fighting half-devils" (p. 182). Perhaps reflecting this, the novel maps a further hardening in Smiley as he considerably exceeds his limited brief and seizes upon Karla's one weakness—his love for his daughter, Alexandra, who is confined to a psychiatric hospital in Switzerland, funded illegally by Karla out of the public purse. This emotional exploitation of Karla neatly mirrors Karla's exploitation of Smiley's troubled marriage to Ann, in which he instructed Haydon to conduct a very public affair with her in order to protect his own identity and to undermine any case Smiley might subsequently make against him. Despite Smiley's hardening, however, le Carré makes clear which are the half-angels and

which the half-devils: Smiley may badger the dying Connie, blackmail Soviet diplomatic bureaucrat Anton Grigoriev, and exploit the mentally ill Alexandra in order to reach Karla, but he would balk at the trail of bodies Karla unblinkingly leaves behind him as he attempts to cover his tracks. Yet the novel's final scene is typically ambiguous. Under the shadow of the Berlin Wall, Karla and Smiley finally stand face to face, each looking into a mirror: "They exchanged one more glance and perhaps each for that second did see in the other something of himself" (p. 334). It is perhaps this recognition that is behind Smiley's understated response to Guillam's exhortation that he had "won": "'Did I?' said Smiley. 'Yes. Yes, well I suppose I did'" (p. 335). But what, le Carré seems to be asking, was the cost?

THE 1980S: OTHER THEATERS, OTHER SPIES

With Karla defeated and Smiley's methods increasingly indistinguishable from those of the enemy, le Carré sensed that it was time to leave his celebrated creation behind. In *The Little Drummer Girl* (1983) his attention would turn toward the Middle East, and in preparation for the novel he visited the region on several occasions, spending time in both the Israeli and Palestinian camps. As was the case in *The Honourable Schoolboy,* the novel explores a complex political landscape geographically removed from Europe but inextricably linked to that more familiar theater. That the West cannot escape its involvement in the Middle East is made clear in the fact that the terrorist attacks with which the novel begins and ends take place on mainland Europe. An even clearer indicator of the West's involvement comes in the shape of Charlie, the novel's protagonist. Modeled in part upon his half-sister Charlotte, Charlie is le Carré's most fully drawn female protagonist. A minor actress, she comes to the Israelis' attention through her abundant, passionately held, and sometimes contradictory radical stances. Le Carré satirizes the tendency of certain types of left-leaning individuals to adopt fashionable allegiances, characterizing Charlie as "a passionate opponent of apartheid ... a militant pacifist, a Sufist, a nuclear marcher, an anti-vivisectionist, and, until she went back to smoking again, a champion of campaigns to eliminate tobacco from theatres and on the public underground" (p. 111).

Charlie's shallow brand of radicalism is exploited by the redoubtable Mossad agent Kurtz, whose ruthless pursuit of the Israeli cause sends Charlie toward her own heart of darkness. She is guided on that journey by the brooding Gadi Becker, like Smiley coaxed out of retirement for an operation of which he does not entirely approve. The section of the novel in which he prepares Charlie for "the theatre of the real" ranks among the most remarkable of any of le Carré's writing. In a segment in which identities become increasingly amorphous (much of it narrated in the second person), Gadi—whom Charlie has christened Joseph—takes the part of Michel, alias for Salim, a Palestinian terrorist killed by the Israelis. In order to ensnare Salim's brother, Khalil, Joseph and Charlie method-act an affair between Charlie and Michel, with the aim of enabling Charlie to infiltrate Salim's family and lead the Israelis to Khalil. The effect of these multiple personas is to blur the distinction between the real world and the fabrication, so that when Charlie "could not tell whether Joseph or Michel was replying, and she knew he did not mean her to" (p. 246), the effect on the reader is equally disorienting. Nor is Joseph immune from the effect. His defense of the Palestinian position (in the guise of Michel) forces him to confront his own sense of history and identity:

> The British gave away my country to the Zionists, they shipped the Jews of Europe to us with orders to turn the East into the West.... The old British colonisers were tired and defeated, so they handed us over to the new colonisers who had the zeal and the ruthlessness to cut the knot.
>
> (p. 243)

But if the novel serves to disorient and to break down polarized views of the conflict, its ultimate message appears ambiguous. The mission's "success" seems to change little—the final chapter presents a sweeping "post-history" which makes clear that the cycle of violence, revenge, and recrimination remains unbroken. Only the sight of the disillusioned Gadi nursing Charlie, who has been left psychologically damaged by the operation, back into the real world offers any small hope of redemption.

Whereas le Carré's preparations for *The Little Drummer Girl* involved copious research and several visits to the Middle East, the subject matter of *A Perfect Spy* (1986) was much closer to home. Recognized (not least by the author himself) as his most autobiographical work, *A Perfect Spy* is the novel in which le Carré directly confronts his own past and his feelings toward his father. The spy of the title is Magnus Pym, but although the early life of this character is modeled on le Carré's own childhood, the truly biographical character is the brilliantly realized Rick Pym, a fictionalization of le Carré's Gatsby-like father, Ronnie. Rick's influence is all-consuming: "All Rick demanded was the totality of your love. The least you could do in return was give it to him blindly" (p. 45). For Magnus, the only escape is into the world of secrets. Even at boarding school, Magnus is preparing for a life of subterfuge, designating the staff lavatory his "safe house" (p. 70) and engaging in "clandestine operation[s]" (p.71) against classmates. One such operation, in which he frames the school bully, Sefton Boyd, gives an early indication of Magnus' capacity for betrayal. In the course of the novel he will betray everyone close to him: his family, his colleagues, his country, his father (Magnus leaks news of Rick's past convictions to thwart his parliamentary candidacy). The final betrayal comes after he is "set free" by the death of his father.

Whereas le Carré paid for but declined to attend the funeral of Ronnie Cornwell in 1975, Magnus does attend Rick's burial. But instead of returning to his post in Vienna he retreats to the English countryside to confront his treacherous past. Magnus' life as a spy is revealed in the form of a memoir, by turns humorous and tragic, which he addresses to his son, Tom. Something of the complex psychology of the character is revealed in the manner in which he records his past now in the first person, now in the third, suggesting that he has been playing so many parts for so long that his true identity is irrevocably lost. These chapters are juxtaposed with others that foreground the hunt for him, and in a finely controlled piece of plotting the two separate narrative strands converge as Magnus' memoir draws toward the present and his pursuers close in on his Dorset hideaway. But as we are coming to realize, for le Carré there can be only one outcome for Pym's brand of treachery. Like Haydon, Pym is a selfish character, possessing no apparent sense of obligation toward anyone but himself. But in the final words he writes to Tom—"I am the bridge … I am what you must walk over to get from Rick to life" (pp. 461–462)—he offers at least a hint at redemption, a hope that the betrayal ends with his death and that his son is spared the legacy that Magnus could not escape from his own father.

The novel's tragic ending invites us to ask just how autobiographical *A Perfect Spy* actually is. Although Rick Pym is clearly a barely disguised fictional version of Ronnie Cornwell, and although there are clear parallels between the early lives of le Carré and Magnus Pym, Magnus' path diverges from that of his creator when he chooses to betray his country. Whereas Magnus' treachery leads him to his eventual destruction, le Carré has, happily, resisted any such fate. And yet a 2008 interview sheds an intriguing sidelight onto the way in which Magnus' story might easily have become le Carré's. The author admits that he was tempted, in the early 1960s, to defect to the Soviet Union: "I wasn't tempted ideologically … but when you spy intensively and you get closer and closer to the border … it seems such a small step to jump … and, you know, find out the rest" (Liddle, p. 1). Read this way, it is possible to view Magnus as another of le Carré's doubles, the spy le Carré might have become had his life taken only a slightly different turn.

As it was, le Carré would finally set foot on Russian soil a quarter-century after he was first tempted to do so. With the Soviet policy of glasnost thawing the frozen relations of the cold war, le Carré was able in 1987 to visit the country he had been writing about from afar for thirty years. The result was *The Russia House* (1989), a novel that looks forward to the end of the cold war even as it retraces and rehearses some of the themes of that conflict. Le Carré's visit to Russia

influenced the novel deeply: whereas in previous novels the Soviets have been represented in terms of a Communist "other," *The Russia House* contains something of the heart and soul of the country and its people. Although the threat of the State remains, the Secret Services brood in the background of *The Russia House*. Instead, the novel gives voice to ordinary people—to the unsophisticated, motherly Katya, to the dissident scientist Yakov, and to the publisher and accidental agent Barley Blair. Blair is a most imperfect spy: "I'm the wrong man. And you're a fool for using me" (p. 130). The "wrong man" is thrust into the great game through his contact with Yakov, a Soviet scientist who passes, through Katya, a manuscript revealing Soviet military might to be a myth. At an earlier meeting, Yakov appeals to Barley, "Promise me that if ever I find the courage to think like a hero, you will act like a merely decent human being" (p. 114). In many ways this is the subject of *The Russia House*—what happens when the bureaucrats are sidelined and the ordinary decent human beings take over. In that respect, the novel looks forward to a post–cold war world that relies more on human values than on competing political and ideological systems. However, the manner in which *The Russia House* ends suggests that such a world remains some way off. Yakov is missing, assumed executed, and Barley trades the American "shopping list" in a bargain to save Katya. The novel ends with Barley restored to his home in Lisbon, trusting that the Russians will keep their part of the bargain and grant Katya permission to join him. But le Carré leaves open the question of whether Barley's gambit has carried the day, the ambiguous ending posing the larger question of whether the new policies inside the Soviet Union would truly bring about a thawing of relations between East and West.

In the second half of 1989, many tens of thousands of people in Eastern Europe acted as much more than decent human beings, bringing about the end of almost a half-century of ideological conflict. In Berlin, crowds from both sides congregated at, traversed, and ultimately dismantled the Wall, which had served not only as the most potent symbol of the cold war but also as the symbolic backdrop for several le Carré novels. For le Carré, as for many writers of espionage fiction, it was a time for reflection, a time to look back and draw conclusions but also a time to look forward to the brave new world that stood before them. *The Secret Pilgrim* (1991) does just that. The novel marks the return from semiretirement of George Smiley, invited back to speak to that year's graduating students. Introduced as "a legend of the Service," Smiley, self-effacing as ever, demurs: "Oh, I don't think I'm a legend at all.... I think I'm just a rather fat old man wedged between the pudding and the port" (p. 13). This neatly encapsulates Smiley's role in *The Secret Pilgrim*. Smiley's brief observations to the group in the primary narrative are wedged between Ned's recollections of cases he has been involved in over the years. Formerly head of the Russia House, Ned has been consigned to heading up Sarratt, the Circus training facility, in the fallout from the Barley Blair affair. The cases he recalls raise familiar le Carréan themes while also looking forward beyond the cold war to speculate on the future of espionage. Predictably, the novel's most enduring moments come in the short passages where Smiley takes center stage. He begins by looking back: "The purpose of *my* life was to end the time I lived in. So if my past were still around today, you could say I'd failed. But it's not around. We won" (p. 19). The doubts, however, quickly surface: "perhaps we didn't win anyway. Perhaps they just lost.... What matters is the hope" (p. 19). The ambiguous mixture of hope and trepidation capture neatly the uneasy peace that the end of the cold war brings. Smiley is, as ever, keen to make a distinction between the individual and the ideology: "I only ever cared about the *man*.... It was *man* who ended the Cold War" (p. 336). But he also cautions, somewhat presciently, that "if a democratic Russia emerges—why then, Russia will have been the winner" (pp. 336–337), inadvertently prefiguring one of the flashpoints that will provide new ground for the spy writer to explore. For the spy writer perhaps, but not for this particular spy—for *The Secret Pilgrim* is the novel in which Smiley finally bids a permanent farewell to the world of espionage. In the most poignant passage of

what is already an elegiac novel, Smiley takes his leave in typically modest fashion: "It's over, and so am I. Absolutely over. Time you rang down the curtain on yesterday's cold warrior. And please don't ask me back ever again. The new time needs new people. The worst thing you can do is imitate us" (p. 336). Smiley's words are aimed at the graduates of the Circus, but it is hard not to think that at this point he is also addressing his creator, imploring le Carré to find new protagonists to negotiate the new age.

THE 1990S: AFTER THE WALL

The subject matter le Carré chose for *The Night Manager* (1993), his first post–cold war novel, was the illicit international trade in arms and narcotics, and the shadowy involvement of supposedly democratic governments in such trade. In selecting Richard "Dickey" Roper, "the worst man in the world" (p. 36), as the novel's chief villain, le Carré signals one possible new direction for espionage fiction, where covert activities are directed not against particular countries with opposing ideological positions but rather toward individuals motivated not by ideology but by greed. Roper and his coterie of misfits and sycophants enjoy a lavish existence funded by their immoral activity. Into this world steps Jonathan Pine, night manager of the prestigious Hotel Meister Palace in Zurich. Pine is another of le Carré's classic misfits, an "orphaned only son of a cancer-ridden German beauty and a British sergeant ... killed in one of his country's many postcolonial wars" (p. 57). A former special forces soldier himself, this "self-exiled creature of the night" (p. 57) slowly comes to realize "that his life had consisted of a run of rehearsals for a play he had failed to take part in" (p. 76). Pine's self-exile is motivated by the slaughter in Cairo of his former mistress, Sophie, at the hands of Roper and Sophie's arms-dealer boyfriend. Recruited by Leonard Burr and a well-meaning but marginal branch of British Intelligence, Pine ingratiates himself into Roper's inner circle, first by rehearsing a past that recalls Charlie's psychological reconditioning in *The Little Drummer Girl* and then by staging an improbable rescue of Roper's son from the hands of violent robbers. Once he is accepted within Roper's world, Pine, like many le Carré protagonists, must become the enemy he seeks to destroy. But unlike protagonists such as Leamas or Charlie, there is no blurring of the line, no sense that Pine may actually have turned. Pine betrays Roper, exposing a major arms-for-drugs deal, but is in turn betrayed by corrupt elements of the British and American Intelligence establishment. In a highly improbable ending, made even more unlikely by le Carré's penchant for dark denouements, Pine is rescued by the heroic Burr and his small intelligence unit. Plucked off the torture table, Pine rides into the sunset with Jed, Roper's mistress. But despite the weak ending, in *The Night Manager* le Carré demonstrates that the end of the cold war did not strip espionage fiction of its subject. Pine may escape but there is no indication at the novel's end that his efforts have harmed, let alone defeated, Roper. Indeed, the end of the cold war appears to have created a world of alliances and rivalries more complex than those that have been left behind.

Le Carré's next novel, *Our Game* (1995), draws even more closely upon the end of the cold war by examining the disintegration of the Soviet Union. The novel is concerned with the fate of the semi-autonomous region of Ingushetia and its attempts to establish its own identity in the face of the Russian bear. The narrative centers around two characters, the former spy Tim Cranmer and his field agent Larry Pettifer. Pettifer is entirely absent from the novel, present only in Cranmer's efforts to track him down, so the reader is left to construct his character from the scraps offered by Cranmer. These scraps are mostly of memory, but Cranmer's narrative is presented in a dizzying variety of past, present, and future tenses to leave the reader grasping for the truth. Cranmer and Pettifer can be read as another of le Carré's doubles, two sides of the same spy. Cranmer claims Pettifer is "my creation and I must have him.... When I send him out into the world I intend that he should come back to me more mine than when he left me" (p. 48), and later Dee, a friend of Cranmer's wayward partner Emma, observes of Cranmer, "I don't

think you wish to *find* your friend, only to *become* him" (p. 329). Like Jonathan Pine in *The Night Manager,* Cranmer discovers his life to have been empty and "finds himself" in the search for Pettifer. At its heart, the novel is about the quest for personal identity, about what becomes of people when the cause they have fought for all their lives is suddenly removed. As Cranmer wonders early in the novel, "What good had it ever done us, this cloak-and-dagger rigmarole? What harm had it done us, this endless wrapping-up and hiding of our identities?" (p. 45). After the too-neat ending of *The Night Manager,* le Carré ends *Our Game* on more familiarly shaky ground. With Pettifer apparently killed fighting the Ingush cause, Cranmer's search appears to have been in vain: "I stood alone, converted to nothing, believing in nothing. I had no world to go back to and nobody left to run except myself. A Kalashnikov lay beside me. Slinging it across my shoulder, I hastened ... down the slope" (pp. 407–408). Yet le Carré seems to suggest that, in slinging the Kalashnikov over his shoulder, Cranmer has found some kind of redemption, that he is at last taking some kind of meaningful action and unwrapping the identity so concealed and constrained by years of cold war service.

All of le Carré's work is concerned to some extent with fabrication. His protagonists have either been fabricators or have been charged with unpicking the fabrications of others. And le Carré himself is a great fabricator, a spinner of stories that draw the reader into the worlds he creates. Fabrication lies also at the heart of *The Tailor of Panama* (1996). The protagonist, Harry Pendel, engages in fabrication on numerous levels. A tailor by trade, his very occupation requires, according to Pendel, the skills of the fabricator, or what he terms "fluence": "Your ideal cutter, he liked to maintain ... is your born impersonator. His job is to place himself in the clothes of whoever he is cutting for and become that person" (p. 28). But Pendel's flair for fabrication extends beyond impersonating his customers: he also tailors his own history, hiding his jailbird past behind a fictional apprenticeship on Savile Row. Pendel's fictional identity is undone by the unscrupulous British operative Andrew Osnard: "When he barged in, Pendel was one person. By the time he barged out again Pendel was another" (p. 13). The ambitious Osnard recruits Pendel, believing that in the course of tailoring to the rich and famous, Pendel will encounter an endless stream of valuable intelligence. And Pendel does indeed cater to the great and the good in post-Noriega Panama, characters that are portrayed in typically satirical style as every bit as corrupt and immoral as the regime they replaced. As Pendel himself puts it, "Panama's not a country, it's a casino" (p. 15). And at stake is control of the Panama Canal.

Only, the stakes are not as high as they seem. In a plot twist which echoes that of Graham Greene's *Our Man in Havana* (the acknowledged inspiration for *Tailor*), Pendel, bereft of any real intelligence, employs his "fluence" to concoct an ever more sinister world of subterfuge, fabricating harmless gossip into concrete conspiracies. With the Americans set to return the canal to Panamanian control, Pendel concocts

> a great plot, though nobody could quite work out what the plot consisted of: except that the French and possibly the Japanese and Chinese and the Tigers of South-East Asia were part of it or might be, and perhaps the drug cartels of Central and South America. And the plot involved selling the Canal out of the back door.
>
> (p. 220)

As is so often the case with le Carré, however, it is the personal betrayals that impact most heavily. Pendel's one true friend, Mickie Abraxas; his wife, Louisa; his family; even Pendel himself as he is left high and dry by the fleeing Osnard—as ever, these real people are the real victims as Pendel's fictions spiral out of control. That these fictions can have such repercussions serves as a commentary on the increasingly chaotic geopolitical landscape of the late twentieth century. But the novel also recalls *The Looking-Glass War* in questioning the extent to which all intelligence is fabrication, a self-perpetuating, self-fulfilling game set quite apart from the real world it purports to protect.

In *Single and Single* (1999), le Carré returns to the dissolution of the Soviet Union and the resultant struggle to fill the power vacuum left behind. Into that vacuum step the Orlov brothers, Yevgeny and Mikhail, "flooding what we used to call the free world with every dirty product they can lay their hands on" (p. 115). From their Georgian homeland the tentacles of their crime syndicate spread around the world, encompassing the House of Single, which provides a laundering service to the Georgians. Theirs is a brutal yet highly organized regime, as demonstrated in the opening chapter by the violent execution of the bank's lawyer, Alfred Winser. The murder, predicated on the betrayal of the Orlovs' shipment of drugs, has two purposes, one rooted in loyalty, the other purely commercial: "Sure, it's a vengeance killing … but also we intend this gesture will be interpreted as formal request for recompense" (p. 19). And yet, for all that the novel has to warn about the perils of globalized crime, at its heart *Single and Single* is a novel about family. Mixed in with the brutality is a warmth and gregariousness that engenders in the reader a certain sense of sympathy toward the Orlovs. Fiercely loyal not only to their Georgian identity but also to their local Mingrelian roots, the Orlovs are, as Tiger Single reminds his son Oliver, family men: "They like fathers, brothers, sons. Send them your son, it's a pledge of good faith" (p. 152). Appropriately, then, the other dominant family relationship in the novel is also a patriarchal one, that between Tiger and Oliver, who become estranged because of Oliver's moral decision to betray his father and the firm's criminal links with the Orlov syndicate. Breaking his cover as a children's magician (another suitable occupation for a fabricator) after Winser's assassination, Oliver tracks down his missing father, who is being held captive by Yevgeny and his group. In order to free his father, Oliver must highlight one final betrayal—that perpetrated by Yevgeny's son-in-law and fixer Alix Hoban and the younger members of both the Orlov's and Tiger's coteries, which results in the death of Mikhail and the ensuing cycle of reprisals. For Oliver, however, as is the case for all of le Carré's "moral" characters, the motivation behind that betrayal is love, loyalty, and duty: "His overriding aim was to magic his father out of here and say sorry to him if he felt it, though he wasn't sure he did" (pp. 409–410).

THE 2000S: SOME THINGS CHANGE, SOME STAY THE SAME

In the decade after the end of the cold war, le Carré, like the spies he had spent his life writing about, was forced to broaden his horizons and look toward the opportunities offered by the new geopolitical landscape. Yet although the resultant novels were commercially successful, they lacked the vital spark of le Carré's earlier work. Did his best years lie behind him, on the other side of the Wall? Fans need not have worried: the new millennium would bring with it new ills that would blow fresh wind into the septuagenarian novelist's sails.

First into le Carré's line of fire, in *The Constant Gardener* (2001), was the exploitation of Africa. The multinational pharmaceutical giant Karel Vita Hudson, through its British ally Three-Bees ("Finger in every African pie.... Hotels, travel agencies, newspapers, security companies, banks, extractors of gold, coal and copper, importers of cars, boats and trucks.... Plus a fine range of drugs," p. 127), uses Africa as a testing ground for trial drugs not yet safe for Western consumption. As the novel's protagonist, Justin Quayle, insists, "Drugs are the scandal of Africa. If any one thing denotes the Western indifference to African suffering, it's the miserable shortage of the right drugs, and the disgracefully high prices that the pharmaceutical firms have been exacting over the last thirty years" (p. 188). Quayle, a career diplomat, is jolted out of his complacency by the murder of his young wife, Tessa, one of the few Westerners who does take an interest in the plight of the local Kenyans. Quayle emerges into the story only slowly. The early chapters of the novel are given over instead to the bureaucrat Sandy Woodrow, whose compassionate handling of Tessa's death at first engenders the reader's sympathy. Woodrow's character begins to come undone in another of le Carré's brilliant interrogation scenes, although it will be much later in the novel before Justin or the reader will stumble upon the love letter he

has sent to Tessa. Tessa's loyalty to her husband ensures that such love is unrequited. It also accounts for her "immoral contract" (p. 153) with Quayle: "She follows her conscience, I get on with my job" (p. 153). But the private and the political are not so easily separated. Quayle explains his acquiescence to such an agreement as a form of betrayal: "I failed her.... By detaching myself.... By letting her go it alone. By emigrating from her in my mind" (p. 153).

Belatedly joining his wife's cause, Quayle follows her trail, discovering the malevolent and global reach of Karel Vita Hudson, which is suppressing the negative test results for its new wonder drug Dypraxa. This reach is reflected in the novel's geographical scope: the narrative ranges out from Kenya to encompass Italy, Germany, the United Kingdom, Canada, and the Sudan before returning to Kenya. As Quayle discovers, the reach also extends into government, in the form of the corrupt Foreign Office diplomat Sir Bernard Pellegrin, who is among those to betray Tessa, suppressing her report to protect his own interest in the company. As Justin awaits his fate by the shores of Lake Turkana, at the same spot at which Tessa was murdered, he reflects: "He had met her betrayers of course, Pellegrin, Woodrow.... He had rewritten her scandalously discarded memorandum for her.... And now, it seemed, he was about to share with her the last of all her secrets" (p. 565). But le Carré rarely does happy endings. Juxtaposed with this redeeming climax, we learn that Pellegrin has "sought early retirement in order to take up a senior managerial post with the multinational pharmaceutical giant Karel Vita Hudson" (p. 549), while, in Kenya, the promotion is announced "of Mr. Alexander Woodrow to the estate of British High Commissioner" (p. 548).

Although there has always been a political edge to le Carré's writing, his work has long been characterized by his ability to balance his own political leanings against alternative points of view. But as the increasingly acquisitive forces of globalization have taken root, so le Carré's neutrality has given way to a more clearly defined political position. In January 2003 he published in the London *Times* a letter savaging the invasion of Iraq and the larger war on terror, accusing the United States of entering "one of its periods of historical madness" and bemoaning the lack of real opposition on either side of the Atlantic. Many of the themes and complaints present in le Carré's impassioned missive are explored in *Absolute Friends* (2004). *Absolute Friends* is an angry book, a tilt against the "old Colonial oil war dressed up as a crusade for Western life and liberty" (p. 272). The novel centers upon the lifelong friendship between Ted Mundy and the radical but well-meaning West German, Sasha. Mundy first meets Sasha in Berlin, where both flirt with student politics. Their friendship is reactivated in the 1980s when Sasha, by now a disillusioned East German agent, passes secrets to the British through his old friend. The pair lose touch until the new millennium, when Sasha reappears in Germany to recruit Mundy—now a tour guide at a Bavarian castle—to his grandiose scheme to combat the divisive effects of the War on Terror. Slowly Mundy comes to realize what his old friend cannot see—that they are being used as pawns to bolster the very cause they purport to stand against.

Mundy was born in India on August 15, 1947, son of a British army major and an Irish chambermaid who died while bringing him into the world. His confused and ambiguous identity thus has its roots in historical circumstance: "When my mother began her labour the sun was still Indian. By the time she was dead it was Pakistani" (p. 313). In making his protagonist one of the "midnight children," those born between 12 A.M. and 1 A.M. on the day the British Partition of India took effect, le Carré links the twenty-first-century "war on terror" to the legacy of Partition. Another political legacy is that of Berlin 1968, where Mundy first meets Sasha and becomes involved in the student protest movement, le Carré using the political activities of Sasha, Mundy, and the other students as a means of highlighting the relative lack of opposition to the contemporary "war on terror."

Just as Smiley reflects, in *The Secret Pilgrim*, that it was man and not ideology that brought down the Wall, so in *Absolute Friends* le Carré suggests that if and when the present-day conflict is resolved, it will be at the human level. Mundy, on the run from his creditors and in search of someplace to call "home" after a failed business venture in nearby Heidelberg, is propositioned by Zara, a Munich call girl. Declining her offer, he instead takes her under his wing and "assumes the role of secular father to a Muslim child and platonic guardian to a traumatized woman in a state of religious shame" (p. 15). Members of Munich's Muslim community initially regard him with suspicion but acceptance soon follows, thanks in large part to the tolerant teachings of their "enlightened young imam" (p. 16). But the hope that such cross-cultural contact brings is fleeting. In a final chapter in which le Carré comes closer than he ever has to outright polemic, Mundy and Sasha are denounced as terrorists, Mundy's "religiously observant" (p. 376) partner is arrested, and the imam is "held indefinitely under investigative detention" (p. 376). One last loyal voice rings out, that of Amory, case officer to Sasha and Mundy during the cold war years in which Sasha was passing to Britain—through Mundy—East German secrets. But Amory's revelations, confined to a "not-for profit website pledged to transparency in politics" (p. 377), are easily drowned out by the jingoistic media as the actions of one of those "closet saboteurs of our nation's good name" (p. 379). The novel ends on a note of venal collusion between governments, private enterprise, and the media, ostensibly in the interests of "freedom."

Notions of abused and manipulated freedom are also central to *The Mission Song* (2006). The novel's concern with the fate of Africa recalls the subject matter of *The Constant Gardener*, but le Carré's narrative approach to that subject is very different. Although the author visited the Democratic Republic of Congo while preparing the novel, and although the novel is concerned with the preparations for a coup in that country, the narrative itself is set exclusively in London and on an unnamed island in the North Sea, venue for a secret and highly illicit conference between the faceless Syndicate and leaders of the Congo's various warring factions. The absence of Africa in the novel speaks something of what le Carré views as the powerlessness of Africans in deciding their own affairs: the unedifying sight of the Congo, and her natural resources, once more being carved up over European conference tables recalls the imperial past and serves to suggest that a century after Joseph Conrad's *Heart of Darkness* the scramble for Africa proceeds unabated.

The Mission Song is narrated entirely in the first person. Le Carré's vehicle of choice is Bruno Salvador, or Salvo, son of a promiscuous Irish missionary father and a Congolese mother. Salvo is an interpreter for the British government, and, with typical attention to detail, le Carré draws his reader convincingly into the world of the "sound thief" who "hear[s] like the blind" (p. 201) and who can pick up on the "subtleties and evasion[s]" (p. 148) of peasant languages indistinguishable to the lay listener. But the first-person narrative has its limitations. Salvo's narrative is peppered with omissions, abstractions, and moments of forgetfulness. Nowhere is the limited perspective more evident than in the novel's most striking scene, in which one of the delegates, the gauche but perceptive Haj, is tortured by members of the Syndicate. Closeted in his basement listening post, Salvo is able to listen illicitly but not to see what is going on. That the torture scene is mediated through Salvo's narrative, allowing him to speculate upon events, fill in the visual gaps, and control what the reader is permitted to know, stands as something of a warning as to the limited perspective of the narrative as a whole.

As ever with le Carré, the twin themes of loyalty and betrayal loom large in *The Mission Song*. Salvo and Penelope's dysfunctional marriage and mutual indiscretions are, by now, stock le Carréan fare. More interesting are the conflicting loyalties shown by two of the novel's minor characters after Salvo is betrayed by the Establishment he once served (the reader discovers only at the end of *The Mission Song* that Salvo narrates the novel from the comfort of a detention center for illegal immigrants, awaiting deportation to the Congo having attempted to blow the whistle on the coup). Salvo's controller, the essentially decent Mr. Anderson, is damned by his inability to successfully negotiate "the

prickly moral labyrinth that is his own preserve: Individual Conscience versus Higher Cause" (p. 339). In a letter he sends to Salvo in the detention center, Anderson hopes "that you will one day remember our collaboration in a more favourable light" (p. 386). But enclosed within Anderson's letter is another from Haj, the tortured delegate, promising Salvo employment and a home in the Congo, and illustrating in the process the deeds that truly good individuals can do when they place morality ahead of politics.

CONCLUSION: A MOST WANTED MAN

In October 2008 John le Carré published the twenty-first novel of a remarkable career. Set in Germany, like so many of le Carré's novels, *A Most Wanted Man* returns to the territory of *Absolute Friends,* examining questions of identity, loyalty, and political chicanery in the aftermath of 9/11 and the subsequent war on terror. It is le Carré at his urgent best, tackling the most pressing issues of our time. And yet it is also vintage le Carré, for if he has made a career out of writing individual novels that capture the zeitgeist of a particular time and place, then his body of work stands in its totality as a searching examination of the very human concerns of loyalty and betrayal and of the questions of self and national identity that go along with negotiating such concerns. That he succeeds in entertaining and thrilling his readers along the way should not disqualify le Carré from the recognition he deserves. He has earned his place alongside Conrad and Greene as a literary writer of seriously good espionage novels.

Selected Bibliography

WORKS OF JOHN LE CARRÉ

Novels

Call for the Dead. London: Gollancz, 1961. London: Sceptre, 2000. (All page citations in the text refer to the most recent editions listed here and below.)

A Murder of Quality. London: Gollancz, 1962, 1983.

The Spy Who Came In from the Cold. London: Gollancz, 1963. London: Pan Books, 1964.

The Looking-Glass War. London: Heinemann, 1965. London: Pan Books, 1966.

A Small Town in Germany. London: Heinemann, 1968. London: Sceptre, 2006.

The Naive and Sentimental Lover. London: Hodder & Stoughton, 1971.

Tinker Tailor Soldier Spy. London: Hodder & Stoughton, 1974. London: Pan Books, 1975.

The Honourable Schoolboy. London: Hodder & Stoughton, 1977. London: Pan Books, 1978.

Smiley's People. London: Hodder & Stoughton, 1980. London: Pan Books, 1980.

The Little Drummer Girl. London: Hodder & Stoughton, 1983. London: Sceptre, 2000.

A Perfect Spy. London: Hodder & Stoughton, 1986. London: Book Club Associates, 1986.

The Russia House. London: Hodder & Stoughton, 1989. London: Coronet, 1990.

The Secret Pilgrim. London: Hodder & Stoughton, 1991. London: Coronet, 1991.

The Night Manager. London: Hodder & Stoughton, 1993. London: Coronet, 1994.

Our Game. London: Hodder & Stoughton, 1995. London: Sceptre, 2006.

The Tailor of Panama. London: Hodder & Stoughton, 1996. London: Coronet, 1997.

Single and Single. London: Hodder & Stoughton, 1999. London: Coronet, 2000.

The Constant Gardener. London: Hodder & Stoughton, 2001. London: Hodder & Stoughton, 2005.

Absolute Friends. London: Hodder & Stoughton, 2004. London: Coronet, 2004.

The Mission Song. London: Hodder & Stoughton, 2006, 2007.

A Most Wanted Man. London: Hodder & Stoughton, 2008.

SHORT STORIES

"You Can't Sack a College Boy." *Spectator,* November 1964, pp. 699–700.

"Dare I Weep, Dare I Mourn?" *Saturday Evening Post,* January 28, 1967, pp. 54–60.

"What Ritual Is Being Observed Tonight?" *Saturday Evening Post,* November 2, 1968, pp. 60–65.

OTHER WORKS

"The Writer and the Spy." *Daily Telegraph,* March 29, 1964, p. 18.

"To Russia with Greetings: An Open Letter to the Moscow *Literary Gazette.*" *Encounter,* May 1966, pp. 3–6.

"In England Now." *New York Times Magazine,* October 23, 1977, pp. 34–35, 86–87.

"England Made Me." *Observer,* November 13, 1977, p. 25.

Introduction to *The Philby Conspiracy,* by Bruce Page, David Leitch, and Phillip Knightley. Rev. ed. London: Deutsch, 1968. Pp. 1–16.

"The Betrayal." *Observer,* July 3, 1983, pp. 23–24.

"Spying on My Father." *Sunday Times,* March 16, 1986, pp. 33–35.

"Why I Came In from the Cold." *New York Times,* September 29, 1989, op-ed.

"Will Spy Novels Come In from the Cold?" *Washington Post,* November 19, 1989, p. D4.

"The Unbearable Peace." *Granta* 35:11–76 (1991).

"Quel Panama!" *New York Times Magazine,* October 13, 1996, pp. 52–55.

"A Lot of Very Greedy People." *Guardian,* February 12, 2001. Available online (http://www.guardian.co.uk/world/ 2001/feb/12/aids.wto).

"The United States of America Has Gone Mad." *Times* (London), January 15, 2003, p. 20.

CRITICAL AND BIOGRAPHICAL STUDIES

Aronoff, Myron J. *The Spy Novels of John le Carré: Balancing Ethics and Politics.* Houndmills, Basingstoke, U.K.: Palgrave, 2001.

Barley, Tony. *Taking Sides: The Fiction of John le Carré.* Milton Keynes, U.K.: Open University Press, 1986.

Beene, LynnDianne. *John le Carré.* New York: Twayne, 1992.

Bloom, Clive, ed. *Spy Thrillers: From Buchan to le Carré.* Houndmills, Basingstoke, U.K.: Macmillan, 1990.

Bloom, Harold, ed. *John le Carré.* New York: Chelsea House, 1987.

Bold, Alan, ed. *The Quest for le Carré.* New York: St. Martin's Press, 1988.

Cobbs, John L. *Understanding John le Carré.* Columbia: University of South Carolina Press, 1998.

Homberger, Eric. *John le Carré.* New York: Methuen, 1986.

Lewis, Peter. *John le Carré.* New York: Frederick Ungar, 1985.

Monaghan, David. *The Novels of John le Carré: The Art of Survival.* Oxford: Basil Blackwell, 1985.

Monaghan, David. *Smiley's Circus: A Guide to the Secret World of John le Carré.* New York: St. Martin's Press, 1986.

Sauerberg, Lars Ole. *Secret Agents in Fiction: Ian Fleming, John le Carré, and Len Deighton.* London: Macmillan, 1984.

Wolfe, Peter. *Corridors of Deceit: The World of John le Carré.* Bowling Green, Ohio: Bowling Green University Press, 1987.

INTERVIEWS

Assouline, Pierre. "John le Carré: Spying on the Spymaster." *World Press Review* 33:59–60 (August 1986).

Barber, Michael. "John le Carré: An Interrogation." *New York Times Book Review,* September 25, 1977, pp. 9, 44–45.

Bragg, Melvin. "The Things a Spy Can Do: John le Carré Talking." *Listener,* January 22, 1976, p. 90.

———. "A Talk with le Carré." *New York Times Book Review,* March 13, 1983, pp. 1, 22.

———. "*The Little Drummer Girl:* An Interview with John le Carré." In *The Quest for le Carré.* Edited by Alan Bold. London: Vision Press, 1988. Pp. 129–143.

Dean, Michael. "John le Carré: The Writer Who Came In from the Cold." *Listener,* September 5, 1974, pp. 306–307.

Hodgson, Godfrey. "The Secret Life of John le Carré." *Washington Post,* October 9, 1977, pp. E1, E6.

Isaacson, Walter, and James Kelly. "We Distorted Our Own Minds." *Time,* July 5, 1993, p. 32f.

Leitch, David. "The Ultimate Spy." *Sunday Times Magazine,* September 13, 1987, pp. 50–51.

Liddle, Rod. "The Old Spy Has a Surprising New Story to Tell." *Sunday Times,* September 14, 2008, pp. 1–3.

McCrum, Robert. "I Don't Miss Smiley." *Observer* (http://www.guardian.co.uk/books/2000/dec/17/fiction.crime), December 17, 2000.

Sanoff, Alvin P. "The Thawing of the Old Spymaster." *U.S. News & World Report,* June 19, 1989, pp. 59–61.

Vaughan, Paul. "Le Carré's Circus: Lamplighters, Moles, and Others of That Ilk." *Listener,* September 13, 1979, pp. 339–340.

Watson, Alan. "Violent Images." *Sunday Times,* March 30, 1969, pp. 55–57.

FILMS BASED ON THE WORK OF JOHN LE CARRÉ

The Spy Who Came In from the Cold. Directed by Martin Ritt. Salem Films, 1965.

The Looking-Glass War. Directed by Frank Pierson. Frankovich Productions, 1969.

Tinker Tailor Soldier Spy. TV miniseries. Directed by John Irvin. British Broadcasting Corporation, 1979.

Smiley's People. TV miniseries. Directed by Simon Langton. British Broadcasting Corporation, 1982.

The Little Drummer Girl. Directed by George Roy Hill. Pan Arts, 1984.

A Perfect Spy. TV miniseries. Directed by Peter Smith. British Broadcasting Corporation, 1987.

The Russia House. Directed by Fred Schepisi. Pathé Entertainment, 1990.

A Murder of Quality. Directed by Gavin Millar. Portobello Productions, 1991.

The Tailor of Panama. Directed by John Boorman. Columbia, 2001.

The Constant Gardener. Directed by Fernando Meirelles. Potboiler Productions, 2005.

ANN RADCLIFFE

(1764—1823)

Frances A. Chiu

To John Keats, Ann Radcliffe was "Mother" Radcliffe. Others dubbed her "the great Enchantress." Although Radcliffe is hardly the progenitor of the gothic novel—a title that belongs more properly to Horace Walpole—she can be rightly credited with the development of the gothic novel: her virginal heroines, tyrannical fathers, corrupt clerics, and dark, decrepit castles invited large-scale imitation over the course of the 1790s while haunting the literary imagination for centuries to come. Just as her literary contemporary William Hazlitt deemed her "unrivalled among her fair country women," admiring her ability to "harrow up the soul with imaginary horrors" and "make the flesh creep, and the nerves thrill with fond hopes and fears" (Miles, p. 6). her literary descendants Edgar Allan Poe, J. Sheridan Le Fanu and M. R. James each paid tribute to her in their short stories and novels.

BIOGRAPHY AND SOCIAL CONTEXT

Ann Ward Radcliffe was born on July 9, 1764, in London to William Ward, a tradesman, and his wife, Ann Oates, both of whom had arrived from the north of England and were "nearly the only persons of their families not living in handsome, or at least easy independence," according to the novelist's husband, William Radcliffe (Norton, p. 13). Ward's mother was the sister of William Cheselden, a surgeon to King George II. Radcliffe's maternal kin were slightly more illustrious. Her mother was a cousin of John Jebb, the father of the famous Unitarian physician and liberal reformer Dr. John Jebb (1736–1786): upon Dr. Jebb's death, Ann Oates Ward subscribed to a copy of *The Complete Works of John Jebb*. Not least, her distant maternal relations included the

Dutch radicals Cornelius and Jan De Witt, who were wrongly accused of conspiring to poison William of Orange before dying courageously in prison.

Details of Radcliffe's early childhood, however, have remained largely, if appropriately, shrouded in mystery, requiring ample detective work on the part of her twentieth-century biographers, Robert Miles and Rictor Norton, to piece together. What gradually emerges is the portrait of a virtual orphan—one not dissimilar from her motherless protagonists—parented by her various relatives when her father was establishing his business (presumably with the assistance of his wife). What also emerges, albeit more hypothetically, is the making of a liberally inclined novelist, one who might have imbibed egalitarian principles and the spirit of Unitarianism well before the arrival of the French Revolution: principles that eventually exerted considerable influence on her fiction. At the age of seven, Radcliffe was sent to stay with her uncle Thomas Bentley (1730–1780), a business partner of Josiah Wedgwood since 1768, at Chelsea and Turnham Green. Bentley was also a founder of a prestigious Protestant Dissenting educational establishment, the Warrington Academy, whose instructors included many of the leading figures of late-eighteenth-century political reform and the Unitarian Church: for instance, the physician and writer John Aikin (1747–1822) and the chemist Joseph Priestley (1733–1804). In later years, Bentley met Benjamin Franklin (1706–1790). It is, of course, unknown as to whether Radcliffe herself was personally acquainted with the members of Bentley's and Wedgwood's politically reformist Dissenting circles. Nonetheless, it would have been difficult for her to escape her uncle's liberal politics: like Wedgwood and many of his Dissenting friends, Bentley was opposed to slavery while supporting the freedom of speech and religion as well as the cause of the American colonies. Perhaps more significantly, it would have been equally difficult for her to escape Bentley's interest in the gothic as he amassed numerous prints of British castles, parks, and ruins.

Even less is known of Radcliffe's immediate whereabouts after the death of Bentley in 1780. She may have resided with any of her maternal uncles, including Samuel Hallifax, the bishop of St. Asaph, and Dr. John Jebb (the two of whom were later involved in a dispute over Jebb's religious principles) and the latter's father. If she stayed with the younger Jebb, she may have been exposed to other liberal reformers, particularly since he was one of the original founders of the Society for Constitutional Information along with Major John Cartwright (1740–1824), the first writer to espouse the idea of American independence and propose universal male suffrage in Britain. What is intriguing at this point is the possible nexus between the younger Jebb and his niece's husband, William Radcliffe, an Oxford graduate. Much speculation has been focused on the fact that William, a nephew of Ebenezer Radcliffe, a Dissenting minister and subscriber of Jebb's complete works, may have met Ann at Jebb's home and discovered their congenial political and social views. It is also possible that William's father, a haberdasher, may have been acquainted with Ann's father, since both lived in fairly close proximity to one another in the Holborn section of London. Whatever the case, Ann Ward and William Radcliffe married in Bath in 1787 and then settled in London, where William had already relinquished his desire to enter the legal profession, choosing instead to embark on journalism. Having already served as a writer for the radical *Gazetteer,* but fallen out of favor with its editors, he worked late into the night as a parliamentary reporter while supplementing his income with editing and translating French publications. In 1792, the "democratically inclined" William (as noted by a visitor; see Norton, p. 136) gained the general editorship of another liberal newspaper, the *English Chronicle.*

Thus left to her own devices in the evenings, Ann began to write her novels in fairly quick succession. A novella, *The Castles of Athlin and Dunbayne,* appeared in 1789, with *A Sicilian Romance* following in 1790 and the more carefully crafted and complex *The Romance of the Forest* in 1791. All three of these first volumes were published anonymously. Her magnum opus, *The Mysteries of Udolpho,* nearly twice as long as *Forest,* appeared in 1794. The stream of novels was only interrupted by a brief hiatus as the Radcliffes traveled to Holland, Germany, and parts of England, yielding a joint collaboration titled *Journey Made in the Summer of 1794* (1795). Her fifth novel, *The Italian; or, The Confessional of the Black Penitents,* was published in 1797. In the winter of 1802, Radcliffe began work on her final novel, *Gaston de Blondeville; or, The Court of King Henry III, Keeping Festival in Ardenne.* That book was not sent to the publishers, however, until 1826, two years after her death.

For the most part, the childless couple enjoyed an uneventful life in London and its outskirts. Although fond of traveling around England, Radcliffe was highly reclusive, making few acquaintances and friends. It was a singularity that came to fuel rumors of insanity, that is, as *The Monthly Review* reported, "a state of mental desolation not to be described" (Norton, p. 245). Radcliffe, however, was reasonably healthy into her fifties, except for her failing lungs. In January 1823, she finally succumbed to a bronchial infection, dying a few weeks later on February 7.

Given the upbringing and marriage of Ann Radcliffe, one steeped in Dissent and political reform, it is difficult to understand the shaping of her novels, particularly their plots, themes, motifs, and even characterization, without some knowledge of the concerns and debates that arose during the last three decades of the eighteenth century. This was a period, after all, that witnessed the sudden rise of popular democracy (particularly regarding issues of civil and human rights), new political parties, and a heightened awareness of British national identity. Protestant Dissenters questioned the justice of having to subscribe to the Test and Corporation Acts as decreed by the Church of England (the Anglican Church), while abolitionists began to lobby more actively to put an end to the slave trade. In turn, the American Revolution, with its rallying cry of "no taxation without representation," subsequently led British reformers to question the equity of British representation itself. Why was enfranchisement limited to propertied men? Why were so many large cities such as Manchester denied representation? These were issues addressed by John Jebb and other founders of the Society of Constitutional Information—and possibly discussed in the presence of the young Radcliffe. Many of the arguments for religious toleration, American independence, the abolition of slavery, and universal (male) enfranchisement fomented a new, populist antiauthoritarianism by attacking ecclesiastical and aristocratic hegemony while creating a new distinction between past and future. Yet, it is equally significant that far from embracing the "natural rights" arguments adopted by Americans, British reformers relied on familiar myths and prejudices to support their new agendas. Dissenters, for instance, deployed a longstanding British tradition of anti-Catholic rhetoric in order to impugn Anglicans as being only slightly more enlightened than the despised, yet dreaded Catholics. Meanwhile, those advocating universal male suffrage reintroduced the concept of the "Norman yoke," contending that native Saxon egalitarianism, which granted a vote to every man, had been destroyed by William the Conqueror with his introduction of feudalism.

What is striking in light of Radcliffe's novels and the development of the gothic genre are the themes and imagery used by Jebb and others in their arguments for political reform—even if there is uncertainty as to the extent to which she was familiar with their writings (that is, since her mother owned a copy of Jebb's works). Just as liberal Whiggish writers were increasingly apt to view King George III (r. 1760–1820) as an arbitrary father of the people (as in Thomas Paine's 1776 argument for American independence, *Common Sense*), other writers, such as Joseph Priestley, challenged the paternalistic wisdom of adhering to anachronistic traditions and customs. The crumbling edifice was another

useful simile for reformers. Priestley, for instance, deplored the retrogressive state of theology in *A History of the Corruptions of Christianity*, stating, "Great buildings do not often fall at once but some apartments will still be thought habitable; after the rest are to be seen in ruins" (pp. 274-275). Priestley's probable acquaintance, Cartwright, later applied the same metaphor in a different context when arguing for the complete revamping of the British legislature. Even more interestingly, blind worship of the past was branded by Jebb and others as "gothic": their prose invoked visions of crumbling abbeys and dark clouds. Not least, reformers drove their agenda for progress by vilifying the church and aristocracy with unprecedented vehemence, accusing the "establishments" of presumption and avarice. Conversely, Dissenters and reformers presented themselves as true Britons. Unlike Anglicans and Catholics, they were plain folk, uninterested in ceremony and hierarchy. Internal dictates of virtue outweighed external ones: there was to be little compunction about disobedience if the rules stipulated by the authorities were morally flawed. Independence of mind and fortitude were everything.

It was not until 1789, however, that these ideas acquired more widespread attention. In that year, a few months after the fall of the Bastille, Richard Price, one of the earliest supporters of Jebb's and Cartwright's Society for Constitutional Information, published *A Sermon on the Love of Our Country*; although it was intended as a centennial commemoration of the English Revolution, he exalted the French Revolution as a "blaze that lays despotism in ashes" and "illuminates Europe!" (p. 196). To Price's astonishment—and likewise to the astonishment of other reformers—Edmund Burke, an erstwhile supporter of the American revolution and other liberal causes, responded angrily with *Reflections on the Revolution in France* (1790), reviling the leaders of the revolution while reiterating the necessity of "an established church, an established monarchy, an established aristocracy, and an established democracy" (p. 91). Comparing the dismantling of ancien-régime France to the destruction of a "noble and venerable castle," he mourned the loss of "Antient chivalry" (p. 76); after all, one might "have repaired those walls" and "have built on those old foundations" (p. 35). In turn, the publication of Burke's *Reflections* quickly unleashed a torrent of rebuttals over the course of the 1790s, attracting the likes of Mary Wollstonecraft (1759–1797), Thomas Paine (1737–1809), Joseph Priestley, and William Godwin (1756–1836). These rebuttals, particularly Paine's *Rights of Man* in 1791, advanced the case for a new, more accountable form of government while articulating a nearly unprecedented empathy for the lower and middle classes. Like Jebb, Priestley, and others, these radical writers also posited a utopian view of the future while demonizing the past. "Government is for the living, and not for the dead" (p. 17) as Paine put it tersely, and "old Governments" were all the worse for being constructed in such a manner as to "exclude knowledge as well as happiness" (p. 109). The Scottish jurist and historian James Mackintosh (1765–1832) called for the "gothic" values of aristocratic military power and conquest to be replaced by the "arts of peace" (p. 295) namely trade, agriculture, and scientific progress. From the perspective of the late-eighteenth-century reformer and radical, modern Britain was not all that removed from the Dark Ages: latter-day aristocrats were merely the successors to the marauding Norman robbers-turned-barons who had plundered from the Saxons, while the modern Anglican Church remained as beholden to the aristocracy and monarchy as did the Roman Catholic Church. Nor was modern Britain all that different from the largely Roman Catholic Continent.

The French Revolution also triggered a new awareness of women's rights. Sympathetic male writers such as the legal reformer Jeremy Bentham had begun to acknowledge the legal inequities faced by daughters and wives, and Mary Wollstonecraft was meanwhile applying her challenging of class injustice to gender injustice: was it fair that one sex should be subjected to another?

With the exponential sales of Paine's *Rights of Man* in 1792 came a strong backlash. Radicals were spied upon, rounded up, and placed on trial as Prime Minister William Pitt the Younger attempted to quell political and religious dissent. He also declared war on France, to the outrage of reformers and radicals who questioned the wisdom and justice of reinstituting the monarchy in France. The sense of national turmoil was further exacerbated during the latter half of the 1790s by a poor economy, food shortages, and increasingly rigorous measures over free speech and organization. In short, the unhappy state of Britain could be summed up in the signs "No George!" "No war!" "Bread!" For reformers and radicals alike, ideas of a "new millennium" and "New Jerusalem" (to arrive in 1800) promised by the dawn of the French Revolution were shattered by the end of the decade.

At first glance, Radcliffe's novels, with their predominantly Continental and historical settings, might appear to be entirely removed from the upheavals of 1790s Britain. Yet, when carefully examined, as scholarship on the gothic since the late twentieth century has demonstrated, Radcliffe's works are anything but conservative (as they were once assumed to be, by scholars such as David Durant). If her predominantly historical and Continental settings seem to recapitulate radical comparisons between 1790s Britain and medieval Europe, her occasional anachronisms—for instance, the presence of coffee and laced coats in *The Mysteries of Udolpho*—indicate that it is the former she had in mind. It is not accidental that Radcliffe's villains are either aristocrats, ecclesiastics, or both. Nor is it accidental that just as their "real-life" counterparts were allegedly guilty of plundering the people (e.g., taxation) and depriving them of their ancient Saxon rights (e.g., enfranchisement), Radcliffe's villains are guilty of comparable crimes. Not least, it is significant too that like Wollstonecraft and other feminist writers, Radcliffe demonstrated a keen awareness of the inequities faced by women. Indeed, as E. J. Clery claimed in a 1995 study of the origins of supernatural fiction, it was perhaps only natural that in a period consumed with anxieties over power, "supernatural suggestions are typically formed in the heroine's imagination like an imprint of the arbitrary excesses of patriarchy" (p. 133).

THE CASTLES OF ATHLIN AND DUNBAYNE

In many respects, Radcliffe's first novel, *The Castles of Athlin and Dunbayne: A Highland Story* (1789), is a true heir to Horace Walpole's *Castle of Otranto* (1764) and Clara Reeve's *Old English Baron* (1777). As the primary plot focuses primarily on the attempts of the young protagonist, Osbert, to exact vengeance on the neighboring chieftain of Dunbayne, Malcolm, for the slaying of his father, the subsidiary plot revolves around the true identity of Osbert's ally, Alleyn. Not unlike Theodore in *Otranto* and Edmund in *Old English Baron,* Alleyn is eventually discovered to be the rightful heir of Dunbayne. Despite the essential similarities, however, the reader can easily detect slight yet salient differences between Radcliffe's works and those of her immediate predecessors. Her talent for atmospheric suspense is already apparent in the opening pages as she describes Malcolm's castle—a description that prefigures the outlines of Dracula's castle more than a century later. It is "built with gothic magnificence upon a high and dangerous rock," with its "lofty towers still frown[ing] in proud sublimity," while "the immensity of the pile stood a record of the ancient consequence of its possessors" (p. 13); indeed, as an architectural embodiment of its owner, with his "frowning defiance" (p. 50) and "frown of insulting power" (p. 63), it might be said to pave the way for the idea of the possessed house. Moreover, in comparison with Walpole, Radcliffe's greater attention to the description of interiors further enhances the impression of preternatural eeriness—despite her general adherence to Johnsonian realism. The combination of rich atmospheric foreboding and sensational action is particularly successful when Osbert's sister, Mary, is kidnapped by the henchmen of her would-be suitor, the Count de Santmorin:

> They pursued their journey over the wilds, and towards the close of day approached the ruins of an abbey, whose broken arches and lonely towers arose in gloomy grandeur through the obscurity of evening. It stood the solitary inhabitant of the waste,—a monument of mortality and of ancient superstition, and the frowning majesty of its aspect seemed to command silence and veneration … She [Mary] was not so ill as to be insensible to the objects around her; the awful solitude of the place, and the solemn aspect of the fabric, whose effect was heightened by the falling glooms of evening, chilled her heart with horror....
>
> (p. 102)

The sense of threat is far more pressing here than when Manfred pursues Isabella in *Otranto*.

Another point of distinction in Radcliffe's novella is its more clearly articulated strain of political and social criticism: like her admirer Percy Bysshe Shelley (1792–1822), Radcliffe might be said to assume the role of a political poet as explicated in his *Defence of Poetry*: that is, an "unacknowledged legislator of the world." This is not to deny the presence of such criticism in *Otranto* and *Old English Baron,* where variations of "tyrant" and "tyranny" pervade the former while class consciousness crops up in the latter. In *Athlin and Dunbayne,* however, both criticisms are brought closer to the forefront. There is revolutionary fervor, as Alleyn denounces "the bad policy of oppression in a chief," adding that his lands "are scarcely sufficient to support his wretched people, who, sinking under severe exactions, suffer to lie uncultivated, tracts which would otherwise add riches to their Lord." It is all too certain that "his clan, oppressed by their burdens, threaten to rise and do justice to themselves by force of arms" (p. 7). Similarly, in a passage that is reminiscent of Jean-Jacques Rousseau, the soldiers fighting for Osbert and Alleyn are "impatient of the yoke of tyranny, only wait[ing] a favourable opportunity to throw it off, and resume the rights of nature" (p. 56). Even Malcolm's sister-in-law, confined in his domains, defies him with comparable rhetoric. Equally pointed are Radcliffe's observations on class. As Osbert's sister, Mary, and the apparent peasant Alleyn fall in love with one another, Osbert finds himself vexed by the prospect of a marriage across class lines—regardless of Alleyn's valiant efforts in the toppling of Malcolm. Here, the narrator deprecates the "hereditary pride" that "chilled the warm feelings of friendship and of gratitude." In another passage, Radcliffe dwells at greater length upon this injustice, this time mentioning "pride" and "prejudice" in close conjunction: Osbert's heart "struggled against the pride of birth" and "wished to reward the services and the noble spirit of the youth," but "the authority of early prejudice silenced the grateful impulse, and swept from his heart the characters of truth" (p. 88). Yet, despite the fact that such markedly antagonistic sentiments on class and hierarchy were more likely to be found in the fiction of the so-called Jacobin novelists, most notably Robert Bage (1728–1801), William Godwin, and Thomas Holcroft (1745–1809), it is nonetheless telling that unlike them, Radcliffe preferred the traditional fairy tale–like endings of Walpole and Reeve by revealing her apparent peasant Alleyn to be a baron.

A SICILIAN ROMANCE

If *Athlin and Dunbayne* can be regarded as the foundation of Radcliffe's novels, where her essential narrative strategies—her plot, characterization, imagery, and themes—appear in embryonic form, her second novel, *A Sicilian Romance* (1790), can be viewed as the framework: a framework not only of her future novels but also of the 1790s gothic novel in general. It is here that Radcliffe refines her techniques in the development of a more varied plot and the crafting of suspense. It is also here that she begins to experiment with the incorporation of embedded tales that form a counterpoint to the main narrative, serving to highlight predominant themes in the shape of tragic alternatives: for instance, the injustice of forced marriages and monastic immurement. Finally, it is here that nearly all of the stock ingredients commonly associated with this genre appear in full profusion: the Roman Catholic Continental historical setting; the young, motherless virginal daughter; the tyrannical, aristocratic father; the bigoted ecclesiastic; the old, decrepit, supposedly haunted edifice; and, most critically, the implied criticism of feudal mores.

The plot is one that centers somewhat loosely on a noble family, especially the youngest daughter, Julia. Already in the first few chapters, the reader is presented with the circumstances of a mysterious light in the supposedly haunted southern wing of the castle, a wing that connects to her new room when she is forced to yield her old one to her father's imperious second wife, Maria de Vellorno. The narrative proceeds at breakneck speed after Julia's father, the marquis of Mazzini, urges her to marry his friend, the duke de Luovo, as one sensational event follows another, including: an aborted elopement, Julia's successful solo escape to an abbey (and away), a capture by banditti, a miraculous rescue, and finally, the resolution to the mystery of the haunted wing. It is Radcliffe's nuanced handling of suspense, however, that takes *A Sicilian Romance* beyond earlier gothics. Unlike Walpole or the anonymous writers of *The Compleat Wizzard* (1770), a collection of supposedly real-life accounts involving ghosts, demons, and other creatures, Radcliffe is able to infuse a sense of dread without recourse to supernatural paraphernalia. The first instance takes place when Julia hears a low hollow sound from below her new room. Excitement builds as her brother, Ferdinand, discovers a small door hidden behind the tapestry in her bedroom and ventures beyond to find a desolate hall, one with "many parts falling to decay" and "wind-shutters shattered" (p. 40). The sound of a distant footstep leads him to pursue it through narrow winding passages encumbered with loose stones, while the menacing combination of darkness, unpredictability, and impending physical harm impels the reader on:

> After a momentary hesitation, he determined to ascend the stair-case, but its ruinous condition made this an adventure of some difficulty. The steps were decayed and broken, and the looseness of the stones rendered a footing very insecure. Impelled by an irresistible curiosity, he was undismayed, and began the ascent. He had not proceeded very far, when the stones of a step which his foot had just quitted, loosened by his weight, gave way; and dragging with them those adjoining, formed a chasm in the stair-case that terrified even Ferdinand, who was left tottering on the suspended half of the steps, in momentary expectation of falling to the bottom with the stone on which he rested.
>
> (p. 41)

Having survived this physical danger, Ferdinand is soon presented with the prospect of a supernatural peril, when his father relates the story behind the supposedly haunted southern building, adding that one night he "had such strong and dreadful proofs of the general assertion, that even at this moment I cannot recollect them without horror" (p. 53).

By the end of the novel, however, the haunting is revealed as a convenient fiction designed by the marquis in order to deter others from discovering his secret: namely, that he has concealed his first wife there for nearly twenty years after having fallen in love with the lascivious Maria de Vellorno. But again, what makes Radcliffe's treatment of this possible haunting distinctive is the tension that builds as the marquis cannily leads the servants to the "haunted" building in order to deter them not only from abandoning his service but also from exploring the forlorn, dilapidated building: he knows that his fearful servants, fond of gossip and rumors, will keep away from his secret even if there is supposedly "nothing." Indeed, over the following decade, the idea of the faked haunting—particularly one designed to deter others from detecting crimes—proved far more popular than the real haunting in the British gothic: as encountered not only in Radcliffe's next three novels but also in Charlotte Smith's *The Old Manor House* (1793), Francis Lathom's *Castle of Ollada* (1795) and *The Midnight Bell* (1798), and the anonymously written *Animated Skeleton* (1798).

Equally noteworthy in Radcliffe's second novel is the establishment of one of the genre's most powerful tropes: the arbitrary father and despot. Unlike Walpole's wildly exaggerated Manfred or even the stiff and opaque Malcolm, the marquis makes use of overt force as well as insinuated threats. Given the perceived downfall of the ancien régime after the fall of the Bastille, it is not entirely coincidental that Radcliffe presents sharp generational conflicts between fathers and children. The former, mired in the past, prove as dangerous to the young protagonists as the dark, unpredictable castles they inhabit; in this respect, Radcliffe resembles her close contemporary, William Blake (1757–1827) in her fixation with abusive fathers, kings, and priests. If the marquis is almost literally guilty of

burying his wife alive in the subterranean apartments, he behaves only slightly better to his children, locking up his two daughters and son (whom he cherishes only as a heir) at various points in the novel, while threatening Julia to either marry the duke de Luovo or "quit this castle for ever, and wander where you will" (p. 56). As a master, no less, he governs his servants with an iron fist, variously mocking and threatening them. In short, the marquis personifies all the dangers posed by a feudal paradigm of the family and world: a view that approximates that of Mary Wollstonecraft's *Vindication of the Rights of Men,* published in the same year.

Similarly, Radcliffe censures the church, alternatively ridiculing and demonizing it in a fashion almost reminiscent of her uncle, the younger John Jebb. Just as "the Superior" encountered by the duke de Luovo serves as a humorous means of ridiculing ecclesiastical hypocrisy, the abbot likewise serves as a more melodramatic means of criticizing ecclesiastical ambition. It is significant that the seemingly prototypical gothic description of the abbey itself at once invokes Radcliffe's familiarity with Dissenting criticisms of the Anglican and Roman Catholic churches. If Jebb disparaged "the craft and cunning of a despotic priesthood" (p. 164) while variously invoking visions of "clouds" (p. 186) and "gloom of popery" (p. 213) in such writings as *Every Man His Own Priest,* Radcliffe does much the same here:

> The view of this building revived in the mind of the beholder the memory of past ages ... Thus do the scenes of life vary with the predominant passions of mankind, and with the progress of civilization. The dark clouds of prejudice break away before the sun of science, and gradually dissolving, leave the brightening hemisphere to the influence of his beams ...
>
> ... The dim glass of the high-arched windows, stained with the colouring of monkish fictions ... spread around a sacred gloom, which inspired the beholder with congenial feelings.
>
> (pp. 116–117)

The very contrast between the ancient and the modern reveals as much a contrast endemic to gothic writing as it is to late-eighteenth-century Enlightenment writing.

ANN RADCLIFFE

THE ROMANCE OF THE FOREST

It is not until her composition of *The Romance of the Forest* (1791), however, that Radcliffe began to approach the height of her powers with a more substantially developed plot and nuanced shaping of character: features that were all remarked upon to varying extents by the *Critical Review, English Review, Monthly Review,* and *Scots Magazine.* Based on an actual story from Charlotte Smith's 1786 translation of François Gayot de Pitaval's *Causes célèbres et intéressantes*—a collection of seventeenth-century French trials—*Forest* tells the tale of a young woman who eventually retrieves her birthright as an heiress after discovering that her father was murdered by his younger brother. But if *Forest* is derived in part from a seventeenth-century tale, it may also have been influenced by events in contemporary Britain. Published in 1791, its plot, themes, and characters can be said to form as much of a response to Burke's *Reflections on the Revolution in France* as did James Mackintosh's *Vindiciae Gallicae* (1791) and Thomas Paine's *Rights of Man.*

The novel opens with a description of Pierre de la Motte and his wife as they leave Paris in order to flee their creditors. Here, Radcliffe reveals the Dissenting and reformist distrust of "city" types obsessed with wealth and rank. La Motte's mixed character—one seldom found in earlier gothic novels—is established from the very beginning. Although "his mind was active, and his imagination vivid," the latter is such that the "force of passion, often dazzled his judgement and subdued principle" (p. 2) The influence of passion is already a troubling one from a Dissenting perspective: that he was once "allured by the gaieties of Paris" (p. 3) to the point where "his fortune and affection were equally lost in dissipation" (p. 3) reinforces his foolish fondness for conspicuous consumption, particularly as "a false pride had still operated against his interest" (p. 3).

In contrast, the protagonist of the novel, Adeline, whom La Motte rescues from her surly captors, claims a number of virtues most lauded by Dissenters. Evincing "artless energy" (p. 6) she thrives in spite of her circumstances as "her mind had not lost by long oppression that elastic energy, which resists calamity" (p. 9): for all that she has suffered thus far, she remains capable of extending beyond her immediate self (unlike the villains in their self-absorption) to appreciate the beauties of nature. This is not to say that the virtues of Adeline are exclusively cerebral. Indeed, Radcliffe might be said to lavish a proto-cinematic attention to her physical charms. If Burke's *Reflections* had created a sexualized image of Marie Antoinette, once "full of life, and splendor" (p. 76) flying "almost naked" (p. 71) from her persecutors in October 1789, Radcliffe goes beyond. La Motte finds himself "impossible to contemplate the beauty and distress of the object before him with indifference" (p. 5) with her "habit of grey camlet, with short slashed sleeves" that "shewed, but did not adorn, her figure" as it "was thrown open at the bosom, upon which part of her hair had fallen in disorder" (p. 7).

To assume any Burkean tendencies on Radcliffe's part, however, is premature, for that illusion quickly evaporates when her description of the abbey and its owner, the polished but treacherous Marquis de Montalt, are taken into account. Just as Dissenters, reformers, and radicals perceived the present government of Britain as a disturbingly anachronistic one, riddled with arbitrariness and unpredictability, the abbey itself—once the site of a murder as Adeline soon discovers in a dusty, occasionally illegible manuscript—conforms to this view. Ancient and desolate, the abbey conveys a distinct feeling of oppression in Madame de La Motte upon arrival, not unlike a collective embodiment of its despotic owners. More significantly, as a feudal edifice that is half-modernized in places, with a "spacious apartment" that "was evidently of a much later date than the other part of the structure" (p. 20) and a vaulted room "built in modern times upon a Gothic plan" (p. 20), it shares a certain affinity with Burke's view of the ideal form of government: one that retained the old walls and "old foundations." This politicized framework is no less reinforced by the history of the abbey itself whereby the very shift in hands from the church to an aristocratic landowner mirrors at one remove the convenient and dangerous alliance between the church and aristocracy that reformers and radicals deplored. In other words, like the Mazzini castle, the abbey embodies the threat of a feudal, ancien-régime government.

Not surprisingly, its owner, Marquis de Montalt, personifies the evils of an ancien-régime aristocracy; one that traces its origins back to the Norman military orders as Paine and Wollstonecraft observed separately. A high-ranking nobleman and colonel, the marquis abuses his social and political privileges, clearly anticipating the lecherous aristocrats and soldiers of Wollstonecraft's *Vindication of the Rights of Woman* (1792): this is made particularly clear not only when he abducts Adeline to his showy, luxurious villa, one filled with wine, women, and song, but also when he explains his philosophy of life to the shocked La Motte. Like the reformist stereotype of the aristocratic authority figure, the marquis is unprincipled, maintaining that "when my life ... requires the sacrifice of another, or even if some passion, wholly unconquerable, requires it, I should be a madman to hesitate" (p. 222). As such, though seemingly "amiable" and elegant—the very personification of Burke's noble "Corinthian column"—the marquis' attractiveness belies his personal decrepitude.

If *Forest* demonstrates a more sophisticated command of themes and tropes from her earlier novels, it also reveals Radcliffe's skilled approach to characterization, particularly in scenes involving conflict. The occasion of the marquis' visit to the La Mottes is a tense one that subtly exhibits the barely repressed emotions of the two men, when the former recognizes the latter as his attacker in the forest. Although this fact is not yet disclosed, the reader detects La Motte's fear and the marquis' instinctive desire for revenge, as well as their mutual efforts to suppress their feelings in front of the women:

> He advanced towards the Marquis with a complacent air,; but ... his limbs trembled, and a ghastly paleness overspread his countenance. The Marquis was little less agitated, and in the first moment of surprize, put his hand upon his sword; but, recollecting himself, he withdrew it, and endeavoured to obtain a command of features. A pause of agonizing silence ensued.

(p. 88)

The uncomfortable exchange of glances that is noticed by Madame de la Motte but awkwardly dismissed by both men raises questions in the reader's mind without actually yielding any real clues as to the wronged party. Nor is Radcliffe any less observant in her delineation of La Motte's growing sense of horror and conflict when the marquis presses him to murder Adeline. Well aware "of having deserved from the Marquis a dreadful punishment," La Motte trembles at the consequences of refusing to "acquiesce in his designs" (p. 227). His conflict between self-preservation and conscience heightens the suspense until he urges Adeline to escape.

There is a distinct narrative lull when Adeline settles in safely with the humble La Lucs. Yet it is one that unequivocally exposes Radcliffe's Dissenting biases, as it pits the virtues of the elderly clergyman, Arnand La Luc, against the corrupt, aristocratic vices of Montalt and to a slightly lesser extent, the La Mottes. Although it is difficult to determine Radcliffe's familiarity with Wollstonecraft's *Vindication of the Rights of Men* (1790), with its praise of Richard Price—a friend of Bentley's and Jebb's—it is striking to discern numerous correspondences in their respective descriptions. Like Wollstonecraft's Price, La Luc is modest, rational, scientific, and paternalistic. The secret of Adeline's identity begins to unravel at what initially begins as La Motte's trial for the attempted murder of Montalt. Discovering that her father was slain by his younger brother, Montalt, near the latter's abbey out of desire for his estate and title, she is suddenly reminded of the recollections of the murdered man at the abbey before determining "if she should recover her rights, to have the manuscript sought for" (p. 346). Significantly enough, this emphasis on the reclamation of rights is a rhetoric shared by the founders of the Society for Constitutional Information and, as such, *The Romance of the Forest* can be interpreted as a variation on the theme of the Norman yoke. Representing the usurping Norman and his corrupt aristocratic descendant alike, Montalt is as much a savage robber-turned-baron as an ostensibly polished and influential contemporary nobleman—just as his ancient, semimodernized abbey represents Britain's semimodernized government: indeed, the struggle faced by Adeline at the abbey might be easily viewed as an allegory of Britannia under a near-feudal government. The vanquishing of aristocratic values is settled by the end of the novel as Adeline and her lover, Theodore, settle in his native (republican) Switzerland, choosing a chateau "characterized by an air of simplicity and taste, rather than of magnificence" (p. 362).

THE MYSTERIES OF UDOLPHO

Expectations ran high for Radcliffe's next novel, *The Mysteries of Udolpho*—so high that she was advanced the considerable sum of £500 by a private publisher rather than a publisher for the circulating libraries. When the book appeared in May 1794, critics rushed to review it. The *British Critic* and *Gentleman's Magazine* variously complained and acknowledged that there was "too much of the terrific," "the adventures do not sufficiently point to one centre," and the plot "admirably kept up" but the reader "held too long in suspense, and the development brought on too hastily in the concluding volume." But *Udolpho* was also hailed by the *Critical Review* as "the most interesting novel in the English language," and ultimately ran through numerous editions, translations, and adaptations (into plays and chapbooks, for instance) in her lifetime. It was certainly popular enough in 1798 for Catherine Morland, the heroine of Jane Austen's *Northanger Abbey*, to mention as "very entertaining."

Although many of the same gothic themes and tropes recur, they do so with far greater intensity. The cold, guarded, yet clearly dominant Montoni, though fundamentally no different from Malcolm and the marquis of Mazzini, is a far more impressive yet credible villain as he threatens, manipulates, and schemes: the death of his wife—the foolish aunt of Emily, the protagonist—even if not the result of a brutal murder but rather of close confinement in a distant part of his castle, renders his cruelty that much more

palpable. The banditti imagined by Paine, Wollstonecraft, and others emerge even more vividly as condottieri: perhaps even more so than the plundering and pillaging counterrevolutionary aristocrats in Charlotte Smith's *Desmond* (1792). Similarly, Montoni's castle is also a far larger entity, not only physically but metaphysically, with its abundant tales of dark crimes and unhappy spirits. Indeed, Radcliffe's growing mastery of the genre is amply demonstrated in her brilliant rendering of atmosphere. One might compare her relatively simple portrait of Dunbayne castle to that of Udolpho:

> The sun had just sunk below the top of the mountains she was descending, whose long shadow stretched athwart the valley, but his sloping rays, shooting through an opening of the cliffs, touched with a yellow gleam the summits of the forest …
>
> "There," said Montoni, speaking for the first time in several hours, "is Udolpho."
>
> Emily gazed with melancholy awe upon the castle, which she understood to be Montoni's; for, though it was now lighted up by the setting sun, the gothic greatness of its features, and its mouldering walls of dark grey stone, rendered it a gloomy and sublime object. As she gazed, the light died away on its walls, leaving a melancholy purple tint, which spread deeper and deeper, as the thin vapour crept up the mountain, while the battlements above were still tipped with splendour. From those too, the rays soon faded, and the whole edifice was invested with the solemn duskiness of evening. Silent, lonely, and sublime, it seemed to stand the sovereign of the scene, and to frown defiance on all who dared to invade its solitary reign. As the twilight deepened, its features became more awful in obscurity …
>
> (p. 216)

More so than Dunbayne, Udolpho is nearly a character in its own right, as if radiating the demonic energies of past and present despots. Here, the interplay of the light on the dark towers adds further touches of the sublime to the building, as if revealing glimpses of its own preternatural life.

However much Radcliffe's characters—most notably St. Aubert, Emily, and Montoni (to some extent)—privilege Dissenting rationality over passion and emotion, it is Radcliffe's burgeoning awareness of psychology that distinguishes her style from other novelists of her period. Even if her first biographer, Thomas Talfourd, correctly conceded that "to develope [sic] character was not within the scope of Mrs. Radcliffe's plan, nor compatible with her style" (p. 120), her delineation of social interactions and the interplay between emotions, reasons, and desires may be said to demarcate a new standard in the development of character. Her careful depictions of the rash and foolish Verezzi, the hotheaded Morano, the pretentious Quesnels, Emily's awkward yet ambitious and stalwart aunt, and finally Emily herself, sensitive, prudent, yet courageous—particularly when accompanied by her wry omniscient commentary—look forward to Jane Austen. While Montoni's exchanges with his men attain a realism uncommon in the gothic novel, the Quesnels' petty attempts at displaying their wealth and social standing (through the subtle jabs at Madame Cheron that go over her head) could easily be scenes from *Pride and Prejudice* (1813) or *Emma* (1816).

More effective still are the renderings of Emily's conflicting emotions as she wavers between melancholy, fear, and determination: paradoxically, her attempts to shake off her melancholy and sense of foreboding subvert the ideal of rational equilibrium instilled in her by her father, St. Aubert—as if Radcliffe were tacitly acknowledging the limitations of human reason. Take for instance, her recollections when staring out of her bedroom window at Udolpho. Gazing at the sky, she notices the same planet she had seen in Languedoc on the night before her father's death, recalling the solemn music that "the tenderness of her spirits" had "in spite of her reason, given a superstitious meaning" (p. 310). She weeps at the memory of that evening before suddenly hearing the music outside of her window; such brings "a superstitious dread" at which "she stood listening, for some moments, in trembling expectation" before "endeavour[ing] to recollect her thoughts, and to reason herself into composure" (p. 310). Likewise, consider the following passage where Radcliffe captures Emily's reactions to the discovery that one of the men conducting her to Tuscany is in fact a murderer:

Emily now breathed with difficulty, and could scarcely support herself. When first she saw these men, their appearance and their connection with Montoni had been sufficient to impress her with distrust; but now, when one of them had betrayed himself to be murderer, and she saw herself, at the approach of night, under his guidance, among wild and solitary mountains, and going she scarcely knew whither, the most agonizing terror seized her, which was the less supportable from the necessity she found herself under of concealing all symptoms of it from her companions. Reflecting on the character and the menaces of Montoni, it appeared not improbable, that he had delivered her to them, for the purpose of having her murdered, and of thus securing to himself, without further opposition, or delay, the estates, for, which he had so long and so desperately contended. Yet, if this was his design, there appeared no necessity for sending her to such a distance from the castle; for, if any dread of discovery had made him unwilling to perpetrate the deed there, a much nearer place might have sufficed for the purpose of concealment. These considerations, however, did not immediately occur to Emily, with whom so many circumstances conspired to rouse terror, that she had no power to oppose it, or to enquire coolly into its grounds; and, if she had done so, still there were many appearances which would too well have justified her most terrible apprehensions. She did not now dare to speak to her conductors …

(p. 383)

The long breathless jumble of gut feelings and rational reflections, not to mention the details of the wild physical surroundings, all serve to heighten the overall sense of agitation. Again, as in the preceding example, fear threatens to overcome any internal exhortation to enlightened self-control.

Not least are there hints of the more complex characterizations of the nineteenth-century bildungsroman, when Emily struggles to defend herself to her various guardians. This becomes apparent in her confrontation with Montoni when he undertakes to coerce her into resigning her estates to him. Despite her earlier prudent advice to Madame Montoni,, she changes her mind upon her newfound desire to save the estates for her lover, Valancourt. It is here that she summons "the latent powers of her fortitude into action" (p. 358)—as if following the advice of Mary Wollstonecraft in *Vindication of the Rights of Woman*—instead of becoming overwhelmed by "despondency" (p. 358). There is even a turning point of sorts when Emily bests Montoni, intimidating him momentarily, such that for the first time "the full extent of her own superiority to Montoni" by which she "despised the authority, which, till now, she had only feared" (p. 360).

By the end of the novel, Radcliffe proceeds to deliver her unexpected explanations for the various mysteries. Just as earlier in the novel nothing was ever quite what it seemed—the black veil did not conceal a portrait, Montoni and his wife were less wealthy than either expected, and Valancourt was not absolutely faithful (in fact, he resembles Montoni in certain respects)—the solutions to the mysteries are as equally unexpected. The woman depicted in the miniature cherished by St. Aubert, Emily's father, is not his lover, but rather his much-pitied sister. The terrifying object behind the black veil is not the remains of Laurentini, or even a true corpse, but rather a waxen memento intended to humble the pride of an earlier Montoni. In short, *Udolpho* might already be said to contain the seeds of its own parody in *Northanger Abbey*. But it may be added that like Radcliffe, Jane Austen was also cognizant that the gothic is never entirely remote from reality either.

JOURNEY MADE IN THE SUMMER OF 1794

Flushed with the success of *Udolpho,* the Radcliffes embarked on a journey to the Continent, intending to travel to Switzerland via Holland and Germany. Given the immense popularity of travel literature during the latter half of the century, it is not surprising that the Radcliffes decided to collaborate on an account of their journey, publishing it under her name. Although Radcliffe took care to credit her husband with observations on economics and politics in her preface, it is more than likely that she must have agreed sufficiently with his views to allow them to pass under her authorship.

Much of *A Journey Made in the Summer of 1794* (published in 1795, with the detailed subtitle*: Through Holland and the Western Frontier of Germany, with a Return down the Rhine; to Which Are Added, Observations During a Tour to the Lakes of Lancashire, Westmoreland, and Cumberland*) reverberates with the political and ethical values of Dissent. When compared with other contemporary British travel writings on Holland, Radcliffe devotes considerable attention to the largely middle-class Dutch struggle for liberation from a feudal, aristocratic Roman Catholic Spain: a conflict that may have borne some resonance for the liberally inclined Radcliffes, particularly as Dutch radicals, like their British counterparts, vowed to reclaim their ancient Batavian liberties. This fascination with the struggle for middle-class Protestant freedom is evident from the Radcliffes' choice of historical sites, including the Doolen, an inn erected in 1565 and a monument otherwise overlooked by other travel writers of Radcliffe's day, that was "used by the burghers of Delft for public purposes, during the struggle of the Provinces against Spain" (p. 19). In turn, when the couple proceeds from a predominantly Protestant Holland to Germany, the lingering presence of Roman Catholic fiefdoms and bishoprics in the latter allow Radcliffe to rehearse Dissenting arguments against ecclesiastical artificiality and coerciveness. There is a touch of melodrama as she reflects upon the order of Clarisse at Cologne and their rules forbidding nuns from seeing their parents ever again. Such are "horrible perversions of human reason" that "make the blood thrill and the teeth chatter" (p. 109). Proceeding to voice "astonishment at the artificial miseries, which the ingenuity of human beings forms for themselves by seclusion, is as boundless as at other miseries" (p. 109), she echoes Joseph Priestley's antimonastic sentiments. It is equally telling that her examples not only recapitulate Dissenting criticism on Catholic and Anglican severity but also anticipate some of the characters and scenarios in her following novel, *The Italian* (which appeared in 1797): the proud and severe abbess of San Stefano in that work may have been inspired by the first abbess of the Ladies' Chapter of Vilich, who delivered blows to any nuns who "neglected to sing in the choir" as a method of "restoring their voices" (*Journey*, p. 324). Likewise, the abbess's obsession with aristocratic lineage may have been inspired by the rules at the exclusive Benedictine abbey of Siegberg, which required "the most strict and ceremonious proof, as to the sixteen quarterings in the arms of the candidate … unblemished by any plebeian symptoms" (*Journey,* p. 325).

In light of the generally accepted knowledge of Dissenting prominence in British manufacturing and trade, it is equally telling that Radcliffe applauds the significance of religious toleration for the improvement of trade. Commending the German elector palatine for "permitting the Calvinists and Lutherans to establish their forms of worship there, under equal privileges with the Roman Catholics" (p. 296) and building the prosperity of Bacharach, she contrasts his tolerance to the "pusillanimity" (p. 329) of his predecessor at the earlier part of the century, a man who allowed bigoted Colognese merchants to persecute Protestant merchants. Similarly, Radcliffe defends the late-thirteenth-century burgesses of Cologne for defying their archbishop by means of "a successful resistance" and thereby obtaining the "enjoyment of some commercial rights, here so rare as to be called privileges" (p. 330).

Not least, the Radcliffes' ambivalence, if not outright opposition, toward the war against France grows steadily apparent during the Continental portion of their tour. While commending the Dutch for their reluctance to enter the war, the Radcliffes deplore the casualties and scenes of carnage. It is significant too that the Radcliffes express more hostility against the allies of Britain—the Germans and particularly the Austrians—in this segment, while remaining relatively silent on the French. Some of the anger, however, may be at least partially attributed to their unfortunate experience at the borders of Switzerland, when an Austrian official hassled them over a mistake in their passport. Fearing possible maltreatment from a man "with a disposition for further injustice," the Radcliffes decided to head back to England and travel to the Lake District instead.

Upon their return to England, they breathe a sigh of relief, "the joy of an escape" from what clearly appeared to them as a state of gothic oppression, particularly in "districts where there was scarcely an [sic] home for the natives" (p. 370). Professing "the love of our own country, greatly enhanced by all that had been seen of others" (p. 370), Radcliffe interestingly links Germany with the masculine sublime—that which can be inferred from the idea of power in Burke's *Sublime and Beautiful* and *Reflections*—and Britain with the feminine virtues of empathy, delicacy, and beauty. The "long corn grounds, the huge stretches of hills, the vast plains, and the wide vallies" in Germany can be contrasted to the "gently swelling slopes, rich in verdure, thick inclosures" in England; in short, "English landscape may be compared to cabinet pictures, delicately beautiful and highly finished" and German scenery to paintings "of bold outline and often sublime, but coarse and to be viewed with advantage from a distance." (pp. 370–371). The unstated conclusion is one that elevates Dissenting and reformist notions of government over hierarchical, ancien-régime feudal governments.

As Radcliffe proceeds to Westmoreland and Cumberland, she makes little attempt to guard her political views, roundly criticizing Liverpool for its participation in "the dreadful guilt of the Slave Trade," one of "robbery, cruelty, and murder" (p. 377). It is a striking remark in the context of contemporary travel literature, which was notable for its relative lack of commentary on slavery. It is equally striking that at Kendal, as Robert Miles points out, Radcliffe stopped to contemplate the obelisk erected in 1788 for the centenary commemoration of the Glorious Revolution. Claiming a tacit kinship with those who recently celebrated the French Revolution as a latter-day counterpart of the Glorious Revolution, she observes the oppressiveness of the French ancien régime, which Englishmen were "once justly taught to believe," while betraying impatience with those critical of the ideals of the French Revolution:

At a time, when the memory of that revolution is reviled, and the praises of liberty itself endeavoured to be suppressed by the artifice of imputing to it the crimes of anarchy, it was impossible to omit any act of veneration to the blessings of this event. Being thus led to ascend the hill, we had a view of the country, over which it presides; a scene simple, great and free as the spirit revered amidst it.

(p. 389)

By condemning "the artifice" of blaming the praises of liberty for "the crimes of anarchy," Radcliffe attacks Tory conservatism.

Dissenting approbation of middle-class simplicity and distrust of the bustling city resonates throughout her travels through the Lake District. Radcliffe found herself "struck by the superior simplicity and modesty of the people" who remain "secluded from great towns and from examples of selfish splendour"; acting "freely ... without interruption from envy or triumph," they behave "without servility" and are "plain but not rude" (pp. 397). At Threlkeld, Radcliffe praises the inhabitants for their "true consciousness of independence," underscoring the advantages of a society with few marks of social inequality and luxury. Since the poor are freed from the "baseness ... of becoming abject before persons of one class" and "insolent to those of another," they do not experience the miseries "that dejected vanity and multiplied wishes inflict upon the pursuers of the higher ranks" (pp. 443-444)

It is also here that Radcliffe delivers some of her most stirring sketches of scenery. Her description of Ullswater would certainly not be out of place in a novel, as she ponders the "glimpses of the gigantic shapes" that leave the imagination "thus elevated, to paint the 'forms of things unseen.'" The dark, broken tops of the fells, spread with a mysterious blue tint, are "of size and shape most huge, bold, and awful" seeming "almost supernatural, though according in gloom and sublimity with the severe features it involved" (p. 408).

THE ITALIAN

Not surprisingly, the publication of *The Italian; or, The Confessional of the Black Penitents* was awaited with high expectations—particularly since it drew an even larger sum of £800. When it finally appeared in late 1796, it was lauded by the *New Monthly Magazine* and the *Analytical Review* for marked improvement in reflection and less diffusiveness. Although still recognizably gothic, with its sinister aristocrats, dark, threatening ruins, and reflections on "holy hypocrisy," *The Italian* is a decidedly different work from *Udolpho*. Its most salient difference is a more sharply focused plot centered on two young lovers, Ellena and Vivaldi, who encounter parental opposition from the latter's haughty mother, the Marchesa. Refusing to allow her son to marry beneath him, the Marchesa seeks the assistance of the diabolical-seeming, larger-than-life monk, Father Schedoni (the "Italian"), in order to prevent their union. After a botched escape with Ellena, Vivaldi falls into the clutches of the Inquisition: scenes that are easily some of the most tense and finely wrought in the history of the gothic novel. But at least equally conspicuous is Radcliffe's meticulous attention to detail regarding character. The opening description of Schedoni, with all of its grotesque singularity, represents a considerable departure from the more generalized gothic villains of other authors, not least the eponymous protagonist of Matthew Lewis' famous novel, *The Monk* (1795), a figure who was widely perceived to be the inspiration for *The Italian*. Of Schedoni, Radcliffe writes:

His figure was striking, but not so from grace; it was tall, and, though extremely thin, his limbs were large and uncouth, and as he stalked along, wrapt in the black garments of his order, there was something terrible in its air; something almost super-human. His cowl, too, as it threw a shade over the livid paleness of his face, encreased its severe character, and gave an effect to his large melancholy eye, which approached to horror ... There was something in his physiognomy extremely singular, and that can not easily be defined. It bore the traces of many passions, which seemed to have fixed the features they no longer animated. An habitual gloom and severity prevailed over the deep lines of his countenance; and his eyes were so piercing that they seemed to penetrate, at a single glance, in the hearts of men ...

(p. 35)

It is here that we begin to find glimpses not only of the brooding Byronic antihero but also the complex and less-than-perfect heroes Heathcliff and Rochester of the Brontë sisters.

Radcliffe's prescient awareness of human psychology is no less perceptible in this novel than before. A dramatic scene by the beach where Schedoni begins to pity Ellena in spite of himself is intensified a few pages later when he approaches her room, ready to stab her. It is a scene not unlike that in *The Romance of the Forest,* as La Motte steadies himself to kill Adeline; however, the agitation in Schedoni's mind is more explicitly detailed as the reader sees him possessed of a "shuddering horror" before coming to himself temporarily, and finally struck again by a "new cause of horror" that "seemed to seize all his frame." For the first time, Radcliffe describes the visceral effects of fright: "His respiration was short and laborious, chilly drops stood on his forehead, and all his faculties of mind seemed suspended" (p. 234).

Likewise, the more even-keeled exchanges between Schedoni and the Marchesa represent a step forward as Radcliffe traces their various desires and wishes with a fair degree of plausibility. The bond between them is no longer merely a bond between the aristocracy and the church but rather is a more complex, humanized connection in which they attempt to manipulate one another. The reader's interest is piqued when Schedoni suspects that Ellena is his daughter before attempting to persuade the Marchesa that Vivaldi's choice may be suitable after all. Here, Schedoni proposes his ideas in such a way that flatters her own self-image—"Trusting to the natural clearness of your perceptions, I doubt not that when you have maturely considered the subject, every objection will yield to a consideration of your son's happiness" (p. 295)—while the Marchesa remains distrustful; instead, she chooses to feign agreement, "not suffering him to suspect that she had withdrawn her confidence, but inducing him to believe that she had relinquished all farther design against Ellena" (p. 298).

Not least in *The Italian* is Radcliffe's full mastery of suspense. Vivaldi's visit to the ruins of Paluzzi might be said to support Radcliffe's claims, in her unpublished sketch "On the Supernatural in Poetry," that if "obscurity leaves something for the imagination to exaggerate," terror is something that is "not distinctly pictured forth, but is seen in glimpses through obscuring shades" tending to "excite the imagination to

complete the rest." The overall darkness, desolation, dimly perceived shapes, and apparent blood stains at Paluzzi all convey danger. Radcliffe cleverly incorporates a few hints of the supernatural when she adds, "Its garments, if garments they were, were dark" and "when he [Vivaldi] reached the head of the stair-case, however, the form, whatever it might be, was gone" (p. 74). Finally, the novel's scenes involving the Inquisition are among the most dramatic ones in fiction of this period, as the natural assumes the aura of the supernatural. The darkness, concealed faces, "shadowy countenances," "uncertain forms," and, above all, the seemingly disembodied voices, lend the trial a palpable nightmarishness not found in her earlier novels, while the gradual revelation of Schedoni's past and misdeeds bring the novel to a potent climax.

GASTON DE BLONDEVILLE

Gaston de Blondeville; or, The Court of Henry III, Keeping Festival in Ardenne (1826) is the only novel that Radcliffe did not publish immediately. Reasons for her hesitation remain unknown; it has been assumed that either she had second thoughts or that the book was turned down by her publisher. The fact that Radcliffe later failed to recognize the novel as her own when perusing it some years later suggests that she may have felt uncomfortable with a work so ostensibly different from her other works: one lacking her familiar Continental settings, a young heroine, and the use of the "explained supernatural." But whatever its differences, it is arguably Radcliffe's most tautly designed novel, where suspense and tension are wound up to the highest pitch until the very end.

The novel begins with King Henry III's arrival at Kenilworth, where the approaching wedding of Gaston de Blondeville, the king's favorite courtier, is about to take place. The festivities are disrupted, however, by the arrival of a merchant, Hugh Woodreeve, who seeks justice for the death of his kinsman Reginald de Folville, slain in a forest by a group of robbers. Upon seeing Gaston by the side of Henry III, Woodreeve recognizes him as none other than the murderer and faints. On the following day, Woodreeve accosts the king, telling him the events of that fatal night. Visibly discomfited, Gaston accuses Woodreeve of lying and after further interrogation, Henry confines Woodreeve to await trial. The odds seem to be decidedly stacked against Woodreeve with the arrival of the Prior, who defends Gaston.

Particularly groundbreaking here is Radcliffe's ingenious use of a doubled plot, of which the first element is the implied revelation of Gaston's guilt to the reader, and the second element the active persecution of Woodreeve. The first four days provide clues that incline the reader to accept Woodreeve's claims, as Gaston finds himself increasingly disturbed not only by the entertainments—the ballads, lays, and pageant—that indicate his uneasy conscience, but also by the presence of a ghostly knight at his wedding and banquet. The narrative pace accelerates in the second half of the novel, as Radcliffe shifts her attention to the active persecution of Woodreeve, particularly when the Prior appears at the merchant's prison on the fifth night, attempting to persuade Woodreeve to escape and drop his accusation. It is at this point that Radcliffe provides a thrilling chase through dark winding corridors, stairways, and subterranean dungeons as Woodreeve follows the Prior with great anxiety, fearing both pursuit by others and treachery at the hands of the Prior. Certainly, Woodreeve's sudden recollection of the Prior as one of Gaston's henchmen that fatal night—a recognition that compels the Prior to pursue him with a dagger—shows Radcliffe at her most effective. Far from subsiding, however, tension continues to escalate again on the following day of the trial, without relenting until the very end of the tale, when Woodreeve is reunited with his wife and amply compensated by the king.

Despite the apparent differences between *Gaston* and the earlier novels—in its English setting, a more meticulous handling of historical accuracy, and structural cogency—*Gaston* itself may be construed as the logical resolution of her novels, not to mention the most direct commentary on the times. Radcliffe's final novel can be read not only as a continued onslaught against the aristocracy, clergy, and feudal mores, but also as a withering critique of William Pitt's repression of radicalism. Here, the bond between Gaston and the Prior—analogous to that between Schedoni and the Marchesa in *The Italian*—once more reproduces the liberal perception that the aristocracy and church were guilty of creating disorder while allied in their oppression of common Britons. Just as Charles Pigott associated the church with "monkish rapacity" and the aristocracy decried as "a monster of rapacity, and an enemy to mankind" in his censored *Political Dictionary* (1795), Gaston and the Prior prove guilty of robbing and attacking Woodreeve and de Folville. The polished yet brutal Gaston, like Montalt and Montoni, again represents the intersection between the Norman robber-cum-baron and the elegant courtier possessed of Burke's "ancient chivalry" in his delicate mannerisms. The Prior's words and actions, meanwhile, appear to affirm popular reformist allegations, as found in Pigott's *Political Dictionary,* whereby the church "will justify any thing that is expedient, whether it is robbery or church." At the same time, Gaston's and the Prior's reactions to Woodreeve's accusations conform to that of the "alarmists" ridiculed by Pigott as "miserable politicians, who have been … terrified by the downfall of aristocracy" and "have joined the conspiracy of courts against the interests of the humanity." Finally, the third member of the dangerous triumvirate is King Henry III. Although the least culpable of the group in his general desire to do right, it is noteworthy that he possesses traits associated with George III, widely caricatured as a dim-witted and inarticulate monarch preyed upon by his ministers: these flaws were also identified by William Godwin as particular disadvantages endemic to a monarchy in *Enquiry Concerning Political Justice* (1794). Not surprisingly, Radcliffe returns to her Dissenting emphasis on conscience and independence of mind—traits conspicuously lacking in Henry III:

his [Woodreeve's] peril arose not from any indifference of the King to do what was right, but from the want of steadiness in his mind, and from that misdirected kindness of heart, which made even a suspicion of guilt in one he had esteemed and trusted so painful, that a conviction of it seemed not to be endured. It is well known, that a weak mind, rather have such a suffering, will turn aside, and take shelter in willing credulity to its first opinion.

(p. 116)

As long as Henry III remains enslaved to his whims and passions rather than to principles, he casts doubt on the intrinsic infallibility of the monarchy: the idea that the king can do no wrong.

In distinct contrast to these three blameworthy characters, Woodreeve might be said to represent not only the common Briton (unlike Julia, Adeline, Emily, and Ellena, with their aristocratic lineage)—but the much-persecuted radical Briton. Not unlike the situation of a typical British radical—whether it be a Joseph Priestley pursued by angry church and king mobs; a Thomas Paine; or any of many other writers accused of sedition—Woodreeve's "crime" in *Gaston* is the equivalent one of exposing the crimes of the authorities as he dares to think for himself and do what is right:

And now, what had he gained by his courageous demand of justice? Suspicion, contempt, fear, grief, a prison, and perhaps, death. Yet did he not repent the effort he had made, so honest was his grief for the fate of his kinsman; so much was his mind possessed with the notion, that he had accused his very murderer; so confident was he, that he was performing a duty; and, what is more, so sure was he, that to perform his duty in this world is the wisest, the most truly cunning thing a man can contrive to do.

(p. 67)

Just as this desire is elevated into a radical "cause of humanity" (p. 199), it is hardly accidental that Woodreeve is also accused of spying for the king's enemies, in much the same way that 1790s English radicals were.

Not fortuitously, the most positively portrayed members of the "establishments" in *Gaston* are the archbishop of York and Prince Edward, both of whom display a critical acumen lacking in Henry III. In particular, the archbishop looks askance at "the wasteful magnificence" of the festival and deplores the king's injustice toward Woodreeve as "a striking instance of blindness to the cause of the oppressed" (p. 162).

Given the general impression that reform in England "was dead and buried" by 1800—particularly with the exile of Paine in 1792, the departure of Priestley for the United States in 1794, and the death of Mary Wollstonecraft in 1797, along with the general cessation of radical activity—it is perhaps not surprising that the liberally inclined feared that nothing short of a miracle could save their goals. This may explain why Radcliffe chose to introduce a ghost for the first time in her fiction: a supernatural character that is easily more Shakespearean than gothic in form and function. It is difficult to avoid a sense of "comeuppance" when Gaston dies from shock with the appearance of the mysterious knight who arrives at the tournament; the fact that the latter wields a sword emblazoned with the word "Justice" directly recalls the ideals of the French Revolution. Only with Gaston's death can the full extent of his crimes—murder, robbery, and bigamy—be revealed. But the ending is not complete without the king's rewards to Woodreeve, making him fully prosperous: as if Radcliffe, like other liberals, believed that the sooner the age of aristocratic militarism and conquest was replaced by one of middle-class trade and "arts of peace" the better. And as such, Radcliffe concludes her novel with a vision of literal and figurative enlightenment. If Thomas Paine had optimistically declared in *Rights of Man*, "There is a morning of reason rising upon man on the subject of government, that has not appeared before," Radcliffe's novel closes with a reflection on the "beams of another day springing on the darkness" and "those first pure tints of light upon the darkness, more touching, more eloquent to the soul, than even the glorious sun-rise" (pp. 205–206).

ASSESSMENT AND LEGACY

By the time *Gaston* was published, Ann Radcliffe's literary star had already fallen. What happened? On one hand, as Rictor Norton explains, the not-so-subtle undermining of the gothic by William Wordsworth and Samuel Taylor Coleridge—who had once been admirers and even envious imitators of Radcliffe—could not but affect her reception adversely. Moreover, as Michael Gamer suggests, the rise of conservatism in the political and literary establishments alike inevitably led to the critical disparaging of the gothic, with its democratic and populist tendencies.

Yet, this is not to say that Radcliffe's novels would remain untouched, entirely relegated to literary oblivion. In fact, they can be said to have retained a ghostly presence in the works of her admirers and their literary descendents centuries later and continents apart. If her themes and use of suspense came to be adopted by the Brontë sisters, Charles Dickens, Wilkie Collins, Sheridan Le Fanu, and Bram Stoker (to name only a few), they were no less eagerly embraced by Nathaniel Hawthorne and Edgar Allan Poe. Hawthorne's *The House of the Seven Gables* (1851), a novel complete with an eerie old house, an ambitious judge, and a recovered birthright, belongs to this tradition as does Poe's "The Fall of the House of Usher" (1839). Even today, it is difficult to find horror or suspense fiction that does not reveal some influence of "Mother Radcliffe." Certainly, the popular "gothic romances" of the 1950s to the 1970s owe more than a bit to her, while Stephen King's 1977 horror classic *The Shining,* with its remotely situated Overlook Hotel, abusive father, and ghosts of the "jet set and royalty," can be recognized as a modern variation on *A Sicilian Romance* and *The Mysteries of Udolpho.* It is perhaps only appropriate that the immense popularity of horror in 1970s America and Britain led literary scholars to return to the history of the gothic, studying the novels of the shy, reclusive woman once acclaimed as "the Great Enchantress."

Selected Bibliography

WORKS OF ANN RADCLIFFE

First Editions

The Castles of Athlin and Dunbayne: A Highland Story. London: Thomas Hookham, 1789. (Published anonymously.)

A Sicilian Romance. London: Thomas Hookham, 1790. (Published anonymously.)

The Romance of the Forest. London: Thomas Hookham. 1791. (Published anonymously.)

The Mysteries of Udolpho. London: G. G. and J. Robinson, 1794.

A Journey Made in the Summer of 1794: Through Holland and the Western Frontier of Germany, with a Return down the Rhine; to Which Are Added, Observations During a Tour to the Lakes of Lancashire, Westmoreland, and Cumberland. London: G. G. and J. Robinson, 1795.

The Italian; or, The Confessional of the Black Penitents. London: T. Cadell and W. Davies, 1797.

Gaston de Blondeville; or, The Court of Henry III, Keeping Festival in Ardenne. London: Henry Colburn, 1826. (The edition also includes *St. Alban's Abbey: A Metrical Romance* and *A Memoir of the Author, with Extracts from Her Journals.*)

Modern Editions

The Italian. Edited by Frederick Garber. Oxford: Oxford University Press, 1968, reprinted, 1981.

The Romance of the Forest. Edited by Chloe Chard. Oxford: Oxford University Press, 1986.

A Sicilian Romance. Edited by Alison Milbank. Oxford: Oxford University Press, 1993.

The Castles of Athlin and Dunbayne. Edited by Alison Milbank. Oxford: Oxford University Press, 1995.

The Mysteries of Udolpho. Edited by Jacqueline Howard. London: Penguin, 2001.

A Journey Made in the Summer of 1794: Through Holland and the Western Frontier of Germany, with a Return down the Rhine; to Which Are Added, Observations During a Tour to the Lakes of Lancashire, Westmoreland, and Cumberland. N.p.: Elibron Classics, 2002. (Facsimile edition.)

Gaston de Blondeville. Edited by Frances Chiu. Chicago: Valancourt, 2006.

BIOGRAPHICAL AND CRITICAL STUDIES

Bohls, Elizabeth. *Women Travel Writers and the Language of Aesthetics, 1716–1818.* Cambridge, U.K.: Cambridge University Press, 1995.

Butler, Marilyn. "The Woman at the Window: Ann Radcliffe in the Novels of Mary Wollstonecraft and Jane Austen." *Women and Literature* n.s. 1:128–148 (1980).

Chiu, Frances. "Dark and Dangerous Designs: Tales of Oppression, Dispossession, and Repossession." *Romanticism on the Net,* no. 28 (November 2002).

———. "Faulty Towers: Reform, Radicalism, and the Gothic Castle, 1760–1800." *Romanticism on the Net,* no. 44 (November 2006).

———. "From Nobodaddies to Noble Daddies: Writing Political and Paternal Authority in English Fiction of the 1780s and 1790s." *Eighteenth-Century Life* 26, no. 2:1–22 (spring 2002).

———. "Introduction." In Ann Radcliffe, *Gaston de Blondeville*. Chicago: Valancourt, 2006.

Clery, E. J. *The Rise of Supernatural Fiction, 1762–1800.* Cambridge, U.K., and New York: Cambridge University Press. 1995.

Durant, David. "Ann Radcliffe and the Conservative Gothic." *Studies in English Literature* 22, no. 3:519–531 (1982).

Ellis, Kate F. *The Contested Castle: Gothic Novels and the Subversion of Domestic Ideology.* Urbana and Chicago: University of Illinois Press, 1989.

Gamer, Michael. *Romanticism and the Gothic: Genre, Reception, and Canon Formation.* Cambridge, U.K.: Cambridge University Press, 2000.

Howard, Jacqueline. *Reading Gothic Fiction: A Bakhtinian Approach.* Oxford: Clarendon Press, 1994.

Johnson, Claudia. *Equivocal Beings: Politics, Gender, and Sentimentality in the 1790s: Wollstonecraft, Radcliffe, Burney, Austen.* Chicago: University of Chicago Press, 1995.

Madoff, Mark. "The Useful Myth of Gothic Ancestry." *Studies in Eighteenth Century Culture* 8:337–350 (1979).

Miles, Robert. *Ann Radcliffe: The Great Enchantress.* Manchester, U.K., and New York: Manchester University Press, 1999.

———.*Gothic Writing 1750–1820: A Genealogy.* London and New York: Routledge, 1993.

Norton, Rictor. *Mistress of Udolpho: The Life of Ann Radcliffe.* London and New York: Leicester University Press, 1999.

Talfourd, Thomas Noon. "Memoir of the Life and Writings of Mrs. Radcliffe." In *Gaston de Blondeville; or, The Court of Henry III Keeping Festival in Ardenne, a Romance.* London: Henry Colburn, 1826.

Watt, James. *Contesting the Gothic: Fiction, Genre, and Cultural Conflict, 1764–1832.* Cambridge, U.K.: Cambridge University Press, 1999.

MANUSCRIPTS

There are no extant collections of Radcliffe's manuscripts or correspondence. Her papers are said to have either been destroyed by her husband or surviving in a French archive unsigned and unattributed.

OTHER PRIMARY SOURCES

Burke, Edmund. *Reflections on the Revolution in France.* Edited by Leslie Mitchell. Oxford: Oxford University Press, 1991.

Jebb, John. *Every Man His Own Priest.* Edited by John Disney in *The Works Theological, Medical, Political and Miscellaneous.* London, 1787. Pp. 159–258.

Mackintosh, James. *Vindiciae Gallicae: Defence of the French Revolution and Its English Admirers, Against the Accusations of the Right Hon. Edmund Burke.* Dublin, 1791.

Paine, Thomas. *Rights of Man.* Edited by Gregory Claeys. Indianapolis: Hackett, 1992.

Pigott, Charles. *A Political Dictionary.* London, 1795.

Price, Richard. *A Discourse on the Love of Our Country.* Edited by D. O. Thomas in *Price: Political Writings.* Cambridge, U.K.: Cambridge University Press, 1991. Pp. 176–196.

Priestley, Joseph. *History of the Corruptions of Christianity.* Birmingham, U.K.: Percy and Jones, 1782.

CHRISTINA ROSSETTI

(1830—1894)

Elizabeth Ludlow

THROUGHOUT THE NINETEENTH century, the parameters of identity and selfhood were incessantly challenged and reconceptualized. According to Isobel Armstrong, "The effort to renegotiate a content to every relationship between self and the world is the Victorian poet's project and carries the poet into new genres and a new exploration of language" (p. 7). As this essay will demonstrate, in her poetry, fiction, and devotional prose, Christina Rossetti engages with this project of renegotiation and creation as she experiments with language and form to introduce a scripturally based understanding of the structures of identity.

Rossetti's first published volume, *Goblin Market and Other Poems,* appeared in 1862. Divided into two sections, nondevotional and devotional poetry, and illustrated by her brother Dante Gabriel, it secured Rossetti's reputation. In addition to its famous title poem, "Goblin Market," it includes "A Birthday," "Up-hill," and "The Convent Threshold." It also comprises several poems about fallen women, notably "Cousin Kate" and "Maude Clare." In 1866 Rossetti published her second volume, *The Prince's Progress and Other Poems.* Included in this are several semipolitical poems such as "A Royal Princess" and "The Iniquity of the Fathers upon the Children," numerous poems about lost love and the pain of memory, and a collection of devotional pieces.

In 1872 Rossetti began writing for children and published *Sing-Song: A Nursery Rhyme Book.* In this, she reflects several of her own personal childhood experiences and seeks to teach young children some lessons about human mortality, life, and the natural world. Two years later she published a collection of prose, also for children. Entitled *Speaking Likenesses,* this volume comprises three fantasy stories that impart moral lessons as well as raising some important questions about personal and social development.

Rossetti's fourth volume, *A Pageant and Other Poems,* published in 1881, includes the sonnet sequences "Monna Innominata" and "Later Life." These explore the formation of individual identity, the formation of love, and the problems that face the female writer and demonstrate Rossetti's familiarity with the writings of Dante and Petrarch.

Following the publication of *A Pageant,* Rossetti concentrated almost solely on producing devotional writings. In 1893 she published *Verses.* This volume consists of the poems she had previously included in three of her books of devotional prose, *Time Flies, Called To Be Saints,* and *The Face of the Deep.*

Following the publication of the first volume of Rebecca Crump's variorum edition of her poetry in 1970, Rossetti has received a considerable amount of critical attention from feminist scholars. Her political and social agenda has been examined and her understanding of women's rights has been explored. However, like Germaine Greer, who asserts that "her grasp of theology was poor" and that "she was unconcerned about the rational basis of dogma" (p. xvi), most critics have neglected to perform a thorough reading of her devotional writings. This neglect has begun to be remedied. As a careful study of Rossetti's entire corpus will demonstrate, her engagement with the theological climate of the mid- to late nineteenth century is indisputable. In 1981 G. B. Tennyson initiated a challenge to the critical dismissal of Rossetti's intellectual prowess in his claim that she was "the true inheritor of the Tractarian devotional mode in poetry" (p. 198). He argues that her poetry brings to fruition much of what the Oxford Movement advocated in theory and sought to put into practice. Added to this, he speaks of the need to read Rossetti's poetry in its Tractarian context and recognizes that her "genesis is of a more conventional kind" (p. 200) than has often been supposed. Over the next couple of decades a number of critics began to develop Tennyson's arguments and to focus on the Tractarian context of Rossetti's work. For instance, Emma Mason claims that recognizing her engagement with Tractarian theology rescues Rossetti "from dismissal as a merely pious poet, contextualizes her secretive poetics and exposes her forceful attempts to communicate a scholarly and perhaps elitist religious movement to a broad audience of believers" (p. 215). This contextualization is essential to understanding the foundations upon which she conceptualizes the nature of personal and communal identity.

EARLY LIFE

Christina Rossetti was born in London on December 5, 1830. She was the fourth child of Gabriele Rossetti, an Italian poet and political exile, and Frances Mary Lavinia Polidori, the daughter of an Italian exile and sister of John Polidori (Lord Byron's physician and the author of the 1819 gothic novella *The Vampyre*). As the chair of Italian at King's College, London, Gabriele Rossetti entertained many scholars and writers at his home. His children grew up speaking both Italian and English and were educated in the importance of the arts. Frances taught Maria, Gabriel, William Michael, and Christina at home. Away from the bustle of London, they enjoyed frequent trips to their maternal grandfather's house in Holmer Green, Buckinghamshire, where they were surrounded by the greenery of orchards and the activity of small animals.

In the 1840s Gabriele Rossetti's health suffered, and the family's financial security collapsed. At this time Maria left home to become a governess. In the early 1850s Frances, with the help of Christina, attempted to establish a day school, but this endeavor never succeeded. It was also at this time that Rossetti began to suffer from the ill health that would torment her for the rest of her life. She declined two offers of marriage for religious reasons and remained single, living with her mother and aunt for most of her life.

All of Rossetti's books of poetry were dedicated to her mother. She acknowledges the shaping influence Frances had on her life and work in the sonnet she wrote for her and uses to preface *A Pageant and Other Poems*.

To my first love, my Mother, on whose knee
I learnt love-lore that is not troublesome;
Whose service is my special dignity,
And she my loadstar while I go and come.
("Sonnets are full of love," *Complete Poems,* p. 267)

CENTRALITY OF THE BIBLE

Frances Rossetti was a strict Anglican and brought up her children according to biblical principles and Christian love. A reading of Rossetti's poetry and prose reveals that, for her, the Bible is the book of life and not merely an instruction manual for how to live. Scripture is, she believes, directly inspired from God and forms the basis upon which humans can reach an understanding of their true identity and their place within the eternal schema. Instead of "clinging to every imaginable particular" and concerning oneself with such things as the "precise architecture of Noah's Ark" or the "astronomy of Joshua's miracle" (*Letter and Spirit,* p. 86) she advocates approaching scripture as the molding force behind each individual believer and the basis upon which a relationship with God can be predicated.

In her 1892 critical study of Revelation, *The Face of the Deep,* Rossetti offers a commentary on St. John's words "These things saith He which hath the sharp sword with two edges" (Revelation 2:12). She begins by quoting Hebrews 4:12.

The word of God is quick, and powerful, and sharper than any two-edged sword, piercing even to the dividing asunder of soul and spirit and of the joints and marrow, and is a discerner of the thoughts and intents of the heart.

Following this, she suggests comprehending the nature of "two-edged sword" by dwelling on the notion that

One cuts asunder the evil servant penally, irremediably, by decree of the Supreme and Just Judge. The other, by tenderness of the Good Physician, wounds us for our own benefit and that afterwards He may heal us.

(The Face of the Deep, pp. 66–67)

Her comments demonstrate her acute dual awareness of the Bible's doctrines of judgment and grace and highlight her belief in the powerful shaping force of scripture to both correct behavior and present the good news of salvation. Throughout all her works of devotional prose, Rossetti relies so heavily on the words of scripture that she conflates herself and her readers with its characters and perceives the eschatological basis on which she believes the Kingdom of God is predicated.

Included in both *The Face of the Deep* and *Verses,* Rossetti's poem "Awake, thou that sleepest" (*Complete Poems,* p. 478) indicates the extent to which she integrated her poetic voice into the words of the Bible. It depicts the journey from the confusing despair of the present condition to the perfect enlightenment that can be found in Heaven. The title is taken from Ephesians 5:14–16, "Awake thou that sleepest, and arise from the dead, and Christ shall give thee light. See then that ye walk circumspectly, not as fools, but as wise, Redeeming the time, because the days are evil." Rossetti's first three lines, however, come word for word from Romans 13:12. The first verse reads,

The night is far spent, the day is at hand:
Let us therefore cast off the works of darkness,
And let us put on the armour of light.
Night for the dead in their stiffness and starkness!
Day for the living who mount in their might
Out of their graves to the beautiful land.

Emphasizing the urgency of becoming one of the "living," prepared to "mount" in "might" (l. 5), Rossetti adds her own hermeneutical direction in the second verse. She contemplates,

Far, far away lies the beautiful land:
Mount on wide wings of exceeding desire,
Mount, look not back, mount to life and to light,
Mount by the gleam of your lamps all on fire

Up from the dead men and up from the night.
The night is far spent, the day is at hand.

In this verse alone, at least three Bible passages can be seen to be interpreted as relating to one another. The line "look not back" (l. 9) resonates with the fatal instruction of the angels to Lot and his wife, "Look not behind thee, neither stay thou all in the plain; escape to the mountain, lest thou be consumed" (Genesis 19:17). The warning can also be read to relate to Jesus' instruction to an enquirer, "No man, having put his hand to the plough, and looking back, is fit for the kingdom of God" (Luke 9:62). The importance of mounting "to life and to light" is reinforced when the poem is considered in its context in *The Face of the Deep.* Here, it appears untitled following a commentary on the words of Revelation 22:10, "the time is at hand." Rossetti writes,

If eighteen hundred years ago the time was "at hand," how urgently at hand must it now be! If then it behoved disciples to read, mark, learn, and inwardly digest the prophecy, how urgently now! If then it was of the Divine Grace and Mercy that the Book was left unsealed, still is it of the Divine Grace and Mercy that it continues unsealed to our own day. If then it was high time to awake out of sleep, truly is it so now.

(p. 532)

Rossetti's perception of the urgency of grasping the salvation offered by Christ forms a mainstay of her devotional writings. Alongside this, her emphasis on the intimate relationship between God and the individual sinner is a shaping force of many of her poems.

Together with her focus on the importance of the relational and personal over the process of academic enquiry, Rossetti's self-effacing claim that she can "but quote" both available translations of the Bible (p. 113) is not, on the surface, a great incentive to engage in a comprehensive study of the hermeneutics of her devotional poetry and prose and has undoubtedly contributed to the critical dismissal of her theology. For the most part, the translation of the Bible that Rossetti quotes from is the 1611 King James Version. Alongside of this, she repeatedly uses the Prayer Book Version of the Psalms. However, once the Revised Version, the only officially authorized revision of the King James Bible, was published in 1885 she utilized it in *The Face of the Deep* so that she could bring fresh understandings to her exegesis of the apocalypse. She writes that "the two translations combined kindle hope, gratitude, confidence, excite emulation" (p. 111). With this in mind, the process of quoting the available translations of the Bible no longer appears trite but instead demonstrates itself to be a complex and hermeneutical practice.

In 1995 the critics Jan Marsh and Mary Arseneau highlighted Rossetti's sensitivity to the "*intra*textuality" within her own work. They suggest that, just as the New Testament comments on the Old, so too does Rossetti use one text to comment on another and encourage readers to consider the ways in which, "within her volumes of poetry individual poems, as well as the two sections of poetry, echo, explicate, and critique each other" (p. 21). Indeed, the model they offer can be extended to offer a means through which to interpret Rossetti's earlier, nondevotional, poetry through the framework of her later devotional writings.

EARLY WRITINGS AND THE INFLUENCE OF THE GOTHIC

In 1847, at the age of seventeen, Rossetti had composed enough poems for her grandfather to print a small volume of her work on his home press. Entitled *Verses: Dedicated to Her Mother,* this volume includes the long narrative poem "The Dead City" (*Complete Poems,* pp. 595–603). In this, the speaker travels into the depths of a wood until she comes across a ruined city. Here, all the houses are empty and all is "deathless desolation" (l. 105). She enters the grounds of a gold palace and there discovers a "splendid banquet" (l. 166) spread out. She is awestruck by the silence of the place but finds that each guest has been turned to stone. Consumed by fear, she looks down. Upon looking back up, she sees that the feast has vanished and that she remains alone. She reflects,

All these things that I have said
Awed me, and made me afraid.

What was I that I should see
So much hidden mystery?
And I straightway knelt and prayed.

(ll. 271–275)

Throughout the poem, several of Rossetti's formative literary influences can be traced. The first line, "Once I rambled in a wood," is reminiscent of the opening of Dante's *Divine Comedy,* which speaks of the pilgrim's journey though a dark wood. The imagery of the castle and of the frozen guests points toward the fairy tale "Sleeping Beauty." In addition, in her 1994 biography of Rossetti, Jan Marsh suggests that the opening passages recall both Tennyson's *The Day Dream* (1842) and the start of Charles Robert Maturin's 1820 Gothic tale *Melmoth the Wanderer,* where Immalee wanders through her paradise island. "Somewhere here too," Marsh suggests, "is a memory of that first visit to Madame Tussauds'" (p. 73).

The horror of insubstantial and artificial masks, along with the anguish of being forced into living the life of an automaton, is a central theme of *Melmoth the Wanderer.* According to Rossetti's early biographer, Mackenzie Bell, William Michael remarked that "When Gabriel, Christina, and I were young we used to read Maturin's novels over and over again, and they took great hold of our imaginations" (p. 14). In spite of this, apart from Diane D'Amico's article "Christina Rossetti: The Maturin Poems," Rossetti scholarship has largely resisted investigating the influence of the Gothic upon her work. Indeed, little has been done to ascertain the correspondences between Rossetti's poetry and the writings of Ann Radcliffe, which Rossetti read in 1883 when she was preparing to write a biography of her life (*Letters,* vol. 3, pp. 112–115). Considering that, alongside their concern with the boundaries of identity, the dramatizations of the recurring motifs of barriers, reflections, and silence that appear in Gothic writings are a feature of Rossetti's poetics, it is surprising that she has not been more closely linked to the Gothic genre in which she was certainly well read.

"GOBLIN MARKET"

Rossetti's concern with the gothic imagery of devilish tempters, death, false appearances, and the disintegration of identity emerges in her long narrative poem "Goblin Market" (*Complete Poems,* pp. 5–20). She composed it in 1859 and first published it in *Goblin Market and Other Poems* in 1862. It is the most widely known and read of all Rossetti's poems, and its publication helped to launch her literary career.

Rossetti's initial title for her poem was "A Peep at the Goblins." Highlighting the implications of this title, Lorraine Janzen Kooistra suggests that "while at first blush the word 'peep' may evoke the innocent playfulness of her cousin Eliza Bray's *A Peep at the Pixies,* in the context of the narrative itself 'peep' becomes overlaid with the connotations of furtive looking, stolen glances at the forbidden, clandestine curiosity" (p. 140).

Indeed, in the narrative itself Rossetti indicates her engagement with these connotations when she writes, "Lizzie covered up her eyes, / Covered close lest they should look" (ll. 50–51) before linking Laura's downfall to the initial act of gazing at the animalistic goblin men and their fruits. The idea that Lizzie is able to mirror Christ as she stands "Like a lily in a flood" (l. 409) and resists the onslaughts of the "Cat-like and rat-like / Ratel- and wombat-like" (ll. 340–341) goblin men suggests that it was not the actual *revelation* of their presence that made Laura feel "deaf and blind" (l. 259) and drove her to "Death's door" (l. 321); it was her vulnerability and her unwillingness to ignore the temptations they offer.

The temptation that the goblins attempt to impart to the two sisters has been interpreted in various ways. Read in terms of eroticism, commercialism, and male imagination, the catalog of fruit they offer, "Sweet to tongue and sound to eye" (l. 30), overwhelms as well as confuses the reader.

Recognizing that "We must not look at goblin men, / We must not buy their fruits" (ll. 42–43), Lizzie runs away from them. She recalls the experience of Jeanie, who, after eating goblin fruits, "pined and pined away" (l. 154) and eventually died. "To this day," Lizzie claims, "no grass will grow" on her grave. The fact that she herself "planted daisies there a year ago / that never blow" (ll. 158–161) suggests the stagnation of Jeanie's soul.

In spite of Lizzie's warning, susceptible to Eve's fault of curiosity (l. 69), Laura lingers behind and wonders why the goblin men possess such a strong resemblance to animals (ll. 71–76). Exchanging a "golden curl" (l. 125) for their fruit, she "Sucked and sucked" the sweet juices (l. 134) before returning home and subsequently pining away. When she appears to be "knocking at Death's door" (l. 321), Lizzie takes her life into her own hands, enters the glen of the goblin men, endures their abuse, and buys from them some fruit that would restore her sister back to health. She recovers. Both sisters grow up to have their own children, whom they warn about the "haunted glen" (l. 552), and Laura

Would tell them how her sister stood
In deadly peril to do her good,
And win the fiery antidote....

(ll. 557–559)

By implicitly associating Lizzie's heroic act with Christ's passion, and by emphasizing the significance of sisterhood, Rossetti's poem has often been interpreted as feminist.

The critic D. M. R. Bentley suggests that the composition of *Goblin Market* did not arise solely from Rossetti's concern with the treatment of "fallen women" but that it was "originally written as an 'exemplary tale made imaginative' to be read aloud by Rossetti to an audience of fallen women, perhaps in the company of the Anglican Sisters with whom she associated herself at the St. Mary Magdalene Home for Fallen Women at Highgate Hill" (p. 58). William Michael recalled that, in the early 1860s, she "used pretty often to go to an Institution at Highgate for redeeming 'Fallen Women'" (Bell, p. 54).

TRACTARIANISM AND THE FIGURE OF THE NUN

Rossetti's recognition of the urgent need the women in the penitentiary had for Christian reclamation can be linked to her increasing concern with the inadequacy with the structures of the established church. In *The Face of the Deep,* she voices a lament at these existing structures when she writes,

> Already in England (not to glance at other countries) the signs of the times are ominous: Sunday is being diverted by some to business, by others to pleasure; Church congregations are often meagre, and so services are chilled. Our solemn feasts languish, and our fasts where are they? Yet each for himself, and God for us all, we can if we choose "remember the Sabbath-day, to keep it holy"; jealous of its essentials, not wedded to its accidents.
>
> (p. 243)

Her longing for a biblical observance of the Sabbath is accordant with the principles upheld by the Tractarian leaders who sought to revitalize the church, draw attention to the import of the scriptures for the nineteenth-century Christian, and highlight the necessity of resolving the problems that they perceived to be corrupting the society in which they lived.

The name "Tractarianism" comes from the series *Tracts for the Times,* which the leaders of the Oxford Movement published between 1833 and 1841. The writers of the ninety tracts that make up this series include John Henry Newman, Edward Pusey, Isaac Williams, and John Keble. The purpose of the tracts was to establish a firm basis upon which the doctrine of the Church of England could be established.

Alongside the tracts, the leaders of the Oxford Movement also used poetry as a means of expressing their Anglican beliefs. Indeed, G. B. Tennyson suggests "that the literary expression of the Movement, and the poetry in particular, is as much cause and symptom as it result of the Movement" (p. 8). With this in mind, it is interesting to consider the extent to which Rossetti's writings *contributed to,* rather than merely echoed, the theological precepts of the Tractarians. In 1827 John Keble published *The Christian Year.* This comprises poems for every day of the year. Upon its publication, it met with immediate success. In his analysis of the volume, G. B. Tennyson suggests that the best way to understand it as a Tractarian work "is to see it in

relation to the worship it was designed to enhance." This, he argues, demands a consideration "of its most visible, and most overlooked feature—its subordination to the liturgical year generally and to the Book of Common Prayer specifically" (p. 75). Following this pattern, many of Rossetti's poems can be similarly considered in terms of the Tractarian methods of worship in which they were deeply rooted.

In 1843 Rossetti, along with her sister and mother, began attending the newly established Christ Church, Albany Street. This was an active High Anglican, Tractarian church that emphasized the importance of ritual and ceremony; the celebration of the festivals included in the liturgical year, the use of sacraments, and the doctrines of the Apostolic Church. In addition to having William Dodsworth as its perpetual curate, it was frequented by Edward Pusey and other prominent leaders of the Oxford Movement.

In 1845 the parish of Christ Church established the first Anglican convent since the Reformation. It did not take long for more convents to be established and grow in numbers. In 1874 Maria Rossetti was professed as a nun into All Saints Sisters of the Poor. Susan Mumm estimates that there were between three thousand and four thousand nuns by 1900 living in around sixty communities. These numbers were much higher than any that had been envisaged in 1845. Throughout the late 1840s and early 1850s, the years that saw the biggest growth in the profession of novices, Rossetti included the figure of the nun in several of her poems as well as her 1850 prose narrative *Maude.*

In her convent poems Rossetti repeatedly uses the scriptural imagery of reflections and shadows to typologically articulate the transformation of believers in both spatial and metaphysical terms. By utilizing biblical allusions to depict the interior life of nuns, she is able to dramatize the complexities that are involved in living a self-sacrificial life.

Rossetti composed "The Convent Threshold" (*Complete Poems,* pp. 55–59) in 1858 and published it in her first volume of poetry, *Goblin Market and Other Poems,* in 1862. Written in the form of a dramatic monologue, it employs several

Gothic motifs to narrate the tale of a penitent woman on the verge of entering a convent. Calling her lover to "Repent, repent, and be forgiven" (l. 79), she emphasizes the urgency of responding to the message of Christ before it is too late. She recalls two dreams she had the previous night. In the first, "A spirit with transfigured face" demonstrated to her the power of love over the desire for knowledge (ll. 86, 105). In the second, her lover returned to her and found her drenched in blood and ready to be "Crushed downwards thro' the sodden earth" (l. 123). In the morning, she claims that she woke to find "My face was pinched, my hair was grey, / And frozen blood was on the sill / Where stifling in my struggle I lay" (ll. 134–136). Concluding the poem, she looks forward to standing in Paradise, meeting her lover, and loving "with old familiar love" (l. 148).

Throughout the poem, the self-discipline needed to repent and "*choose* the stairs that mount above" (l. 4, emphasis added) is highlighted. By breaking the regular iambic tetrameters with opening trochees in the lines "Stair after golden skyward stair" and "Mount with me, mount the kindled stair" (ll. 5, 16), Rossetti highlights the effort needed to break out of the expected patterns set by the world and empty oneself of self-interest in order to reflect Christ more truly. She has her speaker recall the saints who "bore the Cross," "drained the cup," and were "Racked, roasted, crushed, wrenched limb from limb" (ll. 25–26). Entering the convent is spoken of in terms of a battle and a pilgrimage. In order to succeed, the novice must "kneel, wrestle, knock, do violence, pray" (l. 48).

Evelyn Underhill suggests that the "total oblation" required from the nun made the restoration of religious orders "the greatest achievement of the Anglican revival when seen in spiritual regard." This oblation, she writes, "expresses in a living symbolism, the ideal consummation of all worship; the total oblation of the creature to the purposes of God" (p. 254). William Dodsworth, the perpetual curate of Christ Church, speaks of the life of self-immolation that the nun is called to make when he argues that

to live a holy and useful life is one thing, to live a life of self sacrifice is another. It is very aweful [*sic*] to remember the service with which they are consecrated to God and to a life of *entire* self-renunciation. And yet unless there is something of painful labour, theirs is in many respects of worldly comfort a life much to be preferred to that of a governess, and which many might covet for its comfort.

(p. 65)

Indeed, he feared that a well-financed and secure home for life would be too comfortable and would attract the wrong sort of recruit while inhibiting the religious life of the devout.

In her 1850 novella *Maude,* Rossetti narrates various responses to the news that a young girl, Magdalen Ellis, has entered a local "Sisterhood of Mercy" as a novice. Telling her cousin Maude that she would "not like such a life," Mary complains,

They have not proper clothes on their beds, and never go out without a thick veil, which must half-blind them. All day long they are at prayers, or teaching children, or attending the sick, or making things for the poor, or something.

(p. 216)

ROMANTIC INFLUENCES

In their discussion of *Maude,* Susan Gilbert and Sandra Gubar claim, "That Rossetti may have gotten from Keats the idea of burying Maude's own journal with the dead writer herself suggests ... just how masochistically a woman poet may transform male metaphors into female images of anxiety or guilt" (p. 553). Their argument that Rossetti, "banqueting on bitterness," buried "herself alive in a coffin of renunciation" (p. 575) highlights the element of deferral that characterizes Rossetti's convent and devotional poetry but neglects the hope of heavenly fulfillment upon which this deferral is based. In her reading diary, *Time Flies,* Rossetti warns the reader against ignoring the second, hopeful, clause of the proverb "Hope deferred maketh the heart sick: but when the desire cometh, it is a tree of life" (Proverbs 13:12, *Time Flies,* pp. 80–81).

In 1849, a year before she wrote *Maude,* Rossetti composed a sonnet which she titled "On Keats" (*Collected Poems,* p. 700). In this, she uses several Romantic tropes in order to highlight the tension between deferral and fulfillment.

A garden in a garden: a green spot
Where all is green: most fitting slumber-place
For the strong man grown weary of a race
Soon over. Unto him a goodly lot
Hath fallen in fertile ground; there thorns are not,
But his own daisies: silence, full of grace,
Surely hath shed a quiet on his face:
His earth is but sweet leaves that fall and rot.
What was his record of himself, ere he
Went from us? *Here lies one whose name was writ*
In water: while the chilly shadows flit
Of sweet Saint Agnes' Eve; while basil springs,
His name, in every humble heart that sings,
Shall be a fountain of love, verily.

By introducing Keats's grave in terms of "a garden in a garden" (l. 1), by speaking to the "race" (l. 3) of Philippians 3:13–19, and by echoing the Song of Songs 4:12, "A garden inclosed is my sister, my spouse; a spring shut up, a fountain sealed," Rossetti roots her contemplation of Keats in the scriptural narrative of Jesus' burial.

> Now in the place where he was crucified there was a garden; and in the garden a new sepulchre, wherein was never man yet laid. There laid they Jesus therefore because of the Jews' preparation day; for the sepulchre was nigh at hand.
>
> (John 19:41–42)

By implicitly positioning the image of the Keats's burial firmly within a biblical framework while simultaneously linking the place of Jesus' burial and resurrection to both the "goodly lot" (l. 4) that is the Garden of Eden and the enclosed garden of the Song of Songs, Rossetti initiates an interpretation more profound than she has previously been given credit for. Indeed, one might suggest that, rather than upholding a quiet Christian dogma throughout "On Keats," she succeeds in "Christianizing" Keats's atheistic ideology. Although this remains implicit in an isolated reading of the sonnet, when it is read in conjunction with the poems contained within her later volume, *Verses,* Rossetti's Christianizing impulse becomes more apparent.

The symbolism in "On Keats" can be more thoroughly understood in terms of her Christianizing impulse when it is considered together with "Let them rejoice in their beds" (*Complete Poems,* p. 494).

Crimson as the rubies, crimson as the roses,
Crimson as the sinking sun,
Singing on his crimsoned bed each saint reposes,
Fought his fight, his battle won;
Till the rosy east the day of days discloses,
All his work, save waiting, done.
Far above the stars, while underneath the daises,
Resting, for his race is run,
Unto Thee his heart each quiet saint upraises,
God the Father, Spirit, Son;
Unto Thee his heart, unto Thee his praises,
O Lord God, the Three in One.

Although she composed this poem only three years after "On Keats," Rossetti's decision to position it among her later depictions of "New Jerusalem and Its Citizens" enhances it with additional spiritual dimensions. By depicting the saints as "Crimson as the rubies, crimson as the roses" (l. 1), she anticipates her later description of a paradise where "raiment is white of blood-steeped linen slowly spun" ("Before the Throne, and before the Lamb," *Complete Poems,* p. 495, l. 8). Her conflation of this process of cleansing with the space of ultimate rest demonstrates the complexities of her interpretation of the Bible. Indeed, when the proclamation in the King James Version of Psalm 149, "Let the saints be joyful in glory: let them sing aloud upon their beds" (Psalm 149:5), is read in the context of the entire psalm, the suggestion is that the praise of the saints is so continuous that it does not waver through the night. Considered alongside the translation in the Prayer Book Psalter, "Let the faithful be joyful in glory: let them rejoice in their ranks," this understanding of the proclamation becomes more apparent. It is significant that, in the title, by depicting the saints "in" rather than "upon" their beds, Rossetti uses a single word from the Prayer Book Version of the Psalm to give her interpretation of the King James Version an added dimension. Indeed, her depiction of the saints resting "in" their beds can be seen to allude to incorporation *in* the larger body of the united Christian community as well as to the promised state of rest.

In "Let them rejoice in their beds," by speaking of "each saint" (l. 3) rejoicing in God while remaining "underneath the daises, / Resting, for his race is run" (ll. 6–7), Rossetti envisions the space of the grave within an eschatological context. Thus she is able to present the place where the saints are washed with Christ's blood as one of peace but also one of movement. Indeed, the allusion to the process whereby "each saint upraises" (l. 9) to the "Three in One" (l. 12) corresponds to the growth of the daisies upon the grave. When "On Keats" is read in conjunction with these images of spiritual upraising and rejoicing, Rossetti's Christianizing impulse is made apparent. Read in isolation, when Rossetti writes that Keats is buried beneath *his own daisies* (l. 6), she appears to be alluding simply to the daisies of *Endymion,* and, when combined with the implicit reference to the "basil" (l. 12) of "Isabella," it would seem the garden depicted is a straightforward visualization of Keats's own poetic persona. However, the fact that the symbolism of the poem corresponds so closely to Rossetti's utilization of biblical imagery presented in "Let them rejoice in their beds" lends the poem an additional typological interpretation whereby the "daisies" can also be read as symbolic of the activity of the soul.

Such a reading suggests that, rather than simply tracing Keats's influence on Rossetti, a more reciprocal relationship between the two poets can be demonstrated. In her book *Consuming Keats: Nineteenth-Century Representations in Art and Literature,* Sarah Wootton argues against the notion that a stable poetic entity can be recovered. She suggests reading Keats's afterlife as a "series or network of transmutations." "We do not inherit the 'real' Keats or even a cultural construction," she writes, "but a multiplicity of economic, poetic, political, and sexual selves formed through the perpetual dialogue between the past and present" (p. 1). With this in mind, rather than conceiving of Rossetti as a passive recipient of Romantic verse, one can see the way the poet brings the biblical exegesis that consti-

tutes her sense of identity into a lively dialogue with her Romantic predecessors.

By mapping the Romantic conception that identity can be understood as a product of reading onto her own poetic contemplations of the practical translation of biblical precepts, Rossetti suggests that the ideology of the individual is constituted through a "perpetual dialogue" with the words of scripture. In "On Keats," by simultaneously relating individual words to Keats's poetry and the language of the Bible, she is able to speak of enclosed gardens in terms of individual identity and link those in Romantic literature to those in scripture. Building on Rossetti's depiction of the enclosed garden in "On Keats" as a cultivated a picturesque garden, Wootton argues that, through the use of words such as "goodly" and "fertile," she "generates a bodily intimacy with the dead poet." She suggests the fertile ground of the poem can be read as a figurative representation of the Keats, through which Rossetti's desires may be fulfilled (p. 28). Certainly, reading the poem through the framework of the Song of Songs is suggestive of this interpretation and highlights a conflation between the garden and the female body. There can be no doubt that Rossetti was familiar with the Pre-Raphaelite paintings that allude to the continuing role of the garden as a metaphor for femininity, such as Arthur Hughes's 1865 illustration *April Love,* in which the women's situation within the leafy arbor draws on the spiritual representations of the enclosed garden as a symbol of the Virgin Birth and of female virginity.

"HAPPY EQUALS": THE PROBLEM OF GENDER

Although Rossetti actively adheres to the belief that men and women are fundamentally equal in the eyes of God, she holds the view that, on earth God grants each sex very different privileges and rights. When Augusta Webster wrote to her in the late 1870s asking for her support in the suffrage campaign she was advocating, in her reply she refused to support the extension of the rights held by men to women householders. She asks, "Does it not appear as if the Bible was based upon an understood unalterable distinction between men and women, their position, duties, privileges?" (*Letters*, vol. 2, p. 158). In her mind, this "unalterable distinction" was made with Eve and continues throughout the Bible.

Despite acknowledging the essential differences between men and women, Rossetti was acutely aware of the disadvantages faced by the nineteenth-century woman and acknowledges these in many of her poems.

In her preface to "Monna Innominata" (*Complete Poems,* pp. 294–301), she acknowledges the "barrier" that unfulfilled spiritual yearnings establish between the lover and her beloved and highlights the historical and cultural situation in which her sequence is framed.

> Beatrice, immortalized by "altissimo poeta … cotanto amante"; Laura, celebrated by a great tho' an inferior bard,—have alike paid the exceptional penalty of exceptional honour, and have come down to us resplendent with charms, but (at least, to my apprehension) scant of attractiveness.
>
> These heroines of world-wide fame were preceded by a bevy of unnamed ladies "donne innominate" sung by a school of less conspicuous poets;; and in that land and that period which gave simultaneous birth to Catholics, to Albigenses, and to Troubadours, one can imagine many a lady as sharing her lover's poetic aptitude, while the barrier between them might be one held sacred by both, yet not such as to render mutual love incompatible with mutual honour.
>
> Had such a lady spoken for herself, the portrait left us might have appeared more tender, if less dignified, than any drawn even by a devoted friend. Or had the Great Poetess of our own day and nation [i.e., Elizabeth Barrett Browning] only been unhappy instead of happy, her circumstances would have invited her to bequeath to us, in lieu of the "Portuguese Sonnets," an inimitable "donna innominata" drawn not from fancy but from feeling, and worthy to occupy a niche beside Beatrice and Laura.
> (p. 294)

In this preface, Rossetti introduces her implicit technique of working *within* traditional representations and transforming them through biblical typology. Her utilization of this technique means that she is able to engage with the traditional male vision while at the same time offering an ironic commentary on it. Thus, rather than allowing the Petrarchan structure to restrain and

contain her expression, she actually utilizes it as a tool of empowerment.

In an entry she wrote in 1863 for *The Imperial Dictionary of Universal Biography,* Rossetti notes how Francesco Petrarca (Petrarch) describes, with "untiring minuteness," Laura's "bare hand and dainty glove, her sweet speech and sweet laugh, her tears, her paleness, [and] her salutation." Despite falling prey to the "fearful pestilence" that "ravaged Europe" in 1348, she writes that Laura was "ever regarded by him [Petrarca] as invested with the pristine charm" that first "captivated" his heart (*Selected Prose,* pp. 164–166). In her preface to "Monna Innominata," then, rather than rejecting the "pristine charm" of the individual muse and invalidating the "resplendent charms" of Laura and Beatrice, Rossetti is striving to render their charms as prefigurative indications of inner beauty.

Throughout "Monna Innominata," Rossetti challenges preconceived expectations about the nature of love and the place of a woman in a romantic relationship. By ending sonnet 7 with the declaration "love is strong as death" and by beginning sonnet 8 with Esther's words "I, if I perish, perish," Rossetti highlights a shift from earthly to divine contemplations of love and exemplifies the centrality of her belief that divine love overcomes all else and causes the believer to actively desire to forgo her own individual concerns and become one with the Communion of Saints. The strength in taking this step is highlighted and thus the woman's capacity for action and passion is emphasized.

Also in *A Pageant and Other Poems,* the sonnet sequence "The Thread of Life" (*Complete Poems,* pp. 330–331) articulates the movement away from the lamenting speakers of Rossetti's early poetry and toward the joyful and patient believers in *Verses.* Referring to the spiritual ascent from worldly concerns through renunciation and toward deep understanding, it begins with the speaker's acknowledgment of the "irresponsive silence" (sonnet 1, l. 1) of the external world as she struggles to come to terms with her own identity. Anticipating the declaration in *The Face of the Deep* that it is "I who undo, defile, deface myself" (p. 489), the "I" of the speaker is described as a "prison" (sonnet 2, l. 1) that prevents her from continuing on her journey toward God. Confining her to a "flawless band / Of inner solitude" (sonnet 1, ll. 5–6), it is only when she freely forgoes this "I" of her individuality that she is able to reach a realization of herself as an indestructible part of God's kingdom that supersedes the onslaught of "Time's winnowing" (sonnet 3, l. 4). Subsequently she is freed to join in the "sweet new song of His redeemed set free" (sonnet 3, l. 12).

POLITICAL CONCERNS

The political implications of Rossetti's biblically based emphasis on the individual and her freedom to choose whether or not she will forgo her selfish concerns and join the larger Communion of Saints can be highlighted in the context of several of her poems that are rooted in the notion of social protest.

Rossetti composed "A Royal Princess" (*Complete Poems*, pp. 143–146) in 1851 and first published it in 1863 in the fund-raising anthology *Poems: An Offering to Lancashire; Printed and Published for the Art Exhibition for the Relief of Distress in the Cotton Districts.* At this time, workers in the Lancashire cotton districts were being discharged from employment as a result of the American Civil War.

In the poem, the princess perceives herself to be surrounded by superficial and flat reflections. Observing the world from her "ivory throne" (l. 14), she is forced her to see herself as hollow and without any interiority and to consider her home a prison.

All my walls are lost in mirrors, whereupon I trace
Self to right hand, self to left hand, self in every place,
Self-same solitary figure, self-same seeking face.

(ll. 10–12)

After languishing in the palace, she comes to the realization that the men and women her father, the king, treats as though they were cattle, are "human flesh and blood" (l. 35); the realization overwhelms her and initiates her rebellion. When she hears that the poor are "clamouring to be fed" (l. 56) and that "There are families out grazing like cattle in the park" (l. 62), her compassion is aroused. When she hears her father command his troops to "Charge!" (l. 89) against those who rebel at their inhumane treatment, she determines to take action.

With a ransom in my lap, a king's ransom in my hand,
I will go down to this people, will stand face to face,
 will stand
Where they curse king, queen, and princess of this
 cursed land.

(ll. 100–102)

In the next stanza, it emerges that the "ransom" she speaks of is her own life. She declares that the "goal" she "half conceive[s]" is

Once to speak before the world, rend bare my heart
 and show
The lesson I have learned, which is death, is life, to
 know.
I, if I perish, perish: in the name of God I go.

(ll. 106–108)

NEGOTIATING WITH PRE-RAPHAELITE IDEOLOGY

In 1848 Dante Gabriel Rossetti, William Michael Rossetti, James Collinson, John Everett Millais, Frederic George Stephens, Thomas Woolner, and William Holman Hunt founded the Pre-Raphaelite Brotherhood. They sought to model their work on the style of art and poetry that was popular before the time of the Italian artist Raphael. They opposed the accepted art of the Royal Academy by emphasizing their concern with fidelity to nature and employing symbolic and allegorical imagery. Although their ideas flourished and their influence eventually surpassed their expectations, the group did not stay together for long. In 1853, several months before they disbanded, Rossetti composed a sonnet highlighting the reasons for the demise of the group.

The P.R.B. is in its decadence:—
for Woolner in Australia cooks his chops;
And Hunt is yearning for the land of Cheops;
D. G. Rossetti shuns the vulgar optic;

While William M. Rossetti merely lops
His B.s in English disesteemed as Coptic;
Calm Stephens in the twilight smokes his pipe
But long the dawning of his public day;
And he at last, the champion great Millais
Attaining academic opulence
Winds up his signature with A.R.A.:—
So rivers merge in the perpetual sea,
So luscious fruit must fall when over ripe,
And so the consummated P.R.B.

(Complete Poems, p. 755)

Whether or not Rossetti can be described as a Pre-Raphaelite has been a subject of contention since the nineteenth century. In a letter to Edmund Gosse she refers to herself as the "least and last of the group" (Bump, p. 322), and certainly the inclusion of her work in the Pre-Raphaelite periodical *The Germ* and her close links with the original members of the brotherhood point to her status as a fully fledged Pre-Raphaelite. However, because her gender prevents her from being recognized as an official member of the "brotherhood," and considering that her brother William Michael wrote in his introduction to the magazine that her contributions were "produced without any reference to publication," her standing as a Pre-Raphaelite has been a matter for dispute. Her focus on matters of gender and the Christian thematics of her work mean that, for the most part, Rossetti has been aligned with other female poets or with her contemporaries in the Oxford Movement rather than with the members of the Pre-Raphaelite Brotherhood. Instead of identifying her as the leading member or a marginalized observer of the Pre-Raphaelite movement, perhaps a more fruitful way to characterize the relationship is to say that she began her poetic career by identifying herself as a participant of the Pre-Raphaelite school as she worked with their trope of the epipsyche while simultaneously offering an ironic commentary on it.

Rossetti's 1856 sonnet "In an Artist's Studio" (*Complete Poems,* p. 796) reflects the dynamics between interior and exterior identity and concerns itself with the nature of authentic selfhood beyond the mirror's reflection.

One face looks out from all his canvasses,
One selfsame figure sits or walks or leans;
We found her hidden just behind those screens,
That mirror gave back all her loveliness.
A queen in opal or in ruby dress,
A nameless girl in freshest summer greens,
A saint, an angel; every canvass means
The same one meaning, neither more nor less.
He feeds upon her face by day and night,
And she with true kind eyes looks back on him
Fair as the moon and joyful as the light:
Not wan with waiting, not with sorrow dim;
Not as she is, but was when hope shone bright;
Not as she is, but as she fills his dream.

Like the mirrors that surround the "self-same solitary figure" of Rossetti's princess ("A Royal Princess," l. 12), the "screens" and the "mirror" in the studio (ll. 3, 4) reflect a false sense of the model's identity. Perhaps painted with imaginary scenes they, like the princess's chamber, isolate her from the reality of the outside world and cast her as a superfluous other who is so far removed from the humanity of the artist that she cannot threaten or compromise his sense of autonomous identity. By drawing attention to her "one face" and her "selfsame figure" (ll. 1–2) Rossetti reinforces the idea that the women, as seen through men's eyes, do not exist as individuals but as objects.

Critics have often interpreted the model of the poem to represent Dante Gabriel Rossetti's wife, Elizabeth Siddal. Dante Gabriel and Siddal had a very complex and tumultuous relationship. Originally posing as a model for various members of the Pre-Raphaelite Brotherhood, Siddal eventually became Dante Gabriel's muse and model. He painted her "selfsame figure" (l. 2) incessantly.

According to J. B. Bullen, in the poem,

The Pygmalion artist creates an anonymous (nameless) image of undifferentiated femininity, compliantly reciprocal, a prophylactic against the threat of self-disintegration, and the canvas is a "mirror" which reflects back the feminised self of the creator. Here, Christina Rossetti describes a positive, stable situation in which the lunar feminine image reflects back the solar warmth of male desire, and where the male, in turn, is as dependent upon the nutritive potential of that image as the baby who "feeds" upon the good breast. What the female offers, however, is not a reality but a wish-fulfilling dream: "Not as she is, but as she fills his dream."

(pp. 126–127)

Whether or not "In an Artist's Studio" refers directly to Siddal, it undoubtedly presents an ironic commentary on the vampiric relationship that can exist between the active, consuming male and the passive female figure who is not appreciated for who she actually is but who the male wants her to be.

FEMALE POETICS

Rossetti composed "L.E.L." (*Complete Poems*, pp. 147–149) in 1859 and first published it in *Victoria Magazine* in 1863. In 1866 she included it in her second volume of verse, *The Prince's Progress and Other Poems*. In it, she builds on her investigation of outward appearance and inner reality. Like the model in "In an Artist's Studio," L.E.L. is prevented from expressing her true feelings by the mask she is forced to wear.

L.E.L. (Elizabeth Letitia Landon) was born in 1802. She began publishing her poetry at age eighteen and soon attracted recognition, becoming one of the most popular female poets of the nineteenth century. Throughout the 1820s and 1830s she wrote numerous poems and several novels. Her increasing celebrity status caused an intensification of interest in her private life. In 1838, to escape a scandal, she married a governor of the Gold Coast renowned for his cruelty. Three months after arriving in Africa with her new husband, she was found dead with a bottle of prussic acid in her hand. She was only thirty-six. Suspicions were aroused, and a huge amount of speculation about the cause of her death followed. Rossetti was one of several Victorian writers to contemplate the poet "whose heart was breaking for a little love."

Throughout the poem, Rossetti uses images of concealment to highlight the dichotomy between the face L.E.L. presents to the world and her true self. Declaring "I deck myself with silks and jewelry" (l. 22), L.E.L. is shown to use her dresses and her jewels as masks to cover up her loneliness. Although her disguise appears to

be effective ("They praise my rustling show, and never see / My heart is breaking for a little love," ll. 24–25), it intensifies her loneliness. Rossetti contrasts the freedom of the birds, bees, and rabbits (ll. 6, 19, 20) to the confinement suffered by L.E.L., who cannot live a similar life of natural simplicity.

The final verse encourages the avoidance of entanglement with the world by renunciation, disassociation, and solitude. Like the preacher of Ecclesiastes who claims that he has "seen all the works that are done under the sun" and beheld that "all is vanity and vexation of spirit" (Ecclesiastes 1:14, Rossetti's lamenting L.E.L. is taught to reject the illusionary promise that the earthly spring brings and look forward to the ultimate "new spring" which "builds heaven and clean new earth" (l. 42).

Christina Rossetti's "L.E.L." can be contrasted to Elizabeth Barrett Browning's 1839 poem "L.E.L.'s Last Question." In this, Browning has L.E.L. repeatedly ask "Do you think of me as I think of you?" and emphasizes the poet's lonely and darkened heart. She describes her as a "craver of a little love" (l. 39). By choosing L.E.L. as her subject and by positioning her poem alongside Browning's, Rossetti places herself on a continuum of female poets and reinforces the notion of the existence of a poetess network.

DEVOTIONAL PROSE

The importance of the eternal over the earthly that Rossetti hints at in "L.E.L." characterizes her six books of devotional prose published between 1874 and 1893. These include *Annus Domini: A Prayer for Each Day of the Year* (1874); *Seek and Find: A Double Series of Short Studies of the Benedicite* (1879); *Called To Be Saints: The Minor Festivals Devotionally Studied* (1881); *Letter and Spirit: Notes on the Commandments* (1883); *Time Flies: A Reading Diary* (1885); and *The Face of the Deep: A Devotional Commentary on the Apocalypse* (1892). All are concerned with the celebration of saints, the liturgical calendar, and the Apostolic Church. Seeking to edify other Christians, Rossetti used these volumes to reflect upon verses from scripture and explicate their meaning.

In most of her prose writings, poems are combined with commentaries, anecdotes, and excerpts from the Bible. By adopting this mosaic style and by using the Bible to interpret the Bible, or in other words, by illuminating the words of one passage or phrase by quoting extensively from other parts of scripture, and by seamlessly conflating her own words with those of the Psalmists and the Prophets, Rossetti is able to integrate herself and her community into the biblical schema.

Throughout each volume, Rossetti offers constant reminders of her humility. Although these works were incredibly popular at the time she was writing, it is difficult for a modern readership to appreciate, or look beyond, her self-deprecation. An example can be seen in a characteristic remark:

> Should I have readers ... let me remind them that what I write professes to be a *surface* study of an unfathomable depth.... My suggestions do not necessarily amount to beliefs; they may be no more than tentative thoughts compatible with acknowledged ignorance.
>
> (*The Face of the Deep*, p. 365)

That Rossetti, a successful writer of five best-selling volumes of poetry, a number of short stories, and five previous books of devotional prose, felt it necessary to hint that she may not have readers, and to acknowledge an ignorance that she was by no means in possession of, indicates her awareness of her position as a female theologian. Masking a profound theology, she valorizes her self-deprecating remarks by rooting them in biblical precepts. She writes that "to humble ourselves, to repent, to stand alert at the rumour of a Divine message, such acts as these lie within our own power; acts whereby we can all please God" (*The Face of the Deep*, p. 167). The more we humble ourselves, she argues, the more receptive we are to God's blessings and message. Considering her theory of humility and divine inspiration further, it would seem that rather than diminish her spiritual authority, her acknowledgments of ignorance actually reinforce

and give the power of holiness to her as an interpreter.

In conclusion, it is instructive to highlight Rossetti's presentation of herself as a vessel or a conduit for God's word. Emphasizing the fluidity that exists between the self and the Holy Spirit, Rossetti challenges the developing concepts of personhood and individual identity that were being formulated in the latter part of the nineteenth century. Throughout her writings, she implicitly challenges her readers to renegotiate their relationship with the world through an eschatological rather than earthly framework. By reading her nondevotional and devotional writings in conjunction, her emphasis on aligning the worldly with the Heavenly can be clearly identified and her poetic project understood.

Selected Bibliography

WORKS OF CHRISTINA ROSSETTI

POETRY
Verses: Dedicated to Her Mother. Privately printed by G. Polidori, 1847.

Goblin Market and Other Poems. London: Macmillan, 1862.

The Prince's Progress and Other Poems. London: Macmillian, 1866.

A Pageant and Other Poems. London: Macmillan,1881.

Verses: Reprinted from "Called To Be Saints," "Time Flies" and "The Face of the Deep." London: Society for Promoting Christian Knowledge, 1893.

New Poems Hitherto Unpublished or Uncollected. Edited by W. M. Rossetti. London: Macmillan, 1896.

DEVOTIONAL PROSE
Annus Domini: A Prayer for Each Day of the Year. London: James Parker & Co., 1874.

Seek and Find: A Double Series of Short Studies of the Benedicite. London: Society for Promoting Christian Knowledge, 1879.

Called To Be Saints, the Minor Festivals Devotionally Studied. London: Society for Promoting Christian Knowledge, 1881.

Letter and Spirit: Notes on the Commandments. London and Brighton: Society for Promoting Christian Knowledge, 1883.

Time Flies: A Reading Diary. London: Society for Promoting Christian Knowledge, 1885.

The Face of the Deep: A Devotional Commentary on the Apocalypse. London: Society for Promoting Christian Knowledge, 1892.

FOR CHILDREN

Sing-Song: A Nursery Rhyme Book. London: George Routledge, 1872.

Speaking Likenesses. London: Macmillan, 1874.

OTHER WORKS

"Petrarcha, Francesco." In *The Imperial Dictionary of Universal Biography.* 3 vols. Edited by John Francis Waller. London: W. Mackenzie, 1863. Republished in *Selected Prose of Christina Rossetti.* Edited by David A. Kent and P. G. Stanwood. Macmillan: Basingstoke, U.K: Macmillan, 1998. Pp. 163–168.

Maude: A Story for Girls, 1850. Edited by W. M. Rossetti. London: James Bowden and Herbert S. Stone, 1897. Republished in *Christina Rossetti: Poems and Prose.* Edited by Jan Marsh. London: Everyman, 1994. Pp. 251–274.

Commonplace and Other Short Stories. London: F. S. Ellis, 1870.

COLLECTED WORKS

The Letters of Christina Rossetti, 4 vols. Edited by Antony H. Harrison. Charlottesville and London: University Press of Virginia, 1997–2004.

Christina Rossetti: The Complete Poems. Edited by Rebecca W. Crump. Notes and introduction by Betty S. Flowers. London and New York: Penguin, 2001.

JOURNALS, CORRESPONDENCE, AND MANUSCRIPTS

Christina Rossetti's letters are scattered all over the world. However, the largest collections are at the University of British Columbia and at Princeton's Firestone Library.

BIOGRAPHICAL AND CRITICAL STUDIES

Armstrong, Isobel. *Victorian Poetry: Poetry, Poetics, and Politics.* London and New York: Routledge, 1993.

Arseneau, Mary, and Jan Marsh. "Intertextuality and Intratextuality: The Full Text of Christina Rossetti's 'Harmony on First Corinthians XIII' Rediscovered." *Victorian Newsletter* 88:17–26 (fall 1995).

Bell, Mackenzie. *Christina Rossetti: A Biographical and Critical Study.* 4th ed. New York: Haskell House, 1971. (Originally published in 1898).

Bentley, D. M. R. "The Meretricious and the Meritorious in *Goblin Market:* A Conjecture and an Analysis." In *The Achievement of Christina Rossetti.* Edited by David A. Kent. Ithaca, N.Y.: Cornell University Press, 1987. Pp. 57–81.

Bullen, J. B. *The Pre-Raphaelite Body: Fear and Desire in Painting, Poetry, and Criticism.* Oxford and New York: Oxford University Press, 1998.

Bump, Jerome. "Christina Rossetti and the Pre-Raphaelite Brotherhood." In *The Achievement of Christina Rossetti.* Edited by David A. Kent. Ithaca, N.Y.: Cornell University Press, 1987. Pp. 322–343.

D'Amico, Diane. "Christina Rossetti: The Maturin Poems." *Victorian Poetry* 19, no. 2:117–137 (1981).

Dodsworth, William, to E. B. Pusey. Unpublished letter (September 9, 1845), Pusey House, Oxford. Quoted in Martha Vicinus, *Independent Women: Work and Community for Single Women 1850–1920.* London: Virago, 1985.

Gilbert, Sandra M., and Susan Gubar. *The Madwoman in the Attic: The Women Writer and the Nineteenth-Century Imagination.* 2nd ed. New Haven, Conn., and London: Yale University Press, 2000.

Greer, Germaine. Introduction to *Goblin Market.* Stonehill, U.K.: Braziller, 1975.

Kooistra, Lorraine Janzen. "Visualising the Fantastic Subject: Goblin Market and the Gaze." In *The Culture of Christina Rossetti: Female Poetics and Victorian Contexts.* Edited by Mary Arseneau, Lorraine Janzen Kooistra, and Antony H. Harrison. Athens: Ohio University Press, 1999. Pp. 137–169.

Marsh, Jan. *Christina Rossetti: A Literary Biography.* London: Jonathan Cape, 1994.

Mason, Emma. "Christina Rossetti and the Doctrine of Reserve." *Journal of Victorian Culture* 7, no. 2:196–219 (2002).

Maturin, Charles R. *Melmoth the Wanderer: A Tale,* 4 vols. Edinburgh: A. Constable, 1820. Republished, Harmondsworth, U.K.: Penguin, 1977.

Mumm, Susan. *Stolen Daughters, Virgin Mothers: Anglican Sisterhoods in Victorian Britain.* London and New York: Leicester University Press, 1999.

Tennyson, G. B. *Victorian Devotional Poetry: The Tractarian Mode.* Cambridge, Mass., and London: Harvard University Press, 1981.

Underhill, Evelyn. *Worship.* London: James Nisbet, 1936. Reprinted, Guildford, U.K.: Eagle, 1991.

Wootton, Sarah. *Consuming Keats: Nineteenth-Century Representations in Art and Literature.* Basingstoke, U.K., and New York: Palgrave Macmillan, 2006.

WILLIAM SHAKESPEARE

(1564—1616)

Charlotte Scott

WHEN KING HENRY V stands before his troops on the eve of the battle of Agincourt, he says that every soldier who survives this battle will look back upon it in his old age and remember the names of the men who fought beside him, names as "familiar in his mouth as household words." (4.3.52). (All references, unless otherwise stated, are to *The Norton Shakespeare,* edited Stephen Greenblatt, Walter Cohen, Jean E. Howard, Katherine Eisaman Maus, London and New York: W. W. Norton & Company, 1997).When William Shakespeare wrote this in 1598, halfway through his career, he could not have anticipated that he too would become a household word. Probably the most famous writer in the world, Shakespeare wrote 36 plays, 2 narrative poems, and 154 sonnets; his work is second only to the Bible in the scope of its translation. Shakespeare's prodigious career, most of it spent in London, spanned about twenty years, a period that witnessed the rise of public theater, the flourishing of the printed word, the entrenchment of Protestantism, and the reign of two monarchs. When Shakespeare died in 1616 he was part of the throng of a city that was often in crisis, always expanding, and moving into an era that was to see regicide, revolution, and the birth of the modern self.

Nobody could have imagined, least of all Shakespeare, the impact the Warwickshire playwright would have on Western literature: it is estimated that Shakespeare introduced around seventeen hundred words into the English language, many of which we use in ordinary conversation today—"gossip" and "swagger," for example. Shakespeare was popular during his lifetime and died a relatively rich man, owning a portion of land outside Stratford-upon-Avon and a fine house in the town, as well as enough money to leave both his daughters a comfortable sum. But the Shakespeare we know, a "genius" and an icon, is largely a product and legacy of the Romantic period of the eighteenth century. The Romantics sought and reified the complexity of human emotion and, as Shakespeare's work emerged from and articulated the psychological, subjective, political, and social animal that man recognized as his representational self, writers turned again and again to the playwright who, in the words of Harold Bloom, "invented the human."

EARLY YEARS

In April 1564 William arrived as the third of six children born to John and Mary Shakespeare. The exact date of William's birth is not known, but because the baptismal register of the Holy Trinity Church in Stratford records the date of April 26, scholars have long agreed Shakespeare's birthday is April 23, working on the basis that most babies were baptized the first Sunday after they were born, as stipulated in the Book of Common Prayer. William was the oldest surviving son; Joan and Margaret died in infancy, Anne died in 1579, and his brothers Edmund and Gilbert died in 1607 and 1612 respectively. His surviving sister, called Joan after the Shakespeares' first baby, lived well into her seventies, dying in 1646 and leaving two children. It is a notorious fact that little can be known of Shakespeare the man, owing to the lack of surviving documents or evidence; this is true of most lay figures of the sixteenth and seventeenth centuries. Although frustrating, such mystery has provided generations of scholars with imaginative license as they try desperately to recover the man from his art. We do know, for example, that, as the son of an apprentice glover and tanner, Shakespeare likely had some working knowledge of these industries, which is borne out by his knowledge and treatment of such articles in the plays: both symbolic and literal, the "glove" often features at key moments within the drama. Think of Romeo's desirous whisperings to Juliet's hand:

See, how she leans her cheek upon her hand!
O, that I were a glove upon that hand,
That I might touch that cheek!

(2.1.65–67; p. 1696)

Or, in *Twelfth Night*, when Feste the clown wittily declares:

A sentence is but a cheverel glove to a good wit, how
  quickly the wrong side may be turned outward!

(3.1.10–12; p. 672)

Another is the iconic moment when a disguised Henry V challenges his soldiers in defense of the king, throwing down the glove in trial and filling it with money in reward. In any case, the little we have on record for Shakespeare makes it tempting to see his personal story in his plays.

What documentation there is begins with his father buying a house in Stratford in 1552 and some few years later his marriage to Mary Arden in about 1557. Mary Arden was the daughter of a relatively wealthy landowner, Robert Arden, who had a farm just outside Stratford. When the couple married, neither of them was literate, signing their names with marks in the register. Literacy was not common among rural communities: the printing of vernacular literature had yet to take hold outside of the immediate circle of wealthy Londoners, and there was little need to read and write beyond the domestic demands of the household. All this would change, however, over the next fifty years, and Shakespeare's theaters would become places of dynamic exchange for the written and spoken word. Despite his lack of reading and writing skills—and occasional disreputable behavior—John Shakespeare held a range of civic positions, including town alderman, high bailiff, and mayor. Such positions occasionally came with benefits, one of which was education for his children at Stratford grammar school. The King's New School in

Stratford was well established and took boys from about the age of seven, when they were "breeched." (For a male, "breeching" meant that he moved from being an infant to being a child: as babies, both boys and girls wore skirts or dresses until around age seven, when boys were put into breeches, or trousers.) As Bianca says in one of Shakespeare's earliest comedies, *The Taming of the Shrew:*

I am no breeching scholar in the schools;
I'll not be tied to hours nor 'pointed times,
But learn my lessons as I please myself.

(3.1.18–20; p. 555)

Bianca puns on her status as a woman, finding liberty rather than constraint in her sex, but for most children, breeching was a serious matter that marked a rite of passage. We do not know exactly what sort of education Shakespeare would have received at the King's New School, but we can suppose that it offered the basics of humanism in the course of study called the trivium, consisting of grammar, logic, and rhetoric. Shakespeare's education—or lack of it—has always been a focal point for scholarly debate. Those scholars who argue that William Shakespeare did not write the plays and poems we have long thought he did focus on the man's education and suggest that a person without university or classical training could not have produced the material attributed to him. Those who do believe in Shakespeare's hand, however, want to know more about how such a mind as his made the move from schoolboy to unsurpassed poet and playwright. Shakespeare himself is much concerned with education and often satirizes the schoolboy as well as the scholar. In *Love's Labour's Lost,* the pompous Nathaniel dismisses the ignorant Dull:

Sir, he hath never fed of the dainties that are bred
in a book. He hath not eat paper, as it were. He
hath not drunk ink. His intellect is not replenished,
he is only an animal, only sensible in the duller
parts.

(4.2.21–24; p. 330)

In *The Merry Wives of Windsor,* the young pupil William is taken through his Latin grammar:

Evans: *Nominativo, hig, hag, hog.* Pray you, mark: *genitivo, huius.*

Well, what is your accusative case?

William Page: *Accusativo, hinc—*

Evans: I pray you, have your remembrance, child, *accusativo, hing, hang, hog.*

Mistress Quickly: "Hang-hog" is Latin for bacon, I warrant you.

(4.1. 36–41, p. 138)

Shakespeare treats education with a light and humorous touch in his plays, but there is often a more sophisticated discussion at the heart of such moments—the distance between education and experience, for example, and the social significance of learning. Social status was defined for the Elizabethans by birth, but education could and did blur the boundaries between what one was born into and what one could become.

In 1570 John Shakespeare applied for his coat of arms and the title of "gentleman," which he was refused, probably as a result of his increasing debts and capricious sense of responsibility. Over the next twenty years, as William grew up, John's fortunes ebbed and flowed, but not long before he died he found himself in a position to reapply for the status of "gentleman" and was successful. In 1596 the Garter King of Arms awarded the Shakespeares their heraldic badge, which was gold with a black banner bearing a silver spear and sporting the motto *Non sanz droict*—"Not without right." The coat of arms is on William Shakespeare's tomb in Stratford. When this was awarded to John, William was moving into an established career in the theaters of London, but during his time at home little is certain. We know, however, that he married Anne Hathaway in 1582, when he was still a young man and she was twenty-six and several months pregnant.

Much has been imagined over the years of the relationship between Anne and William, not least of all by scholars who have hoped to find what love meant to the man who created some of the most brutal and most beautiful literary lovers. Shakespeare's relationship with his wife notoriously has come to pivot on a clause in his will, which states that he would like Anne to have his "second best bed." Such an apparent demotion from the superlative bed has led many people to assume that Shakespeare felt very little for the wife he left in Stratford. Their relationship was, to a large extent, unconventional in that they appear to have lived separately for the majority of their adult lives, but we also know that the bed Shakespeare left his wife was very probably the one that they had shared and slept in and that it was very usual to bequeath your most costly belongings to your children rather than to your spouse. Shakespeare wrote so compellingly and so conflictingly on love and marriage that it is almost impossible to imagine his private self among his public creations. It is true, however, that very few of Shakespeare's dramatic marriages are sanguine: Macbeth and Lady Macbeth, Gertrude and Claudius, Othello and Desdemona, Richard III and Anne, Antony and Octavia, Leontes and Hermione, Petruchio and Katherina are all profoundly at odds with their loving selves; "the catastrophe is a nuptial" (4.1.73–4; p. 328) as Boyet says in *Love's Labour's Lost,* or as Feste puts it in *Twelfth Night:* "Many a good hanging prevents a bad marriage" (1.5.17, p. 656). Perhaps *Hamlet* most compellingly captures a more sinister ambivalence when Claudius, having married the widow of his murdered brother, says:

With one auspicious and one dropping eye,
With mirth in funeral and with dirth in marriage,
In equal scale weighing delight and dole.

(1.2.11–13; p. 1928)

Whatever Shakespeare may have felt for his wife, he apparently remained loyal to her and returned to Stratford before he died. Anne bore her husband three children: Susanna, who arrived six months after they were married, and the twins, Judith and Hamnet, who were born two years later. Hamnet died in 1596 at age eleven. Hamnet has always played a fascinating, if mysterious, part in Shakespeare's biography. The similarities in name to his most famous creation, Hamlet, are obvious, and it is also clear that at about the same time Hamnet died Shakespeare seemed to undergo a metamorphosis from an accomplished poet-playwright to an extraordinary author. Whether losing a son pushed Shakespeare into a period in his career where his work starkly matured—moving toward the great tragedies, via the "problem plays" from the histories—is debatable, but it is a truism that confronting death leads one to contemplate and even interrogate the conditions of life. Whether or not the ghost of Shakespeare's son is present in his most complex creation, Prince Hamlet, can only be conjecture; from a historical standpoint, however, it is likely that the boy and his twin sister were named after Anne and William's neighbors and presumed friends, Hamnet and Judith Sadler. The twins were baptized in 1585 with the Sadlers as godparents, possibly one of the last occasions Shakespeare was to attend in Stratford.

Very little is known of Shakespeare's movements between 1585 and his arrival in London in the early 1590s, but there are several plausible suggestions. By the time we come across the name William Shakespeare in association with the London theaters it is clear that Shakespeare has gone some way in exploring and developing the actor's and playwright's arts. Although Shakespeare was apparently a peaceable man, staying clear of trouble, brawls, censorship, and notoriety (unlike a number of his peers, including Christopher Marlowe and Ben Jonson), he had ruffled some feathers by the time we first hear of him in connection with the theater. In a pamphlet entitled *Greenes Groats-worth of Wit Bought With A Million of Repentance,* the author, Robert Greene, a prose fiction writer and so-called university wit declares:

> there is an upstart Crow, beautified with our feathers, that with his *Tygers hart wrapt in a Players hyde,* supposes he is as well able to bombast out a blanke verse as the best of you: and being an absolute *Johannes fac totum,* is in his owne conceit the onely Shake-scene in a countrey.
>
> (F1v)

This "upstart Crow," jack-of-all-trades and master of none, actor-playwright who is accused of ignorance, arrogance, and plagiarism is probably Shakespeare. "Shakes-scene" is a witty conflation of Shakespeare's name and the theater, and the "Tygers hart wrapt in a Players hyde" directly recalls a line from *Henry VI, Part 3* when York, repelled and full of vituperation for Queen Margaret, declares, "O, tiger's heart wrapt in a woman's hide" (1.4.138, p. 1249). The play, originally titled *The True Tragedy of Richard Duke of York,* was probably the first play Shakespeare wrote, in about 1590. In 1588, however, Elizabeth I, visiting her troops employed against the Spanish Armada, told them: "I know I have but the body of a weak and feeble woman; but I have the heart of a king, and of a king of England, too" (Marcus, Mueller, and Rose, eds., p. 326).

Elizabeth's speech, now famous for its enthralling evocation of both strength and weakness, lurks, perhaps, beneath York's indictment of Margaret. The powerful images of ambiguity that accompany Shakespeare's great and terrifying women—Tamora (*Titus Andronicus*), Margaret (*Henry VI*), Lady Macbeth (*Macbeth*), Goneril (*King Lear*), the Queen (*Cymbeline*)—are often predicated upon the proximity of strength and weakness, man and woman, good and evil. When, however, Greene published his insult to the "upstart Crow," Shakespeare must already have established himself as something of a fixture in, and indeed a threat to, the developing life of the London theater. Although *Henry VI, Part 3* was not published until 1595, Greene's comment helps us to date its performance and Shakespeare's career. The period, however, between 1585 and 1590 is something of a mystery because there is no material record of Shakespeare's movements between the birth of the twins and the performance of *Henry VI, Part 3.* All we can be sure of is that somewhere in those five years he moved to London and either became or established himself as an actor and playwright.

Where Shakespeare learned his art and what he was doing in the so-called lost years have always been contentious. John Aubrey, a seventeenth-century antiquary, compiled a brief history of more than four hundred people, known as the *Brief Lives*; in his entry for Shakespeare he claimed that the playwright "had been in his younger years a schoolmaster in the country" (MS Bodleian, *Arch.* F, C37). The "country," in this context, has come to mean Lancashire since E. K. Chambers focused our attention on the will of Alexander Houghton Esq of Lea (in Lancashire). Houghton's will, dated August 3, 1581, stipulated that he would like to hand over his players to his brother, Sir Thomas Hesketh, but should Sir Thomas not want a theatrical entourage, Houghton expressed a particular wish for the treatment of two men:

> And I most heartily require the said Sir Thomas to be friendly unto Fulk Gillome & William Shakeshafte now dwelling with me & either to take them unto his service or else to help them to some good master, as my trust is he will.
>
> (quoted by E. A. J. Honigmann, p. 3)

Alexander Houghton was a wealthy Catholic landowner and friend to the arts. Spelling was indeed mutable in this period, and multiple spellings of a single name were very common, but so too was the name Shakespeare—or indeed Shakeshaft. The possibility of Shakespeare living in Lancashire with this family, and being a schoolmaster, has led to further speculation about Shakespeare's denomination. Despite Protestantism being the official religion, there remained, albeit clandestinely, a strong Catholic presence in the north, and for Shakespeare to ally himself with Catholic families, together with the belief that his father, John Shakespeare, may have remained a Catholic throughout his life, has led many to believe that Shakespeare supported this denomination. Shakespeare's plays remain so artfully ambivalent, as well as philosophically sophisticated, that it is very difficult, if very tempting, to trace certain beliefs. What makes this even more compelling is that Shakespeare was writing at a moment and in a city that was both rigorously controlled and always in flux. The Elizabethans witnessed a period that moved through an intense process of change—social, political, religious, scientific, and economic—and although the theater was, like all media, subject to censorship, it was a platform for the trade and exchange of cultural values and sociopolitical negotiations.

LONDON AND THE THEATER

Until the sixteenth century there were no public theaters in England. Before drama moved into the province of public entertainment and spectacle it was exclusively didactic, emerging out of religious teachings to form morality plays and the staging of conversions or miracles. Before the inception of the first theater, the Red Lion Inn, in 1567, dramatic productions were limited to inn yards or private houses. In 1576, however, James Burbage commissioned the Theatre, which was the first building expressly built for the purpose of playing. The Theatre, like the Curtain, also built in about 1576, was situated in the Liberties, which were areas outside of the City of London's control and therefore subject to different, usually more lax, authorities. James Burbage would be an important figure in Shakespeare's life: his son, Richard Burbage, was to become one of the leading actors in Shakespeare's company and central to ways in which the playwright wrote his roles. The theaters developed quickly, and one after the other began to be built in and around London. The earliest theaters were all open-air. These included, along with the Theatre and the Curtain, the Rose, the Fortune, and the Globe, each of which probably housed a play of Shakespeare's at one time or another.

The nature of the outdoor theater and the company of actors had a significant impact on the ways in which plays were written. The construction of the space, for example, meant that there were particular facilities any play could make use of: the gallery, trap door, or "discovery space," for example, where actors could declaim, hide, or reveal. Shakespeare's plays are full of references to the art of playing and the nature of the theater. Both practical and conceptual, the nature of representation and the execution of drama are central to the ways in which he explores his subjects and stories. Two early plays, *The Taming of the Shrew* and *A Midsummer Night's Dream,* are deeply concerned with performance and pretending. Where *The Shrew* is a play within a play, beginning with the duping of a drunkard into believing he is a lord set before his own private entertainment, *Dream* ritualizes the illusion of representation and the art of believing. But where *The Shrew* begins with the staging of its own performance, *Dream* ends with an allusion to the play itself:

If we shadows have offended,
Think but this, and all is mended,
That you have but slumbered here
While these visions did appear.
And this weak and idle theme,
No more yielding but a dream ...

(Epilogue, 1–6, p. 411)

Shakespeare returns again and again to the art of playing and the nature of theater, compelled, as he seemed to be, by the vagaries of representation and the implications of illusion. As media developed toward the end of the sixteenth century—the printed book, broadsides, and pamphlets—the theater became a particularly vibrant place for the mixing of spectacle and entertainment, knowledge and commentary. To its supporters the theater offered an extraordinary and unique synthesis of ribaldry, story, morality, amusement, diversion, and learning. Words, new or fantastic, flew across the stage as gifts to the audience; people could attend a play in order to hear language being used in new ways, to appropriate whole sentences, and to explore ways of communicating in a developing climate of expression. This was the age when the printed word became available to more than the university educated, the Bible had been translated into English for the first time, and the classical theater was being rewritten in the tongues of many. The theater became a trading place for the commodification of language and the celebration of style: it was also a valuable resource for those who could not read. When the theaters closed during the Civil War it was for the state of language that people feared:

The *Stage* ... having much conferd and contributed to the inrichment of [language], it being the *Mint* that daily coyns new *words*, which are presently received and admitted as *currant*, ... the plucking downe of which will I feare, not only *retard* the perfectioning of our Language towards which it was advancing amain, but even quite hinder and *recoyle* it, and make it return to its former *Barbarisme*.

(Richard Flecknoe, *Miscellania*, 1653, pp. 103–104)

But although the theater was intensely popular, and populist, it was also a place of controversy. The very nature of the public space brought people together to mix in close proximity and socialize in excitement, and antitheatricalists seized on such circumstances as license for sin. In 1579 the Puritan and writer Stephen Gosson explained, in *The Schoole of Abuse:*

In our assemblies at playes in *London*, you shall see suche heauing, and shoouing, suche ytching and shouldring, too sitte by women; Suche care for their garments, that they bee not trode on: Such eyes to their lappes, that no chippes light in them: Such pillowes to ther backes, that they take no hurte: Such masking in their eares, I knowe not what: Such giuing the Pippins to passe the time: Suche playing at foote Saunt without Cardes: Such ticking, such toying, such smiling, such winking, and such manning them home, when the sportes are ended, that it is a right Comedie, to marke their behauiour, to watche their conceites, as the Catte for the Mouse, and as good as a course at the game it selfe, to dogge them a little, or followe aloofe by the print of their feete, and so discouer by slotte where the Deare taketh soyle.

(p. 17)

For Gosson, the physical space encouraged a mingling and vanity that was both antisocial and ungodly; for others, however, the plays themselves fostered profanity. As John Northbrooke put it, in *A Treatise Wherein Dicing, Dauncing, Vaine Plaies ... Are Reproved ...* (1579):

I am persuaded that Satan hath not a more speedy way and fitter school to work and teach his desire to bring men and women into his snare of concupiscence and filthy lusts of wicked whoredom, than those places and plays, and theaters are.

(pp. 59–60)

For Shakespeare, the relationship between sin and representation was more complex and certainly subtler. His exploration of playing and performing became central to the ways in which he examined the moral and political fabrics of the play worlds. Hamlet's great invocation of the art of theater is rooted in an obsession with truth, and what that comes to mean in a "seeming" world. When Hamlet stages his play *The Mousetrap* to entrap his murderous uncle, he insists on a heightened realism that will resonate from the play to its audience. Instructing the players, he declares:

> Suit the action to the word, the word to the action, with this special observance: that you o'erstep not the modesty of nature; for anything so overdone is from the purpose of playing, whose end, both at the first and now, was and is to hold as 'twere the mirror up to nature, to show virtue her own feature, scorn her own image, and the very age and body of the time his form and pressure.
>
> (3.2.16–22, p. 1960)

Invoking the theater as a reflective glass, showing us who we are and how we live, exposes it as a powerful tool in the discussion—and understanding—of a society in crisis. The power of theater is nowhere more apparent than in *Hamlet,* where it is precisely constructed for revelation and disclosure. As Claudius sees his crimes dramatized before his very eyes, he will be compelled to react and thereby prove his guilt. In 1612 Thomas Heywood, a fellow playwright and great supporter of the stage, wrote a treatise titled *An Apology for Actors,* which discusses the role and significance of the theater. In support of his argument he describes in some detail an incident that took place involving a widow, a murder, a play, and a conviction: during a performance with "a company of our *English* Comedians," a woman, watching the dramatization of a murder, became "with great gravity strangely amazed," and "with a distracted and troubled brain oft sighed these words: Oh my husband, my husband!" A few days later, the sexton, having discovered the skull of a man whose murder was similar to that of the man in the play, makes it known to the churchwarden, and "the woman, out of the trouble of her afflicted conscience discovered a former murder" (Heywood, G2v, G2r). As Hamlet says, "the play's The thing / Wherein I'll catch the conscience of the king" (2.2.581–2, p. 1956)—or in this case, an ordinary woman.

Shakespeare's use of the play-within-a-play is not unique, and Elizabethan and Jacobean theater is full of this conceit as a way of exploring the arts of representation and the psychologies of guilt and exposure. But Shakespeare is unique in his sophisticated explorations of what

is and what seems; in other words, the complex interrelations between subjective and objective truths. *Hamlet,* perhaps Shakespeare's greatest creation, and certainly his most famous, was composed about halfway though his dramatic career and marked a turning point for the dramatist. As Shakespeare moved through his early career he shifted through different registers of performance, starting, probably, with *The Comedy of Errors* and the three parts of *Henry VI;* he then turned to *The Taming of the Shrew, A Midsummer Night's Dream, Romeo and Juliet, Richard II,* and *Titus Andronicus.* As he was moving between classical comedy, history, and tragedy, Shakespeare was exploring the nature of theater (entertainment and spectacle) as well as the limits of representation (the structure of the space, the role of the imagination, and the contexts of illusion).

Toward the end of the sixteenth century Shakespeare began to write the plays that have become celebrated for their sophisticated understanding of the social and political worlds, through which multiple voices emerge. As the theater itself developed and the nature of entertainment spread through a compelling synthesis of organized executions, bear-baiting, endorsed misrule, royal processions, pageants, and plays, so too did Shakespeare's exploration of the relations between the self and the state, institution and emotion, surveillance and authority. *Richard II,* written in about 1596, is a play that has become inextricably, although perhaps erroneously, linked with the historical moment in which it was performed. An extraordinary play that interrogates the limits of representation, *Richard II* charts the downfall of a king who is single-minded and insincere, brilliant and untrustworthy, emotional and bloody-minded. Alongside the creation of this fragmented king runs the history of fraud and deposition, of rebellion and dishonor. The play dramatizes the deposing of a monarch, something unacceptable on the Elizabethan stage. Legend has it—along with many scholarly editions—that Elizabeth I identified herself with Richard II, and the Earl of Essex, her onetime ally turned detractor, wanted the play performed the night before his planned rebellion. In the event, the rebellion was quashed and the performance aborted, but the radical scene in which Richard is deposed by Bolingbroke (the future Henry IV) was not published in Elizabeth's lifetime. Censorship was a serious business, and all plays were subject to approval by the Master of the Revels, a position appointed by and accountable to the queen, before they could legally be performed. Although plays were to some extent at the whim of the monarch, her patronage, their popularity, and the dynamic between the public and political worlds were all testaments to the power of theater and the potential spaces it could inhabit in the lives of others. Shakespeare was surprisingly canny in avoiding the censors; unlike his fellow playwrights Christopher Marlowe, Ben Jonson, and John Marston, Shakespeare was never directly or specifically censored. Censorship reminds us, however, that plays are always in conversation with their worlds, and that those conversations are not necessarily straightforward or transparent.

Shakespeare's interest in performance reflects not only the medium in which he worked but also a predominantly illiterate society that was deeply rooted in a visual culture and a demonstrative religious and political establishment. Power and authority had emerged from a long history of iconography that needed to speak—with immediacy—through the image to a society largely unschooled in the written word. Teaching, whether the word of God or the monarch, had to be done through the image, and although the Protestant Reformation worked hard to make this shift from the icon to the word, the eye to the intellect, much of Elizabethan state culture remained deeply invested in spectacle. Shakespeare would have walked through a city that displayed the decapitated heads of traitors, preserved in tar, on London Bridge; that supported the scaffolds for public hangings, the spaces for floggings, blocks for the stocks, and ritualized public punishments for brawling, domestic disturbance, and disorderly behavior. This was a city and a society that celebrated both its punishments and rewards in public. Royal progresses, processions, and state funerals were all intended as a visual embodiment of authority, and the theater grew up in a society that recognized the performance of image as didactic. But with the rise and development of Protestantism the image was to undergo a dramatic change, and the trust in a visual culture would become more ambivalent. In his plays Shakespeare repeatedly explores what we see and how we see it, and as his career moved forward into the more intense period of the tragedies he returned again and again to questions of representation and the psychologies of appearance. With a developing awareness of the art of theater in the dynamic between the collective and the individual, Shakespeare became more self-reflexive in his treatment of the stage.

When Shakespeare turned his hand to a history of Henry V, a popular subject for plays in this period, he used the stage as a platform to incite the imagination well beyond the confines of its structure and temporality. As the play opens, the Chorus enters to speak the Prologue:

O, for a muse of fire, that would ascend
The brightest heaven of invention.
A kingdom for a stage, princes to act
And monarchs to behold the swelling scene!
Then should the warlike Harry, like himself,
Assume the port of Mars, and at his heels,
Leashed in like hounds, should famine, sword, and
  fire
Crouch for employment. But pardon, gentles all,
The flat unraisèd spirits that hath dared
On this unworthy scaffold to bring forth
So great an object. Can this cockpit hold
The vasty fields of France? Or may we cram
Within this wooden O, the very casques
That did affright the air at Agincourt?

(Prologue, 1–14.1–14; pp. 1032–1033)

The Chorus wonderfully describes what any play must be able to do—create a kingdom on a stage, princes from players, and history in a heartbeat. But referring back to the structure—"this unworthy scaffold," "this wooden O"—we must imagine that the theater (cockpit) holds "the vasty fields of France" and the armor ("casques") of the soldiers. The Chorus returns at crucial moments within the drama to urge us to travel, geographically or temporally, beyond the remit of the stage:

There is the playhouse now, there must you sit,

And thence to France shall we convey you safe,

And bring you back, charming the narrow seas

To give you gentle pass, for if we may,

We'll not offend one stomach with our play.

(2.0.36–40; p. 1043)

As Shakespeare became more conscious of the limits of drama, he also became more aware of how to manipulate those limits and develop the imagination beyond the requisites of seeing.

Around the time *Henry V* was being composed, James Burbage was running into trouble with the lease on his Theatre in Shoreditch. The lease ran out in April 1598 and it was not renewed. In the winter of that year Burbage and the Theatre's loyal troop, the Lord Chamberlain's Men, which included Shakespeare, dismantled the structure—the "wooden O"—and carried it, piece by piece, over the river to the Liberties, where it could be established with a new license and without such strict regulations. The men erected the theater in the Clink in Southwark, where it became the Globe playhouse, not far from where the current Globe Theatre stands today. The new theater now belonged to five shareholders as well as the Burbages, which included William Shakespeare and John Heminge, the latter of whom would go on to publish Shakespeare's complete works with Henry Condell in 1623. The Globe playhouse was polygonal with a thatched roof, which, in 1613, during a performance of *Henry VIII,* caught fire from the sparks of burning wadding that had been ignited by ceremonial guns and burned down. Looking on at the remnants of the destroyed theater Ben Jonson exclaimed, "See the world's ruins ...!" The Globe had been an extremely popular theater and marked a turning point in Shakespeare's career as he moved from actor to playwright to shareholder, staging some of his best-loved plays at the theater. Jonson's comment draws on the metaphor of the world as a stage and the stage as

a world, and is symptomatic of the space the theater had come to occupy in the language of representation.

Hamlet, written at the turn of the century and performed at the Globe, is more than a great play. It is also a study in the art of performance: performing politics, plays, language, and the self; it is a play that puts objectivity on trial as it searches for meaning. Shakespeare's fascination with the "truth" became more and more complex as he moved into writing the tragedies and what are now called the "problem plays," a term coined by the critic Frederick S. Boas at the end of the nineteenth century. The problem plays, which usually include *Measure for Measure, All's Well That Ends Well,* and *Troilus and Cressida,* are defined as such because they engage their protagonists in specific moral dilemmas and social crises. With the turn of the seventeenth century Shakespeare's plays became increasingly dense and sophisticated in their treatment of the moral fabric of their worlds.

END OF THE BEGINNING

When Elizabeth I died in 1603 the Tudor dynasty that defined so much of the achievement of the sixteenth century came to an end. Since her grandfather, Henry VII, came to the throne in 1485, the Tudors had reigned over England and witnessed—and even encouraged—the great changes that were to take place under the auspices of what we would later call the English Renaissance: humanism, trade, exploration, nationalism, Protestantism, and vernacular literature. Although there was much that was variable in Elizabeth—her refusal to marry and produce an heir, the wars in Ireland, Protestant propaganda, her relationship to Scotland, and capricious politics—she inspired a nation, supported the theater, exploited the power of the arts, and enabled a city to grow through the ceremony of her presence. Elizabeth steadily influenced and supported the leading theatrical companies, the Lord Chamberlain's Men and the Lord Admiral's Men. Under James I, however, royal patronage was granted to the Lord Chamberlain's Men, further cementing the place of theater in London life. James I's endorsement of the Chamberlain's Men, of which Shakespeare was a member, had a number of implications for the playwright and players. James's interest in theater and the stage enabled its development through the other forms of spectacle that became popular in this period, including the masque and pageant, and also reflected a growing fascination with interior spaces as they became a more pronounced feature of the Jacobean court. James I, often described as the monarch of the bedchamber, ruled in a way that was far more internalized, distant, and absolutist than Elizabeth, and as a result the interior space—its intrigue, authority, surveillance, and iconography—became a place of fascination for dramatists. Under James I, Shakespeare's great tragedies emerged with a growing sense of agitation about this absolutist power, the nature of sovereignty, and a complex organization of the psychology of space.

Othello traces the anxiety of identity, of the relationship between power and the self, and *Coriolanus* explores the confrontation between ruler and the state as both the public and the private spaces turn in on the hero. However, it is not only the tragedies that explore this territory. *Cymbeline*, a strange and uneven play, enlists the supernatural in a quest to distinguish right and wrong through the private space and an awkward hero. *Measure for Measure*, a problem play, explores a profoundly complex dynamic between power and fulfillment, abuse and authority, manipulation and morality. Most famously, however, it is *Macbeth* that reveals the anxieties—and desires—of the Stuart king. As with most of his histories, Shakespeare looked to Raphael Holinshed's first volume of the *Chronicles of England, Scotland and Ireland*, first published in 1577, for a version of his plot, and, in this case, the foundations for an account of the reigns of Duncan and Macbeth. But *Macbeth* is particularly immersed in interests at the heart of the king—Scotland, witches, Stuart ancestry, and absolutism. It is commonly held that Shakespeare wrote *Macbeth*, with the help of Thomas Middleton, for James I, and that the Porter's references to equivocation and treason refer to the Gunpowder Plot of 1605–1606.

Although there is no record of a court performance of *Macbeth*, it is more than likely it was played before the king. The apparitions that the witches summon for Macbeth—a parade of Scottish kings descending from Banquo, the eighth and last of whom has a mirror in his hand which may have shown the royal patron his own reflection—directly involves James in a dynastic drama that celebrates him as both the hero and the legacy. As the apparitions vanish the first witch exclaims:

Come, sisters, cheer we up his sprites
And show the best of our delights.
I'll charm the air to give a sound,
While you perform your antic round,
That this great king may kindly say,
Our duties did his welcome pay.

(4.1.143–48; p. 1898)

But where James may have celebrated himself in Banquo, others may have seen shadows in Macbeth and Shakespeare's portrait of monomania and fear.

Shakespeare's interest in the nature of kingship—its absolutism and disintegration, as well as questions of moral responsibility and trial—had already found expression in his most profound tragedy, *King Lear*. Although perhaps not as psychologically complex as *Macbeth*, *Lear* traces the breakdown of authority through the parallel pressures of love and abuse in a world that can find no relief from destruction. *Lear* interrogates a world fragmented by both anxiety and individualism. Tracing the demise of moral and social orders, it explores the conditions on which we base both relationships and reason through a paradigm of loss. At the end of the Folio's *King Lear*, Edgar speaks:

The weight of this sad time we must obey:
Speak what we feel, not what we ought to say.
The oldest hath borne most: we that are young
Shall never see so much, nor live so long.

(5.3.298–301; p. 2073)

Despite the aphoristic structure, Edgar's sentiment is more than morality in cadence: he speaks to a community that is in crisis. Having lost both its hope and its authority, he speaks for a language of change, which is embedded in a future of responsibility and care.

Although Shakespeare's greatest tragedies were written under the reign of James I, we must not assume that this reflects either the playwright's personal circumstances at the time or his attitude toward the king; rather, it reflects the Jacobean period's critical shift in the popularity and horror of human drama as well as a development in the representation of breakdown and despair. The shift in drama that took place under James's reign was not just a question of personal taste. Although the Jacobean period would become famous for its more ostentatious attitudes toward the court, entertainment, and spectacle as it willfully adopted more continental approaches to architecture, fashion, and drama, the theaters themselves were also changing. The growing impulse toward more intimate, exclusive even, theater and the development of set design meant that greater effects could be achieved on the stage. A building called Blackfriars, which was bought by James Burbage in 1596 with the intention of making it the Chamberlain's Men's theater after the lease expired on the Theatre in 1597, eventually became the stage it was destined to be some thirteen years later. The project had suffered a number of obstacles, including objections from the local residents about the noise and disruption a theater would bring to their area; James Burbage's death in 1597; the pouring of most of the Chamberlain's Men's resources and time into the Globe; an interloping company showing a performance that offended the king; and then the plague, which closed the building until the late autumn 1609. Although the company would continue to perform at the Globe in the summer, it would play at Blackfriars in the winter. When it reopened, Blackfriars proved to be something of a new theater: performances were now divided into five acts (partly perhaps based on the classical models but also to provide breaks for candle trimming and musical intervals); the audience was entirely seated, unlike theaters such as the Globe, which had a proportion of standing tickets; and it had the capacity to finesse special effects—quieter descents in a flying machine and subtler ascents through the trap door, for example.

Writing for an indoor theater such as Blackfriars meant that Shakespeare's plays could reflect something of the changing space, the lighting, the intimacy (spectators could pay to sit on the stage), and the scene breaks. Although previous plays, such as *Measure for Measure,* could be adjusted to play the space of Blackfriars, either *The Winter's Tale* or *Cymbeline* were probably the first of Shakespeare's plays to be written specifically with the place in mind. Although both romances would have played at the Globe too, they reflect something of the magical quality that a smaller, seated, candlelit space could give.

POETRY, PRINTING, AND PATRONAGE

In 1609, the same year that Blackfriars opened, a London printer, Thomas Thorpe, published Shakespeare's *Sonnets.* Although this was the first time the sonnets appeared in printed book form, his career as a poet had begun around the same time as his career as a playwright in the early 1590s. For Shakespeare, to separate drama from poetry is misleading. In Sonnet 23, for example, the poet uses the stage to explore the language of expression in poetic form:

As an unperfect actor on the stage,
Who with his fear is put besides his part,
Or some fierce thing replete with too much rage,
Whose strength's abundance weakens his own heart,
So I, for fear of trust, forget to say
The perfect ceremony of love's rite,
And in mine own love's strength seem to decay,
O'ercharged with burden of mine own love's might.

(pp. 1930–31)

And in *Romeo and Juliet*—as well as *Twelfth Night, Love's Labour's Lost, Much Ado About Nothing, Cymbeline,* and *King John,* to name a few—poetic form captures and celebrates a dramatic moment:

Juliet: Good pilgrim, you do wrong your hand too much,

Which mannerly devotion shows in this,

For saints have hands that pilgrims' hands do touch,

And palm to palm is holy palmer's kiss.

Romeo: Have not saints lips, and holy palmers too?

Juliet: Ay, pilgrim, lips that they must use in prayer.

Romeo: O, then, dear saint, let lips do what hands do:

They pray, grant thou, lest faith turn to despair.

Juliet: Saints do not move, though grant for prayers' sake.

Romeo: Then move not, while my prayer's effect I take.

Thus from my lips, by thine, my sin is purged.

Juliet: Then have my lips the sin that they have took.

Romeo: Sin from my lips? O, trespass sweetly urged!

(1.5.94–106)

Here, the lovers, finding each other at the Capulets' masqued ball, weave their desire in and out of each other's language, and together they form the rhythm and fourteen lines of a sonnet, which is itself a model of love. By making the moment dynamic, however, Shakespeare does something unique with the convention.

As indicated earlier, Shakespeare began his first narrative poem probably about the same time he began writing plays, and in many ways he developed the different arts through testing the limits and ambitions of each form. *Venus and Adonis,* published in 1593, tells a passionate, sympathetic, erotic, and witty story of a woman's pursuit of love. By far Shakespeare's most popular work at the time, running through at least ten editions before he died, *Venus and Adonis* was also Shakespeare's first foray into the world of literary patronage. The dedication to Henry Wriothesley, Earl of Southampton, refers to the poem as the "first heir of my invention," which makes an implicit contrast between "legitimate" poetry and "illegitimate" drama. Despite Shakespeare's mercurial ability to move between the two, there is a sense in which he acknowledges the former as more respectable.

The extent to which Shakespeare distinguished his poetic and dramatic careers is always debatable, and recent scholars argue compellingly that Shakespeare did not in fact make the separations that such notions of "legitimacy" suggest; rather, they argue, the author sees both forms as interchangeable; testing and flexing the poet as playwright and vice versa. Those scholars who separate out Shakespeare's literary roles attribute his narrative poems—and indeed the sonnets—to periods when the theaters were closed because of outbreaks of plague. The plague, however, was a relatively frequent occurrence, especially during the summer months, and theaters, being heaving sites of public interaction, were always hothouses for the spread of infection. Although temporary closures of the theaters would have affected Shakespeare as they would any other playwright or actor, it is unlikely that he used the time merely to fill a gap in his creativity or, indeed, become a poet of patronage simply to endorse his career as a playwright.

Each narrative poem was dedicated, like almost all printed and coterie poetry of this period, to a patron, and this system of patronage was fundamental to the ways in which literature was circulated and received. Just as the acting companies needed a patron to legally perform (without one they were classed as vagabonds and liable to prosecution), so literature needed patronage to enter the intellectual and social world of the sixteenth and seventeenth centuries. In practice, however, systems of patronage operated differently for acting companies and poets. Although a royal or noble patron was crucial for the survival, indeed existence, of an acting troop, it was essentially financially and culturally independent, with its members creating and carrying their plays—albeit within the bounds of censorship—however they might choose. For a poet, on the other hand, a patron was a necessary and strategic device. Although art, most scholars would argue, was created by patronage (an aristocrat would commission a painting, sculpture, or poem), as the Renaissance developed and cities like London grew through the weight and movement of trade, exchange, and commerce, aligning oneself with a household or patron became more significant in the reception than in the creation of artistic work. Although most dedications are elaborately constructed to offer praise to the patron and humble self-denigration to the author, many writers never came into contact with the person they so slavishly adopted, and whether they ever recovered any financial reward is debatable.

Examination of such a system tends to indicate how social networks might have operated rather than describe specific personal circumstances. Although the Earl of Southampton was also the dedicatee of Shakespeare's next great narrative poem, *The Rape of Lucrece,* it is unclear what precise role he may have played in Shakespeare's literary life. Southampton was a great fan of the theater, and through his allegiance to the Earl of Essex he was persuaded to join him in his attempts at rebellion in 1601. It was Southampton who sent Shakespeare's company, the Lord Chamberlain's Men, forty shillings at the Globe to perform *Richard II* on the eve of Essex's insurrection in an attempt to garner the city's support for the deposing of a monarch. The project failed with fatal consequences for Essex, and Southampton had his peerage removed and was imprisoned for life.

The Rape of Lucrece, published soon after *Venus and Adonis,* in 1594, tells a brutal story of desire, rape, and suicide through the central figures of the chaste and devoted wife Lucrece and the obsessive assailant Tarquin. One of the ways in which we see how Shakespeare's poetry and drama coincide is in the story of Lucrece and the plays *Titus Andronicus* and *Cymbeline.* In *Titus* and *Lucrece,* written within a few years of each other, the heroines undergo a similar ordeal with similar consequences, and as Shakespeare tells their stories he synthesizes the empathy of poetry with the drama of action. Shakespeare returns again to this literary figure in his late play *Cymbeline.* Here, drawing on Ovid's figure of Philomel (from whom Lucrece and Lavinia emerge) in *Metamorphoses,* an important source for Shakespeare, he dramatizes poetry in action through the story in Imogen's book, her op-

pressed honor, and the dangerous figure of Iachimo. As Iachimo, hidden in a trunk, watches the sleeping Imogen he remembers how "Our Tarquin thus / Did softly press the rushes" (2.2. 12–13; p. 2263). Drawing in Lucrece's assailant to conspire with his own silent approach, he goes on to see the incriminating mole on Imogen's breast and declare: "this secret / Will force him think I have picked the lock, and ta'en / The treasure of her honour" (2.2.40–42; p. 2263). Iachimo's analogy draws us back to the poem and Tarquin's extended assault in his approach to Lucrece's bedchamber, where "his guilty hand plucked up the latch" (line 358; p. 2417). The interrelations between the poetry and the drama are always present—whether in subject matter or style—but particularly so in the classical texts that Shakespeare draws on.

The title page of the sonnets boasts of Shakespeare's name, suggesting that he had become a figure of some distinction by this time. Although we know that the narrative poems were extremely popular, Shakespeare may have had a reputation for his sonnets as early as 1598 when Francis Meres, critic and chronicler, wrote of "his sugared Sonnets among his private friends," implying that they were circulated for a coterie. The 154 sonnets can be roughly divided into movements, and there is some debate as to whether they are to be read as a sequence or as individual poems. The first 126 are taken up with the "fair youth" and the praise of his beauty which, in the first 17, he is encouraged to continue through marriage and children:

Look in thy glass and tell the face thou viewest
Now is the time that face should form another,
Whose fresh repair if now thou not renewest
Thou dost beguile the world, unless some mother.

(Sonnet 3; p. 1924)

As the sonnets progress so too does the relationship between the poet and his subject, celebrating their friendship, fearing its loss, mourning mortality, and rendering the verse as monuments:

So oft have I invoked thee for my Muse
And found such fair assistance in my verse
As every alien pen hath got my use
And under thee their poesy disperse.

Thine eyes that taught the dumb on high to sing
And heavy ignorance aloft to fly,
Have added feathers to the learnèd wing
And given grace a double majesty.
Yet be most proud of that which I compile,
Whose influence is thine and born of thee.
In others' works thou dost but mend the style,
And arts with thy sweet graces gracèd be:
But thou art all my art and dost advance
As high as learning my rude ignorance.

(Sonnet 78; p. 1949).

In Sonnet 127 there is a shift, however, from the fair youth to "the dark lady," as she has become known. These last 28 sonnets not only change their subject but also their tone, as the poet moves between lust, disgust, admiration, and disdain. That the subject is a "dark" lady becomes clear through the poet's almost obsessive attention to the color black, which, in this period, is antithetical to the conventional image of beauty. Although other poets, most notably Philip Sidney in his sonnet sequence *Astrophil and Stella,* had rejected typical notions of beauty as "fair," both literally and descriptively, by making his Muse and heroine have deep, dark eyes, Shakespeare's use of the color black is more ambivalent. Sonnet 127 begins:

In the old age black was not counted fair,
Or if it were, it bore not beauty's name.
But now is black beauty's successive heir
And beauty slandered with a bastard shame …

(p. 1966)

Black is strangely neither beautiful nor ugly but triumphant, having succeeded beauty; taken her place but not her title. Later, however, black returns to her former province: "For I have sworn thee fair and thought thee bright, / Who art as black as hell, as dark as night" (Sonnet 147; p. 1973). The last sonnets are full of Shakespeare's brilliant and witty ambivalence and remind us again and again of how he could use the briefest of moments to capture the heart of an emotion; the lover's silence in anger, for example:

Be wise as thou art cruel, do not press
My tongue-tied patience with too much disdain,

Lest sorrow lend me words and words express
The manner of my pity-wanting pain.

(Sonnet 140; pp. 1970–1971)

The title page of the sonnets holds the dedication "To the only begetter of these insuing sonnets Mr. W. H. all happiness and that eternity promised by our ever-living poet" (p. 2435) as well as Shakespeare's name and the initials of the London printer, Thomas Thorpe. The identity of Mr. W. H. has always been in contention. There are those who assume it must be the Earl of Southampton, Henry Wriothesley, with his initials reversed (and who was in prison when the sonnets were published) and those who believe it to be the Earl of Pembroke, William Herbert, to whom the First Folio is dedicated. There is even a school of thought that thinks they may be the mis-set initials of Shakespeare himself in a dedication that is in fact from the printer to the poet. The title of "Mr." is confusing, since it would be an inappropriate one for either of the earls, yet they still seem the most likely candidates. Whoever W. H. is, he is probably the subject—and object—of many of the sonnets. Although for Shakespeare's contemporaries the sonnets were his least popular works, their publication in this form is indicative of the audience he could expect to receive.

Shakespeare, it has long been assumed, was not interested in publication: in his lifetime only about half of his plays were printed. Those that were, such as the sonnets, were printed in quartos, which were small books with the printed sheet folded in half twice, making eight pages. The first of Shakespeare's plays to be printed was *Titus Andronicus* (1594), and the first on which his name appeared was *Love's Labour's Lost* (1598). Shakespeare's apparent lack of concern with publication may be owing to a number of factors. Theater companies retained the rights to plays so long as they were registered but not published; once they hit the public domain, anybody could perform them. Further, the author did not directly benefit from the sale of the script; rather it was a collaborative recuperation. Playbooks did, however, enter the commercial market in waves, and this may well have been prompted by financial need, marketing, or advertising.

THE FINAL CURTAIN

Around the time that the sonnets were published Shakespeare began to write the plays that we now call "romances." These four plays—*Pericles, Cymbeline, The Winter's Tale,* and *The Tempest*—reflect a different style in their use of language, fabulous recoveries, magical illusions, wonder, and make-believe. The heightened use of illusion and disbelief perhaps makes these plays his most acutely theatrical. A younger dramatist, John Fletcher, with whom Shakespeare was to collaborate, paved the way for this type of comedy with his play *Philaster; or, Love Lies A-Bleeding,* which inspired, we can only assume from the similarities, Shakespeare's *Cymbeline.* Fletcher took over from Shakespeare as the playwright for the King's Men, but before he did they collaborated on a number of plays, including *Henry VIII* (or *All Is True*) and *The Two Noble Kinsmen.* These were to be the last plays that Shakespeare would write.

His last single-author plays, however, were *The Winter's Tale* and *The Tempest. The Winter's Tale,* a story of jealousy and destruction, grief and recovery, wonder and illusion, was played for the wedding of James I's daughter, Princess Elizabeth. Before that, however, it was played at the Globe and is one of the few plays for which we have a contemporary account: Simon Forman, a physician, who saw the play in May 1611, described the character of Autolycus as "the rogue that came in all tattered like colt-pixie.... Beware of trusting feigned beggars or fawning fellows" (Chambers, pp. 340–341) It is perhaps Shakespeare's most programmatic play in that it shifts quite radically from tragedy to pastoral comedy halfway through the drama: it is at this pivotal point that the now infamous stage direction "Exit pursued by a bear" appears. This famous bear was probably a real one: not only did theaters have a history of doubling as bear-baiting arenas (the Hope is an example) but James I had a particular interest in exotic animals and kept his own menagerie in London. James is said to have owned polar bears and tigers, and it is possible that one of his bears was used for the performance for his daughter's marriage. Another defining moment in the play comes toward the end, when a statue appears shrouded in secrecy and magic. This is the statue of the dead queen—presented as though she were living—at which kneels her daughter, having grown up as a shepherdess and been presumed dead. Both women are resurrected—literally and metaphorically—as families are reunited and wounds salved. Shakespeare seems fascinated by the drama of resurrection, of returning and reviving life; it appears in some form in each of the late plays. Healing and revelation become central to the ways in which the dramas evolve and resolutions are reached. Not all of these resolutions, however, seem convincing, and the vast scope of emotion, time, and events that the plays try to incorporate can lead to ambiguities and problems with realism. Shakespeare often leaves many questions unanswered: Where and how had Paulina kept Hermione a secret for sixteen years? How did Thaisa survive after being cast into the sea in a box, apparently having died in childbirth? But part of these mysteries is also their magic, and nowhere is magic more important than in Shakespeare's final play, *The Tempest.*

The first recorded performance of *The Tempest* took place at James I's court on November 1, 1611. It was probably a relatively new play—it relies on three texts that were published only a year before. These three texts were all about travel and discovery and a famous shipwreck, the *Sea-Adventure,* which struck the coast of Bermuda with five hundred colonists onboard, all of whom were initially presumed dead. Most of the passengers and crew, however, eventually turned up in Jamestown, and their stories emerged. The play begins with a storm, conjured from Prospero's magic and with the power of revenge. As the play unfolds through spirits, witches, dukes, princes, islanders, servants, and goddesses, Prospero presides as the enigmatic author, controlling and creating his drama of retribution and recuperation. The play has a compelling opacity through which we are permitted to move for a few hours before we are cast back out of the theater and the fantasy. The elusive sense in which we arrive and leave the island through a moment of its time has given the play a rich afterlife. From Caliban and Ariel to Prospero and Miranda, the play has inspired versions and shadows of its story through many different idioms. The figure of Prospero, the play's magical synthesis of drama and illusion, and the strange air of loss and renouncement has led many critics to identify the magus as Shakespeare himself. Although William Davenant and John Dryden suggested this connection in the prologue to their adaptation of the play, it became a critical commonplace in the eighteenth and nineteenth centuries. When Prospero closes the play, having cast off his magic robes, renounced the island, freed his spirit, Ariel, and made his way toward a return to Italy, he declares:

Now my charms are all o'erthrown,
And what strength I have's mine own,
Which is most faint: now 'tis true,
I must be here confined by you,
Or sent to Naples. Let me not,
Since I have my dukedom got
And pardoned the deceiver, dwell
In this bare island by your spell,
But release me from my bands
With the help of your good hands:
Gentle breath of yours my sails
Must fill, or else my project fails,
Which was to please.

(Epilogue, 1–13)

Directly invoking the audience, Prospero synthesizes the play and the stage, the actor and the author, as the clapping ("good hands") and cheering ("Gentle breath") bring the drama to a close and send the character from the stage. However tempting it may be for us to imagine William Shakespeare as Prospero, casting, creating, and controlling the lives of others through the magic of theater and the illusion of effects as his play unfolds for the "two hours' traffic of our stage" (*Romeo and Juliet*, Prologue, p. 872-3), we are probably mistaken. As Shakespeare began his career with a fascination for the art of theater— its illusions, limits, idiosyncrasies, and power—so too he ends it there. As both a poet and playwright, Shakespeare grew up in a culture that was inventing, developing, exploring, and exploiting its media alongside a new world of words. Shakespeare's theater made new worlds with a depth, sophistication, and subtlety that was to make him the playwright, as Ben Jonson said, "not of an age, but for all time!"

Shakespeare died on April 23, 1616, leaving the bulk of his money to his daughter, Judith, and his property to Susanna; he also left some money to his sister Joan and her three sons. To his granddaughter Elizabeth Hall, he left all his plates (except for a bowl he left to Judith). His wife, Anne Hathaway, of course, got his "second best bed with the furniture." And to "the poor of Stratford" he left £10: the price of ten copies of the First Folio.

THE FIRST FOLIO

At the end of Peter Greenaway's film of *The Tempest,* titled *Prospero's Books* (1991), he shows a large, beautifully bound, watermarked book, its pages being flicked open by wind. The pages settle at the beginning of the book, where we see they are empty; into these pages falls the play of *The Tempest,* and the book is complete. Shakespeare's last play became his first, as it came to mark the beginning of his works. Greenaway's image presents the First Folio as though it were Shakespeare's last breath as well as the culmination of his imagination and art, and to some extent this is also how his friends and cowriters presented the book at the time. Fellow playwright Ben Jonson was the writer of the opening verse "To the Reader," whereupon follows the dedication to William Herbert, Earl of Pembroke, from John Heminge and Henry Condell as well as their epistle "To the great variety of readers," followed by a series of paeans to Shakespeare, including a famous declaration from Jonson:

Shine forth, thou star of poets, and with rage
Or influence chide or cheer the drooping stage,
Which, since thy flight from hence, hath mourned like
  night
And despairs day, but for thy volume's light.

(*A Facsimile of The First Folio,* p. 10)

This "volume" was to become one of the most famous books in the world, of which there are very few left in existence. A folio was an expensive thing to make as well as buy: it is larger than a quarto, with the printed sheet folded in half, making two leaves or four pages; it ran to 907 pages and took nearly two years to complete. The design was generally reserved for books of significance—history or theology, for example. Although Shakespeare was the first to have his plays printed as an entirety in folio, Ben Jonson had, in 1616, his *Workes* printed as such. How and why the folio came about is not clear, but we do know that Shakespeare's fellow actors—led by John Heminges and Henry Condell—pushed through the initiative:

> It had been a thing, we confess, worthy to have been wished that the author himself had lived to have set forth and overseen his own writings. But since it hath been ordained otherwise, and he by death departed from that right, we pray you do not envy his friends the office of their care and pain to have collected and published them, ...
>
> (*A Facsimile of the First Folio*, p. 7)

The folio held thirty-six plays, including eighteen plays previously unpublished. Of the twelve plays that existed in quarto, the title page boasts that they are "published according to the true original copies" and not, as subsequently described, the "divers stolen and surreptitious copies, maimed and deformed by the frauds and stealths of injurious impostors that exposed them" (p. 7). Only three plays were published from the playbooks—*Julius Caesar, Macbeth,* and *As You Like It*—and nine from Shakespeare's "foul papers" (authorial script). The generic divisions that we are now so familiar with—comedy, history, and tragedy—were created as such by Heminges and Condell, who also included a list of the principle actors of the King's Men. When the book went on sale in 1624 it cost £1, four times the cost of a quarto. The First Folio was an immediate success as it ran to a second edition in 1632, a third edition in 1663 (and a second issue in 1664), and a fourth edition in 1685. It is arguably the most important text to be written in the vernacular in the English language and has left the legacy of Shakespeare as the greatest writer we have.

Selected Bibliography

WORKS OF WILLIAM SHAKESPEARE

COMEDIES
The Two Gentlemen of Verona
The Taming of the Shrew
The Comedy of Errors
Love's Labour's Lost
A Midsummer Night's Dream
The Merchant of Venice
The Merry Wives of Windsor
Much Ado About Nothing
As You Like It
Twelfth Night
Measure for Measure
All's Well That Ends Well
The Two Noble Kinsmen

HISTORIES
The First Part of the Contention (2 Henry VI)
Richard Duke of York (3 Henry VI)
1 Henry VI
Richard III
Richard II
King John
1 Henry IV
2 Henry IV
Henry V

TRAGEDIES
Titus Andronicus
Romeo and Juliet
Julius Caesar
Hamlet
Troilus and Cressida
Othello
Timon of Athens
King Lear
Macbeth
Antony and Cleopatra
Coriolanus

ROMANCES
Pericles
The Winter's Tale
Cymbeline
The Tempest

WILLIAM SHAKESPEARE

LOST PLAYS
Love's Labour's Won

Cardenio

UNFINISHED PLAY
Sir Thomas More (coll. Anthony Munday, Thomas Nashe, Thomas Middleton)

POEMS
"Venus and Adonis"

"The Rape of Lucrece*"*

SONNETS
"A Lover's Complaint"

"Epitaph on Elias James"

"Epitaph on John Combe"

"On Ben Jonson"

"The Phoenix and Turtle"

CRITICAL AND BIOGRAPHICAL STUDIES

Aubrey, John. *Brief Lives*. MS Bodleian, Arch. F.

Bate, Jonathan, ed. *The Romantics on Shakespeare*. London and New York: Penguin, 1992.

Bloom, Harold. *Shakespeare: The Invention of the Human*. New York: Riverhead Books, 1998.

Bowers, Fredson T. *Bibliography and Textual Criticism*. Oxford: Clarendon Press, 1964.

Bradbrook, Muriel. *Shakespeare the Poet in His World*. New York: Columbia University Press, 1978.

Bradley, A. C. *Shakespearean Tragedy*. London: Macmillan, 1904.

Chambers, E. K. *William Shakespeare: A Study of the Facts and Problems*. Vol. 2, Oxford: Clarendon Press, 1930.

Chedgzoy, Kate, ed. *Shakespeare, Feminism, and Gender*. Houndmills, Basingstoke, U.K.: Palgrave, 2001.

Cheney, Patrick. *Shakespeare, National Poet-Playwright*. New York: Cambridge University Press, 2004.

Dawson, Anthony B., and Paul Yachnin. *The Culture of Playgoing in Shakespeare's England: A Collaborative Debate*. Cambridge, U.K., and New York: Cambridge University Press, 1995.

Dobson, Michael, and Stanley Wells, eds. *The Oxford Companion to Shakespeare*. Oxford: Oxford University Press, 2001.

Dollimore, Jonathan, and Alan Sinfield, eds. *Political Shakespeare: New Essays in Cultural Materialism*. Ithaca, N.Y.: Cornell University Press, 1985.

Dowden, Edward. *Shakespeare: A Critical Study of His Mind and Art*. London, 1875.

Drakakis, John, ed. *Alternative Shakespeares*. London and New York: Methuen, 1985.

Empson, William. *Essays on Shakespeare*. Edited by David B. Pirie. Cambridge, U.K., and New York: Cambridge University Press, 1986.

Erne, Lukas. *Shakespeare as Literary Dramatist*. Cambridge, U.K., and New York: Cambridge University Press, 2003.

Flecknoe, Richard. *Miscellania*. London, 1653.

Greenblatt, Stephen. *Shakespearean Negotiations: The Circulation of Social Energy in Renaissance England*. Berkeley: University of California Press, 1988.

Greenblatt, Stephen, Walter Cohen, Jean E. Howard, and Katherine Eisaman Maus, eds. *The Norton Shakespeare*. London and New York: W. W. Norton & Company, 1997.

Greene, Robert. *Greenes Groats-worth of Wit Bought With A Million of Repentance. Describing the Follie of Youth, the Falsehoode of Makeshifte Flatterers, the Miserie of the Negligent, and Mischiefes of Deceiving Courtesans*. London: Imprinted for William Wright, 1592.

Gosson, Stephen. *The Schoole of Abuse*. London: Thomas Woodstock, 1579.

Gurr, Andrew. *The Shakespearean Stage, 1574–1642*. 3rd ed. Cambridge, U.K., and New York: Cambridge University Press, 1992.

Hazlitt, William. *Characters of Shakespeare's Plays*. London: Oxford University Press, 1916.

Heywood, Thomas. *An Apology for Actors*. London: Nicholas Okes, 1612.

Honan, Park. *Shakespeare: A Life*. Oxford: Oxford University Press, 1998.

Honigmann, E. A. J., *Shakespeare: The Lost Years*. Manchester, U.K.: Manchester University Press, 1998.

Howard, J. E., and M. F. O'Connor, eds. *Shakespeare Reproduced: The Text in History and Ideology*. New York: Methuen, 1987.

Knight, G. Wilson. *The Wheel of Fire: Essays in Interpretation of Shakespeare's Sombre Tragedies*. London: Oxford University Press, 1930.

Marcus, Leah S., Janel Mueller, and Mary Beth Rose, eds. *Elizabeth I: Collected Works*. Chicago: University of Chicago Press, 2000.

Northbrooke, John. *A Treatise Wherein Dicing, Dauncing, Vaine Plaies ... Are Reproved....* London, 1579.

Parker, Patricia, and Geoffrey Hartman, eds. *Shakespeare and the Question of Theory*. New York: Methuen, 1985.

Pollard, Tanya. *Shakespeare's Theater: A Sourcebook*. Oxford: Blackwell, 2004.

Rossiter, A. P. *Angel with Horns: Fifteen Lectures on Shakespeare*. Edited by Graham Storey. London and New York: Longman, 1989.

Scott, Charlotte. *Shakespeare and the Idea of the Book*. Oxford and New York: Oxford University Press, 2007.

Schwartz, Murray M., and Coppélia Kahn, eds. *Representing Shakespeare: New Psychoanalytic Essays.* Baltimore: Johns Hopkins University Press, 1980.

Stern, Tiffany. *Making Shakespeare: From Stage to Page.* London and New York: Routledge, 2004.

Stone Peters, Julie. *Theatre of the Book 1480–1880: Print, Text, and Performance in Europe.* Oxford and New York: Oxford University Press, 2000.

Wells, Stanley, ed. *Shakespeare in the Theatre: An Anthology of Criticism.* Oxford: Clarendon Press, 1997.

MARY SHELLEY

(1797—1851)

Lisa K. Kasmer

ACCORDING TO ESTHER Schor, for most students Mary Shelley is represented by the single work *Frankenstein* (1818; rev. 1831), usually "read in relation to Percy Bysshe Shelley, Byron, and the so-called Satanic school of British Romanticism," Robert Southey's pejorative designation for these incendiary writers (introduction to the *Cambridge Companion to Mary Shelley*, p. 2). Although this poignant tale of human overreaching continues to resonate with audiences almost two centuries later, critics have not only begun to examine *Frankenstein* through a wider range of thematic and critical approaches but have also brought attention to other works by Shelley. In addition to this classic gothic tale, Shelley wrote travel narratives, biographies, domestic novels, and, most notably, novels that explore singular historical terrain, such as *Valperga* and *The Fortunes of Perkin Warbeck,* and the striking futuristic tale *The Last Man.* Each of these novels speaks to the Romantic ideal of transcendent creative power but also encompasses broader epistemological, social, and political concerns. It was Shelley's familial and literary coterie that helped to shape these ideals.

LIFE

Mary Wollstonecraft Godwin Shelley, born August 30, 1797, was a child of two of the most famous radicals of eighteenth-century Britain, whose thought and work had a profound effect on her writing. Her mother, the protofeminist Mary Wollstonecraft (1759–1797), authored *A Vindication of the Rights of Woman* (1792), which argued that women possessed the same intellectual capabilities as men and, as such, should be educated in a similar manner. The ideas concerning the role of women in this startling,

concise treatise were revolutionary. Wollstonecraft spoke to the cause of human rights more generally in *A Vindication of the Rights of Men* (1790) and her Jacobin history *An Historical and Moral View of the Origins and Progress of the French Revolution, and the Effect It Has Produced in Europe* (1794), written while she lived in revolutionary France. Mary's father, William Godwin (1756–1836), the radical philosopher, based his philosophical tome *An Enquiry Concerning Political Justice, and Its Influence on General Virtue and Happiness* (1793) in Enlightenment rationalism to argue that government in its present form hindered the natural moral progression of humankind and should ultimately be abolished. He maintained that the institutions of marriage and property ownership, in particular, encouraged corruption.

Coupled with the political radicalism of Mary's parents, the ostensibly scandalous nature of their lives—particularly Wollstonecraft's—had a lasting impact on their daughter. Wollstonecraft had enthusiastically embraced her independence as a young woman: she had fallen in love with the painter Henry Fuseli and then the entrepreneur Gilbert Imlay, with whom she had a child, Fanny, out of wedlock; when Imlay took another mistress, Wollstonecraft attempted suicide. Meeting through mutual acquaintances in their intellectual circles, Wollstonecraft and Godwin were drawn to each other and began an affair. When Wollstonecraft became pregnant, the couple only acceded to the convention of marriage to maintain their circle of friends. Tragically, on September 10, 1797, eleven days after giving birth to Mary, Wollstonecraft died of puerperal fever. In an attempt to memorialize his wife, Godwin wrote the forthright *Memoirs of Mary Wollstonecraft* (1798), which celebrated her personal daring as well as her intellectual accomplishments. Instead of enhancing his wife's reputation, however, *Memoirs* merely served to seal her fate as a notorious figure.

The death of her mother influenced Mary's intellectual and emotional development as much as her parents' lives had. The inescapable link between life and death made tangible through Mary's birth particularly haunts *Frankenstein* but seems to echo throughout all her writing. Mary herself would lose four of the five children she would have with Percy Bysshe Shelley (1792–1822). Regular visits to her mother's gravesite at the churchyard in St. Pancras—where, it is said, Mary first learned her letters by tracing the words on the headstone—established a lasting bond between Mary and her mother. Her parents' intellectual legacy solidified that attachment. In her introduction to the 1831 edition of *Frankenstein,* Mary Shelley says that as a young girl she was encouraged to indulge in "waking dreams" or write stories and was given access to her father's extensive library of English authors and, of course, the works of both her parents (2007 edition, p. 186). She would often listen to her father's conversations with famed scientific and literary guests such as William Wordsworth and Samuel Taylor Coleridge. As a little girl, Mary, hidden behind a chair, had heard Coleridge recite *The Rime of the Ancient Mariner* (1798), a memory that emerges within *Frankenstein* through the image of a man disturbed by his horrific acts.

The camaraderie Mary felt within her family home appeared to end at age four with Godwin's marriage to Mary Jane Clairmont, who had two children, Charles and Jane (Clara Mary Jane, later known as Claire Clairmont). Mary had a difficult relationship with her new stepmother, feeling that Mary Jane encroached upon her privacy and her time. In turn, Godwin seemed to withdraw from his daughter once he was married, and Mary blamed her stepmother for the loss of intimacy with her father.

In 1812 Percy Shelley, a young aristocrat who valued the ideals of Godwin and Wollstonecraft as much as Mary did, joined the Godwin household. Godwin was drawn to Percy as a mentor to the younger man, but he also saw in Percy's wealthy family a possible solution to his current financial difficulties. Percy, a radical who had been expelled from Oxford University for writing *The Necessity of Atheism* (1811), was attracted to the concept of revolutionary communities. With Percy, Mary would visit her mother's grave to read Wollstonecraft's works in the shadow of her tombstone.

As the relationship between Percy and Mary burgeoned, Percy, taken by Mary as well as her parentage, urged Mary to elope with him even though he was already married to a woman named Harriet, who was six months pregnant and with whom he also had a year-old daughter, Ianthe. Percy, for his part, had suggested to Mary that Harriet had been unfaithful and was pregnant with another man's child. He also encouraged Harriet to join him and Mary as a sister; instead Harriet turned to a lawyer. Mary, inspired by her own parents' unconventionality, relished Shelley's proclamations of love and stole away with him to France and then Switzerland joined by Jane, her stepsister.

Through her liaison with Percy, Mary gained a new mentor as he compiled a rigorous reading program for her—gothic novels, travel books, philosophy, history, and the classics, as well as the works by her father and mother. As they moved through each country, Percy read aloud to Mary from Wollstonecraft's *Letters Written During a Short Residence in Sweden, Norway, and Denmark* (1796), which provided Mary with a model for her own travel narrative. Mary's journal entries and letters home during this time period subsequently became her account of their travels published as *History of a Six Weeks' Tour Through a Part of France, Switzerland, Germany, and Holland, with Letters Descriptive of a Sail Round the Lake of Geneva, and of the Glaciers of Chamouni* (1817).

Mary's affiliation with Percy also brought scandal to herself and her immediate family, an indignity that pursued her throughout her life. Percy's father, Sir Timothy, enraged by Percy's actions, cut off his allowance, which established a financial hardship that Mary struggled with even after Percy died. Mary's father, also infuriated by his child's behavior, refused to correspond with Mary for three and a half years, which appeared to leave a deep emotional scar upon her. Mary's continued struggle with the loss of her relationship with her father resounds throughout her writing. In 1819 she wrote "The Cave of Fancy," which she later revised as *Matilda,* a novella about incestuous feelings of a father for his daughter. In the tale, the father is confused by the resemblance of Matilda, a young girl whose mother dies giving birth to her, to her mother, and feels ardent love for her. He flees her presence and then drowns himself, leaving Matilda devastated and alone.

Mary's young adulthood also brought the almost continual pain of miscarriage and death of her children, which also impacted her writing. Her first child with Percy, a daughter named Clara, born two months prematurely, died in 1815. Three months earlier Harriet had given birth to Shelley's son, Charles, which wounded the distraught Mary. In 1816 Mary and Percy's son William was born, and the following year Mary gave birth to a baby girl, the baby with whom she was pregnant while writing the novel *Frankenstein,* also named Clara, eerily recalling the child she had lost. Shortly after, however, Clara died from a fever, precipitated by a journey across Italy, and the following summer William died of malaria. Mary and Percy's only child to survive, Percy Florence, would be born in 1819.

In a macabre denouement to Harriet and Percy's estranged marriage, Harriet, pregnant by a new man in her life, committed suicide in December 1816, which allowed the now widowed Percy to wed Mary a few weeks later, on December 30. The inauspicious beginning of the Shelley union augured the subsequent intimations of Percy's infidelity: in 1821 Percy Shelley would devote the opening stanzas of his autobiographical poem *Epipsychidion* (1821) to Emilia Vivani, the daughter of the governor of Pisa, whom he names as his muse rather than Mary.

It was some seven months prior to Mary and Percy's wedding, however, that Mary, Percy, Jane, and the infant William traveled to Switzerland and in June 1816 joined Lord Byron at his rented villa on Lake Geneva for the infamous ghost story writing challenge precipitated by discussions on the principle of life. According to the anecdote, *Frankenstein* emerged from this challenge. Mary published the ghoulish and shocking *Frankenstein* anonymously in January 1818, and, predictably, reviewers regarded the work as absurd and horrific. The intriguing novel, however, soon became universally known.

The Shelley family departed for Italy in March 1818 to aid Percy's health, and Mary began to carry out research for a novel on Castruccio, the medieval Prince of Lucca, published later as *Valperga.* During a time of outbreak of revolutions across Europe, Mary began to pen this historical novel set during the medieval trials of the Ghibelines and Guelphs, Italian city-states that upheld the republican ideal of civic liberty.

Percy Shelley died unexpectedly in a summer squall in July 1822 while out on a boat with a friend off the coast of Italy, and in a truly Romantic gesture of union, Mary ultimately received as a relic the heart from his corpse. In 1823 Mary returned to England as a widow with the hopes of securing a maintenance for her son from her father-in-law and to publish the poetry of her husband, as well as to make her own contribution to the publishing world. However, even though 1823 was in many ways a banner year for Shelley's writing—a second edition of *Frankenstein* was published (this time identifying Shelley by name, thus establishing her fame), a fifth version of the story appeared on the London stage, and her novel *Valperga* was published, albeit to tepid reviews—none of Shelley's ambitions succeeded as she hoped. Her father-in-law disliked and disapproved of Mary, believing that she had kept Percy from accepting his family inheritance, and she received merely a small allowance from him. Even when Sir Timothy died, Mary and her son Percy only inherited the property entailed to Percy Florence, but none of the family's wealth, even though Percy was the last surviving grandchild. That allowance, moreover, was awarded solely under the condition that Mary not bring Percy Shelley's name into the public eye through publication of his work or reference to his family name in her own writings. To support herself, Shelley produced short stories, mainly sentimental tales, for ladies' annuals for the next sixteen years. Dionysius Lardner, a professor of natural philosophy who was superintending a project for a complete *Cabinet Cyclopaedia* and a *Cabinet Library,* also commissioned Shelley to undertake an account of the lives of eminent Italian authors, followed by those of the Spanish, the Portuguese, and the French.

In 1832, with the passage of the Reform Bill and the subsequent transformation of the political climate in Britain, more of Percy Shelley's revolutionary works, such as the *Masque of Anarchy* (1832), a political poem written after the Peterloo Massacre in 1819, were being published and read. A publisher requested that Mary Shelley complete a four-volume collection of Percy Shelley's oeuvre. In her editorial notes to his work, she assiduously attempted to temper Percy's political zeal with his philanthropy. Unfortunately, even though she had anticipated writing her husband's biography since his death, her editing of his work was disparaged as unilluminating.

Her most important literary endeavor, her next two novels, moreover, did not fare well critically. The reviews of *The Last Man* (1826), an apocalyptic vision of the world ended by plague, were dismal. She then wrote *The Fortunes of Perkin Warbeck* (1830), a historical novel set in fifteenth-century England after the Wars of the Roses, which was faulted for not separating fiction from historical fact. In 1831 Shelley wrote a revised edition of *Frankenstein* for Standard Novel. Some critics argue that the 1831 changes in *Frankenstein* reflected a more rigid culture, so that Elizabeth Lavenza, Victor's love, is an orphan, rather than his cousin, and is reduced to the more passive role of sentimental heroines. Shelley also began the novel *Lodore* (1835), which was linked to the social detail of the "silver-fork" genre, followed by *Falkner* (1837). Beginning in 1840 she toured the Continent several times with her son, Percy Florence, who graduated from Trinity College, Cambridge, in 1841; these tours formed the basis of *Rambles in Germany and Italy in 1840, 1842, and 1843,* which was praised upon its publication in 1844

as thoughtful and entertaining. Shelley died in London on February 1, 1851, aged fifty-three.

FRANKENSTEIN; OR, THE MODERN PROMETHEUS

Mary Shelley's prescient novel about a scientist attempting to create life speaks not only to life's genesis but also to its end. With the current scientific community rife with discussion of the ethics of life-altering experimentation, *Frankenstein* speaks directly to contemporary fears as well. Beyond these universal concerns of birth and death, Frankenstein also addresses Shelley's most intimate apprehensions as a woman writer.

In *Literary Women* (1976), Ellen Moers was the first to read *Frankenstein* through Shelley's biography, in particular, her anxieties surrounding pregnancy and mothering. The novel in which Victor Frankenstein creates life necessarily addresses issues of birth, which become more potent with the parallels to the author's own life. Both the death of Shelley's mother shortly after giving birth to her and the death of her baby girl eighteen months before writing *Frankenstein* are seen as influencing Shelley's first novel. Shelley's affecting reaction to her baby's death in her journal reveals a fantasy of reanimation, which delineates her struggle to accept this tragedy: "Dream that my little baby came to life again— that it had only been cold & that we rubbed it by the fire & it lived—I awake & find no baby" (*Journals,* p. 70). The wish for the return of her dead daughter ostensibly emerges directly in her novel, but the juxtaposition of birth and death underlies the novel as a whole.

Through her depiction of Frankenstein's rejection of his creation, Shelley also reveals her trepidation concerning parental responsibility, according to Anne Mellor in *Mary Shelley: Her Life, Her Fiction, Her Monsters* (1989). The entirety of the novel traces Frankenstein's abandonment of his creation after producing this "wretch." Frankenstein labors to give life to this being, through a thoroughly unnatural production, until he observes its "birth." Once he witnesses his creation, he rushes out of the room, repulsed by its abnormality. When the creature follows him, Frankenstein flees. He literally does not view the creature realistically until he has completed constructing him, and only then does he recognize the physical horror of this colossal being—"His yellow skin scarcely covered the work of muscles and arteries beneath ... his watery eyes, that seemed almost of the same colour as the dun white sockets in which they were set, his shriveled complexion, and straight black lips" (*Frankenstein,* ed. 2007, p. 37).

The creature confronts Frankenstein about his parental obligation by alluding to the creation myth of Adam and Eve: "I ought to be thy Adam" (p. 95). Frankenstein not only refuses to acknowledge the creature as his "child" but also fails to provide his creation with a companion, the only request his creation makes of him. Enraged and wounded by his abandonment, the creature willfully avenges himself through acts of terror against Frankenstein's family.

Frankenstein's ambivalence toward his creation emblematizes the artist's own fears and impressions of the creative process. In *The Madwoman in the Attic* (1979), Sandra Gilbert and Susan Gubar discuss the difficulty for the woman writer in finding a voice in a culture that suppresses women's literary productions. As the daughter of two famed intellectuals and the partner of an established poet, Shelley felt pressure to produce and feared that she could not. In her introduction to the 1831 edition of the novel, she relates that after the ghost story challenge was formed, she was asked each morning, "Have you thought of a story?" and was "forced to reply with a mortifying negative" (p. 188). Shelley also broaches the "impropriety" of female authorship through the question frequently asked of her as the author of *Frankenstein:* "How I, then a young girl, came to think of, and to dilate upon, so very hideous an idea?" (p. 186). Shelley signals both her uncertainty and her quiet affection toward her tale by naming it as a "hideous progeny" in her introduction, which echoes Victor's own comments about his creation (p. 191). Within the novel, the complex frame narrative itself, which only allows the reader to glimpse the tale of the creator and creation through Robert Walton's letters to his sister, establishes a self-censoring mechanism for this tale.

In her introduction to *Frankenstein,* Shelley locates the source of the novel not only in a personal moment in her early life but also in an experience thoroughly tied to the literary tradition of Romanticism. On June 16, 1816, she, Percy, Byron, and Byron's doctor John William Polidori, during their stay near Geneva, spent the evening reading ghost stories and agreed to try their own hands at the genre. Through philosophical and scientific discussions, the possibility of creation solely through human endeavor was broached. Influenced by these conversations, Mary began to write *Frankenstein.* Shelley then relates in her introduction that she fell into a dream in which she saw "the pale student of unhallowed arts kneeling beside the thing he had put together" and saw the corpse he had reanimated with a "spark of life" (p. 190). This emergence of the tale in a nightmare connects it both to the gothic tradition and to the Romantic creative process as the "spontaneous overflow of feeling," such as the related origin of Coleridge's "Kubla Khan; or, A Vision in a Dream: A Fragment" (1816), which he says came to him in a dream.

Through the affecting tale of Frankenstein's creation, Shelley further reveals a Romantic vision of humankind and society. The creature stands as a symbol of Jean-Jacques Rousseau's theory of the natural man as a noble savage, born free and only corrupted by society. The creature learns, based on the model of John Locke's *Essay Concerning Human Understanding* (1690), by first distinguishing sensation and then language. Like a lost child, the creature must understand how to recognize the sun and gather food for himself; he then acquires speech by watching the DeLacey family. Through the books he reads, Shelley conveys moral and political ideals foundational to Romanticism. In reading Plutarch's *Lives of the Noble Romans,* the creature learns of public virtue; C. F. Volney's *Ruins; or, Meditation on the Revolutions of Empires; and the Law of Nature* teaches him about political justice; and John Milton's *Paradise Lost* reveals the nature of humanity.

The creature's mistreatment by everyone he meets elucidates the underlying tyranny of society, providing a revolutionary appraisal. In reading Volney, the creature garners a liberal sense of history and government in looking at the ruin of tyrannical empires throughout the centuries. The creature underlines the essential injustice of society through his exploitation of its "bloody" justice system that condemns Justine for his murder of William. Frankenstein's treatment of his creation, moreover, not only touches upon the ethical responsibility of the father but of the ruler as well. The creature names Frankenstein as his "lord" and king" who must "perform thy part, the which thou owest me" (p. 73). The creature notes that his wretched condition originates in his lack of the artificialities shown necessary for sustenance in this society—lineage and property. Since the creature has "no money, no friends, no kind of property" and is "besides, endowed with a figure hideously deformed and loathsome," he is shunned by all (p. 90). His summary rejection, then, discloses the inequitable nature of society that impugns the disenfranchised. That the creature's difference is imprinted on his physical form links the creature's maltreatment with British imperialism and racism.

The novel approaches these Romantic ideals more expansively through the creation myth in Milton's *Paradise Lost,* which Romantic poets such as Percy Shelley and Byron admired. In his interrogation of his creator, the creature broaches epistemological queries that Romantic poets pondered: "Who was I? What was I? Whence did I come?" (p. 97). In allegorizing the creature's journey, Shelley makes him an analogue of Milton's Adam, but unlike God's creation, who is "beautiful and alluring, after his own image," the creature has to recognize that his form "is a filthy type" (p. 99). When the creature asks Frankenstein to provide him with a partner, alluding to the creation of Eve in *Paradise Lost,* Frankenstein destroys the female figure, suggesting that the female "might become ten thousand times more malignant than her mate" (p. 129). The creature is also figured as the mythic Satan, whom Percy Shelley and Byron apotheosized, since he rebels against his "master" Frankenstein as Satan rebels against God in Milton's epic poem.

According to Anne Mellor, however, Shelley can also be seen as critiquing Romantic ideology through the figure of the Promethean hero. Percy Shelley's drama *Prometheus Unbound* (1820) presented Promethean acts of rebellion as heroic. Victor Frankenstein, who is named as the "modern Prometheus" in the title of the novel, imagines that he will be adored by a race as a God through his creation. Just as the hubris of Prometheus in the ancient tale leads him to steal fire for mankind against the orders of the god Zeus, the pride of Frankenstein blinds him to the problems of creating a race himself, which encourages him to overreach his station.

To obtain the knowledge for his experiment, Frankenstein must "penetrate into the recesses of nature, and shew how she works in her hiding places" (p. 29). Here Shelley presents Frankenstein as violently acquisitive in his pursuit. The gendering of nature as female makes this quest even more troubling. In completing his experiment, Frankenstein gathers his materials in the gruesome arena of "the dissecting room and the slaughter-house" (p. 35), and this work makes him grow "pale" (p. 34) as well as turn from his family; Shelley, then, juxtaposes this work with Frankenstein's goal of creation. Indeed, Frankenstein warns Walton that pursuit of knowledge should not "interfere with the tranquility of … domestic affections" and further implies that on a grander scale such quests lead to oppression and domination: Frankenstein relates that if interference with domesticity had not occurred "Greece had not been enslaved; Caesar would have spared his country; America would have been discovered more gradually; and the empires of Mexico and Peru had not been destroyed" (p. 37).

The ingenious narrative in *Frankenstein* highlights this critique of Romantic heroism. The tale of the novel is told by Walton, an explorer who also "prefer[s] glory" (p. 7), making his way with his crew to the North Pole where he hopes to make discoveries that "may regulate a thousand celestial observations" and "confer [benefit] on all mankind to the last generation" (p. 6). Walton, then, provides a corollary to the driven

Frankenstein, who proclaims "what glory would attend the discovery, if I could banish disease from the human frame, and render man invulnerable to any but a violent death!" (p. 23). As the dying Frankenstein relates his history to Walton, however, Walton's men threaten mutiny after the ship becomes endangered by ice, and Walton, chastened, must return home. In fact, it is the creature's speech that we hear last as he eloquently addresses Walton, who naturally feels sympathy for him. The ambiguous ending of the novel with the creature's springing from the "cabin-window" and being "borne away by the waves, and lost in darkness and distance" more clearly complicates Shelley's response to Romantic ideology (p. 179).

HISTORICAL NOVELS

In her two historical novels, *Valperga; or, The Life and Adventures of Castruccio, Prince of Lucca* (1823) and *The Fortunes of Perkin Warbeck* (1830), Shelley presents portraits of imagined political communities that are based on the values of sympathy and rational virtue and that uphold an Enlightenment ideal of personhood and citizenship. In *Valperga,* set in medieval Italy, Shelley concentrates on an individual life in a tale that emerges from the "private chronicles" of Euthanasia, the fictitious protagonist. As Stuart Curran argues, *Valperga* privileges the "private desires" erased by "public histories" and thus revises the male-centered universe of Walter Scott ("Valperga," p. 107). In envisioning "alternative" communities that forward women's essential role in the public sphere, as Kari Lokke (2003) and numerous twentieth-century critics have suggested, Shelley establishes a "feminine" ideology founded on domestic virtue as opposed to a "masculine" rule.

Valperga relates the adventures of the early-fourteenth-century despot Castruccio Castracani (1281–1328), a historical figure who became the Lord of Lucca and conquered Florence. In the novel, his armies threaten the fictional fortress of Valperga, governed by Countess Euthanasia, the woman he loves. He forces her to choose between her feelings for him and political liberty. She chooses the latter and sails off to her death.

Shelley creates the imagined reign of Euthanasia through a historiography that looks to the full range of sentiments contained within individual memory, not just public events. By focusing on Euthanasia's "chronicles," Shelley brings private feeling into the forefront of a historical tale. To Shelley, it is Euthanasia's domain, not the "two opposed Italian factions" of the Ghibelines and the Guelphs, that holds the real political tale of medieval Italy. Domestic life is literally made public because Euthanasia's power centers on her maternal care of the populace in her realm: she makes use of her position primarily to carry out beneficent acts for her people. As Euthanasia refuses to yield her dominion to Castruccio, Shelley implies that this position carries grave political import. Euthanasia believes that her refusal supports "the good of my people, who are happy under my government" (*Valperga,* ed. Tilottama Rajan, p. 291). Here Shelley stresses that women can offer political leadership superior to that established under state rule. In "imagining" this ideal community within a historical context, however, Shelley reveals her pessimism about the possibility of such a community developing.

Shelley's treatment of her sources for *Valperga* underscores the distinct nature of her view of history and politics. In preparing to write *Valperga,* she had read Machiavelli's account of Castruccio Castracani. Castracani spent his early life in exile and in 1320 was made Lord of Lucca. In the political wars that besieged Italy in the fourteenth century, Castruccio led the Ghibelines, waged long campaigns against Florence, and conquered Italian territory, and in 1327 the Holy Roman emperor, Louis I, recognized him as Duke of Lucca. After his death, his principality disappeared. In condemning Castruccio's rule, Shelley is engaged in a critique of Machiavelli's political principles as well. To Machiavelli, Castruccio should be celebrated as a successful "cavalier."

Shelley's historical novel *The Fortunes of Perkin Warbeck,* which forwards the hypothesis that Warbeck was the true Duke of York, the youngest son of Edward IV, contains a similar focus on history. *Perkin Warbeck* begins at the end of the Wars of the Roses with the victory of the Lancastrians over the Yorkists in 1485 and ends after the execution in 1499 of Perkin Warbeck. In this novel, Shelley implicitly criticizes the focus on war in histories and instead situates her tale on the domestic life of Warbeck.

As opposed to Machiavelli's history, Shelley's *Valperga* reveals a commitment to delineating Castruccio's individual moral development rather than assessing his political achievements. In *Valperga* she carefully describes the evolution of Castruccio's moral character, in particular his "miseducation." Initially Shelley depicts the young Castruccio as dismayed by absolutism. However, unscrupulous lords tutor Castruccio in the ways of tyranny. Galeazzo, an Italian nobleman, opens to him the "the artful policy and unprincipled motives" that make him "regard treachery and cruelty as venial faults" (p. 131). Through this tutelage, he comes to hunger for domination. For Castruccio, "ambition had become the ruling passion of his soul" (p. 269) which "smothered" in his mind the "voice of his better reason; and the path of tyranny was smoothed, by his steady resolve to obtain the power, which under one form or other it had been the object of his life to seek" (p. 173).

Unlike Castruccio, Euthanasia gains her principles of "domestic felicity" from a proper classical education. As a young girl, she reads the works of the ancient Romans and of Dante, among other books, to her father. From this learning, she develops an appreciation for liberty: "and I must date my enthusiasm for the liberties of my country, and the political welfare of Italy, from the repetition of these Cantos of Dante's poem. The Romans, whose writings I adored, were free" (p. 146). As part of her education, Euthanasia travels to Rome, which represents a pilgrimage for her. Castruccio, in contrast, has not studied these ancient histories, which for Euthanasia provide moral and political guidance.

When the death of her mother and two brothers compels Euthanasia to become the "queen" of Valperga and the surrounding villages, she establishes a rule based on her ideals of sympa-

thetic rationalism. She views her reign as an opportunity for "doing good" and only "censors" these benevolent acts with her "own reason and the opinion of her fellow-citizens, to whose love and esteem she aspired" (p. 134). Out of care and sympathy for her people, she spends most of her time among her dependents at Valperga, who then become prosperous. Euthanasia implements these principles in her own life by sacrificing her love for Castruccio in order to protect her people. Although she has deeply loved Castruccio since she was a girl, she relies upon reason and conscience to reject her love for him when Castruccio wages war against her people.

In turn, this sympathetic rule fosters a community of happy citizenry: Euthanasia's "undisguised sympathy in their feelings made her adored by her servants and dependents" (p. 170). In particular, Shelley imagines these sympathetic acts as familial and domestic. Euthanasia characterizes her link to the Florentines as being based on "consanguinity and friendship": Euthanasia cannot support the attempt by Castruccio to rule Florence because she has "joined in the social meetings of the Florentines" and "been present at their marriages" (p. 166). Through her learned and reasoned understanding of the horror of Castruccio's tyrannical reign, Euthanasia focuses on the protection of her people once Castruccio sets his sights upon domination of Valperga. Euthanasia insists that the "wish" of her heart "is for peace" but if attacked she will defend her realm (p. 302). When Castruccio's forces batter her castle and she senses the political demise of her dominion, she continues to attend to the wounded soldiers. Through Euthanasia's rule, Shelley emphasizes the necessary moral basis of citizenship and establishes the domestic community as a model reign.

In *Perkin Warbeck* as well, Warbeck's wife, Lady Katherine, expresses that "love, charity or sympathy" is "the best, the angelic portion of us," which "teaches us to feel pain at others' pain" (*The Fortunes of Perkin Warbeck*, ed. Doucet Devin Fischer, p. 398). This historical novel ends with the phrase "to love": Katherine declares she must "love and be loved" within her small circle of friends in the court of Henry VII (p.

400). Shelley defends the loving domestic circle Katherine has formed after the execution of her husband, although that community exists within the court of the tyrannical Henry, the man who has ordered her husband's execution. While Shelley acknowledges that the figure of Lady Katherine Gordon has been vilified throughout history for her ostensible treachery in living at this court, Shelley attempts to exonerate her, emphasizing that she is a "favourite" of hers (*The Fortunes of Perkin Warbeck,* p. 395). Shelley believes that Katherine's conduct in deciding to live in Henry's court was in accordance with the devotion and fidelity with which she attended her husband during his life. Katherine justifies her place in the court by claiming that she is supporting her cousin who resides there: "Where I see suffering, there I must bring my mite for its relief. We are not deities to bestow in impassive benevolence. We give, because we love" (p. 400). For Katherine, her duty to love surpasses any desire she may feel to live apart from Henry's presence. Similarly, Warbeck's love for Katherine sustains him in the face of political failure and disgrace. Thus Shelley codes sympathy as political in nature.

Through a metonymic gesture, Shelley illustrates the destructiveness of leadership that does not encompass sympathy. As Castruccio plots his political ascendancy, he

> had reduced in his own mind his various political plans to a system. He no longer varied either in the end which he desired to attain, or the means by which he resolved to accomplish it. He thought coolly on the obstacles in his way; and he resolved to remove them. His end was the conquest of Tuscany; his means, the enslaving of his native town; and, with the true disposition of a conqueror and an usurper, he began to count heads to be removed, and hands to be used, in the furtherance of his designs.
>
> (*Valperga,* p. 257)

In depicting Castruccio's "reducing" of his plans to a "system," Shelley characterizes his ambition as a rationalistic abstraction thoroughly removed from any consideration for the people he rules or the people he will conquer. To achieve his goal of "enslaving his native town," Castruccio "coolly" vows to remove "obstacles" in his way,

regardless of consequences. As a "conqueror" and "usurper," Castruccio contemplates only "removing heads" and using "hands." His diminishment of other rulers to "heads" and his soldiers to "hands" starkly grounds his actions in Machiavellian strategy.

The portrait of Castruccio's rule emphasizes that a government without sympathetic engagement with its people or the past cannot foster progress. By paralleling scenes from Castruccio's boyhood with those of his current reign, Shelley depicts the regressive nature of his rule. In *Valperga* the scene of disheartened families fleeing Lucca under Castruccio's proclamation echoes the beginning scene in which Castruccio's family faces banishment by the ruling Guelphs: "The troops paraded the streets, and before night-fall three hundred families, despoiled of their possessions, and banished their native town, passed through its gates in mournful procession" (p. 258). Shelley substantiates the cycle of failure promoted by hardness of heart and oppression in her statement that, according to public histories, in the future the Florentines will reconquer Lucca from Castruccio. This regime based on personal ambition, rather than care for its people, creates a cycle of rebellion and violence.

Through her depiction of Castruccio's rule, especially in contrast to Euthanasia's, Shelley implies that the complex power structure of the state is merely a "fiction," a facade concealing the ruler's base and selfish desires. As a sovereign, Castruccio is directly implicated in acts that bring torture and pain to the Guelph faction of Italy. Shelley reveals the nugatory origins of state policy in Castruccio's actions toward Euthanasia. In determining her fate as a traitor to his state, he reveals that his desire to triumph over her serves as retaliation for her rejection of his romantic advances. He considers, "Shall this false girl ... enjoy this triumph over me? ... Let her yield; and she will find the Castruccio whom she calumniates, neither a tyrant nor a monster; but, if she resist, to her be the burthen of the misery that must follow" (*Valperga,* p. 295). Similarly, in *Perkin Warbeck,* through the character of Lady Katherine, Shelley suggests that the outward form of political hierarchy is also only a "vain mask." Katherine reveals that

> she saw ... in the cottage, or in halls of state, felicity resulted from the affections only. It was but being an actor in different scenes, to be a potentate or a peasant; the outward garb is not the livery of the mind: the refinement of taste, which enables us to gather pleasure from simple objects; the warmth of heart which necessitates the exercise of our affections ... these, to her mind, were the only ... ingredients of happiness.
>
> (*The Fortunes of Perkin Warbeck*, p. 291)

In insisting that the "outward garb is not the livery of the mind," Katherine supplants civic status, which to her is merely an appearance, with individual morality and felicity.

Through the figures of Euthanasia and Katherine, Shelley suggests that women, in having the ability to yoke domestic ideals to public action, can excel as citizens and political leaders. In a telling scene, Euthanasia advises Ugo, a member of the conspiracy against Castruccio, to turn to his wife: "Woman's wit is ready; consult with her; she may devise some plan for your safety" (*Valperga*, p. 428). Since for Shelley, women are naturally more sensitive, they have the capacity to be more politically able.

In her fiction Shelley implies, however, that men use their political power against women. In *Perkin Warbeck*, for example, Jane Shore, the former mistress of Edward, stands as an admonition to his treatment of women as "the once lovely mistress of King Edward, now the miserable outcast of the world's scorn" (p. 190). Similarly, Shelley implies that leaders steeped in the patriarchal values of domination at all costs ignore sympathetic engagement to their own detriment. Shelley depicts the explicit intersection of Castruccio's sexual appetites with the violent ambitions of his state in his war against Euthanasia's dominion. Exploiting memories of his boyhood friendship with Euthanasia, Castruccio discovers a hidden path to Euthanasia's castle, which enables his soldiers to conquer her castle. For Shelley, the decisions of the state can annihilate the sanctity and sacredness of human life. The thought that "the man of power" should destroy the life of his fellow-man, especially "the

being, voice, looks, thoughts, affections of our all" by unlocking the "secret chamber" and "rifl[ing] it of all its treasures," is "heart-rending" and "odious" (p. 389).

Literary critics have highlighted the failure of female characters in Shelley's novels to succeed in the public realm. In *Valperga*, Beatrice, a prophetess who believes that she is the chosen vessel of God, represents both feminist power and its inevitable demise. Beatrice is the illegitimate daughter of Wilhelmina of Bohemia, who formed a secret heretical sect. Her followers believed that she was the daughter of the Holy Ghost sent in place of Jesus to redeem humanity. Beatrice's belief in her ascendancy, however, leads the government to label her a heretic and hound her. The narrowness of the domestic community within *Perkin Warbeck* as well—Katherine's "community" consists of herself and her cousin—points to Shelley's uncertainty regarding the viability of women's power.

In *Valperga* it appears that Euthanasia is completely erased from the text after her banishment by Castruccio and her subsequent death:

> Earth felt no change when she died and men forgot her.... Endless tears might well have been shed at her loss; yet for her none wept, save the piteous skies, which deplored the mischief they had themselves committed;—none moaned except the sea-birds that flapped their heavy wings above the ocean-cave wherein she lay;—and the muttering thunder alone tolled her passing bell, as she quitted a life, which for her had been replete with change and sorrow.
>
> (*Valperga*, p. 438)

In delineating the failure of both female and male leaders, Mary Shelley displays her pessimism concerning the progress of mankind in building caring governments.

Because Shelley's historiography excludes the possibility of political change, she can only envision progress within an imaginary community created within her fiction. Ultimately, the alternative history she portrays within *Valperga* and *Perkin Warbeck* is history that is already foreclosed, each novel representing an imagined community created and destroyed within the past. Shelley's unique form of historical fiction allows her to explore political possibilities, especially for women that have never existed and, in her belief, might never exist.

THE LAST MAN

The Last Man (1826) presents a future apocalypse in which the world is devastated by plague. The subject of a surviving "last man" was popular in the early nineteenth century, but Shelley's contribution to the genre was not a critical success. The work was decried for its focus on the horrible and viewed as derivative of the other tales of this genre. In the novel, Shelley presents a fatalistic portrait of Romanticism in illuminating the failure of art, progressive political systems, and the imagination itself.

Shelley wrote this novel between 1824 and 1825 in England. In his introduction to the novel (1998), Morton D. Paley writes that Shelley prepared for the novel's scenes depicting the intrigue at Westminster by visiting Parliament and established the childhood haunts of the character Adrian through rambles in Windsor. She also researched the battle between the Greek and Turkish armies, the only conflict she imagines lasting through future time.

She sets *The Last Man* in the early twenty-first century after the British Empire has almost engaged in civil war, which has led to the abdication of the king and finally the installment of a republic, a state led by the people rather than a hereditary monarch. In the republic, the parliament rules with the agency of a "Protector" elected by its members. Adrian, the hereditary king, who becomes the final leader during the plague, pleads for greater equalization of wealth at home and supports the cause of freedom with the Greeks against the Turks abroad. When England is ravaged by a plague, he becomes Lord Protector of England and leads his countrymen toward a healthier climate in the Alps. He and his fellow Britons die during the journey, and Lionel Verney, the narrator of the tale, is left the last man.

In the introduction to the novel, Shelley depicts an anonymous speaker seeking out the Cave of the Sibyl at Baiae on the Bay of Naples, Italy. The Cave of the Sibyl is associated with the Cumean Sibyl, or ancient prophetess, who wrote her prophecies on leaves that she then left in the mouth of her cave. Virgil's Aeneas visited the priestess of the ancient oracle of Apollo at Cumae to learn how to enter the underworld and return alive; thus the Cave of Sibyl is suggestive of existentialist revelation.

The incident of searching for Sibyl's cave corresponds with Mary and Percy Shelley's own exploration in 1818, so this introduction aligns this tale both with narrow autobiographical and personal experiences and with sweeping epistemological uncertainties. The novel has been noted for the seeming biographical connections between the Romantic figures in Shelley's circle— particularly Shelley's late husband and Lord Byron and the novel's protagonists, Adrian and Lord Raymond. One year after her husband drowned in 1822, Shelley began to write *The Last Man,* and in the novel, Adrian, a political idealist like Percy Shelley, "matured his views for the reform of the English government" (*The Last Man,* ed. Anne McWhir, p. 34). Adrian also disappears at sea as Percy did. Lord Raymond, the megalomaniacal aristocrat, is portrayed as an "adventurer" in the Greek wars (p. 31). Raymond, who stands as the English hero of the Greek people against the Turks, dies a champion of the Greeks. The solipsistic Byron joined the cause for Greek independence as well but died slightly less heroically of fever. Lionel Verney, the narrator whose story is found in a cave by the "editor," is often seen as a corollary for Mary Shelley. In relating his tale, Verney encompasses philosophical and social questions that Shelley broached in her other novels, such as *Frankenstein* and *Valperga.* Verney is also intimately connected to Adrian because he loves Adrian's sister Idris.

There are other incidental parallels between the novel and Shelley's life: Perdita, Lionel's sister and Raymond's wife, drowns herself, as did Harriet, Percy Shelley's first wife. Clara, the name of Perdita and Lord Raymond's child, is the name of Mary Shelley's daughter who died in 1808 and of Clara (Jane) Clairmont, Shelley's stepsister, as well as that of Clara's child by Byron, Clara Allegra.

The novel, however, is more a eulogy than a panegyric of Shelley's circle; most of the figures in the novel were gone from her life when she wrote it. In his introduction, Paley suggests that the novel serves as a paean to Shelley's loneliness and isolation. She exclaimed in her journal, "The Last Man! Yes I may well describe that solitary being's feelings, feeling myself as the last relic of a beloved race, my companions extinct before me" (*Journals,* pp. 476–477). At this point in her life, she had lost four children along with her husband and his coterie of literary companions; this loss diminished both her personal and intellectual life.

The frame of the introduction also points to a larger loss in Shelley's mind—the failure of the Romantic imagination. Whereas, as Paley points out, the Romantics saw the writer's imagination as having liberatory power, Shelley's novel has much to say about its limits. In the introduction, the speaker discovers fragments of the "Sibyllean leaves" and laments that, in the speaker's hands as their "decipherer," these texts have "suffered distortion and diminution of interest and excellence"; the speaker's "only excuse" is that "they were unintelligible in their pristine condition" (p. 4). In delineating the writer's process of interpretation, Shelley acknowledges that a credible interpretation of the historical moment is impossible and that such knowledge can only be accessed through this imperfect method.

The story that the narrator "translates" is that of Lionel Verney, who writes of his life and later struggles with the devastation of the plague. Lionel describes the author as "king," and he views his words as being left to posterity. Ironically his words become a "monument" to the Last Man, a final record of humankind. When Verney traverses Europe searching for any other form of life, he notes the "supreme indifference" of the historic monuments, suggesting the failure of art as well.

To highlight the failure of the creative process, Shelley symbolically aligns the origins of the plague with the feminine. The feminine, associated by Shelley with the creation and nurturance of life, then becomes associated with death instead. Evadne, the daughter of the Greek monarch, intrigues with Raymond while he is married to Perdita. After Raymond abandons her, she vengefully places a curse of plague on him. The plague uncannily takes hold with Evadne's dying curse on Raymond and spreads through Asia, Europe, America, and England. Shelley grounds this malevolence temporally as well: Evadne has conspired with Russia in "bringing the scythe of foreign despotism to cut away the new springing liberties of her country," Greece (p. 88). Ironically, the very source of this tale of destruction can also be viewed as feminine; Sandra Gilbert and Susan Gubar point out in *The Madwoman in the Attic* that Sibyl's cavern, whose ancient feminine tradition empowers the editor of the tale, is a female space.

The Last Man, then, not only laments the loss of Shelley's friends but also questions the Romantic ideals for which they stood. Shelley develops this personal portrait through an enlarged picture of sentimental domesticity that quickly dissolves: after Lionel marries Idris, he joins Adrian at Windsor Castle. Lord Raymond relinquishes his political ambitions and marries Perdita, and they too unite with Lionel, Idris, and Adrian at Windsor Castle. In this happy society, Adrian briefly goes mad after he loses Evadne, whom he loves, but regains his strength. Raymond, however, turns to Evadne in secret and then travels to Greece to join the war, leaving Perdita to mourn the loss of his love. Adrian is subsequently drawn into the position of Protector to fill the political void.

Through the plague's destruction, the novel reveals the political failure of the republican state, which Romantics such as Percy Shelley had supported. Indeed, in the course of the novel, the government is shown to be a failure and all party speeches are "cant." The Austrian mother of Adrian has tried to reinstate the monarchy through a marriage between Lord Raymond and Idris, the sister of Adrian, and Raymond proclaims that inheritance is the natural "splendour of a kingdom" as opposed to the "commercial spirit of republicanism" (p. 47), but the monarchy and the aristocracy collapse in the face of civil war. Although Raymond initially abandons his political ambitions to pursue his love for Perdita, he, as the self-serving aristocrat, cannot "rule" himself when he begins a clandestine relationship with Evadne, forcing Perdita to leave him and to abandon his Protectorate (p. 117).

Ryland, who establishes a republic after Raymond sacrifices his rule, quickly realizes that he needs the assistance of the aristocracy to gain funds necessary to maintain supplies once the plague hinders trade in the empire. Ultimately Ryland is ready to depart England, though, caring more about saving himself than his people. Adrian then takes over the rule and has the most success, leading a nation decimated by the plague. Through peaceful negotiation, he is even able to stop marauding gangs of Americans and Irish who have immigrated to Great Britain. The possibility of this rule is foreclosed by the ultimate demise of its population by the plague. In addition to political systems being leveled, both evil and good, religious and atheist alike fall in this novel. As Adrian and his countrymen traverse Europe, Shelley reveals the attempts of a false prophet to exploit the fear of the plague to gain followers.

As the plague spreads throughout the globe, Shelley takes a larger geographical view, not only following the plague around the world but also presenting the world itself as a map, contained and determined. Indeed, Shelley suggests that we cannot change our nature or the trajectory of our lives. When Lord Raymond and Lionel discuss the nature of free will, they suggest that once we are created, we cannot transform ourselves. Through the metaphor of the web, Shelley elucidates the complex and mostly impenetrable nature of life. Alluding to the classical myth of Theseus trapped in the labyrinth, Shelley delineates the "pathless mazes of society" (p. 48) and life as "that labyrinth of evil" (p. 171). Even humanity itself is described as a "net of love and civilization" (p. 205). Our human condition is not a connection that nurtures and reaffirms our humanity but one that is frightening and inescapable. In the novel's bleak denouement, Verney travels the Mediterranean in hopes of meeting fellow survivors, but he has neither "hope" nor "joy" (p. 367). His status as the last man, filled with loneliness and fear, points to our own isolation and hopelessness as individuals.

Percy Shelley had maintained the lack of security or the capriciousness of life in his poem "Mutability" (1824), in which he laments "Naught may endure but Mutability." In the novel, there seems to be no reason for the failure of the government, no reason behind the personal torment of the characters, and, most importantly, no reason for the plague and its devastation. The plague itself is presented ambiguously as a supernatural force. Evadne appears mysteriously on the Greek battlefield dressed as a soldier and curses Raymond with famine and plague, after which the plague begins to spread throughout the world. This destructive force is inexplicable and unstoppable as, Shelley says, it spreads mysteriously through the air.

CONCLUSION

A deeper and fuller examination of Mary Shelley's oeuvre enhances modern readers' understanding of her contribution to literary history. She is not just the daughter of William Godwin and Mary Wollstonecraft, the wife of Percy Bysshe Percy, and a member of a Romantic coterie. It is especially important to recognize not only her alliances with this literary coterie but also her disagreements. Shelley is certainly part of the Romantic tradition, but she is also a singular author.

Selected Bibliography

WORKS OF MARY SHELLEY

Novels

Frankenstein; or, The Modern Prometheus. London: Lackington, Hughes, Harding, Mavor, and Jones, 1818. Rev. ed., London: Henry Colburn and Richard Bentley, 1831. Rev. ed., edited by Susan J. Wolfson. 2nd ed. New York: Longman, 2007. (Quotations in essay are from the 2007 edition.)

Matilda. (Written 1819; unpublished until 1959.) In *Matilda, Dramas, Reviews & Essays, Prefaces & Notes.* Vol. 2 of *The Novels and Selected Works of Mary Shelley.* Edited by Pamela Clemit. London: Pickering, 1996.

Valperga; or, The Life and Adventures of Castruccio, Prince of Lucca. London: G. and W. B. Whittaker, 1823. Rev. ed, edited by Tilottama Rajan. Peterborough, Ont.: Broadview, 1998. (Quotations in essay are from the 1998 edition.)

The Last Man. London: Henry Colburn, 1826. Rev. ed, edited by Anne McWhir. Peterborough, Ont.: Broadview, 1996. (Quotations in essay are from the 1996 edition.)

The Fortunes of Perkin Warbeck: A Romance. London: Henry Colburn and Richard Bentley, 1830. Vol. 5 of *The Novels and Selected Works of Mary Shelley,* edited by Doucet Devin Fischer. London: Pickering, 1996.

Lodore. London: Richard Bentley, 1835. Vol. 6 of *The Novels and Selected Works of Mary Shelley,* edited by Fiona Stafford. London: Pickering, 1996.

Falkner: A Novel. London: Saunders and Otley, 1837. Vol. 7 of *The Novels and Selected Works of Mary Shelley,* edited by Pamela Clemit. London: Pickering, 1996.

ESSAYS AND TRAVEL

History of a Six Weeks' Tour Through a Part of France, Switzerland, Germany, and Holland with Letters Descriptive of a Sail Round the Lake of Geneva and of the Glaciers of Chamouni. London: T. Hookham, Jr., and C. and J. Ollier, 1817. In *Travel Writing.* Vol. 8 of *The Novels and Selected Works of Mary Shelley,* edited by Jeanne Moskal. London: Pickering, 1996.

Lives of the Most Eminent Literary and Scientific Men of Italy, Spain, and Portugal, 3 vols. London: Longman, Orme, Brown et al., 1835, 1837.

Rambles in Germany and Italy in 1840, 1842, and 1843. London: Edward Moxon, 1844. In *Travel Writing.* Vol. 8 of *The Novels and Selected Works of Mary Shelley,* edited by Jeanne Moskal. London: Pickering, 1996.

LETTERS, JOURNALS, AND MANUSCRIPTS

The Letters of Mary Wollstonecraft Shelley, 3 vols. Edited by Betty T. Bennett. Baltimore and London: Johns Hopkins University Press, 1980.

The Journals of Mary Shelley. Edited by Paula R. Feldman and Diana Scott-Kilvert. Baltimore and London: Johns Hopkins University Press, 1987.

In addition to some pieces in the Carl H. Pforzheimer Collection of Shelley and His Circle in the Rare Books and Manuscripts Division, New York Public Library, the primary archive of Mary Shelley is the Abinger Collection in the Bodleian Library, Oxford University.

COLLECTED WORKS

Mary Shelley: Collected Tales and Short Stories. Edited by Charles Robinson. Baltimore: Johns Hopkins University Press, 1990.

The Novels and Selected Works of Mary Shelley. 8 vols. General editor, Nora Crook. London: William Pickering, 1996.

CRITICAL AND BIOGRAPHICAL STUDIES

Curran, Stuart. *Valperga.* In *The Cambridge Companion to Mary Shelley.* Edited by Esther Schor. Cambridge, U.K., and New York: Cambridge University Press, 2003. Pp. 103–115.

Gilbert, Sandra, and Susan Gubar. *The Madwoman in the Attic.* New Haven, Conn.: Yale University Press, 1979.

Lokke, Kari. "Children of Liberty": Idealist Historiography in Staël, Shelley, and Sand." *PMLA* 118, no. 3:502–520 (2003).

Mellor, Anne K. *Mary Shelley: Her Life, Her Fiction, Her Monsters.* New York and London: Routledge, 1989.

Moers, Ellen. *Literary Women.* Garden City, N.J.: Doubleday, 1976.

Paley, Morton. Introduction to *The Last Man.* Edited by Morton Paley. Oxford: Oxford World Classics, 1998.

Schor, Esther. Introduction to *The Cambridge Companion to Mary Shelley.* Edited by Esther Schor. Cambridge, U.K., and New York: Cambridge University Press, 2003.

Seymour, Miranda. *Mary Shelley.* New York: Grove Press, 2000.

STEVIE SMITH

(1902—1971)

Janet McCann

THE BRITISH POET Stevie Smith had a great deal in common with the American poet Sylvia Plath, including a lifelong fascination with death, the writing of autobiographical novels, and a tendency to pillory friends, relatives, and acquaintances in poetry and prose. Plath described herself as a Smith fan. She wrote to her and made plans to meet her, but Plath's death intervened. It is tempting to wonder if meeting the older, tougher poet might possibly have given Plath something she needed to go on with her life.

EARLY LIFE

Stevie Smith was born Florence Margaret Smith on September 20, 1902 in Hull, Yorkshire, England. Her father, Charles Ward Smith, was a shipping agent who was seldom home; her mother, Ethel Rachel Spear Smith, suffered from permanent ill health. The absent father not providing adequate support for his family, Ethel moved with her two small daughters and her sister to Palmers Green, a suburb of London where Stevie, then called Peggy, was to spend the rest of her life.

Stevie Smith's childhood, spent, as she said, in "a house of women," was shadowed by her father's absence and her own frequent illnesses. When she was five years old, she was diagnosed with tubercular peritonitis and was sent to a convalescent home on the coast, where she lived for a time; this complete separation from her family in childhood contributed to Stevie's sense of herself as an orphan and alone. Her mother's health became worse as Stevie grew up. Parenting was done more by the aunt, Margaret Annie ("Madge") Spear, than by the mother, who became wheelchair-bound and could not travel far from the house. Stevie graduated in 1917 from Palmers Green High School, where she had been a good but not an outstanding student. Her sister Molly had won a scholarship to the North London Collegiate School for Girls, and although she had no scholarship, Stevie attended the school with her. But the school was not the friendly, supportive place Palmers Green High School had been, and she never took to it. There were many minor rules and regulations with which she was always finding herself at odds.

Her mother's illness worsened, and after a series of crises Ethel died in 1919. Charles returned in time to attend her deathbed, but a year later he married a much younger woman and started a poultry farm, and Stevie never visited him after that. Not choosing to go on to university for health and financial reasons, Stevie took a six-month secretarial training course and shortly afterward accepted a position with a consulting engineer. Very slight in stature, she enjoyed horseback riding. She was compared to the jockey Steve Donoghue by a friend, and "Stevie" she became thereafter. After leaving school she educated herself through voracious reading and the mentoring of others; she often used Latin, French, and German in her work, and she was knowledgeable in music and art.

The second job she took would be the position as secretary she held for her entire working life. In 1923 she accepted a post with C. Arthur Pearson Ltd., a publishing firm that later changed its name to Newnes, Pearson Ltd. She soon became secretary to Sir Neville Pearson and Sir Frank Newnes. Her job, though not highly paid, was certainly not onerous, and, with her bosses' permission, she had plenty of time to write during slack periods. She wrote poems and novels at her office desk, using the cheap yellow paper ordinarily used for carbon copies; she often had hours on end for uninterrupted reading and writing.

Early on, her friends encouraged her to publish her poems. However, editors did not know what to make of her poetry, which did not seem to fit any tradition. When Smith sent out her first collection, she was told to try fiction instead. She did, and her first novel, which came out in 1936, was titled *Novel on Yellow Paper.* Her first book of poetry, *A Good Time Was Had by All,* was published the following year. During her lifetime she saw the publication of twelve of her books—three novels and nine poetry collections—as well as several books she edited.

Smith was known for her eccentricity, her sharp mind and equally sharp tongue, and her absolute refusal to compromise. She had many friends and seemed to value friendship above erotic love, yet she was willing to sacrifice friendship to what she saw as truth. *Novel on Yellow Paper* begins with "Good-bye to all my friends, my beautiful and lovely friends" (p. 9) and in fact when some of her intimates found themselves apparently caricatured in the book, they did abandon the friendship. But Smith did not give up the practice. She unashamedly and unabashedly wrote about the people and events in her life and claimed that she could not do otherwise. She could not invent incidents and people but had to use those she knew.

This focus on her own small life makes her work intense and self-reflexive, and the self-image it reflects is that of a brilliant, hyperaware child surrounded by prosaic and less-than-honest adults. She has been accused of faux-naïveté, and yet this voice often appears to reflect her genuine self-perception. The speaker is often someone placed in uncomfortable circumstances by others and by social forces, who has the power to describe vividly but not to change. Although Smith claimed that the characters in the novel and the poems existed within and not outside her work, the novel was so close to a record of her life that it became a major source for the play Hugh Whitemore wrote about Smith, which in turn fed the movie *Stevie.*

In fact, the apparently claustrophobic life Smith lived in the London suburb, together with the startling quality of her writing, combined to make her a figure of interest to the public, both during her later life and after her death. Whitemore's play *Stevie: A Play from the Life and Work of Stevie Smith* was popular in London in 1977; the movie *Stevie,* starring Glenda Jackson, came out in 1978 and was filmed partly in the actual house where Smith had lived. Yet Smith did not disappear into her suburb and never reemerge; she cultivated literary friends, had lovers and a fiancé, and visited on the Continent. But the house in Palmers Green was the place to which she always returned, and her aunt Madge was the person from whom she derived the most love, support, and comfort—even though her aunt was not an intellectual, nor even very much of a reader. The tiny, exclusive family has provided a mystique to Stevie Smith's story.

The voice of Smith's poems does not suggest sexual maturity—she seems a child, pure, untouched. But she did have at least two major love interests, who appear in her novels and poems more as problems to be solved than as love objects. In 1929 and 1931 Smith vacationed in Germany, and during the second trip she met Karl Eckinger, a Swiss-German graduate student who fascinated Smith by his intelligence and intensity. Unfortunately he was also very nationalistic, and when the war loomed Smith found she could not stomach his jingoism and the two parted company. She then met Eric Armitage and became engaged to him; he features in her novels as "Freddie." The affair was not passionate, and he seemed to want a typical 1930s wife, which is not what Smith wanted to be. Their relationship was off-again, on-again, and finally permanently off. It is thought by some that she later had a brief affair with George Orwell; certainly she had a friendship with him. Some believe she also had an affair with a woman. In any case sex did not loom large in Smith's life, despite Pompey's claim in *Novel on Yellow Paper* that she loved sex; the context of the comment suggests that Stevie/Pompey loved playing with sex roles, gender definitions, and the way in which the two sexes interact. Procreation was not high on her list either. She seldom responded positively to children, though she claimed to be fond of them.

In an interview with Kay Dick she said, "Why I admire children so much is that I think all the time, 'Thank heaven they aren't mine'" (Dick, p. 73). Smith apparently had a view of family life similar to that of Sylvia Plath in *The Bell Jar:* she saw women as absorbed and effaced by the demands of husbands and children.

FIRST NOVEL AND FIRST POEMS

Novel on Yellow Paper (1936) hardly seems to be a novel: it is instead a monologue, with a sharp intelligence that goes through details of work, partying, home life, and relationships, sometimes stuffing a whole incident into a single breath. There are no chapters, no titles. There is only a brief break occasionally when the scene changes. The speaker often addresses the reader directly, asking an opinion of something or imagining what the reader is thinking at the moment. The novel is self-referential, aware of itself as an artifact. Smith takes pains within the novel to allow her narrator to explain what she is doing:

> "For my part I will try to punctuate this book to make it easy for you to read, and to break it up, with spaces for a pause, as the publisher has asked me to do. But this I find very extremely difficult.... For this book is the talking voice that runs on, and the thoughts come, the way I said, and the people come too, and come and go, to illustrate the thoughts, to point the moral, to adorn the tale"
>
> (p. 25).

As the speaker implies, there is no real plot. And yet the book compels attention; the apparently endless mocking voice, whose scorn is directed at both the world and the self, commands interest. The narrator, Pompey Casmilus, does call to mind Esther Greenwood, the speaker of *The Bell Jar,* Plath's autobiographical novel. Both protagonists are strongly opinionated women with a vitally humorous vision, and both books have suicide as a theme—if not actually committing it, at least thinking about it.

The main character, Pompey Casmilus, like Stevie, goes by a masculine name, lives with her aunt, and works for a publishing firm that is much like Stevie's. Her name is taken from Roman and Greek sources: Pompey the Great was a Roman general, and Casmilus (or Camilus) was another name for Hermes or Mercury. The people in Smith's life, sometimes renamed and sometimes not, pass through the book. Conversations Smith overheard are recorded verbatim. The narrative, such as it is, is interrupted by quotations in several languages. Her own prejudices are reported seemingly without concern—she tells how she loves being a goy among Jews, for instance. She plays with national stereotypes and the interwar-period tension between Germany and England; she has a German boyfriend, who gives her a badly translated copy of Faust as a present. She also has a fiancé, Freddy, who finally breaks off with her in the novel's climax, to the extent that it has one. Freddy, it seems, wants to get married immediately while Pompey does not really want to change her circumstances—moreover, she does not feel at home in Freddy's "meelyou," as she calls it, nor he in hers.

Her attitudes about the war that was over and the gathering tensions of the war to come are interesting for their complexity and candor but do not show much political acuity; they mostly ridicule public figures. There is little genuine affection in this book, and what there is is directed mainly toward Pompey's aunt, "the Lion," who is of course a portrayal of Smith's own aunt. The time period is caught in swift strokes and telling details, and so is the feeling of being outside it all that is part of the narrator's daily experience. The voice of Pompey expresses itself in long, run-on sentences, great leaps of thought, a semi-surreal stream of consciousness. The reader must sometimes go back to find the connection between elements of a sequence to trace the flight of Pompey's imagination from some minor event in ordinary life. Despite the complex style, the novel remains readable for its difficult, eccentric narrator, who has chosen to exclude most possibilities of action or escape from her life and to be caustic about those that remain. She is cutting about the typical women of her age, "the public on whom we rely to buy and read our twopenny weeklies" (p. 150). Her satire is mostly good-humored, however:

"These are the girls who believe everything our contributors tell them. They put a spot of scent behind the ear, they encourage their young men to talk about football, they are Good Listeners, they are Good Pals, they are Feminine, they Let him Know they Sew their own Frocks, they sometimes even go so far as to Pay Attention to Personal Hygiene"

(p. 151).

These are the readers from whose happy number the narrator is excluded by virtue of her more sophisticated understanding. Yet while the speaker may condescend to them, they clearly have that sense of being part of their society that she does not.

The narrator also indicates that satisfaction and contentment are not within her power. The world is too dark, and her experience of it too unmediated by pleasant illusion. Her vision is too accurate. At the end she recounts a final horror, a dream of the death of "the tigress Flo," who is almost, but not quite, brought back from a drowning death: "Yes, chaps, they worked Flo's chest, and sooner you than me, you'll say, and sooner me than Flo, that couldn't understand and wasn't raised for these high jinks. Back came Flo's fled spirit and set her on uncertain pads. She looked, she lurched, and sensing some last, final outrage, she fell, she whimpered, clawed in vain, and died" (p. 252). The lurching forward and falling back is not only the death of the tiger but the movement of the book, and Stevie identified herself too with the tiger—Florence was Stevie's given name.

Stevie Smith's first book of poems, *A Good Time Was Had by All* (1937), appeared about a year after her first book of autobiographical fiction, although many of the poems were written earlier. The product of ten years' poetry writing, it was well received despite its dissimilarity to most poetry being published then. What is unusual about Smith is that it is not easy to trace changes in her work that came from reading the poetry of her contemporaries and being involved in the London poetry scene, because she did little of either. Her literary friends were, for the most part, fiction writers. She read eccentrically, mostly choosing older works in a variety of languages, and she deliberately avoided reading

her contemporaries' poetry. She spent her life in the same house in the company of her aunt. Her passionate friendships and love affairs made themselves a presence in her work, but by and large her style did not change drastically from her first to her last poem. She did not reflect changes in literary taste. Her subject was her world, which changed little over her writing years.

Her poems from the beginning are gothic, sometimes death-centered in an offhand, cheery way. She uses rhyme and rhythm like a melancholic Ogden Nash, mixing line lengths and employing regular, slant, and mosaic rhyme. Some poems are very spare while others reach for the margins. She invents weird symbolic or suggestive names from beginning to end, and she mingles local people with biblical and mythic persons and events. Her lifelong struggle with religion is present from the beginning—her persistent desire for faith is at war with her anger at what she believes the church has done to human beings, and her work reflects both her longing and her fury.

Her poems throughout her work are unified by the presence of her eccentric cartoon-like sketches which, when it was possible, she insisted accompany the poems. She claimed that sometimes the drawings preceded and inspired the poems, so that the poems, not the drawings, were sometimes the true illustrations. These sketches, often distorted and exaggerated, like children's drawings, contributed to the charge occasionally leveled at Smith that her work is "faux-naïf." However, they are often strangely appealing. Some of them, especially the sketches of women, catch a mood well in a few quick strokes, sometimes by the slant of a shoulder, the tilt of a hat. The sketch that is featured on the cover of her *Collected Poems* is particularly winsome, a scrawled women's face with an alert, observant look.

The first poetry collection introduces a variety of odd characters who came from her life and from peripheral sources such as local news stories and rumors. Her dramatis personae include among many others Mrs. Osmosis and Mrs. Pale, Sholto Peach Harrison, Lord Barrenstock, Louise and Mr. Tease, Major Hawkaby Cole Macroo, Mr. Mounsel, Lawless Lean, and Belvoir, a dog-martyr who appears in more than one poem. She favors short narrative poems with black humorous endings. Her archaisms, her "thee"'s and "thou"'s, at first ennervate the reader but then become a familiar element of her voice. Her carefully constructed rhythms vary. Some poems are written to specific tunes, and others create their own slightly dissonant music. Yet one of the predictable results of reading a number of these poems at once is a sense of claustrophobia: the reader is locked into Smith's suburban life, feeling the sameness of the days and the odd terrors that can come forth in nondescript rooms.

Although her first novel lost her some good friends, which she apparently expected, the poems of *A Good Time Was Had by All* were less bothersome to others because their genesis was better hidden (and perhaps because fewer friends and acquaintances read them). The mixture of wit and pathos, cynicism and romanticism, the gothic and the prosaic, produces poems that are playful and angry at once. Part of the appeal of Smith's work is the glance it provides into middle-class British life and the caricatures produced by someone whose position (unmarried working woman) makes her a permanent outsider. Her preoccupation with death, sometimes as a fear and sometimes as an attraction, weaves through her scenes of the small lives of people and animals. Death appears often in her titles and, especially in the first book, in her sketches, which often feature graveyards or tombstones. Her preoccupation amounts to obsession; it is no wonder that Sylvia Plath was so attracted to her work. Smith's work provides a grotesque vision of death-in-life: the dead speak about having committed suicide or having been killed. These poems often provide disturbingly unexpected endings at which point the reader, who assumes that the urge has been put aside or the accident averted, realizes that the speaker is a corpse or a ghost. Smith's bizarre humor often is based on what she found to be bizarre truth—that death and life are lovers, that all opposites are both tragically and comically combined. In "Sunt Leo-

nes," she describes the role the lions played in the establishment of Christianity:

My point which up to this has been obscured
Is that it was the lions who procured
By chewing up blood gristle flesh and bone
The martyrdoms on which the Church has grown.

(*Collected Poems*, p. 56)

Many of the poems similarly produce a laugh and a shudder at once. Her deflation of Christian myth is something that appears throughout her work.

SHORT FICTION AND ESSAYS

In between poems, Smith was writing short fiction, which she also found hard to place. Smith's short stories are similar to those of Sylvia Plath; while writing poems and novels, she wrote stories that satirized her situation and her friends, dramatized her fears, and struggled with her death obsession. During her lifetime Smith published ten short stories and wrote others that remained unpublished. Like Plath's short fiction, Smith's stories tend to emphasize the exclusion of the main character, who does not belong in her settings and also looks down on them. Moreover, Smith was often a houseguest, and her short stories did not please her friends any more than her novels did. It seems to readers surprising that she would continue to be invited to pass periods of time with people whose characters and circumstances she would then acidly dissect in poems and stories. Indeed, friends were afraid of her sharp tongue and pen. Her attitudes toward Jews were particularly offensive—she sought them out as friends and then stereotyped them in her work. Her depiction of family life was sometimes vitriolic. In "The Herriots" (1939) a young woman lives with her aunt and great aunt in a house of women; she thinks she has escaped into marriage but finds that marriage, complete with martinet mother-in-law, is worse than her original situation. Things get worse: eventually the main character has to take a job as a companion for an old woman because her husband is unemployed. The old woman consoles her that there is still an escape: death.

Another take on marriage, though this one more humorously caustic, is "Sunday at Home" (1949), which satirizes the relationship between a scientist and his unintellectual wife. He is demanding and fey, she is the drudge. Two stories feature a writer named Helen. In "The Story of a Story" (1946) Helen endures Smith's experiences in writing about her friends and being condemned by her friends for it; in "Beside the Seaside: A Holiday with Children" (1949) Helen endures a vacation with Jewish friends, who are of course Smith's friends, and whose badly reared son interferes with impunity with everyone's enjoyment of the seashore. The stories show her hostility toward the institution of marriage and her antipathy toward children, despite her claim to be fond of them. They also project a sense of being the one outside the fold, however the fold is defined—as church, suburban couples life, the academy. The stories lack closure and resemble sketches, but they help to fill in the picture of the poet that emerges in other work. She stopped writing them long before her writing career was over.

Smith's essays, written throughout her life, tend to be friendlier than her stories, but they too are an odd mixture, often tinged with a slightly barbed nostalgia that suggests she is perfectly aware that the idyllic scenes she describes have their flaws. She talks about the richness of life in the suburbs in "A London Suburb," an essay comparing suburbs and city, to the advantage of suburbs. In it she catches the rhythm of speech of her neighbors and concludes with a snapshot description that both praises and condemns the suburban life:

> It smells of lime trees, tar, cut grass, roses, it has clear colours that are not smudged by London soot, as are the heath at Hampstead and the graceful slopes of Primrose Hill. In the streets and gardens are the pretty trees–laburnum, monkey puzzle, mountain ash, the rose, the rhododendron, the lilac. And behind the fishnet curtains in the windows of the houses is the family life—father's chair, uproar, dogs, babies and radio.
>
> (*Me Again*, p. 104)

Other essays are equally clever and ambivalent. As she grew older and found a need for a supplemental income, her essays were largely replaced by her book reviews, which too were witty, opinionated, and graceful.

POETRY AND NOVELS OF HER MIDDLE PERIOD

Over the Frontier (1938) is the sequel to *Novel on Yellow Paper* and takes up Pompey's life where the first novel leaves off. However, this novel is somewhat schizoid in a melting together of realism and apparent fantasy. The first half offers Pompey's sardonic take on the world of Europe and England before the war, as she looks around her with a jaundiced eye after failing to make a go of her relationship with Freddy. The perspective is particularly damning when it comes to the women of the age, who are partly pushed into their stereotypes and partly choose them. Pompey looks with horror on the roles that are offered to her and with much more interest on the men's choices—even though she decries war, she wants to participate.

The second half launches suddenly into a dreamlike adventure, with Pompey joining her new love interest, Tom, as a spy. Their nighttime rides over the countryside to the other side of the border (of what, we never know) are erotic, symbolic, and suggestive to the extent that the reader wonders if the whole adventure is not a dream sequence, and some critics have read it as such. However, the adventure frees Pompey from the fetters of her class and sex and allows her to act on her conscience, even to the point of shooting and killing an ill-defined villain. But after her successful adventures in the world of men, her lover Tom is somewhat jealous and less enthusiastic than formerly about the relationship. It is decided that they will follow their separate callings. Pompey thus has entered into the world of action and adventure and fled the safe confines of British middle-class suburbia, but she has entered it alone. Moreover, having completed her quest—which is never clearly specified—she will return to London and, quite possibly, to the life she left.

Smith attempted to extend the sequence with a third novel about Pompey, which she planned to call "Married to Death," but she was told by her editor, David Garnett, it was unreadable and she destroyed the manuscript. He also told her that she should stop writing about herself. Smith turned away from novel writing for a time to focus on poetry.

Her second poetry collection, *Tender Only to One* (1938), has some death-centered poems, but it also includes weirdly funny gothic touches and quirky flights of fancy. The title poem is a love poem to death. The speaker plays the petal-picking game to find the name of her lover; picking the last petal, she realizes that "His name, his name is Death" (*Collected Poems,* p. 93). "Eulenspiegelei" is another poem both playful and macabre. Till Eulenspiegel is the legendary medieval German trickster who was said to have played practical jokes on his contemporaries, exposing their hypocrisy, foolish pride, and greed. The title suggests his jokes and her angle of vision: sharp, sometimes caustic, but wistful. Eulenspiegel appears too in her prose; the image of the jester who turns society on its ears must have had an appeal for her. The poem includes the tale of the "changeling child" who is stolen away, complete with romantic details that appear to be deliberately gothic exaggerations. Smith's poems often seem like Grimms' fairy tales retold by those children whom they had terrified—and the Grimm collection is one of her sources for both subject and tone.

Another poem, however, "Dear Karl," is far more literal in its narrative. It is atypical in that it is high-humored in its description of an event in Smith's life—the gift of a sixpenny collection of Walt Whitman to her German boyfriend Karl. She imagines him saying,

"I hate these selections
Arbitrarily made to meet a need that is not mine and a
   taste
Utterly antagonistic, wholly alien, egregiously coer-
   cionary
Of individualism's, egotism's, insolence's light-
   fingered traffickings."

She pleads poverty and tells him to hold his scorn, to go forth willingly on "an afternoon's excursion" which will take him on an ironically Whitmanian trek:

Over sixpennyworth of tarmac, blistered by an
   American sun, over irrupted boulders,
And a hundred freakish geology's superimpositions.
                              (*Collected Poems,* p. 125)

This other voice, lighthearted and expansive, is a side of Stevie Smith not often evident in her poems but very much present in her first two novels. She has created a poem about Whitman in Whitman's expansive style, in friendly mockery.

Other poems are quick portraits or self-portraits drawn from odd angles. One is "The Photograph," which gives a sense of inner wildness:

They photographed me young upon a tiger skin
And how I do not care at all for kith and kin,
For oh the tiger nature works within.
                              (*Collected Poems,* p. 145)

Again playfully, she suggests that "Parents of England" avoid taking such photographs because the animal wildness can be absorbed by the seated child, who may "tiger-possessed abandon all things human."

The poems in *Mother, What Is Man?* (1942) have a somewhat different tone and emphasis from the earlier work. They are more directly involved with religious issues, and they veer back and forth between a fragile faith and a vigorous questioning. Some of them are brief, single quatrains and even tercets, and the volume as a whole is slight. The title comes from the very long poem "An Anthem of Earth," by Francis Thompson:

Ay, Mother! Mother!
What is this Man, thy darling kissed and cuffed,
Thou lustily engender'st,
To sweat, and make his brag, and rot,
Crowned with all honour and all shamefulness?
                     (*The Poems of Francis Thompson,* p. 172)

That she has chosen a popular religious poem to name her collection telegraphs its concern—in the Thompson poem belief wars with doubt and wins, whereas in Smith's book the struggle is a draw, veering back and forth—and yet the desire to believe is evident throughout the book. But the element of struggle and question in all Thompson's work would have been congenial. And the Thompson conclusion, despite its roots in faith and acceptance, would have pleased Smith for its death-centeredness:

Here I pluck loose the body's cerementing,
And break the tomb of life; here I shake off
The bur o' the world, man's congregation shun,
And to the antique order of the dead
I take the tongueless vows: my cell is set
Here in thy bosom; my little trouble is ended
In a little peace.

(The Poems of Francis Thompson, p. 178)

For God's peace Smith substitutes death's peace, and yet throughout the collection are echoes of the Thompson attitude. An example is the tiny poem "If I Lie Down":

If I lie down upon my bed I must be here,
But if I lie down in my grave I may be elsewhere.

(Collected Poems, p. 176)

Other echoes of Thompson abound in this collection, suggesting that Smith must have found in him a kindred soul. This book, while not the way to enter Smith's work most happily, does give a close-up of her struggle with and for faith. It seems to represent a vigorous struggle with doubt, in which doubt will eventually become the victor.

Smith considered her third and last novel, *The Holiday* (1949), her favorite. This book was, despite advice, again a story about herself. This time she calls herself Celia, a woman with an office life at "the ministry"—a new equivalent for her work at the publisher—and a home shared with her elderly aunt. Celia takes a train trip to stay with her uncle in the north, and she is accompanied by Casmilus, a cousin she loves. Beginning as preparations are being made for the trip, this novel is even more filled with stories and diversions than is *Novel on Yellow Paper*, and Celia is more mournful and less snappy than Pompey. Smith wrote it during the war but had trouble getting it published, so that when she finally got it out she had to make changes to a vague "postwar" period and adjust some of the political speculations. Some think the original

version was more acute. Many find Celia less engaging than Pompey, who despite her waspishness has a consistent persona, with a perspective that is always an interesting mixture of ingenuousness and spite.

The novel weaves Celia's passions and opinions—despite her stated hatred for opinions—through the slight action of the trip. It details her struggle against the threats and promises of Christianity and the love she had for Casmilus as well has her constant awareness of death, which sometimes appears to her a desirable suitor. Celia attempts to compensate for the tedium and lack of challenge of her job by a stream of observations about her bosses and their habits. When she is not at work she is talking about literature or politics with her friend Lopez the writer or her cousins, Caz, with whom she has always been in love, and Tom, who had suffered a breakdown and had rejected his father, her uncle that she will visit. During the planning stage and the trip itself, Celia quotes some of Smith's poems. This book is harder to read than *Novel on Yellow Paper* or even *Over the Frontier* because Pompey, though perhaps less sympathetic, seems more developed a character than Celia, and there is some confusion resulting from the shift from wartime to the postwar years—some of the opinions and attitudes seem uninformed by recent events that would have been very much in the public eye.

Smith loved this novel for the "melancholy," and this sadness dominates; it has none of the optimism of the postwar period, but then it was actually written during the war. There are many scenes of seemingly unmotivated weeping. The book does, however, frame some of her poems for the reader. The aunt becomes a minor character here, and more is seen of Smith's essential loneliness in the form of Celia, who seems unable to marry either the man she loves or another man, marriage with whom might solve both partners' problems.

BREAKDOWN AND WORK THAT FOLLOWED

Smith's many tales of life at the publishing firm, in both conversations and novels, suggest it was a somewhat lazy, disorganized place, with a lot of socializing and teasing and tea. There were seldom immediate deadlines or complaints about work poorly done, and in fact the business seemed to be a family-like operation in which all employees were content. She even occasionally complained that actually having to do an assignment was interrupting a poem or a novel, but it was generally accepted that when an assignment was not pending, Smith would be writing away on the yellow paper supplied for copies by the firm. If she did not find her work for the firm challenging, for many years she found it comfortable and supportive.

However, at the beginning of the 1950s Smith became more and more depressed, partly due to the constant rejection of her poems both in England and in the United States. She had liked having a dual identity, the homebody and the writer. But the patter of interest awakened by her first publications had died down, and she was constantly being disappointed by editors who at first showed interest in her work and then did not follow through with publishing it. Her tasks at the office of course did not hold her attention, and she became withdrawn, no longer a part of the pleasant chatter at work. She believed that other employees were making fun of her, which may have been true—the simple, old-fashioned style of dress she affected made her look like an old child, and her sometimes snippy or condescending comments wore on others' nerves. For many years her eccentricities had been simply accepted, but when she stopped being cheery and talkative, her coworkers grew wary of her. Her friends did try to help. One friend, Margaret Branch, gave her the writings of St. John of the Cross, hoping to spark her interest. She told Smith that St. John was a depressive as well as a mystic and often felt cut off from God and Man. Smith said she too felt that way, but she did not allow the book to lift her spirits. Rather, at this low point in her life, in April 1953, she wrote the poem most frequently anthologized still, "Not Waving but Drowning."

The crash came shortly thereafter, in July. Smith had a number of personal items in her office that she invested with great significance, and when Sir Neville Pearson picked one up, she apparently became violently upset. Rumor has it that she attacked him with a pair of scissors, and then cut her wrist with them. The suicide attempt resulted in her hospitalization. She remained in the hospital for three weeks after her breakdown, and then on medical recommendation went to the beach for recovery. Her doctor, with the agreement of her aunt, Smith herself, and her employer, affirmed that she should not go back to work. She was pensioned off from the company, though not generously, so that she needed to count on book reviewing to supply her modest needs. Smith, then, effectively retired at age fifty and spent the rest of her life caring for her aunt, who became more and more disabled, and writing, mostly poems and book reviews.

While some phases of Smith's poetic output may seem less cutting and more melancholy, the direction of all the collections is the same. It is true that the wistful-waif sketches become more varied and less funereal as the years pass; those in the last two books are not so much of tombstones and graveyards but of figures and animals, and the most common of them are women's faces projecting a meditative air or women's figures in some sort of athletic leap. Yet the tone of the poems maintains the eerie detachment of the fairytale, and their subjects explore once more the hapless terror of the childlike subject confronted with death. The voice becomes clearer, a little more definite, and some critics find that the two books *Harold's Leap* and *Not Waving but Drowning* represent the apex of her performance. These books were written before and after the breakdown and suicide attempt that resulted in her retirement. Yet whether they are her best or not, they have a fine combination of wit and condemnation, and her major themes are crystallized in them.

Harold's Leap (1950) and *Not Waving but Drowning* (1957) contain most of the anthologized poems. In *Harold's Leap,* a collection of sixty-five poems, the desperate persona seeks a way out of her miasma, which seems to have closed in as the bell jar has closed in on Plath's Esther Greenwood. The poems are suicide-clouded, overcast with an impenetrable fog of unhappiness. In many the bright, terse voice of the sardonic commentator is blurred. Several poems praise someone for suicide or for giving up on life in one form or another. They employ myth and fairy tale but less frequently than others; mythical figures with whom the speaker seems to identify include Antigone and Persephone. Often the dead speak, caught forever in a blurry limbo of semi-awareness. One of the unusual mythical characters who becomes a motif in poem and story for Smith is Titurel, one of the guardians of the Grail who has died but yet lives on in the grave and who gives thanks to the Savior for granting him this extended strange existence. Stevie's dead speakers share Titurel's situation but lack his conviction that sentience is a wonderful gift under whatever circumstances it is experienced. Again and again in this quite lengthy collection death is the lover who is reliable, who must come when called and thus cannot abandon the beloved.

The poems of *Harold's Leap* show the confused despair that overwhelmed their author at the beginning of the 1950s, while those of *Not Waving but Drowning* are more a mixture of hope and despondency. In the poems of *Harold's Leap* the stultifying particulars of existence can be eluded only by the mind, which provides the refuges of madness or death. The persona in the poems has unslakable desires that lead her to desperate remedies. This is the book that preceded Smith's suicide attempt, and the looming presence of her despair darkens the poems. A typical poem is "Deeply Morbid," in which Joan, a sad, lonely typist, attempts to escape her miserable life and finally does, through death; the speaker turns out to be an onlooker who envies Joan her quietus. The theme is echoed in the title poem, which describes another leap and implies again a communication with the dead as she addresses the suicide Harold and commends him for his bravery in undertaking this definitive exit. In some of her poems her dark humor sparkles, but in many, the sense of overwhelming pessimism and depression dominates. However, the sharpness of her questioning enlivens the poems even at their darkest.

The next collection holds her most popular poem, which she wrote around the time of her collapse. The title poem, "Not Waving but Drowning," is based, according to Smith, on a newspaper account of a misunderstanding that resulted in a death, but of course it was Smith's own story as well. It is one of the strange, disturbing poems she wrote in the voice of a dead person, a swimmer whose frantic calls for help are perceived as cheery greetings. The drowned speaker "lay moaning" and explains to the people who did not come to his aid that he was "much further out than you thought" and that he was "not waving but drowning." The group of the onlookers is quick to dismiss him with mild pity: "Poor chap," they call him, and they theorize, "It must have been too cold for him his heart gave way" (*Collected Poems,* p. 303). The dead man explains, though, that it was "too cold always" and that he was "much too far out all my life," and repeats that he was always "not waving but drowning." So the speaker was never able to communicate his torment to the satisfied, conventional world; his inability to signal his situation resulted in his death. It is not strange that Smith wrote this poem at a time when she felt far out and in deep. The alienation, terror, and sadness of the drowning man would have held strong personal appeal.

This frequently read poem has not provoked as much critical discussion as might have been expected. While many writers on Smith quote it and comment on it, it does not lend itself to deep analysis. Its appeal is to the isolated and uncertain in readers and the distance between the speaker, solitary and cruelly misinterpreted, and the ordinary people from whom he is divided by the water, the cold, the lack of communication. The fact that the speaker is dead gives a spooky quality to the poem and suggests that it has always been too late for him—the alien element in which he found himself was not conducive to survival. It is tempting to see the element as life, the uncontrollable world that Smith was reluctant to enter: she clung to her undemanding job and her simple home life with her aunt.

The poems of this collection show wit and flexibility. Her way of giving the twist by indirect allusion is seen in "God the Drinker," which begins:

I like to see him drink the gash
I made with my own knife
And draw the blood out of my wrist
And drink my life.

(*Collected Poems*, p. 340)

The first line evokes Emily Dickinson's "I like to see him lap the miles" and the form recalls the hymn stanzas Dickinson used. But the Smith poem describes the writer's suicide attempt and the horror of this scene is intensified by the comparison with the innocuous Dickinson poem. Other poems in this collection concern death and religion and reiterate Smith's belief that religion is purely escape, as in the poem "Will Man Ever Face Fact and Not Feel Flat" in which the title becomes the last line: the wind "sneered" about "our little Man" and his ability to "Invent fairy stories about everything" and concludes with the rhetorical question (*Collected Poems*, p. 341).

This issue is also raised in her frequently anthologized poem "Was He Married?," which was written later; in this discussion of Christ's life Smith's wit and venom are both turned up high. The poem is a series of questions about Christ's humanity, which are answered with responses stressing how very much his life was not that of a typical human. Smith went to some pains to comment on this poem, which was not typical of her. "It is a poem for two voices," she wrote in *Me Again*. "One voice, the simple, young one, is complaining that Christ could not have known human suffering because human suffering has its roots in imperfection, and he was perfect. The other voice is older, and not very kind" (p. 162). Her discussion of her problems with Christianity center upon the doctrine of redemption and on what she felt to be the duality of Christ as both man and deity. Yet clearly she did wrestle with these issues rather than simply turn away to another source of support, and some poems show a kind of nostalgia for faith. "Was He Married?" begins by asking if Jesus was married and plagued with the common burden of taking care of a family, which would have made their importance greater than his; the answer is in

the negative. The questions grow more probing until finally the questioner concludes that humans "should have a medal" and that "a god could not carry it." This provokes a caustic response that

A god is Man's doll, you ass,
He makes him up like this on purpose.

The questioner then returns to his/her queries, asking if it is not "a little move" to "choose a god of love," and then pushes on toward a conclusion mutually arrived at:

A larger one will be when men
Love love and hate hate but do not deify them?
It will be a larger one.

(*New Selected Poems*, p. 91)

The cleverness of the poem resides in the jaunty rhythms, the question-and-answer counterpoint, the understanding of the human situation, and the human need for divine sanction.

The last collections she published before her death are relatively predictable. Some of her later poems are more discursive, less tormented. Of interest is "Thoughts About the Person from Porlock," which begins with the famous interruption and then decides that Coleridge was "already stuck / With Kubla Khan" (*New Selected Poems*, p. 87). He seized the opportunity to blame the Porlock visitor for not taking the poem further. The poem then gives a life and place to the visitor—and of course a grandmother who was a warlock. The speaker then talks about her own desire for a "Person from Porlock" to end her own thoughts, and it is clear that the visitor is no longer the interruption of worldly business but rather Death himself. Like the interrogator of "A Turn Outside," Smith's radio play, this person too is a desirable companion. The poem shifts to the notion of "One Above" who is "experimenting": "All is interesting for him it is exciting, but not for us" (*New Selected Poems*, p. 88). This poem has the trademark Stevie Smith mixture of high spirits and depression, leaping from one to the other between lines. The poem shares with others written about the same time the notion that God is an experimenter who sets up catch-22 situations for his creation—predestination, eternal damnation, and so on. When she interrogates

God, she gets a variety of contradictory and confusing answers. The same series also features figures from Roman history and myth which sometimes represent a more realistic view of things—and which again underscore the belief that Death is the answer to life's misery, the only savior who will come on command.

LATE WORK AND GROWING REPUTATION

Smith's *A Turn Outside* is a strange, short radio play that was first performed in 1959. It is an interview between "S.S." and "the interlocutor," and at the beginning sounds very much like an ordinary interview with the poet except that the interviewer is oddly intimate with S.S. He calls her "Dear," which S.S. appreciates: "I would rather have 'dear' than a name, it is less personal" (*Me Again,* p. 335). S.S. describes the genesis of some of her poems in the words of an ordinary interviewee and discusses in detail their music, their "hymn-like" rhythms. In fact, her words remind us of the attention given to sound in Smith's work. The interlocutor keeps trying to approach her more closely and to lead her away, but she tells him she just wants to keep reading her poems. They discuss issues of publication as in any talk show.

But Smith begins to recognize her interviewer, as interacting with him recalls to her the scene of the garden where Persephone, heedless, picked flowers, and Hades captured her away. The interlocutor is, it seems, Death—and the two discuss views of death: religious, intellectual, personal. She prefers oblivion to alternatives. And yet when he wants to take her for "a turn outside" she wants to wait, to keep speaking or singing her poems, not to go outside just yet. However, the room begins to frighten and disgust her. Becoming nervous, she tells him to hurry up and open the door. He has the last word. The brief play gives a view into the conflicting attitudes toward death that plagued Smith for a lifetime.

The play was broadcast on BBC in May 1959, with Janet Richer as S.S. and Hugh Burden as the interlocutor. It was later set to music by Simon Rowland-Jones, and he performed it in 2005 to mixed, confused reviews; it premiered in London in 2007. The Rowland-Jones play eliminates the interlocutor to focus on Smith alone—the questioner is suggested by Smith's responses to his invisible presence. The play and the musical adaptation both highlight the attention to music Smith paid in writing her poems: some are based on hymn form, like Emily Dickinson's; others are written after popular and folk songs. In the Rowland-Jones adaptation Smith's poems are sung, some to original music and others to the tunes S.S. spoke of in the "interview." This play gives a vivid impression of Smith's poetic purposes as well as the claustrophobic nature of her life and the attraction and fear she felt for death. In many ways reading or listening to the play is a good way to enter into Stevie Smith's world.

Critical discussion of her is in fact increasing, although commentators tend to want to see Stevie Smith as a whole—the poems, the novels, the life. Thus much discussion of her is biographical criticism or critical biography. Readers often focus on her outsider status—which is ironic considering that she lived and wrote very much within the confines of middle-class suburbia. But she felt like an outsider, someone whose intellect roamed far beyond the standard concerns of her class and place and who always found reasons for not fitting in anywhere. This position too is similar to that of Sylvia Plath, who did not have the drive to throw off the bondage of the middle-class life completely but who resented its burdens and said so again and again. As in Plath's case the absent father figures in the Stevie myth—and although Smith's father is just absent and not dead, his absence seems to cast a dark shade over her. She pictures herself as an orphan, and the fairy-tale orphan looms large in her work.

Smith's last few years were filled with both success and trouble. She had caught on with a fairly large segment of poetry writers and readers at last; it is strange that her most enthusiastic audience seemed to be sixties rebels. Her personal life remained stolidly middle-class, and her persona, the wise child who dressed in such a way to emphasize her smallness and vulnerability, was very unlike the personas popular with followers of Allen Ginsberg and his ilk. Yet she appeared too as an outsider, a small, acute critic. Another widely anthologized poem gives a sense of this persona from within. "To Carry the Child" describes the inner turmoil of one who is fated to do so: "it is never happy, / To carry the child into adulthood," the poem claims, suggesting that children should die innocent and good. The child who does "carry the child" ends up with a twisted vision:

But oh the poor child, the poor child, what can he do,
Trapped in a grown-up carapace,
But peer outside of his prison room
With the eye of an anarchist?

(*Collected Poems*, p. 437)

Smith's anarchist eye caught an answering glint in the rebels of the fifties and sixties. She received an important recognition in these years: in 1969 she received the Gold Medal for Poetry, which was given to her by Queen Elizabeth II in a private audience. (She described her experience at court in an essay published in *Me Again*.) Her books were widely reviewed and discussed. She was invited to many literary evenings, and her readings were filled with enthusiastic listeners.

A distinctive characteristic of her work is her genre-crossing and her defiance of types. She mentioned once that there was not much difference between her poetry and her prose, and in fact they often mingle. She tossed poems into novels, short stories, and even book reviews. She sometimes told the same event as a poem and within a prose piece. Her style in prose was breathless, run-on; whole paragraphs are sometimes stuck together with commas, violating expectations of syntactic weighting and giving a stream-of-consciousness effect. She balked expectations in other ways, mixing humor and tragedy, setting up the reader to expect a particular outcome in a narrative and then sliding off with it in another direction. She injected surreal episodes into seemingly realistic narration so that readers wonder if these strange narrative loops are dreams or fantasy, and different commentators have wildly differing interpretations. These elements of postmodernism were combined with a schoolgirl voice that left the reader wondering

who Stevie Smith really was and what games she was playing. Ogden Nash was very taken with her and described her in a poem:

Who or what is Stevie Smith,
is she woman? Is she myth?
...
Searching out her God to haunt him,
Now to praise him, now to taunt him,
Then to sing at Man's expense
Songs of deadly innocence.

(*Collected Poems*)

Her ability to elude capture was one of the main characteristics that made her an icon of the poetry scene in the sixties. She was the shy performer, the middle-class orphan waif, the child with an adult's sensuous knowledge. It is not surprising that her readings were crowded, and they provoked much discussion.

However, her Aunt Margaret died in 1968 at age ninety-six; despite the increasing burden of her care, Smith was devastated by her loss. In 1970 Smith was mainly concerned about the health of her sister Molly, who had had a stroke. She visited Molly for months in Buckfast, Devon, one of the longest periods spent away from Palmers Green, and then after a return home and giving poetry readings she returned to Molly. She continued to give readings despite increasing tiredness and spells of dizziness; she was concerned about money, and the influx of small sums from the readings was a comfort to her. She was also putting poems together for a new collection, *Scorpion and Other Poems,* and worked with her publisher on a planned reissue of *Selected Poems* and *The Frog Prince* in one volume. By the end of the year, however, it was clear to Smith and those who knew her that something was wrong. She had spells of fainting and aphasia, and kept a record her symptoms in a journal. By January the fits were more frequent; initially diagnosed as petit mal epilepsy, they were eventually revealed to be an advanced brain tumor. Despite increasing disability, she wrote and composed until the end, actually reading her poem "Come Death" to visitors from her hospital bed. She had only a few weeks of disability, and she was a poet until the end, on March 7, 1971.

In fact, she wrote her last poems during her final illness, and these poems show her preoccupation with death without so much of the cheer and wit that accompanied it earlier. Poems about desire for death alternate with nostalgia-touched memories of long-ago scenes. The poems wrestle with the possibility of God's existence and life after death, but these possibilities seem neither likely nor desirable. The speaker, identifying with the scorpion, pleads for her departure: "Scorpion so wishes to be gone" (*Collected Poems*, p. 513).

It is reported that she showed a friend at her deathbed her poem "Come, Death" with the word "death" circled, asking the friend to deliver her. The friend did not do as she requested, but did show the note to the doctor, and after that Smith was given more morphine to alleviate her pain.

After her death, *Scorpion and Other Poems*, the last collection she had worked on, was published in 1972; *The Collected Poems of Stevie Smith* appeared in 1975, and *Me Again: Uncollected Writings of Stevie Smith* (1981) filled in the gaps with poems, stories, essays, reviews, and some letters. *Scorpion* is a slim book that contains some of her earlier work as well as her new poems. Her last poem is the final poem in the book, the second with the title "Come, Death" and the poem she read from her hospital bed:

Ah me, sweet Death, you are the only god
Who comes as a servant when he is called, you know,
Listen then to this sound I make, it is sharp,
Come Death. Do not be slow.

(*Collected Poems*, p. 571)

The poems in this last collection assembled by Smith herself show her old themes of wrestling with religion and desire for death. The comforts of religion she now finds disappointing and deceptive. One strange long poem, "The House of Over-Dew," tells the story of a religious family, the Minnims, falling on hard times and turning foolishly to the minutia of caring for the church, thereby leading the family to ruin rather than restoration. A more serious poem, "How Do You See?" interrogates Christianity and concludes that whatever it may offer, it is neither comforting nor restorative:

Does the beautiful Holy Ghost endorse the doctrine of
  eternal hell?
Love cruelty, enjoin the sweet comforts of religion?
Oh yes, Christianity, yes, he must do this
For he is your God …

(*Collected Poems*, p. 518)

The conclusion is that what religion teaches, or instructs, is cruelty and destruction, and that it must be put aside.

Oh how sad it is to give up the Holy Ghost
He is so beautiful, but not when you look close …

(*Collected Poems*, p. 520)

The six-page poem revisits all her questions and doubts, the stages in her struggle with religion that is a motif in all her work. Her conclusion is that if we do not learn to be good without the help of such a grand narrative, then the dishonesty will be too much for us, and "armed as we are now, we shall kill everybody" (*Collected Poems*, p. 521). Its theme is a reprise on that of the more popular "Was He Married?" but with greater emphasis and less wit. She is no longer playing with ideas and concepts but drawing final conclusions. Unlike so many poets who struggled with religion for a lifetime, her ultimate position on Christianity appears to be rejection: she sees the religion not only as offering false promises but as encouraging dangerous behavior.

Stevie Smith has a permanent place in the canon, both as a poet and as a fiction writer. Speaking from the margins, she shows the restrictions her time and place imposed on a free-spirited woman of intelligence and sensitivity. Her themes and images remain compelling. They continue to remind us of Sylvia Plath and sometimes Emily Dickinson, but they are vitalized by her own stubborn perspective. The overall body of work is a gothic kaleidoscope: night rides on horseback, bodies of water, near-drowning and drowning incidents, early death, weird death. Scenes of dead animals, such as the dead vole that appears in both poetry and prose, are touched with pity, innocence, and death coming together in a kind of perfection. Fairy tales, Greek and Roman figures, orphans and the lonely frequent the poems, and many describe suicides, deathbeds, religious disillusion, graves. Yet these same poems also sparkle with comedy and glitter with defiance. They seem to hide nothing; their effect of honesty is a large part of their appeal.

The collections of her work and retrospective evaluations that appeared after her death enhanced her reputation. Her work has been examined for its presentation of the outsider's perspective, for its wrestling with religion, for its relationship with modernism, and perhaps most tellingly, for the acute sense of time and place it expresses. Her work is so idiosyncratic that it does not fall into a particular area of critical interest; "close readings" of Smith poems are infrequent and tend to be focused on the same handful of poems. However, her work is of a nature to attract more readers than scholars. Nevertheless, few writers have been such careful listeners that they have caught the accents of an age with such acuity, and few have been so closely aware of the exigencies of a particular social class. Her feminism is the kind of reaction to a smothering society that re-creates the society for the contemporary reader as well as providing a clear sense of what it was like to inhabit it. The acute claustrophobia of this society communicates itself painfully, and there seems to be helplessness on the part of the speaker to do anything more than observe precisely and comment critically. She can do nothing to bring about change. The works that do describe some form of rebellion have a fatalism to them; they suggest that this rebellion is all inside. The mind may transcend the limitation of time and place, but behavior conforms. All of Stevie Smith's works in all her genres together create one single, distinctive voice, which cajoles, criticizes, bewails, and entices.

Selected Bibliography

WORKS OF STEVIE SMITH

POETRY
A Good Time Was Had by All. London: Jonathan Cape, 1937.
Tender Only to One. London: Jonathan Cape, 1938.
Mother, What Is Man? London: Jonathan Cape, 1942.
Harold's Leap. London: Chapman & Hall, 1950.
Not Waving but Drowning. London, Deutsch, 1957.

Selected Poems. London: Longman, 1962; Norfolk, Conn.: New Directions, 1964.
The Frog Prince, and Other Poems. London: Longman, 1966.
The Best Beast. New York: Knopf, 1969.
Two in One: Selected Poems; and, The Frog Prince and Other Poems. London: Longman, 1971.
Scorpion and Other Poems. London: Longman, 1972.
New Selected Poems of Stevie Smith. New York: New Directions, 1988.

NOVELS
Novel on Yellow Paper; or, Work It Out for Yourself. London: Jonathan Cape, 1936, reprinted, 1969; New York: Morrow, 1937. (All page citations in the text refer to the most recent edition).
Over the Frontier. London: Jonathan Cape, 1938.
The Holiday. London: Chapman & Hall, 1949.

OTHER WORKS
Some Are More Human than Others. London: Gaberbocchus, 1958. (Drawings and captions.)
A Turn Outside. Radio play. First broadcast on BBC Third Programme May 23, 1959. Published in *Me Again: Uncollected Writings of Stevie Smith.* Edited by Jack Barbera and William McBrien. London: Virago, 1981; New York: Farrar, Straus and Giroux, 1982.
Introduction to *Cats in Colour.* London: Batsford, 1959; New York: Viking, 1960.

AS EDITOR
T. S. Eliot: A Symposium for His 70th Birthday. London: Hart-Davis, 1958.
The Poet's Garden. New York: Viking, 1970. Published in England as *The Batsford Book of Children's Verse.* London: Batsford, 1970.

COLLECTED WORKS
The Collected Poems of Stevie Smith. Edited by James MacGibbon. London: Allen Lane, 1975; New York: Oxford University Press, 1976.
Me Again: Uncollected Writings of Stevie Smith. Edited by Jack Barbera and William McBrien, London: Virago, 1981; Farrar, Straus and Giroux, 1982.
A Very Pleasant Evening with Stevie Smith: Selected Short Prose. New York: New Directions, 1995.

BIBLIOGRAPHY AND PAPERS
Barbera, Jack, William McBrien, and Helen Bajan. *Stevie Smith: A Bibliography.* Westport, Conn.: Meckler, 1987; London: Mansell, 1987.
Many of the Stevie Smith manuscripts and letters are housed in the McFarlin Library, Special Collections Department,

University of Tulsa, Oklahoma. Some letters and manuscripts are housed at the University of Reading Library, Reading, U.K.

CRITICAL AND BIOGRAPHICAL STUDIES

Barbera, Jack, and William McBrien. *Stevie: A Biography of Stevie Smith.* New York: Oxford University Press, 1986.

Bedient, Calvin. *Eight Contemporary Poets: Charles Tomlinson, Donald Davie, R. S. Thomas, Philip Larkin, Ted Hughes, Thomas Kinsella, Stevie Smith, W. S. Graham.* London and New York: Oxford University Press, 1974. Pp. 139–158.

Civello, Catherine A. *Patterns of Ambivalence: The Fiction and Poetry of Stevie Smith.* Columbia, S.C.: Camden House, 1997.

Dick, Kay. *Ivy & Stevie: Ivy Compton-Burnett and Stevie Smith; Conversations and Reflections.* London: Duckworth, 1971.

Dinnage, Rosemary. *Alone! Alone! Lives of Some Outsider Women.* New York: New York Review, 2005.

Huk, Romana. *Stevie Smith: Between the Lines.* Houndmills, Basingstoke, U.K., and New York: Palgrave Macmillan, 2005.

Orr, Peter, ed. *The Poet Speaks: Interviews with Contemporary Poets Conducted by Hilary Morrish, Peter Orr, John Press, and Ian Scott-Kilvert.* London: Routledge, 1966. Pp. 225–231.

Severin, Laura. *Stevie Smith's Resistant Antics.* Madison: University of Wisconsin Press, 1997.

Spalding, Frances. *Stevie Smith: A Biography.* 2nd ed. Stroud, Gloucestershire, U.K.: Sutton, 2002.

Sternlicht, Sanford. *Stevie Smith.* Boston: Twayne, 1990.

Thompson, Francis. *The Poems of Francis Thompson.* Edited by Brigid M. Boardman. London: Continuum International, 2001.

FILMS AND PLAYS BASED ON THE WORKS OF STEVIE SMITH

Stevie. Film, with screenplay by Hugh Whitemore, based on his play of the same name. Directed by Robert Enders. Bowden Productions, 1977.

A Turn Outside. Musical adaptation for the stage by Simon Rowland-Jones of Stevie Smith's 1959 radio play. First performed at First North Norfolk Music Festival, U.K., 2005.

ALFRED TENNYSON

(1809—1892)

Katherine Firth

ALFRED TENNYSON IS the most important of the Victorian poets. He has become synonymous with the era, and his reputation has followed and formed the reputation of the era as a whole. He was, during his life, both a poetic best seller and a critical success. He was granted the highest accolades possible by the British state, given a civil list pension, made poet laureate, granted personal access to Queen Victoria herself, and was the first English writer to be ennobled for his services to literature.

At the same time, he was a man, and a poet, of contrasts. He had a wide and influential group of friends, and he was close to his wife and children. Yet he had come from an extremely difficult family, with an inherited strain of what the family called "black blood"; he was forced to leave university without a degree; his early poems were vilified by the critics and failed to sell. His best friend died suddenly of a brain hemorrhage at the age of twenty-two; his first love refused him to marry a rich, older man; and he had to wait more than a decade to be able to marry the woman who did become his wife. He would use and distance himself from these tragic autobiographical events in his poems throughout his life.

Tennyson was a prolific writer, whose extensive corpus included fourteen individual poetry collections, with an even more extensive background of manuscripts (edited in thirty-one volumes as *The Tennyson Archive* in 1987–1993) and letters (published in three volumes in 1982–1990). He also wrote seven plays, and he created a song cycle, *The Window; or, The Songs of the Wrens,* with Arthur Sullivan (1871). Tennyson is famous for his shorter, memorable lyrics, like "The Charge of the Light Brigade" or "Crossing the Bar"; for the lyrics extracted from longer works, like "Now sleeps the crimson petal now the white" from *The Princess* (1847), and for his extended sequences, including *Maud* (1855), *In Memoriam A.H.H.* (1850)*, and Idylls of the King* (published, revised, and expanded during the period 1856–1885).

Tennyson's poems frequently deal with death and madness, and with thwarted love. He used Greek and Arthurian mythology as the basis for many of his poems, including "Ulysses" (1842) and "The Lady of Shalott" (1832), giving archetypal characters new facets of inner reflection. He used Shakespeare in the same way, taking, for example, a small and ignored character in *Measure for Measure* and exploring her despair and heartbreak in his poem "Mariana" (1830).

The critical reactions to Tennyson are as prolific and diverse as his oeuvre. During his own lifetime, there were those who saw Tennyson's fortunes mirror those of the age in which he lived, with their apex in 1850–1855. This time frame, the height of the Victorian age, was the period in which Tennyson published his two major sequences, *In Memoriam A.H.H.* and *Maud*, and became not only a best seller but Britain's poet laureate. Tennyson's early poetry collections had been derided by critics including John Wilson Croker and "Christopher North" (John Wilson), but at the height of his popularity, Tennyson was praised by eminent intellectual and literary figures such as Edward FitzGerald, the translator of *The Rubáiyát of Omar Khayyám* (1859); Coventry Patmore, the author of *The Angel in the House* (1854–1862); and Benjamin Jowett (Regius Professor of Greek at Oxford University).

By the end of the nineteenth century, however, Tennyson's reputation was again falling with critics—the poets Alfred Austin (who replaced Tennyson as poet laureate), Charles Manley Hopkins, and Algernon Charles Swinburne, for instance, disparaged the later poems, particularly *Idylls of the King,* for being hidebound and derivative. Even his earlier friend and supporter Patmore complained that the later works were merely "Tennysonian."

For some early-twentieth-century critics, including T. S. Eliot and F. R. Leavis, Tennyson's influence on English poetry was comparable to John Milton's: they found his style overwrought, overlong, and stultifying for poets who came after. In *Tennyson: An Introduction and a Selection* (1946), W. H. Auden says that Tennyson's earlier lyrics were where his poetic strengths lay, and he comments that after about 1850 (the year in which Tennyson's masterpiece *In Memoriam* appeared, he was married, and he succeeded William Wordsworth as the British poet laureate) he was more concerned with his public role as a poet than with his writing. However, other critics (like Tennyson's twentieth-century biographer Michael Thorn) suggest that Tennyson improved as he aged and that the last, long poems show a poet at the height of his powers.

The conflicting aspects of Tennyson's life, character, and writing have led to an argument for "two Tennysons," a way of assessing the poet that was first advanced by Harold Nicholson in 1923 and has been developed, repudiated, or multiplied ever since. Tennyson has been seen as prudish (by A. C. Swinburne) and as a womanizer (by Thorn); as morbidly afraid of inheriting the illnesses, both physical and psychological, that ran through his family (by Robert Bernard Martin) and yet as a warm family man with a prosaic interest in lawns (by his son Hallam Tennyson). He was obsessed by his health, but he smoked, drank, and used opium. His manners were vulgar and he was uninterested in social niceties, and yet he frequently visited Queen Victoria. Tennyson has been seen as a deadening influence on poetry, hypocritical and morally hidebound (by Leavis) but also as a champion of truthfulness, vitality, and liberty (by Peter Levi). What therefore becomes clear is that Tennyson was a poet of great range and variety, whose work evolved over his long life and the radical changes of the century through which he lived.

EARLY LIFE

Alfred Tennyson was born August 6, 1809, in Somersby, a tiny hamlet in Lincolnshire, just over twenty miles from the sea in the northeast of England. His father was the vicar of the fifteenth-century St. Margaret's Somersby and of an even older church, also dedicated to St. Margaret, in the even smaller hamlet of Bag Enderby, about half a mile away. Tennyson was his parents' fourth child and the second of ten to be born at Somersby.

Alfred Tennyson's father, George Clayton Tennyson, was the eldest son of one of the richest men in Lincolnshire. But because of a filial argument, George Clayton Tennyson had been deposed as heir to his father's substantial personal fortune, which had been gained through purchase and speculation. Instead, this fortune was inherited by the younger brother, Charles Tennyson-D'Eyncourt (1784–1861), a radical politician. George Clayton Tennyson was therefore forced to take up work in the church. Somersby was a mere sixteen miles south from the ancestral family seat at Bayons Court, in Tealby. Alfred Tennyson's mother, Elizabeth Fych, was the daughter of the vicar of Louth (a larger town about ten miles to the north of Somersby). In 1815, George Clayton Tennyson was also made rector of Grimsby, but the family remained living in Somersby.

The Tennyson family suffered from a range of debilitating illnesses and addictions—from alcoholism, insanity, and opium dependence to "fits" and depression. These were known, collectively, in the family as "black blood." They believed that these illnesses were hereditary, and black blood was understood at the time to be a symptom of melancholy.

The exact nature of this "black blood" has been the source of much critical debate. Some scholars, such as Christopher Ricks in his 1989 study of Tennyson, use the term as a catch-all for the eccentric, argumentative, neurotic, hypochondriac, and otherwise emotionally destructive behavior of the Tennyson family, as well as for the medical symptoms of seizures or depression. On the other hand, Martin in *Tennyson: The Unquiet Heart* (1983), argues that modernly understood "epilepsy," with its associated seizures, headaches, and anxiety disorders, was the "black blood." Jack Kolb, in his "Portraits of Tennyson," points out that the nineteenth-century understanding of epilepsy was broader than current medical definitions and that in Tennyson's time, "black blood" and "epilepsy" were both imprecise terms that related to a view of the body now discounted by modern medicine. Other critics have even more firmly repudiated Martin's suggestion; Peter Levi claims that "there is not the slightest evidence that Alfred had epilepsy" (p. 25).

Whatever the medical basis of the family's ills, the Tennysons were undoubtedly a strange and difficult family. Alfred Tennyson's grandfather had argued with his heir, leading to (or resulting in) George Clayton Tennyson's sense of ill usage, his "unhealthy indulgence in fantasy" (as Kolb describes it in "Review," p. 175), and his abuse of narcotics and alcohol, which contributed to his death at the age of fifty-two. Of Alfred Tennyson's brothers, the eldest, Frederick, had violent disagreements with both his father and his grandfather. On one occasion, the village constable had to be called from his house next door to the vicarage to break up a fight. Of the other brothers: Charles Tennyson suffered from an opium addiction for many years; Arthur was, for some time, an alcoholic; Edward was institutionalized in an asylum; and the youngest, Septimus, suffered from deep depression. Both Arthur and Septimus Tennyson spent some time in Dr. Matthew Allen's sanatorium at High Beech. Tennyson's sister Emily suffered from hypochondria and various nervous disorders. As a young boy, Alfred Tennyson would go out into the graveyard around the church and lie on the graves, "wishing to be dead" (Ricks, *Tennyson*, p. 2). This portrait of an unhappy family has been painted in a 1949 biography by Alfred Tennyson's grandson, Sir Charles Tennyson; by Christopher Ricks in his 1989 study, *Tennyson*; and in

Martin's 1983 biography, all correcting an overly rosy depiction by Tennyson's son Hallam in his 1897 memoir of his father.

EDUCATION

The sons of George Clayton Tennyson were educated at local grammar schools (where Alfred Tennyson was particularly unhappy) and then at home by their father—except for Frederick, the eldest, who was sent to Eton College. All of the family wrote verses, and three of the brothers eventually became published poets: Frederick, Charles, and Alfred published juvenilia collectively in *Poems by Two Brothers* [sic] (1827), written when the brothers were in their teens. Later, Frederick (1807–1898) published four further volumes of verse, little read in his own time or today. Charles Tennyson Turner (1808–1879), as he became known, combined his career as a clergyman with writing sonnets, and collections were published in 1864, 1868, and posthumously in 1880 (with a "Prefatory Poem to My Brother's Sonnets" by Alfred Tennyson in that final volume). However, neither had the talent of their brother Alfred.

The three brothers were all sent to Trinity College, Cambridge University. Alfred Tennyson began his studies there in 1828. This is when he met his friend Arthur H. Hallam (1811–1833). Hallam was the son of an important Whig historian (a member of the liberal party in England), Henry Hallam, whose *Constitutional History of England* was published in 1827. Tennyson and Hallam were both at Trinity College, and both (if in Tennyson's case only briefly) were members of a secret intellectual society called the Apostles.

Before the end of his first term, Tennyson entered a poem, "Timbuctoo," for the university chancellor's medal, which he won. "Timbuctoo" recalled the English Romantic poet John Keats's poem "On First Looking into Chapman's Homer," and its sense of the explorer "on a peak in Darien," and also Percy Bysshe Shelley's "Ode to the West Wind," with its "pumice isle in Baiæ's bay." Yet the poem instead argued the failure of such Romantic values. Tennyson, too, "stood upon the Mountain which o'erlooks / The narrow seas" and surveys "the chasms of deep, deep blue" (*The Poems of Tennyson*, pp. 172–173) However, he is rebuked by the seraph who (in a vision influenced by Milton's *Paradise Lost*) replaces the fairy-tale beauties of Atlantis, Eldorado, and, perhaps, Timbuctoo, with the pragmatic realities of "Low-built, mud-walled, Barbarian settlements" discovered in real life exploration (p. 180).

Tennyson was highly prolific at this time, and he brought out his first independent collection in 1830, *Poems, Chiefly Lyrical*. He was helped by Hallam in arranging the publication, and his friend also provided an adulatory review in the *Englishman's Magazine* of August 1831. When away from Cambridge, Hallam and Tennyson frequently wrote to one another, sharing their ideas on poetry, their concerns for the future, and their struggles with depression and atheism.

In the Easter holidays of 1830, Hallam visited Somersby and met Tennyson's sister Emily. They were both then aged nineteen. That summer Tennyson and Hallam traveled together to the Pyrenees with other university friends (Tennyson's poem "In a Valley of Cauterez" remembered this trip, thirty years later). Hallam returned to Somersby in December, and he and Emily became engaged. The match was, unsurprisingly, considered overly hasty by Hallam's family, and the two were forbidden to see one another for a year. In 1832, Hallam's theological essay, "Theodicaea Novissima" (On a New Natural Theology) was delivered to the Apostles in Cambridge (published 1834 in Arthur Henry Hallam, *Remains in Verse and Prose*, edited by his father).

"Theodicea Novissima" was influenced by Platonic ideas—particularly significant for Tennyson's later poems about Hallam was the concept of Platonic love, which Hallam expounded in his essay. Drawing from Plato's *Symposium*, this argued that the highest form of love between people is the disinterested friendship of men (in contrast to romantic love between men and women, within families, or romantic love between men).

In 1831, George Clayton Tennyson died. His family was permitted to remain at the vicarage in Somersby for another six years, but without a stipend. Tennyson was forced to leave university without having taken a degree. In 1832, Tennyson and Hallam traveled together to the German Rhineland, and Tennyson's second mature collection of poems was published. A review of *Poems* in the *Quarterly Review* by John Wilson Croker in April 1833 was even more derogatory than the earlier review of *Poems, Chiefly Lyrical,* by "Christopher North" (John Wilson) in *Blackwood's Magazine* in May 1832. Tennyson was stung into a verse reply, "To Christopher North" (1832), "You did mingle blame and praise" (*The Poems of Tennyson*, p. 461).

The criticism further prompted Tennyson to heavily revise those poems that he included in his 1842 *Poems*, a number of which are now among his most popular, including "The Lady of Shalott," "The Palace of Art," "The Hespirides," and "The Lotos-Eaters." The revisions greatly strengthened the poems. The first stanza of "The Lady of Shalott" now famously reads, following the 1842 version:

On either side the river lie
Long fields of barley and of rye,
That clothe the wold and meet the sky;
And through the field the road runs by
To many-towered Camelot;
And up and down the people go,
Gazing where the lilies blow
Round an island there below,
The island of Shalott.

In 1832, the second half of the stanza had run:

The yellowleavèd waterlily,
The greensheathèd daffodilly,
Tremble in the water chilly,
Round about Shalott.

(*The Poems of Tennyson*, p. 355)

Not only were the rhymes improved ("daffodilly" / "chilly" is far weaker than "go" / "blow" / "below") and the archaic neologisms removed, but the rhythm was also strengthened. The stress pattern of "The yellowleavèd" (x/x/x) is confusing when laid onto the almost similar "The greensheathèd." The 1842 version was therefore stronger in terms of versification, choice of diction, and assurance. However, the themes, images, and imaginative narrative are already present.

PERSONAL LYRICS

Poems, Chiefly Lyrical (1830) and *Poems* (1832) were written before the poet was yet twenty-four. Even at this early stage, some of Tennyson's abiding concerns and techniques were emerging: among them his use of myth, his narrative flair and his sympathetic female characters. Tennyson's interest in the lyric and in longer sequences was also emerging. Striking a darker note, his poems already describe despair, the wish for death, and the lure of drugs, magic, or art as a retreat from reality (as in the Lady of Shalott's weaving and mirror), the protective walls of the "Palace of Art," or the "lotos" flowers eaten by Ulysses' crew.

The lyric had been understood by Romantic poets as a means to speak of their most intimate and nuanced thoughts in short, compressed poems of emotional intensity. William Wordsworth (1770–1850), then poet laureate, had championed such a view with his *Lyrical Ballads* (1798) and in poems like "Tintern Abbey." Likewise, in his first mature collection Tennyson had exploited the potential of the lyric to explore internal processes, in poems like "A Poet's Mind." At the same time, he showed early on an ambivalence to Romanticism, particularly notable in "Timbuctoo." Already, he was distancing himself from the need to have a straightforward, autobiographical, and confessional attitude in his lyrics, with debate poems like the juvenilia "All Things Will Die" and "Nothing Will Die" or his later poem "The Two Voices," as well as the "Supposed Confessions of a Second-Rate Sensitive Mind Not in Unity with Itself." By only "supposedly" confessing, he maintains distance and artistic license over his poetry.

ARTHUR HALLAM, ROSA BARING, AND EMILY SELLWOOD

In 1832, Henry Hallam took his son on a tour of Europe. While in Vienna, Arthur Hallam suffered a brain hemorrhage and died. Hallam was twenty-two years old, a talented poet, a promising theoretical thinker, Tennyson's closest university friend, and the fiancé of Tennyson's sister Emily, so his early death was a tragic shock.

Immediately, Tennyson began to construct poetic memorials to his friend, and over the next five decades, he began, rewrote, and arranged a large number of fragmentary and separate poems in service to this project. These included individual poems and lyrics that were later used in long sequences, like "Oh! that 'twere possible," rewritten to reflect the love of the speaker for "Maud" in the title poem of his so-named 1855 collection, or "The Death of Arthur," which became a section of *Idylls of the King*.

Most significant, however, were the sonnets Tennyson began to write, that he would later structure as *In Memoriam*. "The sections were written at many different places," Tennyson's son recalled his father explaining the poem, "and as the phases of our intercourse came to my memory and suggested them. I did not write them with any view of weaving them into a whole, or for publication, until I found that I had written so many" (quoted in Ricks, *The Poems of Tennyson*, p. 859). Although the poems were begun soon after Hallam's death, Tennyson did not make any of them public for another five years, when "Oh! that 'twere possible" was published, in an incomplete form (as "Stanzas") in a charity volume of poetry (*The Tribute,* 1837) for the benefit of the family of the Reverend Edward Smedley, a poet who had recently died. Most of the poems written in memory of Hallam were not published until the second volume of *Poems* (1842) was issued. The volume of poems collected as *In Memoriam* did not appear until 1850.

In 1834, meanwhile, Tennyson met Rosa Baring, the stepdaughter of the largest house in the vicinity of Somersby. Ricks claims that the two shared "a brief and frustrated love" that "was never to fade from his memory" (*Tennyson*, p. 137), but Peter Levi sees the relationship as nothing more than "mildly flirtatious" (p. 130). Tennyson wrote "Early Verses of Compliment to Miss Rose Baring," "Thy rosy lips are soft and sweet," and "The Rosebud" in 1834. In 1835 or 1836, he wrote "Three Sonnets to a Coquette" and "To Rosa," which Ricks attributes to "their lovers'-quarrel at a ball" (*The Poems of Tennyson*, p. 648). The references to the ball are slight, however, and clear only when comparing the two sonnets to the rose imagery in the ball scene in part 1 of *Maud*.

The financial situation of the Tennyson family was at that time extremely straightened. Furthermore, Tennyson's poetry was not selling, and he had no training for any other profession. By 1836, Tennyson had met and become engaged to another woman, Emily Sellwood. In 1836, Charles Tennyson had married Louisa Sellwood, and Alfred Tennyson was therefore introduced to Louisa's sister, her bridesmaid. Tennyson marked the occasion with a poem, "The Bridesmaid" (not published until 1872), "O happy bridesmaid, make a happy bride!" (*The Poems of Tennyson*, p. 661). In 1837 Alfred Tennyson and Emily Sellwood became engaged, and the contract was recognized formally by their families in 1838.

The six years of grace given to the Tennysons to stay at the rectory at Somersby ended in 1837, and the family moved to Epping. Three years later, with no amelioration in his financial circumstances, and with his family moving again (to Tunbridge Wells), Tennyson released Emily Sellwood from her engagement. This was followed by another move, to Boxley. The family's financial situation was soon made worse by the failure of an ecclesiastical wood-carving scheme promoted by Dr. Matthew Allen, in which Tennyson had invested his remaining savings (1840–1843).

Tennyson was now suffering from ill health and depression. The circumstances surrounding the breaking off of his engagement to Emily Sellwood were similar to the opposition faced by Hallam and Tennyson's sister, and possibly by Tennyson and Rosa Baring—and the rejection of a young man due to his social, familial, and financial situation became a trope that refracted into Tennyson's poetry, in poems such as "Locksley Hall," "Northern Farmer. New Style," and "Maud."

POEMS *OF 1842*

In 1842, Tennyson brought out a new collection of poetry in two volumes, his first book publication in ten years. In the first volume, he included revised poems from his much-derided earlier collections, *Poems, Chiefly Lyrical* (1930) and *Poems* (1832).

The second volume included new poems, including "Morte d'Arthur," which was his first poem explicitly derived from Sir Thomas Malory's compilation *Le Morte d'Arthur* (1485) and also the first poem written for the later sequence *Idylls of the King* and linked to his meditation on the death of Hallam. Volume 2 of the 1842 *Poems* also included "The Gardener's Daughter"—based on the seventh idyll of Theocritus but mirroring the experience of Hallam (Eustace) and Emily Tennyson (Juliet)—and "Break, break, break," another poem written in memory of Hallam.

For the first time, Tennyson was explicitly playing with dramatic monologues, such as the satirical "Will Waterproof's Lyrical Monologue" (assuming the voice of the British politician George Canning, who died several weeks after assuming the post of prime minister in 1827). "Ulysses," however, was a more complex construction. It was an important early dramatic monologue written soon after Hallam's death, and it expresses private and personal emotions of grief and weariness of life. And yet, here Tennyson is translating lines from book 9 of Homer's *Odyssey* and from canto 26 of Dante's *Inferno*, and taking on the voice of an ancient Greek king who has traveled far and lived long.

Along with other Victorian poets such as Robert Browning (who explored the abnormal psychology of fictionalized, distant characters such as a sixteenth-century Italian duke in "My Last Duchess" and a Spanish monk in "Soliloquy of the Spanish Cloister"), Tennyson had been significant in advancing a new kind of poetry, distinctive for its widely divergent characters and voices, that he would call the "monodrama." As in the Shakespearean soliloquy, where an actor addresses his personal feelings and motivation directly to the audience, the dramatic monologue allowed poets to take fictional characters and speak through them in the first person. Through discussing long ago or far away or merely fictionalized characters, whether in the first or third persons, Tennyson could write poems about murder, madness, adultery, suicide, and depression.

Tennyson's new volume also contained the long poem "Locksley Hall," in which a young man mourns his "cousin Amy," who has spurned him for a wealthier, titled man (*The Poems of Tennyson*, p. 691). Again, this poem is spoken by a character like Tennyson, but not Tennyson. It may also be partly Hallam's voice. Alternatively, "Locksley Hall" may be intended to serve as a more general comment, adapted from Thomas Carlyle's *Sartor Resartus* ("The Tailor Retailored," first published serially in 1833–1834), in which Carlyle discussed his own spiritual experiences in a fashion both serious and satirical (with reference to a fictional philosopher named Teufelsdröckh), and Sir William Jones' 1782 translation of the pre-Islamic Mu'allaqat—*The Moallakát, or Seven Arabian Poems Which Were Suspended on the Temple at Mecca*—collected in the first and second centuries CE, in which the poet Amriolkais supposedly recalls his earlier amours, provides not only some of the narrative but also some of the images in the poem.

Certainly both English and foreign literary influences and imaginative landscapes shape Tennyson's works. Tennyson's poetry, while English and Victorian, was written at a time when the British Empire controlled much of North America, Africa, Asia, and Australasia, with significant holdings in the Middle East and scattered footholds in Central America and South America. Thus, in "Locksley Hall," the speaker's father died "in wild Mahratta-battle" (a reference to the Mahratta war of 1817–1818, which gave the British control of most of present-day India; *The Poems of Tennyson*, p. 697), and later in the poem he imagines life on a Pacific island or in China. The vastness of the British Empire is also the context for the speaker's "Vision of the world" (*The Poetry of Tennyson*, p. 690) in the future, with its successful, peaceful commonwealth. This vision, though, is marred, for modern readers, by its misogyny and racism.

The cultural, religious, and racial imperialism that justified the empire (based on a belief that it was the duty of the industrialized, Christian West to bring civilization to the rest of the world) is expressed in the poem. The speaker turns from his fantasy of escape on a paradisal island by reminding himself, "But I count the gray barbarian lower than the Christian child" (p. 698) and "Better fifty years of Europe than a cycle of Cathay" (p. 699).

"Locksley Hall" made Tennyson's popular reputation. For the first time, his works gained a wider public reception, and the two volumes of *Poems* (1842) sold well. Three years later, he was given a civil list pension (paid by the government) of £200 a year.

TURNING FORTUNES

Tennyson's next project involved a new technical challenge. *The Princess: A Medley* (1847) was a long poem sequence about a women's university, and it was a plea for gradual social reform. The poem was published two years before the first university college for women in Britain was established, at Bedford College, London.

The length of the poem was a problem for readers of Tennyson's day, and it remains so for modern readers. Christopher Ricks, in *The Poems of Tennyson*, records that Elizabeth Barrett Browning wrote to her husband, Robert Browning, "I don't know what to think" (p. 741), and T. S. Eliot wrote, "*The Princess* is a dull poem; one of the poems of which we may say, that they are beautiful but dull" (quoted in Killham, ed., *Critical Essays*, p. 209).

More popular were the song lyrics excerpted from the poem: "Tears, idle tears" and "Now sleeps the crimson petal, now the white." The second edition of *The Princess*, in 1850, was much revised, with additional lyrics. The sequence was later adapted as a comic opera by W. S. Gilbert and Arthur Sullivan, premiering in 1884 as *Princess Ida*.

The poet's growing critical and popular support was associated with greater financial and social security. Tennyson and Emily Sellwood became engaged again in 1849, and they finally married in June of the next year. In 1853 they moved to a house in Farringford, on the Isle of Wight off the south coast of Hampshire, near to Queen Victoria's summer residence, Osbourne House. The Tennysons lived at Farringford for the rest of their lives (although from 1869 on, they would escape the summer tourists by shifting to a home at Blackdown in Sussex). To complete Tennyson's annus mirabilis of 1850, he was made poet laureate following the death of William Wordsworth that year.

But neither his marriage to Emily, delayed for more than a decade, nor the onset of a more settled domestic, financial, and professional period of his life were able to lay Tennyson's earlier ghosts to rest. Instead, he arranged and edited poems he had written about the death of Hallam into the monumental *In Memoriam A.H.H.* (1850), and then in *Maud* (1855), he produced an extended meditation on the hurt of "Locksley Hall."

IN MEMORIAM

The memorial elegy for a poet-friend who has died young is a classical form. Influential Greek pastoral laments from about 150 BCE exist, such as Bion's *Lament for Adonis*. Major English examples include John Milton's "Lycidas" (1637), also written for a Cambridge friend, and Percy Bysshe Shelley's *Adonais,* written for John Keats (1821). Furthermore, Victorian poets in the mid-nineteenth century were experimenting with the sonnet sequence, using Shakespeare's sonnets and the sequences of Renaissance writers in Italy and England as their basis. Elizabeth Barrett Browning's *Sonnets from the Portuguese*, for example, was also published in 1850.

In Memoriam A.H.H. (that is, "in memory of Arthur Henry Hallam") is nonetheless unique within this literary context. It comprises a sequence of 132 cantos of varying length, all using stanzas of four octosyllabic lines, rhymed *abba*. The poems were originally written over a period of seventeen years, but they are arranged into a structure that suggests three years of reflec-

tion as they describe the stages of the poet's grief over three Christmas Eves.

In Memoriam is more than a poem of death and grief. It is also a profound meditation on contemporary life and on faith. The poems are framed by a wider context, in and through which Tennyson's grief and friendship is transformed: "My love is vaster passion now; / Though mixed with God and Nature" (canto 130, *The Poems of Tennyson*, p. 980). Tennyson's awareness of the divine and the world around him both comforts him and assures him of Hallam's continued presence in the word.

The prologue to *In Memoriam* is a prayer, and the epilogue (canto 131) is an epithalamion (a poem celebrating a wedding) on the nuptials of Tennyson's sister Cecilia and Edward Lushington, who had been a friend at Cambridge of both Hallam and Tennyson. Hallam in these final lines of the poem is imagined both as a benevolent, ghostly guest and as

That friend of mine who lives in God,
That God, which ever lives and loves,
One God, one law, one element,
And one far-off divine event
To which the whole creation moves.

(p. 988)

Yet the movement from intense private grief to wider concern is not simply religious and universal. It finds expression in the particular quotidian details of daily life, as in one of the early poems, canto 7:

He is not here; but far away
The noise of life begins again,
And ghastly through the drizzling rain
On the bald streets breaks the blank day

(p. 871)

Tennyson also relates his love for an individual fellow man to the broader love for his fellow men, expressed in political concerns, such as the way he addresses the threats of revolutions and proclaims the need for "social truth ... and justice" in the wake of the 1848 risings across Europe, in one of the last poems (canto 127, p. 977). It was probably on the strength of *In Memoriam* that Tennyson was made poet laureate. The collection was published anonymously, but the authorship seems to have been widely known, and the volume is perhaps Tennyson's greatest achievement. "It is, in my opinion," wrote Eliot, "in *In Memoriam*, that Tennyson finds full expression" (in Killham, ed., p. 211). The poem is as notable for its technical mastery, inventiveness, and variation as for the depth of its feeling, its descriptive honesty, and its epic length. Levi agrees with the judgment that this poem is perhaps Tennyson's greatest work, although he qualified that it can also be viewed as "that entangled shipwreck, that many times started and incoherent lament" (p. 134).

On the other hand, Ricks sees that "there is much in *In Memoriam* that does not carry conviction." Where the poems consider Tennyson's earlier life, politics, or his father, "its language falters or coarsens" (*Tennyson*, p. 212). Most of all, however, the poem lacks conviction when Tennyson claims his "Faith in a God of Love" (*The Poems of Tennyson*, p. 859). Eliot did not see this as a failure, however: *In Memoriam,* he wrote, is "not religious because of the quality of its faith, but because of the quality of its doubt" (Killham, ed., p. 214).

A question of the nature of Tennyson and Hallam's friendship is raised within the poem itself and entered into its criticism from the first. Shakespeare's sonnets were not only an important source for Tennyson's poems; they are one of the most useful means to understand *In Memoriam*. Henry Hallam in his *Introduction to the Literature of Europe* (1839) viewed Shakespeare's sonnets as unmanly and inappropriate declarations of friendship for a fair youth. For Henry Hallam, Shakespeare's sonnets gave the beloved, whether the Young Man and the Dark Lady, a strength of feeling, and an importance that should be retained for God alone. Furthermore, the excess of the emotions in the sonnets were unmasculine. Whether the friendship was sexual or platonic was unimportant to Henry Hallam, who was more concerned that the feelings were an "idolatry" (Ricks' notes to *The Poems of Tennyson*, p. 861).

Tennyson had grown up in the Regency period; he was twenty-six before Victoria came to the throne. While he and his contemporaries were nonetheless generally disapproving of homosexuality, his generation's views on gender were far less based on essentialist notions of sex-role stereotypes than the later Victorians. Instead, many held that men and women were (as Aristophanes described in Plato's *Symposium*) partial expressions of a complete humanity. As Tennyson wrote in the poem "On One Who Affected an Effeminate Manner" (1889): "While man and woman still are incomplete, / I prize that soul where man and woman meet, / Which types all Nature's male and female plan, / But, friend, man-woman is not woman-man. (*The Poems of Tennyson*, p. 1424) In the poem, Tennyson at once records his disapproval of the "effeminate" character, but also points to Christ, who was for Tennyson the most perfect human, who transcended gender differences.

Nonetheless, late-Victorian anxiety surrounding these more flexible definitions of sexuality and gender led Hallam Tennyson to directly and indirectly rebut (through judicious editing) in his memoirs in 1897 (two years after the trial of Oscar Wilde for sodomy) any suggestion that his father had been homosexual. Tennyson's major modern biographers dismiss the suggestion that his friendship with Hallam had a sexual element, largely because such an enormous quantity of Tennyson's manuscripts and letters have survived him (published now in *The Tennyson Archive*, comprising thirty-one volumes) that it seems evidence would have come to light had such an attachment existed. Harold Nicolson's imagined romance, described in his 1923 biography of Tennyson, is now held to have more to do with Nicholson's own sexuality than with any evidence.

The emergence of post-Marxist and feminist theory in the late twentieth century, however, reignited the debate, with critics such as Alan Sinfield arguing that the ambiguities in Tennyson's poems for Hallam, particularly the poems of *In Memoriam*, reflect a suppressed sexual relationship. *In Memoriam* blurs the distinction between language to describe friendship and romantic love, and therefore the love of both Emily and Arthur Tennyson for Hallam:

O Sorrow, wilt thou live with me
No casual mistress, but a wife,
My bosom friend and half of life.

(The Poems of Tennyson, p. 914)

Here, in canto 59 of *In Memoriam,* "Sorrow" is invited to be Tennyson's constant companion, but the metaphors suggest a marriage to Sorrow (like the expected marriage between Hallam and Emily Tennyson) and for Sorrow to be Tennyson's best friend (as Hallam had been his best friend). There is a delicately shaded ambiguity as to whether the "wife" and "friend" is Hallam himself, or the loss of Hallam.

A clear synopsis of both sides of the argument, with helpful quotations that give more context to the most often cited possible suggestions that Hallam or Tennyson may have been homosexual, are given in Jack Kolb's 2000 article, "Hallam, Tennyson, Homosexuality, and the Critics." He concludes that much of the seemingly amorous language in the poems was common to male friendship in Cambridge at the time, and that furthermore, the language lacks the coded references that were included in poems of same-sex desire by Lord Byron or Oscar Wilde. Furthermore, "Theodicicae Novissima" had considered Christian and Platonic ideas of friendship, couched in similarly ardent language.

In Memoriam A.H.H. and the other poems that Tennyson wrote in memory of Hallam were not his only memorials. In 1852, when Tennyson's first son was born, he named the child after his dead friend, and his sister Emily also called one of her sons after Hallam.

In 1854, Tennyson's second son, Lionel, was born. The next year, Tennyson was granted an honorary doctorate in classical literature from the University of Oxford. The young man who had been forced to leave university without a degree, thwarted in love, faced with personal tragedy and financial insecurity, and whose work had been lambasted in the press was now happily married with two children, given the highest title available to a writer in Britain, and was popular and selling well. This cementing of his reputation was paralleled in his private audiences and correspondence with the queen (from 1862) and her

bestowing upon him the title of baron (so thereafter he was titled Alfred, Lord Tennyson).

MAUD

The earlier unhappinesses of his life nonetheless continued to be kept alive in Tennyson's poems. In 1855, he published *Maud and Other Poems,* a volume that not only draws upon the trope of thwarted love used in "Locksley Hall" but that incorporated "Oh! that 'twere possible" (one of the first poems written after Hallam's death) into part 2, section 4, of the new poem.

While Tennyson had used the dramatic monologue form before, *Maud* was the first poem he described as "a monodrama," and it is by far the longest of the poems he wrote in this form. Furthermore, the poem fits a dramatic three-act (or -part) structure. Such long monologues were less usual for drama in verse than were briefer soliloquies, like Robert Browning's depiction of another jealous murderer, "My Last Duchess." The length of Tennyson's poem gave him the opportunity for a more in-depth consideration of the speaker's psychology and for the development of dramatic tension and narrative.

Tennyson wrote of his intentions regarding the first-person form in *In Memoriam*: "'I' is not always the author speaking of himself, but the voice of the human race speaking through him" (*The Poems of Tennyson*, p. 859). Furthermore, Tennyson claimed that *In Memoriam* was structured less as a diary or confession and more as a play: "the different moods of sorrow as in a drama are dramatically given" (p. 859). This is even more true in *Maud,* where the speaker was a madman and a murderer.

The speaker in the title poem of the 1855 volume is a young man obsessively in love with Maud, the daughter of the local landowner. However, her family opposes the match. His beautiful lyrics calling Maud to a secret tryst in the garden—"Come into the garden, Maud, / For the black bat, night, is flown"—are among the best known and most widely quoted sections of the poem (*The Poems of Tennyson*, p. 1075). However, Maud's brother comes to find her; the speaker kills him in a duel and is forced to flee the country. He then takes part in the Crimean War. (Tennyson's most famous poem on that war, "The Charge of the Light Brigade," was written in 1854 and collected in *Maud and Other Poems*.)

The monodrama is told in flashbacks, as the speaker returns to the scene of his crime and his lost love, haunted and burdened by memories that have driven him mad. While Tennyson had the family's "black blood," had suffered from depression, and had experienced family opposition to his romance with Rosa Baring and his engagement to Emily Sellwood—as well as watching the opposition faced by Hallam and Emily Tennyson—Tennyson was never a soldier, nor of course was he a murderer. Instead of wild action, he had waited patiently over a decade from 1840 to 1850, attempting to build up a career as a poet. Dramatic monologue enabled him to explore alternatives to his own life's path. Yet as expressed in *Maud* these alternatives confirm rather than reject social codes. The speaker of *Maud* is punished threefold for his crimes—he goes mad, he suffers the horrors of war, and he is haunted forever. To imagine alternatives was not necessarily to commend them.

RETURN OF THE KING

By the late 1850s, Tennyson was beginning to look backward. While memory and revision had been integral to his poetic since the beginning—for example the revisions of 1832 poems for *Poems* (1842) or the reuse of "Oh! that 'twere possible" from 1833 in *Maud* (1855)—such rewriting seemed only to intensify after the publication of *Maud*. Most significant in this respect was Tennyson's work on what would become a twelve-book sequence: *Idylls of the King* (1891).

Tennyson began writing the first of the *Idylls* in 1855 (with "Merlin and Vivien"), although the final sequence would include material written in 1833, and the collection would not be complete until 1874 nor published in its final arrangement until 1891. *Idylls of the King* thus represents nearly half a century of endeavor. Tennyson published "Enid," "Vivien," "Elaine," and "Guin-

evere" in 1859. For Tennyson, "Elaine" was a rewriting of "The Lady of Shalott" (1832), although the earlier poem had not been written as a version of the Elaine story.

Poems from Tennyson's 1870 volume *The Holy Grail* (1870) were later included in the *Idylls*: "Coming of Arthur," "The Holy Grail," "Pelleas and Ettarre," and "The Passing of Arthur" (including the "Morte d'Arthur," written after Hallam's death and published in *Poems* of 1842). "The Last Tournament" appeared in the *Contemporary Review* in 1871 and was published along with *Gareth and Lynette* the next year. "Balin and Balan" was written in 1872–1874 and published 1885 in *Tiresias and Other Poems*. The *Idylls* eventually comprised twelve books, published in 1891.

Such revision of the Arthurian myths, of Thomas Malory's *Morte d'Arthur,* and of his own poetry to create the *Idylls* was part of the broader pattern Tennyson exercised throughout his career, in which he regularly altered or reused his poems again and again. Moreover, he habitually edited poems between their first manuscript: through reading them aloud to friends and family, by making trial editions before submitting his poems to the press, and by reworking poems through various editions of the published collections. "Tiresias" (the title poem of the 1885 collection), for example, had been begun in the early 1830s, revised after the death of Hallam, and ultimately became the title poem of a collection published nearly fifty years later.

An Imperial Library edition of Tennyson's *Selected Works* (1872) encouraged this reformation of his canon. However, this did not mean that Tennyson was now able to erase early missteps from his oeuvre. Such was his popularity, and such the public demand for poems by him, that an early poem, "The Lover's Tale," which had been circulated in a prepublication form but excluded from *Poems, Chiefly Lyrical,* in 1832, was "mercilessly pirated" (*The Poems of Tennyson*, p. 299). This forced Tennyson to bring out his own edition in 1879. It does not seem to have been Tennyson's practice to suppress poems he no longer felt were print-worthy, but rather he rewrote or revised them.

In the title poem of *Locksley Hall Sixty Years After* (1886), this revisitation is both poetic and (in terms of the story) literal. The poet-speaker returns to Locksley Hall, the place where his cousin Amy had lived with the rich, titled husband she had married in the poet's stead. By now, the poet is sixty years older, Amy and her husband are dead, and the speaker takes his grandson, in a similar situation himself, to visit their graves and give advice.

The speaker looks back at his earlier anger, forgives the earlier hurt, and speaks of his long and happy life with the woman he married instead. He even revises the poem's original angry revulsion toward all women and toward foreigners—suggesting that the earlier invective was due to his dissatisfaction with the world in general. In "Locksley Hall," Tennyson had written, "O my cousin, shallow-hearted! O my Amy, mine no more!" (p. 691), her shallow feelings leading him to conclude, "Woman is the lesser man, and all thy passions, match'd with mine, / Are as moonlight unto sunlight, and as water unto wine" (p. 697). In his manuscript draft, the point had been made even stronger: woman's lesser emotions are "bounded by a shallower brain" (*The Poems of Tennyson*, p. 697). However, in "Locksley Hall Sixty Years After," by comparison, the speaker credits his wife Edith as "She with all the charm of woman, she with all the breadth of man" (p. 1361).

In the first "Locksley Hall" poem, the speaker's anger not only fuels invective and wild promises of convoluted revenge, but also prophecy:

For I dipt into the future, far as human eye could see,
Saw the Vision of the world, and all the wonder that would be:
Saw the heavens fill with commerce, argosies of magic sails,
Pilots of the purple twilight, dropping down with costly bales;

...

Till the war-drum throbbed no longer, and the battle-flags were furled
In the Parliament of man, the Federation of the World.

(pp. 695–696)

Yet sixty years after, the speaker is unable to conjure a second "Vision of the world"; he is old and tired and looks backward rather than into the future. In a letter written in April 1888, Tennyson complained to a friend that "the whole thing [*Locksley Hall Sixty Years After*] is dramatic impersonation, but I find in almost all modern criticism this absurd tendency to personalities. Some of my thought *may* comes out in the poem but am I therefore the hero?" (*Letters*, vol. 3, pp. 366–367).

Tennyson's relationship to his "hero" or speaker remained complex: "Locksley Hall Sixty Years After" is clearly influenced by episodes in Tennyson's autobiography of fifty years before. The earlier poem was written in about 1837–1838, as the engagement to Emily was faltering because of his social and financial standing and as Rosa Baring married a richer, older man. In "Sixty Years After," the speaker describes his later happiness with his wife, "Edith" (Tennyson had later married an Emily), and of his son "Leonard," who died young (Tennyson's second son Lionel had died in 1886—the year that *Locksley Hall Sixty Years After* was published—at the age of thirty-two).

Tennyson was adept at interweaving the personal and the impersonal—drawing equally on dramatic monologues or narratives from ancient Greece, the Orient, and Arthurian myths and on contemporary situations that seemed parallel to Tennyson's own. Tennyson's poems were not the "spontaneous overflow of powerful feeling," as Wordsworth had suggested in the preface to his own *Lyrical Ballads* (1798). Rather, Tennyson's creations were delayed, revised, depersonalized, fictionalized, and invented.

MATURE NEW DIRECTIONS

Tennyson's late revision, and his continued fascination with the past, was in creative tension with new forms. From the mid-1850s, Tennyson had been writing a verse novel, *Enoch Arden* (published in 1864), and from 1875, at the age of sixty-six, Tennyson began to write plays for the stage. Such a development seems obvious for a poet who had always structured his writing "as in a drama" and crafted the voices of his poetry as "dramatic impersonation." The voices of various women and men—as diverse as that of the "Northern Farmer" in the dialect of Lincolnshire, or that of a long-dead king—had been woven in with his own voice throughout his career.

For the next seventeen years, from 1875 right up to his death, Tennyson developed his dramatic writing for the stage, again drawing on historical and semimythological figures from British history. *Queen Mary* (1875) was about Mary I of England, with lute music written by Edward Elgar. *Harold* (1877) was based on the life of King Harold Goodwin (II) who was defeated and killed at the Battle of Hastings in 1066. *The Cup* (1884), a Roman tragedy based on Plutarch, had a run of more than three months at the Lyceum Theatre in London in 1881. *The Falcon* (1884) was developed from the fifth tale of Boccaccio's *Decameron* and performed at St. James' Theatre, London, in 1879. *Becket* (1884) was about St. Thomas Becket (the archbishop of Canterbury martyred in 1170). *The Promise of May* (1886; subtitled "A Village Tragedy"), Tennyson's only prose work, was vilified by the critics, and its run at the Globe Theatre in London lasted for only five weeks in 1882. *The Foresters; or, Robin Hood and Maid Marian,* with music by Arthur Sullivan, was performed successfully in New York in 1892 and less successfully in London the next year.

In his role as poet laureate, Tennyson wrote odes on contemporary events, such as his "Ode on Wellington" in 1852. The most famous of these is "The Charge of the Light Brigade," based on a report from the Crimean War that appeared in the London *Times* newspaper on November 13, 1854. These poems were, on the whole, ephemeral, occasional works on royal birthdays and weddings which had little effect on his reputation or later reception.

As Tennyson aged, he suffered from serious illnesses. In 1889, after he recovered from one of these bouts of ill health, he wrote "Crossing the Bar"—literally a reference to the Solent River on the way from the British mainland to the Isle of Wight (where he had lived for many years) but metaphorically a meditation on death, expressed as "when I put out to sea" (*The Poems of Tennyson*, p. 1458). In line with the poet's own wishes, this poem is usually printed at the end of all selections and editions of his work.

In 1889 Tennyson also published the volume *Demeter and Other Poems.* Tennyson was still using Greek myths (here of the search by the earth goddess Demeter for her daughter Persephone, who had been kidnapped by the god of the underworld, Hades) to make new poetry, but, as Tennyson explained to his son, "It is no use giving a mere *réchauffé* [reheating] of old legends," and so he imagines Demeter the earth goddess looking forward to the coming of Christ (p. 1373).

Tennyson died on October 6, 1892, at the age of eighty-three. Less than a month later, his final volume of poetry, *The Death of Oenone, Akbar's Dream, and Other Poems,* was published. Greek myths here again were of significance (Oenone was the wife Paris abandoned for Helen of Troy), but Eastern influences are also important (Akbar was the Indian Mogul emperor who reigned from 1542 to 1602, famous for his religious and racial tolerance). The next year Tennyson's last play, *The Foresters,* returned from a tour of the United States to open in London. He was buried in Poet's Corner in Westminster Abbey.

LATE AND POSTHUMOUS REPUTATION

Even in his later years, Tennyson's reputation was less elevated that it had been in the mid-nineteenth century. While *Becket* and *The Cup* had long and successful runs on stage, *The Promise of May* and *The Foresters* did not do well in the London theater. While the first *Idylls* sold ten thousand copies in six weeks, the completed *Idylls* had a divided reception from critics. Some found the later poetry overly long, with empty, flowery language. Thomas Carlyle, a longtime friend of Tennyson's, read the poems "with considerable impatience at being treated so very like infants, though the lollipops were so superlative" (Ricks, *Tennyson*, p. 258). Swinburne, in a 1872 pamphlet titled *Under the Micro-*

scope, argued that Tennyson's poetry was hide-bound by his Victorian morals. Henry James in *Mr. Tennyson's Drama* (1875) considered that Tennyson's failure as a poetic dramatist was matched only by his failure in the dramas to write as his did in his dramatic poems.

For his contemporaries Edward FitzGerald and Gerard Manley Hopkins, the late Tennyson was "Parnassian," a parody of himself with his "Tennysonianisms" (Ricks, *Tennyson*, p. 212). Several decades later, in the study *New Bearings on English Poetry* (1932), Leavis wrote of "late Victorian poetastery" (p. 12), in which "Tennysonian" was used as an uncomplimentary epithet to tar a whole generation and "Victorian poetry" became a term of abuse. Eliot's 1936 essay on *In Memoriam* praises that poem but at the expense of *Maud* and *The Princess*. Between the world wars, in fact, Tennyson's reputation was at its nadir. At no time, however, has Tennyson ever been ignored, though aspects of his work—his longer poems, his dramas, his philosophy—have gone in and out of favor.

In 1946, Auden (the preeminent of the poets of the 1930s) edited the volume *Tennyson: An Introduction and Selection*. By extensive quotation, Auden endorsed Harold Nicholson's view (from the 1925 volume *Tennyson: Aspects of His Life, Character, and Poetry*) of a poet of parts: who had come to be defined by his mid-Victorian, prissy, xenophobic, and dull period, exemplified by *Idylls of the King* and the verse novel *Enoch Arden*.

In 1960, John Killham collated some of the most significant twentieth-century criticism on Tennyson, with *Critical Essays on the Poetry of Tennyson*. This book included the essay on *In Memoriam* by Eliot already discussed. Furthermore, Cleanth Brook's chapter on "Tears, Idle Tears" from *The Well Wrought Urn* (1947), is reprinted, alongside Graham Hough's development of Brook's idea of the idleness, the lack of a specific context for the lament in Tennyson's poem, which is disputed in another essay published in the collection by Leo Spizter. The essays on Tennyson show serious attempts to critically engage with Tennyson's poetry, including his midcentury and late-Victorian works, rather than dismissing them. In 1962, the biographer Joanna Richardson claimed for Tennyson the accolade of "pre-eminent Victorian."

The real change in Tennyson's posthumous reputation, however, came in 1969, as the editors George MacBeth, in his influential *Penguin Book of Victorian Verse* (note, not "poetry"), and Isobel Armstrong, in *The Major Victorian Poets: Reconsiderations*, both put Tennyson at the center of the age. In the same year, Christopher Ricks produced the first complete edition of Tennyson's poetry since 1908. In 1972, Ricks produced the fundamental text for Tennyson studies, *Tennyson*. Robert Bernard Martin's biography *Tennyson: The Unquiet Heart* appeared in 1980.

At this point, the reconsideration of Tennyson was gaining momentum. In an essay about the poet for the Britsh Council series *British Writers* in 1981, Brian Southam assessed the situation this way:

> For many years the prevailing image of Tennyson has been of one of the great corruptors of English poetry, of a writer with a style so meretricious and insidiously molding that he misshaped the taste of generations of readers and the practice of generations of poets ... The refreshing challenge for anyone coming to Tennyson in the 1980's precisely is this question, for there is no commonly accepted view of his achievement.
>
> (p. 323)

In the early 1980s, the restrictions on Tennyson's personal manuscripts were lifted, thus giving new impetus to Tennyson studies. Ricks produced new editions of the poems (1987) and also a revision of his critical study (1989) to accommodate manuscript evidence, and with Aidan Day he published the thirty-one volumes of the manuscripts in facsimile (1987–1993). Tennyson's letters were edited by Cecil Y. Lang and Edgar F. Shannon (1982–1990), complementing new work on figures associated with Tennyson, such as the *Letters of Arthur Henry Hallam* (1981), edited by Kolb. New biographies appeared in the 1990s, by Michael Thorn (1992) and Peter Levi (1993).

From the late 1970s, meanwhile, Anglo-American criticism was also being re-formed by post-Marxist and poststructuralist theory. Terry Eagleton's 1978 article "Tennyson: Politics and Sexuality in *The Princess* and *In Memoriam*" encouraged debate of the longer poems according to gender criticism. Alan Sinfield's book for the Blackwell "Rereading Literature" series (1986) was the first book-length critical consideration of the possibility that *In Memoriam* might record Tennyson's romantic love for Hallam. Two years later, Marion Shaw's *Alfred Lord Tennyson* considered the poet's work from a feminist point of view.

The adjective "Victorian" was no longer necessarily an insult (see Kolb, 1983, p. 175), but the late-twentieth-century reevaluations of Tennyson and his time have meant that less effort has been put toward debating the "value" of his works; instead Tennyson studies have become more a means of understanding the Victorian context than literary engagement with his oeuvre. As Brian Southam put it, "No writer has ever dominated his age so completely as Tennyson dominated Victorian England ... His writing entered the consciousness of the age" (p. 323).

As the preeminent poet of his time, that is, Tennyson has become an invaluable tool for understanding the nineteenth century, a period of English world dominance and of unprecedented social, industrial, and scientific change. Roger Ebbatson, for instance, has written on nationalism and art in *Tennyson's English Idylls* (2003); Kathryn Ledbetter on the link between a growing media or newspaper culture and Tennyson's work in *Tennyson and Victorian Periodicals: Commodities in Context* (2007); and Cornelia Pearsall on the link between *In Memoriam* and contemporary religious movements in *Tennyson's Rapture: Transformation in the Victorian Dramatic Monologue* (2008).

Such changes in critical consideration have themselves been subject to scrutiny. Earlier considerations were more concerned with the impact of contemporary views on Tennyson's poetry, as in 1915 with Thomas R. Lounsbury's *The Life and Times of Tennyson*, which considered Tennyson's early criticism in periodicals and correspondence. Edgar Finley Shannon updated this important stage of Tennyson's literary development by looking at the early influence of critics on his writing up to 1851 in *Tennyson and*

the Reviewers: A Study of His Literary Reputation and of the Influence of the Critics upon His Poetry, 1827–1851 (1952). Hugh Sykes Davies gave Tennyson a chapter in the second volume of his work on *The Poets and Their Critics* (1962), and John D. Jump edited a collection of contemporary reviews of Tennyson, including those by Hallam and "Christopher North" on *Poems, Chiefly Lyrical*, in *Tennyson: The Critical Heritage* (1967).

Since the development of critical theory, however, the focus on Tennyson has moved to modern readings of twentieth- and twenty-first-century criticism—for example, Kolb's consideration in philological journals of late-twentieth-century critical "portraits of Tennyson" in an article by that title in 1983 or his article "Hallam, Tennyson, Homosexuality, and the Critics" in 2000. Laurence W. Mazzeno's 2004 volume *Alfred Tennyson: The Critical Legacy* suggests that the reactions of critics to the Victorian laureate reveals as much about themselves and the prejudices of their own times as it does about Tennyson and his poetry.

The many Tennysons projected by the poet and by his critics, and the variety of his voices and modes of writing, however, continues to excite interest. At the same time, the sheer lyric accessibility of his talent enables Tennyson to remain a staple of school and university curricula and remain still widely popular.

Selected Bibliography

WORKS OF ALFRED TENNYSON

FIRST EDITIONS

Poems by Two Brothers. London: Printed for W. Simpkin and R. Marshall ... and J. and J. Jackson, Louth, 1827. (With Frederick and Charles Tennyson.)

Timbuctoo: A Poem, Which Obtained the Chancellor's Medal... M.DCCC.XXIX. Cambridge: Pr. by J. Smith, 1829.

Poems Chiefly Lyrical. London: Effingham Wilson, 1830.

Poems. London: E. Moxon, 1833.

Poems. London: E. Moxon, 1842.

The Princess: A Medley. London: E. Moxon, 1847.

In Memoriam. London: E. Moxon, 1850. (Published anonymously.)

Maud, and Other Poems. London: Edward Moxon, 1855.

Idylls of the King. London:, E. Moxon, 1859 (Includes "Enid", "Vivien", "Elaine" and "Guinevere").

Enoch Arden. London: E. Moxon, 1864.

The Holy Grail and Other Poems. London: Strahan and Co., 1870.

The Window; or, The Song of the Wrens. With music by Arthur Sullivan. London: Strahan, 1871.

Gareth and Lynette [and The Last Tournament]. London: Strahan, 1872.

The Works of Alfred Tennyson London: Strahan & Co., 1872–1873 (Imperial Library edition in 6 vols).

Queen Mary: A Drama. London: Henry S. King, 1875.

Harold: A Drama. London: Henry S. King & Co. 1877.

The Lover's Tale (The Golden Supper). London: C. Kegan Paul, 1879.

Ballads, and Other Poems. London: Kegan Paul & Co., 1880.

The Cup and the Falcon. London: Macmillan & Co., 1884.

Becket. London: Macmillan & Co., 1884.

Tiresias and Other Poems. London: Macmillan & Co., 1885.

Locksley Hall Sixty Years After. London: Macmillan & Co., 1886. (Includes *The Promise of May,* a drama.)

Demeter and Other Poems. London: Macmillan & Co., 1889.

Daphne and Other Poems. London: Macmillan & Co., 1891.

The Death of Oenone, Akbar's Dream, and Other Poems. London: Macmillan & Co., 1892.

The Foresters: Robin Hood and Maid Marian. London: Macmillan & Co., 1892.

CRITICAL EDITIONS

Tennyson: An Introduction and a Selection. Edited by W. H. Auden. London: Phoenix House, 1946.

The Poems of Tennyson. Edited by Christopher Ricks. London: Longmans, 1969. (This essay quotes from the single-volume, 1969 edition; a revised second edition of this collection, 1987, was published in three volumes and incorporates more manuscript evidence.)

The Letters of Alfred Lord Tennyson. 3 vols. Edited by Cecil Y. Lang and Edgar F. Shannon. Oxford: Clarendon Press, 1982–1990.

The Tennyson Archive. Edited by Christopher Ricks and Aiden Day. 31 vols. New York and London: Garland, 1987–1993.

CRITICAL AND BIOGRAPHICAL STUDIES

Armstrong, Isobel, ed. *The Major Victorian Poets: Reconsiderations*, London: Routledge & Kegan Paul, 1969.

Baum, Paull Franklin. *Tennyson: Sixty Years After*. Chapel Hill: University of North Carolina Press, 1948.

Bloom, Harold. "Tennyson: In the Shadow of Keats." In his *Poetry and Repression*. New Haven, Conn.: Yale University Press, 1976. Pp. 143–174.

Davies, Hugh Sykes. *The Poets and Their Critics*. London, Hutchinson Educational, 1962. Vol. 2, pp. 243–295.

Eagleton, Terry. "Tennyson: Politics and Sexuality in *The Princess* and *In Memoriam*." In *1848: The Sociology of Literature*. Edited by Francis Barker et al. Colchester, U.K.: University of Essex, 1978. Pp. 77–106.

Ebbatson, Roger. *Tennyson's English Idylls: History, Narrative, Art*. Lincoln, Nebr.: Tennyson Society, 2003.

Hallam, Arthur Henry. *Remains in Verse and Prose*. Edited by Henry Hallam. London: W. Nichol, 1834. (Including "Theodicaea Novissima.")

James, Henry. *Mr. Tennyson's Drama*. New York: Sheldon, 1875.

Jump, John D. *Tennyson: The Critical Heritage*. London: Routledge & Kegan Paul, 1967.

Killham, John, ed. *Critical Essays on the Poetry of Tennyson*. London: Routledge & Kegan Paul, 1960 (Includes T. S. Eliot, "*In Memoriam*", pp. 208–215; Cleanthe Brooks, "The Motivation of Tennyson's Weeper", pp. 177–185; Graham Hough, "'Tears, Idle Tears,'" pp. 186–191; Leo Spitzer, "'Tears, Idle Tears', Again", pp. 192–203.).

Kolb, Jack. "Emily Tennyson and Arthur Hallam." *Review of English Studies* 28, no. 109:32–48 (1977).

———. "Hallam, Tennyson, Homosexuality, and the Critics." *Philological Quarterly* 79, no. 3:365–396 (summer 2000).

———. "Portraits of Tennyson." *Modern Philology* 81, no. 2:173–190 (November 1983).

Ledbetter, Kathryn. *Tennyson and Victorian Periodicals: Commodities in Context*. Aldershot, U.K.: Ashgate, 2007.

Leavis, F. R. *The Living Principle*. Oxford: Oxford University Press, 1975.

———. *New Bearings in English Poetry: A Study of the Contemporary Situation*. Ann Arbor: University of Michigan Press, 1932. Reprint 1960.

Levi, Peter. *Tennyson*. London: Macmillan, 1993.

Lounsbury, Thomas R. *The Life and Times of Tennyson (from 1809–1850)*. New Haven, Conn.: Yale University Press, 1915.

Martin, Robert Bernard. *Tennyson: The Unquiet Heart*. London: Faber & Faber, 1983.

Mazzeno, Laurence W. *Alfred Tennyson: The Critical Legacy*. Woodbridge, U.K.: Boydell & Brewer, 2004.

Nicholson, Harold. *Tennyson: Aspects of His Life, Character, and Poetry*. London: Constable, 1923.

Pearsall, Cornelia D. J. *Tennyson's Rapture: Transformation in the Victorian Dramatic Monologue*. New York: Oxford University Press, 2008.

Richardson, Joanna. *The Pre-eminent Victorian: A Study of Tennyson*. London: Jonathan Cape, 1962.

Ricks, Christopher Bruce. *Tennyson*. London: Macmillan, 1972. Rev. ed. 1989.

Shannon, Edgar Finley. *Tennyson and the Reviewers: A Study of His Literary Reputation and of the Influence of the Critics upon His Poetry, 1827–1851*. Cambridge, Mass: Harvard University Press, 1952.

Shaw, Marion. *Alfred Lord Tennyson*. Hemel Hempstead, U.K.: Harvester, 1988.

Sinfield, Alan. *Alfred Tennyson*. Oxford: Blackwell, 1986.

Southam, Brian. "Alfred Tennyson." In *British Writers*. Edited by Ian Scott-Kilvert. Vol. 4. New York: Charles Scribner's Sons, 1981.

Swinburne, A. C., *Under the Microscope*. London: D. White, 1871.

Tennyson, Charles. *Alfred Tennyson*. London: Macmillan, 1949. Reprint 1968.

Tennyson, Hallam. *Alfred Lord Tennyson, a Memoir: By His Son*. 2 vols. London: Macmillan, 1897.

———. *Tennyson and His Friends*. London: Macmillan, 1912.

Thorn, Michael. *Tennyson*. London: Little, Brown, 1992.

DYLAN THOMAS

(1914—1953)

J. C. Bittenbender

ONE OF THE most mythologized of writers, Dylan Marlais Thomas has sustained his mystique into the twenty-first century. Thomas's life was as impassioned and as complex as his work, filled with joyful revelry as well as poignant longing and the darkest of despair. A poet of rich lyricism, Thomas also was accomplished as a writer of short fiction, radio and film scripts, and short pieces of criticism. Like many other great modern writers of the twentieth century he shared a love-hate relationship with his country of birth, in his case Wales, which finds expression in his work. As with James Joyce and Ireland, Thomas ultimately reflects a deeply felt connection to Wales and to the Celtic traditions he often addresses and revitalizes for the modern world. Thomas' poetry shows the interconnectedness of the natural world with the often obscure and troubled nature of human consciousness, while his fiction articulates a sense of place, often the life of the small town or village in Wales.

LIFE

Thomas was born on October 27, 1914, at 5 Cwmdonkin Drive in Swansea, Wales. The city of Swansea and surrounding towns of the southwest coast of Wales, such as Laugharne, would figure largely in his work. His father, David John (D.J.) Thomas was a schoolteacher who instilled a profound love of books in Dylan, and especially a love of Shakespeare. His mother, Florence Hannah Thomas, was a seamstress; he also had a sister, Nancy, eight years older than Dylan. As a boy and young man he had a playful nature. Indeed, concealed jokes can be detected in some of his fiction (as well as in the play *Under Milk Wood*). He liked to play tricks on people throughout his life, and misreadings of his intentions,

whether literary or otherwise, became a part of his story. He started writing poetry in school, and some of his juvenile poems found their way into school magazines. Throughout his life he presented an acute sense of his own impending destruction, and this can be seen even in his earliest poetry and fiction. He served for a while as a reporter for the *South Wales Daily Post* and as an amateur actor, cultivating the voice that would become so popular later in his life. In 1932 Thomas left Wales for London, and much of the rest of that decade and the war years would be spent in that city.

In 1934 his first poetry collection, *18 Poems,* based on writing from his notebooks, was published. In 1936 he published his second collection, *Twenty-five Poems.* While in London he met his future wife, Caitlin MacNamara, a dancer whose family was from Ireland. Dylan and Caitlin were married in Cornwall on July 11, 1937. Their tempestuous relationship has become legendary, much like those of other great modernist writers and their spouses such as D. H. Lawrence (whose poetry had an influence on Thomas) and Sylvia Plath. Despite rumors of infidelity assigned to both Dylan and Caitlin, their relationship remained a central focus of Thomas' life and writing. Dylan and Caitlin had two sons, Llewelyn and Colm, and a daughter, Aeronwy. In the early 1940s Thomas began writing scripts in London for Strand Films. In 1939 he produced his third collection of poetry, *The Map of Love,* which includes seven prose pieces, and he published a collection of roughly autobiographical stories, *A Portrait of the Artist as a Young Dog,* in 1940. An unfinished prose work, *Adventures in the Skin Trade,* was attempted at this time as well, but found publication only in 1955, after Thomas' death. During and shortly after the war years in London, Thomas worked as a radio broadcaster for the BBC, a documentary scriptwriter, and a creator of other film scripts. He eventually made a number of return trips to Wales, and many of his final poems were composed in his "writing shed" at the Boat House, the Thomases' home overlooking the Bristol Channel in Laugharne, Wales.

In 1950 Thomas began visiting the United States and going on lecture and poetry reading tours. This would lead to the production in 1953 of his "play for voices," *Under Milk Wood* (in an unfinished form), in New York shortly before his death. His reputation for drinking has become mythologized, as has his death in New York on November 5, 1953, after supposedly saying, "I've had eighteen straight whiskies. I think that's the record." As a number of critics have pointed out, these were not his last words, and the causes of Thomas's death are more complicated than the legend. However, his tragic ending (the official cause was an "insult to the brain") and the lyricism of his verse have contributed to a cult following that to some extent lives on in the twenty-first century.

THE COLLECTED POEMS

Although Thomas published a number of individual volumes of poems, the most widely accepted and authoritative collection of his work is *The Collected Poems of Dylan Thomas, 1934–1952* (1953). This volume includes poems that were selected by Thomas as representative of his poetic work (page references to poems reflect the pagination in *The Collected Poems* and not pagination from the individual volumes). The book is notable for its inclusion of "Author's Prologue," which Thomas describes in a note that precedes the poem as a "prologue in verse, written for this collected edition of my poems … intended as an address to my readers, the strangers" (p. xiii). The poem immediately announces to the first-time reader of Thomas the beauties and complexities of his verse style and themes:

This day winding down now
At God speeded summer's end

In the torrent salmon sun,
In my seashaken house
On a breakneck of rocks …

(p. xv)

Like his life, Thomas' poetry, as represented in these lines, often seems to present a voice on the threshold between the natural world and what can only ever be a tentative sense of human certainty. There is often something of Gerard Manley Hopkins in Thomas' verse, and it is evident here in lines such as "God speeded summer's end." Alliteration is part of Thomas' style and indicates his ever keen appreciation of the modulations of language. His verse is often sound-driven and exhibits a profound appreciation for the oral. His poetry is meant to be spoken aloud, and the voices of his poems seem directed at both the ear and the heart simultaneously. There is much in Thomas's best poetry that displays those talents that served him well as a scriptwriter for radio, a medium that depends on sound alone to convey meaning. Later lines in the prologue address the readers/strangers themselves:

At poor peace I sing
To you strangers (though song
Is a burning and crested act,
The fire of birds in
The world's turning wood,
For my sawn, splay sounds),
Out of these seathumbed leaves
That will fly and fall
Like leaves of trees and as soon
Crumble and undie
Into the dogdayed night.

(pp. xv–xvi)

As one becomes familiar with Thomas' personal life, the "poor peace" resonates as a form of resignation, especially considering that the poem, as well as the collection itself, was prepared a year before the poet's tragic death in 1953. The "sawn, splay sounds" hint at that irregular yet rhythmic quality of Thomas' poetry that unites lyric beauty and thematic complexity. Here as well are the portmanteau words that he crafts throughout his verse work, such as "seathumbed leaves" and "dogdayed night." As the poem progresses it becomes a song of invitation to the reader to the rest of Thomas' work as well as a tribute to Wales and the larger, natural world. By the end the speaker and, seemingly, the reader inhabit an ark that acts as a conduit between the human and natural world:

We will ride out alone, and then,
Under the stars of Wales,
Cry, Multitudes of arks! Across
The water lidded lands,
Manned with their loves they'll move,
Like wooden islands, hill to hill.
Huloo, my prowed dove with a flute!
Ahoy, old, sea-legged fox,
Tom tit and Dai mouse!
My ark sings in the sun
At God speeded summer's end
And the flood flowers now.

(p. xviii)

18 POEMS

In *The Collected Poems,* the order in which the poems are presented often reflects the order in which they were originally published in separate, earlier editions. One of the most powerful poems from *18 Poems* (1934) is "The force that through the green fuse drives the flower." Here, the passage of time and mortality merge and an unknown energy surges through the natural world, joining it with the human:

The force that through the green fuse drives the flower
Drives my green age; that blasts the roots of trees
Is my destroyer. And I am dumb to tell the crooked rose
My youth is bent by the same wintry fever.

(p. 10)

A theme of the impossibility of articulation suggests itself here, as the speaker is "dumb" (as elsewhere in the poem) to tell of his experience of how the two worlds of experience inform one another: "And I am dumb to tell the lover's tomb / How at my sheet goes the same crooked worm" (p. 10). Thomas' world is often a haunted, mystical world, which reflects to an extent his early interest in the supernatural and the Welsh folklore and stories that he absorbed as a young

boy. These same interests serve their purpose in his stories and in *Under Milk Wood.* The poem expresses the vulnerability of the individual soul in a condition that may possibly result in destruction: "The force … is my destroyer."

Criticism of Thomas often focuses on the complexity, if not the outright obscurity, of his work. Thomas believed in the vitality of paradox, and contradictions and tensions increased in his poems as his career progressed. He articulated his philosophy of poetic complexity in a letter to his friend Charles Fisher: "I like things that are difficult to write and difficult to understand.… contradicting my images, saying two things at once in one word, four in two words and one in six" (quoted in Ferris, 2000, p. 83). Another poem that bears out this interest is "Light breaks where no sun shines," another piece from *18 Poems.* Here, natural imagery is used to suggest a cosmic connection between the form of the human body and the mystical, inexplicable workings of the external world:

Light breaks where no sun shines;
Where no sea runs, the waters of the heart
Push in their tides;
And, broken ghosts with glow-worms in their heads,
The things of light
File through the flesh where no flesh decks the bones.

(p. 29)

An almost epiphanic understanding is achieved in the poem through the illumination of the body, and the intersection of the flesh, eye sockets, and skull are infused with a light of spiritual proportions. There is plenty of water imagery in Thomas's poetry, which may in some ways be a reflection of the importance the coast of Wales played in his life and work.

A focus on the body can be detected as well in the poem "Before I knocked," in which Thomas attempts to formulate a metaphysical connection between the physical human body and the forces of nature:

Before I knocked and flesh let enter,
With liquid hands tapped on the womb,
I who was shapeless as the water
That shaped the Jordan near my home

339

Was brother to Mnetha's daughter
And sister to the fathering worm.

(p. 8)

Another Thomas characteristic seen here is engagement with a mythology of the human soul. References to Blake's "Mnetha" and the river Jordan implicate the body in a larger, universal mythology that transcends time. It is as if nature and myth coalesce to create the physical human form. The speaker of the poem projects his future through signs from both the natural and the mythic worlds. Notable too is Thomas' predilection for metapoetics. The poem adds that which is human to the script of what is to be read upon the face of nature:

As yet ungotten, I did suffer;
The rack of dreams my lily bones
Did twist into a living cipher,
And flesh was snipped to cross the lines
Of gallow crosses on the liver
And brambles in the wringing brains.

(p. 8)

Here the speaker is "yet ungotten" but writes himself alive on the natural landscape. The final two stanzas further bring into focus Thomas' interest in joining the notion of a preconceived state of existence with another abstract state of "nonexistence," death:

I, born of flesh and ghost, was neither
A ghost nor man, but mortal ghost.
And I was struck down by death's feather.
I was mortal to the last
Long breath that carried to my father
The message of his dying christ.
You who bow down at cross and altar,
Remember me and pity Him
Who took my flesh and bone for armour
And doublecrossed my mother's womb.

(p. 9)

Thomas aligns his image of a potential fleshless birth and death with the condition of Christ's own substantiation. God ("Him") here seems to assume the "armour" of Christ as he "doublecrossed" the womb of Mary in establishing a metaphysical birth. Thomas' attitudes toward religion often seem shrouded in mystery, but, as

displayed in this poem, he was able to tap into the power of mystery that religion offers to serve his poetic purposes.

Another early poem that engages with the bodily as well as the mystical is "Where once the waters of your face." Here the body aligns itself with a world in which myth and the rhythms of nature are merged:

Where once the waters of your face
Spun to my screws, your dry ghost blows,
The dead turns up its eye;
Where once the mermen through your ice
Pushed up their hair, the dry wind steers
Through salt and root and roe.

(p. 12)

The ebb and flow of the ocean, as represented in the poem, lends a hypnotic quality to the verse and highlights a rhythm that may also suggest human love. The speaker is addressing an auditor, and the forces of nature appear at times to connect the two individuals despite the actions of the natural world that may either bind or separate them from one another: "Invisible, your clocking tides / Break on the lovebeds of the weeds; / The weed of love's left dry" (p. 12). The poem questions, or at the very least reevaluates, faith, indicating again the anxieties of modern consciousness:

Dry as a tomb, your coloured lids
Shall not be latched while magic glides
Sage on the earth and sky;
There shall be corals in your beds,
There shall be serpents in your tides,
Till all our sea-faiths die.

(p. 12)

Here the elements of the natural world appear to be dependent on the "magic" that may or may not be related to traditional religious belief but which certainly seems at one with a larger "sea-faith" that combines the metaphysical and the natural.

TWENTY-FIVE POEMS

Thomas' second collection of poetry, *Twenty-five*

340

Poems, was published in 1936, but most of its poems had been written before those that made up his first volume (Ferris, 2000, p. 77). Though poems from the second volume continue to exhibit complexity, and Thomas' meditative flow can still be detected, the collection contains some early poems, such as "Ears in the turrets hear" and "The hand that signed the paper," that are easier for the reader to comprehend. Readers of these poems, and especially "Ears in the turrets hear," who come to them with the recognition of the strange publishing chronology, will further understand Thomas' interest in anatomical metaphors.

Ears in the turrets hear
Hands grumble on the door,
Eyes in the gables see
The fingers at the locks.
Shall I unbolt or stay
Alone till the day I die
Unseen by stranger-eyes
In this white house?
Hands, hold you poison or grapes?

(p. 67)

The tension between the embodied "white house" or fortress and the "Hands" that attempt to enter soon transforms into a broader, natural image. In the two stanzas that follow, the body becomes identified with an island:

Beyond this island bound
By a thin sea of flesh
And a bone coast,
The land lies out of sound
And the hills out of mind.
No birds or flying fish
Disturbs this island's rest.
Ears in this island hear
The wind pass like a fire,
Eyes in this island see
Ships anchor off the bay.
Shall I run to the ships
With the wind in my hair,
Or stay till the day I die
And welcome no sailor?
Ships, hold you poison or grapes?

(p. 67)

The earlier, mysterious "Hands" now translate into the sailor and ships that may offer the vital-ity of grapes or the dangers of poison. The island and its elements become one with the senses as they calculate the risk of interaction with an unknown other. The concluding lines of the poem offer a coalescing of images where the speaker (now more identifiable as such because of his questioning voice) contemplates admitting the sailor/stranger into/onto the house/island:

Hands grumble on the door,
Ships anchor off the bay,
Rain beats the sand and slates.
Shall I let in the stranger,
Shall I welcome the sailor,
Or stay till the day I die?
Hands of the stranger and holds of the ships,
Hold you poison or grapes?

(p. 68)

At some level the poem seems to be a meditation on the risks of intimacy or the unknowable dangers to the self through interaction with an external and potentially threatening other. With the question "Or stay till the day I die?" the speaker also seems to hint that the consequences of isolation might be even more damaging than those resulting from engagement with another.

A hand also appears in "The hand that signed the paper," another early poem that found its way into *Twenty-five Poems.* The synecdoche of the poem works to focus on the power of writing and its potential abuses by humans:

The hand that signed the paper felled a city;
Five sovereign fingers taxed the breath,
Doubled the globe of dead and halved a country;
These five kings did a king to death.

(p. 71)

Throughout the poem, Thomas focuses on the finality of the written word as a force that has the ability to compromise other forms of peaceful communication: "A goose's quill has put an end to murder / That put an end to talk" (p. 71). The quill, fashioned from an animal, has been used by "Man" to silence fruitful discussion. The danger that a writing implement can hold in the hand of a particular person increases as the poem progresses: "Great is the hand that holds dominion over / Man by a scribbled name" (p. 71). For

DYLAN THOMAS

Thomas, a larger and more spirited force can be detected in the inscriptions of the natural world. Here, though, interaction of pen and hand suggests a threat that is more manufactured and less organic. The implied critique is of forms of writing that exert tyranny not only in a political sense but a religious one as well, for writings that lay claim to absolute truth are also subject to scrutiny. This point is emphasized in a broad sense in the final lines: "A hand rules pity as a hand rules heaven; / Hands have no tears to flow" (p. 71). Perhaps Thomas is suggesting that pity and heaven are beyond the dictates of human forms of writing. Hands may use the ink from the pen; but true spirit and soul, as represented by tears, reside outside the power of written forms of control as represented by the word "dominion."

The word "dominion" figures elsewhere in Thomas' work, notably in another poem from *Twenty-five Poems,* "And death shall have no dominion." In this poem, one of Thomas's most popular, he displays his style of repeating lines to create a lilting, oral effect as the mantra "And death shall have no dominion" recurs at the beginning and end of each stanza. The poem conveys a meditative tone, and death is represented as another force seeking to conquer the human and natural worlds. Scholars suggest that the predominance of the theme of death in Thomas poems can often be traced to periods when his father was suffering from life-threatening illnesses; "Do not go gentle into that good night" is the best-known example. Defying death is central to "And death shall have no dominion" as well:

And death shall have no dominion.
Dead men naked they shall be one
With the man in the wind and the west moon;
When their bones are picked clean and the clean bones
  gone,
They shall have stars at elbow and foot;
Though they go mad they shall be sane,
Though they sink through the sea they shall rise again;
Though lovers be lost love shall not;
And death shall have no dominion.

(p. 77)

Though death will come, it will not be victorious. Thomas positions human integration with the natural world as a certain way of denying death the territorial possessions it seeks. The durability of the human power to withstand death is seen throughout the poem: "Faith in their hands shall snap in two, / And the unicorn evils run them through; / Split all ends up they shan't crack" (p. 77). Death is as much a theoretical concept as religion and mythology and holds no power over the substantial nature of being human.

The final poem in *Twenty-five Poems,* "Altarwise by owl-light," is a ten-part sonnet sequence that is often cited as being one of Thomas' most popular poems. The title alone signifies the poet's continuing interest in combining symbols taken from human concepts, such as religion, and those taken from the natural world. The interweaving of specifically Christian imagery with philosophical considerations of birth and death dominate the poem. In one of the most powerful sonnets (VII) from the sequence, Thomas again engages with notions of how writing serves to bring together different forms of human experience:

Now stamp the Lord's Prayer on a grain of rice,
A Bible-leaved of all the written woods
Strip to this tree: a rocking alphabet,
Genesis in the root, the scarecrow word,
And one light's language in the book of trees.
Doom on deniers at the wind-turned statement.
Time's tune my ladies with the teats of music,
The scaled sea-sawers, fix in a naked sponge
Who sucks the bell-voiced Adam out of magic,
Time, milk, and magic, from the world beginning.
Time is the tune my ladies lend their heartbreak,
From bald pavilions and the house of bread
Time tracks the sound of shape on man and cloud,
On rose and icicle the ringing handprint.

(pp. 83–84)

Here again, the importance of reading the inscribed world becomes paramount to Thomas' poetic metaphysics. That act of reading is complex and inclusive of signs that are not typically recognized as markers of meaning. For Thomas the idea of text is greater than the page and includes a canvas that encompasses and unifies "time, milk, and magic." Here even the senses transcend the limited powers they traditionally command as "Time tracks the sound of shape on man and cloud, / On rose and icicle the ringing handprint."

THE MAP OF LOVE

Thomas' next collection of poems, *The Map of Love,* was published in 1939 and includes both poems and short stories. This volume explores some new themes that expand on his earlier interests in nature, death, and the act of writing. The impending war in Europe can be felt in the background of many of the poems, as can the complexity of Thomas' love for his wife, Caitlin, whom he had married in 1937. The collection also offers poems with a local Welsh geographical flavor, an interest his earlier published poems largely avoided. Thomas's fiction and radio plays mostly concern life in small-town Wales and specifically areas that were familiar to him, such as Swansea and Laugharne. With the increasing use of notebook material from earlier periods in his life to fill out volumes of poetry, Thomas's abiding love for Wales and his special interest in conveying a sense of place become more recognizable in poetic form.

"I make this in a warring absence" is a poem that concerns itself with the absence of love, specifically the love that Caitlin provided for Thomas. Originally titled "Poem for Caitlin," the lost object of love is figured as a ship that has wandered out to sea:

I make this in a warring absence when
Each ancient, stone-necked minute of love's season
Harbours my anchored tongue, slips the quaystone,
When, praise is blessed, her pride in mast and fountain
Sailed and set dazzling by the handshaped ocean,
In that proud sailing tree with branches driven
Through the last vault and vegetable groyne, ...

(p. 87)

Critics suggest that the poem refers to Caitlin's infidelity, tendencies of which were being diagnosed by Thomas even shortly after their marriage (Ferris, 2000, p. 154). This is a sexually charged poem, rife with potential Freudian interpretations. There is, however, a quality of deeply felt loss, as if the idealized love that Dy-

lan and Caitlin shared has suffered a tremendous blow, and all of nature, as represented by a wealth of sea imagery, has suffered devastation as well. In the end, though, there is a note of return and forgiveness as the speaker seems to swallow his pain in the renewed presence of his altered, but now no longer absent, love:

Now in the cloud's big breast lie quiet countries,
Delivered seas my love from her proud place
Walks with no wound, nor lightning in her face,
A calm wind blows that raised the trees like hair
Once where the soft snow's blood was turned to ice.
And though my love pulls the pale, nippled air,
Prides of to-morrow suckling in her eyes,
Yet this I make in a forgiving presence.

(p. 89)

Another Thomas poem that makes use of water imagery is "We lying by seasand." The "we" of this poem may or may not be Caitlin, but it is in any case someone who seems to share the unique vision of the speaker, who attempts to perceive a unity of experience that brings together the illusions of difference represented by sea and land, sound and silence. Like Hopkins, Thomas in this poem makes much use of alliteration and a form of sprung rhythm to capture the ebb and flow of the sea and its interaction with the landscape:

We lying by seasand, watching yellow
And the grave sea, mock who deride
Who follow the red rivers, hollow
Alcove of words out of cicada shade,
For in this yellow grave of sand and sea
A calling for colour calls with the wind
That's grave and gay as grave and sea
Sleeping on either hand.

(p. 91)

One of Thomas' first "local" poems is "After the funeral," in which he pays tribute to his aunt, Ann Jones, a resident of Fernhill, the farm where Thomas spent a good portion of his time as a boy and which figures prominently in his short stories as well as in the beautiful poem "Fern Hill." In "After the funeral," Thomas makes Ann the subject of the poem and elevates her from his own position as "Ann's bard" (p. 96). He remembers her for the way in which her "fountain heart once fell in puddles / Round the parched worlds of Wales" (p. 96). He praises Ann as a benefactor to the natural world:

But I, Ann's bard on a raised hearth, call all
The seas to service that her wood-tongued virtue
Babble like a bellbuoy over the hymning heads,
Bow down the walls of the ferned and foxy woods ...

(p. 96)

Where earlier in the poem there appeared a "stuffed fox and a stale fern," here, through the vitality of the language used to praise her, these dead objects from nature are revivified by what seems to be the life-giving power of verse. Though Ann is dead and "monumental," the memory of her, as preserved in the poem, is able to resurrect the fox and the fern:

And sculptured Ann is seventy years of stone.
These cloud-sopped, marble hands, this monumental
Argument of the hewn voice, gesture and psalm,
Storm me forever over her grave until
The stuffed lung of the fox twitch and cry Love
And the strutting fern lay seeds on the black sill.

(p. 97)

A rather opaque poem from *The Map of Love,* "How shall my animal," returns Thomas to a poetry of the self that is more in keeping with his usual subject matter. Here, though, he links a consideration of the self with that of poetic inspiration. In the poem the "animal" appears to be the creative force inside the writer/Thomas that is seeking a valid and fulfilling outlet of expression. The poem becomes a metapoetic meditation on how the inner life of the poet might become lost or radically altered once the ideas and the spirit behind the words become committed to the page:

How shall my animal
Whose wizard shape I trace in the cavernous skull,
Vessel of abscesses and exultation's shell,
Endure burial under the spelling wall,
The invoked, shrouding veil at the cap of the face,
Who should be furious,
Drunk as a vineyard snail, flailed like an octopus,
Roaring, crawling, quarrel
With the outside weathers,

The natural circle of the discovered skies
Draw down to its weird eyes?

(p. 100)

To be buried under the "spelling wall" suggests that a certain freedom is sacrificed by the writer who has to harness inspiration (the "animal") in order to share it with the outside world. Here language may be considered as a type of "wall" that contains the imagination through definition, tradition, and conformity to certain types of interpretation. Later, in the third stanza of the poem, the speaker draws an analogy between the work of a fisherman and his own poetic project as he "angles" for a particular vision of the world:

Fishermen of mermen
Creep and harp on the tide, sinking their charmed, bent pin
With bridebait of gold bread, I with a living skein,
Tongue and ear in the thread, angle the temple-bound
Curl-locked and animal cavepools of spells and bone,
Trace out a tentacle, ...

(p. 101)

The writer's net is "living" as long as the inspiration is not killed by the sterility of an intransigent meaning. In the final stanza the "animal" becomes fully realized in the shape of a "bird" and ultimately a "beast" that seems to take over from the writer and in some ways turn against him: "Lie dry, rest robbed, my beast. / You have kicked from a dark den, leaped up the whinnying light, / And dug your grave in my breast" (p. 101). There seems to be a return to the source with these lines. Perhaps Thomas is signaling the sense that the work/poem comes home to be refurbished by the poet and offered new life. It may also suggest the artistic sacrifice that is made when the living language runs the risk of dying on the page.

Two more personal poems appear toward the end of *The Map of Love.* "A saint about to fall" weaves together the anticipation of a new child and the impending war in Europe (Ferris, 2000, p. 164). In this haunting poem Thomas places images of birth and nourishment alongside those of destruction and death. The threat of the falling bombs is joined with the joy of the baby to be "dropped" from the womb. In "Twenty-four years," Thomas offers the reader one of the many "birthday" poems that he would write in moments of fearful self-reflection:

Twenty-four years remind the tears of my eyes.
(Bury the dead for fear that they walk to the grave in
  labour.)
In the groin of the natural doorway I crouched like a
  tailor
Sewing a shroud for a journey
By the light of the meat-eating sun.

(p. 110)

A poem such as this one highlights the often tragic relationship that Thomas had with himself. The self-doubt and foreboding in this and other poems show that as Thomas' career progressed he was less sure of the future, particularly in terms of his life and creative ability. Here the speaker is preparing to set out but is not doing so with any sense of joyful anticipation. Instead there is uncertainty yet also a sense of the unavoidable, as in these final lines:

Dressed to die, the sensual strut begun,
With my red veins full of money,
In the final direction of the elementary town
I advance for as long as forever is.

(p. 110)

The fatalism of these lines does not suggest a poet who is optimistically setting out on the road to success. Rather, these are the words of a depressed individual resigned to follow the road to that "elementary town" because it is the only avenue available.

DEATHS AND ENTRANCES

Another "birthday poem," though one of quite a different nature, is "Poem in October," which appears early in Thomas' penultimate poetry volume, *Deaths and Entrances*, published in 1946. This poem exudes the themes of personal memory that characterize his short fiction and that find voice as well in classic Thomas poems such as "Fern Hill" and "Over Sir John's Hill." One of his more accessible poems, it moves from moments of reflection on the speaker's thirtieth birthday to memories of his youth. Though not as

depressing as "Twenty-four years," the poem does open with a slightly morbid view of life as a journey to death:

It was my thirtieth year to heaven
Woke to my hearing from harbour and neighbour
  wood
And the mussel pooled and the heron
Priested shore
The morning beckon
With water praying and the call of seagull and rook
And the knock of sailing boats on the net webbed
  wall
Myself to set foot
That second
In the still sleeping town and set forth.

(p. 113)

Here again we have a birthday speaker setting forth on a journey, but in this poem the itinerary includes a journey to a happier time in youth. Thomas' boyhood memories are displayed with great merit in his short stories, particularly his early stories and those in the collection *Portrait of the Artist as a Young Dog*. Additionally, his finely tuned sense of place, character, and the nature of small-town coastal Wales is to be later capitalized upon in the "play for voices," *Under Milk Wood*, and stories such as "A Child's Christmas in Wales" and "Quite Early One Morning." Perhaps more than any other collection of poems, *Deaths and Entrances* serves as a poetic journey of memory to Thomas' past and the places that concerned him as a youth. Poems such as "The Hunchback in the Park" and "Fern Hill" characterize Thomas' shift toward writing memory poems that attempt at some level to reclaim the beauty and innocence of his lost youth.

He introduces that atmosphere of return with "Poem in October," where the speaker's interactions with nature are less metaphysical and more in touch with a sensed experience that is not intellectualized or approached by way of a stream-of-consciousness style of composition. However, the interconnectedness of the natural world and that of the mystic and sacred is still palpable in lines such as "the heron / Priested shore." A raw, lyrical worship of nature through the eyes of the young speaker becomes evident in this poem as he moves from his thirtieth year to a much earlier period of discovery and inspiration. In the fourth stanza "the weather turned around":

It turned away from the blithe country
And down the other air and the blue altered sky
Streamed again a wonder of summer
With apples
Pears and red currants
And I saw in the turning so clearly a child's
Forgotten mornings when he walked with his mother
Through the parables
Of sun light
And the legends of the green chapels ...

(p. 114)

The speaker returns to his youth and sees the "forgotten mornings" as well as the "woods the river and sea / Where a boy / In the listening / Summertime of the dead whispered the truth of his joy" (p. 115). The fifth stanza is one of pure joyful memory of a past that was aligned with nature and the mysteries of what the future might hold. Closely following upon this, however, is the return, through another change in weather, to reality of the final stanza: "And there I could marvel my birthday / Away but the weather turned around. And the true / Joy of the long dead child sang burning / In the sun" (p. 115). If the speaker is Thomas reflecting on the occasion of his birthday, it is to look back at the "dead" child of his youth, a romantic Thomas who is not the same in his thirtieth year: "It was my thirtieth / Year to heaven stood there then in the summer noon / Though the town below lay leaved with October blood" (p. 115). There are sacrifices made by the violence of this return to the past. The mixing of life and the immanence of death is a theme that will carry over into more of Thomas' poems in this volume.

Many of the poems from *Deaths and Entrances* are dedicated to family members or refer to them indirectly. In addition to "This Side of the Truth," dedicated to Thomas's six-year-old son Llewelyn (who was also the subject of Thomas' earlier poem "A saint about to fall"), there is "On a Wedding Anniversary," with allusions to his marriage to Caitlin, and of course what is perhaps the most famous of Thomas' poems, "Do not go gentle into that good night."

In "This Side of the Truth," Thomas appears to be passing along rather grim advice to his son when he writes of the "unminding skies" (p. 116). Later in the poem he suggests that darkness can be both guilty and innocent and death both good and bad. If the inevitability of death is one of the themes of the poem, it is the power of unconditional love that seems to claim victory by the end: "And all your deeds and words, / Each truth, each lie, / Die in unjudging love" (p. 117).

In "On a Wedding Anniversary," Thomas brings together images of a living love and death when he alludes to the air raids in London of the early 1940s and brings them to represent symbolically the assaults on a marriage: "The sky is torn across / This ragged anniversary of two / Who moved for three years in tune / Down the long walks of their vows" (p. 138). Once again Thomas turns to nature to supply a number of images that are to be confronted by the destructiveness of human activity. Here the wholeness of the sky is torn, as is the purity of a love that was seemingly intact for three years. "From every true or crater / Carrying cloud, Death strikes their house" (p. 138). The blissful union seems shattered by Death's arsenal. As in "I make this in a warring absence," Thomas in the final stanza of the poem seems to hint at a reconciliation that is yet stained by some affliction and remains damaged: "Too late in the wrong rain / They come together whom their love parted: / The windows pour into their heart / And the doors burn in their brain" (p. 138). The structure of the marriage is salvaged but is still beyond full repair.

Thomas' best known poem, and the one that is most taught and listened to on recordings, is his poetic exhortation "Do not go gentle into that good night," written with his dying father in mind. A villanelle, the poem uses the alternating two-rhyme scheme to great effect as the repetitions of lines serve to mesmerize the reader and lend potency to the message of resistance. As in "And death shall have no dominion" and other poems, Thomas forcefully attempts to deny death the finality it seeks: "Do not go gentle into that good night, / Old age should burn and rave at close of day; / Rage, rage against the dying of the light" (p. 128). The speaker supplicates the

346

father gradually, though strongly, by identifying those types of "men" who have faced death and, though cognizant of its inevitability, yet find the energy to resist in their own particular fashions. Here "wise men," "Good men," "Wild men," and "Grave men" all serve as examples to the father of how to approach and treat the impending finality of death. They do not go gently into death but rather rage against it. The lines that treat these types of men elaborate on the ways in which the men perhaps have been lulled into a sense of immortality; yet when the certainty of death confronts them, they find enlightenment in the force of their resistance to the outcome that will ultimately complete the definition of their mortal existence. The final lines, however, are full of both love and anger as the son/speaker builds his argument upon tensions and oppositions that lend intensity to his own most powerful wish:

And you, my father, there on the sad height,
Curse, bless, me now with your fierce tears, I pray.
Do not go gentle into that good night.
Rage, rage against the dying of the light.

(p. 128)

It is as if any emotional resistance, be it curse or blessing, will serve to fend off death, or at the very least the ultimate victory and dominion of death. The ungentle rage that the speaker urges onto his father serves to rob death of its claim to finality.

Deaths and Entrances contains a wide variety of poems in which Thomas reveals not only a growing concern with mortality but also an interest in stylistic experimentation. In addition to "On a Wedding Anniversary," Thomas' experiences in 1940s war-torn London are recalled in "Ceremony After a Fire Raid," "A Refusal to Mourn the Death, by Fire, of a Child in London," "Among Those Killed in the Dawn Raid was a Man Aged a Hundred," and the title poem, "Deaths and Entrances," in which fears of invasion by Germany mix with larger philosophical issues surrounding the interplay of life and death:

On almost the incendiary eve
Of several near deaths,
When one at the great least of your best loved
And always known must leave

Lions and fires of his flying breath,
Of your immortal friends
Who'd raise the organs of the counted dust
To shoot and sing your praise,
One who called deepest down shall hold his peace
That cannot sink or cease
Endlessly to his wound
In many married London's estranging grief.

(p. 129)

The poem includes a number of "incendiary" images, and there is a pervasive sense of impending disaster that will come from the skies over London and bring with it the complex emotion of an "estranging grief."

In "A Winter's Tale," Thomas offers the reader a narrative poem that explores overarching issues of life, death, and rebirth. Interweaving images of fire and water again signify the tensions between emotional states. Thomas offers a stylistic experiment with "Vision and Prayer," a pattern poem in which the first six stanzas appear in diamond form and the final six appear in the shape of wings. The wing-shaped stanzas are reminiscent of "Easter Wings" by George Herbert, and critics have suggested that the poem perhaps represents his most significant attitudes toward Christianity (Ferris, 2000, p. 193). Another narrative poem that has generated much critical interest is "The Ballad of the Long-legged Bait," in which a fisherman uses a living woman as bait and, as William York Tindall puts it, "catches the church and the village green" (p. 248). Tindall and other Thomas scholars have seen this poem as a meditation on the snares of love that lead from naive sexual attraction to the sober and sometimes less pleasurable consequences of marriage: "Land, land, land, nothing remains / Of the pacing, famous sea but its speech, / And into its talkative seven tombs / The anchor dives through the floors of a church" (p. 176). Here the fisherman, at the end of the poem, seems to be enslaved by his now lifeless "bait" through marriage (by way of the church).

The final poem in *Deaths and Entrances* is "Fern Hill," one of Thomas's most beautiful poems that involve his memories from childhood. The title refers to the farm owned by Thomas' uncle and aunt, and it figures largely in his fiction, mainly in the stories that would make up *A Portrait of the Artist as a Young Dog.*

Now as I was young and easy under the apple boughs
About the lilting house and happy as the grass was
  green
The night above the dingle starry,
Time let me hail and climb
Golden in the heydays of his eyes,
And honoured among wagons I was prince of the
  apple towns
And once below a time I lordly had the trees and
  leaves
Trail with daisies and barley
Down the rivers of the windfall light.

(p. 178)

In some ways a companion poem to "Poem in October," "Fern Hill" serves as a memory of a lost "green and carefree" past (p. 178). Here too are a few indicators of how nature served so many sacred purposes for Thomas, much as it did for Emily Dickinson, who found her faith through the nontraditional and noninstitutionalized offerings of garden and orchard. Though Thomas takes his cue from the Celtic pre-Christian sense of divinity in nature, he aligns it with the Christian imagery of modern Wales: "And the sabbath rang slowly / In the pebbles of the holy streams" (p. 178). These are not only youthful reminiscences but recollections of the writer's devotion to a theology of nature that has become more complex as he has aged. Thomas reflects on the simple purity of an earlier faith that was not complicated by the hardships of his adult life. Toward the end of the poem, however, the poet realizes it was inevitable that time's "tuneful turning" would eventually bring an end to youthful innocence: "Nothing I cared, in the lamb white days, that time would / take me / Up to the swallow thronged loft by the shadow of my hand" (pp. 179–180). Looking back, he sees that there was always a threat to the ideal of "Fern Hill," perhaps through his own actions ("by the shadow of my hand"). Time was always there, though he may not have realized it at such an early age: "Time held me green and dying / Though I sang in my chains like the sea" (p. 180).

IN COUNTRY SLEEP

Thomas's final volume of poetry published before the *Collected Poems* is *In Country Sleep* (1952). These late poems have a mystical quality and Thomas, in keeping with some of the themes that appear in *Deaths and Entrances,* continues an exploration of a type of Celtic Christian vision of the world. The title poem, "In country sleep," is a dreamlike poem in which the speaker addresses a "girl" (perhaps Thomas' daughter?) and leads her through a night in which he wishes to instill a sense of faith that is strengthened and informed by a full and soulful experience of nature:

The country is holy: O bide in that country kind,
Know the green good,
Under the prayer wheeling moon in the rosy wood
Be shielded by chant and flower and gay may you
Lie in grace.

(pp. 182–183)

By the end of the poem, the speaker seems to break the spell of sleep with a forecast of a sustained faith he would wish the sleeping girl to have taken from her sleep journey: "And you shall wake, from country sleep, this dawn and each / first dawn, / Your faith as deathless as the outcry of the ruled sun" (p. 186). Bird symbolism is prevalent in this poem and continues in "Over Sir John's hill," in which nature, particularly through references to a variety of birds, again assumes a sacred quality. Here we have the "fishing holy stalking heron," "saint heron hymning in the shell-hung distant // Crystal harbour vale" (p. 188). This poem, as well as "Poem on his birthday," were written when Thomas was living in Laugharne in the Boat House, where he would sit in his writing shed and look out over the estuary where the rivers Taf, Towy, and Gwendraeth meet in the Bristol Channel. He records in these poems the birds he could see along the coast from the vantage point of the shed (Ferris, 2000, pp. 239–230). The tone of "Over Sir John's hill," as in Thomas' final "birthday poem" titled "Poem on his birthday," is one of sad resignation that nonetheless signifies a union of the speaker with the natural world he is witnessing. The heron and the speaker are brought together through the verse of the one who captures the song of the other in a lament of longing. Birds figure largely in "Poem on his birthday" as well:

In the mustardseed sun,
By full tilt river and switchback sea
Where the cormorants scud,
In his house on stilts high among beaks
And palavers of birds
This sandgrain day in the bent bay's grave
He celebrates and spurns
His driftwood thirty-fifth wind turned age;
Herons spire and spear.

(p. 190)

Another Hopkinsesque poem, with lines such as "In the thistledown fall" (p. 190), Thomas writes of how his gaze out from the writing shed lends itself to his meditations on life and mortality as he turns thirty-five years of age. With lines such as the following, one might be tempted to see Thomas as one who approaches death with a sense of hope:

That the closer I move
To death, one man through his sundered hulks,
The louder the sun blooms
And the tusked, ramshackling sea exults;
And every wave of the way
And gale I tackle, the whole world then,
With more triumphant faith
Than ever was since the world was said,
Spins its morning of praise.

(p. 193)

However, as Paul Ferris points out (2000, p. 272), this poetic hopefulness is belied by Thomas' sense of despair and foreboding in his final years. Yet, in the context of the poem, the culminating unity of self and nature it expresses may represent the true nature of faith for Thomas, one that is articulated most clearly in his later poems.

Notable final poems from *In Country Sleep* include the haunting "In the White Giant's Thigh," with its imagery of a giant carved in the chalk hillside of Wales by an ancient Celt; and "Elegy," an incomplete poem that appears in *Collected Poems* as edited by Vernon Watkins. "Elegy" serves as a companion poem to "Do not go gentle into that good night" as Thomas pays tribute once more to his father, now dead: "Too

proud to die, broken and blind he died / The darkest way, and did not turn away, / A cold kind man brave in his narrow pride" (p. 200). The final line of the poem, "Until I die he will not leave my side" (p. 201), reveals again the reverence Thomas had for his father.

Though the published poetry spans the years 1934–1952 it is important to note that Thomas often worked from notebooks that included poems that had been written much earlier and then later found their way into publication. He would often hit dry spells with his poetic work and at times found his inspiration more driven to the writing of fiction and drama, especially in the form of radio plays and film scripts. However, Thomas' poetic sensibility is perhaps his finest, and the imprint of his poetic self is apparent in all of his work, most notably in his short fiction and in *Under Milk Wood.*

FICTION AND ESSAYS

Thomas was an accomplished writer of shorter fiction and wrote one comic novel, *The Death of the King's Canary* (published in 1976 and coauthored with John Davenport), as well as a novel based on a film script, *Rebecca's Daughters* (1965). However, most of Thomas' important pieces of fiction are to be found in his early stories and those that form the collection *A Portrait of the Artist as a Young Dog,* first published in 1940. The majority of his short fiction has been collected in a volume titled *The Collected Stories,* published by New Directions in 1984.

Thomas' early stories display his interest in Welsh locales as well as a fascination with the extraordinary and fantastical. Often supernatural in quality, these stories exhibit a number of fairytale elements that go a long way toward explaining the often magical and surreal nature of Thomas' mind; the stories depend at times on the spontaneity of imagination reflected through a stream-of-consciousness style of writing. Further, the prose often is marked by a metafictional element. In one of the early stories, "The Mouse and the Woman," Thomas writes through the voice of a madman who perhaps is driven by the same force as the early Thomas: "I have a devil, but I do not tell it what to do. It lifts my hand. I write. The words spring into life" (*Collected Stories,* p. 77). Yet a prominent hallmark of Thomas' early short fiction, as well as the stories that make up *A Portrait of the Artist as a Young Dog,* is a concern with portraying small-town Wales in a sympathetic and realist light, much in the way Joyce treats his characters and sense of place in *Dubliners.* This is especially true of *A Portrait of the Artist as a Young Dog,* in which Thomas blends the realism of rural and small-town Wales with the distinct impressions he gathered as a young boy growing up in Swansea. In stories such as "The Peaches" and "A Visit to Grandpa's," Thomas places himself in the text and works off of childhood memories to frame his brief glimpses into a world where human life and nature are closely connected. Here, as well as in his poetry, Thomas is driven by fond recollections of his youthful experiences at Fernhill. In "The Peaches," Thomas' poetic imagination allows different realms of experience to blend into one another as he visits a farm based on Fernhill and encounters his Aunt Annie and Uncle Jim: "The front of the house was the single side of a black shell, and the arched door was the listening ear" (*Collected Stories,* p. 124). "He sat down on his special chair, which was the broken throne of a bankrupt bard" (p. 125).

Examples of Thomas' later prose include *Adventures in the Skin Trade,* an unfinished novel that was finally published in 1969. In this work a character named Sam (based no doubt on Thomas) travels from a small town to London, where he becomes involved in a number of fantastical scenarios reminiscent of Flann O'Brien's or Mikhail Bulgakov's stories that engage with magic realism. Other important prose pieces include "Quite Early One Morning," a predecessor to *Under Milk Wood,* and "A Child's Christmas in Wales." Both these works provide poignant reflections on life in rural and small-town Wales and give the reader a fine sense of the voices of its inhabitants. Thomas is a great practitioner of voice and offers readers and listeners alike a strong sense of the "overheard"

polyphony of identities that constitute town and village life. In addition to fiction and various pieces of memoir, Thomas also contributed essays on poetry and writers such as Wilfred Owen, which can largely be found at the end of the volume titled *Quite Early One Morning.*

RADIO PLAYS, RECORDINGS, AND OTHER SCRIPTS

Thomas' highly developed ear for voice was an important factor in his work on radio plays and film scripts. A significant part of his working life was spent in London working for the BBC (especially during and after the war years of the 1940s). Thomas helped to write scripts and even lent his voice to a variety of parts in radio productions sponsored by the BBC, such as a radio version of the long poem *In Parenthesis* by the Welsh poet David Jones, which also featured the voice of the actor Richard Burton. In addition to lending his talents to radio documentaries and other voice-oriented projects, Thomas also wrote and collaborated on film scripts. Among the titles he helped to develop were film versions of *The Beach of Falesá* by Robert Louis Stevenson, *The Doctor and the Devils* (based on the Scottish body snatchers Burke and Hare), and *Twenty Years A-Growing* by the Irish writer Maurice O'Sullivan. Many of these scripts were never developed into films, but Thomas gained a reputation as a proficient screenwriter.

Thomas was far more successful with his radio talents, and this led him to develop what is perhaps his finest individual piece of long work, *Under Milk Wood,* a "play for voices," which was first performed in New York shortly before Thomas' death in 1953. This play, with its rich and varied voices of characters from the fictional town of Llareggub, Wales, is one of Thomas' finest achievements, and in 1973 it was turned into a film production starring Richard Burton, Peter O'Toole, and Elizabeth Taylor. In addition to the rich interplay of voices that represent the life of the town from before sunrise (in the shape of dreams and ghosts) to the end of the day, the play gained some notoriety from Thomas' playful use of Welsh place names (read "Llareggub" backwards).

Toward the end of his life, Thomas was in much demand as a speaker and reader of his own work. His powerful and lilting voice was much admired, and Caedmon Records and other studios prepared a number of recordings of Thomas reading his works including famous poems such as "Do not go gentle into that good night," "Fern Hill," and "Poem on his birthday." Additionally, *Under Milk Wood* and "A Child's Christmas in Wales" are available as recordings. In 2008 a film based on events in Thomas' life, *The Edge of Love,* was released starring Matthew Rhys (as Dylan), Keira Knightley, Sienna Miller, and Cillian Murphy.

Although his life was tragic in many regards, Dylan Thomas remains one of the most original voices of the twentieth century. His fascination with the intersections between the human and natural worlds and his development of a modern poetic theology that joins landscapes and seascapes with the sacred is unsurpassed. His ability to create a reality from the world of the imagined and fantastical is a significant contribution to modernist literature. He has been called the last Romantic poet in British literature, but his writing clearly shows engagement with a realistic understanding of the self and the psychology of a modern psyche in search of hope, forgiveness, and love.

Selected Bibliography

WORKS OF DYLAN THOMAS

POETRY
18 Poems. London: Fortune Press, 1934.

Twenty-five Poems. London: Dent, 1936.

The Map of Love. London: Dent, 1939.

Deaths and Entrances. London: Dent, 1946.

In Country Sleep, and Other Poems. New York: New Directions, 1952.

The Collected Poems, 1934–1952. London: Dent, 1953; New York: New Directions, 1953. (All page citations in the text refer to the New York edition.)

Dylan Thomas: The Poems. Edited by Daniel Jones. London: Dent, 1971.

Dylan Thomas: The Notebook Poems, 1930–1934. Edited by Ralph Maud. London: Dent, 1989.

FICTION, MEMOIR, AND PROSE WRITINGS
Portrait of the Artist as a Young Dog. London: Dent, 1940.

Quite Early One Morning. London: Dent, 1954; New York: New Directions, 1954.

Adventures in the Skin Trade, and Other Stories. Norfolk, Conn.: New Directions, 1955.

A Prospect of the Sea, and Other Stories and Prose Writings. Edited by Daniel Jones. London: Dent, 1955.

Rebecca's Daughters. London: Triton, 1965.

Poet in the Making: The Notebooks of Dylan Thomas. Edited by Ralph Maud. London: Dent, 1968.

Dylan Thomas: Early Prose Writings. Edited by Walford Davies. London: Dent, 1971.

The Death of the King's Canary. With John Davenport. New York: Viking, 1976.

Dylan Thomas: The Collected Stories. Edited by Walford Davies. Introduction by Leslie Norris. London: Dent, 1983; New York: New Directions, 1984. (Page citations in the text refer to the later edition.)

LETTERS
Letters to Vernon Watkins. Edited by Vernon Watkins. London: Dent and Faber, 1957.

Dylan Thomas: The Collected Letters. Edited by Paul Ferris. London: Dent, 1985. New ed., 2000. (Page citations in the text refer to the later edition.)

FILM/RADIO SCRIPTS AND RECORDINGS
Under Milk Wood. London: Dent, 1954; New York: New Directions, 1954.

The Beach of Falesá. London: Cape, 1964.

Twenty Years A-Growing. London: Dent, 1964.

The Doctor and the Devils and Other Scripts. New York: New Directions, 1966.

The Broadcasts. Edited by Ralph Maud. London: Dent, 1991.

Dylan Thomas: The Filmscripts. Edited by John Ackerman. London: Dent, 1995.

CRITICAL AND BIOGRAPHICAL STUDIES
Bold, Alan, ed. *Dylan Thomas: Craft or Sullen Art.* London: Vision Press; New York: St. Martin's Press, 1990.

Brinnin, John Malcolm. *Dylan Thomas in America.* Boston: Little, Brown, 1955. Reprinted, New York: Paragon House, 1989.

Davies, James A. *A Reference Companion to Dylan Thomas.* Westport, Conn., and London: Greenwood Press, 1998.

Ferris, Paul. *Caitlin: The Life of Caitlin Thomas.* London: Pimlico/Random House, 1993.

————. *Dylan Thomas: The Biography.* New ed. Washington, D.C.: Counterpoint, 2000.

Fryer, Jonathan. *Dylan: The Nine Lives of Dylan Thomas.* London: Kyle Cathie, 1993.

Hardy, Barbara. *Dylan Thomas: An Original Language.* Athens, Ga., and London: University of Georgia Press, 2000.

Lycett, Andrew. *Dylan Thomas: A New Life.* Woodstock and New York: Overlook Press, 2004.

Maud, Ralph. *Where Have the Old Words Got Me?: Explications of Dylan Thomas's Collected Poems.* Montreal and Kingston, Ont.: McGill-Queens Press, 2003.

McKenna, Rollie. *Portrait of Dylan: A Photographer's Memoir.* Introduction by John Malcolm Brinnin. Owings Mills, Md.: Stemmer House, 1982.

Seymour, Tryntje Van Ness. *Dylan Thomas' New York.* Owings Mills, Md.: Stemmer House, 1978.

Sinclair, Andrew. *Dylan the Bard: A Life of Dylan Thomas.* London: Constable, 1999.

Thomas, Caitlin. *Leftover Life to Kill.* London: Putnam, 1957.

————. *Not Quite Posthumous Letter to My Daughter.* London: Putnam, 1963.

————. *Double Drink Story: My Life with Dylan Thomas.* Toronto: Viking, 1997.

Thomas, David N. *Dylan Thomas: A Farm, Two Mansions, and a Bungalow.* Bridgend, Wales: Seren/Poetry Wales Press, 2000.

Tindall, William York. *A Reader's Guide to Dylan Thomas.* New York: Noonday Press, 1962.

MASTER INDEX

The following index covers the entire British Writers series through Retrospective Supplement III. All references include volume numbers in boldface Roman numerals followed by page numbers within that volume. Subjects of articles are indicated by boldface type.

"Across the Estuary" (Nicholson), **Supp. VI:** 216

"Across the Moor" (Adcock), **Supp. XII:** 8

Across the Plains (Stevenson), **V:** 389, 396

"Act, The" (Harrison), **Supp. V:** 161–162

Act of Creation, The (Koestler), **Supp. I:** 37, 38

Act of Grace (Keneally), **Supp. IV:** 347

"Act of Reparation, An" (Warner), **Supp. VII:** 380

Act of Terror, An (Brink), **Supp. VI: 55–56,** 57

Act of Worship, An (Thompson), **Supp. XIV:** 291

Act Without Words I (Beckett), **Supp. I:** 46, 55, 57

Act Without Words II (Beckett), **Supp. I:** 46, 55, 57

Actaeon and Diana (Johnson), **I:** 286

Acte (Durrell), **Supp. I:** 126, 127; **Retro. Supp. III:** 85

Actions and Reactions (Kipling), **VI:** 204

Acton, John, **IV:** 289, 290; **VI:** 385

"Actor's Farewell, The" (Conn), **Supp. XIII:** 81

"Acts of Restoration" (Fallon), **Supp. XII:** 107

"Ad Amicam"sonnets (Thompson), **V:** 441

Ad Patrem (Milton), **Retro. Supp. II:** 272

Adam and Eve and Pinch Me (Coppard), **VIII:** 85, 88, 89, 91–93

"Adam and Eve and Pinch Me" (Coppard), **VIII:** 90

Adam and Eve and Pinch Me (Rendell), **Supp. IX:** 189, 195

Adam and the Sacred Nine (Hughes), **Supp. I:** 357, 363

Adam Bede (Eliot), **V:** xxii, 2, 191–192, 194, 200; **Retro. Supp. II:** 104–106

"Adam confesses an infidelity to Eve" (Constantine), **Supp. XV:** 72

"Adam Pos'd" (Finch), **Supp. IX:** 68

"Adam Tempted" (Thomas), **Supp. XII:** 290

Adams, Henry, **VI:** 65

Adam's Breed (Hall), **Supp. VI:** 120, 122, 128

"Adam's Curse" (Yeats), **III:** 184; **VI:** 213

"Adam's Dream" (Muir), **Supp. VI:** 207–208

"Adapting *Nice Work* for Television" (Lodge), **Supp. IV:** 373, 381

Adcock, Fleur, **Supp. XII: 1–16**

"Adders' Brood" (Powys), **VIII:** 248, 249

Addison, Joseph, **II:** 195, 200; **III:** 1, 18, 19, **38–53,** 74, 198; **IV:** 278, 281, 282

"Additional Poems" (Housman), **VI:** 161

"Address to the Deep" (Jewsbury), **Supp. XIV:** 161

Address to the Deil (Burns), **III:** 315, 317

Address to the Irish People, An (Shelley), **IV:** 208; **Retro. Supp. I:** 245

"Address to the Ocean" (Jewsbury), **Supp. XIV:** 152, 153

"Address to the Unco Guid" (Burns), **III:** 319

"Addy" (Blackwood), **Supp. IX:** 12

Adéle: Jane Eyre's Hidden Story (Tennant), **Supp. IX:** 239

Adelphi, **Supp. XIII:** 191

Adelphi (Cowper), **Retro. Supp. III:** 39–40

Adepts of Africa, The (Williams, C. W. S.), *see Black Bastard, The*

"Adieu to Fancy" (Robinson), **Supp. XIII:** 204

"Adina" (James), **VI:** 69

Administrator, The (MacNeice), **VII:** 401

Admirable Bashville, The (Barker), **VI:** 113

Admiral Crichton, The (Barrie), **Supp. III:** 6, 9, **14–15**

Admiral Guinea (Stevenson), **V:** 396

"Admonition on a Rainy Afternoon" (Nye), **Supp. X:** 203

Adolphe (Constant), **Supp. IV:** 125, 126, 136

Adonais (Shelley), **I:** 160; **VI:** 73; **IV:** xviii, 179, 196, 205–206, 207, 208; **Retro. Supp. I:** 255

Adonis and the Alphabet (Huxley), **VII:** 206–207

Adonis, Attis, Osiris: Studies in the History of Oriental Religion (Frazer), **Supp. III:** 175, 180

Adoption Papers, The (Kay), **Supp. XIII:** 99, 100, 102–103, 108

"Adoption Papers, The" (Kay), **Supp. XIII:** 102–103

Adored One, The (Barrie), **Supp. III:** 5, 9

Adorno, Theodor, **Supp. IV:** 29, 82

"Adrian and Bardus" (Gower), **I:** 54

"Adultery" (Gunn), **Retro. Supp. III:** 125

"Advanced Lady, The" (Mansfield), **VII:** 172

Advancement of Learning, An (Hill, R.), **Supp. IX:** 122

Advancement of Learning, The (Bacon), **I:** 261–265; **II:** 149; **IV:** 279

Advantages Proposed by Repealing the Sacramental Test, The (Swift), **III:** 36

"Adventure of Charles Augustus Milverton, The" (Doyle), **Supp. II:** 173

"Adventure of Charles Wentworth" (Brontë), **V:** 118–119

"Adventure of the Abbey Grange, The" (Doyle), **Supp. II:** 168, 173, 176

"Adventure of the Blanched Soldier, The" (Doyle), **Supp. II:** 168

"Adventure of the Blue Carbuncle, The" (Doyle), **Supp. II:** 173

"Adventure of the Bruce–Partington Plans, The" (Doyle), **Supp. II:** 170, 175

"Adventure of the Copper Beeches, The" (Doyle), **Supp. II:** 168

"Adventure of the Creeping Man, The" (Doyle), **Supp. II:** 165

"Adventure of the Devil's Foot, The" (Doyle), **Supp. II:** 167, 176

"Adventure of the Empty House, The" (Doyle), **Supp. II:** 160

"Adventure of the Engineer's Thumb, The" (Doyle), **Supp. II:** 170

"Adventure of the Golden Pince–Nez, The" (Doyle), **Supp. II:** 175

"Adventure of the Illustrious Client, The" (Doyle), **Supp. II:** 169

"Adventure of the Lion's Mane, The" (Doyle), **Supp. II:** 168–169

"Adventure of the Missing Three–Quarter, The" (Doyle), **Supp. II:** 165, 171

"Adventure of the Norwood Builder, The" (Doyle), **Supp. II:** 169, 170, 173

"Adventure of the Retired Colourman, The" (Doyle), **Supp. II:** 172

"Adventure of the Second Stain, The" (Doyle), **Supp. II:** 175, 176

"Adventure of the Six Napoleons, The" (Doyle), **Supp. II:** 170–171, 174–175

"Adventure of the Speckled Band, The" (Doyle), **Supp. II:** 165–166

"Adventure of the Sussex Vampire, The" (Doyle), **Supp. II:** 169

"Adventure of the Three Garridebs, The" (Doyle), **Supp. II:** 165

"Adventure of Wisteria Lodge, The" (Doyle), **Supp. II:** 168

Adventure Story (Rattigan), **Supp. VII:** 316–317

Adventures Aboard the Maria Celeste (Carey), **Supp. XII:** 52

Adventures in the Skin Trade (Thomas), **Supp. I:** 182

Adventures in the Skin Trade, and Other Stories (Thomas), **Retro. Supp. III:** 335, 348

Adventures of Caleb Williams, The (Godwin), **III:** 332, 345; **IV:** 173

Adventures of Covent Garden, The (Farquhar), **II:** 352, 354, 364

Adventures of Eovaai, Princess of Ijaveo, The (Haywood), **Supp. XII:** 135, 141–142, 146

Adventures of Ferdinand Count Fathom, The (Smollett), *see Ferdinand Count Fathom*

Adventures of Harry Richmond, The (Meredith), **V:** xxiii, 228, 234

Adventures of Johnny Walker, Tramp, The (Davies), **Supp. XI:** 93

Adventures of Peregrine Pickle, The (Smollett), *see Peregrine Pickle*

Adventures of Philip on His Way Through the World, The (Thackeray), **V:** 19, 29, 35, 38

Adventures of Robina, The (Tennant), **Supp. IX:** 239

Adventures of Roderick Random, The (Smollett), *see Roderick Random*

Adventures of Sir Launcelot Greaves, The (Smollett), *see Sir Launcelot Greaves*

Adventures of the Black Girl in Her Search for God, The (Shaw), **VI:** 124, 127, 129

Adventures of Ulysses, The (Lamb), **IV:** 85

"Adventurous Exploit of the Cave of Ali Baba, The" (Sayers), **Supp. III:** 340

Advice: A Satire (Smollett), **III:** 152n, 158

Advice to a Daughter (Halifax), **III:** 40

Aiken, Conrad, **VII:** 149, 179; **Supp. III:** 270

Aimed at Nobody (Graham), **Supp. VII:** 106

Ainger, Alfred, **IV:** 254, 267

Ainsi va la monde (Robinson), **Supp. XIII:** 202, 205

Ainsworth, Harrison, **IV:** 311; **V:** 47

"Air" (Traherne), **Supp. XI:** 267

Air and Angels (Hill), **Supp. XIV:** 116, 125

"Air and Angels" (MacCaig), **Supp. VI:** 185

"Air Disaster, The" (Ballard), **Supp. V:** 33

Air Show, The (Scupham), **Supp. XIII:** 224–225

"Aire and Angels" (Donne), **II:** 197

Airship, The (Caudwell), **Supp. IX:** 35

"Aisling" (Delanty), **Supp. XIV:** 67

"Aisling" (Muldoon), **Supp. IV:** 418–419

"Aisling Hat, The" (McGuckian), **Supp. V:** 286, 288, 289

Aissa Saved (Cary), **VII:** 185

"Akbar's Bridge" (Kipling), **VI:** 201

Akerman, Rudolph, **V:** 111

Akhenaten Adventure, The (Kerr), **Supp. XII:** 198

Akhmatova, Anna, **Supp. IV:** 480, 494

"Al Som de l'Escalina" (Eliot), **VII:** 152

Alaham (Greville), **Supp. XI:** 110, 120

Alamanni, Luigi, **I:** 110–111

Alamein to Zem–Zem (Douglas), **VII:** xxii, 441

Alarcos (Disraeli), **IV:** 306, 308

Alaric at Rome (Arnold), **V:** 216

"Alas, Poor Bollington!" (Coppard), **VIII:** 94–95

"Alaska" (Armitage), **VIII:** 5

Alastair Reid Reader, An: Selected Poetry and Prose (Reid), **Supp. VII:** 333, 336

Alastor (Shelley), **III:** 330, 338; **IV:** xvii, 195, 198, 208, 217; **Retro. Supp. I:** 247

Albatross, and Other Stories, The (Hill), **Supp. XIV:** 118–119

"Albatross, The" (Hill), **Supp. XIV:** 115, 118–119

"Albergo Empedocle" (Forster), **VI:** 399, 412

Albert's Bridge (Stoppard), **Supp. I:** 439, 445

Albigenses, The (Maturin), **VIII:** 201, 207, 208

"Albinus and Rosemund" (Gower), **I:** 53–54

Albion! Albion! (Hill, R.), **Supp. IX:** 111

"Albion & Marina" (Brontë), **V:** 110

Albion and Albanius (Dryden), **II:** 305

Album, The (Jewsbury), **Supp. XIV:** 157

Album Verses (Lamb), **IV:** 83, 85

Alcazar (Peele), *see Battle of Alcazar, The*

Alcestis (Euripides), **IV:** 358

Alchemist, The (Jonson), **I:** 304–341, 342; **II:** 4, 48; **Retro. Supp. I:** 163

"Alchemist in the City, The" (Hopkins), **V:** 362

Alchemist's Apprentice, The (Thompson), **Supp. XIV:** 286, 291, 292–293

"Alchemy of Happiness, The" (Kureishi), **Supp. XI:** 163

Alcott, Louisa May, **Supp. IV:** 255

Aldington, Richard, **VI:** 416; **VII:** xvi, 36, 121

Aldiss, Brian, **III:** 341, 345; **Supp. V:** 22

Aldous Huxley (Brander), **VII:** 208

Alentejo Blue (Ali), **Supp. XIII:** 6–10, 11

Alexander, Peter, **I:** 300n, 326

Alexander, William (earl of Stirling), **I:** 218; **II:** 80

"Alexander and Zenobia" (Brontë), **V:** 115

Alexander Pope (Sitwell), **VII:** 138–139

Alexander Pope (Stephen), **V:** 289

Alexander Pope as Critic and Humanist (Warren), **II:** 332n

Alexander's Feast; or, The Power of Musique (Dryden), **II:** 200, 300, 304; **Retro. Supp. III:** 77

Alexanders saga, **VIII:** 237, 242

Alexandria: A History and Guide (Forster), **VI:** 408, 412

Alexandria Quartet (Durrell), **Supp. I:** 94, 96, 97, 98, 100, 101, **104–110,** 113, 122; **Retro. Supp. III:** 83, 85, 87, 88–90, 91, 92, 95

"Alfieri and Salomon the Florentine Jew" (Landor), **IV:** 91

"Alford" (Crawford), **Supp. XI:** 78–79

Alfred (Thomson and Mallet), **Supp. III:** 412, 424–425

Alfred Lord Tennyson: A Memoir (Tennyson), **IV:** 324, 338

Alfred the Great of Wessex, King, **Retro. Supp. II:** 293, 295–297

Algernon Charles Swinburne (Thomas), **VI:** 424

Ali, Monica, **Supp. XIII: 1–12**

Ali the Lion: Ali of Tebeleni, Pasha of Jannina, 1741–1822 (Plomer), **Supp. XI:** 225

Alice (Potter, D.), **Supp. X:** 228, 230–233

Alice Fell (Tennant), **Supp. IX:** 235, 236

Alice in Wonderland (Carroll), *see Alice's Adventures in Wonderland*

Alice Sit–by–the–Fire (Barrie), **Supp. III:** 8, 9

Alice's Adventures in Wonderland (Carroll), **V:** xxiii, 261–265, **266–269,** 270–273

Alice's Adventures Under Ground (Carroll), **V:** 266, 273; *see Alice's Adventures in Wonderland*

"Alicia's Diary" (Hardy), **VI:** 22

"Alien, The" (Delanty), **Supp. XIV:** 74

Alien (Foster), **III:** 345

"Alien Corn, The" (Maugham), **VI:** 370, 374

Alien Sky, The (Scott), **Supp. I:** 261–263

"Alien Soil" (Kincaid), **Supp. VII:** 221, 229

All About Mr. Hatterr (Desani), **Supp. IV:** 445

"All Alone" (Robinson), **Supp. XIII:** 212

"All blue and bright, in glorious light" (Brontë), **V:** 115

"All Catches Alight" (Larkin), **Retro. Supp. III:** 204

"All Day It Has Rained" (Lewis), **VII:** 445

All Day on the Sands (Bennett), **VIII:** 27

"All Flesh" (Thompson), **V:** 442

All Fools (Chapman), **I:** 235, 238, 244

All for Love (Dryden), **II:** 295–296, 305; **Retro. Supp. III:** 79

All for Love (Southey), **IV:** 71

All Hallow's Eve (Williams, C. W. S.), **Supp. IX:** 281, 282, 284, 285

"All Legendary Obstacles" (Montague), **Supp. XV:** 212, 215, 216

All My Eyes See: The Visual World of G. M. Hopkins (ed. Thornton), **V:** 377n, 379n, 382

All My Little Ones (Ewart), **Supp. VII:** 36

All on a Summer's Day (Inchbald), **Supp. XV:** 155

All Ovid's Elegies (Marlowe), **I:** 280, 291, 293

"All philosophers, who find" (Swift), **IV:** 160

All Quiet on the Western Front (Remarque), **VII:** xvi

All Religions Are One (Blake), **III:** 292, 307; **Retro. Supp. I:** 35

"All Roads Lead to It" (Scupham), **Supp. XIII:** 228

"All Saints: Martyrs" (Rossetti), **V:** 255

"All Souls Night" (Cornford), **VIII:** 112

All That Fall (Beckett), **Supp. I:** 58, 62; **Retro. Supp. I:** 25

All the Conspirators (Isherwood), **VII:** 310

"All the hills and vales along" (Sorley), **VI:** 421–422

"All the Inventory of Flesh" (Raine), **Supp. XIII:** 164

All the Usual Hours of Sleeping (Redgrove), **Supp. VI:** 230

All the Year Round (periodical), **V:** 42

"All Things Ill Done" (Cameron), **Supp. IX:** 23–24

"All Things Will Die" (Tennyson), **Retro. Supp. III:** 321

All Trivia (Connolly), **Supp. III:** 98

"All Washed Up" (Jamie), **Supp. XIV:** 138

All What Jazz: A Record Diary, 1961–1968 (Larkin), **Supp. I:** 286, 287–288; **Retro. Supp. III:** 200

"All Wraiths in Hell are single" (Constantine), **Supp. XV:** 70

Allan Quatermain (Haggard), **Supp. III:** 213, 218

"Allegiance, An" (Wallace–Crabbe), **VIII:** 315

Allegory of Love: A Study in Medieval Tradition (Lewis), **Supp. III:** 248, 249–250, 265

Allen, John, **IV:** 341, 349–350, 352

Allen, Walter Ernest, **V:** 219; **VI:** 257; **VII:** xvii, xxxvii, 71, 343

Allestree, Richard, **III:** 82

Allott, Kenneth, **IV:** 236; **VI:** xi, xxvii, 218

Allott, Miriam, **IV:** x, xxiv, 223n, 224, 234, 236; **V:** x, 218

All's Well That Ends Well (Shakespeare), **I:** 313, 318; **Retro. Supp. III:** 275

All You Who Sleep Tonight (Seth), **Supp. X:** 283–284, 288

"Allusion to the Tenth Satire of the Second Book of Horace" (Rochester), **II:** 259

Almayer's Folly (Conrad), **VI:** 135–136, 148; **Retro. Supp. II:** 70–71

Almeria (Edgeworth), **Supp. III:** 158

Almond Tree, The (Stallworthy), **Supp. X:** 293–294

"Almond Tree, The" (Stallworthy), **Supp. X:** 293–294, 302

"Almswoman" (Blunden), **Supp. XI:** 42

"Aloe, The" (Mansfield), **VII:** 173–174

Alone (Douglas), **VI:** 293, 294, 297, 304, 305

"Along the Terrace" (Conn), **Supp. XIII:** 74–75

Alpers, Antony, **VII:** 176

"Alphabetical Catalogue of Names . . . and Other Material Things Mentioned in These Pastorals, An" (Gay), **III:** 56

Alphabetical Order (Frayn), **Supp. VII:** 60

"Alphabets" (Heaney), **Retro. Supp. I:** 131

Alphonsus, King of Aragon (Greene), **VIII:** 139–140

Alps and Sanctuaries (Butler), **Supp. II:** 114

"Alps in Winter, The" (Stephen), **V:** 282

Alroy (Disraeli), **IV:** 296, 297, 308

"Altar, The" (Herbert), **II:** 128

"Altar of the Dead, The" (James), **VI:** 69

"Altarwise by owl–light" (Thomas), **Supp. I: 174–176**; **Retro. Supp. III:** 340–341

Alteration, The (Amis), **Supp. II:** 12–13

"Alternative to Despair, An" (Koestler), **Supp. I:** 39

Althusser, Louis, **Supp. IV:** 90

Alton, R. E., **I:** 285

Alton Locke (Kingsley), **V:** vii, xxi, 2, 4; **VI:** 240

"Altruistic Tenderness of LenWing the Poet, The" (Cameron), **Supp. IX:** 19

Altus Prosator (tr. Morgan, E.), **Supp. IX:** 169

Alvarez, A., **II:** 125n

Alvíssmál, **VIII:** 231

Amadeus (Shaffer), **Supp. I:** 326–327

Amadis of Gaul (tr. Southey), **IV:** 71

Amado, Jorge, **Supp. IV:** 440

Amalgamemnon (Brooke–Rose), **Supp. IV:** 99, 110–111, 112

Amaryllis at the Fair, A Novel (Jefferies), **Supp. XV:** 176–178

Amateur Emigrant, The (Stevenson), **V:** 389, 396

"Amateur Film–Making" (Fuller), **Supp. VII:** 73

Amateur Poacher, The (Jefferies), **Supp. XV:** 166–168

Amazing Marriage, The (Meredith), **V:** 227, 232, 233, 234

Ambarvalia: Poems by T. Burbidge and A. H. Clough, **V:** 159–160, 161, 170

Ambassadors, The (James), **VI:** 55, 57–59; **Supp. IV:** 371

"Amber Bead, The" (Herrick), **II:** 106

Amber Spyglass, The (Pullman), **Supp. XIII:** 150, 151, 153, 157–158

Amberley, Lady, **V:** 129

"Ambiguities" (Fuller), **Supp. VII:** 73

Ambition and Other Poems (Davies), **Supp. XI:** 102

"Ambitious Squire, An" (Jefferies), **Supp. XV:** 169–170

Ambler, Eric, **Supp. IV: 1–24**

Amboyna (Dryden), **II:** 305

"Ambulances" (Larkin), **Retro. Supp. III:** 207

"Ambush" (Conn), **Supp. XIII:** 72

Amelia (Fielding), **III:** 102–103, 105; **Retro. Supp. I:** 81, 89–90

"Amen" (Rossetti), **V:** 256

Amendments of Mr. Collier's False and Imperfect Citations (Congreve), **II:** 339, 340, 350

America. A Prophecy (Blake), **III:** 300, 302, 307; **Retro. Supp. I:** 39, 40–41

America I Presume (Lewis), **VII:** 77

American, The (James), **VI:** 24, 28–29, 39, 67

"American Boy" (Gunn), **Retro. Supp. III:** 129

"American Dreams" (Carey), **Supp. XII:** 54, 55, 56

American Ghosts and Other World Wonders (Carter), **Supp. III:** 91

American Journal of Religious Psychology, **Supp. XIII:** 44

American Notes (Dickens), **V:** 42, 54, 55, 71

American Scene, The (James), **VI: 54, 62–64,** 67

American Senator, The (Trollope), **V:** 100, 102

American Visitor, An (Cary), **VII:** 186

American Wake (Delanty), **Supp. XIV:** 67–69–71, 72, 75

"American Wife, The" (O'Connor), **Supp. XIV:** 226

"Americans in My Mind, The" (Pritchett), **Supp. III:** 316

"Ametas and Thestylis Making Hay–Ropes" (Marvell), **II:** 211

Aminta (Tasso), **II:** 49

"Amir's Homily, The" (Kipling), **VI:** 201

Amis, Kingsley, **Supp. II: 1–19; Supp. IV:** 25, 26, 27, 29, 377; **Supp. V:** 206

Amis, Martin, **Supp. IV: 25–44,** 65, 75, 437, 445

"Among All Lovely Things My Love Had Been" (Wordsworth), **IV:** 21

Among Muslims: Everyday Life on the Frontiers of Pakistan (Jamie), **Supp. XIV:** 129, 135, 144

"Among School Children" (Yeats), **VI:** 211, 217

Among the Believers: An Islamic Journey (Naipaul), **Supp. I:** 399, 400–401, 402

Among the Cities (Morris, J.), **Supp. X:** 183

"Among the Ruins" (Malouf), **Supp. XII:** 220

Among the Walls (Fallon), **Supp. XII:** 102

"Among Those Killed in the Dawn Raid was a Man Aged a Hundred" (Thomas), **Retro. Supp. III:** 345

Amores (tr. Marlowe), **I:** 276, 290

Amoretti and Epithalamion (Spenser), **I:** 124, 128–131

Amorous Cannibal, The (Wallace–Crabbe), **VIII:** 319, 320–321

"Amorous Cannibal, The" (Wallace–Crabbe), **VIII:** 319

Amorous Prince, The; or, The Curious Husband (Behn), **Supp. III:** 26

"Amos Barton" (Eliot), **V:** 190

"Amour de l'impossible, L'" (Symonds), **Supp. XIV:** 252

Amours de Voyage (Clough), **V:** xxii, 155, 156, 158, 159, 161–163, 165, 166–168, 170

Amphytrion; or, The Two Sosias (Dryden), **II:** 296, 305

"Ample Garden, The" (Graves), **VII:** 269

Amrita (Jhabvala), **Supp. V:** 224–226

"Amsterdam" (Murphy), **Supp. V:** 326

Amusements Serious and Comical (Brown), **III:** 41

"Amy Foster" (Conrad), **VI:** 134, 148

An Duanaire: An Irish Anthology, Poems of the Dispossessed, 1600–1900 (Kinsella), **Supp. V:** 266

An Giall (Behan), **Supp. II:** 71–73

Anacreontiques (Johnson), **II:** 198

"Anactoria" (Swinburne), **V:** 319–320, 321

"Anahorish" (Heaney), **Retro. Supp. I:** 125, 128

Anand, Mulk Raj, **Supp. IV:** 440

"Anarchist, An" (Conrad), **VI:** 148

Anathemata, The (Jones), **Supp. VII:** 167, 168, 169, 170, 175–178

Anatomy of Exchange–Alley, The (Defoe), **III:** 13

Anatomy of Frustration, The (Wells), **VI:** 228

Anatomy of Melancholy (Burton), **II:** 88, 106, 108; **IV:** 219

Anatomy of Oxford (eds. Day Lewis and Fenby), **Supp. III:** 118

Anatomy of Restlessness: Selected Writings, 1969–1989 (Chatwin), **Supp. IV:** 157, 160; **Supp. IX:** 52, 53, 61

"Ancestor" (Kinsella), **Supp. V:** 274

"Ancestor to Devotee" (Adcock), **Supp. XII:** 12–13

Ancestors (Brathwaite), **Supp. XII:** 33, 41–42, 45, 46

"Ancestors" (Cornford), **VIII:** 106

Ancestral Truths (Maitland), **Supp. XI:** 170–172

Anchises: Poems (Sisson), **Supp. XI:** 257

"Anchored Yachts on a Stormy Day" (Smith, I. C.), **Supp. IX:** 211

Ancient Allan, The (Haggard), **Supp. III:** 222

Ancient and English Versions of the Bible (Isaacs), **I:** 385

"Autumn Chapter in a Novel" (Gunn), **Retro. Supp. III:** 120

"Autumn Evening" (Cornford), **VIII:** 102, 103, 112

Autumn Journal (MacNeice), **VII:** 412

Autumn Midnight (Cornford), **VIII:** 104, 105, 109

"Autumn Morning at Cambridge" (Cornford), **VIII:** 102, 103, 107

"Autumn 1939" (Fuller), **Supp. VII:** 69

"Autumn 1942" (Fuller), **VII:** 430–431

"Autumn on Nan–Yueh" (Empson), **Supp. II:** 191–192

Autumn Sequel (MacNeice), **VII:** 407, 412, 415

"Autumn Sunshine" (Trevor), **Supp. IV:** 504

"Autumn Walk" (Conn), **Supp. XIII:** 80

"Autumnall, The" (Donne), **II:** 118

Available for Dreams (Fuller), **Supp. VII:** 68, 79, 80, 81

Avatars, The (Russell), **VIII:** 277, 285, 290–291, 292

Ave (Moore), **VI:** 99

"Ave Atque Vale" (Swinburne), **V:** 314, 327

"Ave Imperatrix" (Kipling), **VI:** 201

Aveling, Edward, **VI:** 102

Avignon Quintet (Durrell), **Supp. I:** 100, 101, **118–121**; **Retro. Supp. III:** 86, 87, 92–94

"Avising the bright beams of those fair eyes" (Wyatt), **I:** 110

Avoidance of Literature, The: Collected Essays (Sisson), **Supp. XI:** 247,

"Avoirdupois" (Burnside), **Supp. XIII:** 19

Avowals (Moore), **VI:** 97–98, 99

"Awake, my heart, to be loved" (Bridges), **VI:** 74, 77

"Awake, thou that sleepest" (Rossetti), **Retro. Supp. III:** 253

Awakened Conscience, The (Dixon Hunt), **VI:** 167

"Awakening, The" (Brathwaite), **Supp. XII:** 39

Awakening Conscience, The (Holman Hunt), **V:** 45, 51, 240

"Away with the Birds" (Healy), **Supp. IX:** 107

Awesome God: Creation, Commitment and Joy (Maitland), **Supp. XI:** 164, 165

Awfully Big Adventure, An (Bainbridge), **Supp. VI:** 18, **23–24**

Awkward Age, The (James), **VI:** 45, 56, 67

"Axeing Darkness / Here Below" (Dutton), **Supp. XII:** 94

"Axel's Castle" (Mahon), **Supp. VI:** 177

Ayala's Angel (Trollope), **V:** 100, 102

Ayckbourn, Alan, **Supp. V:** **1–17**

Ayesha: The Return of She (Haggard), **Supp. III:** 214, 222

Aylott & Jones (publishers), **V:** 131

"Ayrshire Farm" (Conn), **Supp. XIII:** 71, 72

"**B**aa, Baa Black Sheep" (Kipling), **VI:** 166

"Babby" (Crawford), **Supp. XI:** 76

Babees Book, The (Early English Poems and Treatises on Manners and Meals in Olden Time) (ed. Furnival), **I:** 22, 26

Babel Tower (Byatt), **Supp. IV:** 139, 141, 149–151

"Babes" (Fallon), **Supp. XII:** 102

Babes in the Darkling Wood (Wells), **VI:** 228

"Baby Nurse, The" (Blackwood), **Supp. IX:** 5, 9

"Baby's cradle with no baby in it, A" (Rossetti), **V:** 255

Babylon Hotel (Bennett), *see Grand Babylon Hotel, The*

"Babysitting" (Galloway), **Supp. XII:** 126

Bachelors, The (Spark), **Supp. I:** 203, 204

Back (Green), **Supp. II:** 254, 258–260

Back at the Spike (Constantine), **Supp. XV:** 66

"Back of Affluence" (Davie), **Supp. VI:** 110

"Back to Cambo" (Hartley), **Supp. VII:** 124

Back to Methuselah (Shaw), **VI:** **121–122,** 124; **Retro. Supp. II:** 323

"Backfire" (Delanty), **Supp. XIV:** 68

"Background Material" (Harrison), **Supp. V:** 155

Background to Danger (Ambler), **Supp. IV:** 7–8

Backward Look, The (O'Connor), **Supp. XIV:** 217

Backward Place, A (Jhabvala), **Supp. V:** 229

Backward Son, The (Spender), **Supp. II:** 484, 489

Backwater (Richardson), **Supp. XIII:** 182–183

Bacon, Francis, **I:** **257–274; II:** 149, 196; **III:** 39; **IV:** 138, 278, 279; annotated list of works, **I:** 271–273; **Supp. III:** 361

Bad Boy (McEwan), **Supp. IV:** 400

"Bad Dreams in Vienna" (Malouf), **Supp. XII:** 220

"Bad Five Minutes in the Alps, A" (Stephen), **V:** 283

"Bad Girl, The" (Pitter), **Supp. XIII:** 141

Bad Land: An American Romance (Raban), **Supp. XI:** 236, 239, 241

"Bad Night, A" (Auden), **Retro. Supp. I:** 14

Bad Sister, The (Tennant), **Supp. IX:** 229, 230, 231–234, 235–236, 238, 239, 240

"Back" (Scupham), **Supp. XIII:** 225

Bagehot, Walter, **IV:** 289, 291; **V:** xxiii, 156, 165, 170, 205, 212

"Baggot Street Deserta" (Kinsella), **Supp. V:** 259–260

Bagman, The; or, The Impromptu of Muswell Hill (Arden), **Supp. II:** 31, 32, 35

"Bagpipe Music" (MacNeice), **VII:** 413

Bailey, Benjamin, **IV:** 224, 229, 230, 232–233

Bailey, Paul, **Supp. IV:** 304

Baillie, Alexander, **V:** 368, 374, 375, 379

Bainbridge, Beryl, **Supp. VI:** **17–27**

Baines, Jocelyn, **VI:** 133–134

Baird, Julian, **V:** 316, 317, 318, 335

"Bairns of Suzie: A Hex" (Jamie), **Supp. XIV:** 138

"Bairnsang" (Jamie), **Supp. XIV:** 141–142

"Baite, The" (Donne), **IV:** 327

Bajazet (tr. Hollinghurst), **Supp. X:** 132–134

Bakerman, Jane S., **Supp. IV:** 336

"Baker's Dozen, The" (Saki), **Supp. VI:** 243

Bakhtin, Mikhail, **Supp. IV:** 114

"Balakhana" (McGuckian), **Supp. V:** 284

"Balance, The" (Waugh), **Supp. VI:** 271

Balance of Terror (Shaffer), **Supp. I:** 314

Balaustion's Adventure (Browning), **IV:** 358, 374; **Retro. Supp. II:** 30; **Retro. Supp. III:** 30

"Balder Dead" (Arnold), **V:** 209, 216

Baldrs draumar, **VIII:** 231

Baldwin, Edwin, *see Godwin, William*

Baldwin, Stanley, **VI:** 353, 355

Bale, John, **I:** 1, 3

Balfour, Arthur, **VI:** 226, 241, 353

Balfour, Graham, **V:** 393, 397

"Balin and Balan" (Tennyson), **Retro. Supp. III:** 327

Balin; or, The Knight with Two Swords (Malory), **I:** 79

Ball and the Cross, The (Chesterton), **VI:** 338

Ballad at Dead Men's Bay, The (Swinburne), **V:** 332

"Ballad of Bouillabaisse" (Thackeray), **V:** 19

"Ballad of Death, A" (Swinburne), **V:** 316, 317–318

Ballad of Jan Van Hunks, The (Rossetti), **V:** 238, 244, 245

"Ballad of Kynd Kittok, The" (Dunbar), **VIII:** 126

"Ballad of Life, A" (Swinburne), **V:** 317, 318

Ballad of Peckham Rye, The (Spark), **Supp. I:** 201, 203–204

Ballad of Reading Gaol, The (Wilde), **V:** xxvi, 417–418, 419; **Retro. Supp. II:** 372–373

Ballad of Sylvia and Ted, The (Tennant), **Supp. IX:** 239, 240

"Ballad of the Investiture 1969, A" (Betjeman), **VII:** 372

"Ballad of the Long–legged Bait" (Thomas), **Supp. I:** 177; **Retro. Supp. III:** 345

"Ballad of the Red–Headed Man" (Beer), **Supp. XIV:** 5

"Ballad of the Three Spectres" (Gurney), **VI:** 426

"Ballad of the Two Left Hands" (Dunn), **Supp. X:** 73

"Ballad of the Underpass" (Beer), **Supp. XIV:** 6

"Ballad of the White Horse, The" (Chesterton), **VI:** 338–339, 341

"Ballad of Villon and Fat Madge, The" (tr. Swinburne), **V:** 327

Fille du Policeman (Swinburne), **V:** 325, 333

Film (Beckett), **Supp. I:** 51, 59, 60

Filostrato (Boccaccio), **I:** 30

Filthy Lucre (Bainbridge), **Supp. VI:** 23

Final Demands (Reading), **VIII:** 271, 273

Final Passage, The (Phillips), **Supp. V:** 380–383

"Final Problem, The" (Doyle), **Supp. II:** 160, 172–173

Final Unfinished Voyage of Jack Aubrey, The (O'Brian), **Supp. XII:** 259

"Finale" (Dutton), **Supp. XII:** 99

Finch, Anne, **Supp. IX: 65–78**

Finden's Byron Beauties (Finden), **V:** 111

Finding the Dead (Fallon), **Supp. XII:** 104

Findings (Jamie), **Supp. XIV:** 129, 139, 144–145

"Findings" (Jamie), **Supp. XIV:** 145

Findlater, Richard, **VII:** 8

Fine Arts, The (Symonds), **Supp. XIV:** 256–257, 257–259

Fine Balance, A (Mistry), **Supp. X:** 142, 145–149

Finer Grain, The (James), **VI:** 67

Fingal (Macpherson), **VIII:** 181–182, 186–189, 190, 191, 192, 193, 194

"Fingal's Visit to Norway" (Macpherson), **VIII:** 186

Finished (Haggard), **Supp. III:** 214

"Finistére" (Kinsella), **Supp. V:** 268

Finnegans Wake (Joyce), **VII:** 42, 46, 52–54; critical studies, **VII:** 58; **Supp. III:** 108; **Retro. Supp. I:** 169, 179–181; **Retro. Supp. III:** 168, 177–179

Firbank, Ronald, **VII:** 132, 200; **Supp. II: 199–223**

"Fire and Ice" (Kinsella), **Supp. V:** 261

Fire and the Sun, The: Why Plato Banished the Artists (Murdoch), **Supp. I:** 230, 232

"Fire and the Tide" (Stevenson), **Supp. VI:** 260

Fire Down Below (Golding), **Retro. Supp. I:** 104–105

"Fire, Famine and Slaughter" (Coleridge), **Retro. Supp. II:** 53

Fire from Heaven (Renault), **Supp. IX:** 184–185

Fire in the Wood, The (Welch), **Supp. IX:** 267

Fire of the Lord, The (Nicholson), **Supp. VI: 219**

Fire on the Mountain (Desai), **Supp. V:** 53, 55, 64–65, 73

"Fire Sermon, The" (Eliot), **Retro. Supp. II:** 127–128

Fires of Baäl, The (Clarke), **Supp. XV:** 18

Firework–Maker's Daughter, The (Pullman), **Supp. XIII:** 152

"Fireworks Poems" (Cope), **VIII:** 81

"Firing Practice" (Motion), **Supp. VII:** 251, 254, 257, 260

"Firm of Happiness, Ltd., The" (Cameron), **Supp. IX:** 25–26

"Firm Views" (Hart), **Supp. XI:** 129

First Affair, The (Fallon), **Supp. XII:** 101, 102–103

First and Last Loves (Betjeman), **VII:** 357, 358, 359

First & Last Things (Wells), **VI:** 244

First and Second Poems (Pitter), **Supp. XIII:** 133, 137–139

First Anniversary, The (Donne), **I:** 188, 356; **Retro. Supp. II:** 94

"First Anniversary of the Government under O. C., The" (Marvell), **II:** 210, 211; **Retro. Supp. II:** 262–263

First Book of Odes (Bunting), **Supp. VII:** 5, 13

First Book of Urizen, The (Blake), **III:** 299, 300, 306, 307; **Retro. Supp. I:** 43–44

"First Countess of Wessex, The" (Hardy), **VI:** 22

First Earthquake, The (Redgrove), **Supp. VI: 236**

First Eleven, The (Ewart), **Supp. VII:** 41

First Episode (Rattigan), **Supp. VII:** 308

First Flight, The (Heaney), **Supp. II:** 278

First Folio (Shakespeare), **I:** 299, 324, 325

First Grammatical Treatise, **VIII:** 236

First Gun, The (Jefferies), **Supp. XV:** 166

First Hundred Years of Thomas Hardy, The (Weber), **VI:** 19

"First Hymn to Lenin" (MacDiarmid), **Supp. III:** 119; **Supp. XII:** 211

"'First Impression' (Tokyo), A" (Blunden), **Supp. XI:** 35

"First Impressions" (Austen), *see Pride and Prejudice*

"First Journey, The" (Graham), **Supp. VII:** 109

First Lady Chatterley, The (Lawrence), **VII:** 111–112

First Language (Carson), **Supp. XIII:** 54, 59–60

First Light (Ackroyd), **Supp. VI:** 1, 8

"First Light" (Kinsella), **Supp. V:** 263

First Life of Adamastor, The (Brink), **Supp. VI: 54–55,** 57

"First Love" (Beckett), **Retro. Supp. I:** 21

"First Love" (Beer), **Supp. XIV:** 5

First Love, Last Rites (McEwan), **Supp. IV:** 390–392

"First Man, The" (Gunn), **Supp. IV:** 264–265

First Men in the Moon, The, (Wells), **VI:** 229, 234, 244

"First Men on Mercury, The" (Morgan, E.), **Supp. IX:** 169

First Ode of the Second Book of Horace Paraphras'd, The (Swift), **III:** 35

"First Place, A: The Mapping of a World" (Malouf), *Supp. XII: 218*

First Poems (Muir), **Supp. VI:** 198, **204–205**

First Poems (Pitter), **Supp. XIII:** 132, 134

First Satire (Wyatt), **I:** 111

First Satire of the Second Book of Horace, Imitated, The (Pope), **III:** 234

First Steps in Reading English (Richards), **Supp. II:** 425

First Things Last (Malouf), **Supp. XII:** 220

"First Things Last" (Malouf), **Supp. XII:** 220

"First Things, Last Things" (Scupham), **Supp. XIII:** 228

"First Winter of War" (Fuller), **Supp. VII:** 69

First World War, see World War I

First Year in Canterbury Settlement, A (Butler), **Supp. II:** 98, 112

Firstborn, The (Fry), **Supp. III:** 195, 196, 198–199, 207

Firth, Sir Charles Harding, **II:** 241; **III:** 25, 36; **IV:** 289, 290, 291

Fischer, Ernst, **Supp. II:** 228

"Fish" (Lawrence), **VII:** 119

"Fish, The" (Brooke), **Supp. III:** 53, 56, 60

Fish Preferred (Wodehouse), **Supp. III:** 460

"Fishermen, The" (Mangan), **Supp. XIII:** 122

"Fisherman, The" (Yeats), **VI:** 214; **Retro. Supp. I:** 331

"Fishermen with Ploughs: A Poem Cycle (Brown), **Supp. VI:** 63

"Fishes in a Chinese Restaurant" (Carson), **Supp. XIII:** 56

"Fishing" (Thomas), **Supp. XII:** 287

Fishing for Amber (Carson), **Supp. XIII:** 54, 56, 63–65

Fishmonger's Fiddle (Coppard), **VIII:** 89, 95

"Fishmonger's Fiddle" (Coppard), **VIII:** 95

"Fishy Waters" (Rhys), **Supp. II:** 401

Fit for the Future: The Guide for Women Who Want to Live Well (Winterson), **Supp. IV:** 542

"Fitz–Boodle Papers, The" (Thackeray), **V:** 38

FitzGerald, Edward, **IV:** xvii, xxii, xxiii, 310, **340–353; V:** xxv

Fitzgerald, Penelope, **Supp. V: 95–109**

Fitzgerald, Percy, **III:** 125, 135

Five (Lessing), **Supp. I:** 239, 240, 241, 242

Five Autumn Songs for Children's Voices (Hughes), **Supp. I:** 357

"Five Dreams" (Nye), **Supp. X:** 205

"Five Dreams and a Vision" (Pitter), **Supp. XIII:** 144

"Five Eleven Ninety Nine" (Armitage), **VIII:** 9–11, 15

Five Finger Exercise (Shaffer), **Supp. I:** 313, **314–317,** 319, 322, 323, 327

Five Looks at Elizabeth Bishop (Stevenson), **Supp. VI:** 264–265

"Five Minutes" (Nicholson), **Supp. VI:** 216

Five Metaphysical Poets (Bennett), **II:** 181, 202

Five Nations, The (Kipling), **VI:** 204; **Retro. Supp. III:** 194

Five Novelettes by Charlotte Brontë (ed. Gérin), **V:** 151

"Five Orange Pips, The" (Doyle), **Supp. II:** 174

"Five Poems on Film Directors" (Morgan, E.), **Supp. IX:** 163

Five Red Herrings, The (Sayers), **Supp. III:** 334, 343–344

Five Rivers (Nicholson), **Supp. VI: 213–215,** 216

Five Sermons on the Errors of the Roman Catholic Church (Maturin), **VIII:** 197, 208

"Five Songs" (Auden), **Retro. Supp. I:** 11–12

"Five Students, The" (Hardy), **VI:** 17

Five Tales (Galsworthy), **VI:** 276

Five Uncollected Essays of Matthew Arnold (ed. Allott), **V:** 216

Five Years of Youth (Martineau), **Supp. XV:** 185

Fivefold Screen, The (Plomer), **Supp. XI:** 213

Five-Year Plan, A (Kerr), **Supp. XII:** 194, 195

Fixed Period, The (Trollope), **V:** 102

Flag on the Island, A (Naipaul), **Supp. I:** 394

Flame, The: A Play in One Act (Clarke), **Supp. XV:** 24

Flame in Your Heart, A (Jamie), **Supp. XIV:** 129, 131–134, 143

Flame of Life, The (Sillitoe), **Supp. V:** 410, 421, 424

Flame Tree (Hart), **Supp. XI:** 126–127

"Flaming Heart Upon the Book and Picture of the Seraphicall Saint Teresa, The" (Crashaw), **II:** 182

"Flaming sighs that boil within my breast, The" (Wyatt), **I:** 109–110

Flare Path (Rattigan), **Supp. VII:** 311–312, 313, 314

Flatman, Thomas, **II:** 133

"Flatting Mill, The" (Cowper), **Retro. Supp. III:** 48

Flaubert, Gustave, **V:** xviii–xxiv, 340, 353, 429; **Supp. IV:** 68, 69, 136, 157, 163, 167

Flaubert's Parrot (Barnes), **Supp. IV:** 65, 67, 68–70, 72, 73

Flaws in the Glass: A Self-Portrait (White), **Supp. I:** 129, 130, 132, 149

Flea, The (Donne), **I:** 355; **Retro. Supp. II:** 88

"Fleckno, an English Priest at Rome" (Marvell), **II:** 211

"Fleet" (Coppard), **VIII:** 88

Fleetwood; or, The New Man of Feeling (Godwin), **Supp. XV:** 125–126

Fleming, Ian, **Supp. IV:** 212

Fleming, Ian, **Supp. XIV:** 81–98

Flesh & Blood (Roberts), **Supp. XV:** 270–271, 273

Fleshly School of Poetry, The (Buchanan), **V:** 238, 245

Fletcher, Ian, **V:** xii, xiii, xxvii, 359

Fletcher, Ifan Kyrle, **Supp. II:** 201, 202, 203

Fletcher, John, **II: 42–67,** 79, 82, 87–88, 90, 91, 93, 185, 305, 340, 357, 359

Fletcher, Phineas, **II:** 138

Fletcher, Thomas, **II:** 21

Fleurs du Mal (Baudelaire), **V:** xxii, 316, 329, 411

Fleurs du Mal (Swinburne), **V:** 329, 331, 333

"Flickerbridge" (James), **VI:** 69

"Flight" (Conn), **Supp. XIII:** 72

Flight from the Enchanter, The (Murdoch), **Supp. I: 220–222**

Flight into Camden (Storey), **Supp. I:** 408, 410–411, 414, 415, 419

"Flight of the Duchess, The" (Browning), **IV:** 356, 361, 368; **Retro. Supp. II:** 24; **Retro. Supp. III:** 22, 23

"Flight of the Earls, The" (Boland), **Supp. V:** 36

Flight of the Falcon, The (du Maurier), **Supp. III:** 139, 141

Flight to Africa and Other Poems (Clarke), **Supp. XV:** 27–28

Flint Anchor, The (Warner), **Supp. VII:** 376, 378–379

"Flitting, The" (McGuckian), **Supp. V:** 281

Flood, A (Moore), **VI:** 99

Flood, The (Rankin), **Supp. X:** 244, 246–247, 250

"Flooded Meadows" (Gunn), **Supp. IV:** 267; **Retro. Supp. III:** 122

Floor Games (Wells), **VI:** 227

"Flora" (Dutton), **Supp. XII:** 88

Flora Selbornesis (White), **Supp. VI:** 282–283

"Florent" (Gower), **I:** 55

Florentine Painting and Its Social Background (Antal), **Supp. IV:** 80

Flores Solitudinis (Vaughan), **II:** 185, 201

Floud, Peter, **V:** 296, 307

"Flower, The" (Herbert), **II:** 119n 125; **Retro. Supp. II:** 177–178

Flower Beneath the Foot, The (Firbank), **Supp. II:** 202, 205, **216–218**

Flower Master, The (McGuckian), **Supp. V:** 277, 278, 281–282

"Flower Master, The" (McGuckian), **Supp. V:** 281

Flower Master and Other Poems, The (McGuckian), **Supp. V:** 281

"Flower Poem" (Hope), **Supp. VII:** 154

Flowers and Shadows (Okri), **Supp. V:** 347–348, 350, 352, 354–355

Flower of Courtesy (Lydgate), **I:** 57, 60, 62

"Flowering Absence, A" (Montague), **Supp. XV:** 210, 217

Flowering Death of a Salesman (Stoppard), **Supp. I:** 439

Flowering Rifle (Campbell), **VII:** 428

Flowering Wilderness (Galsworthy), **VI:** 275, 282

Flowers and Insects (Hughes), **Retro. Supp. II:** 214

"Flowers of Empire, The" (Kincaid), **Supp. VII:** 229

"Flowers of Evil" (Kincaid), **Supp. VII:** 219

Flowers of Passion (Moore), **VI:** 85, 98

Flurried Years, The (Hunt), **VI:** 333

Flush: A Biography (Woolf), **Retro. Supp. I:** 308, 320–321

Flute-Player, The (Thomas), **Supp. IV:** 479–480, 481

"Fly, The" (Blake), **III:** 295–296

"Fly, The" (Chatwin), **Supp. IV:** 158

"Fly, The" (Mansfield), **VII:** 176

Fly Away Peter (Malouf), **Supp. XII:** 217, 224–225

"Flying Above California" (Gunn), **Supp. IV:** 263

"Flying Ace, The" (Redgrove), **Supp. VI:** 236

"Flying Bum, The" (Plomer), **Supp. XI:** 222

Flying Hero Class (Keneally), **Supp. IV:** 347

Flying in to Love (Thomas), **Supp. IV:** 486–487

Flying Inn, The (Chesterton), **VI:** 340

"Flying to Belfast, 1977" (Raine), **Supp. XIII:** 167

"Flyting of Crawford and Herbert, The" (Crawford and Herbert), **Supp. XI:** 68

"Flyting of Dunbar and Kennedie, The" (Dunbar), **VIII:** 117, 118, 126–127

"Focherty" (MacDiarmid), **Supp. XII:** 205

Foe (Coetzee), **Supp. VI:** 75–76, **83–84**

Foe-Farrell (Quiller-Couch), **V:** 384

"Foetal Monitor Day, The" (Delanty), **Supp. XIV:** 74

Folding Star, The (Hollinghurst), **Supp. X:** 120–122, 128–134

"Folie à Deux" (Burnside), **Supp. XIII:** 29

"Folk Wisdom" (Kinsella), **Supp. V:** 263

"Folklore" (Murray), **Supp. VII:** 276

Folk-Lore in the Old Testament (Frazer), **Supp. III:** 176

Follow My Leader (Rattigan), **Supp. VII:** 310

"Follower" (Heaney), **Supp. IV:** 410

"Followers, The" (Thomas), **Supp. I:** 183

Following a Lark (Brown), **Supp. VI:** 72

"Folly" (Murphy), **Supp. V:** 327

Folly of Industry, The (Wycherley), **II:** 322

"Fond Memory" (Boland), **Supp. V:** 35

Fontaine amoureuse, **I:** 33

"Food of the Dead" (Graves), **VII:** 269

Food, Sex, and God: On Inspiration and Writing (Roberts), **Supp. XV:** 259, 270, 273

Fool, The (Bond), **Supp. I:** 423, 434, 435

Fool of the World and Other Poems, The (Symons), **Supp. XIV:** 279

"Fool's Song" (Cornford), **VIII:** 107

Fools of Fortune (Trevor), **Supp. IV:** 502, 503, 512–514, 517

Foot of Clive, The (Berger), **Supp. IV:** 79, 84–85

"Football at Slack" (Hughes), **Retro. Supp. II:** 210–211

Foote, Samuel, **III:** 253; **V:** 261

Footfalls (Beckett), **Retro. Supp. I:** 28

Footnote to History, A: Eight Years of Trouble in Samoa (Stevenson), **V:** 396

"Footsteps of Death, The" (Steel), **Supp. XII:** 269

"For a Five-Year-Old" (Adcock), **Supp. XII:** 5

"For a Greeting" (MacCaig), **Supp. VI:** 185

"For a Young Matron" (McGuckian), **Supp. V:** 284–285

"Great Lover, The" (Brooke), **Supp. III:** 556

"Great Man, The" (Caudwell), **Supp. IX:** 35, 37

"Great Man, The" (Motion), **Supp. VII:** 256

"Great McEwen, Scottish Hypnotist, The" (Crawford), **Supp. XI:** 71

"Great men have been among us" (Wordsworth), **II:** 208

Great Moments in Aviation (film), **Supp. IV:** 542

Great Port: A Passage through New York, The (Morris, J.), **Supp. X:** 182

"Great Ship, The" (Delanty), **Supp. XIV:** 75

Great Short Stories of Detection, Mystery and Horror (ed. Sayers), **III:** 341; **Supp. III:** 340, 341

"Great Spirits Now on Earth Are Sojourning . . . A (Keats), **IV:** 214

"Great Spunky Unflincher: Laurence Sterne, B. S. Johnson, and Me: The 2004 Laurence Sterne Memorial Lecture" (Coe), **Supp. XV:** 52

Great Trade Route (Ford), **VI:** 324

Great Tradition, The (Leavis), **VI:** 68, 149; **VII:** 234, **248–251**; **Retro. Supp. I:** 90

"Great Unknown, The" (Hood), **IV:** 267

Great Victorian Collection, The (Moore, B.), **Supp. IX:** 143–144, 154

Great War and Modern Memory, The (Fussell), **Supp. IV:** 57

Great World, The (Malouf), **Supp. XII:** 218, 226–227

Greater Lakeland (Nicholson), **Supp. VI:** 223

"Greater Love" (Owen), **VI:** 450

Greater Trumps, The (Williams, C. W. S.), **Supp. IX:** 281

"Greatest TV Show on Earth, The" (Ballard), **Supp. V:** 28

Greatness of the Soul, A, . . . (Bunyan), **II:** 253

Greber, Giacomo, **II:** 325

Grecian History, The (Goldsmith), **III:** 181, 191

Greek Christian Poets, The, and the English Poets (Browning), **IV:** 321

"Greek Interpreter, The" (Doyle), **Supp. II:** 167

Greek Islands, The (Durrell), **Supp. I:** 102; **Retro. Supp. III:** 84

Greek Studies (Pater), **V:** 355, 357

Greeks have a word for it, The (Unsworth), **Supp. VII:** 354, 355–356, 357, 359

Green Fool, The (Kavanagh), **Supp. VII:** 183, 186, 187, 188, 194, 199

Green, Henry, **Supp. II: 247–264**

"Green Hills of Africa, The" (Fuller), **Supp. VII:** 69

"Greenhouse Effect, The" (Adcock), **Supp. XII:** 12

Green, Joseph Henry, **IV:** 57

Green, Roger Lancelyn, **V:** 265n, 273, 274

Green Crow, The (O'Casey), **VII:** 13

"Green Geese" (Sitwell), **VII:** 131

"Green, Green Is Aghir" (Cameron), **VII:** 426; **Supp. IX:** 27

Green Helmet, The (Yeats), **VI:** 222

"Green Hills of Africa" (Fuller), **VII:** 429, 432

"Green Leaf, The" (Smith, I. C.), **Supp. IX:** 223

Green Man, The (Amis), **Supp. II:** 13–14

"Green Mountain, Black Mountain" (Stevenson), **Supp. VI:** 256–257, 261–262, 266

"Green Room, The" (Delanty), **Supp. XIV:** 75

Green Shore, The (Nicholson), **Supp. VI: 219–220**

Green Song (Sitwell), **VII:** 132, 135, 136

"Green Tea" (Le Fanu), **III:** 340, 345

"Greenden" (Gibbon), **Supp. XIV:** 104, 105

Greene, Graham, **VI:** 329, 370; **VII:** xii; **Supp. I: 1–20**; **Supp. II:** 311, 324; **Supp. IV:** 4, 10, 13, 17, 21, 157, 365, 369, 373–374, 505; **Supp. V:** 26; **Retro. Supp. II: 151–167**

Greene, Robert, **I:** 165, 220, 275, 286, 296, 322; **II:** 3; **VIII: 131–146**

Greene's Arcadia (Greene). *See Menaphon*

Greenlees, Ian Gordon, **VI:** xxxiii

"Greenshank" (MacCaig), **Supp. VI:** 192

Greenvoe (Brown), **Supp. VI:** 64, **65–66**

"Greenwich—Whitebait" (Thackeray), **V:** 38

Greenwood, Edward Baker, **VII:** xix, xxxvii

Greenwood, Frederick, **V:** 1

Greer, Germaine, **Supp. IV:** 436

Greg, W. R., **V:** 5, 7, 15

Greg, W. W., **I:** 279

Gregory, Lady Augusta, **VI:** 210, 218, **307–312, 314–316**, 317–318; **VII:** 1, 3, 42

Gregory, Sir Richard, **VI:** 233

Greiffenhagen, Maurice, **VI:** 91

Gremlins, The (Dahl), **Supp. IV:** 202, 211–212

"Grenadier" (Housman), **VI:** 160

Grenfell, Julian, **VI:** xvi, 417–418, 420

"Greta Garbo's Feet" (Delahunt), **Supp. XIV:** 52–53

"Gretchen" (Gissing), **V:** 437

"Gretna Green" (Behan), **Supp. II:** 64

Grettis saga, **VIII:** 234–235, 238, 241

Greuze, Jean–Baptiste, **Supp. IV:** 122

Greuze: The Rise and Fall of an Eighteenth Century Phenomenon (Brookner), **Supp. IV:** 122

Greville, Fulke, **I:** 160, 164; **Supp. IV:** 256; **Supp. XI: 105–119**

Grey Area (Self), **Supp. V:** 402–404

Grey Eminence (Huxley), **VII:** 205

"Grey Eye Weeping, A" (tr. O'Connor), **Supp. XIV:** 221

Grey of Fallodon (Trevelyan), **VI:** 383, 391

Grey Granite (Gibbon), **Supp. XIV:** 102, 106, 111–113

"Grey Woman, The" (Gaskell), **V:** 15

Greybeards at Play (Chesterton), **VI:** 336

Greyhound for Breakfast (Kelman), **Supp. V:** 242, 249–250

"Greyhound for Breakfast" (Kelman), **Supp. V:** 250

Grid, The (Kerr), **Supp. XII:** 194, 195

Gridiron, The (Kerr), **Supp. XII:** 194, 195

"Grief" (Browning), **IV:** 313, 318

Grief Observed, A (Lewis), **Supp. III:** 249

"Grief on the Death of Prince Henry, A" (Tourneur), **II:** 37, 41

Grierson, Herbert J. C., **II:** 121, 130, 196, 200, 202, 258; **Retro. Supp. II:** 173

Grigson, Geoffrey, **IV:** 47; **VII:** xvi

Grim Smile of the Five Towns, The (Bennett), **VI:** 250, 253–254

Grímnismál, **VIII:** 230

Grimus (Rushdie), **Supp. IV:** 435, 438–439, 443, 450

"Grip, The" (Delahunt), **Supp. XIV:** 59

Gris, Juan, **Supp. IV:** 81

"Grisly Folk, The" (Wells), **Retro. Supp. I:** 96

Groatsworth of Wit, A (Greene), **I:** 275, 276; **VIII:** 131, 132

Grænlendinga saga, **VIII:** 240

Grosskurth, Phyllis, **V:** xxvii

Grote, George, **V:** 289

Group of Noble Dames, A (Hardy), **VI:** 20, 22

"Grove, The" (Muir), **Supp. VI:** 206

"Growing, Flying, Happening" (Reid), **Supp. VII:** 328

"Growing Old" (Arnold), **V:** 203

Growing Pains: The Shaping of a Writer (du Maurier), **Supp. III:** 135, 142, 144

Growing Points (Jennings), **Supp. V:** 217

Growing Rich (Weldon), **Supp. IV:** 531, 533

Growth of Love, The (Bridges), **VI:** 81, 83

Growth of Plato's Ideal Theory, The (Frazer), **Supp. III:** 170–171

"Grub First, Then Ethics" (Auden), **Retro. Supp. I:** 7, 13

Grünewald, Mathias, **Supp. IV:** 85

Gryffydh, Jane, **IV:** 159

Gryll Grange (Peacock), **IV:** xxii, 166–167, 170

Grylls, R. Glynn, **V:** 247, 260; **VII:** xvii, xxxviii

Guardian (periodical), **III:** 46, 49, 50; **Supp. XIII:** 1

Guardian, The (Cowley), **II:** 194, 202

Guardian, The (Massinger), **Supp. XI:** 184

Guarini, Guarino, **II:** 49–50

Gubar, Susan, **Retro. Supp. I:** 59–60

"Gude Grey Katt, The" (Hogg), **Supp. X:** 110

"Guerrillas" (Dunn), **Supp. X:** 70–71

Guerrillas (Naipaul), **Supp. I:** 396–397

Guest from the Future, The (Stallworthy), **Supp. X:** 298–302

"Guest from the Future, The" (Stallworthy), **Supp. X:** 298

Guest of Honour, A (Gordimer), **Supp. II:** 229–230, 231

Medal: A Satyre Against Sedition, The (Dryden), **II:** 299, 304; **Retro. Supp. III:** 62

Medea (Seneca), **II:** 71

Medea: A Sex–War Opera (Harrison), **Supp. V:** 164

"Medico's Song" (Wallace–Crabbe), **VIII:** 324

Medieval Heritage of Elizabethan Tragedy (Farnham), **I:** 214

"Meditation of Mordred, The" (Williams, C. W. S.), **Supp. IX:** 283

Meditation upon a Broom–Stick, A (Swift), **III:** 35

"Meditation with Mountains" (Wallace–Crabbe), **VIII:** 317–318

Meditations Collected from the Sacred Books . . . (Richardson), **III:** 92

"Meditations in Time of Civil War" (Yeats), **V:** 317; **VII:** 24; **Retro. Supp. I:** 334–335

Meditations of Daniel Defoe, The (Defoe), **III:** 12

"Meditations with Memories" (Wallace–Crabbe), **VIII:** 317

"Mediterranean" (Redgrove), **Supp. VI:** 231

Mediterranean Scenes (Bennett), **VI:** 264, 267

"Medussa's Ankles" (Byatt), **Supp. IV:** 154–155

Medwin, Thomas, **IV:** 196, 209

Mee, Arthur, **Supp. IV:** 256

Meet My Father (Ayckbourn), **Supp. V:** 2

"Meet Nurse!" (Hope), **Supp. VII:** 151

Meeting by the River, A (Isherwood), **VII:** 317

"Meeting My Former Self" (Cameron), **Supp. IX:** 24

"Meeting of David and Jonathan, The" (Symonds), **Supp. XIV:** 252

"Meeting of Minds, The" (Coe), **Supp. XV:** 54

Meeting Place (Kay), **Supp. XIII:** 100

Meeting the British (Muldoon), **Supp. IV:** 421–424

Meeting the Comet (Adcock), **Supp. XII:** 8

"Megaliths and Water" (Scupham), **Supp. XIII:** 221

"Melancholia" (Bridges), **VI:** 80

"Melancholy" (Bridges), **VI:** 80

"Melancholy Hussar of the German Legion, The" (Hardy), **VI:** 20, 22; **Retro. Supp. I:** 116

"Melbourne" (Wallace–Crabbe), **VIII:** 313

"Melbourne in 1963" (Wallace–Crabbe), **VIII:** 313–314

Melbourne or the Bush (Wallace–Crabbe), **VIII:** 313–314, 319, 320

Melchiori, Giorgio, **VI:** 208

Meleager (Euripides), **V:** 322, 323

Melincourt (Peacock), **IV:** xvii, 162, 163–164, 165, 168, 170

Melly, Diana, **Supp. IV:** 168

Melmoth Reconciled (Balzac), **III:** 334, 339

Melmoth the Wanderer (Maturin), **III:** 327, 333–334, 335, 345; **VIII:** 197–200, 201–205, 208–209; **Supp. III:** 384–385

Melnikov, Konstantin, **Supp. IV:** 174

"Melon" (Barnes), **Supp. IV:** 75

Melville, Herman, **IV:** 97; **V:** xvii, xx–xxi, xxv, 211; **VI:** 363; **Supp. IV:** 160

Memento Mori (Spark), **Supp. I:** 203

"Memoir" (Scott), **IV:** 28, 30, 35–36, 39

"Memoir of Bernard Barton" (FitzGerald), **IV:** 353

"Memoir of Cowper: An Autobiography" (ed. Quinlan), **III:** 220

"Memoir"of Fleeming Jenkin (Stevenson), **V:** 386, 395

Memoir of Jane Austen (Austen–Leigh), **III:** 90

"Memoir of My Father, A" (Amis), **Supp. II:** 1

Memoir of the Author's Life and Familiar Anecdotes of Sir Walter Scott (Hogg), **Supp. X:** 105

Memoir of the Bobotes (Cary), **VII:** 185

Mémoire justificatif etc. (Gibbon), **III:** 233

Mémoires littéraires de la Grande Bretagne (periodical), **III:** 233

Memoirs (Amis), **Supp. IV:** 27

Memoirs (Robinson), **Supp. XIII:** 196–197, 198, 199, 200, 201, 203, 204, 207, 213

Memoirs (Temple), **III:** 19

Memoirs of a Cavalier, The (Defoe), **III:** 6, 13; **VI:** 353, 359; **Retro. Supp. I:** 66, 68, 71–72

Memoirs of a Certain Island Adjacent to the Kingdom of Utopia (Haywood), **Supp. XII:** 135, 141

Memoirs of a Midget (de la Mare), **III:** 340, 345

Memoirs of a Physician, The (Dumas père), **III:** 332

Memoirs of a Protestant, The (tr. Goldsmith), **III:** 191

Memoirs of a Survivor, The (Lessing), **Supp. I:** 249–250, 254

Memoirs of Barry Lyndon, Esq., The (Thackeray), *see Barry Lyndon*

Memoirs of Doctor Burney (Burney), **Supp. III:** 68

Memoirs of Himself (Stevenson), **V:** 396

"Memoirs of James Boswell, Esq." (Boswell), **III:** 248

Memoirs of John Addington Symonds, The: The Secret Homosexual Life of a Leading Nineteenth–Century Man of the Letters (Symonds), **Supp. XIV:** 250, 251, 252, 253, 262–263

Memoirs of Jonathan Swift (Scott), **IV:** 38

Memoirs of Lord Byron, The (Nye), **Supp. X:** 195–196

Memoirs of Martin Scriblerus, (Pope), **III:** 24, 77; **Retro. Supp. I:** 234

"Memoirs of M. de Voltaire" (Goldsmith), **III:** 189

Memoirs of My Dead Life (Moore), **VI:** 87, 88, 95, 96, 97, 98–99

"Memoirs of Percy Bysshe Shelley" (Peacock), **IV:** 158, 169, 170

Memoirs of the Author of "A Vindication of the Rights of Woman" (Godwin), **Supp. III:** 465; *Supp. XV:* 123

Memoirs of the Baron de Brosse (Haywood), **Supp. XII:** 135

Memoirs of the Late Thomas Holcroft . . . (Hazlitt), **IV:** 128, 139

Memoirs of the Life of Edward Gibbon, The (ed. Hill), **III:** 221n, 233

Memoirs of the Life of Sir Walter Scott, Bart. (Lockhart), **IV:** 27, 30, 34, 35–36, 39

Memoirs of the Life of William Collins, Esp., R.A. (1848) (Collins), **Supp. VI:** 92, 95

Memoirs of the Navy (Pepys), **II:** 281, 288

"Memoirs of the World" (Gunn), **Supp. IV:** 264

Memoirs Relating to . . . Queen Anne's Ministry (Swift), **III:** 27

"Memorabilia" (Browning), **IV:** 354–355

Memorable Masque of the Middle Temple and Lincoln's Inn, The (Chapman), **I:** 235

Memorial, The (Isherwood), **VII:** 205, 310–311

"Memorial for the City" (Auden), **VII:** 388, 393; **Retro. Supp. I:** 8

Memorials of a Tour on the Continent (Wordsworth), **IV:** 24–25

Memorials of Edward Burne–Jones (Burne–Jones), **V:** 295–296, 306

"Memorials of Gormandising" (Thackeray), **V:** 23, 24, 38

Memorials of Thomas Hood (Hood and Broderip), **IV:** 251, 261, 267

Memorials of Two Sisters, Susanna and Catherine Winkworth (ed. Shaen), **V:** 149

Memories and Adventures (Doyle), **Supp. II:** 159

Memories and Hallucinations (Thomas), **Supp. IV:** 479, 480, 482, 483, 484, 486

Memories and Portraits (Stevenson), **V:** 390, 395

"Memories of a Catholic Childhood" (Lodge), **Supp. IV:** 363–364

"Memories of a Working Women's Guild" (Woolf), **Retro. Supp. I:** 311

Memories of the Space Age (Ballard), **Supp. V:** 24

"Memories of the Space Age" (Ballard), **Supp. V:** 33

Memories of Vailiona (Osborne and Strong), **V:** 393, 397

"Memories of Youghal" (Trevor), **Supp. IV:** 501

"Memory, A" (Brooke), **Supp. III:** 55

"Memory and Imagination&rdqo; (Dunn), **Supp. X:** 77

"Memory Man" (Ewart), **Supp. VII:** 41

Memory of Ben Jonson Revived by the Friends of the Muses, The (Digby), **Retro. Supp. I:** 166

"Memory Unsettled" (Gunn), **Supp. IV:** 277; **Retro. Supp. III:** 127, 128

"Midsummer Ice" (Murray), **Supp. VII:** 278

"Midsummer Night's Dream, A" (Scupham), **Supp. XIII:** 223

Midsummer Night's Dream, A (Shakespeare), **I:** 304–305, 311–312; **II:** 51, 281; **Supp. IV:** 198; **Retro. Supp. III:** 271–272, 273

"Mid–Term Break" (Heaney), **Retro. Supp. I:** 125

Mid–Victorian Memories (Francillon), **V:** 83

"Midwich Cuckoos, The" (Wyndham), **Supp. XIII:** 291–292

"Mightier than Mammon, A" (Carpenter), **Supp. XIII:** 39

Mightier Than the Sword (Ford), **VI:** 320–321

Mighty and Their Full, The (Compton–Burnett), **VII:** 61, 62

Mighty Magician, The (FitzGerald), **IV:** 353

"Migrants" (Thomas), **Supp. XII:** 290

Miguel Street (Naipaul), **Supp. I:** 383, 385–386

"Mike: A Public School Story" (Wodehouse), **Supp. III:** 449

Mike Fletcher (Moore), **VI:** 87, 91

"Mildred Lawson" (Moore), **VI:** 98

Milesian Chief, The (Maturin), **VIII:** 201, 207

Milestones (Bennett), **VI:** 250, 263, 264

Milford, H., **III:** 208*n*

"Milford: East Wing" (Murphy), **Supp. V:** 328

Military Memoirs of Capt. George Carleton, The (Defoe), **III:** 14

Military Philosophers, The (Powell), **VII:** 349

"Milk–cart, The" (Morgan, E.), **Supp. IX:** 168

"Milk–Wort and Bog–Cotton" (MacDiarmid), **Supp. XII:** 212

Mill, James, **IV:** 159; **V:** 288

Mill, John Stuart, **IV:** 50, 56, 246, 355; **V:** xxi–xxii, xxiv, 182, 279, 288, 343

Mill on the Floss, The (Eliot), **V:** xxii, 14, 192–194, 200; **Supp. IV:** 240, 471; **Retro. Supp. II:** 106–108

Millais, John Everett, **V:** 235, 236, 379

Miller, Andrew, **Supp. XIV:** 179–192

Miller, Arthur, **VI:** 286

Miller, Henry, **Supp. IV:** 110–111

Miller, J. Hillis, **VI:** 147

Miller, Karl, **Supp. IV:** 169

"Miller's Daughter, The" (tr. Mangan), **Supp. XIII:** 127

"Miller's Daughter, The" (Tennyson), **IV:** 326

Miller's Tale, The (Chaucer), **I:** 37

Millet, Jean François, **Supp. IV:** 90

Millett, Kate, **Supp. IV:** 188

Millionairess, The (Shaw), **VI:** 102, 127

"Millom Cricket Field" (Nicholson), **Supp. VI:** 216

"Millom Old Quarry" (Nicholson), **Supp. VI:** 216

Mills, C. M., pseud. of Elizabeth Gaskell

Millstone, The (Drabble), **Supp. IV:** 230, 237–238

Milne, A. A., **Supp. V:** 295–312

"Milnes, Richard Monckton" (Lord Houghton), *see* Monckton Milnes, Richard

Milton, Edith, **Supp. IV:** 305–306

Milton (Blake), **III:** 303–304, 307; **V:** xvi 330; **Retro. Supp. I:** 45

Milton (Meredith), **V:** 234

"Milton" (Macaulay), **IV:** 278, 279

"Milton as Muse" (Hill), **Retro. Supp. III:** 142

Milton in America (Ackroyd), **Supp. VI:** 11–12, 13

Milton, John, **II:** 50–52, 113, 158–178, 195, 196, 198, 199, 205, 206, 236, 302; **III:** 43, 118–119, 167*n*, 211*n*, 220, 302; **IV:** 9, 11–12, 14, 22, 23, 93, 95, 185, 186, 200, 205, 229, 269, 278, 279, 352; **V:** 365–366; **Supp. III:** 169; **Retro. Supp. II:** 269–289

Milton's God (Empson), **Supp. II:** 180, 195–196

Milton's Prosody (Bridges), **VI:** 83

Mimic Men, The (Naipaul), **Supp. I:** 383, 386, 390, 392, 393–394, 395, 399

"Mina Laury" (Brontë), **V:** 122, 123, 149, 151

Mind at the End of Its Tether (Wells), **VI:** xiii; **VI:** 228, 242

Mind Has Mountains, The (Jennings), **Supp. V:** 213, 215–216

Mind in Chains, The (ed. Day Lewis), **Supp. III:** 118

"Mind Is Its Own Place, The" (Wallace–Crabbe), **VIII:** 316

Mind of the Maker, The (Sayers), **Supp. III:** 345, 347

Mind to Murder, A (James), **Supp. IV:** 319, 321, 323–324

Mind's Eye, The (Blunden), **Supp. XI:** 35

"Mine old dear enemy, my froward master" (Wyatt), **I:** 105

"Miner's Hut" (Murphy), **Supp. V:** 328

"Miners" (Owen), **VI:** 452, 454

"Minerva's Bird, Athene Noctua" (Thomas), **Supp. XII:** 289

"Minimal" (Dutton), **Supp. XII:** 90, 91

Minister, The (Thomas), **Supp. XII:** 283, 284

"Ministrations" (Conn), **Supp. XIII:** 80

Ministry of Fear, The (Greene), **Supp. I:** 10–11, 12; **Retro. Supp. II:** 157

Minor Poems of Robert Southey, The (Southey), **IV:** 71

Minpins, The (Dahl), **Supp. IV:** 204, 224

Minstrel, The (Beattie), **IV:** 198

Minstrelsy of the Scottish Border (ed. Scott), **IV:** 29, 39

"Mint" (Heaney), **Retro. Supp. I:** 133

Mint, The (Lawrence), **Supp. II:** 283, 291–294

Minute by Glass Minute (Stevenson), **Supp. VI:** 261

Minute for Murder (Day Lewis), **Supp. III:** 130

"Minutes of Glory" (Ngũgĩ), **VIII:** 220

Minutes of the Negotiations of Monsr. Mesnager, . . . (Defoe), **III:** 13

"Mirabeau" (Macaulay), **IV:** 278

"Miracle, The" (Gunn), **Retro. Supp. III:** 125, 129

"Miracle Cure" (Lowbury), **VII:** 432

"Miracle of Purun Bhagat, The" (Kipling), **Retro. Supp. III:** 192, 194

Miracles (Lewis), **Supp. III:** 248, 255, 258–259

"Miraculous Issue, The" (Dutton), **Supp. XII:** 89

Mirèio (Mistral), **V:** 219

"Mirror, The" (Delanty), **Supp. XIV:** 70

Mirror for Magistrates, The, **I:** 162, 214

"Mirror for Poets, A" (Gunn), **Retro. Supp. III:** 118

"Mirror in February" (Kinsella), **Supp. V:** 262

Mirror in the Roadway, The: A Study of the Modern Novel (O'Connor), **Supp. XIV:** 211, 219

Mirror of the Mother, The: Selected Poems, 1975–1985 (Roberts), **Supp. XV:** 261, 262

Mirror of the Sea: Memories and Impressions, The (Conrad), **VI:** 138, 148

Mirror Wall, The (Murphy), **Supp. V:** 313, 329–330

Mirrour; or, Looking–Glasse Both for Saints and Sinners, A (Clarke), **II:** 251

Misadventures of John Nicholson, The (Stevenson), **V:** 396

Misalliance (Shaw), **VI:** xv, 115, 117, 118, 120, 129; **Retro. Supp. II:** 321

Misalliance, The (Brookner), **Supp. IV:** 129

Misanthrope, The (tr. Harrison), **Supp. V:** 149–150, 163

"Misanthropos" (Gunn), **Supp. IV:** 264–265, 268, 270; **Retro. Supp. III:** 121

"Misapprehension" (Traherne), **Supp. XI:** 266

Miscellanea (Temple), **III:** 40

Miscellaneous Essays (St. Évremond), **III:** 47

Miscellaneous Observations on the Tragedy of Macbeth (Johnson), **III:** 108, 116, 121

Miscellaneous Poems (Marvell), **II:** 207

Miscellaneous Studies (Pater), **V:** 348, 357

Miscellaneous Works of the Duke of Buckingham, **II:** 268

Miscellaneous Works . . . with Memoirs of His Life (Gibbon), **III:** 233

Miscellanies (Cowley), **II:** 198

Miscellanies (Martineau), **Supp. XV:** 186

Miscellanies (Pope and Swift), **II:** 335

Miscellanies (Swinburne), **V:** 332

Miscellanies; A Serious Address to the People of Great Britain (Fielding), **III:** 105

Miscellanies, Aesthetic and Literary . . . (Coleridge), **IV:** 56

Miscellany (Tonson), **III:** 69

Miscellany of New Poems, A (Behn), **Supp. III:** 36

Miscellany Poems (Wycherley), **II:** 321

Miscellany Poems, on Several Occasions (Finch), **Supp. IX:** 65, 67, 74, 77

Miscellany Tracts (Browne), **II:** 156

Mrs. Perkins's Ball (Thackeray), **V:** 24, 38

Mrs. Shakespeare: The Complete Works (Nye), **Supp. X:** 196

"Mrs. Silly" (Trevor), **Supp. IV:** 502

"Mrs. Simpkins" (Smith), **Supp. II:** 470

"Mrs. Temperley" (James), **VI:** 69

Mrs. Warren's Profession (Shaw), **V:** 413; **VI:** 108, 109; **Retro. Supp. II:** 312–313

Mistressclass, The (Roberts), **Supp. XV:** 271, 272–273

Mistry, Rohinton, **Supp. X: 137–149**

"Mists" (Redgrove), **Supp. VI:** 228

Mist's Weekly Journal (newspaper), **III:** 4

Mitchell, David, **Supp. XIV: 193–209**

Mitchell, James Leslie, *see* Gibbon, Lewis Grassic

Mitford, Mary Russell, **IV:** 311, 312

Mitford, Nancy, **VII:** 290; **Supp. X: 151–163**

Mithridates (Lee), **II:** 305

Mixed Essays (Arnold), **V:** 213n, 216

"Mixed Marriage" (Muldoon), **Supp. IV:** 415

Mnemosyne Lay in Dust (Clarke), **Supp. XV:** 28–29

Mo, Timothy, **Supp. IV:** 390

"Moa Point" (Adcock), **Supp. XII:** 6

Mob, The (Galsworthy), **VI:** 280, 288

Moby–Dick (Melville), **VI:** 363

Moby Dick: A Play for Radio from Herman Melville's Novel (Reed), **Supp. XV:** 245, 248, 251, 252, 254, 255

Mock Doctor, The (Fielding), III 105

Mock Speech from the Throne (Marvell), **II:** 207

Mock–Mourners, The: . . . Elegy on King William (Defoe), **III:** 12

Mockery Gap (Powys), **VIII:** 251, 256

"Model Prisons" (Carlyle), **IV:** 247

Mock's Curse: Nineteen Stories (Powys), **VIII:** 251, 252, 256

Modern Comedy, A (Galsworthy), **VI:** 270, 275

Modern Fiction (Woolf), **VII:** xiv; **Retro. Supp. I:** 308–309

Modern Husband, The (Fielding), **III:** 105

Modern Irish Short Stories (ed. O'Connor), **Supp. XIV:** 226

"Modern Love" (Meredith), **V:** 220, 234, 244

Modern Love, and Poems of the English Roadside . . . (Meredith), **V:** xxii, 220, 234

Modern Lover, A (Moore), **VI:** 86, 89, 98

Modern Manners (Robinson), **Supp. XIII:** 207

"Modern Money–Lending, and the Meaning of Dividends: A Tract for the Wealthy" (Carpenter), **Supp. XIII:** 40

Modern Movement: 100 Key Books from England, France, and America, 1880–1950, The (Connolly), **VI:** 371

Modern Painters (Ruskin), **V:** xx, 175–176, 180, 184, 282

Modern Painting (Moore), **VI:** 87

Modern Poet, The: Poetry, Academia, and Knowledge Since the 1750s (Crawford), **Supp. XI:** 82–83

Modern Poetry: A Personal Essay (MacNeice), **VII:** 403, 404, 410

Modern Poetry in Translation, **Supp. XV:** 67

"Modern Science: A Criticism" (Carpenter), **Supp. XIII:** 41

Modern Theatre, The (ed. Inchbald), **Supp. XV:** 149, 160, 161

"Modern Times" (Delanty), **Supp. XIV:** 70

"Modern Times" (Wallace–Crabbe), **VIII:** 324

Modern Utopia, A (Wells), **VI:** 227, 234, 241, 244

"Modern Warning, The" (James), **VI:** 48, 69

Modernism and Romance (Scott–James), **VI:** 21

Modes of Modern Writing: Metaphor, Metonymy, and the Typology of Modern Literature, The (Lodge), **Supp. IV:** 365, 377

"Modest Proposal" (Ewart), **Supp. VII:** 46

Modest Proposal, A (Swift), **III:** 21, 28, 29, 35; **Supp. IV:** 482

"Moestitiae Encomium" (Thompson), **V:** 450

Moffatt, James, **I:** 382–383

Mogul Tale, The (Inchbald), **Supp. XV:** 148, 153, 154, 156

Mohocks, The (Gay), **III:** 60, 67

Mohr, Jean, **Supp. IV:** 79

Moi, Toril, **Retro. Supp. I:** 312

"Moisture–Number, The" (Redgrove), **Supp. VI:** 235

Molière (Jean Baptiste Poquelin), **II:** 314, 318, 325, 336, 337, 350; **V:** 224

Moll Flanders (Defoe), **III:** 5, 6, 7, 8, 9, 13, 95; **Retro. Supp. I:** 72–73

Molloy (Beckett), **Supp. I:** 51–52; **Supp. IV:** 106; **Retro. Supp. I:** 18, 21–22

Molly Sweeney (Friel), **Supp. V:** 127

"Molly Gone" (Hardy), **Retro. Supp. I:** 118

Moly (Gunn), **Supp. IV:** 257, 266–268; **Retro. Supp. III:** 116, 117, 120, 122–123, 125, 129, 130

"Moly" (Gunn), **Supp. IV:** 267; **Retro. Supp. III:** 116, 117, 122, 123

Molyneux, William, **III:** 27

"Moment, The: Summer's Night" (Woolf), **Retro. Supp. I:** 309

"Moment in Eternity, A" (MacDiarmid), **Supp. XII:** 204

Moment Next to Nothing, The: A Play in Three Acts (Clarke), **Supp. XV:** 25

"Moment of Cubism, The" (Berger), **Supp. IV:** 79

Moment of Love, A (Moore), see *Feast of Lupercal, The*

Moments of Being (Woolf), **VII:** 33; **Retro. Supp. I:** 305, 315

Moments of Grace (Jennings), **Supp. V:** 217–218

Moments of Vision, and Miscellaneous Verses (Hardy), **VI:** 20

Monastery, The (Scott), **IV:** xviii, 39

Monckton Milnes, Richard (Lord Houghton), **IV:** 211, 234, 235, 251, 252, 254, 302, 351; **V:** 312, 313, 334; **Retro. Supp. I:** 185–186

"Monday; or, The Squabble" (Gay), **III:** 56

Monday or Tuesday (Woolf), **VII:** 20, 21, 38; **Retro. Supp. I:** 307

Mondo Desperado (McCabe), **Supp. IX:** 127, 136–137

Money: A Suicide Note (Amis), **Supp. IV:** 26, 32–35, 37, 40

Money in the Bank (Wodehouse), **Supp. III:** 459

"Money–Man Only" (Smith, I. C.), **Supp. IX:** 213–214

"Money Singing" (Motion), **Supp. VII:** 261

Monk, The (Lewis), **III:** 332–333, 335, 345; **Supp. III:** 384

Monkfish Moon (Gunesekera), **Supp. X:** 85–88, 95, 100

Monks and the Giants, The (Frere), *see Whistlecraft*

Monks of St. Mark, The (Peacock), **IV:** 158, 169

Monk's Prologue, The (Chaucer), **II:** 70

Monk's Tale, The (Chaucer), **I:** 31

Monk's Tale, The (Lydgate), **I:** 57

"Monna Innominata" (Rossetti), **V:** 251; **Retro. Supp. III:** 251, 260

"Mono–Cellular" (Self), **Supp. V:** 402

Monody on the Death of the Right Hon. R. B. Sheridan . . . (Byron), **IV:** 192

"Monody to the Memory of Chatterton" (Robinson), **Supp. XIII:** 206

"Monody to the Memory of Sir Joshua Reynolds" (Robinson), **Supp. XIII:** 202

"Monody to the Memory of the Late Queen of France" (Robinson), **Supp. XIII:** 202

"Monologue, or The Five Lost Géricaults" (Constantine), **Supp. XV:** 79

Monro, Harold, **VI:** 448

"Mons Meg" (Crawford), **Supp. XI:** 81–82

Monsieur (Durrell), **Supp. I:** 118, 119; **Retro. Supp. III:** 86, 87, 92–93, 94

Monsieur de Pourceaugnac (Molière), **II:** 325, 337, 339, 347, 350

Monsieur d'Olive (Chapman), **I:** 244–245

"M. Prudhomme at the International Exhibition" (Swinburne). **V:** 333

Monsieur Thomas (Fletcher), **II:** 45, 61, 65

Monsignor Quixote (Greene), **Supp. I:** 18–19; **Retro. Supp. II:** 166

Monster (Beamish and Galloway), **Supp. XII:** 117

Monstre Gai (Lewis), **VII:** 72, 80

"Mont Blanc" (Shelley), **IV:** 198; **Retro. Supp. I:** 248

Montagu, Lady Mary Wortley, **II:** 326

Montague, John, **VI:** 220; **Supp. XV: 209–225**

Montaigne, Michel Eyquem de, **II:** 25, 30, 80, 104, 108, 146; **III:** 39

"Setteragic On" (Warner), **Supp. VII:** 380

Setting the World on Fire (Wilson), **Supp. I:** 165–166

"Settlements" (Burnside), **Supp. XIII:** 24

"Settlers" (Adcock), **Supp. XII:** 8

"Seven Ages, The" (Auden), **Retro. Supp. I:** 11

Seven at a Stroke (Fry), **Supp. III:** 194

Seven Cardinal Virtues, The (ed. Fell), **Supp. XI:** 163

"Seven Conjectural Readings" (Warner), **Supp. VII:** 373

Seven Days in the New Crete (Graves), **VII:** 259

Seven Deadly Sins, The (ed. Fell), **Supp. XI:** 163

"Seven Deadly Sins: A Mask, The" (Nye), **Supp. X:** 202

"Seven Good Germans" (Henderson), **VII:** 426

Seven Journeys, The (Graham), **Supp. VII:** 111

Seven Lamps of Architecture, The (Ruskin), **V:** xxi, 176, 184

Seven Lectures on Shakespeare and Milton (Coleridge), **IV:** 56

"Seven Letters" (Graham), **Supp. VII:** 111

Seven Men (Beerbohm), **Supp. II:** 55–56

Seven Men and Two Others (Beerbohm), **Supp. II:** 55

Seven Men of Vision: An Appreciation (Jennings), **Supp. V:** 217

"7, Middagh Street" (Muldoon), **Supp. IV:** 411, 422, 424

"7 Newton Road, Harston, Cambridge" (Scupham), **Supp. XIII:** 224

Seven Pillars of Wisdom (Lawrence), **VI:** 408; **Supp. II:** 283, 284, 285, 286, **287–291**

"Seven Poets, The" (Brown), **Supp. VI:** 69

Seven Poor Men of Sydney (Stead), **Supp. IV:** 461–464

"Seven Rocks, The" (Nicholson), **Supp. VI: 216–217**

"Seven Sages, The" (Yeats), **Supp. II:** 84–85

Seven Seas, The (Kipling), **VI:** 204

Seven Short Plays (Gregory), **VI:** 315

Seven Types of Ambiguity (Empson), **I:** 282; **II:** 124, 130; **VII:** 260; **Supp. II:** 179, 180, 183, **185–189**, 190, 197

Seven Winters (Bowen), **Supp. II:** 77–78, 91

Seven Women (Barrie), **Supp. III:** 5

Sevenoaks Essays (Sisson), **Supp. XI:** 249, 256

"1740" (Kinsella), **Supp. V:** 271

"1738" (Stallworthy), **Supp. X:** 297

Seventh Man: Migrant Workers in Europe, A (Berger), **Supp. IV:** 79

Several Perceptions (Carter), **Supp. III:** 80, 81, 82–83

"Several Questions Answered" (Blake), **III:** 293

"Severe Gale 8" (Kay), **Supp. XIII:** 99

Severed Head, A (Murdoch), **Supp. I:** 215, 224, 225, 228

Severn and Somme (Gurney), **VI:** 425

"Sewage Pipe Pool, The" (Nye), **Supp. X:** 203

"Sex That Doesn't Shop, The" (Saki), **Supp. VI:** 246

Sexing the Cherry (Winterson), **Supp. IV:** 541, 542, 545, 547, 549, 552, 554, 556, 557

"Sex–Love: And Its Place in Free Society" (Carpenter), **Supp. XIII:** 41

"Sexton's Hero, The" (Gaskell), **V:** 15

Sexual Inversion (Ellis and Symonds), **Supp. XIV:** 261–262

Sexual Politics (Millett), **Supp. IV:** 188

Seymour-Smith, Martin, **VII:** xviii, xxx-viii

Shabby Genteel Story, A (Thackeray), **V:** 21, 35, 37

"Shack, The" (Cameron), **Supp. IX:** 27

Shade Those Laurels (Connolly), **Supp. III:** 111–112

Shadow Dance (Carter), **III:** 345; **Supp. III:** 79, 80, 81, 89

Shadow in the North, The (Pullman), **Supp. XIII:** 151

Shadow in the Plate, The (Pullman), **Supp. XIII:** 151

Shadow of a Gunman, The (O'Casey), **VI:** 316; **VII:** xviii, 3–4, 6, 12

"Shadow of Black Combe, The" (Nicholson), **Supp. VI:** 218

Shadow of Cain, The (Sitwell), **VII:** xvii, 137

Shadow of Dante, A (Rossetti), **V:** 253n

Shadow of Hiroshima, The (Harrison), **Supp. V:** 164

Shadow of Night (Chapman), **I:** 234, 237

Shadow of the Glen, The (Synge), **VI:** 308, 309, 310, 316

Shadow of the Sun, The (Byatt), **Supp. IV:** 140, 141, 142–143, 147, 148, 149, 155

Shadow Play (Coward), **Supp. II:** 152–153

"Shadow Suite" (Brathwaite), **Supp. XII:** 35

Shadow–Line, The: A Confession (Conrad), **VI:** 135, 146–147, 148

"Shadows" (Lawrence), **VII:** 119

"Shadows in the Water" (Traherne), **II:** 192; **Supp. XI:** 269

Shadows of Ecstasy (Williams, C. W. S.), **Supp. IX:** 279–280

Shadows of the Evening (Coward), **Supp. II:** 156

Shadowy Waters, The (Yeats), **VI:** 218, 222

Shadwell, Thomas, **I:** 327; **II:** 305, 359

"Shadwell Stair" (Owen), **VI:** 451

Shaffer, Anthony, **Supp. I:** 313

Shaffer, Peter, **Supp. I: 313–328**

Shaftesbury, earl of, **Supp. III:** 424

Shaftesbury, seventh earl of, **IV:** 62

Shaftesbury, third earl of, **III:** 44, 46, 198

Shahnameh (Persian epic), **Supp. IV:** 439

Shakes Versus Shav (Shaw), **VI:** 130

Shakespear, Olivia, **VI:** 210, 212, 214

Shakespeare, William, **I:** 188, **295–334; II:** 87, 221, 281, 302; **III:** 115–117; **IV:** 149, 232, 352; **V:** 41, 328; and Collins, **IV:** 165, 165n, 170; and Jonson, **I:** 335–337, **II:** 281; **Retro. Supp. I:** 158, 165; and Kyd, **I:** 228–229; and Marlowe, **I:** 275–279, 286; and Middleton, **IV:** 79–80; and Webster, **II:** 71–72, 74–75, 79; influence on English literature, **II:** 29, 42–43, 47, 48, 54–55, 79, 82, 84; **III:** 115–116, 167n; **IV:** 35, 51–52; **V:** 405; **Supp. I:** 196, 227; **Supp. II:** 193, 194; **Supp. IV:** 158, 171, 283, 558; **Retro. Supp. III: 267–285**

Shakespeare (Swinburne), **V:** 333

"Shakespeare and Stage Costume" (Wilde), **V:** 407

Shakespeare and the Allegory of Evil (Spivack), **I:** 214

Shakespeare and the Goddess of Complete Being (Hughes), **Retro. Supp. II:** 202

Shakespeare and the Idea of the Play (Righter), **I:** 224

"Shakespeare and the Stoicism of Seneca" (Eliot), **I:** 275

"Shakespeare as a Man" (Stephen), **V:** 287

Shakespeare Wallah (Jhabvala), **Supp. V:** 237–238

Shakespeare Wrote for Money (Hornby), **Supp. XV:** 145

Shakespeare's Predecessors in the English Drama (Ellis and Symonds), **Supp. XIV:** 262

Shakespeare's Sonnets Reconsidered (Butler), **Supp. II:** 116

Shall I Call Thee Bard: A Portrait of Jason Strugnell (Cope), **VIII:** 69

Shall We Join the Ladies? (Barrie), **Supp. III:** 6, 9, 16–17

Shaman (Raine), **Supp. XIII:** 173

"Shamdev; The Wolf–Boy" (Chatwin), **Supp. IV:** 157

Shame (Rushdie), **Supp. IV:** 116, 433, 436, 440, 443, 444–445, 448, 449

Shamela (Fielding), **III:** 84, 98, 105; **Retro. Supp. I:** 80; **Retro. Supp. I:** 82–83

Shamrock Tea (Carson), **Supp. XIII:** 63–65

Shape of Things to Come, The (Wells), **VI:** 228, 241

"Shape–Changer, The" (Wallace–Crabbe), **VIII:** 318–319

"Shapes and Shadows" (Mahon), **Supp. VI:** 178

SHAR: Hurricane Poem (Brathwaite), **Supp. XII:** 35–36

Sharawaggi: Poems in Scots (Crawford and Herbert), **Supp. XI:** 67–71, 72

Shards of Memory (Jhabvala), **Supp. V:** 233, 234–235

"Shark! Shark!" (Kay), **Supp. XIII:** 109

"Sharp Trajectories" (Davie), **Supp. VI:** 116

Sharp, William, **IV:** 370

Sharpeville Sequence (Bond), **Supp. I:** 429

Sharrock, Roger, **II:** 246, 254

Shaving of Shagpat, The (Meredith), **V:** 225, 234

MATIGNON HIGH SCHOOL
LIBRARY